Information Systems Today

Managing in the Digital World

Information Systems Today

FIFTH EDITION

Managing in the Digital World

Joe Valacich
Washington State University

Christoph Schneider
City University of Hong Kong

Prentice Hall

Boston   Columbus   Indianapolis   New York   San Francisco   Upper Saddle River
Amsterdam   Cape Town   Dubai   London   Madrid   Milan   Munich   Paris   Montreal   Toronto
Delhi   Mexico City   São Paulo   Sydney   Hong Kong   Seoul   Singapore   Taipei   Tokyo

Editorial Director: Sally Yagan
Editor in Chief: Eric Svendsen
Executive Editor: Bob Horan
Editorial Project Manager: Kelly Loftus
Director of Marketing: Patrice Lumumba Jones
Senior Marketing Manager: Anne Fahlgren
Marketing Assistant: Melinda Jensen
Senior Managing Editor: Judy Leale
Production Project Manager: Kelly Warsak
Senior Operations Supervisor: Arnold Vila
Operations Specialist: Cathleen Petersen
Creative Director: Christy Mahon

Senior Art Director/Design Supervisor: Janet Slowik
Interior and Cover Designer: Michael Fruhbeis
Cover Art: Michael Fruhbeis
Manager, Rights and Permissions: Hessa Albader
Media Project Manager: Lisa Rinaldi
Media Editor: Denise Vaughn
Full-Service Project Management: Tiffany Timmerman/S4Carlisle Publishing Services
Composition: S4Carlisle Publishing Services
Printer/Binder: R.R. Donnelley/Roanoke
Cover Printer: Lehigh-Phoenix Color/Hagerstown
Text Font: 9/11 Times

Credits and acknowledgments borrowed from other sources and reproduced, with permission, in this textbook appear on appropriate page within text.

Microsoft® and Windows® are registered trademarks of the Microsoft Corporation in the U.S.A. and other countries. Screen shots and icons reprinted with permission from the Microsoft Corporation. This book is not sponsored or endorsed by or affiliated with the Microsoft Corporation.

Library of Congress Cataloging-in-Publication Data

Valacich, Joseph S.
  Information systems today: managing in the digital world/Joe Valacich,
Christoph Schneider.—5th ed.
      p. cm.
  Includes bibliographical references and indexes.
  ISBN-13: 978-0-13-706699-5
  ISBN-10: 0-13-706699-6
  1. Information technology.   2. Information storage and retrieval systems—Business.
I. Schneider, Christoph   II. Title.
  T58.5.J47 2012
  658.4'038011—dc22

                                                              2010043082

10 9 8 7 6 5 4 3 2 1

Prentice Hall
is an imprint of

www.pearsonhighered.com

ISBN 10:   0-13-706699-6
ISBN 13: 978-0-13-706699-5

Dedication

To Jackie, Jordan, and James for your sacrifices, love, and support.
—**Joe**

To Birgit for your love and support.
—**Christoph**

About the Authors

Joe Valacich is the George and Carolyn Hubman Distinguished Professor of MIS and was the inaugural Marian E. Smith Presidential Endowed Chair at Washington State University. He has had visiting faculty appointments at the University of Arizona, City University of Hong Kong, Buskerud College (Norway), and the Helsinki School of Economics and Business. He currently teaches in summer programs for the Norwegian University of Life Sciences and Riga Technical University (Latvia). He received the PhD degree from the University of Arizona (MIS) and the MBA and BS (computer science) degrees from the University of Montana. Prior to his academic career, Dr. Valacich worked in the software industry in Seattle in both large and start-up organizations.

Dr. Valacich has served on various national task forces designing model curricula for the information systems discipline, including *IS '97, IS 2002,* and *IS 2010: The Model Curriculum and Guidelines for Undergraduate Degree Programs in Information Systems,* where he was cochairperson. He also served on task force that designed *MSIS 2000* and *2006: The Master of Science in Information Systems Model Curriculum.* He served on the executive committee, funded by the National Science Foundation, to define the *IS Program Accreditation Standards* and served on the board of directors for CSAB (formally, the Computing Sciences Accreditation Board) representing the Association for Information Systems (AIS). He was the general conference cochair for the 2003 International Conference on Information Systems (ICIS) in Seattle, and was the vice chair of ICIS 1999 in Charlotte, North Carolina. He is the general conference cochair for the 2012 Americas Conference on Information Systems (AMCIS) in Seattle.

Dr. Valacich has conducted numerous corporate training and executive development programs for organizations, including AT&T, Boeing, Dow Chemical, EDS, Exxon, FedEx, General Motors, Microsoft, and Xerox. He is currently a senior editor at *MIS Quarterly* and is on the editorial boards at *Decision Sciences* and *Small Group Research.* He was previously an associate editor (two terms) at *Information Systems Research.* His primary research interests include human–computer interaction, technology-mediated collaboration, mobile and emerging technologies, e-business, and distance education. He has published more than 80 scholarly articles in numerous prestigious journals, including *MIS Quarterly, Information Systems Research, Management Science, Academy of Management Journal, Journal of MIS, Decision Sciences, Journal of the AIS, Communications of the ACM, Organizational Behavior and Human Decision Processes,* and *Journal of Applied Psychology.* He is a coauthor of the best-selling textbooks *Modern Systems Analysis and Design* (6th ed.), *Essentials of Systems Analysis and Design* (4th ed.), *Object-Oriented Systems Analysis and Design* (2nd ed.), and *Information Systems Project Management* (1st ed.); all are published by Prentice Hall.

Dr. Valacich was awarded the 2009 Outstanding Alumnus Award by the School of Business Administration, University of Montana. Also, in 2009, *MIS Quarterly* selected his 2008 paper "Media, Tasks, and Communication Processes: A Theory of Media Synchronicity" as its Paper of the Year, and he was ranked as one of 25 most prolific scholars in the history of *MIS Quarterly* over the 32-year life of the journal (1977–2008). Also in 2009, he was named a Fellow of the Association for Information Systems. He has won the Outstanding Researcher Award in 2006 and again in 2008 by the College of Business, Washington State University.

Christoph Schneider is an assistant professor in the Department of Information Systems at City University of Hong Kong and previously held a visiting faculty appointment at Boise State University. He earned a Swiss Higher Diploma in hotel management at the University Centre César Ritz in Brig, Switzerland, and a BA in hotel and restaurant administration at Washington State University. Following extensive experience in the international hospitality industry, he studied information systems at the Martin Luther University in Halle, Germany, before joining the information systems department at Washington State University to earn his PhD degree. His teaching interests include the management of information systems, business intelligence, and enterprise-wide information systems.

Dr. Schneider is an active researcher. His primary research interests include human–computer interaction, electronic commerce, and computer-mediated collaboration. His research has appeared in peer-reviewed journals, such as *Information Systems Research, Management Information Systems Quarterly, Management Science,* and *IEEE Transactions on Professional Communication;* further, he has presented his research at various national and international conferences, such as the International Conference on Information Systems, the European Conference on Information Systems, and the Hawaii International Conference on System Sciences. He is a member of the International Advisory Committee of the International Conference on Information Systems Development.

Brief Contents

Contents

Approach

The world is *flat*. Companies are focusing on the *long tails*. New business models based on concepts of *freeconomics* are flourishing. Change is the norm in the digital world. Globalization, downsizing, outsourcing, and offshoring are a way of life for today's organizations and tomorrow's managers. What does all this mean? What are the catalysts of these concepts and of all this change? More important, how can organizations thrive in this dynamic and highly competitive marketplace? The answer to these and many similar questions is that information systems and related information technologies are driving globalization, new business models, and hypercompetition. It is little wonder that teaching an introductory course on information systems has never been more crucial—or more challenging.

One of the greatest challenges that we face in teaching information systems courses is how to keep pace in the class with what is happening out in the real world. Being relevant to students while at the same time providing the necessary foundation for understanding the breadth, depth, and complexity of information systems has never been more difficult. We wrote *Information Systems Today,* Fifth Edition, with this overarching goal in mind, to be both rigorous *and* relevant. To accomplish this, we want students not only to learn about information systems but also to clearly understand the importance of information systems for individuals, organizations, and society. Additionally, we do not want to simply spoon-feed students with technical terms and the history of information systems. Instead, students must understand exactly what innovative organizations are doing with contemporary information systems and, more important, where things are heading. Finally, we want to empower students with the essential knowledge needed to be successful in the use and understanding of information technology in their careers.

To this end, we wrote *Information Systems Today,* Fifth Edition, so that it is contemporary, fun to read, and useful, focusing on what business students need to know about information systems to survive and thrive in the digital world.

Audience

Information Systems Today, Fifth Edition, is primarily for the undergraduate introductory information systems course required of all business students. The introductory information systems course typically has a diverse audience of students majoring in many different areas, such as accounting, economics, finance, marketing, general management, human resource management, production and operations, international business, entrepreneurship, and information systems. This book also was written for students studying topics outside of business, especially in the growing and broad area of information sciences. Given the range of students taking this type of course, we have written this book so that it is a valuable guide to all students and provides them with the essential information they need to know. Therefore, this book has been written to appeal to a diverse audience.

Information Systems Today, Fifth Edition, can also be used for the introductory course offered at the graduate level—for example, in the first year of an MBA program. Such usage would be especially appropriate if the course heavily focused on the diverse set of cases provided in each chapter.

What's New to the Fifth Edition

Our primary goal for *Information Systems Today,* Fifth Edition, was to emphasize the importance of information systems to all business students as the role of information technology and systems continues to expand within organizations and society. Most notably, we extensively examine how information systems are fueling globalization—making the world smaller and more competitive—in virtually every industry and at an ever-increasing pace. Given this clear focus, we are better able to identify those topics most critical to students and future business professionals. Consequently, we have made substantial revisions to the basic content of the chapters and pedagogical elements that we believe achieve this goal. New or expanded chapter topics include the following:

- An extensively revised chapter—Chapter 1, "Managing in the Digital World"—focuses on defining not only what an information system consists of but also the role of technology as a catalyst for tremendous change, as evidenced by the rise of globalization and emerging ethical issues.
- An updated chapter—Chapter 3, "Managing the Information Systems Infrastructure and Services"—continues to cover essential infrastructure concepts related to hardware, software, networking and the Internet, and databases but also extends this discussion by examining the growth in various technology services, such as utility, cloud, grid, edge, and green computing, which help organizations better manage the rapid obsolescence, ongoing maintenance, energy usage, and demand fluctuations when deploying a modern technology infrastructure.
- In Chapter 6, "Enhancing Business Intelligence Using Information Systems," we sharpen our focus on various topics related to business intelligence by discussing how databases serve as a foundation for gaining business intelligence and examining three components of business intelligence: information and knowledge discovery, business analytics, and information visualization.
- In Chapter 7, "Enhancing Business Processes Using Enterprise Information Systems," we greatly expand our coverage on the core business processes of most organizations in order to better inform students of the complexities of modern organizations. Using this foundation, enterprise systems are introduced as a powerful mechanism to improve business processes.
- In Chapter 8, "Improving Supply Chains and Strengthening Customer Relationships Using Enterprise Information Systems," we greatly expand our coverage of supply chain management and customer relationship management, focusing on both upstream and downstream business relationships.
- In Chapter 10, "Securing Information Systems," we consolidate content that was spread over two chapters, providing content on both computer crime, cyberwar, and cyberterrorism as well as issues related to information systems security, control, auditing, and disaster recovery planning.
- An updated and expanded Technology Briefing covers foundational concepts related to various information technologies. The Technology Briefing provides the groundwork for a deeper understanding of the topics introduced in Chapter 3 and is intended for use in more technically oriented courses. Each section of this briefing was designed to be stand-alone— it can be read with or without the other sections.

Beyond the chapter content and features, we have also made substantial changes and refinements to the end of each chapter. First, we carefully revised the end-of-chapter problems and exercises to reflect content change and new material. Second, we have carefully revised the end-of-chapter cases about real, contemporary organizations and issues to illustrate the complexities of the digital world. Each case mirrors the primary content of its chapter to better emphasize its relevancy within the context of a real organization. All these elements are discussed more thoroughly next.

Our goal has always been to provide only the information that is relevant to all business students, nothing more and nothing less. We believe that we have again achieved this goal with *Information Systems Today,* Fifth Edition. We hope you agree.

Key Features

As authors, teachers, developers, and managers of information systems, we understand that in order for students to best learn about information systems with this book, they must be motivated to learn. To this end, we have included a number of unique features to help students quickly and easily assess the true value of information systems and their impact on everyday life. We show how today's professionals are using information systems to help modern organizations become more efficient and competitive. Our focus is on the application of technology to real-world, contemporary situations. Next, we describe each of the features that contribute to that focus.

A Multitiered Approach

Each chapter utilizes cases in a variety of ways to emphasize and highlight how contemporary organizations are utilizing information systems to gain competitive advantage, streamline organizational processes, or improve customer relationships.

Opening Case—Managing in the Digital World All chapters begin with an opening case describing a real-world company, technology, and/or issue to spark students' interest in the chapter topic. We have chosen engaging cases that relate to students' interests and concerns by highlighting why information systems have become central for managing in the digital world. Each opening case includes a series of associated questions the students will be able to answer after reading the chapter contents. The organizations, technologies, or issues highlighted in these cases include the following:

- Apple Computer's rise, fall, and reemergence as a global technology giant
- How TiVo, Sling Media, and other innovative technologies are transforming the television and movie industries
- Google's meteoric rise and the challenges associated with maintaining its success
- How social media sites like Twitter and YouTube are being used by business to connect and provide services to customers
- How Facebook has emerged as one of the most successful and powerful Web 2.0 sites
- eBay's use of business intelligence to battle its ongoing struggles with counterfeit products and fraudulent buyers and sellers
- Amazon.com's use of its sophisticated infrastructure to automate the supply chain for both large and small customers
- How a recent volcanic eruption in Iceland disrupted the global supply chains of countless organizations throughout the world
- How the Nintendo Wii created tremendous demand by purposefully being different than the Sony PlayStation or Microsoft Xbox
- The vulnerability of your information systems and networks to hacker attacks via wireless networks

Brief Case Each chapter also includes a brief case that discusses important issues related to companies, technologies, or society. These are embedded in the text of the chapter and highlight concepts from the surrounding chapter material. Discussion questions are provided to seed critical thinking assignments or class discussions. The organizations, trends, and products highlighted in these cases include the following:

- How some are sharing their Internet connection to help others
- How domainers—those who buy and sell lucrative domain names on the Internet—have grown into a multi-billion-dollar industry.
- How the ongoing battle between Microsoft and Apple is fueling rapid innovation in the computing industry
- How the human-powered search engine ChaCha makes any mobile phone smarter
- How organizations can best utilize instant messaging to aid the collaboration of an increasingly distributed workforce
- How the Internet Movie Database (IMDb) provides comprehensive information on films, television, and video games to enhance and change the entertainment industry
- How the complexity of modern manufacturing creates innovative but also highly vulnerable products
- How McDonald's is outsourcing drive-through order placement
- How Microsoft aids hackers by releasing security update patches
- How it may now be possible to hack into airplanes that rely more and more on internal computers and networks

End-of-Chapter Case To test and reinforce chapter content, we present two current real-world cases at the end of each chapter. Sources for these cases include *InformationWeek, BusinessWeek, CIO* magazine, and various Web sites. Like the Brief Cases within the chapter, these are taken from the news and are contemporary. However, these are longer and more substantive than the Brief Cases. They too are followed by discussion questions that help the student apply and master the chapter content. The organizations and products highlighted in these cases include the following:

- How the One Laptop per Child program is attempting to bridge the digital divide
- How PayPal created a global currency to enable worldwide collaboration and commerce
- How NetFlix is transforming the movie industry
- How LinkedIn, a social networking site for professionals, can help people find jobs, useful business contacts, and business opportunities
- How broadband Internet access in airplanes has evolved and will soon become common
- How Facebook's infrastructure has evolved to support social games like FarmVille and Mafia Wars
- How the picture exchange site Flickr aids in the globalization movement
- How YouTube has grown into a mainstream Web marvel
- How Wikipedia has become both a useful and a sometimes controversial Web resource
- How Digg.com is changing how news is delivered to consumers
- How Netflix is utilizing crowdsourcing to improve its ability to make movie recommendations to customers
- How online mapping services like Google maps are enabling many innovative products and services
- How enterprise resource planning systems transform business processes but often do not satisfy the needs of the users and the organization
- How organizations are managing their computing applications, costs, and delivery using service-oriented architectures
- How customer relationship management is evolving to include social media capabilities
- How the automobile industry is expanding their supply chains as cars become more reliant on information technologies for information services, navigation, and communication
- How the advent of open source software systems, such as the Linux operating system, Apache Web server, and Firefox Web browser, are transforming the software industry
- How the FBI is developing a comprehensive database of biometric information to better track and apprehend criminals
- How and why cybercriminals target eBay, PayPal, and other popular Web sites and resources
- How China limits information exchange within its society through its "great firewall"

Common Chapter Features

Throughout every chapter, a variety of short pedagogical elements are presented to highlight key information systems issues and concepts in a variety of contexts. These elements help to show students the broader organizational and societal implications of various topics.

Industry Analysis

Every industry is being transformed by the Internet and the increasing use of information systems by individuals and organizations. To give you a feel for just how pervasive and profound these changes are, each chapter presents an analysis of a specific industry to highlight the new rules for operating in the digital world. Given that no industry or profession is immune from these changes, each Industry Analysis highlights the importance of understanding information systems for *every* business student, not only for information systems majors. Discussion questions help students better understand the rapidly changing opportunities and risks of operating in the digital world. Chapter 1 examines how the digital world is transforming the opportunities for virtually all business professions. Subsequent chapters examine how globalization and the digital world have eliminated or forever transformed various industries, including banking, movie, retail, travel, health care, automobile, manufacturing, broadcasting, and law enforcement. Clearly, we are in a time of tremendous change, and understanding this evolution will better equip students to not only survive but also thrive in the digital world.

Coming Attractions

We worked to ensure that this book is contemporary. We cover literally hundreds of different current and emerging technologies throughout the book. This feature, however, focuses on an innovation that is likely to soon have an impact on organizations or society. Topics include the following:

- Real-time language translation
- Television for the visually impaired
- Autonomic computing
- Very smart phones and services of the future
- Future of TV
- Medical records of the future
- Swarm intelligence learned from ants, bees, termites, and wasps
- Simplifying the recharging of gadgets
- Microsoft's Surface computerized table
- Brain sensors to improve market research

When Things Go Wrong

Textbooks don't usually describe what not to do, but this can be very helpful to students. This feature enables students to learn about a real-world situation in which information systems did not work or were not built or used well. Topics include the following:

- Apple Computer's numerous product and strategy failures
- eWaste and what to do with all our old computers and gadgets
- Google Buzz, a privacy fiasco for the search giant
- Apple Computers' resistance to Adobe's Flash in its browsers and devices
- Nestlé's social media fiasco after blocking a YouTube video posted by Greenpeace
- How the Internet can quickly disseminate false information with unforeseen consequences
- How the failure of the Federal Aviation Administration's computer system grounded hundreds of flights
- How Apple mismanaged initial complaints about the iPhone 4 antenna
- How spam and spyware are creating traffic jams on the information superhighway
- Unusual cyberthreats, such as accidentally (or purposely) digging up largely unprotected fiber-optic networks

Net Stats

The Internet is now a significant part of every organization as well as our personal lives. Net Stats provide interesting, important trends and forecasts related to Internet usage within a variety of contexts. These insights help students better understand the Internet's role in fueling globalization and transforming the digital world. Topics include the following:

- Global Internet usage
- Online search market share
- Broadband access
- Top Internet advertisers
- Most popular Facebook fan pages
- Demise of broadcast television
- Changing value of social media in the workplace
- Growth of radio-frequency identification
- Lagging information technology adopters
- Top cyberthreats

Ethical Dilemma

Ethical business practices are now a predominant part of contemporary management education and practice. This feature examines contemporary dilemmas related to the chapter content and highlights the implications of these dilemmas for managers, organizations, and society. Topics include the following:

- Differences in online rights throughout the world
- An underground gaming industry selling virtual goods for "real" money
- The collection and easy dissemination of public information over the Web
- Monitoring productive employees
- Virtual reality people
- Stealing WiFi
- Privacy of radio-frequency identification
- Using customer relationship management systems to target or discriminate
- Genetic testing and discrimination
- Ethical hacking

Powerful Partnerships

A variety of key collaborations have shaped the information technology industry. While there are countless people who have contributed to today's digital world, this feature presents some of the more prominent teams that have significantly advanced technologies or lead important companies. These partnerships include the following:

- Apple's Steve Jobs and Steve Wozniak
- Skype's Niklas Zennström and Janus Friis
- Google's Sergey Brin and Larry Page
- YouTube's Steve Chen and Chad Hurley
- Digg's Kevin Rose and Jay Adelson
- Adobe's John Warnock and Chuck Geschke
- SAP's Dietmar Hopp, Hans-Werner Hector, Hasso Plattner, Klaus Tschira, and Claus Wellenreuther
- Flickr's Caterina Fake and Stewart Butterfield
- Microsoft's Bill Gates and Paul Allen
- Netscape's James H. Clark and Marc Andreessen

End-of-Chapter Material

Our end-of-chapter material is designed to accommodate various teaching and learning styles. It promotes learning beyond the book and the classroom. Elements include the following:

- *Key Terms*—Highlight key concepts within the chapter.
- *Review Questions*—Test students' understanding of basic content.
- *Self-Study Questions*—Enable students to assess whether they are ready for a test.
- *Matching Questions*—Check quickly to see if students understand basic terms.
- *Problems and Exercises*—Push students deeper into the material and encourage them to synthesize and apply it.
- *Application Exercises*—Challenge students to solve two real-world management problems using spreadsheet and database applications from a running case centered on a university travel agency. Student data files referenced within the exercises are available on the book's Web site: www.pearsonhighered.com/valacich.
- *Team Work Exercise*—Enable students to work in teams to solve a problem and/or address an issue related to the chapter material.

We have extensively updated these elements to reflect new chapter content and the natural evolution of the material.

Pedagogy

In addition to the features described above, we provide a list of learning objectives to lay the foundation for each chapter. At the end of the chapter, the Key Points Review repeats these learning objectives and describes how each objective was achieved. A list of references is located at the end of the text, organized by chapter.

Organization

The content and organization of this book are based on our own teaching as well as on feedback from reviewers and colleagues throughout the field. Each chapter builds on the others to reinforce key concepts and allow for a seamless learning experience. Essentially, the book has been structured to answer three fundamental questions:

1. What are contemporary information systems, and how are they being used in innovative ways?
2. Why are information systems so important and interesting?
3. How best can we build, acquire, manage, and safeguard information systems?

The ordering and content of our chapters was also significantly influenced by a recent article, "What Every Business Student Needs to Know About Information Systems."[1] This article was written by forty prominent information systems scholars to define the information systems core body of knowledge for all business students. By design, the content of *Information Systems Today,* Fifth Edition, carefully follows the guidance of this article. We are, therefore, very confident that our book provides a solid and widely agreed-on foundation for any introductory information systems course.

The chapters are organized as follows:

- *Chapter 1: Managing in the Digital World*—This chapter helps the student understand what information systems are and how they have become a vital part of modern organizations. We walk the student through the technology, people, and organizational components of an information system, and we lay out types of jobs and career opportunities in information systems and in related fields. We also focus on how technology is driving globalization and creating countless ethical concerns. We use a number of cases and examples, such as that of Apple Computers, to show the student the types of systems being used and to point out common "best practices" in systems use and management.

- *Chapter 2: Gaining Competitive Advantage Through Information Systems*—Here, we discuss how companies, such as TiVo, can use information systems for automation, organizational learning, and strategic advantage. Given the rapid advancement of new technologies, we also explain why and how companies are continually looking for innovative ways to use information systems for competitive advantage.

- *Chapter 3: Managing the Information Systems Infrastructure and Services*—In this chapter, we provide an overview of the essential information systems infrastructure components and describe why they are necessary for satisfying an organization's informational needs. With the ever-increasing complexity of maintaining a solid information systems infrastructure, it becomes increasingly important for organizations, such as Google, to design a reliable, robust, and secure infrastructure. We also examine the rapid evolution toward the delivery of infrastructure capabilities through a variety of technology services.

- *Chapter 4: Enabling Commerce Using the Internet*—Perhaps nothing has changed the landscape of business more than the use of the Internet for electronic commerce. In this extensively updated chapter, we describe how a number of firms, such as Alaska Air, Timbuk2, or the Boeing Company, use the Internet to conduct commerce in cyberspace. Further, we explain how organizations build intranets to support internal processes and build extranets to interact with other firms. We then describe the stages of business-to-consumer electronic commerce and discuss emerging trends in consumer-to-consumer e-commerce, mobile commerce, and Internet marketing. Finally, we explain different forms of e-government and show how governmental regulations can become a threat to e-commerce.

---

[1]Ives, B., Valacich, J., Watson, R., Zmud, R. (2002). What every business student needs to know about information systems. *Communications of the Association for Information Systems,* 9(30). Other contributing scholars to this article include Maryam Alavi, Richard Baskerville, Jack J. Baroudi, Cynthia Beath, Thomas Clark, Eric K. Clemons, Gordon B. Davis, Fred Davis, Alan R. Dennis, Omar A. El Sawy, Jane Fedorowicz, Robert D. Galliers, Joey George, Michael Ginzberg, Paul Gray, Rudy Hirschheim, Sirkka Jarvenpaa, Len Jessup, Chris F. Kemerer, John L. King, Benn Konsynski, Ken Kraemer, Jerry N. Luftman, Salvatore T. March, M. Lynne Markus, Richard O. Mason, F. Warren McFarlan, Ephraim R. McLean, Lorne Olfman, Margrethe H. Olson, John Rockart, V. Sambamurthy, Peter Todd, Michael Vitale, Ron Weber, and Andrew B. Whinston.

- *Chapter 5: Enhancing Collaboration Using Web 2.0*—Web 2.0 has given rise to various different social media, which have forever changed how people interact. In addition to enabling various business opportunities, Web 2.0 technologies have also enabled companies to better harness the power and creativity of their workforce. In this chapter, we examine how different social media can enhance communication, collaboration, cooperation, and connection within organizations but also between organizations and their customers. Further, we discuss the importance of carefully managing an Enterprise 2.0 strategy. Finally, using examples such as Twitter and Facebook, we describe how companies can deal with potential pitfalls associated with Web 2.0.

- *Chapter 6: Enhancing Business Intelligence Using Information Systems*—Given how many different types of information systems organizations use to run their business and gain business intelligence, in this chapter we use examples from eBay.com and other firms to describe the various types of systems. In this extensively updated chapter, we describe key business intelligence concepts and explain how databases serve as a foundation for gaining business intelligence. Further, we discuss three components of business intelligence: information and knowledge discovery, business analytics, and information visualization.

- *Chapter 7: Building Organizational Partnerships Using Enterprise Information Systems*—In this chapter, we focus on enterprise systems, which are a popular type of information system used to integrate information and span organizations' boundaries to better connect a firm with customers, suppliers, and other partners. We walk students through various core business processes and then examine how enterprise resource planning systems can be applied to improve these processes and organizational performance.

- *Chapter 8: Improving Supply Chains and Strengthening Customer Relationships Using Enterprise Information Systems*—In this chapter, we continue our focus on enterprise systems by examining the complexities of supply networks and how they can be managed more effectively using supply chain management systems. Additionally, customer relationship management systems and their role in the attraction and retention of customers are examined.

- *Chapter 9: Developing and Acquiring Information Systems*—In this chapter, we begin by describing how to formulate and present the business case to build or acquire a new information system. We then walk the student through the traditional systems development approach and explain that numerous other approaches, such as prototyping, rapid application development, and object-oriented analysis and design, can be utilized depending on the situation. Finally, we examine the steps followed to request and acquire an information system from an outside vendor.

- *Chapter 10: Securing Information Systems*—With the pervasive use of information systems, new dangers have arisen for organizations, and information security has become a paramount issue within the context of global information management. In this chapter, we define computer crime and contrast several types of computer crime. Next, given its growing relevance to managing and living in the digital world, we examine the growing significance of cyberwar and cyberterrorism. This is followed by an examination of the primary threats to information systems security and how systems can be compromised. Using real-world examples, we show how companies can implement both technological and human-based safeguards to better manage information systems, The chapter concludes with a discussion of the role of auditing, information systems controls, and the Sarbanes-Oxley Act.

In addition to these ten chapters, we include a Technology Briefing that focuses on foundational concepts regarding hardware, software, networking and the Internet, and databases. While Chapter 3, "Managing the Information Systems Infrastructure and Services," provides a more managerial focus to these enabling technologies, this foundational material is intended to provide a more in-depth examination of these topics. By delivering this material as a Technology Briefing, we provide instructors the greatest flexibility in how and when they can apply it.

Supplement Support

Online Instructor's Resource Center

The convenient Online Instructor's Resource Center is accessible from www.pearsonhighered .com/valacich by choosing the "Instructor Resources" link from the catalog page. The online center includes the following supplements: Instructor's Manual, Test Item File, PowerPoint presentations, and Image Library (text art). The online center also contains TestGen and TestGen conversions in WebCT and BlackBoard-ready files.

The Instructor's Manual includes answers to all review and discussion questions, exercises, and case questions. The Test Item File (Test Bank) includes multiple-choice, true-or-false, and essay questions for each chapter. The Test Bank is delivered in Microsoft Word as well as in the form of TestGen. The PowerPoint presentations highlight text learning objectives and key topics. Finally, the Image Library is a collection of the figures and tables from the text for instructor use in PowerPoint slides and class lectures.

CourseSmart eTextbooks Online

CourseSmart is an exciting new choice for students looking to save money. As an alternative to purchasing the print textbook, students can purchase an electronic version of the same content. With a CourseSmart eTextbook, students can search the text, make notes online, print out reading assignments that incorporate lecture notes, and bookmark important passages for later review. For more information or to purchase access to the CourseSmart eTextbook, visit www.coursesmart .com.

myMISlab

myMISlab is now available to bring a greater software applications emphasis to your class. Included is myitlab, a Microsoft Office simulation currently used by thousands of students allowing them to gain practical skills in the use of spreadsheet and database software. End-of Chapter applications are tied to this unique tutorial.

A turnkey collaboration application in the form of **Microsoft's SharePoint** is ready for your class. No need to worry about coordinating through your school's computer lab and server. Monitor your students' activities as they work through their teamwork assignments—all from within **myMISlab.**

Please visit www.mymislab.com and contact your local rep for more details.

Reviewers

We wish to thank the following faculty who participated in reviews for this and previous editions:

Lawrence L. Andrew, *Western Illinois University*
Karin A. Bast, *University of Wisconsin–La Crosse*
David Bradbard, *Winthrop University*
Rochelle Brooks, *Viterbo University*
Brian Carpani, *Southwestern College*
Amita Chin, *Virginia Commonwealth University*
Jon D. Clark, *Colorado State University*
Paul Clay, *Washington State University*
Thomas Engler, *Florida Institute of Technology*
Roy H. Farmer, *California Lutheran University*
Mauricio Featherman, *Washington State University*
David Firth, *University of Montana*
Frederick Fisher, *Florida State University*
James Frost, *Idaho State University*
Frederick Gallegos, *California State Polytechnic University–Pomona*
Dale Gust, *Central Michigan University*
Albert Harris, *Appalachian State University*
Michelle Hepner, *University of Central Oklahoma*
Traci Hess, *University of Massachusetts*
Bruce Hunt, *California State University–Fullerton*

Carol Jensen, *Southwestern College*
Bhushan Kapoor, *California State University–Fullerton*
Elizabeth Kemm, *Central Michigan University*
Beth Kiggins, *University of Indianapolis*
Chang E. Koh, *University of North Texas*
Brian R. Kovar, *Kansas State University*
Kapil Ladha, *Drexel University*
Linda K. Lau, *Longwood University*
Cameron Lawrence, *University of Montana*
Martha Leva, *Penn State University–Abington*
Weiqi Li, *University of Michigan–Flint*
Clayton Looney, *University of Montana*
Dana L. McCann, *Central Michigan University*
Richard McCarthy, *Quinnipiac University*
Patricia McQuaid, *California State Polytechnic University*
Michael Newby, *California State University–Fullerton*
Kathleen Noce, *Penn State University–Erie*
W. J. Patterson, *Sullivan University*

Timothy Peterson, *University of Minnesota–Duluth*

Lara Preiser-Houy, *California State Polytechnic University, Pomona*

Eugene Rathswohl, *University of San Diego*

Rene F. Reitsma, *Oregon State University*

Bonnie Rohde, *Albright College*

Kenneth Rowe, *Purdue University*

Dana Schwieger, *Southeast Missouri State University*

G. Shankaranarayanan, *Boston University*

James Sneeringer, *St. Edward's University*

Cheri Speier, *Michigan State University*

Bill Turnquist, *Central Washington University*

Craig K. Tyran, *Western Washington University*

William Wagner, *Villanova University*

Minhua Wang, *State University of New York–Canton*

John Wells, *University of Massachusetts*

Nilmini Wickramasinghe, *Cleveland State University*

Yue Zhang, *California State University–Northridge*

Acknowledgments

Although only our two names are listed as the authors for this book, this was truly a team effort that went well beyond the two of us. Prentice Hall has been an outstanding publishing company to work with. They are innovative, have high standards, and are as competitive as we are.

Among the many amazingly helpful people at Prentice Hall, there are a handful of people we wish to thank specifically. First, Kelly Loftus, our editorial project manager, helped to whip us and this book into shape and get it finished on time. Additionally, Kelly Warsak, our production project manager, and Tiffany Timmerman of S4Carlisle Publishing Services helped in getting approval for photos, figures, Web sites, and other graphics as well as coordinating refinements as the book moved through the stages of production. Finally, our executive editor, Bob Horan, guided the book and us from its inception, and he dared us to dream of and to write the best introductory information systems textbook ever.

In addition to our colleagues at Prentice Hall, several individuals have been particularly instrumental in making the fifth edition the best ever. First, Karen Judson did an outstanding job on drafting several of our case elements; Tracy Hess from the University of Massachussetts and Mauricio Featherman from Washington State University provided valuable inputs into our revision of Chapters 7 and 8. Likewise, Ryan Wright from the University of San Francisco provided many ideas that shaped the current edition. Also, two Washington State University PhD students, Nathan Johnson and Fengchun Tang, provided many ideas for updating various cases throughout the book. Thanks, team! We could not have done it without you.

Most important, we thank our families for their patience and assistance in helping us to complete this book. Joe's wife Jackie, daughter Jordan, and son James were a constant inspiration, as was Christoph's wife Birgit. This one is for all of you.

Information
Systems Today
Managing in the Digital World

After reading this chapter, you will be able to do the following:

1. Describe the characteristics of the digital world and the advent of the information age.

2. Define globalization, describe how it evolved over time, and describe the key drivers of globalization.

3. Explain what an information system is, contrasting its data, technology, people, and organizational components.

4. Describe the dual nature of information systems in the success and failure of modern organizations.

5. Describe how computer ethics impact the use of information systems and discuss the ethical concerns associated with information privacy, accuracy, property, and accessibility.

Preview

Today, organizations from Apple Computer to Zales Jewelers use computer-based information systems (IS) to better manage their operations in the digital world. These organizations use information systems to provide high-quality goods and services as well as to gain or sustain competitive advantage over rivals. In addition to helping organizations to be competitive, information systems have contributed to tremendous societal changes. Our objective for Chapter 1 is to help you understand the role of information systems as we move into the digital world and how they have helped fuel globalization. We then highlight what information systems are, how they have evolved to become a vital part of modern organizations, and why this understanding is necessary for you to become an effective manager in the digital world. We conclude by discussing ethical issues associated with the use of information systems.

Managing in the Digital World: Apple Computer

It happened on April Fools' Day 1976, but history has shown it was no joke. On that date, Stephen "Woz" Wozniak and Steven Paul Jobs officially formed the Apple Computer Company. The two friends had been fascinated with computers since their days as students at Homestead High School in Cupertino, California. Wozniak graduated first, in 1967, because he is five years older than Jobs, but their shared interest in anything digital kept bringing the two together, both before Jobs graduated from high school and then after he graduated in 1972.

The two Steves both dropped out of college to work on building computers—first in Jobs's bedroom, then in his garage when the bedroom got too crowded. (Wozniak later returned to school at the University of California in Berkeley and graduated with a degree in engineering in 1986.) At first, they were interested just in building circuit boards, but later decided to build entire computers and sell them to home users.

The Apple I debuted shortly after the company was formed and sold for $666.66, paving the way for profound changes in the way everyday people would use computers. Shortly after the introduction of the Apple I, the Apple II debuted with a keyboard, a floppy disk drive, and color graphics. Because of its jazzy appearance and ease of use (which can't be compared with today's personal computers [PCs]), consumers liked the Apple II, and the company eventually sold 50,000 units. It continued to be Apple's dominant product until 1993. To date, the Apple II's 17-year life span is a record within the computer industry.

The working relationship between Wozniak and Jobs was key to Apple's success. Wozniak, the engineer, was concerned primarily with a computer's function, while Jobs focused on ease of use and design. Thanks to the two-Steves team, the Apple II was an attractive and functional addition to a family's living room. Apple continues to offer products that are a blend of engineering and aesthetics, and many consumers are devoted to its products. The history of Apple Computers, however, includes a series of high highs and low lows. For example, the Lisa, introduced in 1983, was a commercial disaster; and the Apple III, introduced shortly after the Apple II, was discontinued after only a year on the market when it failed to entice consumers. In 1984, Apple once again had a hit when it introduced the popular Macintosh 128K, featuring the AppleMouse II (the first computer mouse introduced to the mass market) and the first true graphical user interface. When Apple introduced the Macintosh Portable (an early laptop), it had only limited success, but after it was redesigned and renamed, the PowerBook proved a marketplace success. Other near failures for Apple included the Apple Newton (an early personal digital assistant [PDA]) and the G3 enterprise server computer (for more on Apple's failures, see When Things Go Wrong later in this chapter).

Jobs left Apple in 1985 amid employee complaints that he was an erratic and tempestuous manager; Wozniak left Apple for good in 1986. Jobs was so disgruntled when he left Apple that he sold all but one share of his stock in the company. Jobs then started another computer company, NeXT Computer,

FIGURE 1.1

The iPad is Apple's latest gadget.

Dreamstime LLC –Royalty Free

which designed and marketed a technologically advanced computer that did not sell well because of its high price. Apple's leadership foundered for a while, but the company purchased NeXT for $402 million in 1996, and Jobs again took over the helm. Jobs brought Apple back to profitability by revamping its product line. The iMac, a PowerBook featuring a 14-inch display, and Mac OS X—a new operating system—were the most successful units in the 1998 product line.

In late 2001, Apple introduced the iPod, the now universally familiar MP3 music player. Selling for $250 and offering 4 GB of hard drive storage for music files, the player went mainstream in 2003. The simple user interface and small size made the iPod one of the most sought after digital music players. Apple soon began offering the device in a range of sizes and colors, including the iPod mini, iPod color, iPod shuffle, and iPod nano. Although competitors have released their own digital music players, none have achieved Apple's market share.

To build on the iPod's success, Apple created an online music store called iTunes, where users could download digital music for 99 cents per track. iTunes soon expanded into the video market, providing portable movies and television shows to media-hungry users. The combination of product (the iPod) and service (online iTunes store) resulted in massive profits for Apple.

Apple continued its success with new products in 2007 when it introduced the iPhone—a smart phone with Internet access and a touch-screen interface. The iPhone sold 1.4 million units the first 90 days after its introduction. Not only could iPhone users make phone calls and surf the Internet, they could do a large variety of other things via software downloaded from the "App Store," a new wing of iTunes. Users could download both pay and free applications—or "apps"—to enhance the utility and entertainment value of their iPhones. As the App Store grew in popularity, users could find something for almost any occasion, from games to grocery list generators. The diversity and range of apps available to users spawned Apple's famous "There's An App for That" marketing campaign. Building on this success, Apple released the iPod touch, which offered most of the iPhone's capabilities, minus the phone. Two years after its initial launch, the third iteration of the iPhone went on sale. Not to be outdone by its predecessors, the iPhone 3GS sold over 1 million units in its first *weekend* on sale. In 2010, iPhone 4G was released. Although many consumers complained about problems with the phone's antenna, the iPhone 4 was another sales hit for Apple. The iPhone has continued to outsell other smart phones on the market, while analysts and fans alike look to the horizon to see what Apple's next generation handset will bring to the world of smart phones.

Barely as thick as your index finger and weighing a mere three pounds, the MacBook Air, introduced in 2008, also proved popular with consumers. The lightweight laptop boasted 2 GB of built-in RAM, an 80-GB hard drive, and a 1.6- to 1.8-GHz Intel Core 2 dual processor. Apple continued wowing computer enthusiasts in 2010 with the release of one of its latest gadgets, the tablet-like iPad (see Figure 1.1). Touted by Jobs as a "third-category" device between smart phones and laptops, the iPad measured just under 8.5 by 11 inches and half an inch thick. Sporting Wi-Fi, Bluetooth, and optional cellular network connectivity, the 1.5-pound iPad shipped with a specially designed 1-GHz processor and up to 64 GB of internal storage. In addition, the iPad utilized a touch-screen keyboard similar to those found on the iPhone and iPod touch. Integration with iTunes and the App Store allowed users to download music, e-books, and games into the ultraportable and light-weight computer.

While Apple Computers was enjoying a long list of successful products, in 2005 environmentalists criticized the company for its lack of an e-waste recycling policy. Jobs was at first defiant, dismissing such complaints as trivial. However, shortly after Apple's annual meeting in April 2005, he announced that Apple would take back used iPods for free. In 2006, he further expanded Apple's recycling programs to any customer who buys a new Mac. This program includes shipping and "environmentally friendly disposal" of customers' old systems. In late 2007, Apple once again came under scrutiny from Greenpeace, this time for the use of toxic chemicals in the iPhone. Only a few days later, Apple announced that in addition to recycling its old products, toxic chemicals would be removed from new products.

Environmental issues haven't been Apple's only concern. In 2004, Jobs underwent surgery for pancreatic cancer. A few years later, public speculation spread over the status of Jobs's health, as he began to experience severe weight loss from a hormone imbalance. In early 2009, Jobs took an extended leave of absence as Apple's chief executive officer (CEO) because of his health. During this time, Apple's stock began to drop as uncertainty surrounded the future direction of the company. After receiving a liver transplant and successfully recovering, Jobs returned to actively steering the company and marketing new products.

Thanks to innovative product design, clever marketing tactics, and a swift response to environmental concerns, Apple Computer's profits have consistently risen over the past several years, and financial analysts see more of the same in the company's future.

After reading this chapter, you will be able to answer the following:

1. Given the pace at which technology is converging (e.g., phones, music players, cameras, and so on), what do you think is next for Apple?
2. Apple has had many "near-death" experiences throughout its history. Is Apple now here to stay?
3. Jobs has been the catalyst for many of Apple's successes (and failures). Can Apple survive without Jobs?

Based on:

Anonymous. (n.d.). Apple-history.com: Recent changes. Retrieved May 17, 2010, from http://www.apple-history.com.

Anonymous. (2009, April 12). WSJ: Apple's Jobs still closely tied to company. *PCMag.com*. Retrieved May 20, 2010, from http://www.pcmag.com/article2/0,2817,2345154,00.asp.

Anonymous. (2010, February 1). Apple iPad: Welcome to the new world of computing! *MacDailyNews*. Retrieved May 20, 2010, from http://macdailynews.com/index.php/weblog/comments/23880.

Carew, S. (2009, June 22). Apple sells more than 1 million iPhone 3GS. *Reuters*. Retrieved May 20, 2010, from http://www.reuters.com/article/idUSTRE55I2FK20090622.

Flynn, L. J. (2003, April 17). Profits at Apple computer are down 65% in quarter. *New York Times*. Retrieved May 17, 2010, from http://query.nytimes.com/gst/fullpage.html?res=9A05E3DD16 3AF934A25757C0A9659C8B63.

Keizer, G. (2010, May 20). 1-in-5 U.S. consumers plan to buy Apple's iPad. *SFGate*. Retrieved May 20, 2010, from http://www.sfgate.com/cgi-bin/article.cgi?f=/g/a/2010/05/20/urnidgns852573C4006938800025772900 5E6546.DTL.

Weyhrich, S. (2008, April 8). Apple II history chap 1. Retrieved May 17, 2010, from http://apple2history.org/history/ah01.html.

Information Systems Today

In 1959, Peter Drucker predicted that information and of information technology (IT) would become increasingly important, and at that point, over four decades ago, he coined the term **knowledge worker.** Knowledge workers are typically professionals who are relatively well educated and who create, modify, and/or synthesize knowledge as a fundamental part of their jobs.

Drucker's predictions about knowledge workers were very accurate. As he predicted, they are generally paid better than their prior agricultural and industrial counterparts; they rely on and are empowered by formal education, yet they often also possess valuable real-world skills; they are continually learning how to do their jobs better; they have much better career opportunities and far more bargaining power than workers ever had before; they make up about a quarter of the workforce in the United States and in other developed nations; and their numbers are rising quickly.

Drucker also predicted that, with the growth in the number of knowledge workers and with their rise in importance and leadership, a **knowledge society** would emerge. He reasoned that, given the importance of education and learning to knowledge workers and the firms that need them, education would become the cornerstone of the knowledge society. Possessing knowledge, he argued, would be as important as possessing land, labor, or capital (if not more so) (see Figure 1.2). Indeed, research shows that people equipped to prosper in the knowledge society, such as those with a college education, earn far more on average than people without a college education, and that gap is increasing. In fact, the most recent information from the U.S. Census Bureau (2008 data) reinforces the value of a college education: workers 18 and over with a bachelor's degree earn an average of $57,181 a year, while those with a high school diploma earn $31,286. Workers with a master's degree make an average of $70,186, and those without a high school diploma average $21,484. Additionally, getting a college degree will qualify you for many jobs that would not be available to you otherwise and will distinguish you from other job candidates. Finally, a college degree is often a requirement to qualify for career advancement and promotion opportunities once you do get that job.

People generally agree that Drucker was accurate about knowledge workers and the evolution of society. While people have settled on Drucker's term "knowledge worker," there are many alternatives to the term "knowledge society." Others have referred to this phenomenon as the knowledge economy, new economy, the digital society, the network era, the Internet era, and other names. We simply refer to this as the *digital world*. All these ideas have in common the premise that information and related technologies and systems have become very important to us and that knowledge workers are vital.

Some have argued, however, that there is a downside to being a knowledge worker and to living in the digital world. For example, some have argued that knowledge workers will be the first to be replaced by automation with information technology. Others have argued that in the new economy there is a *digital divide,* where those with access to information technology have great advantages over those without access to information technology (discussed later in this chapter).

To be sure, there is a downside to overreliance on information technology, but one thing is for certain: Knowledge workers and information technologies are now critical to the success of

FIGURE 1.2

In the knowledge society, information has become as important as—and many feel more important than—land, labor, and capital resources.

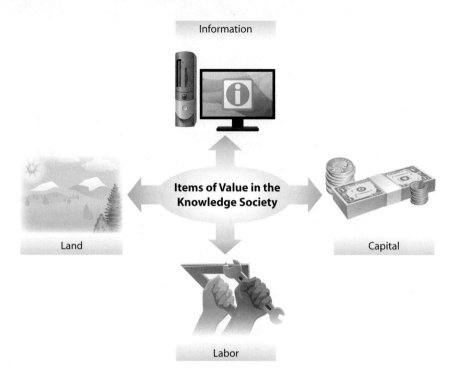

modern organizations, economies, and societies. What are some of the characteristics of the digital world? This is examined next.

Characteristics of the Digital World

Computers are the core component of information systems. Over the past decade, the advent of powerful, relatively inexpensive, easy-to-use computers has had a major impact on business. To see this impact, look around your school or place of work. At your school, you may register for classes online, use e-mail to communicate with fellow students and your instructors, and complete or submit assignments on networked PCs. At work, you may use a PC for e-mail and many other tasks. Your paychecks are probably generated by computer and automatically deposited in your checking account via high-speed networks. Even in your spare time, information technology is ubiquitous: you use social networking sites like Facebook to stay connected with your friends and family, you watch videos on YouTube, you upload pictures taken with your cell phone or digital camera to picture sharing sites like Flickr, and you use your smart phone for playing games, sending e-mails, or even reading books. Chances are that each year you see more information technology than you did the year before, and this technology is a more fundamental and important part of your learning and work than ever before.

When you stop and think about it, it is easy to see why information technology is important. Increasing global competitiveness has forced companies to find ways to be better and to do things less expensively. The answer for many firms continues to be to use information systems to do things better, faster, and cheaper. Using global telecommunications networks, companies can more easily integrate their operations to access new markets for their products and services as well as access a large pool of talented labor in countries with lower wages. In the next section, we will discuss how information technologies became pervasive throughout our lives and throughout society.

In his book *The Third Wave,* futurist Alvin Toffler describes three distinct phases, or "waves of change," that have taken place in the past or are presently taking place within the world's civilizations (see Figure 1.3). The first wave—a civilization based on agriculture and handwork— was a comparatively primitive stage that replaced hunter-gatherer cultures and lasted for thousands of years. The second wave of change—the industrial revolution—overlapped with the first wave. The industrial revolution began in Great Britain toward the end of the eighteenth century and continued over the next 150 years, moving society from a predominantly agrarian culture to the urbanized machine age. Where once families supported themselves by working the land or handcrafting items for sale or trade, now mothers, fathers, and children left home to work in factories. Steel mills, textile factories, and eventually automobile assembly lines replaced farming and handwork as the principal source of family income.

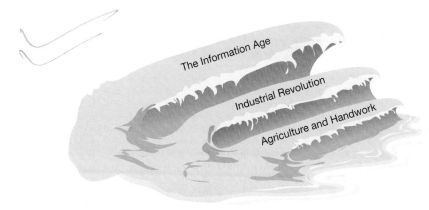

FIGURE 1.3

The information age is the biggest wave of change.

As the industrial revolution progressed, not only did occupations change to accommodate the mechanized society, but so did educational, business, social, and religious institutions. On an individual level, punctuality, obedience, and the ability to perform repetitive tasks became qualities to be instilled and valued in children in public schools and, ultimately, in workers. Although industrialization has brought about many positive changes, technology introduced challenges for individuals, societies, and the environment. Many felt threatened by these changes, and some—called **Luddites**—resorted to protesting against the technology; some others even resorted to destroying the technology that they felt threatened their livelihoods.

The Information Age Arrives

In a much shorter period of time than it took for civilization to progress past the first wave, societies worldwide moved from the machine age into the **information age**—a period of change Toffler has dubbed the "third wave." As the third wave gained speed, information became the currency of the realm. For thousands of years, from primitive times through the Middle Ages, information, or the body of knowledge known to that point, was limited. It was transmitted verbally within families, clans, and villages, from person to person and generation to generation. Then came Johannes Gutenberg's invention of the printing press with movable type in the middle of the fifteenth century, and a tremendous acceleration occurred in the amount and kinds of information available to populations (see Figure 1.4). Now knowledge could be imparted in written form and sometimes came from distant locations. Information could be saved, absorbed, debated, and written about in publications, thus adding to the exploding data pool.

FIGURE 1.4

The printing press gave birth to the information age.

Shutterstock

WHEN THINGS GO WRONG

Failure: The Path to Success?

Management consultant Tom Peters, author or coauthor of 10 international best-sellers, including *In Search of Excellence*, *Thriving on Chaos*, *The Pursuit of Wow!*, and his latest, *Re-Imagine! Business Excellence in a Disruptive Age*, often tells business managers that a company's survival may depend on those employees who fail over and over again as they try new ideas. There's little that is more important to tomorrow's managers than failure, Peters maintains.

Apparently Apple Computers lives by Peters's philosophy. In January 2008, to help celebrate 24 years of the Mac, first introduced to consumers in 1984, *Wired* magazine recalled some of Apple's more infamous failures.

One of Apple's most visible flops was the Newton, actually the name of a newly conceived operating system that stuck to the product as a whole. The Newton, which Apple promised would "reinvent personal computing," fell far short of its hype when it was introduced in 1993 as a not-so-revolutionary PDA. The Newton was on the market for six years—a relatively long time for an unsuccessful product—but one of Steve Jobs's first acts when he returned to Apple's helm in 1997 was to cut the Newton Systems Group.

Other Apple product failures include the following:

- The Pippin, introduced in 1993, an inexpensive game player/network computer that couldn't compete with Nintendo's N64 or the Sony PlayStation.
- The TAM (Twentieth Anniversary Macintosh), which debuted in 1997 and lasted only a year. The sleek design was contemporary and attractive, but the machine was panned as overpriced and underpowered.
- The Macintosh television, of which only 10,000 units were produced, from 1993 to 1994. It tanked because it was incapable of showing television feeds in a desktop window.
- The PowerMac G4 Cube, an eight- by eight- by eight-inch designer machine. It failed because it was seen as

overpriced and needed a separate monitor (as opposed to the popular iMac series).

- The Apple IIc (the "c" is for "compact"), which was meant to be the world's first portable computer and came complete with carrying case. It lacked internal expansion slots and direct access to the motherboard, however, and thus was less popular than other Apple II models that allowed users to upgrade.
- The puck mouse that came with the iMac G3. Apple made the mouse popular but miscued when it expected consumers to adapt to this too-small, awkward-to-control device that users often mistakenly used upside down. The puck was soon replaced with the Mighty Mouse—a consumer favorite.
- The Lisa, introduced in 1983, was intended for business use; but its whopping $9,995 price tag (more than $20,000 in current dollars) made it too rich for most businesses, which could buy IBM PCs at much lower prices. The Lisa was retired in 1986 after the Mac had captured consumers' attention.

Apple continues to produce innovative products that consumers stand in line to get. In the spring of 2010, many watched the launch of the Apple iPad to see if it would be the next success or if it would flop for the company. Like the other products in the list, time will tell if the iPad survives. Although Apple's failures are often cited by its competitors, the company has proved Peters right time and time again: Any company without an interesting list of failures probably isn't trying hard enough.

Based on:

Claburn, T. (2010, April 8). Can 300,000 iPads equal failure? *Information Week*. Retrieved April 20, 2010, from http://www.informationweek.com/news/security/management/showArticle.jhtml?articleID=224202035.

Gardiner, B. (2008, January 24). Learning from failure: Apple's most notorious flops. *Wired*. Retrieved April 20, 2010, from http://www.wired.com/gadgets/mac/multimedia/2008/01/gallery_apple_flops.

Most modern-day high school and university students have grown up in a computerized world. If by some chance they do not know how to operate a computer by the time they graduate from high school, they soon acquire computer skills, because in today's work world, knowing how to use a computer—called **computer literacy** (or information literacy)—can mean the difference between being employed and being unemployed. Knowing how to use a computer can also open up myriad sources of information to those who have learned how to use the computer as a device to gather, store, organize, and otherwise process information. In fact, some fear that the information age will not provide the same advantages to "information haves"—those computer-literate individuals who have unlimited access to information—and "information have-nots"—those with limited or no computer access or skills.

Shutterstock

FIGURE 1.5

Computers are used in countless types of jobs and industries, including the medical field.

The first computer-related occupations have evolved as computers became more sophisticated and more widely used. Where once we thought of computer workers as primarily programmers, data entry clerks, systems analysts, or computer repairpersons, today many more job categories in virtually all industries, from accounting to the medical field (see Figure 1.5), involve the use of computers. In fact, today there are few occupations where computers are not somehow in use. Computers manage air traffic, perform medical tests, monitor investment portfolios, control construction machinery, and more. Since they are especially adept at processing large amounts of data, they are used extensively by universities and public schools, in businesses of all sizes, and in all levels and departments of government. Engineers, architects, interior designers, and artists use special purpose computer-aided design programs. Musicians play computerized instruments, and they write and record songs with the help of computers. Not only do we use computers at work, we also use them in our personal lives. We teach our children on them, manage our finances, do our taxes, compose letters and term papers, create greeting cards, send and receive electronic mail, surf the Internet, purchase products, and play games on them. With the increasing use of computers in all areas of society, many argue that being computer literate—knowing how to use a computer and use certain applications—is not sufficient in today's world; rather, **computer fluency**—the ability to independently learn new technologies as they emerge and assess their impact on your work and life—is what will set you apart in the future.

Today, in most developed societies, information technologies have become pervasive—information technologies are in fact used throughout society (see the end of this chapter for a discussion of issues surrounding the digital divide). The development of sophisticated Web technologies has brought about a fundamental shift in types of information technologies that are being used; whereas traditionally each user would install applications for various tasks—from composing documents to listening to music—on his or her computer, Web technologies enable using the Internet as the platform for applications, a phenomenon termed Web 2.0. Now, much of the functionality previously offered by applications installed on a computer is offered by applications "in the cloud," accessed via your Web browser. In fact, many regard **cloud computing** as the beginning of the "fourth wave," where not only the applications but also the data reside in the cloud, to be accessed anytime from anywhere. A good example of cloud computing are various services offered by Google, such as Gmail (e-mail), Google docs (word processing), or Google Calendar, all of which are accessed via a Web browser, freeing users from the task of installing or updating traditional desktop applications or worrying about storing or backing up data.

In addition to changing the way people work and interact, information technology has also enabled *globalization,* the integration of economies throughout the world, fundamentally changing how not only people but also organizations and countries interact. In the next section, we examine the evolution of globalization and the effects on our daily lives.

FIGURE 1.6

Visible economic, cultural, and
technological changes are fueled
by globalization.

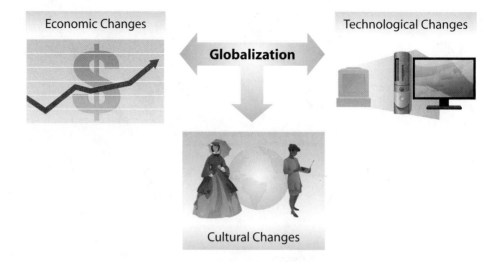

Evolution of Globalization

You can see the effects of globalization in many ways, such as the greater international movement of
commodities, money, information, and labor, as well as the development of technologies, standards,
and processes to facilitate this movement (see Figure 1.6). Specifically, a more global and competitive world includes visible economic, cultural, and technological changes, including the following:

- *Economic Changes.* Increases in international trade, in the development of global
  financial systems and currency, and in the outsourcing of labor
- *Cultural Changes.* Increases in the availability of multiculturalism through television and
  movies; the frequency of international travel and tourism, and immigration; the availability
  of ethnic foods and restaurants; and the frequency of worldwide fads and phenomena such
  as Facebook, FarmVille, Twitter, and YouTube
- *Technological Changes.* The development of low-cost computing platforms and communication technologies; the availability of low-cost communication systems such as e-mail,
  Skype, and instant messaging; the ubiquitous nature of a low-cost global telecommunications
  infrastructure like the Internet; and the enforcement of global patent and copyright laws to
  spur further innovation

Through the convergence of economics and culture, fueled by a robust global technology infrastructure, the world has forever changed.

Over the past centuries, **globalization**—the integration of economies throughout the world,
enabled by innovation and technological progress (International Monetary Fund, 2002)—has
come a long way, from separate nation-states on different continents to what we see today, a world
where people and companies can enjoy worldwide communication and collaboration, with fewer
and fewer barriers. In his book *The World Is Flat*, *New York Times* foreign affairs columnist
Thomas L. Friedman has characterized the evolution of globalization as having three distinct
phases (see Figure 1.7), differing in the focal point and primary drivers of this evolution (see Table 1.1
for an overview of each phase). While it had taken humankind thousands of years to discover that
the world is round, Friedman argues that forces of globalization are now creating a "flat," level
playing field such that competitors in many areas of the world now have equal opportunities to
access the global marketplace. As technologies have evolved and diffused broadly throughout the
world, the pace and scope of globalization have accelerated. Next, we examine this evolution.

Globalization 1.0

The first stage, termed **Globalization 1.0** by Friedman, began in the late fifteenth century and
ended about 1800. During those times, for example, India was famous for its wealth of spices and
other goods; however, getting there by traveling east was very cumbersome and dangerous, as no
sea route had been discovered until the end of the fifteenth century. Even then, sailing to India
going east included circumnavigating the entire continent of Africa, including a dangerous
passage around the Cape of Good Hope (South Africa). When Christopher Columbus set sail in

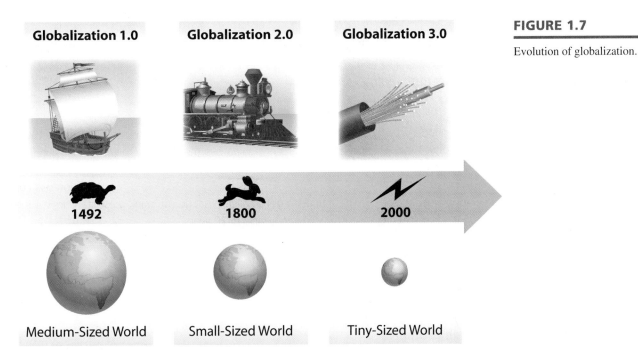

FIGURE 1.7

Evolution of globalization.

August 1492 to discover a westward route to India, he was convinced, contrary to popular belief at that time, that the earth was round. However, instead of discovering a new route to India, he discovered the Americas, opening up new areas for discovery and new sources for resources.

During Globalization 1.0, mainly European countries were globalizing, attempting to extend their territories into the New World. Power—from domesticated horses (for transportation and agriculture), wind (for grinding grain and sailing), and, in the late stages, steam (then used primarily for mining)—was the primary driver of this stage of globalization. Collectively, this evolution brought continents closer together, shrinking the world "from size large to size medium." During those times, industries changed slowly, and any change took generations. While many industries (such as the apparel industry) changed, most people didn't notice how it affected their lives because of the slow pace of change.

Globalization 2.0

In 1800, **Globalization 2.0** started, lasting until 2000 (being interrupted only by the Great Depression and the two world wars). During Globalization 2.0, the world shrunk from "size medium to size small," as companies (rather than just countries) started to globalize. While people were constantly innovating, changes still took quite some time. For example, it took more than a generation before people felt the effects of the industrial revolution. In the early stages of Globalization 2.0, the steam engine led to falling costs for the transportation of goods, both on land using railroads and on sea using steamships. Technological innovations such as the telegraph and, later, telephones, PCs, satellites, and early forms of the Internet tremendously reduced telecommunication costs. The reduction of transportation and telecommunication costs spurred a growing market for products and labor. However, it was still mainly Americans and Europeans driving globalization.

TABLE 1.1 Phases of Globalization

Globalization Phase	Time	Primary Entities Globalizing	Regions Globalizing
1.0	1492–1800	Countries	Europe and America
2.0	1800–2000	Companies	Europe and America
3.0	2000–now	Individuals and small groups	Worldwide

NET STATS

Worldwide Internet Usage

In January 2010, 14.4 percent of the world's active Internet users were located in North America. As the rest of the world is getting online, this is about half of the nearly 30 percent share of 2004. Overall, it was estimated that there were over 1.8 billion active Internet users worldwide in early 2010: over 764 million users in Asia, 425 million in Europe, and 259 million in North America (about 220 million active users in the United States alone) (see Table 1.2). The Internet is most heavily used in North America, with 76.2 percent of the total population going online; Africa has the lowest penetration (percentage of a region's population using the Internet) with 8.7 percent. China has the most users with 384 million, followed by the United States. As the world continues to embrace the Internet, it is inevitable that the U.S. proportion will continue to get smaller. What do you think these statistics will look like in 10 years? In 20 years?

Based on:

Anonymous. (n.d.). World Internet usage statistics. Retrieved May 20, 2010, from http://www.internetworldstats.com/stats.htm.

TABLE 1.2 World Internet Usage Estimates

World Regions	Population (2009 estimates)	Internet Usage, Estimate	% Population (penetration)	Usage (% of world)
Africa/Middle East	1.1 billion	144 million	13.1%	8.0%
Asia	3.8 billion	764 million	20.1%	42.4%
Europe	800 million	426 million	53.2%	23.6%
North America	341 million	260 million	76.2%	14.4%
Latin America/Caribbean	587 million	187 million	31.8%	10.4%
Oceania/Australia	35 million	21 million	60.0%	1.2%
World total	6.7 billion	1.8 billion	26.9%	100.0%

Note: Internet usage and world population statistics were updated for December 31, 2009.
Source: Based on http://www.internetworldstats.com/stats.htm.

Globalization 3.0

Around 2000, **Globalization 3.0** began, with individuals and small groups from virtually every nation joining the globalization movement, shrinking the world from "size small to size tiny." Not only did the world shrink, but this shrinking brought with it an even faster pace of change. People now feel the effects of industry changes within decades, and new industries have emerged that no one would have imagined only a few decades ago. For example, Google, the company that now dominates the search engine market and is one of the world's largest companies, was only incorporated in 1998. In the next sections, we discuss the factors enabling Globalization 3.0 and how these factors have forever transformed the world.

Key Factors Enabling Globalization 3.0 In the last decade of the twentieth century, a number of technological and societal changes took place, ushering in Globalization 3.0. In his book, Friedman provides a list of 10 forces enabling the transition from Globalization 2.0 to Globalization 3.0. While the list of enablers could be extended almost endlessly (or be debated as to their ultimate significance), we focus on those discussed by Friedman given their broad popularity.

Enabler 1: November 9, 1989—The Fall of the Berlin Wall. The fall of the Berlin Wall marked the end of the Cold War between communist and capitalist countries and the breakup of the Eastern bloc, freeing millions of people. At once, people in many former communist countries could enjoy greater freedoms. For many companies, this meant a tremendous increase in potential customers as well as access to a huge, talented labor pool in the former Eastern bloc countries. Around the same time, Microsoft released the first version of the Windows operating

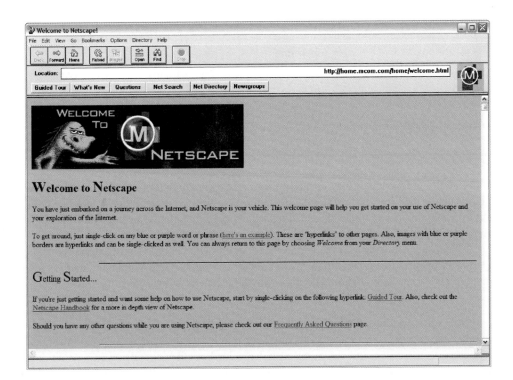

FIGURE 1.8

The Netscape browser was a
cornerstone in giving individuals
easy access to the Internet.

Source: © Netscape Communications
Corporation. Used with permissions.

system, which over time became the de facto world standard in PC operating systems, enabling
people from all over the world to use a common computing platform.

Enabler 2: August 9, 1995—The Release of the Netscape Web Browser. The second big
flattener was the Internet browser—the "killer app" that enabled everyone who had a computer
and a modem to view Web pages (see Figure 1.8). A company called Netscape released the first
mainstream Web browser in 1994 and went public on August 9, 1995. In addition to opening up
the possibilities of the Internet for the general public, Netscape helped set a standard for the
transport and display of data that other companies and individuals could build on, making the
Internet even easier to use and more powerful than ever.

In the final years of Globalization 2.0, companies supplying the network infrastructure saw
the need to provide more and faster connections, leading to a tremendous *overinvestment* in
telecommunications infrastructure, such as fiber-optic cable, which is used to transmit very large
amounts of data at the speed of light. With the bursting of the dot-com bubble, the plummeting
demand for telecommunications infrastructure (that had been installed just a few years before)
led to an oversupply, causing infrastructure providers to fail; and much of the infrastructure had
to be sold for a fraction of the cost. The most notable long-term consequence was falling telecommunications costs, enabling the collaboration of individuals and small groups that we see today.

Enabler 3: Work Flow Software. What Friedman broadly calls **work flow software** is a variety
of software applications that allow for software-to-software interaction. Whereas the Netscape
browser enabled people to access the Internet, other standards allowed different companies all over
the world to communicate seamlessly. For example, eXtensible Markup Language (see Chapter 8,
"Improving Supply Chains and Strengthening Customer Relationships Using Enterprise Information
Systems") enabled computer programs to "talk" to other programs so that, for example, a computer
in an automobile manufacturing plant could automatically order a new shipment of windshield wipers
from a supplier once the inventory fell to a certain level. This and a variety of other transactions could
be handled without human intervention, thanks to standards allowing different computers from different computer manufacturers to communicate even though running different operating systems.

Enabler 4: Uploading. The fourth enabler of Globalization 3.0 Friedman calls **uploading,** or
the ability of individuals and companies to actively participate in content generation on the Web,
enabling everyone to be a producer of information instead of merely a consumer. This enabler encompasses open source software, wikis, and blogs (see Chapter 5, "Enhancing Collaboration
Using Web 2.0," for a more detailed discussion of these Web 2.0 tools).

TABLE 1.3 Outsourcing, Offshoring, and Offshore Outsourcing

Concept	Description	Example
Outsourcing	Business processes performed by another company	Payroll processing by a specialized provider, such as ADP
Offshoring	Business processes performed in-house but in a different country	Boeing having aircraft design work performed at a Boeing design center in Moscow, Russia
Offshore outsourcing	Business processes performed by another company in a different country	A U.S. company having software developed by an Indian software firm such as Wipro

The ability to upload has been a catalyst for the growing popularity of open source software products such as the Linux operating system, the Firefox Web browser, or the OpenOffice.org Productivity Suite. Another example of uploading is the successful online encyclopedia *Wikipedia,* the content of which can be created and updated by anyone with an Internet connection. The term **wiki** refers to Web sites allowing users to add, remove, or edit content and is now often used synonymously with open source dictionaries. Within a wiki community like Wikipedia, there is a huge number of people throughout the world reviewing all recent additions and edits; flaws in the content are usually quickly detected and fixed.

Enabler 5: Outsourcing. **Outsourcing** is the moving of business processes or tasks (such as accounting or security) to another company (outsourcing is discussed in detail shortly). The tremendous decrease in communication costs has added another dimension to outsourcing, as now companies can outsource business processes on a global scale (also referred to as **offshore outsourcing**). For example, companies commonly outsource customer service functions (such as call centers) or accounting to companies specializing in that service. Often, companies located in countries such as India can provide these services much cheaper because of lower labor costs.

Enabler 6: Offshoring. As opposed to outsourcing, **offshoring** refers to having certain functions performed by the same company but in a different country (see Table 1.3). For example, aircraft manufacturer Boeing offshored design work (such as computational fluid dynamics) for its new 787 Dreamliner aircraft to Russia, making use of the availability of highly skilled aeronautical engineers.

When China officially joined the World Trade Organization in 2001, it agreed to follow certain accepted standards of trade and fair business practices. Now, instead of just offshoring production to Mexico or Canada, companies set up entire factories in emerging countries in order to mass-produce goods at a fraction of the price it would cost to produce these goods in the United States, Canada, or even in Mexico (see Figure 1.9).

FIGURE 1.9

Companies are offshoring production to overseas countries (such as China) to utilize talented workers or reduce costs.

Shutterstock

Enabler 7: Supply Chaining. Supply chaining refers to the use of information systems to tightly integrate retailers, their suppliers, and their customers. One of the best-known examples is the supply chain of the giant retailer Walmart. Walmart leverages the other enablers to create a seamless supply chain (see Chapter 7) to get the goods from the manufacturers to the customers. Not only does Walmart receive the information about its stores' sales, but it also transmits this vital data to the manufacturers so that they can anticipate when the next shipment is needed, how their products sell, and what products may need improvement to increase sales.

Enabler 8: In-Sourcing. The eighth major enabler is **in-sourcing,** which refers to the delegation of a company's logistics operations to a subcontractor that specializes in that operation, or to transferring a previously outsourced function to an in-house department. For example, United Parcel Service (UPS) is becoming a leading in-sourcing provider. In addition to providing their traditional service offering of delivering packages to worldwide destinations, UPS started offering complete supply chain solutions to companies. Traditionally, online retailers, such as Nike .com, would handle all online customer orders themselves. However, through an in-sourcing arrangement, UPS manages Nike's warehouse and handles product packing and shipping as well as payment collection from customers so that Nike can concentrate on its core competencies, such as the design of new athletic shoes.

Enabler 9: In-Forming. For the individual, **in-forming** allows individuals to utilize powerful search engines on the Internet, such as Google, Yahoo!, or Bing, to build their "own personal supply chain of information, knowledge, and entertainment" (Friedman, 2007, p. 178).

Enabler 10: The Steroids. The last group of enablers, which Friedman (2007) calls "the steroids," are technologies that make different forms of collaboration "digital, mobile, virtual, and personal" (p. 187). This group of technologies amplifies all the enablers discussed previously. By digitizing content—books, music, photographs, or virtually any business document—people can collaborate easier than ever before, benefiting from lightning-fast transmission of information. Similarly, the collaboration becomes virtual in that people using these technologies never have to think about the underlying standards or technologies enabling the collaboration; greater mobility enables collaboration from a wide variety of locations without being tied to one's office or desk. Finally, certain enablers, such as in-forming, are available to everyone with an Internet connection, making the new forms of collaboration very personal.

Triple Convergence Although any one of these enablers may be powerful alone, it's their *convergence* that makes Globalization 3.0 possible; Friedman refers to this as a "triple convergence." First, between 2000 and 2003, the enablers started working together, making new forms of collaboration possible, such as the sharing of knowledge and work without regard to distance or geography and soon even language. Second, this convergence enabled the move from vertical to horizontal collaboration, facilitating value creation and innovation. For example, employees of a global organization represent a vast global pool of specialists that can be assembled (and disassembled) as needed. Finally, people from countries such as China, India, or the former Soviet Union could enter the playing field and connect and collaborate with others all over the world, enabling more people than ever to participate in new forms of collaboration. However, different countries and regions are at various stages of participation in the global village, so clearly we are only at the *beginning* of Globalization 3.0—the deep and pervasive impacts of this phase are in their infancy.

The Rise of Outsourcing

Many organizations that are **downsizing**, or rightsizing as some call it, are looking for ways to streamline business functions and, in some cases, to slash costs and replace people. Often, these organizations try to use the IS function and technology as the lever for simultaneously shrinking the organization by reducing personnel head count and making the organization more productive (i.e., doing more with less). Although this approach may not be fair for the people who lose their jobs, many firms are forced to do this to remain competitive and, in some cases, to continue to exist.

COMING ATTRACTIONS

Real-Time Language Translation

If you ever watched *Star Trek*, you may have wished for a universal language translator as used in the movie. In reality, such a universal language translator maybe is not so far away from us. In July 2009, Sakhr Software and Dial Directions introduced a new iPhone app designed to translate Arabic speech into English and vice versa. This application promises to be extremely useful for diplomats, aid workers, and troops who don't speak Arabic.

The application works just like Google's iPhone app. You simply hold down a button and speak aloud a sentence in English or Arabic. The software then beams a resulting voice sample to an online application, where voice recognition algorithms parse digital data into raw text. The online application then returns the translation, which can be read or played back on your device.

More recently, the search giant Google told the British daily *The Times* that they are working on a new translation technology that can convert spoken words into a different language in real time. The idea behind this application is to allow users to easily communicate in other languages using a smart phone. Using Google Translate technology, along with the voice recognition system used within Android smartphones, the system will "listen" to the speaker until it understands the full meaning of the words/phrases being spoken. Once translated by Google's servers, the system sends a voice translation to the person at the other end of the line. According to Google, the technology could be ready within a few years.

Despite "huge progress recently," it's still difficult to recognize various accents, explained Franz Och, Google's head of translation services. Google aims to solve this problem by having the software learn the users' style of talking.

Based on:

Ionescu, D. (2010, February 8). Google's next venture: Universal translator. *PC World*. Retrieved March 20, 2010, from http://www.pcworld.com/article/188777/googles_next_venture_universal_translator.html.

Zibreg, C. (2009, July 2). The future is now: Star Trek-like language translator debuts on the iPhone. *geek.com*. Retrieved March 20, 2010, from http://www.geek.com/articles/mobile/the-future-is-now-star-trek-like-language-translator-debuts-on-the-iphone-2009072.

Similarly, as discussed previously, one phenomenon that has seen a huge increase because of the decrease in telecommunication costs is *outsourcing,* both onshore (domestically) and offshore. Traditionally, organizations (domestically) outsourced many of the more routine jobs or entire business functions, such as accounting, to other companies. In 2008, the global market for outsourcing was $326 billion, and was projected to be worth more than $412 billion by the end of 2010. Companies are choosing to outsource business activities for a variety of reasons; the most important reasons include the following (King, 2003):

- To reduce or control costs
- To free up internal resources
- To gain access to world-class capabilities
- To increase revenue potential of the organization
- To reduce time to market
- To increase process efficiencies
- To be able to focus on core activities
- To compensate for a lack of specific capabilities or skills

Early examples of offshore outsourcing included the manufacturing of goods in countries such as Mexico to take advantage of lower wages and less stringent regulations. Then, in the years leading to Globalization 3.0, companies started to introduce offshore outsourcing of *services,* starting with the development of computer software and the staffing of customer support and telemarketing call centers. Today, a wide variety of services—ranging from telephone support to tax returns—are candidates for offshore outsourcing to different countries, be it Ireland, China, or India. Even highly specialized services, such as reading X-rays by skilled radiologists, are outsourced by U.S. hospitals to doctors around the globe, often while doctors in the United States are sleeping. However, companies operating in the digital world have to carefully choose offshore outsourcing locations, considering factors such as English proficiency, salaries, or geopolitical risk. While countries such as India remain popular for offshore outsourcing, other formerly popular countries (such as Singapore, Canada, or Ireland) are declining because of rising salaries. With these shifts, outsourcers are constantly looking at nascent and emerging countries such as Bulgaria, Egypt, Ghana, or Vietnam, each of which has some particular benefits to offer (see Table 1.4). Obviously, organizations have to weigh the potential benefits (e.g., cost savings) and drawbacks (e.g., higher geopolitical risk or less experience) of offshore outsourcing to a particular country.

Fueled by Globalization 2.0 and 3.0, outsourcing is now a fact of life, and no matter which industry you're in, you will likely feel the effects of outsourcing (see Table 1.5). With Globalization 3.0, individuals will have to ask themselves how they can seize the global opportunities and how they will be able to compete with individuals from all over the world who might be able to do their job at the same quality but at a lower cost.

TABLE 1.4 Popular Offshore Outsourcing Destinations

Country	Ranking	English Proficiency	Yearly Entry-Level Programmer Salary (in U.S. $1,000)	Relative Geopolitical Risk
Asia				
India	Leading	Very good	5–10	Moderate
China	Up and coming	Poor	5–10	Moderate
Malaysia	Up and coming	Fair	10–15	Moderate
Philippines	Up and coming	Very good	5–10	High
Vietnam	Nascent	Fair	<5	Moderate
Thailand	Nascent	Poor	5–10	Moderate
Singapore	Declining	Fair	15–20	Low
Europe				
Czech Republic	Up and coming	Good	10–15	Moderate
Poland	Up and coming	Good	10–15	Moderate
Hungary	Up and coming	Poor	10–15	Moderate
Russia	Up and coming	Poor	10–15	Moderate
Romania	Emerging	Good	5–10	Moderate
Bulgaria	Emerging	Fair	5–10	Moderate
Ukraine	Emerging	Poor	5–10	Moderate
Ireland	Declining	Excellent	>20	Low
Middle East				
Egypt	Emerging	Very good	<5	High
Israel	Declining	Very good	15–20	Moderate
Africa				
South Africa	Challenging	Very good	10–15	Moderate
Ghana	Nascent	Very good	5–10	High
The Americas				
Mexico	Up and coming	Poor	10–15	Moderate
Costa Rica	Emerging	Very good	10–15	Moderate
Brazil	Emerging	Poor	5–10	High
Argentina	Nascent	Fair	5–10	Moderate
Canada	Declining	Excellent	>20	Low

Source: Based on Overby (2006).

TABLE 1.5 Examples of Offshoring and Offshore Outsourcing

Industry	Examples	Offshoring/Offshore Outsourcing
Airlines	British Airways moves customer relations and passenger revenue accounting to India.	Offshoring
	Delta outsources reservation functions to India.	Offshore outsourcing
Airplane design	Parts of Airbus and Boeing airplanes are designed and engineered in Moscow, Russia.	Offshoring
Consulting	McKinsey moves global research division to India.	Offshoring
	Ernst & Young moves part of its tax preparation to India.	Offshoring
Insurance	British firm Prudential PLC moves call center operations to India.	Offshoring
Investment banking	J.P. Morgan moves investment research to India.	Offshoring
Retail banking	Worldwide banking group HSBC moves back-office operations to India.	Offshoring
Credit card operations	American Express moves a variety of services to India.	Offshoring
Government	The Greater London Authority outsources the development of a road toll system to India.	Offshore outsourcing
Telecommunications	T-mobile outsources part of its content development and portal configuration to India.	Offshore outsourcing

Source: Based on http://www.ebstrategy.com (2006).

However, offshore outsourcing does not always prove to be the best approach for an organization. For example, only about a decade ago, German companies manufacturing highly specialized products such as large crankshafts, ship cranes, or road-paving equipment offshored parts of their operations to Eastern European countries in order to cut costs. However, the cost savings have turned out to be negligible because of added overhead, such as customs, shipping, or training, and quality problems ran rampant, leading to a reversal of this trend. Today, many companies are moving production back to Germany in order to better control production quality and costs. Similarly, *InformationWeek,* a leading publication targeting business IT users, found that 20 percent of the 500 most innovative companies in terms of using IT took back previously offshored projects. Another recent trend is **nearshoring**—the use of locations closer to the home country in terms of geographical, political, linguistic, economic, or cultural distance. Nearshoring is thus the reversal of offshoring, such that, for example, U.S. companies move work from India back to Mexico or British Columbia in order to address some of the challenges associated with overseas offshoring destinations. Similarly, the noted technology author Nicholas Carr recently suggested that cloud computing may contribute to a decline in outsourcing; because much of an IT outsourcer's business is built around managing complex internal systems, a shift to a simpler cloud-based IT infrastructure (see Chapter 3, "Managing the Information Systems Infrastructure and Services") should reduce the need for outsourcers.

The next sections will outline some opportunities made possible by increasing globalization.

Opportunities of Operating in the Digital World

Clearly, globalization has opened up many opportunities, brought about by falling transportation and telecommunication costs. Today, shipping a bottle of wine from Australia to Europe merely costs a few cents, and using the Internet, people can make PC-to-PC phone calls around the globe for free. To a large extent fueled by television and other forms of media, the increasing globalization has moved cultures closer together—to the point where people now talk about a "global village." Customers in all corners of the world can receive television programming from other countries or watch movies produced in Hollywood, Munich, or Mumbai (sometimes called "Bollywood"), helping to create a shared understanding about forms of behavior or interaction, desirable goods or services, or even forms of government. Over the past decades, the world has seen a democratization of many nations, enabling millions of people to enjoy freedoms they had never experienced before. All this makes operating in the digital world much easier than ever before.

Opportunities for Reaching New Markets After the fall of communism, new markets opened up for countless companies. The fall of communism in Eastern bloc countries such as Poland, Romania, and the former Soviet Union enabled the sales of products to literally millions of new customers.

Opportunities of a Global Workforce With the decrease in communication costs, companies can now draw on a large pool of skilled professionals from all over the globe. Many countries, such as Russia, China, and India, offer high-quality education, leading to an ample supply of well-trained people at low cost. While enrollment in the sciences or engineering is dropping in the United States, other countries are producing engineering graduates at an unprecedented pace (Mallaby, 2006). In 2005, for example, 200,000 young engineers graduated from Indian universities, while the United States produced only about a third as many; likewise, Europe produced only about half the number of India. Some countries are actively building entire industries around certain competencies, such as software development or tax preparation in India and call centers in Ireland. For companies operating in the digital world, this can be a huge opportunity, as they can "shop" for qualified, low-cost labor all over the world. On the other hand, the consulting company McKinsey believes that out of the 2.5 million Indian university graduates, only 10 to 25 percent (depending on the field of study) are considered employable by multinational companies, mainly because of differences in the quality of the education and the differences in language skills (Farrell, Kaka, & Stürze, 2005).

Challenges of Operating in the Digital World

The factors discussed in this section translate into a number of direct opportunities for companies, including greater and larger markets to sell products and larger pools of qualified labor. Nevertheless, while globalization has brought tremendous opportunities to companies, they also face a number of daunting challenges when operating in the global marketplace.

Traditionally, companies acquired resources and produced and sold goods or services all within the same country. Such domestic businesses did not have to deal with any challenges posed by globalization but also could not leverage the host of opportunities. The challenges faced can be broadly classified into governmental, geoeconomic, and cultural challenges. See Table 1.6 for a summary of the challenges of operating in the digital world.

TABLE 1.6 Challenges of Operating in the Digital World

Broad Challenges	Specific Challenges	Examples
Governmental	Political system	Market versus planned economy; political instability
	Regulatory	Taxes and tariffs; embargoes; import and export regulations
	Data sharing	European Union Data Protection Directive
	Standards	Differences in measurement units, bar code standards, address conventions, academic degrees, and so on
	Internet access and individual freedom	Internet censorship in various countries
Geoeconomic	Time zone differences	Videoconferences across different time zones
	Infrastructure-related reliability	Differences in network infrastructures throughout the world
	Differences in welfare	Migration and political instability caused by welfare differences between rich and poor countries
	Demographic	Aging population in the United States and Western Europe; younger workforce in other countries
	Expertise	Availability of labor force and salary differences
Cultural	Working with different cultures	Differences in power distance, uncertainty avoidance, individualism/collectivism, masculinity/femininity, concept of time, and life focus; differences in languages, perceptions of aesthetics, beliefs, attitudes, religion, or social organizations
	Challenges of offering products or services in different cultures	Naming and advertising for products; intellectual property

ETHICAL DILEMMA

Online Rights Not Always Universal

American Internet users have been fortunate in that online content is not censored, and U.S.-based bloggers, journalists, and e-mailers are generally not subject to government intrusion or harassment. As the world becomes flatter, however, and the Internet becomes available to users in diverse countries, the question of who owns and/or controls Web-published data becomes an issue.

China has often been in the news for alleged violations of human rights. Since American companies have provided software and hardware for China's Internet infrastructure, the question arises, When China restricts online rights for its citizens, should U.S. companies providing services be cooperative? Consider the following:

- U.S.-based Cisco built the entire Chinese Internet infrastructure and allegedly agreed to supply equipment that allows the Chinese government to monitor Internet users.
- Chinese Internet users use Microsoft's blog tool, Windows Live Spaces. Microsoft censors the Chinese version of its software using a blacklist supplied by Beijing. Among words that will be automatically rejected by the Chinese system are "democracy" and "capitalism."
- In order to do business in China, in 2004 Google agreed to censor "subversive" articles from Google News China or from their search results.
- In 2005, Yahoo! was said to have aided the conviction of a Chinese journalist, Shi Tao, when employees of Yahoo!'s China office supplied details about Shi's e-mail address to local authorities. Mr. Shi, one of five journalists whose convictions for "revealing state secrets" Yahoo! allegedly aided, is currently serving a 10-year prison term in China.
- During the 2008 Olympic Games in Beijing, journalists were initially unable to access Web sites such as www.amnesty.org (the restrictions were later lessened after international protests).
- In 2009, to control news about an ethnic clash, China temporally blocked many social networking Web sites, such as Facebook, YouTube, and Twitter.

Similar to Mr. Shi's situation, a Chinese journalist in Beijing recently posted content that, although probably factually correct, was deemed inappropriate by the Chinese government. The government then requested that Microsoft shut down the blog, and Microsoft complied. The Chinese government monitors all online activity, shutting down "dissident" Web sites and deleting "subversive" postings. Since Chinese bloggers often write under pseudonyms, the Chinese government has recently asked Internet access provider firms to reveal the identities of bloggers who post "inappropriate" content. As a result, several Chinese bloggers have been arrested and sentenced to lengthy jail terms after their identities were revealed.

Reporters Without Borders and other critics have called such censorship agreements unethical. Cisco, Microsoft, Google, and Yahoo! have replied that they are simply following local laws. Opponents argue, however, that online product and service providers based outside of China should not assist the Chinese government in its campaign against Internet users' online rights.

In reference to the company's involvement in Shi Tao's conviction and sentencing, Yahoo! twice faced congressional hearings and was denounced by human rights organizations and others in support of Shi Tao. Consequently, in 2007 Yahoo! settled a legal complaint filed by Shi's family for an undisclosed amount, and Yahoo! CEO Jerry Yang made a public apology to Shi's mother at a congressional hearing. In addition, Yahoo! established a Human Rights Fund to "provide humanitarian and legal assistance to persons in the People's Republic of China who have been imprisoned or persecuted for expressing their views using the Internet."

For human rights activists, the major issue is that American companies, such as Microsoft, Google, and Yahoo!, that profess to value free speech are acting unethically when they cooperate with governments that curtail Internet users' rights to freedom of expression. The fact that Article 19 of the Universal Declaration of Human Rights supports freedom of expression lends legitimacy to this argument.

In 2010, Google decided to stop censoring its search results after it was hacked by people who tried to spy on Chinese dissidents' e-mail, eventually redirecting all Chinese-based searches through servers located in Hong Kong. However, Google's decision got mixed responses from other companies. For instance, Microsoft, which is also promoting its search engine Bing, said they'll stay in China; domain registrar GoDaddy.com, in contrast, sided with Google and stopped registering domain names in China.

Another question that arises in such situations is, Who owns Web-posted data? Since the data is often not physically present in the local country supplying Internet access, do the local authorities have the right to censor the data? (Local authorities would probably argue that the impact of the content posted online is felt locally.) Do local authorities have a right to regulate online content when Internet access is hosted by companies located outside a country?

Most important, is the online environment independent of the digital world we live in, or is it subject to all the rules and regulations of countries the Internet passes through? Should the Internet adapt its own laws that all hosting companies must follow?

These are questions that will need to be answered in the twenty-first century as the world gets smaller and the Internet becomes an integral service in all countries.

Based on:

Barboza, D., & Zellar, T., Jr. (2006, January 8). Microsoft's shutdown of Chinese blog is condemned. *International Herald Tribune.* April 10, 2010, from http://www.iht.com/articles/2006/01/06/technology/web.0107msft.php.

Cohen, R. (2010, March 30). Google's lonely stand for human rights in China. *Washington Post.* Retrieved April 10, 2010, from http://www.washingtonpost.com/wp-dyn/content/article/2010/03/29/AR2010032901890.html.

Jacobs, A. (2010, March 30). Journalists' e-mails hacked in China. *New York Times.* Retrieved April 10, 2010, from http://www.nytimes.com/2010/03/31/world/asia/31china.html.

Johnson, B., Branigan, T., & Nasaw. D. (2010, March 25). We're staying in China, says Microsoft, as free speech row with Google grows. *Guardian.* Retrieved April 10, 2010, from http://www.guardian.co.uk/technology/2010/mar/25/china-microsoft-free-speech-google.

McKinnon, R. (2008, April). Asia's fight for web rights. *Far Eastern Economic Review.* Retrieved April 10, 2010, from http://feer.com/essays/2008/april/asias-fight-for-web-rights.

Information Systems Defined

Information systems are combinations of **hardware, software,** and **telecommunications networks** that *people* build and use to collect, create, and distribute useful *data,* typically in organizational settings. Hardware refers to physical computer equipment, such as the computer monitor, central processing unit, or keyboard. Software refers to a program or set of programs that tell the computer to perform certain tasks. Telecommunications networks refer to a group of two or more computer systems linked together with communications equipment. Although we discuss the design, implementation, use, and implications of hardware, software, and telecommunications throughout the chapters, the specifics on hardware, software, and telecommunications are discussed in detail in Chapter 3 and the Technology Briefing. Often, you will hear the term **information technology** used to refer to the hardware, software, and networking components of an information system; when looking at degree programs or job opportunities, you will find that IT programs or jobs are a bit more technical in nature, whereas IS programs have a stronger managerial focus. However, the difference is shrinking, with many using the terms IS and IT synonymously. In Figure 1.10, we show the relationships among these IS components.

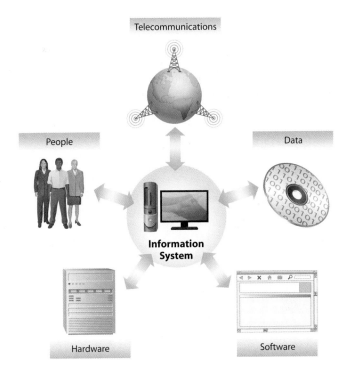

FIGURE 1.10

An information system is a combination of five key elements: people, hardware, software, data, and telecommunications networks.

People in organizations use information systems to process sales transactions, manage loan applications, or help financial analysts decide where, when, and how to invest. Product managers also use them to help decide where, when, and how to market their products and related services, and production managers use them to help decide when and how to manufacture products. Information systems also enable us to get cash from ATMs, communicate by live video with people in other parts of the world, and buy concert or airline tickets. (Note that the term "information systems" is also used to describe the field comprising people who develop, use, manage, and study information systems in organizations.)

It is important to note that people use various terms to describe the field of information systems, such as management information systems, business information systems, computer information systems, and simply "systems." Next, we more thoroughly examine each of the key components of the IS definition.

Data: The Root and Purpose of Information Systems

Earlier, we defined information systems as combinations of hardware, software, and telecommunications networks that people build and use to collect, create, and distribute useful data, typically in organizational settings. We begin by talking about data, the most basic element of any information system.

Data Before you can understand how information systems work, it is important to distinguish between data and information, terms that are often erroneously used interchangeably. **Data** is raw material—recorded, unformatted information, such as words and numbers. Data has no meaning in and of itself. For example, if we asked you what 465889727 meant or stood for, you could not tell us (see Figure 1.11). However, if we presented the same data as 465-88-9727 and told you it was located in a certain database, in John Doe's file, in a field labeled "SSN," you might rightly surmise that the number was actually the Social Security number of someone named John Doe.

Information Data formatted with dashes or labels is more useful than unformatted data. By adding context, it is transformed into **information,** which can be defined as a representation of reality. In the previous example, 465-88-9727 was used to represent and identify an individual person, John Doe (see Figure 1.11). Contextual cues, such as a label, are needed to turn data into information that is familiar to the reader. Think about your experience with ATMs. A list of all the transactions at a bank's ATMs over the course of a month would be fairly useless data. However, a table that divided ATM users into two categories, bank customers and non–bank customers, and compared the two groups' use of the machine—their purpose for using the ATMs and the times and days on which they use them—would be incredibly useful information. A bank manager could use this information to create marketing mailings to attract new customers. Without information systems, it would be difficult to make data useful by turning it into information.

Knowledge In addition to data and information, knowledge is also important. **Knowledge** is the ability to understand information, form opinions, and make decisions or predictions based on the information. For example, you must have knowledge to be aware that only one Social

FIGURE 1.11

Data, information, and knowledge.

Data	Information	Knowledge
465889727	465-88-9727	465-88-9727 → John Doe
Unformatted Data	Formatted Data	Data Relationships
Meaning: ------------ ???	Meaning: ------------ SSN	Meaning: ------------ SSN → Unique Person

Security number can uniquely identify each individual (see Figure 1.11). Knowledge is a body of governing procedures, such as guidelines or rules, that are used to organize or manipulate data to make it suitable for a given task.

Understanding the distinctions between data, information, and knowledge is important because all are used in the study, development, and use of information systems.

Hardware, Software, and Telecommunications Networks: The Components of Information Systems

When we use the term "information system," we are talking about **computer-based information systems.** Remember that we defined an information system as a combination of hardware, software, and telecommunications networks that people build and use to collect, create, and distribute data. Ever since the dawn of mankind, there was a need to transform data into useful information for people, and people have invented various calculating devices, such as the abacus or the slide rule. Before the introduction of the first computers (which worked on a mechanical basis using punch cards), almost all business and government information systems consisted of file folders, filing cabinets, and document repositories. Computer hardware has replaced these physical artifacts, providing the technologies to input and process data and output useful information; software enables organizations to utilize the hardware to execute their business processes and competitive strategy by providing the computer hardware with instructions on what processing functions to perform. Finally, the telecommunications networks allow computers to share information and services, enabling the global collaboration, communication, and commerce we see today.

People: The Builders and Managers of Information Systems

The IS field includes a vast collection of people who develop, maintain, manage, and study information systems. The career opportunities for a person with IS training continue to be strong, and they are expected to continue to improve over the next 10 years. For example, in 2008, the U.S. Bureau of Labor Statistics predicted that employment for computer and IS managers will grow faster than the average for all occupations through 2016. This boost in employment will occur in nearly every industry, not just computer hardware and software companies, as more and more organizations rely more heavily on IS professionals. Likewise, *Money* magazine (http://money.cnn.com/magazines/moneymag/bestjobs) ranked "IT Project Manager" as one of its top 10 best jobs in America (see Table 1.7); also, *FastCompany* magazine (http://www.fastcompany.com/articles/2009/01/top-jobs-2009.html) rated computer-related jobs as the second-best job, stressing that the industry is looking for people who can balance business and technology.

TABLE 1.7 Best Jobs in America

Rank	Career	Job Growth (10-year forecast)	Median Pay
1	Systems engineer	45%	$87,100
2	Physician assistant	27%	$90,900
3	College professor	23%	$70,400
4	Nurse practitioner	23%	$85,200
5	**IT project manager**	16%	$98,700
6	Certified public accountant	18%	$74,200
7	Physical therapist	27%	$74,300
8	Computer/network security consultant	27%	$99,700
9	Intelligence analyst	15%	$82,500
10	Sales director	10%	$140,000

Source: Based on http://money.cnn.com/magazines/moneymag/bestjobs.

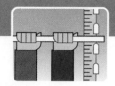

POWERFUL PARTNERSHIPS

The Two Steves—Jobs and Wozniak

Steve Jobs, born in 1955, and Steve Wozniak, born in 1950—one of the most famous partnerships in the history of computing—combined their separate talents to form one of the most successful companies in information technology—Apple Computers (see Figure 1.12). The two actually knew each other in high school but renewed the friendship while Wozniak was working at Hewlett-Packard and Jobs took a summer job there. They visualized and designed the first marketable Apple computer (the Apple I), working first out of Jobs's bedroom and then out of a garage, and founded a company to sell their invention in 1976. A third person, Ron Wayne, helped form the company. As Apple's "adult-in-chief," Wayne's role was to mediate disputes between the two Steves. However, not willing to take the risks of being involved in a startup, Wayne sold his 10% share and left the company after only 12 days, receiving a total of U.S.$2,300 in return. The partners realized early on that they could probably sell 1,000 computers a month, but as Wozniak recently wrote on his Web site, "That took a lot of money. We had none, so we went looking. We met Mark Markkula, and he launched us. I had to leave Hewlett Packard and that was tough."

The infusion of much-needed capital came just in time for Jobs and Wozniak to enter their product in the first West Coast Computer Faire. They rented a prime booth location and even managed to rent a video projector, a feat that Wozniak describes as follows: "This was such an early year that such projectors were virtually unknown. It was a BIG deal." The partners' professional business presentation at the Faire—far above other amateur efforts at the time—earned them several contracts for orders, and Apple Computers was off and running.

Both men left the company in 1985, less than 10 years after founding it. Wozniak left to return to college, where he finally received his engineering degree under the pseudonym Rocky Clark. Steve Jobs, who stayed with Apple, persuaded John Sculley, the former CEO of Pepsi, to come aboard as captain. Ironically, Jobs and Sculley did not get along, and Sculley fired Jobs. Disillusioned, Jobs started his own company, called NeXT, which Apple eventually purchased, and in 1996 a wiser and less erratic Jobs again became Apple's chief executive. (Jobs was also the CEO and major shareholder of Pixar Animation Studios until Walt Disney Studios acquired the company in 2006.)

While Jobs and Wozniak differed widely in personality type and management style, the partners' abilities complemented each other and were an asset to the company they founded. Jobs, somewhat flamboyant and intuitive in anticipating which new concepts will capture consumers' imaginations, is still Apple Computer's CEO. Wozniak, a talented engineer, is more introverted and less willing than Jobs to assume center stage, although in 2009 he had an unsuccessful run on the television show *Dancing with the Stars*. "Woz" has founded several companies since leaving Apple, has taught children, and sponsors music festivals and charitable events. Furthermore, Wozniak is actually still on the payroll as an Apple employee. (He appreciates the 10 percent discount he gets when he buys Apple products.)

Many biographies have been written about the two Steves (*Inside Steve's Brain* by Leander Kahney is a recent one about Jobs), and Wozniak has written his autobiography, *iWoz*. The books offer firsthand accounts of the fabled partnership and glimpses into the creation of one of the world's most successful computer companies. Ron Wayne's share of the company would now be worth U.S.$2.2 billion.

FIGURE 1.12

Steve Jobs (left) and Steve Wozniak (right) of Apple Computer in the 1980s.

AP Wide World Photos

Based on:

Anonymous. (n.d.). Woz.org . . . Everyone is welcome. Retrieved April 16, 2010, from http://www.woz.org.

Bellis, M. (n.d.). Inventors of the modern computer: The invention of the Apple Macintosh—Apple Computers—Steve Jobs and Steve Wozniak. *About.com*. Retrieved April 16, 2010, from http://inventors.about.com/library/weekly/aa051599.htm.

Hoyer, S. (2007, May 14). Interview: Steve Wozniak. *Macnotes.de*. Retrieved April 16, 2010, from http://www.macnotes.de/2007/05/14/interview-steve-wozniak-english-version.

Keizer, G. (2009, April 1). Dancing with the Stars dumps Wozniak. *Computerworld*. Retrieved April 16, 2010, from

http://www.computerworld.com/s/article/9130883/_i_Dancing_with_the_Stars_i_dumps_Wozniak.

Newman, B. (2010, June 5). Apple's lost founder: Jobs, Woz and Wayne. *San Jose Mercury News*. Retrieved July 26, 2010, from http://www.mercurynews.com/bay-area-news/ci_15214122.

Steve Jobs. (2010, May 20). In *Wikipedia, the free encyclopedia*. Retrieved May 21, 2010, from http://en.wikipedia.org/w/index.php?title=Steve_Jobs&oldid=363276938.

Steve Wozniak. (2010, May 20). In *Wikipedia, the free encyclopedia*. Retrieved May 21, 2010, from http://en.wikipedia.org/w/index.php?title=Steve_Wozniak&oldid=363277720.

Finally, in 2010, *US News & World Report* selected being a systems analyst as one of its 50 best careers.

In addition to an ample supply of jobs, earnings for IS professionals will remain strong. According to the U.S. Bureau of Labor Statistics, median annual earnings of these managers in May 2009 were $113,720. The middle 50 percent earned between $89,240 and $143,590. Also, according to Salary.com, the median salary in 2009 for IT managers was $104,297. According to a 2010 survey by the National Association of Colleges and Employers, starting salary offers for IS majors, with one year or less of experience, averaged $54,038, making it one of the 10 top-paid bachelor's degrees. Finally, computer and IS managers, especially those at higher levels, often receive more employment-related benefits—such as expense accounts, stock option plans, and bonuses—than do nonmanagerial workers in their organizations.

Even with lower-level, highly technical jobs (such as systems programmers) being outsourced to organizations in other countries, there continues to be a very strong need for people with IS knowledge, skills, and abilities—in particular, people with advanced IS capabilities, as we describe here. In fact, IS careers are regularly selected as not only one of the fastest growing but also a career with far-above-average opportunities for greater personal growth, stability, and advancement. Although technology continues to become easier to use, there is still and is likely to continue to be an acute need for people within the organization to have the responsibility of planning for, designing, developing, maintaining, and managing technologies. Much of this will happen within the business units and will be done by those with primarily business duties and tasks as opposed to systems duties and tasks. However, we are a long way from the day when technology is so easy to deploy that a need no longer exists for people with advanced IS knowledge and skills. In fact, many people believe that this day may never come. Although increasing numbers of people will incorporate systems responsibilities within their nonsystems jobs, there will continue to be a need for people with primarily systems responsibilities. In short, IS staffs and departments will likely continue to exist and play an important role in the foreseeable future.

Given that information systems continue to be a critical tool for business success, it is not likely that IS departments will go away or even shrink significantly. Indeed, all projections are for long-term growth of information systems in both scale and scope. Also, as is the case in any area of business, those people who are continually learning, continuing to grow, and continuing to find new ways to add value and who have advanced and/or unique skills will always be sought after, whether in information systems or in any area of the firm.

The future opportunities in the IS field are likely to be found in a variety of areas, which is good news for everyone. Diversity in the technology area can embrace us all. It really does not matter much which area of information systems you choose to pursue—there will likely be a promising future there for you. Even if your career interests are outside information systems, being a well-informed and capable user of information technologies will greatly enhance your career prospects.

Careers in Information Systems   The field of information systems includes those people in organizations who design and build systems, those who use these systems, and those responsible

TABLE 1.8 Some IS Management Job Titles and Brief Job Descriptions

IS Activities	Job Title	Job Description	Salary Ranges in Percentiles (25%–75%)
Develop	Systems analyst	Responsible for analyzing business requirements and selecting information systems that meet those needs	$54,000–$87,000
	Programmer	Responsible for coding, testing, debugging, and installing programs	$50,000–$80,000
	Systems consultant	Provide IS knowledge to external clients	$80,000–$120,000
Maintain	IS auditor	Responsible for auditing information systems and operating procedures for compliance with internal and external standards	$45,000–$75,000
	Database administrator	Responsible for managing database and database management software use	$75,000–$100,000
	Webmaster	Responsible for managing the firm's Web site	$50,000–$83,000
Manage	IS manager	Responsible for the management of an existing information system	$60,000–$90,000
	IS security manager	Responsible for managing security measures and disaster recovery	$55,000–$85,000
	Chief information officer	Highest-ranking IS manager; responsible for strategic planning and IS use throughout the firm	$150,000–$180,000
Study	University professor	Teach undergraduate and graduate students; study the use of information systems in organizations and society	$70,000–$180,000
	Government scientist	Research and development of information systems for homeland security, intelligence, and other related applications	$60,000–$200,000

Source: Based on http://www.salary.com; http://cnnmoney.com and http://www.payscale.com.

for managing these systems. The people who help develop and manage systems in organizations include systems analysts, systems programmers, systems operators, network administrators, database administrators, systems designers, systems managers, and chief information officers. In Table 1.8 we describe some of these careers. This list is not exhaustive; rather, it is intended to provide a sampling of IS management positions. Furthermore, many firms will use the same job title, but each is likely to define it in a different way, or companies will have different titles for the same basic function. As you can see from Table 1.8, the range of career opportunities for IS managers is very broad, and salary expectations are very high.

What Makes IS Personnel So Valuable? In addition to the growing importance of people in the IS field, there have been changes in the nature of this type of work. No longer are IS departments in organizations filled only with nerdy men with pocket protectors (Figure 1.13). Many

FIGURE 1.13

IS personnel are no longer nerds.

Past

Present

TABLE 1.9 IS Professional Core Competencies

Domain	Description
Technical Knowledge and Skills	
Hardware	Hardware platforms, infrastructure, virtualization, peripherals
Software	Operating systems, application software, drivers
Networking	Network operating systems, cabling and network interface cards, local area networks, wide area networks, wireless, Internet, security
Business Knowledge and Skills	
Business integration, industry	Business processes, functional areas of business and their integration, industry characteristics
Managing people and projects	Planning, organizing, leading, controlling, managing people and projects
Social	Interpersonal, group dynamics, political
Communication	Verbal, written, and technological communication and presentation
Systems Knowledge and Skills	
Systems integration	Connectivity, compatibility, integrating subsystems and systems
Development methodologies	Steps in systems analysis and design, systems development life cycle, alternative development methodologies
Critical thinking	Challenging one's and others' assumptions and ideas
Problem solving	Information gathering and synthesis, problem identification, solution formulation, comparison, choice

more women are in IS positions now. Also, it is now more common for an IS professional to be a polished, professional systems analyst who can speak fluently about both business and technology. IS personnel are now well-trained, highly skilled, valuable professionals who garner high wages and prestige and who play a pivotal role in helping firms be successful.

Many studies have been aimed at helping us understand what knowledge and skills are necessary for a person in the IS area to be successful (see, for example, Todd, McKeen, & Gallupe, 1995). Interestingly, these studies also point out just what it is about IS personnel that makes them so valuable to their organizations. In a nutshell, good IS personnel possess valuable, integrated knowledge and skills in three areas—technical, business, and systems—as outlined in Table 1.9.

Technical Competency. The technical competency area includes knowledge and skills in hardware, software, networking, and security. In a sense, this is the "nuts and bolts" of information systems. This is not to say that the IS professional must be a high-level technical expert in these areas. On the contrary, the IS professional must know just enough about these areas to understand how they work and how they can and should be applied. Typically, the IS professional manages or directs those who have deeper, more detailed technical knowledge.

The technical area of competency is, perhaps, the most difficult to maintain because the popularity of individual technologies is so fleeting. With the economy rebounding, organizations are starting new projects or are reviving projects put on hold during the economic downturn; hence, while it once appeared as if most programming jobs or support jobs would be outsourced to third-party providers abroad (Collett, 2006), there is an increased demand in many companies for people with application development skills, especially in combination with sound business analysis and project management skills (Brandel, 2009). In fact, many of the hot skills listed in Table 1.10 are focused on the business domain, which is discussed next.

Business Competency. The business competency area is one that sets the IS professional apart from others who have only technical knowledge and skills, and in an era of increased outsourcing, it may well save a person's job. For example, even though some low-level technology jobs may be outsourced, MSNBC.com recently reported (http://www.msnbc.msn.com/id/5077435)

TABLE 1.10 Hot Skills for 2010 and Beyond

Domain	Hot Skills
Business	• Business–IT alignment • Business analysis • Enterprise solutions • Project management • Business process modeling • Project planning, budgeting, and scheduling • Third-party provider management • Web 2.0 business models
Technology infrastructure and services	• Virtualization • Systems analysis • Systems design • Network design • Systems auditing • Wireless • Telecommunications/VoIP (Voice over Internet Protocol) • Data center
Security	• IT security planning and management
Applications	• Customer-facing application development • Web development, open source, portal technologies • Legacy systems integration
Internet	• Web 2.0 • Customer-facing Web application systems • Mobile applications • Search engine optimization • Artificial intelligence • Web mining
Business intelligence	• Business intelligence • Data warehousing • Data mining

Source: Based on Brandel (2009), Leung (2009), and Veritude (2009).

that IS management is one of 10 professions that is not likely to be outsourced. As a result, it is absolutely vital for IS professionals to understand the technical areas *and* the nature of the business as well. IS professionals must also be able to understand and manage people and projects, not just the technology. These business skills propel IS professionals into project management and, ultimately, high-paying middle- and upper-level management positions.

Systems Competency. Systems competency is another area that sets the IS professional apart from others with only technical knowledge and skills. Those who understand how to build and integrate systems and how to solve problems will ultimately manage large, complex systems projects as well as manage those in the firm who have only technical knowledge and skills.

Perhaps now you can see why IS professionals are so valuable to their organizations. These individuals have a solid, integrated foundation in technical, business, and systems knowledge and skills. Perhaps most important, they also have the social skills to understand how to work well with and motivate others. It is these core competencies that continue to make IS professionals valuable employees.

Given how important technology is, what does this mean for your career? Technology is being used to radically change how business is conducted—from the way products and services are produced, distributed, and accounted for to the ways they are marketed and sold. Whether you are majoring in information systems, finance, accounting, operations management, human resource management, business law, or marketing, knowledge of technology is critical to a successful career in business.

Finding Qualified Personnel Unfortunately, given the increased sophistication of modern information systems, organizations can often have a difficult time finding qualified personnel, and attracting the right people with the right skills is not possible in some areas. Consequently, many technology-focused organizations tend to cluster in areas where talented workers are available. Such areas are often characterized by a high quality of life for the people living there, and it is no surprise that many companies in the IT sector within the United States are headquartered in Silicon Valley, California; Boston, Massachusetts; Austin, Texas; or Seattle, Washington. With increasing globalization, other regions throughout the world are boasting about their highly skilled personnel. One such example is the Indian city of Bangalore, where, over a century ago, Maharajas started to lure talented technology-oriented people to the region, building a world-class human resource infrastructure that attracted companies from around the world. In other areas, organizations may have to find creative ways to attract and retain people, such as by offering favorable benefits packages that include educational grants or expense-matching programs to encourage employees to improve their education and skills. Other human resource policies, such as telecommuting, flextime, and creative benefit packages, can also help to attract and retain the best employees.

Organizations: The Context of Information Systems

We have talked about data versus information, the technology side of information systems, and the people side of information systems. The last part of our IS definition is the term "organization." People use information systems to help their organizations be more productive and profitable, to help their firms gain competitive advantage, to help their firms reach more customers or to improve service to their customers. This holds true for all types of organizations—professional, social, religious, educational, and governmental. In fact, not too long ago, the U.S. Internal Revenue Service launched its own site on the Web for the reasons just described (see Figure 1.14). The Web site was so popular that approximately 220,000 users visited it during the first 24 hours and more than a million visited it in its first week—even before the Web address for the site was officially announced. Today, popular Web sites like Facebook.com and Yahoo.com receive millions of visitors every day.

Types of Information Systems Throughout this book, we explore various types of information systems commonly used in organizations. It makes sense, however, for us to describe briefly here the various types of systems used so that you will better understand what we mean by the term "information system" as we use it throughout the rest of the book. Table 1.11 provides a list of the major types of information systems used in organizations.

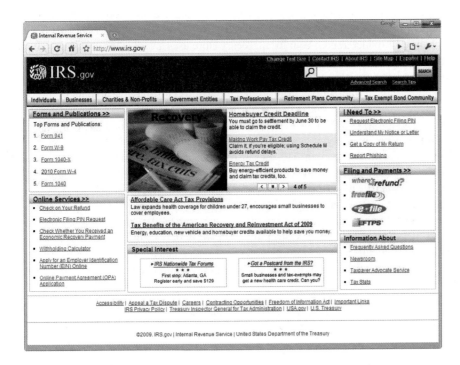

FIGURE 1.14

Web site of the U.S. Department of the Treasury, Internal Revenue Service, http://www.irs.gov.

TABLE 1.11 Types of Information Systems Used in Organizations

Type of System	Purpose	Sample Application
Transaction processing system	Process day-to-day business event data at the operational level of the organization	Grocery store checkout cash register with connection to network
Management information system	Produce detailed information to help manage a firm or a part of the firm	Inventory management and planning system
Decision support system	Provide analysis tools and access to databases in order to support quantitative decision making	Product demand forecasting system
Intelligent system	Emulate or enhance human capabilities	Automated system for analyzing bank loan applications
Data mining and visualization system	Methods and systems for analyzing data warehouses to better understand various aspects of a business	Market analysis
Office automation system (personal productivity software)	Support a wide range of predefined day-to-day work activities of individuals and small groups	Word processor
Collaboration system	Enable people to communicate, collaborate, and coordinate with each other	Electronic mail system with automated, shared calendar
Knowledge management system	Collection of technology-based tools to enable the generation, storage, sharing, and management of knowledge assets	Knowledge portal
Geographical information system	Create, store, analyze, and manage spatial data	Site selection for new shopping mall
Functional area information system	Support the activities within a specific functional area of the firm	System for planning for personnel training and work assignments
Customer relationship management system	Support interaction between the firm and its customers	Sales force automation
Enterprise resource planning system	Support and integrate all facets of the business, including planning, manufacturing, sales, marketing, and so on	Financial, operations, and human resource management
Supply chain management system	Support the coordination of suppliers, product or service production, and distribution	Procurement planning
Electronic commerce system	Enable customers to buy goods and services from a firm's Web site	Amazon.com

Topping the list in the table are some of the more traditional, major categories that are used to describe information systems. For example, **transaction processing systems (TPS)** are used by a broad range of organizations to not only more efficiently processes customer transactions, but also generate a tremendous amount of data that can be used by the organization to learn about customers or ever-changing product trends. Your local grocery store uses a TPS at the checkout that scans bar codes on products; as this occurs, many stores will print discount coupons on the backs of receipts for products related to current purchases. Every hour, online retailer Amazon.com's website processes thousands of transactions from around the world. This massive amount of information is fed into large data warehouses and is then analyzed to provide purchase recommendations to future customers. In addition, TPS data is sorted and organized to support a broad range of managerial decision making, using a variety of systems; the most common of these is generally referred to as a **management information system**. TPS data also fuels the use of a vast variety of information systems within organizations, including *decision support systems, intelligent systems, data mining and visualization systems, knowledge management systems, geographic information systems,* and *functional area information systems.* Five to 10 years ago, it would have been typical to see systems that fell cleanly into one of these categories. Today, with **internetworking**—connecting host computers and their networks together to form even larger networks like the Internet—and **systems integration**—connecting separate information systems and data to improve business processes and decision making—it is difficult to say that any given information system fits into only one of these categories (e.g., that a system is a management information system only and nothing else). Modern-day information systems tend to span several of these categories of information systems, helping not only to collect data from throughout the firm and from customers but also to integrate all that diverse data and present it to busy decision makers, along with tools to manipulate and analyze those data. *Customer relationship management, supply chain management,* and *enterprise resource planning* systems are good examples of these types of systems that encompass many features and types of data and cannot easily be categorized.

Office automation systems such as Microsoft Office and the OpenOffice.org Productivity Suite provide word processing, spreadsheet, and other personal productivity tools, enabling knowledge workers to accomplish their tasks; **collaboration systems,** such as Microsoft's Exchange/Outlook and Lotus Notes, provide people with e-mail, automated calendaring, and online, threaded discussions, enabling close collaboration with others, regardless of their location.

Systems for electronic commerce, such as corporate Web sites, are also very popular and important. These systems are typically Internet-based and enable (1) consumers to find information about, and to purchase goods and services from, each other and from business firms and (2) business firms to electronically exchange products, services, and information. In Chapter 4, "Enabling Commerce Using the Internet," we talk about business-to-business electronic commerce and its variants as well as how people are using the Internet to conduct electronic commerce.

While many modern-day information systems span several of these IS categories, it is still useful to understand these categories. Doing so enables you to better understand the myriad approaches, goals, features, and functions of modern information systems.

We have talked about each of the parts of our definition of information systems, and we have talked about different types of information systems. In the next section, we focus on how information systems can be managed within organizations.

Organizing the IS Function   The current emphasis on the use of technology within businesses is not a fad. Indeed, all indicators point to the increased use of technology and to organizations' continued awareness of the importance of technology, both as a tool for productivity and as a vehicle for achieving competitive advantage and organizational change. Just as information systems have evolved over the past several years, so too has the IS function. Next, we briefly review the evolution of the IS function within organizations.

Early History: Poor Service and Worse Attitudes. Early IS departments typically had huge project backlogs, and IS personnel would often deliver systems that were over budget, were completed much too late, were difficult to use, and did not always work well. In addition, many of these old-school IS personnel believed that they owned and controlled the computing resources, that they knew better than users did, and that they should tell users what they could and could not do with the computing resources. Needless to say, this was not a recipe for success and good relationships. Indeed, relations between IS personnel and users within a firm were often sour and were sometimes bitter.

The Rise and Fall of End-User Development. In the early years of information systems within organizations, users were often forced to put up with the poor service and the poor attitude. Then technology started to become significantly better—faster, easier to build and use, and cheaper—with the advent of the PC and standard software packages (see Figure 1.15). As a result, end users began to develop their own computing applications using PC-based spreadsheet packages (e.g., Visicalc), database management systems (e.g., dBase), and programming languages (e.g., BASIC). Disgruntled users simply said, "If the IS staff cannot or will not do this for us, then we will build our own systems." In many cases, they did just that, and they did it well, much to the dismay of some of the IS managers. Although end-user development clearly has strengths and still exists in some organizations, it also has serious weaknesses (see Chapter 9, "Developing and Acquiring Information Systems"); thus, today, most organizations leave the systems development to the professionals.

The Modern IS Organization. Business managers soon became more savvy about technology and the possibilities and opportunities that it offered, and they reasoned that the possibilities and opportunities were too great to let the IS function simply wither away as end-user development took over. In addition, smart, concerned IS personnel realized that they needed an attitude adjustment. Some people believe that the changes in the nature of technology forced people to cooperate more. For example, the shift from large "mainframe" computers to a "server-centric" model (i.e., relatively powerful PCs spread throughout the organization that share data, applications, or peripherals that are hosted by more powerful server computers) may have forced people within the IS function to improve their operations and their relationships with people in other units of

FIGURE 1.15

The advent of the IBM PC and early applications packages led to end-user development.

Courtesy of IBM Archives

the firm. The client-server model required a new kind of relationship between information systems and other people throughout the firm (Stevens, 1994). As a result of these forces, in modern IS units that do a good job, the atmosphere, attitude, and culture are very different and much more sensitive and responsive than they used to be.

In these more responsive IS units, the personnel have taken on more of a consulting relationship with their users. The IS personnel believe that, fundamentally, they are there to help the users solve problems and be more productive. Indeed, in many cases, the IS personnel do not even refer to the users as "users." They are "clients" or "customers," or, even better, they are "colleagues" within the organization. This new attitude is a major change from the old days, when IS personnel did not want to be bothered by users and thought that the techies knew better than users. It is unfortunate that this old-school mentality still exists in some organizations.

The new IS culture is much like that found in successful service organizations. Think of how customers are treated by service organizations, such as Citigroup's Smith Barney or Ernst & Young, or by product-based organizations where service is also important, such as McDonald's or Nordstrom. Great service to the customer is absolutely critical, and employees do everything they can to please customers. They often live by the credo that "the customer is always right."

The same holds for IS units that have taken on this new **service mentality.** The IS personnel do everything they can to ensure that they are satisfying their systems customers within the firm. They reach out to customers and proactively seek their input and needs rather than waiting for customers to come in with systems complaints. They modify the systems at a moment's notice just to meet customer needs quickly and effectively. They celebrate the customer's new systems ideas rather than putting up roadblocks and giving reasons that the new ideas cannot or will not work. They fundamentally believe that the customers own the technology and the information and that the technology and information are there for the customers, not for the systems personnel. They create help desks, hotlines, information centers, and training centers to support customers. These service-oriented IS units structure the IS function so that it can better serve the customer.

The implications of this new service mentality for the IS function are staggering. It is simply amazing how unproductive a company can be when the IS personnel and other people within the firm are at odds with one another. On the other hand, it is even more amazing how productive and enjoyable work can be when people in the IS function work hand in hand with people throughout the organization. Technology is, potentially, the great lever, but it works best when people work together, not against each other, to use it.

The Spread of Technology in Organizations Another phenomenon that shows how integral and vital information systems and their proper management have become to organizations is the extent to which the technology is firmly integrated and entrenched within the various business units (such as accounting, sales, and marketing).

In many organizations today, you will find that the builders and managers of a particular information system or subsystem spend most of their time out in the business unit, along with the users of that particular system. Many times, these systems personnel are permanently placed—with an office, desk, phone, and PC—in the business unit along with the users.

In addition, it is not uncommon for systems personnel to have formal education, training, and work experience in information systems as well as in the functional area that the system supports, such as finance. It is becoming increasingly more difficult to separate the technology from the business or the systems staff from the other people in the organization. For this reason, how information systems are managed is important to you, no matter what career option you pursue.

As information systems are used more broadly throughout organizations, IS personnel often have dual-reporting relationships—reporting both to the central IS group and to the business function they serve. Therefore, at least some need for centralized IS planning, deployment, and management continues—particularly with respect to achieving economies of scale in systems acquisition and development and in optimizing systems integration, enterprise networking, and the like. Even in organizations that are decentralizing technology and related decisions, a need to coordinate technology and related decisions across the firm still persists. This coordination is likely to continue to happen through some form of a centralized (or, at least, centrally coordinated) IS staff. Organizations are likely to continue to want to reap the benefits of IS decentralization (flexibility, adaptability, and systems responsiveness), but it is equally likely that they will not want to—and will not be able to—forgo the benefits of IS centralization (coordination, economies of scale, compatibility, and connectivity).

Given the trend toward pushing people from the IS staff out into the various business units of the firm and given the need for people within each of the functional areas of the business to have technology skills, there is clearly a need for people who know the technology side *and* the business side of the business. We suspect that the need for people to play these boundary-spanning roles will continue.

The Dual Nature of Information Systems

Given how important and expensive information systems have become, information technology is like a sword—you can use it effectively as a competitive weapon, but, as the old saying goes, those who live by the sword sometimes die by the sword. The two following cases illustrate this dual nature of information systems.

Case in Point: An Information System Gone Awry: Software Glitch Stops Hybrid Vehicle (or Doesn't?)

What happens when an information system does not function as planned? An example of an information system gone wrong that made the news in early 2010 is the computer-controlled braking system of the Toyota Prius hybrid vehicle. Even more than today's "conventional" gasoline-driven vehicles, hybrid vehicles rely on sophisticated information systems to control the interaction of the different engines, the braking systems, batteries, and so on (see Figure 1.16). Typically a hybrid vehicle uses, in addition to hydraulic brakes, a regenerative braking system to recharge the battery while slowing down the vehicle. Depending on factors such as driving speed and pressure on the brake pedal, the car's computer controls when the hydraulic brakes are applied and when the antilock braking system is activated. In early 2010, it became known that a software glitch could cause a delay in the response of the brakes under a certain combination of conditions. Although no fatalities were linked to the software glitch, this incident severely blemished the automaker's reputation for safety and quality, which had already suffered because of another model's problems with the accelerator pedal.

This story has a happy ending—or beginning, as it were—as Toyota's dealerships could easily upload the new software to the affected vehicles. Increasingly sophisticated systems, intended to make driving safer by assisting the drivers in various ways, are one of many ways that this organization is attempting to be innovative and to outdo the competition, and Toyota will be even

Hybrid vehicles rely on information technology to control the interaction between various systems.

more vigilant about the performance of such systems. However, this is still useful as an example of how a problematic information system can adversely affect the performance of an organization.

Case in Point: An Information System That Works: FedEx

Just as there are examples of information systems gone wrong, there are many examples of information systems gone right. FedEx, now a $32 billion family of companies (2010 data), is the world's largest express transportation company and delivers millions of packages and millions of pounds of freight to 220 countries and territories each business day (see Figure 1.17). FedEx uses extensive, interconnected information systems to coordinate more than 140,000 employees, hundreds of aircraft, and tens of thousands of ground vehicles worldwide.

To improve its services and sustain a competitive advantage, FedEx offers extensive services on the Internet. FedEx.com has more than 15 million unique visitors per month and over 3 million tracking requests per day. FedEx.com has become the information hub for a business where managing information *is the business*. In addition to shipment tracking, customers use the site for

FedEx is an innovator in successfully using information systems.

finding out about delivery options and costs, use tools to prepare their own packages, verify them online, and print bar-coded shipping documents. These and other information systems have positioned FedEx as the global leader in express transportation.

Information Systems for Competitive Advantage

Toyota's automotive electronics systems and FedEx's Web site are typical of systems that are pervasive in today's life or used in large, complex organizations. These systems are so large in scale and scope that they are difficult to build. It is important to handle the development of such systems the right way the first time around. These examples also show that as we rely more and more on information systems, the capabilities of these systems are paramount to business success.

Not only were these systems large and complicated, but they were—and continue to be—critical to the success of the firms that built them. The choices made in developing the systems at both Toyota and FedEx were **strategic** in their intent. These systems were not developed solely because managers in these organizations wanted to do things faster or because they wanted to have the latest, greatest technology. These organizations developed these systems strategically to help gain or sustain some **competitive advantage** (Porter, 1985; Porter & Millar, 1985) over their rivals. Let us not let this notion slip by us—while the use of technology can enable efficiency and while information systems must provide a return on investment, technology use can also be strategic and can be a powerful enabler of competitive advantage.

Although we described the use of information systems at two relatively large organizations, firms of all types and sizes can use information systems to gain or sustain a competitive advantage over their rivals. Whether it is a small mom-and-pop boutique or a large government agency, every organization can find a way to use information technology to beat its rivals. In Chapter 2, "Gaining Competitive Advantage Through Information Systems," we talk more about this opportunity to use information systems strategically.

Why Information Systems Matter

On May 1, 2003, Nicholas Carr published an article titled "IT Doesn't Matter" in *Harvard Business Review* that created quite a stir. He argued that as information technology becomes more pervasive, it will become more standardized and ubiquitous, more of a commodity that is absolutely necessary for every company. He reasoned, then, that companies should focus information technology strictly on cost reduction and risk mitigation and that investing in information technology for differentiation or for competitive advantage is futile. Many experts in academia, in the popular press, and within technology companies not only disagreed with that argument but also felt that, if taken literally, such a line of thinking could hurt companies' competitiveness.

Given the debate that this article caused, on May 1, 2004, *CIO* magazine's editor in chief, Abbie Lundberg, published an interview with Carr on the subject, along with an invited counterpoint essay titled "The Engine That Drives Success: The Best Companies Have the Best Business Models Because They Have the Best IT Strategies" by noted technology and business strategy author Don Tapscott. Tapscott argued that companies with bad business models tend to fail regardless of whether they use information technology or not. On the other hand, companies that have good business models and use information technology successfully to carry out those business models tend to be very successful. He described many examples, across a variety of industries, where firms dominate their respective markets; have superior customer relationships, business designs, and differentiated offerings; and are well known for their superior use of information technology in supporting a unique business strategy. His examples included Amazon.com, Best Buy, Citigroup, PepsiCo, Herman Miller, Cisco, Progressive Casualty Insurance, Marriott, FedEx, GE, Southwest Airlines, and Starbucks.

We tend to side with Tapscott on this one. We believe that information systems are a necessary part of doing business, that they can be used to create efficiencies, and that they can also be used as an enabler of competitive advantage. We do agree with Carr, however, that the competitive advantage from the use of information systems can be fleeting, as competitors can eventually do the same thing. Also, given how expensive IS projects have become and given how cost conscious and competitive businesses now are, nearly every IS project today must show a clear return on investment. Again, we talk more about the role of information systems in competitive advantage in Chapter 2 and about return on investment issues in Chapter 9.

IS Ethics

A broad range of ethical issues have emerged through the use and proliferation of computers. Just as the Luddites opposed technological progress during industrialization, **neo-Luddites** oppose information systems, fearing negative impacts such as social decay, increased consumerism, or loss of privacy. **Computer ethics** is used to describe the issues and standards of conduct as they pertain to the use of information systems. In 1986, Richard O. Mason wrote a classic article on the issues central to this debate—information privacy, accuracy, property, and accessibility. These issues are still at the forefront of most ethical debates related to how information systems store and process information (see Figure 1.18). Next, we examine each of these issues.

Information Privacy

If you use the Internet regularly, sending e-mail messages and visiting Web sites, you may have felt that your personal privacy is at risk. Several Web sites where you like to shop greet you by name and seem to know which products you are most likely to buy (see Figure 1.19). Every day, the in-box in your browser's mail program is full to overflowing with messages urging you to buy something. As a result, you may feel as though eyes are on you every time you go online. **Information privacy** is concerned with what information an individual should have to reveal to others in the workplace or through other transactions, such as online shopping.

While the information age has brought widespread access to information, the downside is that others may now have access to personal information that you would prefer to keep private. Personal information, such as Social Security numbers, credit card numbers, medical histories,

FIGURE 1.18

Information privacy, accuracy, property, and accessibility are central to most ethical concerns about information technology.

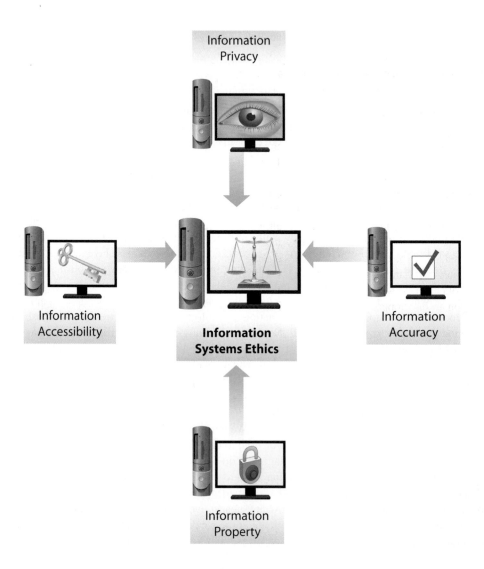

FIGURE 1.19

Amazon.com is famous for personalizing its Web site to individual customers.

and even family histories, is now available on the Internet. Using search engines, your friends, coworkers, current or future employers, or even your spouse can find out almost anything that has been posted by or about you on the Internet. For example, it is very easy to locate your personal blog, your most recent party pictures posted on Facebook, or even sensitive questions you asked in a public discussion forum about drug use or mental health. Moreover, many of these pages are stored in the search engines' long-term cache, so they remain accessible for a long time even after they have been taken off the Web.

How to Maintain Your Privacy Online   When you make Web purchases, vendors are not required by law to respect your privacy. In other words, a vendor can track what pages you look at, what products you examine in detail, which products you choose to buy, what method of payment you choose to use, and where you have the product delivered. After collecting all that information, unscrupulous vendors can sell it to others, resulting in more direct-mail advertising, electronic spam in your e-mail in-box, or calls from telemarketers.

When surveyed about concerns related to online shopping, most consumers list issues of information privacy as a top concern. As a result, governments have pressured businesses to post their privacy policies on their Web sites. Unfortunately, these policies do not often protect the privacy of consumers. To protect yourself, you should always review the privacy policy of all companies you do business with and refuse to do business with those that do not have a clear policy or do not respect your privacy. According to the Consumer Protection Working Group of the American Bar Association at safeshopping.org, a seller's privacy policy should indicate at least the following:

- What information the seller is gathering from you
- How the seller will use this information
- Whether and how you can "opt out" of these practices

To make sure your shopping experience is a good one, you can take a few additional steps to maintain your privacy:

- ***Choose Web Sites That Are Monitored by Independent Organizations.*** Several independent organizations monitor the privacy and business practices of Web sites (e.g., www .truste.com).
- ***Avoid Having "Cookies" Left on Your Machine.*** Many commercial Web sites leave cookies on your machine so that the owner of the site can monitor where you go and what you do on the site. To enhance your privacy, you should carefully manage your browser's cookie settings or get special "cookie management" software (see Chapter 10, "Securing Information Systems," for more on cookies).

■ *Visit Sites Anonymously.* There are ways to visit Web sites anonymously. Using services provided by companies such as Anonymizer (www.anonymizer.com), you have a high degree of privacy from marketers, identity thieves, or even coworkers when surfing the Web.

■ *Use Caution When Requesting Confirmation E-Mail.* When you buy products online, many companies will send you a confirming e-mail message to let you know that the order was received correctly. A good strategy is to have a separate e-mail account, such as one that is available for viewing via a Web browser, that you use when making online purchases.

Of course, there are no guarantees that all your online experiences will be problem free, but if you follow the advice provided here, you are much more likely to maintain your privacy.

Information Accuracy

The issue of **information accuracy** has become highly charged in today's wired world. Information accuracy is concerned with ensuring the authenticity and fidelity of information as well as with identifying who is responsible for informational errors that harm people. With all the computerization that has taken place, people have come to expect to receive and retrieve information more easily and quickly than ever before. In addition, because computers "never make mistakes," we have come to expect this information to be accurate. A case in point is at the bank. The combination of automated teller machines, computerized record systems, and large, electronic client and transaction databases should provide customers with quick and accurate access to their account information. However, we continue to hear about and experience record-keeping errors at banks.

An error of a few dollars in your banking records does not seem significant. However, what if it were an error of hundreds or thousands of dollars in the bank's favor? What if the error caused one of your important payments (such as a home mortgage payment) to bounce? Bank errors can have quite significant consequences.

Now, imagine how significant a data accuracy error might be in other settings. Hospitals use similar automation and computer-intensive record keeping. What would happen if prescription information appeared incorrectly on a patient's chart and the patient became fatally ill as a result of the medicine that was mistakenly dispensed to him? The significance of such a data accuracy error could be tremendous. Furthermore, it would not be clear who was to blame. Would this be the fault of the doctor, the pharmacist, the programmer, the data entry clerk, or maybe some combination of errors by the system designer, the system analyst, the system programmer, the database administrator, and the vendor? It would be too easy simply to blame the computer; some one person would need to be found at fault. As a case in point, in late 2000, a software flaw in a radiation therapy device in a cancer treatment center in Panama City, Panama, increased exposure levels by up to 100 percent, causing multiple deaths and countless injured patients. Blame was placed on the software and also on the doctors who didn't manually double-check the device's settings. As the device and the software were manufactured in the United States, the U.S. Food and Drug Administration filed an injunction to force the manufacturer to stop manufacturing and distributing software for radiation therapy devices; but the physicians involved were indicted for murder under Panama law.

Computer-based information systems and the data within those systems are only as accurate and as useful as they have been made to be. This suggests the need for better precautions and greater scrutiny when modern information systems are designed, built, and used. This means that everyone must be concerned with data integrity, from the design of the system, to the building of the system, to the person who actually enters data into the system, to the people who use and manage the system. Perhaps more important, when data errors are found, people should not blame the computer. After all, people designed it, built it, and entered data into it in the first place.

Information Property

It happens to all of us. Nearly every day in the mail, we receive unwanted solicitations from credit card companies, department stores, magazines, or charitable organizations (see Figure 1.20). Many of these envelopes are never opened. We ask the same question over and over again: "How did I get on another mailing list?" Your name, address, and other personal information were most likely sold from one company to another for use in mass mailings. You probably did not give anyone permission to buy or sell information about you, but that is not a legal issue or a matter of concern for some firms. **Information property** focuses on who owns information about individuals and how that information can be sold and exchanged.

Shutterstock

FIGURE 1.20

Selling personal information has become big business.

Data Privacy Statements Who owns the computerized information about people—the information that is stored in thousands of databases by retailers, credit card companies, and marketing research companies? The answer is that the company that maintains the database of customers or subscribers legally owns the information and is free to sell it. Your name, address, and other information are all legally kept in a company database to be used for the company's future mailings and solicitations. However, the company can sell its customer list or parts of it to other companies who want to send similar mailings.

There are limits, however, to what a company can do with such data. For example, if a company stated at one time that its collection of marketing data was to be used strictly internally as a gauge of its own customer base and then sold that data to a second company years later, it would be unethically and illegally breaking its original promise. Companies collect data from credit card purchases (by using a credit card, you indirectly allow this) or from surveys and questionnaires you fill out when applying for a card. They also collect data when you fill in a survey at a bar, restaurant, supermarket, or the mall about the quality of the service or product preferences. By providing this information, you implicitly agree that this data can be used as the company wishes (within legal limits, of course).

What is even more problematic is the combination of this survey data with transaction data from your credit card purchases. Using the demographic data (Who am I, and where do I live?) and the psychographic data (What are my tastes and preferences?), companies can create a highly accurate profile of customers. How do you know who is accessing these databases? This is an issue that each company must address at both a strategic/ethical level (Is this something that we should be doing?) and a tactical level (If we do this, what can we do to ensure the security and integrity of the data?). The company needs to ensure proper hiring, training, and supervision of employees who have access to the data and implement the necessary software and hardware security safeguards.

In today's interconnected world, there are even more dangers to information property. Although more and more people are concerned about their privacy settings on social networks such as Facebook, there are things that you may not be able to control. For example, if one of your friends tags you on a photo posted on Facebook, a notice about you being in the photo will be on your Facebook "Wall" whether you like it or not. By the time you realize it, most of your friends, coworkers, and family members may have already seen it. Similarly, in early 2010, Google made a huge public relations blunder when it launched its Google Buzz social networking application: by default, this service exposed all of one's Gmail (Google's e-mail service) contacts to others, revealing sensitive information such as lawyers' clients or doctors' patients. After much uproar,

Google quickly changed the settings, but the damage was done, and Google is now facing a class-action lawsuit about this breach of personal rights. At other times, you may divulge sensitive information (such as your address or date of birth) when signing up for yet another social network; as newer, more exciting applications come up, you abandon your profile, but your information stays out there. Sometimes, you may forget who's following your activities at the various social networking sites, and you may tell people things you never wanted them to know. As these examples show, there are many more threats to your privacy than you may have thought.

Information Accessibility

With the rapid increase in online databases containing personal information and the surge in the use of computer-based communication between individuals, ethical concerns have been raised concerning who has the right to access and monitor this information. **Information accessibility** focuses on defining what information a person or organization has the right to obtain about others and how this information can be accessed and used.

For example, almost everyone sends and receives electronic mail, whether or not they have a PC. All that is needed to participate is access to the Internet, whether through a home PC, a school's computer lab, a wireless phone, a handheld computer, or any of several other devices that provide Internet access. E-mail is one of the most popular software applications of all time, and projections are that its use will only continue to increase. However, recent court cases have not supported computer privacy for employee e-mail transmissions and Internet usage. For example, although most companies provide employees with access to the Internet and other outside e-mail systems, many periodically monitor the e-mail messages that employees send and receive. Monitoring employee behavior is nothing new, and for many businesses it was a natural extension to monitor employee e-mail messages.

Surprisingly, there is little legal recourse for those who support e-mail privacy. In 1986, Congress passed the Electronic Communications Privacy Act (ECPA), but it offered far stronger support for voice mail than it did for e-mail communications. This act made it much more difficult for anyone (including the government) to eavesdrop on phone conversations. E-mail privacy is, therefore, much harder to protect. In addition, no other laws at the federal or state levels protect e-mail privacy. However, some states, most notably California, have passed laws that define how companies should inform their employees of this situation and in which situations monitoring is legal. Even so, this law is more of a guideline for ethical practice than a protection of privacy (Sipior & Ward, 1995).

Fortunately, the ECPA and the court case judgments thus far on e-mail monitoring suggest that companies must be prudent and open about their monitoring of e-mail messages and Internet usage. Companies should use good judgment in monitoring e-mail and should make public their policy about monitoring messages. One primary reason that employees perceive their e-mail to be private is the fact that they are never told otherwise (Weisband & Reinig, 1995). In addition, employees should use e-mail only as appropriate, based on their company's policy and their own ethical standards. Given recent actions and rulings on the capture and usage of e-mail messages over the Internet, it appears that online privacy is in jeopardy both in and out of business organizations. As a general rule, we all need to realize that what we type and send via e-mail in and out of the workplace is likely to be read by others for whom the messages were not intended. It is wise to generate only those e-mail messages that would not embarrass us if they were made public.

The Need for a Code of Ethical Conduct

Not only has the Internet age found government playing catch-up to pass legislation pertaining to computer crime, privacy, and security, it has also created an ethical conundrum. For instance, the technology exists to rearrange and otherwise change photographs, but is the practice ethical? If you can use a computer at your school or workplace for professional purposes but "steal" computer time to do personal business, is this ethical? Is it ethical for companies to compile information about your shopping habits, credit history, and other aspects of your life for the purpose of selling such data to others? Should guidelines be in place to dictate how businesses and others use information and computers? If so, what should the guidelines include, and who should write them? Should there be penalties imposed for those who violate established guidelines? If so, who should enforce such penalties?

Many businesses have devised guidelines for the ethical use of information technology and computer systems; similarly, most universities and many public school systems have written guidelines for students, faculty, and employees about the ethical use of computers. EduCom, a nonprofit organization of colleges and universities, has developed a policy for ethics in information technology that many universities endorse. In part, the EduCom statement concerning software and intellectual rights says,

> Because electronic information is volatile and easily reproduced, respect for the work and personal expression of others is especially critical in computer environments. Violations of authorial integrity, including plagiarism, invasion of privacy, unauthorized access, and trade secret and copyright violations, may be grounds for sanctions against members of the academic community.

Most organization and school guidelines encourage all system users to act responsibly, ethically, and legally when using computers and to follow accepted rules of online etiquette as well as federal and state laws.

Responsible Computer Use The Computer Ethics Institute is a research, education, and policy study organization that studies how advances in information technology have impacted ethics and corporate and public policy. The institute has issued widely quoted guidelines for the ethical use of computers. The guidelines prohibit the following:

- Using a computer to harm others
- Interfering with other people's computer work
- Snooping in other people's files
- Using a computer to steal
- Using a computer to bear false witness
- Copying or using proprietary software without paying for it
- Using other people's computer resources without authorization or compensation
- Appropriating other people's intellectual output

The guidelines recommend the following:

- Thinking about social consequences of programs you write and systems you design
- Using a computer in ways that show consideration and respect for others

Responsible computer use in the information age includes following the guidelines mentioned here. As a computer user, when in doubt, you should review the ethical guidelines published by your school, place of employment, and/or professional organization. Some users bent on illegal or unethical behavior are attracted by the anonymity they believe the Internet affords. But the fact is that we leave electronic tracks as we wander through the Web, and many perpetrators have been traced and successfully prosecuted when they thought they had hidden their trails. The fact is, too, that if you post objectionable material on the Internet and people complain about it, your Internet service provider can ask you to remove the material or remove yourself from the service.

The Digital Divide

Unfortunately, there are still many people in our society who are being left behind in the information age. The gap between those individuals in our society who are computer literate and have access to information resources like the Internet and those who do not is referred to as the **digital divide.** The digital divide is one of the major ethical challenges facing society today when you consider the strong linkage between computer literacy and a person's ability to compete in the information age. For example, access to raw materials and money fueled the industrial revolution, "but in the informational society, the fuel, the power, is knowledge," emphasized John Kenneth Galbraith, an American economist who specialized in emerging trends in the U.S. economy. "One has now come to see a new class structure divided by those who have information and those who must function out of ignorance. This new class has its power not from money, not from land, but from knowledge."

The good news is that the digital divide in America is rapidly shrinking, but there are still major challenges to overcome. In particular, people in rural communities, the elderly, people with disabilities, and minorities lag behind national averages for Internet access and computer literacy. Outside the United States, the gap gets even wider, and the obstacles get much more difficult to overcome, particularly in the developing countries, where infrastructure and financial resources

Brief Case ⊘

GUERILLA WI-FI HELPS TO BRIDGE THE DIVIDE

The digital divide refers to the "haves" and "have-nots" in the IT world. One Laptop per Child (OLPC), a nonprofit organization formed in 2005, attempts to overcome the digital divide, in part by providing low-cost computers to children who could otherwise not afford to buy them. However, just having a computer is not enough to join the club of the haves, and even households that have computers do not always have access to affordable Internet connection services. One company addressing this problem is Meraki Networks, Inc., headed by Sanjit Biswas. Biswas, a student at Massachusetts Institute of Technology, is taking time off from working on his doctoral degree in computer science to help bridge the digital divide. (*Meraki* is a Greek word meaning "inserting yourself into something you create.")

It has been determined that at least 1 billion people now connect to the Internet. Biswas's goal is to help the next billion— and the next after that—connect. The company sells small wireless routers (about the size of two iPhones stacked up), which feature software that allows them to "piggyback," so that one Meraki router connected to the Internet can relay the connection through other Meraki devices, thus forming a large network for Internet users. According to Biswas, devices within line of sight (approximately 700 feet) allow a single DSL connection to accommodate up to fifty Internet users. In this way, a network administrator can provide Internet connection service at nominal cost—perhaps as low as $1 per month. The drawback is that some Internet connection providers, such as Verizon and Time Warner, forbid subscribers from sharing connections. Less well known providers, such as Speakeasy and bway.net, have no such restrictions.

Thanks to Meraki, the so-called Guerilla Wi-Fi phenomenon is spreading and helping former Internet connection have-nots become connected—and part of the Internet community.

Mobile technology may be a promising way to reduce the digital divide. Compared to fixed-line Internet services, mobile Internet is much cheaper, is easier to acquire, and covers a larger geographic area. More important, mobile services allow users to access the Internet while on the move. In fact, mobile technology shows great promise for reducing the digital divide. Statistics from the Communications Commission of Kenya show that the country has 3.5 million Internet users. However, driven by mobile access, the number will increase to 10 million by 2012.

While people in developed countries often use mobile media for entertainment and social activities, people in developing countries use their mobile device as tools to acquire information, knowledge that can help them reshape their lives, families, and societies. For instance, in Kenya, RSS feeds from the Internet are fed into mobile phones to educate and inform people. In this southern African country, the Guardian's Activate 09 project sends out headlines to tens of thousands of citizens through text messages.

Questions

1. Should Internet providers be pressured to allow customers to share their connections with "nonpaying" customers?
2. Would you share your connection with a total stranger even if it meant that you would sometimes experience a slowdown to your connection speed?

Based on:

Anonymous. (2009, December 21). Combating the digital divide in the developing world with mobile phones. *Online Journalism Blog.* Retrieved April 1, 2010, from http://onlinejournalismblog.com/2009/12/21/combating -the-digital-divide-in-the-developing-world-with-mobile-phones.

Mims, C. (2007, August 6). Meraki's guerilla Wi-Fi to put a billion more people online. *Scientific American.* Retrieved April 1, 2010, from http://www.sciam.com/article.cfm?id=merakis-guerilla-wi-fi-to-put -billion-people-online.

Okuttah, M. (2010, February 4). Mobile phone the new driver of Internet access. *Business Daily.* Retrieved April 01, 2010, from http://www .businessdailyafrica.com/-/539444/854972/-/t2ckye/-/index.html.

Wakefield, J. (2010, March 19). World wakes up to digital divide. *BBC News.* Retrieved April 1, 2010, from http://news.bbc.co.uk/2/hi/ technology/8568681.stm.

are lacking. For example, most developing countries are lacking modern informational resources such as affordable Internet access or efficient electronic payment methods like credit cards. In an attempt to shrink the digital divide, a global project called **One Laptop per Child (OLPC)** is attempting to distribute low-cost laptop computers to children in developing countries around the world (see Figure 1.21). The initial goal was to price these computers at $100 each for governments and charitable organizations to purchase and distribute. The project is making progress, but there are numerous obstacles to providing a low-cost computer to children throughout the developing world (e.g., the price is still around $200; for more on OLPC and other efforts to develop computers for children in the developing world, see Case 1, "Bridging the Digital Divide," at the end of this chapter). Clearly, the digital divide is a major ethical concern facing the information age.

FIGURE 1.21

One Laptop per Child (OLPC) laptop.

fuseproject

INDUSTRY ANALYSIS

Business Career Outlook

Today, organizations are increasingly moving away from focusing exclusively on local markets. For example, Price-WaterhouseCoopers is focusing on forming overseas partnerships to increase its client base and to better serve the regions located away from its U.S. home. This means that it is not only more likely that you will need to travel overseas in your career or even take an overseas assignment, but also extremely likely that you will have to work with customers, suppliers, or colleagues from other parts of the world. Given this globalization trend, there is a shortage of business professionals with the necessary "global skills" for operating in the digital world. Three strategies for improving your skills include the following:

1. ***Gain International Experience.*** The first strategy is very straightforward. Simply put, by gaining international experiences, you will more likely possess the necessary cultural sensitivity to empathize with other cultures, and, more important, you will be a valuable asset to any global organization.

2. ***Learn More Than One Language.*** A second strategy is to learn more than your native language. Language problems within global organizations are often hidden beneath the surface. Many people are embarrassed to admit when they don't completely understand a foreign colleague. Unfortunately, the miscommunication of

important information can have disastrous effects on the business.

3. ***Sensitize Yourself to Global Cultural and Political Issues.*** A third strategy focuses on developing greater sensitivity to the various cultural and political differences within the world. Such sensitivity and awareness can be developed through course work, seminars, and international travel. Understanding current events and the political climate of international colleagues will enhance communication, cohesiveness, and job performance.

In addition to these strategies, prior to making an international visit or taking an international assignment, there are many things you can do to improve your effectiveness as well as enhance your chances of having fun, including the following:

1. Read books, newspapers, magazines, and Web sites about the country.

2. Talk to people who already know the country and its culture.

3. Avoid literal translations of work materials, brochures, memos, and other important documents.

4. Watch locally produced television and monitor the local news through international news stations and Web sites.

(continued)

5. After arriving in the new country, take time to tour local parks, monuments, museums, entertainment locations, and other cultural venues.

6. Share meals and breaks with local workers and discuss more than just work-related issues such as current local events and issues.

7. Learn several words and phrases in the local languages.

Regardless of what business profession you choose, globalization is a reality within the digital world. In addition to globalization, the proliferation of information systems is having specific ramifications for all business careers. This is discussed next.

For Accounting and Finance. In today's digital world, accounting and finance professionals rely heavily on information systems. Information systems are used to support various resource planning and control processes as well as to provide managers with up-to-date information. Accounting and finance professionals use a variety of information systems, networks, and databases to effectively perform their functions. In addition to changing the ways internal processes are managed and performed, information systems have also changed the ways organizations exchange financial information with suppliers, distributors, and customers. If you choose a career in accounting or finance, it is very likely that you will be working with various types of information systems every day.

For Operations Management. Information systems have also greatly changed the operations management profession. In the past, orders for supplies had to be placed over the phone, production processes had to be optimized using tedious calculations, and forecasts were sometimes only educated guesses. Today, enterprise resource planning and supply chain management systems have eliminated much of the "busywork" associated with making production forecasts and placing orders. Additionally, with the use of corporate extranets, companies are connecting to their suppliers' and distributors' networks, helping to reduce costs in procurement and distribution processes. If you choose operations management as your profession, the use of information systems will likely be a big part of your workday.

For Human Resources Management. The human resources management profession has experienced widespread use of information systems for recruiting employees via Internet job sites, distributing information through corporate intranets, or analyzing employee data stored in databases. In addition to using information systems within your daily work activities, you will also have to deal with other issues related to IS use and misuse within your organization. For example, what are the best methods for motivating employees to use a system they do not want to use? What policies should you use regarding monitoring employee productivity or Internet misuse? If you choose human resource management as a profession, information systems have become an invaluable addition to the recruitment and management of personnel.

For Marketing. Information systems have changed the way organizations promote and sell their products. For example, business-to-consumer electronic commerce, enabled by the Internet, allows companies to directly interact with their customers without the need for intermediaries; likewise, customer relationship management systems facilitate the targeting of narrow market segments with highly personalized promotional campaigns. Marketing professionals must therefore be proficient in the use of various types of information systems in order to attract and retain loyal customers.

For Information Systems. Information systems have become a ubiquitous part of organizational life, where systems are used by all organizational levels and functions. Because of this, there is a growing need for professionals to develop and support these systems. To most effectively utilize the investment in information systems, professionals must be proficient in both business—management, marketing, finance, and accounting—and technology. In other words, IS professionals must understand the business rationale for implementing a particular system as well as how organizations can use various systems to obtain a competitive advantage. Being able to understand both the business needs of the organization and the way in which IS-based solutions can meet these needs will provide you with a competitive advantage in the job market.

Based on:

Treitel, R. (2000, October 9). Global success. *Gantthead.com*. Retrieved April 23, 2010, from http://www.gantthead.com/articles/articlesPrint .cfm?ID=12706.

Key Points Review

1. *Describe the characteristics of the digital world and the advent of the information age.* Today, we live in a knowledge society, and information systems have become pervasive throughout our organizational and personal lives. The information age refers to a time in the history of civilization when information became the currency of the realm. Being successful in many careers today requires that people be computer literate, because the ability to access and effectively operate computing technology is a key part of many careers.

2. *Define globalization, describe how it evolved over time, and describe the key drivers of globalization.* A more global and competitive world includes visible economic, cultural, and technological changes. Globalization is the integration of economies throughout the world, fueled by technological progress and innovation. Over the past centuries, globalization has come a long way; starting with Columbus's discovery of America, Globalization 1.0 was fueled by power. Then, in 1800, Globalization 2.0 started, fueled mainly by a fall in transportation and telecommunications costs. Globalization 3.0 started in 2000 and was enabled by the convergence of a number of enablers, namely, the fall of the Berlin Wall, Netscape going public, work flow software, uploading, outsourcing, offshoring, supply chaining, insourcing, in-forming, and "the steroids." This has led to a rise in outsourcing and has helped to shape the world as we know it today. Companies operating in the digital world see a number of opportunities, many of which are enabled by Globalization 3.0, such as access to new markets and access to a talented labor pool in countries with lower wages. In addition to the opportunities, operating in the digital world also poses a number of challenges to companies. These challenges are of a governmental, geoeconomic, and cultural nature.

3. *Explain what an information system is, contrasting its data, technology, people, and organizational components.* Information systems are combinations of hardware, software, and telecommunications networks that people build and use to collect, create, and distribute useful data, typically in organizational settings. When data are organized in a way that is useful to people, these data are defined as information. The term "information systems" is also used to represent the field in which people develop, use, manage, and study computer-based information systems in organizations. The field of information systems is huge, diverse, and growing, and encompasses many different people, purposes, systems, and technologies. The technology part of information systems is the hardware, software, and telecommunications networks. The people who build, manage, use, and study information systems make up the people component. They include systems analysts, systems programmers, IS professors, and many others. Finally, information systems typically reside and are used within organizations, so they are said to have an organizational component. Together, these four aspects form an information system.

4. *Describe the dual nature of information systems in the success and failure of modern organizations.* If information systems are conceived, designed, used, and managed effectively and strategically, then together with a sound business model they can enable organizations to be more effective, to be more productive, to expand their reach, and to gain or sustain competitive advantage over rivals. If information systems are not conceived, designed, used, or managed well, they can have negative effects on organizations such as loss of money, loss of time, loss of customers' goodwill, and, ultimately, loss of customers. Modern organizations that embrace and manage information systems effectively and strategically and combine that with sound business models tend to be the organizations that are successful and competitive.

5. *Describe how computer ethics impact the use of information systems and discuss the ethical concerns associated with information privacy, accuracy, property, and accessibility.* Information privacy is concerned with what information an individual should have to reveal to others through the course of employment or through other transactions, such as online shopping. Ensuring authenticity and fidelity of information, as well as identifying who is responsible for informational errors that harm people, is information accuracy. Information property focuses on who owns information about individuals and how information can be sold and exchanged. Information accessibility refers to what information a person or organization has the right to obtain about others and how this information can be accessed and used. While the information age has brought widespread access to information, the downside is that others may now have access to personal information that you would prefer to keep private. Because there are few safeguards for ensuring the accuracy of information, individuals and companies can be damaged by informational errors. Additionally, because information is so easy to exchange and modify, information ownership violations readily occur. Likewise, with the rapid increase in online databases containing personal information and the increase in the use of computer-based communication between individuals, the question of who has the right to access and monitor this information has raised many ethical concerns. Finally, the digital divide between people who are computer literate and have access to information resources and those who do not is one of the major ethical challenges facing society today. While the digital divide is shrinking in the United States, it continues to be a major challenge elsewhere, especially in developing countries.

Key Terms

cloud computing 9
collaboration system 31
competitive advantage 35
computer-based information
  system 23
computer ethics 36
computer fluency 9
computer literacy 8
data 22
digital divide 41
downsizing 15
globalization 10
Globalization 1.0 10
Globalization 2.0 11
Globalization 3.0 12
hardware 21
information 22

information accessibility 40
information accuracy 38
information age 7
information privacy 36
information property 38
information system 21
information technology 21
in-forming 15
in-sourcing 15
internetworking 30
knowledge 22
knowledge society 5
knowledge worker 5
Luddite 7
management information
  system 30
nearshoring 18

neo-Luddite 36
office automation system 31
offshore outsourcing 14
offshoring 14
One Laptop per Child (OLPC) 42
outsourcing 14
service mentality 32
software 21
strategic 35
systems integration 30
telecommunications network 21
transaction processing system
  (TPS) 30
uploading 13
wiki 14
work flow software 13

Review Questions

1. Define the term "knowledge worker." Who coined the term?
2. Describe and contrast the economic, cultural, and technological changes occurring in the digital world.
3. List the 10 factors that led to Globalization 3.0.
4. Describe work flow software. How did this technology drive the flattening of the world?
5. Compare outsourcing, offshoring, and offshore outsourcing.
6. Describe in-sourcing and provide examples of how organizations use in-sourcing.
7. List and describe several reasons why companies are choosing to outsource business activities.
8. List and contrast several challenges of operating in the digital world.
9. Define the term "information systems" and explain its data, technology, people, and organizational components.
10. Define and contrast data, information, and knowledge.

11. Describe three or four types of jobs and career opportunities in information systems and in related fields.
12. List and define three technical knowledge and/or skills core competencies.
13. List and define four business knowledge and/or skills core competencies.
14. List and define four of the systems knowledge and/or skills core competencies.
15. List and define five types of information systems used in organizations.
16. Describe the evolution of the information systems function within organizations.
17. How are the digital divide and computer literacy related?
18. Compare and contrast information privacy, accuracy, property, and accessibility.

Self-Study Questions

1. Information systems today are _____.
   A. slower than in the past
   B. continuing to evolve with improvements to the hardware and software
   C. utilized by only a few select individuals
   D. stable and should not change
2. Whereas data are raw unformatted pieces or lists of words or numbers, information is _____.
   A. data that has been organized in a form that is useful
   B. accumulated knowledge
   C. what you put in your computer
   D. what your computer prints out for you

3. Computer-based information systems were described in this chapter as _____.
   A. any complicated technology that requires expert use
   B. a combination of hardware, software, and telecommunications networks that people build and use to collect, create, and distribute data
   C. any technology (mechanical or electronic) used to supplement, extend, or replace human, manual labor
   D. any technology used to leverage human capital

4. Other terms that can be used to represent the knowledge society include _____.
A. the new economy
B. the network society
C. the digital world
D. all of the above

5. Which of the following was *not* discussed as a common type, or category, of information system used in organizations?
A. transaction processing
B. decision support
C. enterprise resource planning
D. Web graphics

6. What stage of globalization started with expansion of trade to India, where the horse and wind and, in later stages, steam were the primary drivers?
A. Globalization 0.5
B. Globalization 1.0
C. Globalization 2.0
D. Globalization 3.0

7. The release of the Netscape Web browser had the following effects on the flattening of the world *except* _____.
A. helping setting standards for the display of Web data
B. providing easy access to the Internet
C. providing integrated e-mail
D. helping setting standards for the transport of Web data

8. Which of the following is *not* considered an enabler of a flat world by Friedman?
A. uploading
B. supply chaining
C. in-forming
D. customer service software

9. Which of the following is *not* considered open-source software?
A. Microsoft Office
B. OpenOffice.org
C. Firefox
D. Linux

10. Being _____, or knowing how to use the computer as a device to gather, store, organize, and process information, can open up myriad sources of information.
A. technology literate
B. digitally divided
C. computer literate
D. computer illiterate

Answers are on page 49.

Problems and Exercises

1. Match the following terms with the appropriate definitions:

i.   Information
ii. Downsizing
iii. Information systems
iv. Information accuracy
v.   Computer fluency
vi. Globalization 3.0
vii. Offshore outsourcing
viii. Digital divide
ix. Information privacy
x.   Computer ethics

a. The issues and standards of conduct as they pertain to the use of information systems
b. Data that have been formatted in a way that is useful
c. Stage of globalization encompassing virtually every nation and shrinking the world from "size small to size tiny"
d. The ability to independently learn new technologies as they emerge and assess their impact on one's work and life
e. The practice of slashing costs and streamlining operations by laying off employees
f. Combinations of hardware, software, and telecommunications networks that people build and use to collect, create, and distribute useful data, typically in organizational settings
g. The outsourcing of business processes on a global scale
h. An area concerned with what information an individual should have to reveal to others through the course of employment or through other transactions, such as online shopping
i. The gap between those individuals in our society who are computer literate and have access to information resources, such as the Internet, and those who do not
j. An area concerned with ensuring the authenticity and fidelity of information as well as identifying who is responsible for informational errors that harm people

2. Peter Drucker has defined the knowledge worker and knowledge society. What are his definitions? Do you agree with them? What examples can you give to support or disprove these concepts?

3. Of the several information systems listed in the chapter, how many do you have experience with? What systems would you like to work with? What types of systems do you encounter at the university you are attending? The Web is also a good source for additional information.

4. Identify someone who works within the field of information systems as an IS instructor, professor, or practitioner (e.g., as a systems analyst or systems manager). Find out why this individual got into this field and what this person likes and dislikes about working within the field of information systems. What advice can this person offer to someone entering the field?

5. As a small group, conduct a search on the Web for job placement services. Pick at least four of these services and find as many IS job titles as you can. You may want to try monster.com or careerbuilder.com. How many did you find? Were any of them different from those presented in this chapter? Could you determine the responsibilities of these positions based on the information given to you?

6. Visit Walmart China (www.wal-martchina.com/english/index.htm). Compare and contrast www.walmart.com with Walmart China's site. What is the focus of Walmart China's Web site? Discuss how the focus differs from www.walmart.com. What are possible reasons for the differences?

7. What digital news media do you use to get your news? According to this textbook's definitions, are you in-forming? If you are in-forming, describe how. What other ways could you in-form?

8. What are some examples of key technologies that utilize "steroids"? Using the technology definition provided by this textbook, how do you use technological steroids in your everyday life?

9. Should the U.S. government allow companies to use offshore outsourcing if qualified U.S. citizens are willing and able to do a job? Should the government regulate the amount that can be outsourced by any company? Why or why not?

10. Work flow software allows an organization to move documents and/or tasks through a work process. Using your own experiences and observations, either professionally or personally, describe how the work flow software worked.

11. As outlined in the chapter, UPS provides in-sourcing services for many businesses. Visit www.ups.com and identify some examples of UPS providing in-sourcing services and include a listing of some of UPS's in-sourcing customers.

12. List 10 reasons why you would (or would not) be a good global manager.

13. Global outsourcing appears to be here to stay. Use the Web to identify a company that is providing low-cost labor from some less developed part of the world. Provide a short report that explains who the company is, where it is located, who its customers are, what services and capabilities it provides, how long it has been in business, and any other interesting information you can find in your research.

14. The Electronic Frontier Foundation (www.eff.org) has a mission of protecting rights and promoting freedom in the "electronic frontier." The organization provides additional advice on how to protect your online privacy. Review its suggestions and provide a summary of what you can do to protect yourself.

15. Do you consider yourself computer literate? Do you know of any friends or relatives who are not computer literate? What can you do to improve your computer literacy? Is computer literacy necessary in today's job market? Why or why not?

16. Complete the computer ethics quiz at http://web.cs.bgsu.edu/maner/xxicee/html/welcome.htm and visit www.onlineethics.org/Resources/19049.aspx for more issues on computer ethics and social implications of computing. Should ethical codes apply to all professions?

17. Find your school's guidelines for ethical computer use on the Internet and answer the following questions: Are there limitations as to the type of Web sites and material that can be viewed (e.g., pornography)? Are students allowed to change the programs on the hard drives of the lab computers or download software for their own use? Are there rules governing personal use of computers and e-mail?

18. Do you believe that there is a need for a unified information systems code of ethics? Visit www.albion.com/netiquette/corerules.html. What do you think of this code? Should it be expanded, or is it too general? Search the Internet for additional codes for programmers or Web developers. What did you find?

Application Exercises

 Note: The existing data files referenced in these exercises are available on the Student Companion Web site: **www.pearsonhighered.com/valacich**.

 Spreadsheet Application: Ticket Sales at Campus Travel

The local travel center, Campus Travel, has been losing sales. The presence of online ticketing Web sites, such as Travelocity.com and Expedia.com, has lured many students away. However, given the complexity of making international travel arrangements, Campus Travel could have a thriving and profitable business if it concentrated its efforts in this area. You have been asked by the director of sales and marketing to help with analyzing prior sales data in order to design better marketing strategies. Looking at these data, you realize that it is nearly impossible to perform a detailed analysis of ticket sales given that it is not summarized or organized in a useful way to inform business decision making. The spreadsheet TicketSales.csv contains the ticket sales data for spring 2011. Your director has asked you for the following information regarding ticket sales. Modify the TicketSales.csv spreadsheet to provide the following information for your director:

1. The total number of tickets sold.
    a. Select the data from the "tickets sold" column.
    b. Then select the "autosum" function.
2. The largest amount of tickets sold by a certain salesperson to any one location.
    a. Select the appropriate cell.
    b. Use the "MAX" function to calculate each salesperson's highest ticket total in one transaction.
3. The least amount of tickets sold by a certain salesperson to any one location.
    a. Select the appropriate cells.
    b. Use the "MIN" function to calculate the "least tickets sold."
4. The average number of tickets sold.
    a. Select the cells.
    b. Use the "AVERAGE" function to calculate the "average number of tickets sold" using the same data you had selected in the previous steps.

Database Application: Tracking Frequent-Flier Miles at the Campus Travel Agency

The director of sales and marketing of the travel agency would like to increase the efficiency of handling those who have frequent-flier accounts. Often, frequent fliers have regular travel routes, preferred seating area, or meal category. In the previous years, the data has been manually entered in a three-ring binder. In order to handle the frequent fliers' requests more efficiently, your director has asked you to build an Access database containing the following information:

- Name (first and last name)
- Address
- Phone number
- Frequent-flier number
- Frequent-flier airline
- Meal category
- Preferred seating area

To do this, you will need to do the following:

1. Create an empty database named "frequent flier."
2. Import the data contained in the file FrequentFliers.txt. Use "Text File" under "Import" in the "External Data" tab. Hint: Use tab delimiters when importing the data; note that the first row contains field names.

After importing the data, create a report displaying the names and addresses of all frequent fliers by doing the following:

1. Select "Report Wizard" under "Report" in the "Create" tab.
2. Include the fields "first name," "last name," and "address" in the report.
3. Save the report as "frequent fliers."

Answers to the Self-Study Questions

1. B, p. 6
2. A, p. 22
3. B, p. 23
4. D, p. 5
5. D, p. 30
6. C, p. 11
7. C, p. 13
8. D, p. 12
9. A, p. 14
10. C, p. 8

Case 1

Bridging the Digital Divide

An important ethical issue related to computer use is the *digital divide,* which refers to the unequal access to computer technology within various populations. The divide occurs on several levels: socioeconomic (rich or poor), racial (majority/minority), and geographical (urban/rural and developed/undeveloped countries). Studies have shown that as the information age progresses, those individuals who have access to computer technology and to opportunities for learning computer skills generally have an educational edge.

To even the divide, Nicholas Negroponte, an architect and computer scientist who founded the Massachusetts Institute of Technology's Media Lab, announced the creation of One Laptop per Child (OLPC), a nonprofit organization, in 2005 at the World Economic Forum in Davos, Switzerland. As part of the project, the OX-1, a $100 computer, was designed expressly for child use. With $2 million start-up contributions, the OLPC began distributing the computers to children around the world, including locations within the United States. The computers were given to children at an early age, were designed for child ownership and use, had built-in Internet access, were intended to accompany children from school to homes, and were designed for free and open programming access.

The project's goal was to close the digital divide and transform education by providing access to computers to children who would otherwise not have the opportunity to fully participate in the information age.

Critics of the program, however, claimed that Negroponte's policy of dealing only with heads of state and of requiring countries to purchase machines in lots of 1 million seemed in direct opposition to stated goals. (These requirements have since been modified.) In 2007, when Intel mounted competitive campaigns to sell the Classmate PC, a low-cost computer also designed for individuals previously underserved in the computer market, Negroponte complained about the competition, calling Intel's efforts "shameless." The competition, however, is proving beneficial to those who would otherwise not have had access to low-cost, educationally focused, top-of-the-line computer technology.

Despite criticisms, the OLPC campaign continues to provide laptops to children around the world. Amazon.com gave the program a boost when they announced a program in which they would sell the XO laptop through their online marketplace. For $399, a shopper could buy the XO laptop for themselves, and an additional XO laptop was given to the program. In six weeks, over 100,000 laptops were given to children through the Amazon initiative.

In October 2009, every child in the country of Uruguay received a laptop, making Uruguay the first country to fulfill the mission of the OLPC program. As of 2010, over 1.5 million children in 30 countries had received the XO laptop. In Australia, the program is just taking off, and only around 1,500 laptops have been handed out there. However, the country plans to distribute over 400,000 in the next few years. The program has recently begun delivery of 100,000 laptops to Rwanda and, as of March 2010, even delivered 3,700 XOs to war-torn Afghanistan. Countries on the list to receive laptops in the near future include Uganda, Zanzibar, and Sierra Leone.

The next version of the XO laptop is already being designed and is expected to ship in 2011. The XO-1.75 will consume less than two watts of power. Using a crank on the side of the computer, a child will be able to "wind" the laptop for a minute (using a small crank) and get 10 minutes of use out of it. For countries with little to no electrical resources, the XO-1.75 will allow children to use the laptop anywhere. In addition, an XO-3 model will also focus on low power consumption but will be in the form of a tablet instead of a laptop.

Clearly, the OLPC program continues to innovate and find ways to bring technology to children around the world. With every laptop delivered, the digital divide is lessened.

Questions

1. Why does the digital divide matter to children and their families?
2. Do you think the OLPC project will be successful? Why or why not?
3. Identify and discuss what you feel is the major challenge for making the OLPC a success. How can this challenge be overcome?

Based on:

Hernandez, C. (2010, February 8). Computers in Haiti and Afghanistan: One Laptop per Child expands its reach. *Smartplanet.com*. Retrieved April 12, 2010, from http://www.smartplanet.com/people/blog/pure-genius/computers-in-haiti-and-afghanistan-one-laptop-per-child-expands-its-reach/1813.

Nicholas Negroponte (n.d.). Retrieved May 21, 2010, from http://web.media.mit.edu/~nicholas.

OLPC Blog. (2010, March 9). OLPC breaks new ground in Kandahar. *One Laptop Per Child Blog*. Retrieved April 12, 2010, from http://blog.laptop.org/2010/03/09/olpc-provides-children-of-afghanistan-access-to-a-modern-education.

Parrack, D. (2008, November 17). OLPC relaunches "give one get one" offer through Amazon. *Tech.Blorge.com*. Retrieved on April 12, 2010, from http://tech.blorge.com/Structure:%20/2008/11/17/olpc-relaunches-give-one-get-one-offer-through-amazon.

Vota, W. (2007, May 21). OLPC XO vs. Intel Classmate PC, a beneficial competition. *OLPC News*. Retrieved July 26, 2010, from http://www.olpcnews.com/sales_talk/countries/olpc_xo_intel_classmates.html.

Case 2

Enabling Global Payments at PayPal

If you have used eBay (and who hasn't?), you know how easy it is to pay for items you buy and to receive payment for items you have sold. Checks, credit card charges, and money orders are unnecessary. Instead of these traditional methods of payment, digital money is easily and effortlessly zapped to and from accounts at PayPal, the most frequently used digital money transfer service online.

Peter Thiel, a hedge fund manager, and Max Levchin, an online security specialist, founded what was to become PayPal—it was first named Field Link and then Confinity and finally, in 2001, PayPal. The company went online rather naively in 1999. The founders' vision was to create a digital currency exchange service free of government controls, but the site quickly became a target for hackers, con artists, and organized crime groups, who used the site for scams and money laundering. Tighter security measures halted criminal activity and helped assuage customer complaints, but government regulators moved in. Attorneys general in several states investigated PayPal's business practices, and New York and California levied fines for violations. Louisiana banned the company from operating in that state. (The ban has since been lifted.)

When PayPal began, payment for Web products was made through credit card charges at the purchase site and via checks and money orders sent through the U.S. Postal Service. Other companies, such as Beenz.com and Flooz.com, had tried to establish electronic payment systems based on a special digital currency, but merchants, banks, and customers were hesitant to accept "money" that wasn't based on real dollars. Thiel and Levchin saw the need for an electronic payment system that relied on real currency, especially when eBay became popular, and PayPal filled that niche.

After PayPal solved its security and customer support problems, customers liked the convenience and ease of using the service, and its client base grew. Buyers like not having to reveal their credit card numbers to every online merchant, and merchants appreciate having PayPal handle payment collection. New PayPal clients establish an account with a user name and password and fund the account by giving PayPal a credit card number or bank account transaction information. Although PayPal prefers the latter (because bank account transactions are cheaper than credit card transactions), half of PayPal's accounts are funded via credit cards.

eBay bought PayPal in 2002 for $1.5 billion and since then has also been a major source of income for the money transfer site. At the same time, PayPal has expanded its client base both in the United States and abroad and is generating much revenue by charging fees for payment processing for a wide variety of online vendors, auction sites, and corporations.

Services to buyers are free, but sellers are charged a fee, which is generally lower than fees charged by major credit card companies. PayPal now offers special merchant accounts for transferring larger amounts of money and also offers a donation box feature for blogs and other Web sites where visitors can make donations.

PayPal spawned many rivals after its initial launch, but most have since died, including Citigroup's C2it and Bank One's Email Money. As of 2010, PayPal operates in 190 worldwide markets, has localized Web sites in 17 countries, and manages over 78 million active accounts. PayPal allows customers to send, receive, and hold funds in 19 currencies worldwide. PayPal handled over $70 billion in transactions during 2009.

PayPal has recently expanded its services into the realm of social media by partnering with Facebook. Facebook Credits, the social site's virtual online currency, can now be bought using PayPal. Facebook Credits allow Facebook users to buy virtual goods in their online gift shop and are used in social games and various other applications. Users who don't have access to a credit or debit account but do have access to a PayPal account will be able to purchase the virtual credits. It's an important move for many since the Credit Card Accountability, Responsibility and Disclosure Act of 2009 made it illegal for anyone under the age of 21 to be issued a credit card without a parent, guardian, or spouse's cosignature (or showing that they have the income to cover the credit obligation). The law hits at one of Facebook's key demographics: college students between the ages of 18 and 21. Since social gaming generated over $500 million in 2009, PayPal sees virtual credits and, more important, a presence on Facebook as a revenue-generating opportunity. Additionally, the collaboration allows advertisers to buy self-serve ads on Facebook's pages using PayPal.

Another key element of PayPal's business is mobile payments. In 2009, PayPal's mobile transactions topped $140 million, nearly a sixfold increase from their 2008 mobile transaction figures. According to many analysts, the increasing number of mobile smart phone applications is responsible for the increase. More and more mobile users are conducting business on eBay using their smart phones. With PayPal's mobile apps, sending money on the winning bid is easy and can be handled from nearly anywhere. PayPal's latest iPhone app allows users to "bump" their phones together to transfer money between one another. The app also allows a user to request money from a group of people for things like a going-away gift at the office, a fundraiser, or other event where money needs to be pooled. Additionally, the app gives users the ability to "split the ticket" at a restaurant and send their portion of the check total to whoever paid the bill—including tax and tip!

While the company has had its share of problems with fraud and phishers (scamsters who send fraudulent e-mail messages and duplicate legitimate Web sites), PayPal continues to innovate and be the number one method of payment for the world's buyers and sellers.

Questions

1. Why do you think PayPal has been so successful throughout the world?
2. How has PayPal acted to increase globalization?
3. Do you use PayPal? Why or why not?

Based on:

Anonymous. (n.d.). PayPal—About us. Retrieved May 24, 2010, from https:// www.paypal-media.com/aboutus.cfm.

Anonymous. (n.d.). PayPal company history. Retrieved May 24, 2010, from http://www.fundinguniverse.com/company-histories/PayPal-Inc-Company-History .html.

Anonymous. (n.d.). Under 21? No credit card for you. Retrieved May 24, 2010, from http://articles.moneycentral.msn.com/Banking/YourCreditRating/under-21-no-credit-card-for-you.aspx.

Anonymous. (2010, March 18). PayPal smartphone transactions: Increasingly important for eBay. Retrieved May 24, 2010, from http://seekingalpha.com/article/ 194339-paypal-smartphone-transactions-increasingly-important-for-ebay.

Arellano, N. E. (2010, March 17). Bump, split and collect with PayPal's mobile payment iPhone app. *itbusiness.ca*. Retrieved May 24, 2010, from http://www .itbusiness.ca/it/client/en/home/News.asp?id=56825.

Grabianowski, E. (n.d.). How PayPal works. Retrieved May 24, 2010, from http:// computer.howstuffworks.com/paypal3.htm.

PayPal. (2010, May 21). In *Wikipedia, the free encyclopedia*. Retrieved May 21, 2010, from http://en.wikipedia.org/w/index.php?title=PayPal&oldid=363422981.

Walker, L. (2005, May 19). PayPal looks to evolve beyond its auction roots. *Washingtonpost.com*. Retrieved May 24, 2010, from http://www.washingtonpost .com/wp-dyn/content/article/2005/05/18/AR2005051802187.html.

Walsh, M. (2010, February 18). Facebook and PayPal become payment pals. *Online Media Daily*. Retrieved May 24, 2010, from http://www.mediapost .com/publications/?fa=Articles.showArticle&art_aid=122775.

Gaining Competitive Advantage Through Information Systems

After reading this chapter, you will be able to do the following:

1. Discuss how information systems can be used for automation, organizational learning, and strategic advantage.

2. Describe international business and IS strategies used by companies operating in the digital world.

3. Explain why and how companies are continually looking for innovative ways to use information systems for competitive advantage.

4. Describe freeconomics and how organizations can leverage digital technologies to provide free goods and services to customers as a business strategy for gaining a competitive advantage.

Preview

This chapter examines how organizations evaluate information systems (IS) investments and how these investments can be used strategically, enabling firms to gain or sustain competitive advantage over their rivals. As described in Chapter 1, "Managing in the Digital World," a firm has competitive advantage over rival firms when it can do something better, faster, more economically, or uniquely. We will show why it is vital but sometimes difficult for people to determine the value of an IS investment. In this chapter, we begin by examining how organizations can gain the greatest strategic value from their IS investments. We then examine international business strategies that shape how information systems can be designed to support how data and controls flow across national borders. Finally, we talk about the continual need to find innovative ways to succeed with and through information systems.

Managing in the Digital World:
Home Media—You're in Control

"You've got a life. TiVo gets it." With that catchy motto, TiVo Incorporated introduced in 1999 a service that gave users unprecedented control over television viewing. Did you have to miss a football game for your sister's wedding? TiVo could record it for you so that you could watch it at your convenience. Were there certain shows you always had to miss because you worked late hours? TiVo solved the problem again. Since TiVo's initial entrance into the consumer market, an explosion of digital video recorder (DVR) devices and options for recording live TV have become available. DVR technology is incorporated into many cable boxes, satellite dish receivers, and computers. Some televisions are even appearing with DVR technology onboard from the factory. For many people, the phrase "DVR it" has become part of their common vocabulary when talking how they watch TV. DVR technology allows users to watch recorded video in a "time-shifted" environment. Similar to podcasts, where live audio programming is recorded for later listening, time shifting television programs allows users to watch shows at their convenience.

While early set-top boxes like TiVo allowed consumers to record several hours of TV shows, modern DVR devices allow users to record over 200 hours of their favorite shows, movies, and sporting events—all in high definition. A DVR is basically a simple computer with a hard drive recorder that incorporates the following capabilities:

- Your favorite shows can be automatically recorded whenever they are on.
- A search engine can find and automatically record the shows that match your interests (by title, actor, director, category, and even key word).
- Many DVR devices let you transfer shows to your laptop or portable device or easily burn them to DVD.
- Some DVR providers allow you to connect to your DVR remotely via the Internet or smart phone to schedule last-minute shows from anywhere in the world.

DVRs make TV watching an interactive experience in that you can pause the action if the phone rings; you can answer the phone and then either return to the show exactly where you left off or fast-forward to the story where it is when you return. You can also do instant replay without missing a moment of the action.

DVR functionality varies depending on the manufacturer and the package users choose to pay for, but the following abilities are common to many devices:

- You can select a genre of movies, such as comedy, mystery, or romance, and request that your DVR record them.
- You can select only those shows for recording that have your favorite actor.

Getty Images –IStock Exclusive RF

FIGURE 2.1

DVR and other media technologies are putting you in control of your viewing.

- You can select specific types of shows that have your favorite actor.
- Some DVR devices allow you to connect your home computer network, allowing you to play music and view photos from your computer through your DVR system.
- TiVo users have exclusive access to Amazon's Video On Demand service, a catalog of over 50,000 television shows and movies—the first single-box solution that intermingles downloadable broadband video and traditional TV in one place.

Advances in technology continue to push the envelope in terms of how people view and interact with entertainment. Although time shifting has become an everyday occurrence for DVR users, another idea is emerging—*place* shifting. Users of Sling Media's "Slingbox" are able to connect a small box to their cable or satellite receivers and in turn connect that box to their home network. Once set up, Slingbox users can view their home TV channels from anywhere in the world where a broadband Internet connection is available.

If users have a DVR-capable satellite, cable, or TiVo box, the Slingbox can even handle time-shifted, recorded programs. Sling Media even offers a Sling Player application for mobile phones, allowing playback of content from almost anywhere.

Tired of watching your favorite Hulu or YouTube video on the computer? Sling Media even offers a free downloadable utility for your computer that will "sling" any computer window to their "Sling Catcher" box. Users can also sling their favorite music to the next room (or the next state) by connecting an audio source to their Slingbox and "catching" it with a Sling Catcher.

Clearly, technology is evolving to put consumers in control of how they use and interact with media. Companies will continue innovating and competing with one another to meet customer needs and preferences.

After reading this chapter, you will be able to answer the following:

1. How does a DVR help you automate, learn, and strategize regarding your home entertainment?
2. In what way was DVR technology a disruptive innovation?
3. How would you forecast the future of DVR in regard to the advent of on-demand video where any type of video content is available at any time on any device?

Based on:

Digital video recorder. (2010, May 15). In *Wikipedia, the free encyclopedia*. Retrieved May 20, 2010, from http://en .wikipedia.org/w/index.php?title=Digital_video_recorder& oldid=362342888.

DirecTV.com. (2010, April 23). Retrieved April 23, 2010 from http://www.directv.com/DTVAPP/global/article.jsp?assetId=P 5980155.

Lam, B. (2007, February 7). Breaking: Tivo boxes to download Amazon unboxed videos. *Gizmodo.com*. Retrieved April 23, 2010, from http://gizmodo.com/gadgets/home-entertainment/ breaking-tivo-boxes-to-download-amazon-unboxed-videos -234557.php.

McCarthy, C. (2007, October 10). No fast-forwarding at TiVo, Rhapsody party. *CNET News.com*. Retrieved April 23, 2010, from http://www.news.com/8301-13577_3-9794674-36.html.

Olsen, S. (2006, February 14). Love in the time of TiVo. *CNET News.com*. Retrieved April 23, 2010, from http://news.com .com/Love+in+the+time+of+TiVo/2100-1041_3-6039433 .html.

Reardon, M. (2006, March 7). TiVo looks to Verizon phones for TV recording. *CNET News.com*. Retrieved April 23, 2010, from http://news.com.com/TiVo+looks+to+Verizon+ phones+for+TV+recording/2100-1039_3-6046759.html.

Sling Catcher. (2010, April 23). *Slingbox.com*. Retrieved April 23, 2010, from http://www.slingbox.com/go/ slingcatcher-slingplayer.

Spring, T. (2008, January 9). TiVo boosts service, supports video podcasts. *PCWorld.com*. Retrieved April 23, 2010, from http://blogs.pcworld.com/staffblog/archives/006244.html.

Time shifting. (2010, May 7). In *Wikipedia, the free encyclopedia*. Retrieved May 20, 2010, from http://en.wikipedia .org/w/index.php?title=Time_shifting&oldid=360663201.

TiVo DVR: Your ultimate source for entertainment. (n.d.). Retrieved April 23, 2010, from http://www.tivo.com.

What is placeshifting? (2010, April 23). *Slingmedia.com*. Retrieved April 23, 2010, from http://www.slingmedia.com/ go/placeshifting.

Enabling Organizational Strategy Through Information Systems

In Chapter 1, we introduced the notion that information systems can have strategic value to an organization. Because organizations are composed of different levels and functions, a broad range of information is needed to support an organization's business processes. **Business processes** are the activities organizations perform in order to reach their business goals, including core activities that transform inputs and produce outputs, and supporting activities that enable the core activities to take place. As a review, we briefly describe how organizations are generally structured as well as the common functional areas of most modern organizations. Understanding how organizations are structured helps to illustrate how different types of information systems can support various business processes and provide different levels of value to the organization.

Organizational Decision-Making Levels

Every organization is composed of decision-making levels, as illustrated in Figure 2.2. Each level of an organization has different responsibilities and, therefore, different informational needs.

Operational Level At the **operational level** of a firm, the routine, day-to-day business processes and interactions with customers occur. Information systems at this level are designed

FIGURE 2.2

Organizations are composed of different decision-making levels.

to automate repetitive activities, such as sales transaction processing, and to improve the efficiency of business processes and the customer interface. Operational planning typically has a time frame of a few hours or days, and the managers at the operational level, such as foremen or supervisors, make day-to-day decisions that are highly structured and recurring. **Structured decisions** are those in which the procedures to follow for a given situation can be specified in advance. Because structured decisions are relatively straightforward, they can be programmed directly into operational information systems so that they can be made with little or no human intervention. For example, an inventory management system for a shoe store in the mall could keep track of inventory and issue an order for additional inventory when levels drop below a specified level. Operational managers within the store would simply need to confirm with the inventory management system that the order for additional shoes was needed. At the operational level, information systems are typically used to optimize processes and to better understand the underlying causes of any performance problems. Using information systems to optimize processes at the operational level can offer quick returns on the IS investment, as activities at this level are clearly delineated and well focused. Figure 2.3 summarizes the general characteristics of the operational level.

Managerial/Tactical Level At the **managerial level** (or tactical level) of the organization, functional managers (e.g., marketing managers, finance managers, manufacturing managers, human resource managers, and so on) focus on monitoring and controlling operational-level activities and providing information to higher levels of the organization (see Figure 2.4). Managers at this level, referred to as midlevel managers, focus on effectively utilizing and deploying organizational resources to achieve the strategic objectives of the organization. Midlevel managers

Who: Foremen and Supervisors

What: Automate Routine and Repetitive Activities and Events

Why: Improve Organizational Efficiency

FIGURE 2.3

Information systems at the operational level of an organization help to improve efficiency by automating routine and repetitive activities.

FIGURE 2.4

Information systems at the managerial level of an organization help to improve effectiveness by automating the monitoring and controlling of operational activities.

typically focus on problems within a specific business function, such as marketing or finance. Here, the scope of the decision usually is contained within the business function, is moderately complex, and has a time horizon of a few days to a few months (also referred to as tactical planning). For example, a marketing manager at Nike may decide how to allocate the advertising budget for the next business quarter or some other fixed time period.

Managerial-level decision making is not nearly as structured or routine as operational-level decision making. Managerial-level decision making is referred to as semistructured decision making because solutions and problems are not clear-cut and often require judgment and expertise. For **semistructured decisions,** some procedures to follow for a given situation can be specified in advance but not to the extent where a specific recommendation can be made. For example, an information system could provide a production manager at Nike with performance analytics and forecasts about sales for multiple product lines, inventory levels, and overall production capacity. The metrics deemed most critical to assessing progress toward a certain goal (referred to as **key performance indicators [KPIs]**) are displayed on performance *dashboards* (described later in Chapter 6, "Enhancing Business Intelligence Using Information Systems"). The manager could use this information to create multiple hypothetical production schedules. With these schedules, the manager could then perform predictive analyses to examine inventory levels and potential sales profitability, depending on the order in which manufacturing resources were used to produce each type of product.

Executive/Strategic Level   At the **executive level** (or strategic level) of the organization, managers focus on long-term strategic questions facing the organization, such as which products to produce, which countries to compete in, and what organizational strategy to follow (see Figure 2.5).

FIGURE 2.5

Information systems at the executive level of an organization help to improve strategy and planning by providing summaries of past data and projections of the future.

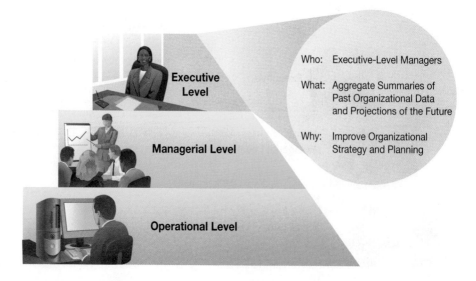

Managers at this level include the president and chief executive officer, vice presidents, and possibly the board of directors; they are referred to as "executives." Executive-level decisions deal with complex problems with broad and long-term ramifications for the organization. Executive-level decisions are referred to as unstructured decisions because the problems are relatively complex and nonroutine. In addition, executives must consider the ramifications of their decisions in terms of the overall organization. For **unstructured decisions,** few or no procedures to follow for a given situation can be specified in advance. For example, top managers may decide to develop a new product or discontinue an existing one. Such a decision may have vast, long-term effects on the organization's levels of employment and profitability. To assist executive-level decision making, information systems are used to obtain aggregate summaries of trends and projections of the future. At the executive level, information systems provide KPIs that are focused on balancing performance across the organization, such that, for example, product launches are staggered to smooth out the effects of spikes in demand on the supply chain. Other KPIs are used to benchmark the organization's performance against its competitors.

In summary, most organizations have three general decision-making levels: operational, managerial, and executive. Each level has unique activities and business processes, each requiring different types of information. In other words, it is common that each decision-making level is supported by different types of information systems.

Organizational Functional Areas

In addition to different decision-making levels within an organization, there are also different functional areas. A functional area represents a discrete area of an organization that focuses on a specific set of activities. For example, people in the marketing function focus on the activities that promote the organization and its products in a way that attracts and retains customers; people in the accounting and finance functions focus on managing and controlling capital assets and financial resources of the organization. Table 2.1 lists various organizational functions and lists examples of the types of information systems that are commonly used. These **functional area information systems** are designed to support the unique business processes of specific functional areas (see Figure 2.6).

When deploying information systems across organizational levels and functions, there are three general ways the information system can provide value: to automate, to learn, and to

TABLE 2.1 Organizational Functions and Representative Information Systems

Functional Area	Information System	Examples of Typical Systems
Accounting and finance	Systems used for managing, controlling, and auditing the financial resources of the organization	• Accounts payable • Expense accounts • Cash management • Payroll processing
Human resources	Systems used for managing, controlling, and auditing the human resources of the organization	• Recruiting and hiring • Education and training • Benefits management • Employee termination • Workforce planning
Marketing	Systems used for managing new product development, distribution, pricing, promotional effectiveness, and sales forecasting of the products and services offered by the organization	• Market research and analysis • New product development • Promotion and advertising • Pricing and sales analysis • Product location analysis
Production and operations	Systems used for managing, controlling, and auditing the production and operations resources of the organization	• Inventory management • Cost and quality tracking • Materials and resource planning • Customer service tracking • Customer problem tracking • Job costing • Resource utilization

FIGURE 2.6

Business process supported
by various functional area
information systems.

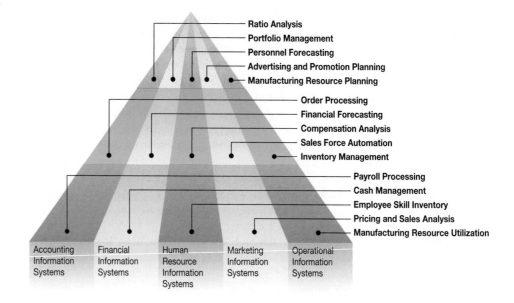

execute organizational strategy (see Figure 2.7). These three ways are not necessarily mutually exclusive, but we believe that each is progressively more useful to the firm and thus adds more value to the business. This is examined next.

Information Systems for Automating: Doing Things Faster

Someone with an **automating** perspective thinks of technology as a way to help complete a task within an organization faster, more cheaply, and perhaps with greater accuracy and/or consistency. Let us look at a typical example. A person with an automating mentality would take a loan application screening process and automate it by inputting the loan applications into a computer database so that those involved in decision making for the loans could process the applications faster, more easily, and with fewer errors. Such a system might also enable customers to complete the loan application online. A transition from a manual to an automated loan application process might enable the organization to deploy employees more efficiently, leading to even more cost savings (see Table 2.2). Information systems at the operational level of an organization often help in automating repetitive activities, but they can also help to gather valuable information for higher decision-making levels within the organization.

Information Systems for Organizational Learning: Doing Things Better

We can also use information systems to learn and improve. Shoshana Zuboff (1988) described this as **informating.** Zuboff explained that a technology informates when it provides information about its operation and the underlying work process that it supports. The system helps us not only to automate a business process but also to learn to improve the day-to-day activities within that process.

The learning mentality builds on the automating mentality because it recognizes that information systems can be used as a vehicle for **organizational learning**—the ability of an organization to use past behavior and information to improve its business processes—and for change as

FIGURE 2.7

The business value added from
automating, learning, and strategizing with information systems.

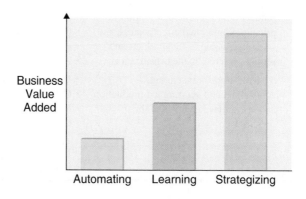

TABLE 2.2 Activities Involved Under Three Different Loan Application Processes and the Average Time for Each Activity

Primary Activities of Loan Processing	Manual Loan Process (Time)	Technology-Supported Process (time)	Fully Automated Process (time)
1. Complete and submit loan application	Customer takes the application home, completes it, and returns it (1.5 days)	Customer takes the application home, completes it, and returns it (1.5 days)	Customer fills out application from home via the Web (15 minutes)
2. Check application for errors	Employee does this in batches (2.5 days)	Employee does this in batches (2.5 days)	Computer does this as it is being completed (3.5 seconds)
3. Input data from application into the information system	Applications are kept in paper form, although there is handling time involved (1 hour)	Employee does this in batches (2.5 days)	Done as part of the online application process (no extra time needed)
4. Assess loan applications under $250,000 to determine whether to fund them	Employee does this completely by hand (15 days)	Employee does this with the help of the computer (1 hour)	Computer does this automatically (1 second)
5. Committee decides on any loan over $250,000	(15 days)	(15 days)	(15 days)
6. Applicant notified	Employee generates letters manually in batches (1 week)	Employee generates letters with the help of a computer (1 day)	System notifies applicant via e-mail (3.5 seconds)
Total time	Anywhere from 25 to 40 days, depending on size of loan	Anywhere from 5 to 20 days, depending on size of loan	Anywhere from 15 minutes to 15 days, depending on size of loan

Many online loan application services can now give you instant "tentative" approval pending verification of data you report in your online application. Also, only some of the activities within the manual and technology-supported processes can occur in parallel.

well as for automation. In a 1993 *Harvard Business Review* article, David Garvin described a **learning organization** as one that is "skilled at creating, acquiring, and transferring knowledge, and at modifying its behavior to reflect new knowledge and insights."

To illustrate a learning mentality, let us think again about our loan processing example. Figure 2.8 shows how a computer-based loan processing system tracks types of loan applications by date, month, and season. The manager easily sees the trends and can plan for the timely staffing and training of personnel in the loan department. The manager can also more efficiently manage the funds used to fulfill loans. Such computer-based loan processing system, focusing on learning, is an example of an information system used at the managerial level of an organization.

A learning approach allows people to track and learn about the types of applications filed by certain types of people at certain times of the year (e.g., more auto loan applications in the fall, mostly from men in their twenties and thirties), the patterns of the loan decisions made, or the subsequent performance of those loans. This new system creates data about the underlying business process that can be used to better monitor, control, and change that process. In other words, you *learn* from this information system about loan applications and approvals; as a result, you can do a better job at evaluating loan applications.

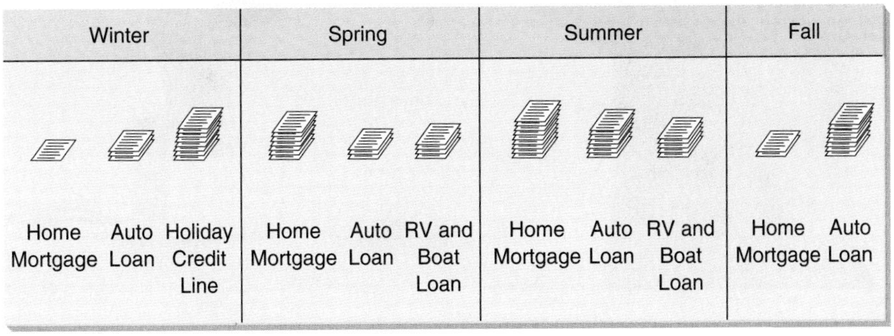

FIGURE 2.8

A computer-based loan processing system enables the bank manager to identify trends in loan applications.

A combined automating and learning approach, in the long run, is more effective than an automating approach alone. If the underlying business process supported by technology is inherently flawed, a learning use of the technology might help you detect the problems with the process and change it. For instance, in our loan processing example, a learning use of technology may help us uncover a pattern among the accepted loans that enables us to distinguish between low- and high-performing loans over their lives and subsequently to change the criteria for loan acceptance.

If, however, the underlying business process is bad and you are using technology only for automating (i.e., you would not uncover the data that would tell you this process is bad), you are more likely to continue with a flawed or less-than-optimal business process. In fact, such an automating use of technology may mask the process problems.

With a bad underlying set of loan acceptance criteria (e.g., rules that would allow you to approve a loan for someone who had a high level of debt as long as they had not been late on any payments recently), a person might manually review four applications in a day and, because of the problematic criteria used, inadvertently accept on average two "bad" applications per week. If you automated the same faulty process, with no learning aspects built in, the system might help a person review 12 applications per day, with six "bad" applications accepted per week on average. The technology would serve only to magnify the existing business problems (see Figure 2.9). Without learning, it is more difficult to uncover bad business processes underlying the information system.

Information Systems for Supporting Strategy: Doing Things Smarter

Using information systems to automate or improve processes has advantages, as described previously. In most cases, however, the best way to use an information system is to support the organization's strategy in a way that enables the firm to gain or sustain competitive advantage over rivals. To understand why, think about **organizational strategy**—a firm's plan to accomplish its mission and goals as well as to gain or sustain competitive advantage over rivals—and how it relates to information systems. When senior managers—at the executive level of the organization—conduct **strategic planning,** they form a vision of where the organization needs to head, convert that vision into measurable objectives and performance targets, and craft a strategy to achieve the desired results. In Figure 2.10, we show some common organizational strategies. An organization might decide to pursue a **low-cost leadership strategy,** as does Walmart, by which it offers the best prices in its industry on its goods and/or services. Alternatively, an organization might decide to pursue a **differentiation strategy,** as do Porsche, Nordstrom, and IBM, by which it tries to

FIGURE 2.9

Automating a loan processing system requires sound underlying business processes.

Yanik Chauvin\Shutterstock

Brief Case ⊙

FOR SALE BY OWNER: YOUR COMPANY'S NAME.COM

They don't sell houses or land, but they do deal in Internet real estate, and most turn a handsome profit. "They" are called domainers, and the real estate they buy and sell consists of domain names. Although they keep a low profile and usually don't flaunt their success, domainers participated in a virtual land grab worth $9 billion in 2006 and $23 billion in 2009, with no end in sight.

As you know, every Web site on the Internet has a domain name, also called a Uniform Resource Locator (URL), or Web address. For large companies such as Amazon.com, the domain name is an extremely valuable asset, as it clearly identifies the owner of the Web site.

Domainers trade on the fact that many businesses, organizations, and celebrities want domain names for their Web sites that clearly identify the site's owner and are, therefore, easy for Internet surfers to find. A domainer might buy the domain name "fordmotorcompany.com," for instance, and then try to sell it to the Ford Motor Company; that is exactly how the domain-buying business operated in the 1990s: buy a name, hold it, and wait for a buyer who wanted it to make an offer. But when pay-per-click advertising was developed, the game changed. Currently, domainers can profit most by renting advertising space on the domain names they hold to marketers. Here is how the domainer makes his or her profit from renting ad space:

1. Buy and hold a general domain name, such as "candy.com" or "cellphones.com." Alternatively, domainers buy domain names that represent common misspellings of popular domains (such as amazo.com), hoping to benefit from Web surfers' typos.
2. Direct Web traffic to a middleman, called an aggregator, who designs a Web site and then taps into Yahoo!, Google, or Microsoft's advertising networks and lists the best-paying clients. When a searcher enters the domain name, such as "cellphone.com," the "cellphone.com" Web page comes up with a list of cell phone Web site URLs.
3. Each time a searcher clicks on one of the URLs listed on the domain name's page, the search engine owner (Yahoo!, Google, or Microsoft) or advertiser pays the domainer a fee.

Renting domain names is a secondary market for domainers that can bring in hundreds of dollars per day. The key to this market is not necessarily search engine traffic; rather, it is type-in traffic or user-directed navigation, because millions of Internet users type what they are looking for directly in the address bar of their browser, such as "candy.com." (Candy.com was recently sold for $3 million to an online candy retailer.)

Figures are not available for this type of URL type-in traffic since the larger search engines, such as Yahoo! and Google, do not disclose how much of their revenue comes from domain name rental. Experts report, however, that as much as 15 percent of Google's and Yahoo!'s revenue may come from per-click advertising.

Domainers could face a loss of revenue if, as has been suggested, Google, Yahoo!, and Microsoft cut out the domainer in the middle and serve Internet browser type-in traffic directly. But until that happens, domainers are raking in the cash.

In March 2008, *Domainer's Magazine* editor Mike St. John expressed concern over the Anti-Phishing Consumer Protection Act of 2008, introduced in Congress but not yet passed. If the bill were to become law, St. John warned, domainers found to have purloined trademarked or government names, such as FordsRUs.com or IRS.com, would face prosecution by the Federal Trade Commission and the U.S. attorney general, and fines of up to $6 million for each violation, plus attorneys' fees. St. John thought the punishment outlined in the bill was excessive. Others may disagree.

In fact, some actions have been taken to curb domainers. For instance, a number of large international corporations including Dell, DIRECTV, Hilton, Nike, and Verizon joined together and formed the Coalition Against Domain Name Abuse, Inc. (CADNA), which aims to build awareness and stop this practice.

Questions

1. How do you feel about domainers? Is it an ethical business?
2. Discuss the pros and cons of having Google, Yahoo!, Bing, and others "cut out" domainers as middlemen in the Web search process.

Based on:

Anonymous (2010). CADNA—The Coalition Against Domain Name Abuse. Retrieved August 4, 2010, from http://www.cadna.org.

Siegler, M. G. (2009, June 5). Candy.com sells for a sweet $3 million. *TechCrunch*. Retrieved May 20, 2010, from http://techcrunch.com/2009/06/05/candycom-sells-for-a-sweet-3-million.

Sloan, P. (2005, December 1). Masters of their domains. *CNN Money.com*. Retrieved August 4, 2010, from http://money.cnn.com/magazines/business2/business2_archive/2005/12/01/8364591/index.htm.

FIGURE 2.10

Five general types of organizational strategy: broad differentiation, focused differentiation, focused low-cost leadership, overall low-cost leadership, and best-cost provider.

Source: A. A. Thompson and A. J. Strickland, III, 1995. *Strategic Management: Concepts and Cases*, 13E, Blurr Ridge, IL: Irwin McGraw-Hill, 2003, p. 151.

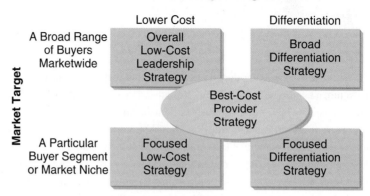

provide better products or services than its competitors. A company might aim that differentiation broadly at many different types of consumers, or it might focus on a particular segment of consumers, as Apple did for many years with its focus on high-quality computers for home and educational markets. Still other organizations might pursue a middle-of-the-road strategy, following a **best-cost provider strategy,** offering products or services of reasonably good quality at competitive prices, as does Dell.

A person with a strategic mentality toward information systems goes beyond mere automating and learning and instead tries to find ways to use information systems to achieve the organization's chosen strategy. This individual wants the benefits of automating and learning but also looks for some strategic, competitive advantage from the system. In fact, in today's business environment, if a proposed information system isn't going to clearly deliver some strategic value (i.e., help to improve the business so that it can compete better) while also helping people to work smarter and save money in the process, then it isn't likely to be funded.

 **NET STATS**

Online Searching

The Google search engine has become so popular with Internet users that the word "Google" is often used as a verb ("I 'Googled' the restaurant to see its reviews"), but there are other well-known search engines, such as Yahoo! and Microsoft's Bing (formerly Microsoft Live). Table 2.3 compares the percentage of Internet surfers who used each search engine (i.e., the search engines' market share) in April 2010 as compared to April 2008.

TABLE 2.3 Top Search Engines by Market Share, April 2008 Compared with April 2010

Search Engine	April 2008 Market Share (%)	April 2010 Market Share (%)	Change (percentage points)
Google	81.4	86.3	4.9
Yahoo!	9.8	5.3	−4.5
Bing	2.5*	3.1	0.6
Other	8.8	5.3	−3.5

*Note: April 2008 market share is for Microsoft Live Search.
Source: Based on http://marketshare.hitslink.com/search-engine-market-share.aspx?qprid=5.

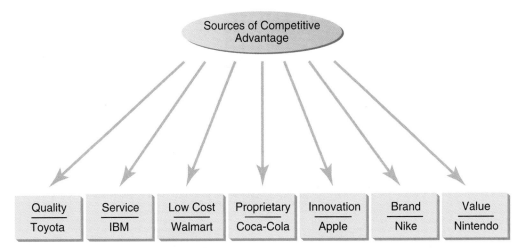

FIGURE 2.11

Sources of competitive advantage.

Sources of Competitive Advantage

How do business firms typically get a competitive advantage? An organization has competitive advantage whenever it has an edge over rivals in attracting customers and defending against competitive forces (Porter, 1985, 2001). In order to be successful, a business must have a clear vision, one that focuses investments in resources such as information systems and technologies to help achieve a competitive advantage. Some sources of competitive advantage include the following (see Figure 2.11):

- Having the best-made product on the market
- Delivering superior customer service
- Achieving lower costs than rivals
- Having a proprietary manufacturing technology, formula, or algorithm
- Having shorter lead times in developing and testing new products
- Having a well-known brand name and reputation
- Giving customers more value for their money

Companies can gain or sustain each of these sources of competitive advantage by effectively using information systems. Returning to our loan example, a person with a strategic view of information systems would choose a computer-based loan application process because it can help achieve the organization's strategic plan to process loan applications faster and better than rivals and to improve the selection criteria for loans. This process and the supporting information system add value to the organization and match the organization's strategy. It is, therefore, essential to the long-term survival of the organization. If, on the other hand, managers determine that the organization's strategy is to grow and generate new products and services, the computer-based loan application process and the underlying system might not be an efficient, effective use of resources, even though the system could provide automating and learning benefits.

Identifying *Where* to Compete: Analyzing Competitive Forces

Organizations struggle with identifying the best uses of their resources to execute their strategy. Given that every industry is different, organizations can better understand where to focus their resources by analyzing the competitive forces within their industry. One framework often used to analyze the competition within an industry is Porter's (1979) notion of the five primary competitive forces: (1) the rivalry among competing sellers in your industry, (2) the threat of potential new entrants into your industry, (3) the bargaining power that customers have within your industry, (4) the bargaining power that suppliers have within your industry, and (5) the potential for substitute products from other industries (see Figure 2.12). Table 2.4 provides examples of how information systems can have an impact on the various competitive forces in an industry. Porter's five-forces model of competition can help you determine which specific technologies will be more or less useful, depending on the nature of your industry. You can then use this knowledge as the basis for identifying particular investments.

FIGURE 2.12

Five forces influence the level of competitiveness in an industry.

Identifying *How* to Compete: Analyzing the Value Chain

Managers use value chain analysis to identify opportunities to use information systems for competitive advantage (Porter, 1985, 2001; Shank & Govindarajan, 1993). Think of an organization as a big input/output process. At one end, supplies are purchased and brought into the organization (see Figure 2.13). The organization integrates those supplies to create products and services that it markets, sells, and then distributes to customers. The organization provides customer service after the sale of these products and services. Throughout this process, opportunities arise for employees to add value to the product or service by acquiring supplies in a more effective manner, improving products, and selling more products. This set of activities that add value throughout the organization is known as the **value chain** within an organization.

Value chain analysis is the process of analyzing an organization's activities to determine where value is added to products and/or services and what costs are incurred for doing so. Because information systems can automate many activities along the value chain, value chain analysis has become a popular tool for applying information systems for competitive advantage. In

TABLE 2.4 IS Impact on Competitive Forces

Competitive Force	Implication for Firm	Potential Use of Information Systems to Combat Competitive Force
Traditional rivals within your industry	Competition in price, product distribution, and service	Implement enterprise resource planning system to reduce costs and be able to act and react more quickly; implement Web site to offer better service to customers.
Threat of new entrants into your market	Increased capacity in the industry, reduced prices, and decreased market share	Improve Web site to reach customers and differentiate product; use inventory control system to lower costs and better manage excess capacity.
Customers' bargaining power	Reduced prices, need for increased quality, and demand for more services	Implement customer relationship management system to serve customers better; implement computer-aided design and/or computer-aided manufacturing system to improve product quality.
Suppliers' bargaining power	Increased costs and reduced quality	Use Internet to establish closer electronic ties with suppliers and to create relationships with new suppliers located far away.
Threat of substitute products from other industries	Potential returns on products, decreased market share, and losing customers for life	Use decision support system and customer purchase database to better assess trends and customer needs; use computer-aided design systems to redesign products.

Source: Based on Applegate, Austin, and McFarlan (2007).

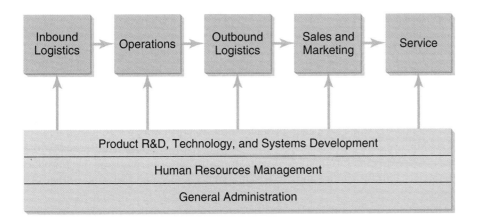

FIGURE 2.13

A sample generic organizational value chain.

value chain analysis, you first draw the value chain for your organization by fleshing out each of the activities, functions, and processes where value is or should be added. Next, you determine the costs—and the factors that drive costs or cause them to fluctuate—within each of the areas in your value chain diagram. You then benchmark (compare) your value chain and associated costs with those of your competitors. You can then make changes and improvements in your value chain to either gain or sustain competitive advantage.

The Role of Information Systems in Value Chain Analysis

The use of information systems has become one of the primary ways that organizations improve their value chains. In Figure 2.14, we show a sample value chain and some ways that use of information systems can improve productivity within it. For example, many organizations use the Internet to connect businesses with one another electronically so that they can exchange orders, invoices, and receipts online in real time. Using the Internet has become a popular method for improving the front end of the organizational value chain. In fact, many firms now use the Internet for such business-to-business interactions; these systems are called *extranets* (described in greater detail in Chapter 4, "Enabling Commerce Using the Internet").

The Technology/Strategy Fit

You might be asking, If any information system helps do things faster and better and helps save money, who cares whether it matches the company's strategy? Good question. If money grew on trees, you probably would build and use just about every information system you could imagine. Organizations could build many different valuable systems, but they are constrained by time and money to build only those that add the most value: those that help automate and learn as well as have strategic value. In other words, organizations are trying to maximize **business/IT alignment,** and in most cases, you do not want systems that do not match the strategy, even if

FIGURE 2.14

Sample value chain and corresponding sample uses of information systems to add value.

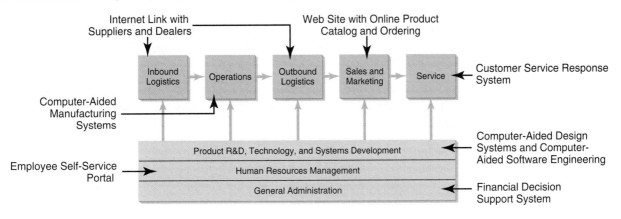

they offer automating and learning benefits. Further, while spending on information systems is rising, most companies are willing to spend money on projects only when they can see clear, significant value. Often, however, organizations have no choice in making some types of investments that may or may not coincide with their overall strategy. Such investments are called a **strategic necessity**—something the organization must do in order to survive.

Given this focus on the value that the system will add, you probably do not want a system that helps differentiate your products based on high quality when the organizational strategy is to be the overall industry low-cost leader. In other words, if a firm were pursuing a strategy for low-cost leadership, investments to help drive costs down would be valued over those that didn't. In Chapter 3, "Managing the Information Systems Infrastructure and Services," we introduce various technologies, infrastructures, and services that can help to support an organization's competitive strategy.

We should also caution that merely choosing and implementing an emerging information system is not sufficient to gain or sustain competitive advantage. In any significant IS implementation, there must be commensurate, significant organizational change. This typically comes in the form of *business process management* and other similar methods of improving the functioning of the organization, as opposed to merely dropping in an information system with no attempts at changing and improving the organization. We will talk more in Chapter 7, "Enhancing Business Processes Using Enterprise Information Systems," about the role of business process management for transforming organizational business processes.

Assessing Value for the IS Infrastructure

Howard Rubin, executive vice president of Meta Group, argued that we should take a more holistic view when assessing IS value (*CIO*, June 2004), particularly in areas such as IS infrastructure, where assessing tangible value may be difficult. IS infrastructure includes an organization's hardware, software, personnel, and so on. While these things are important and expensive to acquire and maintain, they are often difficult to place a value on. Rubin suggested four categories for assessing investments in regard to their value to the overall infrastructure.

Economic Value First, economic value is the contribution an investment makes toward improving the infrastructure's ability to enhance the profitability of the business. Rubin recommended that we use important business metrics in order to gauge the economic value of a given investment. An airline, for example, might use a metric such as revenue per passenger mile to determine effectiveness. To assess an investment, the airline could then calculate the IS infrastructure cost per passenger mile and observe how investments in the infrastructure over time have an impact on profitability.

Architectural Value Second, architectural value is derived from an investment's ability to extend the infrastructure's capabilities to meet business needs today and in the future. To measure architectural value, "before-and-after" assessments of infrastructure characteristics such as interoperability, portability, scalability, recoverability, and compatibility can be taken. Rubin recommended that for each area of the business, infrastructure characteristics be rated on a scale of 1 to 10 as to how well various investments influence the infrastructure's ability to meet those needs.

Operational Value Third, operational value is derived from assessing an investment's impact on enabling the infrastructure to better meet business processing requirements. To assess this, Rubin recommended that we measure the impact of not investing in a particular project. For example, what would be the cost of not investing in a new customer relationship management system in terms of lost staff productivity, lost business revenue, or even lost customers?

Regulatory and Compliance Value Fourth, regulatory and compliance value is derived from assessing the extent to which an investment helps to meet requirements for control, security, and integrity as required by a governing body or a key customer. For example, what is the impact of, say, noncompliance with government reporting requirements necessitated by the Sarbanes-Oxley Act of 2002?

Rubin also argues that, where possible, all evaluation measures should be compared with external benchmarks. In any event, these provide a useful framework for more broadly evaluating a particular investment.

Changing Mind-Sets About Information Systems

Perhaps the most significant change in the IS field has been in mind-sets about technology rather than in technology itself. The old way for managers to think about information systems was that information systems were a necessary service, a necessary evil, and a necessary, distasteful expense that was to be minimized. Managers cannot afford to think this way anymore. Successful managers now think of information systems as a competitive asset to be nurtured and invested in. This does not mean that managers should not require a sound business case for every IS investment. Nor does this mean that managers should not also need to have facts as part of a business case for a system (see Chapter 9, "Developing and Acquiring Information Systems"). It does mean, however, that managers must stop thinking about systems as an expense and start thinking about systems as an asset to invest in wisely. Managers have to become strategic about information systems and have to think of them as an enabler of opportunities.

International Business Strategies in the Digital World

Before the era of globalization, most companies were solely operating in the domestic arena, conducting their activities exclusively in one country, starting from the acquisition of raw materials to the selling of final products. Although such businesses are likely to benefit from the enablers that also spurred Globalization 3.0 (see Chapter 1), many **domestic companies** also feel some negative effects brought about by globalization.

In today's digital world, the number of exclusively domestic companies is continually shrinking, with most domestic companies being relatively small (often local) businesses, such as local service providers, restaurants, farms, or independent grocery stores (and even those have international customers, suppliers, or products). Most of today's large companies, no matter if they are in car manufacturing (such as GM, Toyota, or Daimler), insurance (Allianz or Munich Re), or consumer goods (Nestlé or Procter & Gamble), have some **international business strategy** for competing in different global markets.

Such companies pursue either a home replication, multidomestic, global, or transnational strategy, depending on the degree of supply chain integration and necessary local customer responsiveness (Hitt, Ireland, & Hoskisson, 2009; Prahalad & Doz, 1987). On the one hand, businesses strive for global integration to realize economies of scale; on the other hand, a company's local subunits may benefit strongly from being able to quickly respond to changing conditions in local markets. Different international business strategies are suited better for different situations (see Figure 2.15 and Table 2.5).

Organizations use a variety of business strategies to manage international operations most effectively. For example, Nestlé, one of the world's largest food producers, with over 500 factories and operations in more than 70 countries, uses a transnational business strategy, supported by multiple distributed systems and Internet-enabled applications. In the following sections, we describe each of these various business strategies, along with the appropriate IS strategies.

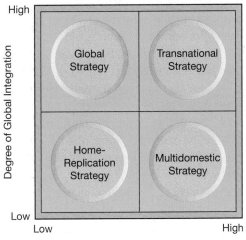

FIGURE 2.15

International business strategies.

TABLE 2.5 When to Use International Business Strategies

Strategy	Description	Strengths	Weaknesses	When to Use
Home replication	International business seen as extension of home business	Focus on core competencies in home market	Inability to react to local market conditions	Homogeneous markets
Global	Centralized organization with standardized offerings across markets	Standardized product offerings allow achieving economies of scale	Inability to react to local market conditions	Homogeneous markets
Multidomestic	Federation of associated business units; decentralized	Ability to quickly react to local conditions	Differing product offerings limit economies of scale, and limited interunit communication limits knowledge sharing	Very heterogeneous markets
Transnational	Some aspects centralized, others decentralized; integrated network	Can achieve benefits of multidomestic and global strategies	Difficult to manage; very complex	Integrated global markets

WHEN THINGS GO WRONG

e-Waste Is a Global Problem

Americans bought an estimated $164 billion worth of consumer electronics in 2009—computers, monitors, cell phones, personal digital assistants, DVD players, microwave ovens, and so on—and that number was projected to increase another billion dollars in 2010. When consumers replace old electronic products with newer versions, many of the discarded products could end up in landfills. This is an environmental concern because electronic products contain a mix of toxic components, such as lead, mercury, cadmium, or polyvinyl chlorides, which are released into the environment when incinerated or buried in a landfill. A conventional computer monitor alone, for example, contains four to eight pounds of lead, and newer LCD screens contain mercury. And with upward of 300 million computers and 1 billion cell phones manufactured each year, the problem is not going away. According to UN figures, around 40 million tons of e-waste are produced each year globally.

So what happens to electronic gadgets when consumers no longer need or want them? Some owners hand them down to someone else or pack them away in the back of a closet or garage. Others donate the items—whether they still function or not—to a charitable organization, but when the products are hopelessly outdated, the donations probably aren't so welcome. Unfortunately, since local landfills generally won't take hazardous waste, some consumers bury discarded electronic products in ordinary household garbage, where they end up in landfills or incinerators despite the ban. In fact, an estimated 70 percent of discarded computers and monitors and over 80 percent of old TVs end up in landfills.

Currently, only 20 percent of e-waste is channeled through municipal dropoff sites or companies that offer disposal service, and even if such services are used, there's no guarantee that the waste will be disposed of properly. Drawing attention to this growing problem, the organizers of the 2010 Winter Olympic Games used some precious metals recovered from e-waste to fashion the gold, silver, and bronze medals given to the athletes.

Although federal law in the United States prevents businesses from improperly disposing of e-waste, this law does not extend to households. Many consumers end up discarding their unwanted electronics in their curbside trash, sending it directly to a landfill. The need for stricter regulations concerning e-waste disposal has been recognized in the United States, and in March 2008, Congress appointed a working group to determine a course of action. In February 2009, the House Committee on Science and Technology held hearings on the e-waste problem, but legislation at the federal level has yet to be enacted. In fact, there are no federal laws that apply to individuals covering consumer electronics recycling. As a result, many states have taken action to regulate e-waste. As of 2010, there were 20 states and one municipality (New York City) that had some type of e-waste laws. Unfortunately, although the export of hazardous waste to developing countries was banned in 1992, between 50 and 80 percent of America's e-waste continues to be shipped to Third World countries, where environmental standards are less strict. So much e-waste has been deported that, in 2002, China banned its import. Now e-waste is smuggled into China, however, where resident scavengers know it is illegal but continue to earn payment for the precious metals and other materials extracted. The waste that doesn't reach China is diverted to other parts of Asia or is sent to West African countries such as Ghana, Nigeria, and the Ivory Coast.

To reduce the environmental impact and to facilitate recycling efforts, the European Union (EU) has banned toxic ingredients, such as lead, mercury, cadmium, and so on, from electronics, appliances, lighting equipment, medical equipment, and other consumer products. Prior to the EU mandate, few companies were concerned with the production of "green" hardware. Now, however, since Europe represents about 30 percent of the world market for electronic equipment, manufacturers are rushing to comply with the EU directive.

While Congress debates the problem, the U.S. Environmental Protection Agency estimates that 30 million to 40 million PCs will be ready for "end of life management" in each of the next few years. And computers are not the only electronic product heading for obsolescence. As of 2009, as digital broadcasting became the norm, American TVs that receive only analog signals no longer function without a set-top box meaning that about 25 million TVs will be taken out of service annually. Add to those numbers the 98 million cell phones that have become unfashionable since 2005, and the garbage heap will grow exponentially. All told, the UN Environment Program estimates that over the next 10 years, e-waste from old computers alone is set to increase 400 percent in China and South Africa and 500 percent in India.

Goodwill Industries, the charitable organization found in many cities and towns across the world, is working to help solve the e-waste problem. The charity has partnered with IT giants Dell and Microsoft to form the Reconnect program, a free recycling program that lets consumers drop off used computer equipment for recycling at over 1,900 locations across the United States. The program accepts any brand of computer equipment for recycling as well as Microsoft products like Xbox, Zune, and their accompanying accessories. Equipment collected through the program is either resold at Goodwill store locations, refurbished, or broken down and recycled. According to the Reconnect Web site, the program has redirected over 96 million pounds of e-waste from landfills and created over 250 "green" jobs.

Clearly, disposing properly of e-waste is a problem begging for a solution if the environment and human health are to be protected.

Based on:

Anonymous. (n.d.) Current electronics recycling laws in effect. Retrieved April 25, 2010, from http://www.ecyclingresource.org/ContentPage.aspx?Pageid=28.

Anonymous. (n.d.). The eWaste crisis introduction. Retrieved April 25, 2010, from http://e-stewards.org/the-e-waste-crisis.

Anonymous. (2005, May 15). Waste electrical and electronic equipment. Retrieved April 30, 2010, from http://europa.eu.int/scadplus/leg/en/lvb/l21210.htm.

Anonymous. (2006, January 6). Is America exporting a huge environmental problem? *ABC News*. Retrieved April 30, 2010, from http://www.abcnews.go.com/2020/Technology/story?id=1479506.

Anonymous. (2008, January 7). 2008 consumer electronics sales seen up. *Reuters.com*. Retrieved April 30, 2010, from http://www.reuters.com/article/businessNews/idUSN0740878220080108.

Anonymous. (2010, April 21). Dell and Goodwill expand free recycling program to include Microsoft products. Retrieved April 25, 2010, from http://www.goodwill.org/press-releases/dell-goodwill-expand-free-consumer-recycling-program-to-include-microsoft-products.

Blouin, G. (n.d.). Is Canadian e-waste an environmental disaster in waiting? *Canada.com*. Retrieved April 30, 2010, from http://www.canada.com/topics/technology/story.html?id=e8def77a-3a8f-420b-ad29-a9e08d03fca0.

Carroll, C. (2008, January). High tech trash. *National Geographic*. Retrieved April 30, 2010, from http://ngm.nationalgeographic.com/2008/01/high-tech-trash/carroll-text.

Irvine, D. (2010, February 24). Can e-waste be turned into gold? Retrieved April 25, 2010, from http://www.cnn.com/2010/TECH/02/23/eco.ewaste.gold.

Mayfiel, K. (2003, January 10). E-waste: Dark side of digital age. *Wired*. Retrieved April 30, 2010, from http://www.wired.com/news/technology/0,57151-1.html.

Watkins, S. (2006, January 2). E-waste epidemic. *Government Technology*. Retrieved April 30, 2010, from http://www.govtech.net/magazine/channel_story.php/97724.

Williams, M. (2010, January 7). U.S. consumer electronics revenue dropped 8% in 2009. *ITWorld*. Retrieved April 25, 2010, from http://www.itworld.com/personal-tech/91854/us-consumer-electronics-revenue-dropped-8-2009.

Home-Replication Strategy

The **home-replication strategy** (sometimes called export strategy or just international strategy) is the most basic form of going global. Companies using this strategy view international operations as secondary to their home operations. Thus, companies pursuing a home-replication strategy focus on their domestic customers' needs and wants and merely export their products to generate additional sales. This allows companies to focus on their core competencies in their respective domestic markets. In some cases, selling products internationally is used as a way to extend the life of products nearing the end of their life cycles domestically (e.g., last year's tennis shoe may still be considered "hip" in some countries). As the company places only secondary emphasis on international operations, there is no expectation of obtaining additional knowledge from foreign operations. For example, it can be argued

TABLE 2.6 International IS Strategies

Business Strategy	Systems	Communications	Data Resources
Home replication	Domestic systems (if any)	Limited (if any)	Local databases (if any)
Global	Centralized systems	Multiple networks between home office and subsidiaries	Data sharing between central home office and subsidiaries
Multidomestic	Decentralized systems	Direct communication between home office and subsidiaries	Local databases
Transnational	Distributed/shared systems; Internet-enabled applications	Enterprise-wide linkages	Common global data resources

Source: Based on Alavi and Young (1992), Karimi and Konsynski (1991), and Ramarapu and Lado (1995).

that German automaker Porsche pursues a home-replication strategy. Specifically, Porsche designs very high performance automobiles geared toward driving on German Autobahns (many of which have no speed limits); although this style of driving is almost impossible in most countries, Porsche sells their cars with the promise of high performance, making only minor modifications for local markets. With a home-replication strategy, the organization provides a relatively low level of local responsiveness and requires a relatively low level of global integration. As such, information systems play a minor role in facilitating this strategy (see Table 2.6).

Global Business Strategy

Companies pursuing a **global business strategy** attempt to achieve economies of scale by producing identical products in large quantities for a variety of different markets. In contrast to the home-replication strategy, where a product is developed for the home country and then exported (with little or no modifications), companies pursuing a global strategy (such as Sony) develop products for the global market.

A global business strategy works much more in a centralized fashion. As the decisions are made at the headquarters, the organization can be characterized as a centralized hub (Bartlett & Goshal, 1998). The headquarters gives the overall strategic direction and thus has tight control of the entire company as well as the knowledge that is generated within the company. However, the need to achieve economies of scale prohibits implementation of local strategies, and thus a global company cannot quickly react to local challenges and opportunities. Here, data flows extensively from the subsidiaries to the home location, and the home location exerts strong control on the subsidiaries (see Figure 2.16). As the home office coordinates most of the strategic decisions of the local subsidiaries, companies pursuing a global business strategy utilize multiple networks between the home office and the subsidiaries to facilitate both communication and data sharing. The data does not stay at the local subsidiaries, reducing the potential for duplication but at the same time introducing issues related to transborder data flows (primarily in EU countries) (see Table 2.6).

Multidomestic Business Strategy

The **multidomestic business strategy** is particularly suited for operations in markets differing widely. The multidomestic business strategy uses a loose federation of associated business units, each of which is rather independent in their strategic decisions. In other words, the degree of integration is very low, and the individual subunits can respond quickly to their respective market demands (Ghoshal, 1987). Multidomestic companies can thus be extremely flexible and responsive to the needs and demands of local markets, and any opportunities arising in local markets can be quickly seized. An example of a multidomestic company is the international arm of General Motors, the national subsidiaries of which produce cars that are customized to the specific local markets (e.g., Opel in Germany and Vauxhall in Great Britain). However, working in a decentralized fashion, much of the knowledge generated is retained at the local subsidiaries, and knowledge transfer between the individual subsidiaries is often limited, leading to inefficiencies and

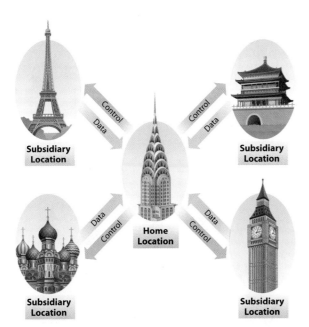

FIGURE 2.16

Global business strategy.

mistakes that potentially can be repeated across subsidiaries (Bartlett & Ghoshal, 1998). In sum, for companies following a multidomestic business strategy, very little data and control information flows between the home and subsidiary locations (see Figure 2.17).

In order to support the loose confederacy of various different local subsidiaries and the decentralized nature of the decision making within companies utilizing a multidomestic business strategy, each organizational subsidiary has its own decentralized information systems. Although the systems within the different business units may be integrated, there is no centralized IS infrastructure. The communications take place primarily between the different subsidiaries and the home office; thus, there is no focus on the communication between the different subsidiaries (this is why there is only limited knowledge transfer among the subsidiaries). As the different subsidiaries are very independent, they retain the decentralized local data processing centers that are responsive to local needs and regulations and at the same time use information technology to integrate them loosely into the framework of the parent organization (see Table 2.6).

FIGURE 2.17

Multidomestic business strategy.

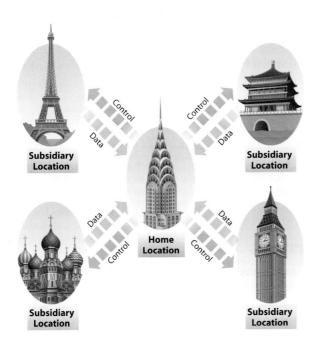

FIGURE 2.18

Transnational business strategy.

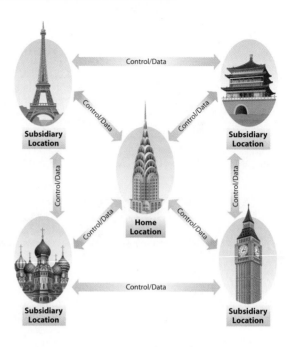

Transnational Business Strategy

An emerging strategy is the **transnational business strategy.** Having realized the benefits and drawbacks of multidomestic and global business strategies, companies using a transnational business strategy selectively decide which aspects of the organization should be under central control and which should be decentralized. This business strategy allows companies to leverage the flexibility offered by a decentralized organization (to be more responsive to local conditions) while at the same time reaping economies of scale enjoyed by centralization. An example of a transnational company is Unilever, which decides when to centralize and when to decentralize, depending on the products and the local markets. However, this business strategy is also the most difficult, as the company has to strike a balance between centralization and decentralization. In contrast to global organizations, where most of the resources are centralized in a company's home country, different resources in a transnational company can be centralized in different countries, depending on where the company can achieve the greatest returns or cost savings. Further, different decentralized resources are interdependent; this is in contrast to the other organizational forms, where there is usually one direction of the flow of resources. In a transnational company, for example, semiconductors for computer chips might be produced in a state-of-the-art factory in Dresden, Germany; shipped to a Southeast Asian country to be assembled into a final product; and then shipped back to Western Europe to be sold to an individual customer. Bartlett and Ghoshal (1998) characterize transnational companies as integrated networks requiring a great deal of effort in terms of managing the different interdependencies, tasks, and communication among the different units. In sum, both data and control can flow in any direction, depending on the specific business process (see Figure 2.18).

Companies utilizing a transnational business strategy need to create integrated networks between the home office and the multiple local subsidiaries. Because of this requirement, there is much communication among the different subunits as well as between the home office and the subunits. Many systems are distributed and/or shared; in this way, a subsidiary can access the systems and resources of other subsidiaries. Similarly, key data is shared throughout the company to enable a seamless integration of processes. Much of the communication, data, and application sharing is enabled by intranet, extranet, and Web-based applications (see Table 2.6).

Valuing Innovations

To differentiate itself, an organization often must deploy new, state-of-the-art technologies to do things even better, faster, and more cheaply than rivals that are using older technologies. Although firms can choose to continually upgrade older systems rather than investing in new systems, these improvements can at best give only a short-lived competitive edge. To gain and sustain significant

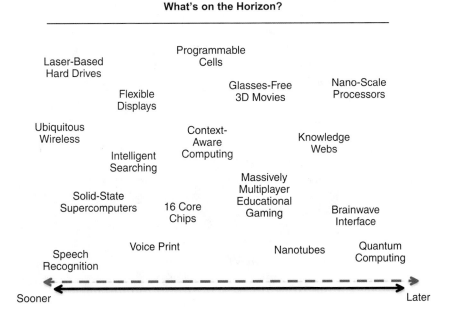

FIGURE 2.19

Some enabling technologies on the horizon.

competitive advantage, firms must often deploy the latest technologies or redeploy and reinvest in existing technologies in clever, new ways.

But with the plethora of new information technologies and systems available, how can you possibly choose winners? Indeed, how can you even keep track of all the new breakthroughs, new products, new versions, and new ways of using technologies? For example, in Figure 2.19 we present a small subset of some new information technologies and systems, ranging from some that are here now and currently being used to some that are easily a decade away from being a reality. Which one is important for you? Which one will make or break your business? Does this list even include the one that you need to be concerned about?

The Need for Constant IS Innovation

Sir John Maddox, a physicist and the editor of the influential scientific journal *Nature* for 22 years, was quoted in *Scientific American* in 1999 as saying "The most important discoveries of the next 50 years are likely to be ones of which we cannot now even conceive." Think about that for a moment. Most of the important discoveries of the next 50 years are likely to be things that, at present, we have no clue about. To illustrate that point, think back to just a short decade ago about what the state of the Internet was. Then, the Internet was not on the radar screens of many business organizations. Those that had Web sites were mostly providing an electronic brochure to customers and weren't exploiting the technology to streamline business processes as is the norm today. Look now at how the Internet has transformed modern business. How could something so transformational not have been easier for businesses to imagine or predict a decade earlier? It is difficult to see these things coming. Next, we examine how you can improve your ability to spot and exploit new innovations.

Successful Innovation Is Difficult

As we hinted at previously, there are limits to using emerging information systems to gain or sustain a competitive advantage. Information systems are often bought from or built by someone else. They are often either purchased from a vendor or developed by a consultant or outsourcing partner. In these situations, the information systems are usually not proprietary technologies owned by the organization. For example, although a soft-drink company can patent the formula of a cola or a pharmaceutical company can patent a new drug, an organization typically cannot patent its use of an information system, particularly if someone else developed it. The data in the system may be proprietary, but the information system typically is not. One classic counterexample, however, is Amazon.com's patented "one-click" ordering process that has been successfully defended in the courts.

Innovation Is Often Fleeting Given the pace of change in the digital world, advantages gained by innovations often have a limited life span. For example, even in situations where an organization has developed an innovative information system in-house, they usually do so with

FIGURE 2.20

Blu-ray has become the industry standard for high-definition DVD players.

Shutterstock

hardware, software, and networking components that others can purchase. In short, rivals can copy emerging information systems, so this form of competitive advantage can be short lived. Indeed, if use of the new system causes one organization to gain a significant advantage over others, smart rivals are quick to duplicate or improve on that use of the system.

Innovation Is Often Risky   Developing innovative information systems always entails risk. The classic example from consumer electronics is the choice of a VCR in the early days of that technology and the competing Betamax (developed by Sony) and VHS (developed by JVC) designs. Most experts agreed that the Betamax had superior recording and playback quality, but VHS ultimately won the battle in the marketplace. People who made the "smart" choice at the time probably would have chosen a VCR with the Betamax design. Ultimately, however, that turned out to be an unfortunate choice. Recently, consumers again had to choose between two competing formats, namely, for high-definition (HD) DVD players, where the Blu-ray and HD DVD format competed to become the industry standard. In this battle, Microsoft, Toshiba, and many others backed the HD DVD format, while Sony led the fight for Blu-ray (and even incorporated it into its PlayStation 3 gaming console). This time around, Sony (and the Blu-ray format) won the "format war," with the dissolution of the HD DVD Promotion Group in early 2008, effectively making Blu-ray the dominant format for HD video discs (see Figure 2.20).

Innovation Choices Are Often Difficult   Choosing among innovative IS-related investments is just as difficult as choosing consumer electronics. In fact, for organizations, choosing among the plethora of available innovative technologies is far more difficult, given the size and often mission-critical nature of the investment. Choosing a suboptimal DVD player, although disappointing, is usually not devastating.

Choosing new technologies in the IS area is like trying to hit one of several equally attractive fast-moving targets. You can find examples of the difficulty of forecasting emerging technologies in the experiences that many organizations have had in forecasting the growth, use, and importance of the Internet. The 1994 Technology Forecast prepared by the major consulting firm Price Waterhouse (now PriceWaterhouseCoopers) mentioned the word "Internet" on only five pages of the 750-page document. The next year, more than 75 pages addressed the Internet. Only three years later, in the 1997 briefing, the Internet was a pervasive topic throughout. Back in 1994, it would have been difficult, perhaps even foolish, to forecast such pervasive, rapidly growing business use of the Internet today. Table 2.7 illustrates how many people and organizations have had difficulty making technology-related predictions.

Given the pace of research and development in the IS and components area, staying current has been nearly impossible. Probably one of the most famous metrics of computer evolution has been "Moore's Law." Intel founder Gordon Moore predicted that the number of transistors that could be squeezed onto a silicon chip would double every 18 months, and this prediction has proven itself over the past 40 years (see Chapter 3). In fact, some computer hardware and

TABLE 2.7 Some Predictions About Technology That Were Not Quite Correct

Year	Source	Quote
1876	Western Union, internal memo	"This 'telephone' has too many shortcomings to be seriously considered as a means of communication. The device is inherently of no value to us."
1895	Lord Kelvin, president, British Royal Society	"Radio has no future. Heavier-than-air flying machines are impossible. X-rays will prove to be a hoax."
1899	C. H. Duell, commissioner, U.S. Office of Patents	"Everything that can be invented has been invented."
1927	H. M. Warner, Warner Brothers	"Who the hell wants to hear actors talk?"
1943	Thomas Watson, chairman, IBM	"I think there is a world market for maybe five computers."
1949	*Popular Mechanics*	"Where a calculator on the ENIAC is equipped with 18,000 vacuum tubes and weighs 30 tons, computers in the future may have only 1,000 vacuum tubes and weigh only 1.5 tons."
1957	Editor, business books, Prentice Hall	"I have traveled the length and breadth of this country and talked with the best people, and I can assure you that data processing is a fad that won't last out the year."
1968	*BusinessWeek*	"With over 50 foreign cars already on sale here, the Japanese auto industry isn't likely to carve out a big slice of the U.S. market."
1977	Ken Olsen, president, Digital Equipment Corporation	"There is no reason anyone would want a computer in their home."

software firms roll out new versions of their products every three months. Keeping up with this pace of change can be difficult for any organization.

Organizational Requirements for Innovation

Certain types of competitive environments require that organizations remain at the cutting edge in their use of information systems. For example, consider an organization that operates within an environment with strong competitive forces (Porter, 1979). The organization has competitive pressures coming from existing rival firms or from the threat of entry of new rivals. It is critical for these organizations to do things better, faster, and more cheaply than rivals. These organizations are driven to deploy innovative information systems.

These environmental characteristics alone, however, are not enough to determine whether an organization should deploy a particular information system. Before an organization can deploy any new system well, its processes, resources, and risk tolerance must be capable of adapting to and sustaining the development and implementation processes.

Process Requirements To deploy innovative information systems well, people in the organization must be willing to do whatever they can to bypass and eliminate internal bureaucracy, set aside political squabbles, and pull together for the common good. Can you imagine, for example, a firm trying to deploy a Web-based order entry system that enables customers to access inventory information directly, when people in that firm do not even share such information with each other?

Resource Requirements Organizations deploying innovative information systems must also have the human capital necessary to deploy the new systems. The organization must have enough employees available with the proper systems knowledge, skills, time, and other resources to deploy these systems. Alternatively, the organization must have resources and able systems partners available to outsource the development of such systems if necessary.

Risk Tolerance Requirements The last characteristic of an organization ready for the deployment of innovative information systems is that its members must have the appropriate tolerance for risk and uncertainty as well as the willingness to deploy and use new systems that may not be as proven and pervasive as more traditional technologies. If people within the organization desire low risk in their use of information systems, then gambling on cutting-edge systems will probably not be desirable or tolerable for them.

Predicting the Next New Thing

As you can see, using innovative information systems toward a strategic end will be difficult to identify, implement, and sustain. As Bakos and Treacy (1986) and others have argued, if you are

COMING ATTRACTIONS

TV and Mobile Content for the Visually Impaired

According to the American Macular Degeneration Foundation, approximately 10 million Americans over age 55 have macular degeneration; it is the leading cause of severe vision loss. Since the disease most often affects older individuals, that number will increase as the number of aging citizens continues to increase.

Patients who suffer from macular degeneration find that gray or blank spots mask the center of their vision, but peripheral vision is usually not affected. They may need more light to read newspapers and magazine print that is now harder to see, road signs are fuzzy, and television images are blurred and distorted. What has happened is that with age the tissue in the macula—the part of the retina responsible for central vision—deteriorates. The damage can't be reversed, but early diagnosis and treatment often helps reduce the degree of vision loss.

High-frequency waves in the visible spectrum are most difficult for people with macular degeneration to see—a major reason that they see distorted television images. Now researchers at the Schepens Eye Research Institute, an affiliate of Harvard Medical School, have developed software that lets users manipulate the contrast to create specially enhanced images that are easier for viewers with macular degeneration to see. The researchers designed an algorithm that specifically increases contrast over the middle- and low-frequency ranges that macular degeneration patients can still detect. Once installed in a television set, the system can be adjusted much like one adjusts a volume knob.

In mid-2008, at least one company, Analog Devices, was building a prototype utilizing the algorithm. Researchers who have developed the system hope that one day it will be installed as an option in all television sets. Ideally, visually impaired viewers with macular degeneration will have an option to enhance images much like hearing-impaired viewers can opt for closed captioning.

Similarly, in March 2010, IBM launched a research project with two universities to develop mobile devices for the elderly, blind, and illiterate. The goal of the project is to develop an open, common user interface platform for these people so that they too can use their mobile devices to exploit the information and services available to Internet users.

Based on:

Anonymous. (n.d.). American macular degeneration foundation. Retrieved March 16, 2010, from http://www.macular.org.

Anonymous. (n.d.). Schepens eye research institute. Retrieved March 16, 2010, from http://www.schepens.harvard.edu.

Sauser, B. (2008, January 28). TV for the visually impaired. *Technologyreview.com.* Retrieved March 16, 2010, from http://www.technologyreview.com/Infotech/20117.

Schaffhauser, D. (March 15, 2010). IBM researching mobile device accessibility with universities. *Campus Technology.* Retrieved March 16, 2010, from http://campustechnology.com/articles/2010/03/15/ibm-researching-mobile-device-accessibility-with-universities.aspx.

using information systems to gain a competitive advantage in the area of operating efficiencies, it is likely that your rivals can just as easily adopt the same types of information systems and achieve the same gains. For example, you might set up a Web site that enables customers to check on the status of their order without requiring help from a customer service representative, and this might enable you to cut costs. Rivals could, however, easily copy this approach and match your cost reductions. The competitive advantage thus turns into strategic necessity for anyone in this industry.

On the other hand, there are ways to use information systems to gain a competitive advantage in a way that is easier to sustain; Bakos and Treacy argued that, if you can use information systems to make your products or services unique or to cause your customers to invest so heavily in you that their switching costs are high (i.e., if switching to a competitor's product involves significant investment in terms of time and/or money for the customer), then you are better able to develop a competitive advantage that is sustainable over the long haul. For example, you might combine heavy investments in computer-aided design systems with very bright engineers in order to perfect your product and make it unique and something relatively difficult to copy. Alternatively, you might use a customer relationship management system to build an extensive database containing the entire history of your interaction with each of your customers, and then use that system to provide very high quality, intimate, rapid, and customized service that would convince customers that if they switched to a rival, it would take them years to build up that kind of relationship with the other firm.

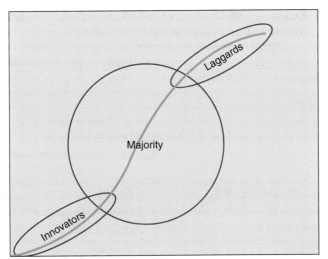

Cumulative
Adoptions

Laggards

Majority

Innovators

Over Time

FIGURE 2.21

Diffusion of innovations.

Source: Based on Rogers (1962).

The Innovator's Dilemma

Deciding which innovations to adopt and pursue has never been easy. In fact, there are many classic examples where so-called industry leaders failed to see the changing opportunities introduced by new innovations (see Table 2.7). In his influential book *Diffusion of Innovations*, Everett Rogers (2003) theorized that the adoption of innovations usually follows an S-shaped curve (see Figure 2.21). When an innovation is brought to market, initially only a small group of "innovators" will adopt that innovation. After some time, sales pick up as the innovators are followed by the "early adopters" and the "early majority," and the increase in sales is strongest. Then sales slowly level off when the "late majority" starts adopting the innovation. Finally, sales stay level as only the "laggards" are left to adopt the innovation.

However, some innovations are more disruptive, turning entire industries upside down. Clayton Christensen's (1997) *The Innovator's Dilemma* outlines how *disruptive innovations* undermine effective management practices, often leading to the demise of an organization or an industry. **Disruptive innovations** are new technologies, products, or services that eventually surpass the existing dominant technology or product in a market (see Table 2.8). For example, retail giant Sears nearly failed in the early 1990s when it did not recognize the transformational power of the disruptive innovation discount retailing; today, discounters like Walmart and segment-specific stores like Home Depot dominate retailing.

Within every market, there are customers who have relatively high, moderate, or low performance requirements from the existing product offerings. For example, within the mobile phone industry today, some low-performance customers demand very basic phones and services (e.g., no text messaging, camera, or data services), whereas high-performance customers use devices and services that rival the capabilities of some personal computers with high-speed Internet connections. Over time, as disruptive innovations and incremental improvements are introduced into an industry, the capabilities of the products in all segments (i.e., low to high performance) improve; as product capabilities improve at the high-performance end of the market, the number of potential customers for these products gets relatively smaller. At the same time, as the low-end products also improve, they are increasingly able to capture more and more of the mainstream marketplace.

To illustrate this progression, Christensen provides compelling examples within several industries. In particular, the collapse of 1970s midrange computer giant Digital Equipment Company (DEC) (and the entire midrange industry for that matter) clearly illustrates the innovator's dilemma. DEC was ultimately surpassed in the marketplace by microprocessor-based computers, with the microprocessor being the disruptive innovation.

In the 1970s, when microcomputers were first introduced, DEC (and its customers) deemed them to be toys and ignored their potential. It is important to note that DEC was a well-run company and was touted as having one of the finest executive teams in the world. Additionally, DEC used leading management techniques, such as conducting extensive market research with its existing customers and industry (i.e., they put "marketing" ahead of technology; for a divergent

TABLE 2.8 Examples of Disruptive Innovations and Their Associated Displaced or Marginalized Technology

Disruptive Innovation	Displaced or Marginalized Technology
Digital photography	Chemical photography
Mobile telephony	Wire-line telephony
Smart phones	Notebook computers
Xbox, Play Station	Desktop computers
Online stock brokerage	Full-service stock brokerages
Online retailing	Bricks-and-mortar retailing
Free, downloadable greeting cards	Printed greeting cards
Distance education	Classroom education
Unmanned aircraft	Manned aircraft
Nurse practitioners	Medical doctors
Semiconductors	Vacuum tubes
Desktop publishing	Traditional publishing
Automobiles	Horses
Airplanes	Trains
Compact discs	Cassettes and records
MP3 players and music downloading	Compact discs and music stores

view, see the discussion of the e-business innovation cycle later in this chapter). When surveyed, none of DEC's customers indicated a need for microcomputers, and thus DEC concluded that developing improved capabilities within its *existing* midrange computer product line is where they should focus. At this time, DEC's goal was to serve the needs of "high-" and "mid"-performance users, which made up the largest part of the total market for computers (see Figure 2.22). The increasing performance of DEC's products started meeting the needs of customers who would traditionally purchase mainframe computers, so DEC could try to "up sell" to mainframe customers of IBM, Burroughs, and Honeywell, where the margins were even greater than in the midrange computer industry.

FIGURE 2.22

Innovator's dilemma view of the evolution of the computing industry.

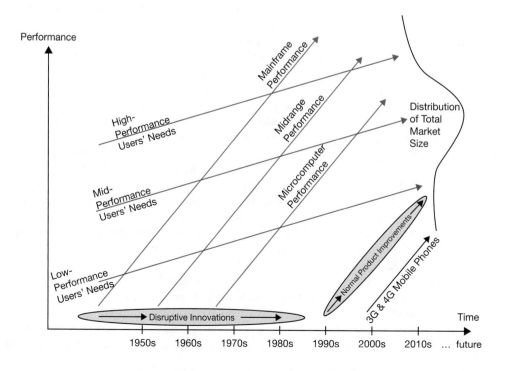

Initially, there were virtually no competitive product offerings serving the needs of the low-performance users; in other words, current product offerings by established computer manufacturers, such as DEC, were either too powerful or too expensive (or both) for these low-end customers. In the 1980s, the microcomputer industry was launched by Apple, and the (disruptive) microprocessor, developed in the 1970s, was now being turned into a product that had the capabilities and price for users in the low-performance category of the marketplace. DEC was not alone in ignoring the introduction of microcomputers; virtually all established players in the computing industry continued to focus on their existing customers and existing product lines, incrementally improving their products over time. Meanwhile, in just a few years, the microcomputer industry grew and matured, going from toy to office automation device (e.g., a replacement for the typewriter or adding machine) to a multipurpose business computer for many small and medium-sized businesses that could never before afford a computer. As the low end of the market took shape in the 1980s, DEC continued to focus on its existing customers and business model (e.g., direct selling, personal service, and so on). Rapidly, the capabilities of the "disruptive" microcomputers improved, meeting the needs of not only the low end but also the mid-performance range of the marketplace, which was traditionally served by DEC's midrange computers. Being far more inexpensive than DEC's products, the microcomputers took over the bulk of the market. Sadly, DEC continued to ignore the microcomputer industry until it was too late, and DEC could do nothing but watch the loss of its biggest traditional market segment. By January 26, 1998, what was left of DEC was sold to Compaq Computers; in 2002, Compaq was acquired by Hewlett-Packard.

Today, microprocessor-based computers from Dell, Sony, Apple, and others meet or exceed the needs of much of the *entire* marketplace; additionally, only a handful of high-end computer manufacturers remain. So what is next for this industry? Many believe that the next disruptive innovations are 3G and 4G mobile phones from companies like Apple, Motorola, and HTC (see the Technology Briefing, "Foundations of Information Systems Infrastructure"). So, the **innovator's dilemma** refers to how disruptive innovations, typically ignored by established market leaders, cause these established firms or industries to lose market dominance, often leading to failure. What DEC experienced, so too have countless other companies in numerous industries. Table 2.9 summarizes the typical progression and effects of a disruptive innovation on an industry.

Organizing to Make Innovation Choices Given the evolution of industries outlined in the innovator's dilemma, how do organizations make decisions on which innovations to embrace and which to ignore? In his follow-up book, *The Innovator's Solution,* Christensen (2003) outlines a process called the *disruptive growth engine,* which all organizations can follow to more effectively respond to disruptive innovations in their industry. This process has the following steps:

1. ***Start Early.*** To gain the greatest opportunities, become a leader in identifying, tracking, and adopting disruptive innovations by making these processes a formal part of the organization (i.e., budgets, personnel, and so on).

TABLE 2.9 Typical Progression and Effects of Disruptive Innovations on an Industry

1. The first mover introduces a new technology. It is expensive, focusing on a small number of high-performance, high-margin customers.
2. Over time, the first mover focuses on improving product capabilities to meet the needs of higher-performance customers in order to continue to reap the highest margins.
3. Later entrants, using a disruptive innovation, have an inferior market position, focusing on lower-performance, lower-margin customers.
4. Over time, later entrants focus on incremental product improvements to serve the needs of more lower-performance customers, also focusing on cost efficiencies to offset the lack of margins with economies of scale.
5. As the market matures, all products improve, competition increases, and margins diminish; the first mover rarely learns the efficiencies of the later entrants and is entrenched in high-margin business practices; the first mover's market share rapidly erodes as that of the later entrants rapidly grows.
6. Ultimately, the later entrants' products meet or exceed the requirements for the vast majority of the marketplace; they "win" with efficient, low-cost business processes demanded by the majority of the marketplace.

2. ***Executive Leadership.*** To gain credibility as well as to bridge sustaining and disruptive product development, visible and credible leadership is required.
3. ***Build a Team of Expert Innovators.*** To most effectively identify and evaluate potential disruptive innovations, build a competent team of expert innovators.
4. ***Educate the Organization.*** To see opportunities, those closest to customers and competitors (e.g., marketing, customer support, and engineering) need to understand how to identify disruptive innovations.

In addition to formalizing the identification of innovations with the organization, shifts in business processes and the fundamental thinking about disruptive innovations are needed. Next, we examine how to implement the innovation identification process.

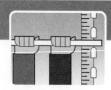

POWERFUL PARTNERSHIPS

The Disruptive Duo: Niklas Zennström and Janus Friis

Niklas Zennström was born in Sweden in 1966 and was educated at Uppsala University in Sweden and the University of Michigan in Ann Arbor. Zennström met Janus Friis, 10 years his junior, in 1996, when both men were working in Denmark, Friis's native country.

Zennström and Friis developed a peer-to-peer file sharing service called KaZaA, which could be used to exchange many file types, such as video, music, applications, and documents (peer-to-peer software uses the combined network bandwidth of the users of the software to improve performance). KaZaA soon became the application of choice for illegally downloading and sharing music files, and Zennström and Friis's company was sued in the Netherlands by the music recording industry for copyright infringement. Further, KaZaA has been accused of being bundled with various programs considered adware and spyware, drawing much criticism from computer security experts. In 2001, the duo sold KaZaA, and KaZaA's user base has dwindled since tight restrictions were implemented into the software to prevent illegal file sharing.

In 2003, Zennström and Friis created Skype, a program that lets users make voice calls over the Internet using peer-to-peer technology. Calls are free to other Skype users, but there are charges for calls to landlines and mobile phones, based on location. Voice mail, call forwarding, instant messaging, file transfer, and videoconferencing services are also available to users. In 2005, eBay bought Skype for $2.6 billion. In 2008, Skype released "Skype for Your Mobile"—a downloadable miniversion of Skype that works on the most popular Java-based mobile phones, followed by an iPhone application. In late 2009, eBay sold a 65 percent interest in Skype to a group of investors for about $2 billion; eBay's vision that buyers and sellers from their popular auction site would discuss transactions via Skype was never realized.

As of early 2010, Skype reported 560 million registered users globally, growing at about 40 million new users each quarter; Skype also estimates that they handle 12 percent of all international calls. Customer service and security have reportedly been issues of concern for users, but user testimonials

FIGURE 2.23

The disruptive duo: Niklas Zennström and Janus Friis.

Atomico

Atomico

posted at Skype.com are, of course, enthusiastic about the service.

In 2007, CNNMoney.com rated the two entrepreneurs twenty-seventh on the publication's list of "The 50 Who Matter Now." "Call them the disruptive duo," the article began. "First they undermined the music industry by unleashing the KaZaA file-sharing network. Then they rattled the telephone industry by creating Skype, a free Internet phone network." The duo's most recent creation, Joost, is a legal streaming video service that brings professionally produced video entertainment to people around the world. In late 2009, Joost was sold to Adconion Media Group for an undisclosed amount. In 2010, Joost reported that each month, more than 67 million people viewed their managed video content, such as advertisements, customer support videos, and entertainment. These videos are not typically viewed at Joost's Web site, where they are hosted; they are viewed primarily as embedded videos on customers' Web sites, much in the way YouTube videos are embedded into various sites throughout the Web. Having made their fortune with various disruptive innovations, Zennström and Friis founded Atomico, a venture capital group to invest in disruptive entrepreneurs working in the consumer Internet technology sector.

Which industry will the "disruptive duo" transform next? Who knows?

Based on:

Ilett, D. (2004, November 26). CA slaps spyware label on Kazaa. *CNET News.com*. Retrieved April 18, 2010, from http://news.cnet.com/CA-slaps-spyware-label-on-Kazaa/2100-1025_3-5467539.html.

Interview: Janus Friis. (2008, January 15). *Netmag.co.uk*. Retrieved April 18, 2010, from http://www.netmag.co.uk/zine/discover-interview/janus-friis.

Janus Friis. (2010, March 23). In *Wikipedia, the free encyclopedia*. Retrieved May 20, 2010, from http://en.wikipedia.org/w/index.php?title=Janus_Friis&oldid=351564174.

Joost. (2010, March 11). In *Wikipedia, the free encyclopedia*. Retrieved May 20, 2010, from http://en.wikipedia.org/w/index.php?title=Joost&oldid=349211667.

Joost. (2010, May 2). Retrieved May 2, 2010, from http://www.joost.com/faq.

Kazaa. (2006, March 22). *Stopbadware.org*. Retrieved April 18, 2010, from http://www.stopbadware.org/reports/reportdisplay?reportname=kazaa.

Naraine, R. (2006, March 32). Spyware trail leads to Kazaa, big advertisers. *eWeek.com*. Retrieved April 18, 2010, from http://www.eweek.com/c/a/Security/Spyware-Trail-Leads-to-Kazaa-Big-Advertisers.

Niklas Zennström. (2010, April 7). In *Wikipedia, the free encyclopedia*. Retrieved May 20, 2010, from http://en.wikipedia.org/w/index.php?title=Niklas_Zennstr%C3%B6m&oldid=354443501.

Skype. (n.d.). Retrieved April 18, 2010, from http://www.skype.com.

Skype. (2010, May 19). In *Wikipedia, the free encyclopedia*. Retrieved May 20, 2010, from http://en.wikipedia.org/w/index.php?title=Skype&oldid=363080172.

The 50 who matter now: Janus Friis and Niklas Zennstrom. (n.d.). *CNNMoney.com*. Retrieved April 18, 2010, from http://money.cnn.com/galleries/2007/biz2/0706/gallery.50whomatter.biz2/24.html.

Wauters, R. (2010, April 14). Joost video network stuns with big reach: 67 million viewers per month. *Washington Post*. Retrieved May 2, 2010, from http://www.washingtonpost.com/wp-dyn/content/article/2010/04/14/AR2010041400730.html.

Implementing the Innovation Process Executives today who are serious about using information technology in innovative ways have made it a point to have their people be continually on the lookout for new disruptive innovations that will have a significant impact on their business. Wheeler (2002) has summarized this process nicely as the **e-business innovation cycle** (see Figure 2.24). Like the term "e-commerce," "e-business" refers to the use of information technologies and systems to support the business. Whereas "e-commerce" generally means the use of the Internet and related technologies to support commerce, **e-business** has a broader meaning: the use of nearly any information technologies or systems to support every part of the business. The model essentially holds that the key to success for modern organizations is the extent to which they use information technologies and systems in timely, innovative ways. The vertical dimension of the e-business innovation cycle shows the extent to which an organization derives value from a particular information technology, and the horizontal dimension shows time. Next, we examine the cycle.

Choosing Enabling/Emerging Technologies. The first bubble left of the graph shows that successful organizations first create jobs, groups, and processes that are all devoted to scanning the environment for new emerging and **enabling technologies** (i.e., information technologies that enable a firm to accomplish a task or goal or to gain or sustain competitive advantage in some way; also called disruptive innovations) that appear to be relevant for the organization. For example, an organization might designate a small group within the IS department as the "Emerging Technologies" unit and charge them with looking for new technologies that will have an impact on the business. As part of their job, this group will pore over current technology magazines,

FIGURE 2.24

The e-business innovation cycle.

Source: Based on Wheeler (2002).

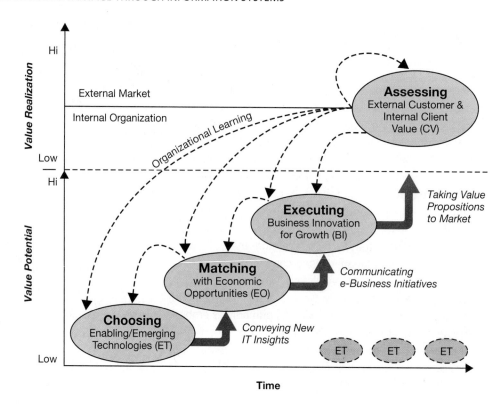

participate in Internet discussion forums on technology topics, go to technology conferences and conventions, and have strong, active relationships with technology researchers at universities and technology companies.

Matching Technologies to Opportunities. Next, in the second bubble, the organization matches the most promising new technologies with current **economic opportunities.** For example, the Emerging Technologies group might have identified advances in database management systems (and a dramatic drop in data storage costs) as a key enabling technology that now makes a massive data warehouse feasible. In addition, managers within the marketing function of the firm have recognized that competitors have really dropped the ball in terms of customer service and that there is an opportunity to gain customers and market share by serving customers better.

Executing Business Innovation for Growth. The third bubble represents the process of selecting—among myriad opportunities to take advantage of—the database and data storage advances and then addressing the current opportunity to grab customers and market share. The organization decides to implement an enterprise-wide data warehouse that enables them to have at their fingertips integrated corporate-wide data and an unparalleled capability to understand, react to, and better serve customers.

Assessing Value. The fourth bubble represents the process of assessing the value of that use of technology, not only to customers but also to internal clients (i.e., sales representatives, marketing managers, the chief operating officer, and so on).

The e-business innovation cycle suggests three new ways to think about investments in disruptive innovations:

1. *Put Technology Ahead of Strategy.* This approach says that technology is so important to strategy and to success that you have to begin with technology. Notice that the first bubble involves understanding, identifying, and choosing technologies that are important. The first bubble does not begin with strategy, as a traditional approach to running a business organization would suggest. In fact, many would argue that given how important technology is today and how fast it changes, if you start with a strategy and then try to retrofit technology into your aging strategy, you are doomed. This approach argues that

you begin by understanding technology and develop a strategy from there. This approach is admittedly very uncomfortable for people who think in traditional ways and/or who are not comfortable with technology. We believe, however, that for many modern organizations, thinking about technology in this way is key.

2. *Put Technology Ahead of Marketing.* The second way that this approach turns conventional wisdom on its head is that, like strategy, marketing also takes a backseat to the technology. Think about it carefully, and you will see that marketing does not come into play until later in this model. A very traditional marketing-oriented approach would be to go first to your customers and find out from them what their needs are and what you ought to be doing with technology (as did DEC). The trouble with this approach is that, given the rapid evolution of technology, your customers are not likely to know about new technologies and their capabilities. In some sense, they are the last place you ought to be looking for ideas about new technologies and their impact on your business. Indeed, if they know about the new technology, then chances are your competitors already do too, meaning that this technology is not the one to rest your competitive advantage on. As Steve Jobs of Apple put it, "You can't just ask people what they want and then try to give that to them. By the time you get it built, they'll want something new."

3. *Innovation Is Continuous.* The third way that this approach is interesting—and potentially troubling—is that the process has to be ongoing. As shown along the time dimension along the bottom of the graph, the first bubble repeats over and over again as the Emerging Technologies group is constantly on the lookout for the "next new thing" that will revolutionize the business. The rate of information technology evolution is not likely to slow down, and innovative organizations truly cannot—and do not—ever rest.

Today, dealing with rapid change caused by disruptive innovations is a reality for most industries. If you are a leader in an industry, you must continually learn to embrace and exploit disruptive innovations, potentially *destroying* your existing core business while at the same time building a new business around the disruptive innovation. If you fail to do this, your competition may do it for you.

Freeconomics: Why Free Products Are the Future of the Digital World

Chris Anderson (2009), editor in chief of *Wired Magazine,* has put forth a provocative idea that charging customers nothing for products and services may be the future of business in the digital world. In fact, he argues that this strategy is a viable approach for making a fortune in virtually any industry. Of course, obvious examples not likely to be easily replicated include Google making billions from its free search engine or Yahoo! making millions from its free Web e-mail service. Anderson convincingly argues, however, that such moneymaking principles are not limited to Google and Yahoo!, but can be applied to countless industries. Here we examine how **freeconomics**—the leveraging of digital technologies to provide *free* goods and services to customers as a business strategy for gaining a competitive advantage—can be utilized by organizations from virtually any industry in the highly competitive digital world.

How Freeconomics Works

According to basic economics within a competitive marketplace, the price of something is set by its marginal cost—the cost of producing an additional unit of output. Given the push toward globalization, the world has never been more competitive (see Chapter 1). Likewise, given the exponential increases in processing power (see Moore's Law in Chapter 3), along with even greater increases in storage and networking capacity, the prices of computer processing, storage, and bandwidth are in a free fall. For example, after Yahoo! has built its Web e-mail environment, the cost to provide this service for each additional person is nearly zero. Consequently, the marginal cost for Web e-mail services is essentially zero. At the same time, huge profits are made giving away this service to more and more customers. For every additional customer, Yahoo! receives payments from companies placing banner advertisements on pages within the Web e-mail service (see Figure 2.25).

ETHICAL DILEMMA

Underground Gaming Economy

The economy in real life is still not in good shape. The unemployment rate is still high, and the real estate market has been in dire straits, forcing many home owners (and speculators) into bankruptcy. Although health care reform has been approved in the United States, health care costs continue to spiral out of control. It's the real world, and those of us who live and work in it develop skills to cope.

Things in Entropia Universe, a virtual world with a real cash economy, aren't much better. Colonists on Calypso must still fight off dangerous enemies, the PED (Project Entropia Dollar) is still worth only 10 cents against the U.S. dollar, and the price of ore-rich property is rising.

Entropia Universe is one of many massively multiplayer online role-playing games (MMORPGs). Other online role-playing games include but are not limited to Sony's Everquest, George Lucas's Star Wars Galaxies, Second Life, and Ultima Online. Players pay monthly subscription fees and assume virtual identities called avatars. Statistics show that the total virtual goods market in the United States was approximately $1.6 billion in 2010 ($6 billion worldwide), up from $500 million in 2008.

In most MMORPGs, gamers slay enemies, build houses and businesses, choose professions, pick up mystical attributes, and fill their virtual bank accounts with gold and cash. Each player's avatar "lives" in the game's virtual community. A recent trend, however, is for serious players to play to collect virtual tools, gold, or cash and then sell the booty for real cash. The dollar amounts involved are usually relatively small, say, $70 for 10 million gold sets in Ultima Online, but there have been notable exceptions. In November 2005, for example, Jon Jacobs, a film producer from Miami, Florida, paid $100,000 for a virtual resort in Entropia Universe. "I have invested in a business that offers numerous opportunities for generating revenue," Jacobs said. He pointed out that the digital resort includes 1,000 hotel rooms that could be sold for $100 each, a stadium for hosting hunting or combat competitions, and a nightclub.

The practice of buying and selling assets from MMORPGs has become so prevalent that the virtual moguls have a name: "farmers." The popular auction site eBay.com daily lists thousands of items taken from MMORPGs under its "Internet Games" category. Items for sale range from characters that have advanced to higher levels of a game to weapons, gold, and other items captured in a game.

Farming has become especially popular in China, where companies employ rows of gamers who play for up to 12 hours

at a time, collecting virtual assets and ascending to the highest levels of a game—all of which the companies will sell. Today, it is estimated that more than 400,000 people worldwide are employed as gold farmers, with nearly 90 percent from China. Like real farmers, these gold farmers work long hours, from 10- to 12-hour shifts, earning around $250 per month, including room and board.

Critics of this new virtual economy say that it penalizes gamers who play strictly for fun but allows those with cash to spend to advance through levels of a game they have not mastered. Others say there is nothing wrong with players buying advantages that let them play at higher levels without putting in large amounts of time.

Some game companies have banned farmers from the playing field. For example, Blizzard Entertainment, the makers of World of Warcraft, a game that boasts more than 6 million subscribers, has permanently banned over 5,000 users following its investigation into cheaters and farmers. By 2008, another 10,700 accounts were suspended for violations of the game's terms of use. Similarly, *PC Gamer*, America's largest gaming magazine, stopped taking advertisements from companies that trade in virtual goods and characters from MMORPGs; and in early 2007, eBay banned the sale of virtual goods such as currency or avatars.

The companies cite ethical reasons for penalizing farmers, but they also realize that farmers can eventually impact revenues, as gamers who don't buy and sell attributes refuse to play with those who do.

Based on:

Entropia Universe. (2010, May 18). In *Wikipedia, the free encyclopedia*. Retrieved May 20, 2010, from http://en.wikipedia.org/w/index.php?title=Entropia_Universe&oldid=362888883.

Gold farming. (2010, May 18). In *Wikipedia, the free encyclopedia*. Retrieved May 20, 2010, from http://en.wikipedia.org/w/index.php?title=Gold_farming&oldid=362816995.

Lyons, D. (2010, March 29). Money for nothing. *Newsweek*. Retrieved April 10, 2010, from http://www.newsweek.com/id/235170.

Millard, E. (2006, January 4). Inside the underground economy of computer gaming. *Newsfactor*. Retrieved April 10, 2010, from http://www.newsfactor.com/story.xhtml?story_id=40592.

Spohn, D. (2006, April 12). Thousands banned from World of Warcraft. *About.com*. Retrieved April 10, 2010, from http://internetgames.about.com/b/2006/04/12/thousands-banned-from-world-of-warcraft.htm.

Wrolstad, J. (2005, November 11). Virtual resort sells for $100,000. *Newsfactor*. Retrieved April 10, 2010, from http://www.newsfactor.com/story.xhtml?story_id=39369.

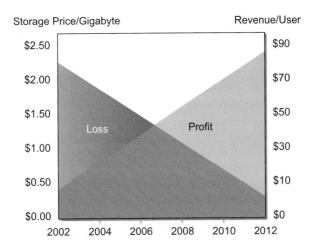

FIGURE 2.25

How Yahoo! makes millions of dollars from its *free* Web-based e-mail service—as the cost of storage has dropped, revenue per user has increased.

It is important to note that *any* industry that utilizes digital technologies (not just those like Google or Yahoo!) is on a path toward increasingly lower costs, ultimately toward a price of free—or at least "free" for consumers. As digital technologies increase in capabilities and at the same time decrease in cost, the industry as a whole will see rapid cost reductions. As costs are reduced, prices for consumers will drop. Moreover, as that industry relies more and more on digital technologies to further reduce costs and to further increase efficiencies, the competitiveness of the industry will further increase, pushing the price closer and closer toward its marginal cost. In other words, as an industry relies more and more on digital technologies, free becomes the inevitable price.

The Freeconomics Value Proposition

Within freeconomics, just because products are free to consumers doesn't mean that someone, somewhere, isn't paying for it and, most important, that someone else isn't also making a lot of money. For example, Google gets paid ad revenue from companies when someone using a Google search clicks on a sponsored link. Here the **value proposition**—what a business provides to a customer and what that customer is willing to pay for that product or service—is larger than simply buyers and sellers. For Google, the value proposition includes a broad ecosystem of many participants, only some of which exchange payments (see Figure 2.26). This value proposition is very similar to that of the radio and television broadcast industries, where consumers receive free content, while advertisers make payments to stations to broadcast commercials. Freeconomics is therefore an extension of this basic advertising model and can be applied to virtually any industry. Additionally, this basic model can be applied in a variety of creative ways beyond advertising.

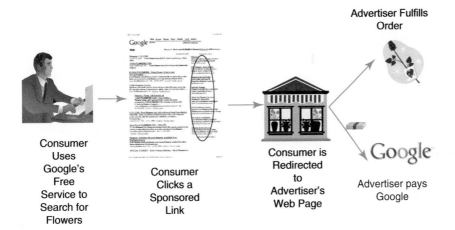

FIGURE 2.26

Google uses a value proposition similar to that of television and radio broadcasting advertising.

Source: www.google.com

Applying Freeconomics in the Digital World

To demonstrate how freeconomics can be applied to a variety of industries beyond Web e-mail or online searches, Anderson explains how cable TV giant Comcast gave a free DVR to millions of its customers, leading to huge profits for the company. The DVR cost Comcast around $250 each, so giving them away needed to stimulate some other type of revenue. Specifically, once consumers had the DVR, they were charged a monthly subscription fee to utilize its capabilities. Comcast was also able to create a stronger relationship with its customers, leading to other revenue streams, including high-speed Internet access, digital telephony services, and pay-per-view movies. In the end, this free DVR is generating tremendous revenue and profits for Comcast.

In another example, the music icon Prince gave away 2.8 million copies of his 2007 CD *Planet Earth,* retail value $19, inside the Sunday edition of London's *Daily Mail.* Although Prince lost money on the giveaway—he received 36 cents per disc from the newspaper while the cost to produce each disc was around $2—he more than made up for this loss through the sale of concert tickets. After the giveaway, he sold out a record-breaking 21 shows in the O_2 Arena in London, netting the entertainer nearly $19 million in revenue after expenses. Indeed, there are many approaches for making money by giving things away.

Table 2.10 outlines six general approaches for applying the concepts of freeconomics to a broad range of industries. For example, the online photo sharing application Flickr (owned by Yahoo!) allows users to store, share, organize, and tag a limited number of pictures for free; applying the *freemium* approach, users can upgrade to a paid "pro account," providing additional features, such as unlimited storage and advertisement-free browsing, or can use other paid services, such as printing through Hewlett-Packard's print services, creating photo gifts, or creating books using Blurb.com. Understanding how to leverage the value of IS investments is fundamental to thriving in the digital world.

TABLE 2.10 General Approaches for Applying Freeconomics to Various Industries

Approach	What It Means	Examples
Advertising	Free services are provided to customers and paid for by a third party.	• Yahoo!'s banner ads • Google's pay-per-click • Amazon's pay-per-transaction "affiliate ads"
Freemium	Basic services are offered for free, but a premium is charged for special features.	• Flickr • Skype • FreeDrive.com • Trillian
Cross subsidies	Sale price of one item is reduced in order to sell something else of value.	• Comcast DVR • Free theater ticket for those willing to buy a large popcorn and beverage • Free Wii to those willing to buy five new games • Free cell phone with two-year contract
Zero marginal cost	Products are distributed to customers without an appreciable cost to anyone.	• Online music distribution at iTunes • Software distribution • Video content on YouTube
Labor exchange	Services are provided to customers; the act of using the services creates value for the company.	• Yahoo! Answers • Google's 411 service • Digg rating services
Gift economy	Environments are created that allow people to participate and collaborate to create something of value for everyone.	• Open source software development • Wikipedia • Freecycle—free secondhand goods to anyone willing to haul them away

Source: Based on Anderson (2009).

INDUSTRY ANALYSIS

Banking Industry

Like many other industries moving into the Internet age, the banking business is changing. Since the nineteenth century, banks in the United States have been heavily regulated. Federal and state laws passed in the 1800s and the 1930s have limited banks to certain geographic locations and have determined the services they could offer. For example, in many states each bank could maintain locations for accepting deposits in only that one state, and in some states they were allowed to maintain offices in just one county. Banks could offer traditional banking services, including deposits and loans, but little more. Insurance services were banned, and securities underwriting was limited. The many banking laws and regulations were intended to limit the number of bank failures after the Great Depression and to make banks safer, but they also limited services that banks could provide to customers, preventing them from competing with stockbrokers and insurance companies.

Nearly all these banking restrictions were eased or eliminated from the 1970s to the present, when banking deregulation took place. Deregulation resulted in increased acquisitions and consolidations, integration across state lines, and a larger market share for better-run banks as they gained ground over their less efficient rivals. As a result, banks could offer more customer services at lower prices, benefiting the country's overall economy.

Today, the Internet provides banks with another way to serve customers and another venue for competition. Banks can now offer customers the convenience and security of online banking services—from account management to loan applications and certificate-of-deposit purchases. No longer do customers judge banks simply according to hours open, ATM locations, fees charged, or travel distance to a brick-and-mortar site. Now banks offering online services can also expect potential customers to judge them according to the following:

1. The degree to which the online banking experience can be personalized
2. Ease of use
3. Responsiveness of the site

Online banking has become the norm, with millions of people logging onto their bank's Web site to pay bills, transfer money, or review transactions. Given the advent of 4G mobile networks, phones, and devices, the next wave of technology innovation within the banking industry will be mobile banking. Mobile banking will provide customers the convenience of conducting any banking service from virtually anywhere while at the same time providing increased security through the application of various encryption and authentications capabilities within the advanced 4G communication networks. For example, USAA, which provides financial services to members of the U.S. armed forces, created an application for the iPhone and Android-based smart phones that allows its customers to deposit a check by simply taking a photo of the endorsed check; the deposit will be instantly credited to the user's bank account.

Although mobile banking seems promising, it still has a ways to go. For instance, today, most banks provide only a limited set of mobile services, such as viewing balances or receiving text alerts about payments or overdrafts. Many mobile devices are not 4G compatible, and advanced 4G networks are only slowly extending outside major cities and population areas. Of course, banks are beginning to provide more advanced services, but there is still a substantial gap between what has been promised and what is reality. Nevertheless, it is clear that this industry is in a state of transition to provide enhanced services to customers that will lower costs and improve convenience, ultimately making the process of paying a bill as easy as sending a text message to a friend.

Questions

1. What are your biggest security concerns related to online banking? How does/should your bank address these concerns?
2. Deregulation of the banking industry allowed banks to more freely operate across state lines; should international banks be allowed to operate in domestic markets? Why or why not?

Based on:

Anonymous. (2005, November 15). Delivering on the promise to change the banking experience. Retrieved April 24, 2010, from http://www .microsoft.com/presspass/features/2005/nov05/11-15Banking.mspx.

Gardner, N. (2009, September 28). The evolution of banking—From the web to phones. *News.com.au*. Retrieved April 24, 2010, from http:// www.news.com.au/money/banking/internet-banking-moves-onto-your -phone/story-e6frfmcr-1225780500924.

Strahan, P. E. (2003, July). The real effects of banking deregulation. Retrieved April 24, 2010, from http://research.stlouisfed.org/ publications/review/03/07/Strahan.pdf.

Whitney, L. (2009, August 11). USAA app lets iPhone users deposit checks. *CNET News.com*. Retrieved August 4, 2010, from http://news. cnet.com/8301-13579_3-10307182-37.html.

Key Points Review

1. *Discuss how information systems can be used for automation, organizational learning, and strategic advantage.* Automating business activities occurs when information systems are used to do a business activity faster or more cheaply. Information systems can be used to help automate and can also be used to improve aspects of an operation in order to gain dramatic improvements in the operation as a whole. When this occurs, technology is said to help us learn because it provides information about its operation and the underlying work process that it supports. Using information systems to automate and learn about business processes is a good start. However, information systems can add even more value to an organization if they are conceived, designed, used, and managed with a strategic approach. To apply information systems strategically, you must understand the organization's value chain and be able to identify opportunities in which you can use information systems to make changes or improvements in the value chain to gain or sustain a competitive advantage. This requires a change in mind-set from thinking about information systems as an expense to be minimized to thinking of information systems as an asset to be invested in.

2. *Describe international business and IS strategies used by companies operating in the digital world.* Companies operating in the digital world can use different business strategies. Some companies pursue a home-replication strategy, which entails selling products developed for the home market internationally. In contrast, other companies develop products for the global market. This strategy, known as global business strategy, includes having a centralized organization to offer standardized products in different markets. This helps to achieve economies of scale and is best suited for homogeneous markets. Information systems used by organizations pursuing this strategy are very centralized, and much data flows from the subsidiaries to the headquarters. The multidomestic business strategy is best suited for heterogeneous markets, as it allows companies to quickly respond to changing local conditions; this strategy includes having a decentralized federation of loosely associated business units in different countries. Companies pursuing this strategy employ decentralized systems, and data sharing is very limited. The transnational business strategy is very well suited for operating in the digital world, as it combines the benefits of the multidomestic and the global business strategies by enabling economies of scale while being responsive to local market conditions. In a transnational business strategy, some aspects of the company are centralized, while others are decentralized. The information systems used are distributed, allowing for increased communication between the headquarters and the subsidiaries as well as between the subsidiaries and for common access

to critical data. Transnational information systems are enabled primarily by intranets, extranets, and the Internet.

3. *Explain why and how companies are continually looking for innovative ways to use information systems for competitive advantage.* Organizations are finding innovative ways to use new technologies to help them do things faster, better, and more efficiently than rivals. Being at the technological cutting edge has its disadvantages and is typically quite difficult to execute. Given that new technologies are not as stable as traditional ones, relying on innovative information systems and technologies can be problematic. Because constantly upgrading to newer and better systems is expensive, relying on emerging systems can hurt a firm financially. In addition, using innovative information systems for competitive advantage can provide short-lived advantages; competitors can quickly jump on the technological bandwagon and easily mimic the same system. Not every organization should deploy innovative information systems. Those organizations that find themselves in highly competitive environments probably most need to deploy new technologies to stay ahead of rivals. To best deploy these new technologies, organizations must be ready for the business process changes that will ensue, have the resources necessary to deploy new technologies successfully, and be tolerant of the risk and problems involved in being at the cutting edge. Deploying emerging information systems is essentially a risk/return gamble: The risks are relatively high, but the potential rewards are great. Organizations successfully utilizing innovative systems and technologies today have people (and in some cases, special units) who scan the environment, looking out for emerging and enabling (and potentially disruptive) technologies that can help their firm. They then narrow down the list to technologies that match with the challenges the firm faces or that create economic opportunities. Next, they choose a particular technology or a set of technologies and implement them in a way that enables them to gain or sustain a competitive advantage. Finally, they assess these technology projects in terms of their value, not only to internal people and groups but also to external clients and partners. This process is ongoing, as information technologies and systems continually evolve.

4. *Describe freeconomics and how organizations can leverage digital technologies to provide free goods and services to customers as a business strategy for gaining a competitive advantage.* Freeconomics refers to the leveraging of digital technologies to provide *free* goods and services to customers as a business strategy for gaining a competitive advantage. Virtually *any* industry that utilizes digital technologies (not just those like Google or Yahoo!) is on a path toward increasingly lower costs, ultimately toward a price of free—or at least "free" for consumers. Industries

can apply freeconomics in a variety of ways to gain a competitive advantage, including using advertising (e.g., Yahoo! banner ads), using a freemium approach (e.g., Flickr providing limited storage for free to gain customers and then charging a fee to those customers who need additional storage and features), having one product cross subsidize another (e.g., Comcast giving away DVRs to charge for programming), having zero marginal costs for additional product offerings (e.g., constant expansion of content on iTunes), gaining labor exchanges for services (e.g., Yahoo!'s answer service), or facilitating a gift economy where people freely collaborate to create something of value to everyone (e.g., open source software development).

Key Terms

automating 58
best-cost provider strategy 62
business/IT alignment 65
business process 54
differentiation strategy 60
disruptive innovation 77
domestic company 67
e-business 81
e-business innovation cycle 81
economic opportunity 82
enabling technology 81
executive level 56
freeconomics 83

functional area information
  system 57
global business strategy 70
key performance indicator (KPI) 56
home-replication strategy 69
informating 58
innovator's dilemma 79
international business strategy 67
learning organization 59
low-cost leadership strategy 60
managerial level 55
multidomestic business strategy 70
operational level 54

organizational learning 58
organizational strategy 60
semistructured decision 56
strategic necessity 66
strategic planning 60
structured decision 55
transnational business strategy 72
unstructured decision 57
value chain 64
value chain analysis 64
value proposition 85

Review Questions

1. Compare and contrast the characteristics of the operational, managerial, and executive levels of an organization.
2. Compare and contrast automating and learning.
3. Describe the attributes of a learning organization.
4. List five general types of organizational strategy.
5. Describe competitive advantage and list six sources.
6. Describe the multidomestic business strategy and how it affects the flow of control information.
7. Why is successful application of innovative technologies and systems often difficult?
8. What is the "innovator's dilemma"?
9. Using past examples, explain what is meant by a disruptive innovation.
10. Describe the e-business innovation cycle.
11. What is freeconomics, and what are several approaches for applying its concepts to various industries?

Self-Study Questions

1. _____ is using technology as a way to help complete a task within an organization faster and, perhaps, more cheaply.
   A. automating
   B. learning
   C. strategizing
   D. processing
2. What are new technologies, products, or services that eventually surpass the existing dominant technology or product in a market called?
   A. surpassing event
   B. disruptive innovation
   C. innovative technology
   D. technology change
3. Which of the following is *not* improving the value chain?
   A. improving procurement processes
   B. increasing operating costs
   C. minimizing marketing expenditures
   D. streamlining production processes
4. A company is said to have _____ when it has gained an edge over its rivals.
   A. monopoly
   B. profitability
   C. competitive advantage
   D. computer advantage
5. Each of the following was described in this chapter as a source of competitive advantage except for _____.
   A. delivering superior customer service
   B. achieving lower cost than rivals
   C. being the subject of a hostile takeover
   D. having shorter lead times in developing and testing new products

6. _____ refers to the emergence of disruptive innovations that undermine effective management practices, often leading to the demise of an organization or an industry.
   A. Moore's law
   B. Technological obsolescence
   C. Life cycle analysis
   D. Innovator's dilemma
7. What is a process of choosing, matching, executing, and assessing innovative technologies called?
   A. environmental scanning
   B. e-business innovation cycle
   C. strategic planning
   D. none of the above
8. What international business strategy is employed by companies that carefully decide which aspect should be under central control and which should be decentralized?
   A. global business strategy
   B. transnational business strategy
   C. multidomestic business strategy
   D. operational business strategy

9. At the _____ level of the organization, functional managers (e.g., marketing managers, finance managers, manufacturing managers, and human resource managers) focus on monitoring and controlling operational-level activities and providing information to higher levels of the organization.
   A. operational
   B. managerial
   C. organizational
   D. executive
10. A supervisor's having to decide when to reorder supplies or how best to allocate personnel for the completion of a project is an example of a(n) _____ decision.
   A. structured
   B. unstructured
   C. automated
   D. delegated
   Answers are on page 92.

Problems and Exercises

1. Match the following terms with the appropriate definitions:
   i. value chain analysis
   ii. freeconomics
   iii. learning organization
   iv. value chain
   v. e-business innovation cycle
   vi. disruptive innovations
   vii. innovator's dilemma
   viii. transnational business strategy
   ix. multidomestic business strategy
   x. operational level

   a. The notion that disruptive innovations can cause established firms or industries to lose market dominance, often leading to failure
   b. The process of analyzing an organization's activities to determine where value is added to products and/or services and the costs that are incurred for doing so
   c. New technologies, products, or services that eventually surpass the existing dominant technology or product in a market
   d. An organization that is able to learn, grow, and manage its knowledge well
   e. A model suggesting that the extent to which modern organizations use information technologies and systems in timely, innovative ways is the key to success.
   f. The leveraging of digital technologies to provide free goods and services to customers as a business strategy for gaining competitive advantage
   g. The set of primary and support activities in an organization where value is added to a product or service
   h. An international business strategy employed to be flexible and responsive to the needs and demands of heterogeneous local markets
   i. An international business strategy that allows companies to leverage the flexibility offered by a decentralized organization (to be more responsive to local conditions) while at the same time reaping economies of scale enjoyed by centralization
   j. The bottom level of an organization, where the routine day-to-day interaction with customers occurs

2. Using a business or organization that you are familiar with, contrast the operational, managerial, and executive levels by contrasting each level's typical activities, types of decisions, and information needs.

3. Using your own life, contrast several structured versus unstructured decisions that you regularly have to make.

4. Identify a company utilizing the distinct competitive strategies shown in Figure 2.10; provide evidence to support your selections.

5. Of the five industry forces presented in the chapter (Porter's model), which is the most significant for an organization in terms of making IS investment decisions? Why? Which is the least significant? Why?

6. Using a company or organization that you are familiar with, map their various business processes into a value chain.

7. Find an international organization not discussed in this chapter that is operating in multiple countries using a home-replication business strategy. Provide evidence and examples that help to support your selection.

8. Find an international organization not discussed in this chapter that is operating in multiple countries using a multidomestic business strategy. Provide evidence and examples that help to support your selection.

9. Find an international organization not discussed in this chapter that is operating in multiple countries using a

global business strategy. Provide evidence and examples that help to support your selection.

10. Find an international organization not discussed in this chapter that is operating in multiple countries using a transnational business strategy. Provide evidence and examples that help to support your selection.

11. Why shouldn't every organization deploy innovative information systems? What are some of the recommended characteristics of an organization that are necessary in order for that organization to successfully deploy innovative technologies?

12. Identify examples not discussed in the chapter of disruptive innovations that successfully displaced or marginalized an industry or technology.

13. Apply the progression and effects of disruptive innovation on an industry (see Table 2.8), describing the evolution of a disruptive technology to a product or industry.

14. Find an example not discussed in the book that demonstrated the freeconomics concept of freemium.

15. Find an example not discussed in the book that demonstrated the freeconomics concept of cross subsidy.

16. Find an example not discussed in the book that demonstrated the freeconomics concept of zero marginal cost.

17. Find an example not discussed in the book that demonstrated the freeconomics concept of labor exchange.

Application Exercises

 Note: The existing data files referenced in these exercises are available on the Student Companion Web site: **www.pearsonhighered.com/valacich.**

 ## Spreadsheet Application: Valuing Information Systems

The cost of maintaining information systems is high for Campus Travel. You have been assigned to evaluate the total cost of ownership (TCO) of a few systems that are currently in use by Campus Travel employees. Take a look at the TCO.csv file to obtain the list of systems that are in use and the costs associated with maintaining the software, hardware, and the associated personnel for each type of system. Calculate the following for your operations manager:

1. The costs for server hardware by adding a new row to include Web servers. This includes $4,500 for the main campus and $2,200 for the other campuses.

2. The TCO for the entire information system in Campus Travel. Hint: Sum all the values for all the systems together.

3. The TCO for servers and network components of the information system.

4. Make sure that you format the table, including using the currency format, in a professional manner.

Database Application: Building a System Usage Database

To understand the assets in Campus Travel, the IS manager has asked you to design a database that would be able to store all the assets. Your manager asks you to do the following:

1. Create a new blank database called asset.mdb.

2. Create a new table called "assets" in the asset database with the following fields:
   a. Item ID (Text field)
   b. Item Name (Text field)
   c. Description (Memo field)
   d. Category (hardware, software, other)
   e. Condition (new, good, fair, poor)
   f. Acquisition Date (Date field)
   g. Purchase Price (Currency field)
   h. Current Value (Currency field)

Team Work Exercise: Pizza, Anyone?

Compare with your classmates your experiences with ordering pizza over the phone for delivery to your home. When you call to order the pizza, do you have to give them your full name, address, and phone number every time you call them, or do they merely ask your phone number and then automatically know who you are and where you live? If it is the latter, then they are using an information system to keep track of you so that they do not continually have to annoy you by asking you for your name, address, and phone number every time you call. How important is this to you? Is this giving the pizza company a competitive advantage? Is it as important to you as the price of the pizza or how fast it is delivered? Are there conditions under which superior use of information systems can compensate for inferior products (also think about products other than pizza)?

Answers to the Self-Study Questions

1. A, p. 58
2. B, p. 77
3. B, p. 65
4. C, p. 60
5. C, p. 63
6. D, p. 79
7. B, p. 81
8. B, p. 72
9. B, p. 55
10. A, p. 55

Case 1

LinkedIn

YouTube is for video entertainment; iTunes services music lovers; Facebook is primarily for socializing; Flickr is for photo exchange; Second Life and World of Warcraft are for participating in virtual communities; Gamezone and Shockwave are for gamesters; and so on and so on. It would seem that the Web has anticipated all of our needs and responded. But wait, what's out there for those of us who want to further our professional lives—to visit with others in our field of expertise, to look at jobs that are available in other parts of the world, to find out what's happening in the business world outside our own familiar circle, and to garner introductions to those who might help us succeed? LinkedIn is an online service that fills this niche. LinkedIn advertises itself as "an interconnected network of experienced professionals from around the world, representing 150 industries and 200 countries. You can find, be introduced to, and collaborate with qualified professionals that you need to work with to accomplish your goals." As of 2010, LinkedIn had over 60 million members, half of whom were from countries outside the United States, and has executives from all Fortune 500 companies in its ranks.

LinkedIn is growing rapidly, with a new member joining approximately every second.

Reid Hoffman, a former executive vice president of PayPal, founded LinkedIn in 2002; the service was launched in May 2003. Hoffman remains chairman of the board at LinkedIn, which is based in Mountain View, California, but also has offices in Omaha, New York, and London. His LinkedIn profile is available at http://www.linkedin.com/in/reidhoffman.

Joining LinkedIn is free; upgrading to a paid account with additional "tools" is optional. Newcomers to LinkedIn create a profile, listing professional accomplishments. Each newcomer then links trusted colleagues, contacts, and clients—called *connections*—by inviting them to join and linking to him or her. In this way, LinkedIn participants create their own professional networks, where contacts may number in the thousands. Connections can be used in many ways:

- Users list trusted contacts, who then list their contacts, called second-degree connections. Second-degree connections list their trusted contacts, called third-degree connections. In this way, the original LinkedIn user brings together thousands of professionals, gaining many valuable contacts.
- Users can then find jobs, people, and business opportunities recommended by someone in the network.
- Employers using the network can list jobs and search for available candidates to fill job openings.
- Job seekers can search the connections of potential employers and find mutual connections who might introduce them.

A free feature called "LinkedIn Answers" lets users ask business-related questions for the community to answer. LinkedIn Groups is another free feature that allows users to make additional contacts by joining alumni, professional, or other job-related groups.

A mobile version of LinkedIn is available in six languages. LinkedIn continues to push mobile use with their latest updated iPhone application and has also announced better integration with Microsoft Outlook and Lotus software—a clear move to better align themselves with business users.

There are ways to enhance one's use of professional profile sites such as LinkedIn, writes Kevin Donlin for the *Minneapolis–St. Paul Star Tribune*. First, enhance your profile. One way to do this is to jazz up your profile with a few pertinent details and statements from colleagues. For example, staff members at LinkedIn advised Guy Kawasaki, managing director of Garage Technology Ventures in San Francisco, California, to add the following statement from a former colleague at Apple Computers, where Guy said he was "chief evangelist." "Spirited and exceptionally bright with a highly developed sense of humor, Guy continues to be one of the most gifted marketing executives I know."

Enhance your profile, Donlin advises, but "keep your dirt to yourself. According to NBC News, 77 percent of employers will search the Internet to check your background, and 35 percent of employers have eliminated a candidate for consideration after finding 'digital dirt' about them online." So don't post that video of yourself imbibing too much at a party on Facebook, and remember that potential employers may not appreciate the video of the tasteless practical joke you played on a friend, so keep it off YouTube.

Like some other social media sites, LinkedIn has come under recent criticism for its threats to business and corporate security. According to the latest annual Security Threat Report by Sophos, an information security firm, LinkedIn is increasingly being used as a conduit for hackers and other malicious entities to develop "road maps" attacks. According to the report, LinkedIn is providing what amounts to a corporate directory of who works at a firm and what their responsibilities are as well as corporate e-mail addresses. Armed with this type of knowledge, hackers can easily devise a social engineering attack—the act of manipulating people into divulging confidential information—and target who and what they want to attack to effectively meet their sinister goals.

Security concerns aside, LinkedIn is clearly a valuable technological tool for Internet users and entrepreneurs alike who are looking for better ways to network.

Questions

1. Do you think it is ethical for employers to search the Internet for information on potential employees?
2. Do you believe that you can gain a competitive advantage by joining a network such as LinkedIn? Why or why not?
3. Have you joined or do you plan to join LinkedIn (or a similar type of site)? Why or why not?

Based on:

Donlin, K. (2008, April 9). Three ways to get found and hired. *Star Tribune*. Retrieved May 12, 2010, from http://www.startribune.com/jobs/career/15116626.html.

Kawasaki, G. (2010, January 16). LinkedIn profile extreme makeover. Retrieved May 12, 2010, from http://blog.guykawasaki.com/2007/01/linkedin_profil.html.

LinkedIn. (2010, April 23). In *Wikipedia, the free encyclopedia*. Retrieved April 23, 2010, from http://en.wikipedia.org/w/index.php?title=LinkedIn&oldid=210484559.

Linkedin.com. (n.d.) Retrieved April 23, 2010, from http://www.linkedin.com/static?key=what_is_linkedin&trk=hb_what.

Muncaster, P. (2010, February 15). LinkedIn hits 60 million global users. *CRN*. Retrieved April 23, 2010, from http://www.crn.com.au/News/167245,linkedin-hits-60-million-global-users.aspx.

Sophos.com. (2010, February 1). Malware and spam rise 70% on social networks, security report reveals. Retrieved April 23, 2010 from http://www.sophos.com/pressoffice/news/articles/2010/02/security-report-2010.html.

Case 2

Netflix

Remember the old brick-and-mortar movie rental services? You drove to the physical location, scanned shelves for your movie of choice (too frequently, it wasn't in), paid the clerk, and left. The flick was due back in 24 hours (or, at most, three to five days later), or you were billed a hefty late fee. In some cases, forgetful customers answered the door to find a police officer asking why they hadn't returned a rental movie.

Movie rental stores still exist, of course—Blockbuster may come to mind first, although many of its stores have closed—but now there are alternatives.

Pay-per-view is an option for cable and satellite dish TV subscribers, but choices are limited to the services' picks and are available only after movies have been offered as rental DVDs and videos for 30 days. Since customers are not always satisfied with limits inherent in these options—late fees, unavailability of newer films, short turnaround times, and so on—it had to follow that someone would come up with the idea to offer a click-based online movie rental service.

Enter Netflix in 2002, the first and now the world's largest online movie rental service. As of 2010, Netflix offered 12 million subscribers over 100,000 movie choices. The term "subscriber" is the key to Netflix's unique idea. Movie aficionados subscribe to the Netflix service by paying a monthly fee for the movie delivery service. Although there are several subscription plans available, the basic plan is $8.99 per month, giving customers access to DVD rentals through the mail on a one-at-a-time basis with unlimited rentals per month and access to Netflix streaming content. With over 100 distribution locations across the United States, the turnaround time to receive the DVD is typically one business day after shipping. Movies are available in standard DVD format and many in Blu-ray, although an additional $2 is charged for renting Blu-ray discs. There are no late fees involved, you can keep the disc as long as you want, and postage is paid both ways. When one movie is returned, a second is mailed from the customer's tailored list of queued movies. On average, the company ships 1.9 million DVDs a day!

An "on-demand" type service was added in 2007 allowing customers to view movies immediately on their PCs or Macs. In 2008, Netflix introduced a service that allowed subscribers to instantly watch streaming movies and TV shows on their television through Netflix-ready devices such as Internet-enabled Blu-ray players or Microsoft's Xbox 360. As of 2010, Netflix streaming has become very popular in part because the service is bundled in the monthly subscription charge. Additionally, the streaming choices are ever growing, with over 17,000 items currently available in Netflix's "Watch Instantly" library. Netflix-ready devices have also expanded, flooding the market with multiple streaming-ready gadgets. Along with top gaming consoles and Blu-ray players, televisions, DVR devices, and home theater components have joined the growing number of devices that can serve up your favorite movie on the fly.

Soon after Netflix's inception in 2002, Blockbuster, the nation's largest movie rental chain, and Walmart, the largest business in the United States, began to offer in-store subscription services similar to Netflix's model. By 2006, however, Walmart had dropped its movie rental subscription service. As of 2010, Blockbuster's subscription service, Blockbuster Online, and their digital download service, Blockbuster on Demand, continue to provide competition to Netflix in some markets.

However, Netflix's extraordinary and, therefore, popular service has outpaced competitive movie rental services, including pay-per-view, because it personalizes a customer's movie rental experience to a degree previously not possible. This personalized service asks the customer to rate up to 40 movies. From this information, software called Cinematch creates a profile of each customer and a list of recommended movies. If, for example, a customer liked *Ironman,* he or she may also like *The Dark Knight Returns,* and that movie will be included in a list the customer accesses by clicking on "recommendations." The customer can then opt to place any of the recommended movies in his or her queue. Customers manipulate the movies listed in the queue by adding new titles to the list, removing titles, and moving titles to the top or to other locations on the list. Netflix's Cinematch system allows customers to tap a wide database of movies, many of which they may not have been aware of at all since it will move to the next movie in a customer's queue if a more recent and popular listing is not immediately available.

Netflix is not without critics. It turns out that the service "rewards" customers with the fewest monthly rentals and "punishes" those with the most rentals in terms of popular movie availability and promptness of shipping. This policy is spelled out in the company's terms of service, published on the Netflix Web site:

> In determining priority for shipping and inventory allocation, we may utilize many different factors, including without limitation, the number and type of DVDs you rent through our service, the subscription plan you select, as well as other uses of our service by you. For example, if all other factors are the same, we give priority to those members who receive the fewest DVDs through our service.

According to the Netflix site, when you add a popular movie that is currently unavailable, you are added to the internal list that rates customers according to profitability. There is an assumption by the customers that the service is linear, meaning that the first customer to request the movie would be the first customer to get the movie—or first in, first out. In reality, the priority service equation selects customers on the basis of their profitability. With shipping being the major cost for the online movie distributor, customers who cost the most in terms of shipping may not receive popular movies first.

What does this mean for the customers? If you are a customer who uses the service infrequently, then you are highly profitable for Netflix since your shipping costs are low. Therefore, your selections are prioritized. The customers who use the service frequently or what Netflix would deem "overfrequently" are seen as not as profitable and therefore do not receive priority.

In 2004, this policy caused a "frequent" Netflix customer to sue the company in a class-action lawsuit titled *Chavez v. Netflix, Inc.* The plaintiff in the case, Frank Chavez, claimed that Netflix's claims that a subscriber could rent "unlimited" DVDs each month and receive them in "a day's time" were false. (Chavez had attempted to rent hundreds of DVDs a month but sued when he found he could not.) Although Netflix denied any wrongdoing, they settled the suit in 2005. Chavez received $2,000, and his lawyers got over $2.5 million. Certain Netflix customers who joined the class-action suit were upgraded to a different rental plan for a short period, and Netflix instituted a limited try-the-plan-for-three-months-free offer. Although some customers have expressed dissatisfaction with the apparent "throttling" of their account, Netflix customer numbers continue to increase rather than decrease.

What's next for the online movie rental company? According to reports, Netflix will soon add 1080p high definition and 5.1-channel surround sound to their streaming video content. Analysts predict that by mid-2011, two-thirds of subscribers will be watching Netflix content through online streaming. Will online content delivery replace the physical DVD and Blu-ray media that the company was founded on? Many in the industry (as well as satisfied streamers) think so, but only time will tell.

Questions

1. Can local video stores survive in the digital world? Contrast their evolution with that of local bookstores. What is similar? What is unique?

2. Forecast the future of Netflix in regard to the advent of on-demand video where any type of video content is available at any time on any device.

3. Discuss whether and how Netflix can maintain its competitive advantage.

Based on:

Elgan, M. (2006, January 30). How to hack Netflix. *Information Week*. Retrieved April 23, 2010, from http://www.informationweek.com/news/showArticle.jhtml?articleID=177105341.

Frauenfelder, M. (2005, November 2). Netflix settlement details. *Boing Boing*. Retrieved April 23, 2010, from http://www.boingboing.net/2005/11/02/netflix_lawsuit_sett.html.

Mullaney, T. J., & Hof, R. (2005, November 10). Netflix starring in merger story? *BusinessWeek*. Retrieved April 23, 2010, from http://www.businessweek.com/technology/content/nov2005/tc20051110_143721.htm.

Netflix. (n.d.). Retrieved April 23, 2010, from http://www.netflix.com.

Netflix. (2010, May 19). In *Wikipedia, the free encyclopedia*. Retrieved May 20, 2010, from http://en.wikipedia.org/w/index.php?title=Netflix&oldid=363071143.

O'Brien, J. M. (2002, December). The Netflix effect. *Wired*. Retrieved April 23, 2010, from http://www.wired.com/wired/archive/10.12/netflix.html.

Portnoy, S. (2010, February 8). Netflix will add 1080p, 5.1-channel surround sound streaming to its online video service later in 2010. *ZDNet*. Retrieved April 23, 2010, from http://blogs.zdnet.com/home-theater/?p=2641.

Managing the Information Systems Infrastructure and Services

After reading this chapter, you will be able to do the following:

1. List the essential IS infrastructure components and describe why they are necessary for satisfying an organization's informational needs.

2. Discuss managerial issues associated with managing an organization's IS infrastructure.

3. Describe current trends that can help an organization address IS infrastructure–related challenges.

Preview

Just as any city depends on a functioning infrastructure, companies operating in a digital world are relying on a comprehensive information systems (IS) infrastructure to support their business processes and competitive strategy. With ever-increasing speed, transactions are conducted; likewise, with ever-increasing amounts of data to be captured, analyzed, and stored, companies have to thoroughly plan and manage their infrastructure needs in order to gain the greatest returns on their IS investments. When planning and managing their IS architectures, organizations must answer many important and difficult questions. For example, how will we utilize information systems to enable our competitive strategy? What technologies and systems best support our core business processes? Which vendors should we partner with, which technologies do we adopt, and which do we avoid? What hardware, software, or services do we buy, build, or have managed by an outside service provider? How can the organization get the most out of the data captured from internal and external sources? Clearly, effectively managing an organization's IS infrastructure is a complex but necessary activity in today's digital world.

This chapter focuses on helping managers understand the key components of a comprehensive IS infrastructure and why its careful management is necessary. With an increasing complexity of an organization's information needs and an increasing complexity of the systems needed to satisfy these requirements, the topic of infrastructure management is fundamental for managing in the digital world.

Managing in the Digital World: "I Googled You!"

You're researching a paper for a physics class, and you need information on quarks. Google it (see Figure 3.1). You'd like to locate a high school classmate, but no one in your graduating class knows where she is. Google her. You're watching a movie, and a character says she "googled" a blind date. The term "google" has become so familiar to Internet users that it's often used as a verb. In fact, the term has become so common that Google is becoming concerned that its use as a verb is a copyright infringement, asking dictionaries such as *Merriam-Webster* to change their definition of the verb *google* to "to use the Google search engine to obtain information . . . on the World Wide Web."

According to Google lore, company founders Larry Page and Sergey Brin argued about everything when they first met as Stanford University graduate students in computer science in 1995. Larry was a 24-year-old University of Michigan alumnus on a weekend visit; Sergey, 23 at that time, was among a group of students assigned to show him around. Both had strong opinions and divergent viewpoints, but they eventually found common ground in a unique approach to solving one of computing's biggest challenges: retrieving relevant information from a massive set of data.

By January 1996, Page and Brin had begun collaboration on a search engine called BackRub, named for its unique ability to analyze the "back links" pointing to a given Web site. Page took on the task of creating a new kind of server environment that used low-end PCs instead of big expensive machines. Afflicted by the perennial shortage of cash common to graduate students everywhere, the pair took to haunting the department's loading docks in hopes of tracking down newly arrived computers that they could borrow for their network.

When Page and Brin first started work on their search engine, they probably had no idea they were creating an Internet-age phenomenon. When they saw the infinite possibilities for their brainchild, however, the two changed the name of their project to "Google." According to Google's Web site, "Google is a play on the word googol, which was coined by Milton Sirotta, nephew of American mathematician Edward Kasner, and was popularized in the book *Mathematics and the Imagination* by

Kasner and James Newman. It refers to the number represented by the numeral 1 followed by 100 zeros. Google's use of the term reflects the company's mission to organize the immense, seemingly infinite amount of information available on the Web."

In 1998, Page and Brin were still operating out of a dorm room. They maxed out credit cards

FIGURE 3.1

Google search page inside Google's Chrome browser.

Source: www.google.com

buying a terabyte of memory to hold their data and went looking for investors to help them further develop their search engine technology. David Filo, a friend and one of the developers of Yahoo!, told the two that their technology was solid and convinced them to start up their own company. Page and Brin put out feelers for investors and found Andy Bechtolsheim, a friend of a faculty member, who wrote them a check for $100,000 after one brief meeting. Since the check was made out to "Google Inc.," Page and Brin scrambled to establish a corporation so they could deposit the check. Other investors joined, and Google Inc. began operations in September 1998 in Menlo Park, California—in a friend's garage that included a washer and dryer and a hot tub.

From the start, Google, still in beta in 1998, handled 10,000 search queries a day. The company soon captured the attention of the press and was extolled in *USA Today*, *Le Monde*, and *PC Magazine*, which named Google the best search engine of

1998. Google quickly outgrew its garage location, and by February 1999 the company had moved into an office in Palo Alto, California, and now had eight employees and was handling more than 500,000 search queries a day. The company continued to expand, removed the "beta" label from the search engine in 1999, and that same year they moved into the Googleplex, its current headquarters in Mountain View, California. In May 2000, Google was already the world's largest search engine, answering 18 million queries a day, and was awarded a Webby Award and a People's Voice Award for technical achievement. (By the end of 2000, Google was answering 100 million search queries a day.)

On April 29, 2004, Google filed with the Securities and Exchange Commission for its initial public offering (IPO). In an unprecedented move, the IPO was sold at auction in order to make the shares more widely available. Shares were priced at $85, and Google hoped to raise $3 billion from the initial offering. Expert opinions on the success of the auction were mixed. Some said the stock price was inflated; others said the stock would eventually tank. Experts who warned of doomsday, however, were eventually proved wrong. In May 2010, Google's stock was selling for $500 a share and was expected to rise even further. As of March 2010, Google employed more than 20,000 full-time employees. Having about 65 percent of the search engine market share in the United States and 90 percent in Europe, Google reached $23.65 billion in revenue and $6.52 billion in profit in 2009.

Google has continued to innovate far beyond its 1996 beginning and it continues to move beyond the search engine market, following its mission "to organize the world's information and make it universally accessible and useful." The company offers e-mail, instant messaging, and mobile text messaging services. Other Google services include an automated news site, a Web blogging site, free imaging software, and a site for programmers interested in creating new applications. The highest revenue generator for Google is its AdSense program. This program allows any Web site to publish advertisements on its pages. The Web site publisher is paid every time someone clicks on an ad originating from that page. The AdSense program also lets Web site publishers analyze how many people look at the site, the cost per click, click-through rates, and so on. The AdSense program can tailor the type of ads that are placed on a Web site—that is, publishers can block ads they don't want to appear, such as competitor ads, ads concerning death or war, and ads for "adult" material.

Another Google service hugely popular with users is Google Maps, which provides street maps, topographic maps, and satellite images for most regions of the world. In addition to locating addresses of businesses, users can (depending on the region and coverage) access features such as "Street View" to see images taken by Google and get driving, biking, and walking directions, traffic and transit information, driving costs, and other information.

All these services have come out of Google's "20-percent time" program, which allows its engineers to spend one day per week on a project that they're passionate about. Many other services are the result of such projects; during its history, Google has launched a variety of such services, some of which have become huge successes, while others have failed. Google has launched projects such as Google News, Google Scholar, Google Finance, or Google Translate, and continues to add to its list of services:

- 2006: Google Docs—a suite of applications used for creating text documents, spreadsheets, and presentations. Created files can be stored online for free, and the user can make them available to others for collaboration. Google Docs manages the collaboration, keeping track of changes in the documents.
- 2007: GOOG-411—a free telephone directory service that uses an automated Google search to retrieve results, and directly routes calls to the business, or sends results via text message or Google Maps to the user's phone.
- 2007: Knol—a service that combines aspects of Wikipedia and Squidoo to create a user-generated knowledge base of everything. While Knol has never sparked the interest Google had hoped for, an active community of contributors continues to contribute "knols" about a variety of topics.
- 2007: OpenSocial—a set of application programming interfaces that allow developers to create applications that work on all social networks that support OpenSocial and thus eliminates the necessity for social network developers to learn and maintain yet another markup language for each additional social network.
- 2008: Android—an open source operating system for mobile phones, directly competing against Apple's iPhone, Research in Motion's BlackBerry, and Microsoft's Windows Phone mobile operating systems.
- 2008: Chrome—a browser lauded for its speed and unique features, starting yet another "browser war."
- 2009: Google Voice—a telecommunication service allowing users to consolidate their phone numbers, giving them control over when and where a phone rings when their number is dialed.
- 2009: Google Wave—a collaboration tool allowing users to build documents called "waves" from conversations. Multiple users can work on waves adding conversational chat, documents, hyperlinks, photos, and other interactive content—all in real time. Wave's developer Lars Rasumussen described Wave as "what e-mail would look like if it were invented today." Lacking user acceptance, Google shut down Wave in late 2010, but many of the innovative technologies have since been

integrated into other Google products, such as Google docs.

- 2010: Nexus One—an Android-powered mobile phone that, along with the typical host of smart phone features, boasts a geotagging five-megapixel flash camera and high-definition video recording and playback.

What's next for the search giant? Google has plans to introduce a computer operating system based on its Chrome browser in late 2010. Initially, the operating system will target the netbook market, but will also run on desktop and laptop computers. To compete with the popular and well-known operating systems from Microsoft and Apple, Google's Chrome operating system will focus on being intuitive, light on system requirements, and extremely fast. Most importantly, the operating system will be completely free. Google also intends to enter the broadband Internet delivery market by building a high-speed fiber-optic network. In its initial testing phase, Google plans on servicing 500,000 people with broadband speeds of up to one gigabit per second (current cable/DSL providers typically offer their customers Internet service with speeds between 5 and 10 megabits per second).

Google has clearly become a significant player on the Internet and in users' daily lives. Look for new Google products and services at http://labs.google.com/.

After reading this chapter, you will be able to answer the following:

1. What are the infrastructure needs for Google if it continues expanding at its current pace?
2. How does Google benefit from a well-functioning infrastructure?
3. How would you rank order the various infrastructure components described in this chapter in their importance to Google's success? Explain your rationale.

Based on:

Ager, M. (2010, May 4). Pedal to the Chrome metal: Our fastest beta to date for Windows, Mac and Linux. *Google Chrome Blog.* Retrieved June 4, 2010, from http://chrome.blogspot.com/2010/05/pedal-to-chrome-metal-our-fastest-beta.html.

Anonymous. (n.d.). About Google Wave. Retrieved August 6, 2010, from http://wave.google.com/about.html.

Anonymous. (n.d.). Company overview. Retrieved June 4, 2010, from http://www.google.com/intl/en/corporate/.

Anonymous. (n.d.). Google milestones. Retrieved June 4, 2010, from http://www.google.com/corporate/history.html.

Arrington, M. (2007, April 6). Google launches free 411 service. *TechCrunch.* Retrieved June 4, 2010, from http://www.techcrunch.com/2007/04/06/google-launches-free-411-business.

Cauley, L. (2008, January 13). Introducing the first Android prototype. *USA Today.* Retrieved June 4, 2010, from http://www.usatoday.com/money/industries/technology/2008-01-13-android-google_N.htm.

Google Chrome OS. (2010, June 3). In *Wikipedia, the free encyclopedia.* Retrieved June 4, 2010, from http://en.wikipedia.org/w/index.php?title=Google_Chrome_OS&oldid=365832864.

Guynn, J., & Hsu, T. (2010, February 10). Google plans to build high-speed broadband service. *Los Angeles Times.* Retrieved June 4, 2010, from http://articles.latimes.com/2010/feb/10/business/la-fi-google11-2010feb11.

Jackson, T. (2010, February 9). Introducing Google Buzz. *The Official Google Blog.* Retrieved August 6, 2010, from http://googleblog.blogspot.com/2010/02/introducing-google-buzz.html.

Queiroz, M. (2010, January 5). Our new approach to buying a mobile phone. *The Official Google Blog.* Retrieved August 6, 2010, from http://googleblog.blogspot.com/2010/01/our-new-approach-to-buying-mobile-phone.html.

Riley, D. (2007, December 14). Google Knol: A step too far? *TechCrunch.* Retrieved June 4, 2010, from http://www.techcrunch.com/2007/12/14/google-knol-a-step-too-far.

The IS Infrastructure

Most people expect a variety of basic municipal services, such as sanitation, security, transportation, provision of energy and water, and so on, to be provided by the city they live in. Any area where people live or work needs a supporting **infrastructure,** which entails the technical structures enabling the provision of services (see Figure 3.2). The infrastructure of a city, for example, includes not only components such as streets and power, telephone, water, and sewage lines, but also schools, retail stores, and law enforcement. Both the area's inhabitants and businesses depend on the services provided by that infrastructure; cities with a good infrastructure, for example, are considered more livable than cities with poorer infrastructure and are much more likely to attract businesses and residents. Likewise, valuable employees often choose firms with better facilities, management, and business processes.

FIGURE 3.2

Infrastructure components
of a city enable the provision
of basic services.

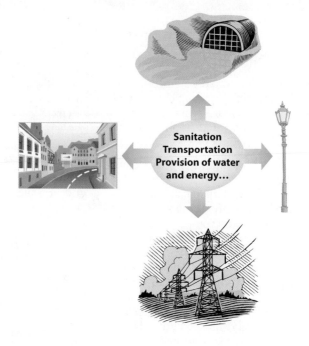

For organizations, many decisions are based on the provision of such services, such as when choosing a site for a new manufacturing plant or company headquarters. Indeed, many municipalities attempt to attract new businesses and industries by setting up new commercial zones with a well-planned infrastructure. In some cases, specific infrastructure components are of special importance. One such example is search engine giant Google, which has data centers located all over the world to offer the best performance to its users. One of Google's newest data center was built in the small town of The Dalles, Oregon, located on the banks of the Columbia River. Why would a company such as Google choose such a rural location? First, the location offered connectivity, using a state-of-the-art fiber-optic network to provide high-speed data transfer to the Internet backbone. Second—and maybe more important—the location on the river would give the data center access to water for its cooling needs (as a large number of computers generates a tremendous amount of heat) as well as uninterrupted power from a nearby hydroelectric dam; in addition to being relatively inexpensive, this renewable source of energy contributes to Google's efforts to be carbon neutral. Indeed, as energy is one of the most important resources for Google, the company attempts to reduce consumption and use renewable sources whenever possible (see Figure 3.3). As you can see from this example, companies such as Google must consider far more than just the need for increased data storage space and processing power.

For organizations operating globally, managing a comprehensive, worldwide infrastructure poses additional challenges. This is particularly acute when operating in developing nations. For example, in many parts of the world, organizations cannot count on an uninterrupted supply of water or electricity. Consequently, many of the large call centers in India that support customers around the world for companies like Dell Computers or Citibank have installed massive power generators to minimize the effects of frequent power outages or have set up their own satellite links to be independent from the local, unreliable communications networks.

Just as people and companies rely on basic municipal services to function, businesses rely on an **information systems infrastructure** (consisting of hardware, software, communication and collaboration networks, databases, facilities, and human resources) to support their decision making, business processes, and competitive strategy. On the highest level, organizations rely on three basic capabilities supported by information systems: processing, storage, and transmission of data (see Figure 3.4). Hence, almost all of an organization's business processes depend on the underlying IS infrastructure, albeit to different degrees. For example, an organization's management needs an infrastructure to support a variety of activities, including reliable communication networks to support collaboration between suppliers and customers, accurate and timely data and knowledge to gain business intelligence, and information systems to aid decision making and support business processes. In sum, organizations rely on a

FIGURE 3.3

Google uses solar energy to power its main campus in Mountain View, California.

complex, interrelated IS infrastructure to effectively thrive in the ever-increasingly competitive digital world.

To get a better understanding of an IS infrastructure, we first provide a brief overview of how computers work and how the following components interact to form an organization's IS infrastructure:

- Hardware
- Software
- Communications and collaboration networks
- Databases

Another component, human resources, has been discussed in Chapter 1, "Managing in the Digital World." To dig deeper into the technical aspects of the various infrastructure components, refer to the Technology Briefing, "Foundations of Information Systems Infrastructure."

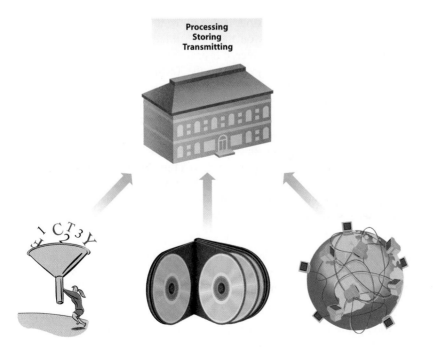

FIGURE 3.4

The IS infrastructure enables processing, storing, and transmitting of data.

FIGURE 3.5

A CPU performs all operations
of a computer.

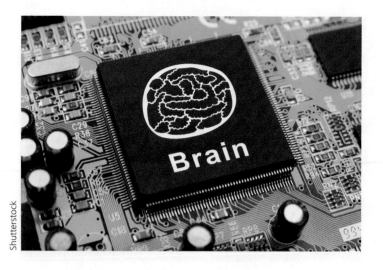

Shutterstock

How a Computer Works: IS Hardware and Software

IS hardware is an integral part of the IS infrastructure and is broadly classified into three types: input, processing, and output technologies. **Input technologies** are used to enter information into a computer using devices such as a keyboard and mouse on your personal computer, a biometric fingerprint reader to authenticate a person entering a secure laboratory, or RFID scanners to track valuable inventory in a warehouse. **Processing technologies** transform inputs into outputs, encompassing both storage and computational resources, such as mobile handheld devices and supercomputers. Finally, **output technologies,** such as a computer monitor and printer, deliver information to you in a usable format.

How a Computer Works   The main component of a computer is the **central processing unit (CPU)** or **microprocessor,** often called the computer's brain, as it is responsible for performing all the operations of the computer (see Figure 3.5). Its job includes loading the *operating system* (e.g., Windows 7, Mac OS X, or Ubuntu) when the machine is first turned on and performing, coordinating, and managing all the calculations and instructions relayed to it while the computer is running. Any input your computer receives (say, a keystroke) is **digitized,** or translated into binary code (i.e., the 0s and 1s that your computer understands) and then is processed by the CPU. The CPU, a small device made of silicon, is composed of millions of tiny transistors arranged in complex patterns that allow it to interpret and manipulate data. In addition to the number of transistors on the CPU, three other factors greatly influence its speed—its system clock speed (the number of instructions a CPU can execute in a fixed amount of time), registers, and cache memory; refer to the Technology Briefing for more details on these factors. As its inner workings are very complex, for most of us, it is easiest to think of a CPU as being a "black box" where all the processing occurs. The CPU uses **primary storage** (such as **random-access memory [RAM]**) as temporary storage space for data that is currently being processed. Because instructions and work stored in RAM are lost when the power to the computer is turned off or when new data are placed there, it is referred to as **volatile memory.** The CPU interacts with **secondary storage** (such as a **hard drive, optical disk,** or **flash drive**) for permanently storing data; secondary storage is **nonvolatile memory,** which means that it retains the data when the power to the computer is shut off. As primary storage is considerably faster than secondary storage, the amount of primary storage greatly influences a computer's performance.

Software   **Software** refers to programs, or sets of instructions, that allow all the hardware components in your computer system to speak to each other and to perform the desired tasks. The two basic types of IS software are systems software and application software.

Systems Software/Operating System.   **Systems software** is the collection of programs that control the basic operations of computer hardware. The most prominent type of systems software, the **operating system,** coordinates the interaction between hardware devices (e.g., the CPU and the monitor), peripherals (e.g., printers), application software (e.g., office programs),

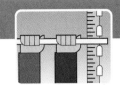

POWERFUL PARTNERSHIPS

Google's Larry Page and Sergey Brin

Before working on the "BackRub" project, Google co-founders Sergey Brin and Larry Page had little in common (see Figure 3.6). Page was raised in a family of computer scientists—his father was a Michigan State University computer science professor, and his mother taught programming classes at college. In his early years, Page discovered his interest in taking things apart, learning to understand how they worked.

Brin was born in Russia. His father, barred by the U.S.S.R. from becoming an astronomer due to his Jewish heritage, earned a Ph.D. in mathematics, while his mother earned a degree from the School of Mechanics and Mathematics at Moscow State University. When Sergey was six, his family emigrated to the United States, where his father became a mathematics professor at the University of Maryland, and his mother a research scientist at NASA.

Brin earned a bachelor's degree in mathematics and computer science from the University of Maryland at College Park, and was a Ph.D. student in computer science at Stanford University when he first met Page.

Page earned a bachelor's degree in engineering at the University of Michigan. He met Brin at an orientation session for new Ph.D. candidates at Stanford; Brin, 23 at that time, was among a group of students assigned to show him around. Both Larry and Sergey are currently on leave from the Ph.D program and hold honorary MBA degrees from IE Business School in Madrid, Spain; Larry holds an honorary Ph.D. from the University of Michigan.

According to Google lore, company founders Larry Page and Sergey Brin argued about everything when they first met in 1995. Both had strong opinions and divergent viewpoints, but they eventually joined forces to develop a search engine that ranked pages based on the number of other pages linking to them. Similar to academic citations, where a paper has a higher impact the more it is cited, Brin and Page argued that a Web page is more important the more other pages link to it.

Google's unique corporate culture has revolved around the personal and business philosophy of the founding partners; having a "healthy disregard for the impossible," the company has worked hard to maintain a "flat" organization with no hierarchy and a collaborative environment that encourages innovation. At Google headquarters, for instance, there are no cubicles, and employees often sit on exercise balls in front of computers. Dogs roam the halls at will and seem as congenial as the company's human employees. In 2006, fearful that the company's growth was hindering its "anticorporate" environment, Google hired a chief culture officer who also serves as human relations director. Since 2007, Google has placed in the top five of Fortune magazine's "100 Best Companies to Work For."

The unique history of Google's co-founders has influenced many other personal and business decisions. For example, following their corporate motto "Don't be evil," Brin and Page foster green projects; in spring of 2009, Google decided to use goats instead of lawnmowers to clear weeds and brush from fields around the company's headquarters. Brin and Page both drive Toyota Prius hybrid vehicles, and financially back Tesla Motors, a manufacturer of premium electric vehicles (yet they also co-own a Boeing 767 for their private use, and Brin was among the first to have booked a space flight). Likewise, Google's stance towards censorship in China can be traced back to the experiences Brin's family had under communism and the founders' insistence on putting principles before profit, as stated in the 2004 IPO letter: "we believe strongly that in the long term, we will be better served—as shareholders and in all other ways—by a company that does good things for the world even if we forgo some short-term gains."

Brin and Page were ranked as the fifth most powerful people by Forbes magazine in 2009, and shared rank 24 of the world's billionaires in 2010.

FIGURE 3.6

Google's Larry Page and Sergey Brin.

Ben Margot/AP Wide World Photos

(continued)

Based on:

Anonymous. (2009). The world's most powerful people: #5 Sergey Brin and Larry Page. *Forbes.com.* Retrieved August 6, 2010, from http://www.forbes.com/lists/2009/20/power-09_Sergey-Brin-and-Larry-Page_D664.html.

Anonymous. (2010). Google management. Retrieved August 6, 2010, from http://www.google.com/corporate/execs.html.

Anonymous. (2010). The world's billionaires. *Forbes.com.* Retrieved August 6, 2010, from http://www.forbes.com/lists/2010/10/billionaires-2010_The-Worlds-Billionaires_Rank.html.

Anonymous. (2010, January 14). Google's threat to China traces back to founders. *Msnbc.com.* Retrieved August 6, 2010, from http://www.msnbc.msn.com/id/34860435.

Anonymous. (n.d.). The Google culture. Retrieved April 19, 2010, from http://www.google.com/corporate/culture.html.

Hoffman, D. (2009, May 1). Mowing with goats. *The Official Google Blog.* Retrieved August 6, 2010, from http://googleblog.blogspot.com/2009/05/mowing-with-goats.html.

Kowalowski, N. (2009, March 28). Tesla Motors Model S backed by Google founders Brin, Page. *eWeek.com.* Retrieved August 6, 2010, from http://www.eweek.com/c/a/Green-IT/Tesla-Motors-Model-S-Backed-By-Google-Founders-Brin-Page-336717.

Malseed, M. (2007, February). The story of Sergey Brin. *Moment.* Retrieved August 6, 2010, from http://www.momentmag.com/Exclusive/2007/2007-02/200702-BrinFeature.html.

Page, L., & Brin, S. (2004, August 18). 2004 Founders' IPO Letter. Google Investor Relations. Retrieved August 6, 2010, from http://investor.google.com/corporate/2004/ipo-founders-letter.html.

Schwartz, J. (2008, June 11). Google co-founder books a space flight. *New York Times.* Retrieved August 6, 2010, from http://www.nytimes.com/2008/06/11/technology/11soyuz.html.

and users, as shown in Figure 3.7. Additionally, given that microprocessors are embedded in countless devices including cell phones, digital video recorders like TiVo, and automobiles, you are likely interacting with operating systems more than you realize. For example, automakers Fiat, Ford, and Kia use a Microsoft operating system for their in-car infotainment systems. Likewise, the onboard passenger entertainment systems within many aircraft are powered by the Linux operating system.

Operating systems are often written in assembly language, a very low level computer programming language that allows the computer to operate quickly and efficiently. The operating system is designed to insulate you from this low-level language and make computer operations unobtrusive. The operating system performs all of the day-to-day operations that we often take

FIGURE 3.7

Operating systems coordinate the interaction between users, application software, hardware, and peripherals.

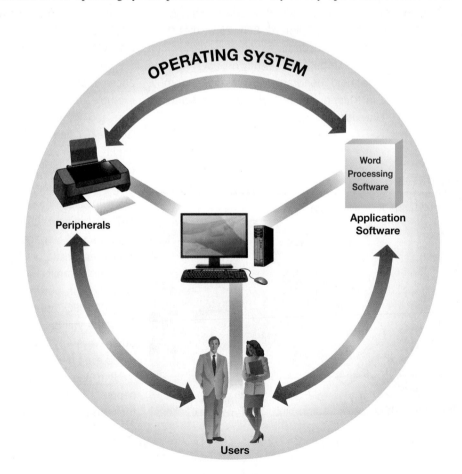

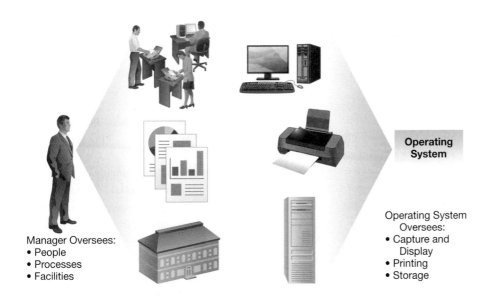

FIGURE 3.8

A manager oversees organizational resources, whereas an operating system oversees computer resources.

for granted when using a computer, such as updating the system clock, printing documents, or saving data to a disk. Just as our brain and nervous system control our body's breathing, heartbeat, and senses without our conscious realization, the systems software transparently controls the computer's basic operations.

Common Systems Software Functions. Many tasks are common to almost all computers. These include getting input from a keyboard or mouse, reading from and/or writing to a storage device (such as a hard disk drive), and presenting information to you via a monitor. Each of these tasks is performed by the operating system, just as a manager of a firm oversees people and processes (as depicted in Figure 3.8). For example, if you want to copy a word processing file from a flash drive onto your computer, the operating systems make this very easy for you, as all it takes is simply using the mouse to point at a graphic icon of the word processing file on the flash drive, then clicking and dragging it onto an icon of your hard disk. The operating system makes this process appear easy. However, underlying the icons and simple dragging operations is a complex set of coded instructions that tell the electronic components of the computer that you are transferring a set of bits and bytes located on the flash drive to a location on your internal hard disk. Imagine if you had to program those sets of instructions every time you wanted to copy a file from one place to another. The operating system manages and executes these types of system operations so that you can spend your time on more important tasks.

Application Software. Unlike systems software, which manages the operation of the computer, **application software** lets a user perform specific tasks, such as writing a business letter, processing payroll, managing a stock portfolio, or manipulating a series of forecasts to come up with the most efficient allocation of resources for a project. As discussed in Chapter 1, application software includes personal productivity software such as Microsoft Office 2010; supply chain management systems to support the coordination of suppliers, product or service production, and distribution; or customer relationship management (CRM) systems to help companies win and retain customers, gain marketing and customer insight, and focus on customers. Application software interacts with the systems software, which, in turn, interacts with the computer hardware.

Open Source Software. Open source is a philosophy that promotes developers' and users' access to the source of a product or idea. Particularly in the area of software development, the open source movement has taken off with the advent of the Internet; and people around the world are contributing their time and expertise to develop or improve software, ranging from operating systems to applications software. As the programs' source code is freely available for use and/or modification, this software is referred to as **open source software.** Open source software owes its success to the inputs from a large user base, helping to fix problems or improve the software; with large open source projects, such as different variants of the operating system Linux, a small group of contributors is responsible for ensuring the quality and stability of the software. Linux, one of the most prevalent examples of open source software, was developed as a hobby by the Finnish university student Linus

Brief Case 🌐

THE BATTLE OF THE GIANTS

When you make the choice to buy a new computer or laptop, you'll have to decide on which operating system to use. Microsoft has traditionally been the leader in the operating system market, with a market share of more than 90 percent. By far the most new computers for home or office use come with a version of Windows 7, Microsoft's newest operating system. In contrast, Apple's Mac desktops and laptops come with Apple's OS X operating system, which is optimized for Apple's hardware. Whereas Microsoft's operating systems can be purchased as retail versions and customers can install Windows on any system that meets the technical requirements, Apple has taken a much more closed approach, allowing its operating systems to be run only on Apple hardware.

Although Apple's operating systems had never gained much market share, Apple's followers were highly loyal, often refusing to purchase any device with a Microsoft operating system. In 2007, however, the tides turned for Apple. In the early 2000s, smart phones (i.e., mobile phones that offer computing capabilities including e-mail, the Internet, and even basic office applications) had gained popularity. Most smart phones came with operating systems developed by Symbian (e.g., many Nokia or Sony Ericsson phones), RIM (BlackBerry), or Windows Mobile (now Windows Phone, e.g., HTC or LG phones). One key challenge for developers of smart phone hardware and software was to ensure the usability of a small device with a small screen, a low-powered processor, and small keys (if any). For Apple, whose strengths are in optimizing its operating systems to work smoothly and flawlessly with its own hardware, as well as in usability and product design, this challenge proved to be an opportunity. Launched in 2007, Apple's iPhone has become hugely successful, with 1 million handsets sold within 74 days after its launch. Apple's iPhone owed its success largely to its highly responsive touch screen, ease of use, and the tight coupling of hardware and operating system. Further, iPhone users can download thousands of different applications from Apple's "App Store." In 2010, the iPhone had the second-highest market share in the United States (28 percent), behind RIM's BlackBerry (35 percent) and before smart phones powered by Microsoft's mobile operating systems (19 percent), Android-based phones (9 percent), and others.

Over time, Apple fine-tuned the iPhone operating system, enabling the use of various hardware capabilities such as a built-in camera, GPS, and so on. In early 2010, Apple introduced the iPad, a highly portable tablet computer, running the iPhone operating system rather than a traditional desktop operating system. As the iPhone, the iPad was an instant success, with 2 million units sold within the first two months. In its latest version, dubbed iOS 4, the operating system supports multitasking, allows connecting wireless keyboards, includes a spell checker, and more. Clearly, Apple has hit the sweet spot with many mobile users, leaving its traditional competitor, Microsoft, trailing behind.

Slowly but surely, another powerful player has entered the operating system arena. Google, famous for its search engine technology, backs the development of the Android mobile phone operating system and is actively involved in developing Google Chrome OS, an open source desktop operating system designed to exclusively use Web applications.

Questions

1. With mobile operating systems being used in tablet PCs, where do you see the future of operating systems heading?
2. Who will win the operating systems battle? Will Google or Apple manage to push Microsoft off the operating systems throne? If so, what will be the "killer capability"?

Based on:

Anonymous. (2010, June 8). Top operating system share trend. *Netmarketshare.com*. Retrieved June 8, 2010, from http://www .netmarketshare.com/os-market-share.aspx?qprid=9.

Dalrymple, J. (2010, June 5). iPhone triples Android in mobile market share. *CNET news.com*. Retrieved June 8, 2010, from http://news.cnet .com/8301-13579_3-20006889-37.html.

Harrison, N., & Pope, S. (2010, May 31). Apple sells two million iPads in less than 60 days. *Apple.com*. Retrieved June 8, 2010, from http:// www.apple.com/pr/library/2010/05/31ipad.html.

Kerris, N., & Dowling, S. (2007, September 10). Apple sells one millionth iPhone. *Apple.com*. Retrieved June 8, 2010, from http://www.apple.com/pr/library/2007/09/10iphone.html.

Torvalds in 1991. Having developed the first version himself, he made the source code of his operating system available to everyone who wanted to use it and improve on it. Since then, various Linux distributions (such as Ubuntu, Red Hat, and Debian) have been released; each distribution integrates the core part of the Linux operating system with different utilities and software applications, depending on the intended use (e.g., desktop computer, netbook, Web server, embedded system, and so on). With most distributions, users can only *suggest* modifications for official releases; for example, users can contribute to program code or provide new designs for the system's user interface, but only a small group of carefully selected "committers" can implement these modifications into

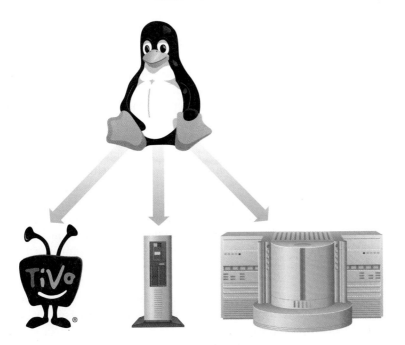

FIGURE 3.9

Linux is the operating system of choice for embedded systems, Web servers, and supercomputers (the penguin "Tux" is the official logo of Linux).

the official releases of the software. Because of its unrivaled stability, Linux has become the operating system of choice for Web servers, **embedded systems** (such as TiVo boxes and network routers; see Figure 3.9), and supercomputers alike (as of 2010, 91 percent of the world's 500 fastest supercomputers ran Linux operating systems; Top 500, 2010). In addition to the Linux operating system, other open source software has been gaining increasing popularity because of its stability and low cost. For example, in 2010, 55 percent of all Web sites were powered by the Apache Web server, another open source project (Netcraft, 2010). Other popular examples of open source application software include the Firefox Web browser (see Figure 3.10) and the office productivity suite OpenOffice. While there are many benefits to open source software, vendors of proprietary software are still highlighting "hidden" costs of running open source software, such as obtaining reliable customer support. On the other hand, however, commercial open source vendors are providing customer support, installation, training, and so on to their paying customers. H&R Block, AVIS Sweden, and many other large companies are using a CRM system offered by SugarCRM, Inc., a commercial open source vendor that offers free "community editions" as well as other, more feature-rich paid editions of its software. Further, many open source projects are now backed by major information technology (IT) companies such as IBM, which gives money and human resources to Linux projects, or Oracle, which sponsors the OpenOffice productivity suite.

FIGURE 3.10

The Firefox Web browser.

Source: Courtesy Washington State University.

Types of Computers Depending on their computing needs, individuals and organizations can choose between a variety of different types of computers. The five general classes of computers are supercomputer, mainframe, server, workstation, and microcomputer. A **supercomputer** is the most expensive and most powerful kind of computer; it is used primarily to assist in solving massive scientific problems. In contrast, a **mainframe,** while being very large, is used primarily as the main, central computing system for major corporations, such as Alamo Rent A Car or Bank of America, or governmental agencies, such as the Internal Revenue Service. A **server** is any computer on a network that makes access to files, printing, communications, and other services available to users of the network. Servers are used to provide services to users within large organizations or to Web users. Typically, each server is dedicated to a certain function, e.g., as a Web server, a database server, or a file server. A server is optimized for access by many concurrent users and has a more advanced microprocessor, more memory, a larger cache, and more disk storage than a single-user computer. As servers for mission-critical applications require ample power, cooling, and security, large organizations use large server rooms or data centers to house hundreds or thousands of servers. A **workstation** offers lower performance than mainframes but higher performance than microcomputers. Designed for medical, engineering, or animation and graphics design uses, workstations are optimized for visualization and rendering of three-dimensional models. A **microcomputer** is used for personal computing and small business computing. Portable computers—notebook computers, tablet PCs, netbooks, handheld computers, and smart phones—are a special type of microcomputer designed to support mobility (see Table 3.1).

Data and Knowledge Infrastructure

Data and knowledge are probably among the most important assets an organization has, as data and knowledge are essential for both executing business processes and gaining business intelligence. Information once taken for granted or never collected at all is now used to make organizations more productive and competitive. Stock prices in the market, potential customers who meet a company's criteria for its products' target audiences, as well as the credit rating of wholesalers and customers are all types of information that organizations collect and analyze. Further, governmental regulations such as the Sarbanes-Oxley Act mandate archiving business documents and relevant internal communication, including e-mail and instant messages. Hence, organizations are faced with the need to reliably store tremendous amounts of data, and this storage requirement is growing at an increasing rate.

As the data are being stored for operational, backup, or archival purposes, organizations have to evaluate and implement various storage technologies. For example, operational data are typically stored in databases (e.g., data from transaction processing systems or customer data) or files (e.g., business documents, images, or company brochures) using disk-based storage media such as hard drives. Hard drives offer high access speeds and are thus preferred for data that are

TABLE 3.1 Characteristics of Computers Currently Being Used in Organizations

Type of Computer	Number of Simultaneous Users	Physical Size	Typical Use	Memory	Typical Cost Range
Supercomputer	One to many	Like an automobile to as large as multiple rooms	Scientific research	5,000+ GB	Low: $1 million; high: more than $20 million
Mainframe	1,000+	Like a refrigerator	Large general purpose business and government	Up to 1,500+ GB	Low: $500,000; high: $10 million
Server	10,000+	Like a DVD player and mounted in a rack to fitting on a desktop	Providing Web sites or access to databases, applications, or files	Up to 512 GB	Low: $300; high: $50,000
Workstation	Typically one	Fitting on a desktop to the size of a file cabinet	Engineering, medical, graphic design	Up to 192 GB	Low: $750; high: $100,000
Microcomputer	One	Handheld to fitting on a desktop	Personal productivity	512 MB to 4 GB	Low: $200; high: $5,000

frequently accessed or where response time is of the essence (as in an e-commerce Web site). To ensure continuous business operations in case disaster strikes, organizations periodically back up their data to a secure location; often, companies have completely redundant systems so as to be able to seamlessly continue business if the primary systems fail (see Chapter 10, "Securing Information Systems"). Storing backup data on hard drives enables quick recovery without slowing the company's operations. Data that are no longer used for operational purposes (such as old internal e-mails) are archived for long-term storage, typically on magnetic tapes. As data are stored sequentially on magnetic tapes, access speed can be very slow; however, magnetic tape has a shelf life of up to 30 years, is very low cost as compared to other storage media, and is removable, meaning that it is highly expandable and tapes can be easily stored in a secure, remote location (see the Technology Briefing for more on different storage technologies).

Databases **Databases,** which are collections of related data organized in a way that facilitates data searches, are vital to an organization's operations and often are vital to competitive advantage and success. For example, Adidas uses databases to design and produce its clothing catalog and to market and sell products. Companies such as Adidas also use databases to gather and store information about customers and their purchasing behavior. Companies such as Nordstrom and Victoria's Secret even produce tailor-made catalogs and other mailings for specific individuals based on the purchasing information stored in corporate databases. Additionally, database technology fuels electronic commerce, from tracking available products for sale to providing customer service. As these examples make clear, databases have become an integral part of the total IS infrastructure for most organizations. In order to harness the power of the data contained in the databases, organizations use **database management systems,** which are a type of application program that allow organizations to more easily store, retrieve, and analyze data.

Modern organizations are said to be drowning in data but starving for information. Despite being a mixed metaphor, this statement seems to portray quite accurately the situation in many organizations. The advent of Internet-based electronic commerce has resulted in the collection of an enormous amount of customer and transactional data. How these data are collected, stored, and manipulated is a significant factor influencing the success of a commercial Internet Web site. In Chapter 6, "Enhancing Business Intelligence Using Information Systems," we talk more about the details of effectively and efficiently collecting, storing, and manipulating data stored in databases.

Communications and Collaboration

One of the reasons why information systems have become so powerful and important is the ability to interconnect, allowing internal and external constituents to communicate and collaborate with each other. The infrastructure supporting this consists of a variety of components, such as the networking hardware and software that facilitate the interconnection of different computers, enabling collaboration literally around the world.

Human Communication and Computer Networking Human communication involves the sharing of information and messages between senders and receivers. The sender of a message formulates the message in his brain and codes the message into a form that can be communicated to the receiver—through voice, for example. The message is then transmitted along a communication pathway to the receiver. The receiver, using her ears and brain, then attempts to decode the message, as shown in Figure 3.11. This basic model of human communication helps us to understand

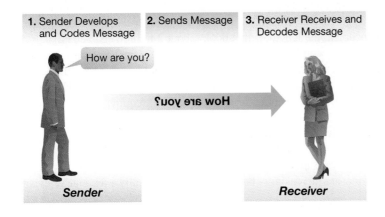

1. Sender Develops and Codes Message
2. Sends Message
3. Receiver Receives and Decodes Message

How are you?

Sender

Receiver

FIGURE 3.11

Communication requires senders, a message to share, and receivers.

FIGURE 3.12

Coding, sending, and decoding a message.

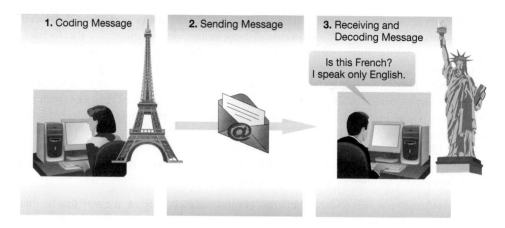

telecommunications or computer networking. **Computer networking** is the sharing of data or services. As with human communication, all computer networks require three things:

- Senders and receivers that have something to share
- A pathway or transmission medium, such as a cable, to send the message
- Rules or protocols dictating communication between senders and receivers

The easiest way to understand computer networking is through the human communication model. Suppose you are applying for a job in France after graduation. You need information about different employers. The first requirement for a network—information to share—has now been met. After contacting a few potential employers, a company sends you information about their hiring process (the encoded message) via e-mail. This is the second requirement: a means of transmitting the coded message. The Internet is the pathway or transmission medium used to contact the receiver. **Transmission media** refers to the physical pathway—cable(s) and wireless—used to carry network information. At this point, you may run into some difficulties. If the potential employer has sent you information in French, you may not understand what they have written—i.e., decode their message—because you don't speak French. Although you have contacted the receiver, you and the receiver of your message must meet the third requirement for successful communication: you must establish a language of communication—the rules or protocols governing your communication. **Protocols** define the procedures that different computers follow when they transmit and receive data. You both might decide that one communication protocol will be that you communicate in English. This communication session is illustrated in Figure 3.12.

Computer Networks A fundamental difference between human and computer communication is that human communication consists of words, whereas computer communication consists of bits, the fundamental information units of computers, as depicted in Figure 3.13. Virtually all types of information can be transmitted on a computer network—documents, art, music, or film—although each type of information has vastly different requirements for effective transmission. For example, a single screen of text is approximately 14 KB of data, whereas a publication-quality photograph could be larger than 200 MB of data. To transmit either the screen of text or the picture in a timely manner from one location to another, adequate bandwidth is needed. **Bandwidth** is the transmission capacity of a computer or communications channel, measured in bits per second (bps) or multiples thereof, and represents how much binary data can be reliably transmitted over the medium in one second. To appreciate the importance of bandwidth for speed, consider how long it would take to transmit a document the length of this book (about 2 million characters, or 16 million bits). It would take about 1.6 seconds at 10 megabits per second (Mbps) and .16 seconds at 100 Mbps. In contrast, using an old-fashioned PC modem that transmits data at a rate of 56 kilobits per second (Kbps), it would take nearly five minutes to transmit the same document. Hence, different types of information have different communication bandwidth requirements (see www.numion.com/Calculators/Time.html for a tool that helps you calculate download times). Typical local area networks have a bandwidth of 10 Mbps to 1 Gbps.

Telecommunications advances have enabled individual computer networks—constructed with different hardware and software—to connect together in what appears to be a single network. Networks are increasingly being used to dynamically exchange relevant, value-adding

ETHICAL DILEMMA

The Ethics of Collecting Public Data

By now, you've probably used Google's mapping service, Google Maps. One of the most powerful aspects of Google's mapping services is the "Street View," which allows a user to zoom down to an actual 360-degree photographic view of the street. Google has been collecting imagery for Street View since 2007, originally starting in big cities and slowly moving across the globe.

The service provides great value to users in that one can actually see what a street looks like without actually going there: those unfamiliar with a destination can "drive" to the location first using Street View to familiarize themselves with the area, eager house hunters can look at potential properties and neighborhoods to narrow their search, and users can share views of their hometown with friends. However, since launching the service, Google has repeatedly come under fire for what many see as an invasion of privacy.

The problem many privacy advocates have with Street View photos is what's in the picture besides the street. Many Street View images capture people walking down the street, children playing in front of their house, and sunbathers laying out for a tan. The people that happen to be in these images are often unknowingly photographed along with the street details. Some of the imagery has been less than ordinary and put people in compromising positions, such as entering adult bookstores, leaving strip clubs, and engaging in prostitution. In addition, car license plates, military base perimeters, and a house on fire have been collected by the Street View cameras. In early 2009, a Street View car hit a deer while taking pictures in upstate New York, an incident not uncommon in this area; while Google sincerely apologized for this, many criticized that the images actually appeared on Street View (the footage has since been replaced). Although all the Street View imagery has been taken from public streets, many people have complained that not everything done in public should be accessible to everyone, everywhere, and at any time. In a recent survey from the United Kingdom, many respondents said the Street View photography was "intrusive," with others going further, calling it a "service for burglars." Parents have also raised concerns that having pictures of their children on Street View images helps child predators locate and target victims.

In response to critics, Google has taken steps to help ease privacy concerns. Using various photo technologies, Google has blurred the faces of people, license plates, and house numbers in Street View photos. In addition, people may request that their pictures be removed from the imagery altogether. Google has also complied with government requests to remove imagery of military installations and other sensitive areas.

In May 2010, Google ran into bigger trouble with its Street View technology—only this time the photos weren't the problem. While collecting imagery for Street View, Google photography vehicles were also mapping the location of open, unsecured Wi-Fi networks to create a database of open Wi-Fi locations. While collecting these data, they were also unknowingly collecting snippets of e-mails and Web surfing data. Since the Wi-Fi project started, Google has collected nearly 600 GB of information in over 30 different countries. Google says that the data collection was happening inadvertently because of an experimental piece of code that was running in the Wi-Fi database project software.

Many are questioning Google's stance that its collection of the data was not premeditated. Computer scientist Dr. Jim Aman believes that Google knew exactly what they were collecting all along. "It had to have been an intentional capture of the signals and not accidental," he said. "I would like to know how they thought it was inadvertent." Ginger McCall, an attorney for EPIC.org, an electronic privacy advocacy group, agreed: "It's difficult to believe they could be both collecting and storing this information without having any knowledge of it."

What will happen as a result of Google's Street View problem remains to be seen, but the discussions surrounding the ethics and privacy ramifications of the technology will undoubtedly continue into the future.

Based on:

Anonymous. (2010, May 14). Google grabbed personal info off Wi-Fi networks. *CBS2Chicago.com*. Retrieved June 4, 2010, from http://cbs2chicago.com/technology/Google.personal.information.2.1695589.html.

Barnett, E. (2010, March 12). Google Street View: Survey raises privacy concerns. *Telegraph.co.uk*. Retrieved June 4, 2010, from http://www.telegraph.co.uk/technology/google/7430245/Google-Street-View-survey-raises-privacy-concerns.html.

Google Street View privacy concerns. (2010, May 29). In *Wikipedia, the free encyclopedia*. Retrieved June 5, 2010, from http://en.wikipedia.org/w/index.php?title=Google_Street_View_privacy_concerns&oldid=364871895.

Parker, M. (2010, May 26). Watchdogs slam Google's Street View WiFi breach. *CBS2Chicago.com*. Retrieved June 4, 2010, from http://cbs2chicago.com/local/google.wifi.breach.2.1717568.html.

FIGURE 3.13

In human communication, words are spoken and transmitted in the air. In computer communication, digital data are transmitted over some type of communication medium.

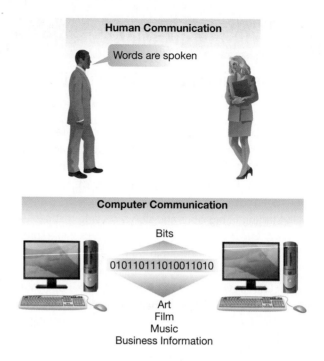

information and knowledge throughout global organizations and institutions. The following sections take a closer look at the fundamental building blocks of these complex networks and the services they provide.

Servers, Clients, and Peers. A **network** consists of three separate components—servers, clients, and peers—as depicted in Figure 3.14. A server is any computer on the network that makes access to files, printing, communications, and other services available to users of the network. Servers only provide services. A **client** is any computer, such as a user's PC or laptop, on the network, or any software application, such as a word processing application, that uses the services provided by the server. Clients only request services. A client usually has only one user, whereas many different users share the server. A **peer** is any computer that may both request and provide services. The trend in business is to use **server-centric networks,** in which servers and clients have defined roles. However, **peer-to-peer networks** (often abbreviated as P2P) that enable any computer or device on the network to provide and request services can be found in small offices and homes. In P2P networks, all peers have equivalent capabilities and responsibilities; this is the network architecture behind the Internet telephony service Skype and popular file sharing applications such as BitTorrent, where peers are able to connect directly to the hard drives of other peers on the Internet that are utilizing the software.

FIGURE 3.14

A server is a computer on the network that enables multiple computers (or "clients") to access data. A peer is a computer that may both request and provide services.

TABLE 3.2 Types of Networks

Type	Usage	Size
Private branch exchange (PBX)	Telephone system serving a particular location	Within a business
Personal area network (PAN)	Wireless communication between devices, using technologies such as Bluetooth	Under 10 meters
Local area network (LAN)	Sharing of data, software applications, or other resources between several users	Typically within a building
Campus area network (CAN)	Connect multiple LANs, used by single organization	Spanning multiple buildings, such as a university or business campus
Metropolitan area network (MAN)	Connect multiple LANs, used by single organization	Larger than LAN or CAN, such as covering the area of a city
Wide area network (WAN)	Connect multiple LANs, distributed ownership and management	Large physical distance, up to worldwide (Internet)

Types of Networks. Computing networks are commonly classified by size, distance covered, and structure. The most commonly used classifications are a **private branch exchange, personal area network, local area network, campus area network, metropolitan area network,** and **wide area network** (see Table 3.2). In addition, high-frequency radio-wave technology is increasingly being used to support **wireless local area networks (WLANs).** WLANs based on a family of standards called 802.11 are also referred to as **Wi-Fi networks (wireless fidelity).** The ease of installation has made WLANs popular for business and home use, and public WLANs can be found in many coffee shops, airports, or university campuses. For more on the different types of networks, see the Technology Briefing.

Internet and World Wide Web One global network that has enabled organizations and individuals to interconnect in a variety of ways is the **Internet,** which is a large worldwide collection of networks that use a common protocol to communicate with each other. The name "Internet" is derived from the concept of *internetworking,* which means connecting host computers and their networks together to form even larger networks.

How Did the Internet Get Started? You can trace the roots of the Internet back to the late 1960s, when the U.S. **Defense Advanced Research Projects Agency** began to study ways to interconnect networks of various kinds. This research effort produced the **Advanced Research Projects Agency Network (ARPANET),** a large wide area network (WAN) that linked many universities and research centers. The first two nodes on the ARPANET were the University of California, Los Angeles, and the Stanford Research Institute, followed by the University of California, Santa Barbara, and the University of Utah.

ARPANET quickly evolved and was combined with other networks. For example, in 1986, the U.S. **National Science Foundation** initiated the development of the **National Science Foundation Network,** which became a major component of the Internet. Other networks throughout the United States and the rest of the world were interconnected and/or morphed into the growing "Internet." Throughout the world, support for the Internet has come from a combination of federal and state governments, universities, national and international research organizations, and industry.

The Internet Uses Packet-Switching Technology. The Internet relies on packet-switching technology to deliver data and information across networks. **Packet switching** is based on the concept of turn taking and enables millions of users to send large and small chunks of data across the Internet concurrently. To minimize delays, network technologies limit the amount of data that a computer can transfer on each turn. Consider a conveyor belt as a comparison. Suppose that the conveyor belt connects a warehouse and a retail store. When a customer places an order, it is sent from the store to the warehouse, where a clerk assembles the items in the order. The items are placed on the conveyor belt and delivered to the customer in the store. In most situations, clerks finish sending items from one order before proceeding to send items from another order. This process works well when orders are small, but when a large order with many items comes in, sharing a conveyor belt can introduce delays for others. Consider waiting in the store for your one item while another order with 50 items is being filled.

FIGURE 3.15

Computers A and B use packet switching to send messages or files to computers C and D.

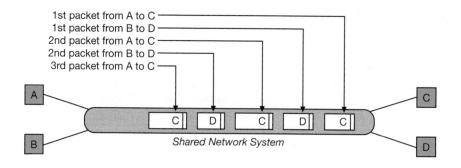

Local area networks (LANs), WANs, and the Internet all use packet-switching technologies so that users can share the communication channel and minimize delivery delays. Figure 3.15 illustrates how computers use packet switching. Computer A wants to send a message to computer C; similarly, computer B wants to send a message to computer D. For example, computer A is trying to send an e-mail message to computer C, while computer B is trying to send a word processing file to computer D. The outgoing messages are divided into smaller packets of data, and then each sending computer (A and B) takes turns sending the packets over the transmission media. The incoming packets are reassembled at their respective destinations, using previously assigned packet sequence numbers.

For packet switching to work, each packet being sent across a network must be labeled with a header. This header contains the network address of the source (sending computer) and the network address of the destination (receiving computer). Each computer attached to a network has a unique network address. As packets are transmitted, network hardware detects whether a particular packet is destined for a local machine. Packet-switching systems adapt instantly to changes in network traffic. If only one computer needs to use the network, it can send data continuously. As soon as another computer needs to send data, packet switching, or turn taking, begins. Now let us see how the Internet handles this packet switching.

Transmission Control Protocol/Internet Protocol. Organizations use diverse network technologies that may or may not be compatible with the technologies of other organizations. Because so many different networks are interconnected today, they must have a common language, or protocol, to communicate. The protocol used by the Internet is called **Transmission Control Protocol/Internet Protocol (TCP/IP).** The first part, TCP, breaks data into small chunks called data packets and manages the transfer of those packets from computer to computer (via packet switching, as described previously). For example, a single document may be broken into several packets, each containing several hundred characters, as well as a destination address (the IP part of the protocol). The IP defines how a data packet must be formed and to where a **router** (an intelligent device used to connect two or more individual networks) must forward each packet. Packets travel independently to their destination, sometimes following different paths and arriving out of order. The destination computer reassembles all the packets on the basis of their identification and sequencing information. Together, TCP and IP provide a reliable and efficient way to send data across the Internet.

A data packet that conforms to the IP specification is called an **IP datagram.** Datagram routing and delivery are possible because, as previously mentioned, every computer and router connected to the Internet is assigned a unique address, called its **IP address.** When an organization connects to the Internet, it obtains a set of IP addresses that it can assign to its computers. TCP helps IP guarantee delivery of datagrams by performing three main tasks. First, it automatically checks for datagrams that may have been lost en route from their source to their destination. Second, TCP collects the incoming datagrams and puts them in the correct order to re-create the original message. Finally, TCP discards any duplicate copies of datagrams that may have been created by network hardware.

World Wide Web One of the most powerful uses of the Internet is something that you probably use almost every day—the World Wide Web. The **World Wide Web** is a system of interlinked documents on the Internet, or a graphical user interface to the Internet that provides users with a simple, consistent interface to access a wide variety of information. A **Web browser** is a software application that can be used to locate and display Web pages, including text, graphics, and multimedia content.

History of the World Wide Web. Prior to the invention of the Web by Tim Berners-Lee in 1991, content posted on the Internet could be accessed through the Internet tool **Gopher.** Gopher provided a menu-driven, hierarchical interface to organize files stored on servers, allowing to tie together related files from different Internet servers across the world. The Web took Gopher one step further by introducing **hypertext.** A hypertext document, otherwise known as a **Web page,** contains not only information but also **hyperlinks,** which are references or links to other documents. The standard method of specifying the format of Web pages is called **Hypertext Markup Language (HTML).** Specific content within each Web page is enclosed within codes, or markup tags, that stipulate how the content should appear to the user. These Web pages are stored on **Web servers,** which process user requests for pages using the **Hypertext Transfer Protocol.** Web servers typically host a collection of interlinked Web pages (called a **Web site**) that are owned by the same organization or by an individual. Web sites and specific Web pages within those sites have a unique Internet address. A user who wants to access a Web site enters the address, and the Web server hosting the Web site retrieves the desired page from its hard drive and delivers it to the user.

The introduction of the Web was the first of three events that led to its proliferation. The second event was the Information Infrastructure Act, passed by the U.S. government in 1992, which opened the Web for commercial purposes (Berghel, 1996). Prior to this legislation, universities and government agencies were the Web's primary users. The third event was the arrival of a graphical Web browser, Mosaic, which quickly transcended Gopher by adding a graphical front end to the Web. Mosaic's graphical interface allowed Web pages to be constructed to deliver an extended range of content, including images, audio, video, and other multimedia, all of which could be included and displayed within the same Web page. Mosaic was the basis for popular browsers such as Internet Explorer and Mozilla Firefox.

Web Domain Names and Addresses. A **Uniform Resource Locator (URL)** is used to identify and locate a particular Web page. For example, www.google.com is the URL used to find the main Google Web server. The URL has three distinct parts: the domain, the top-level domain, and the host name (see Figure 3.16).

The **domain name** is a term that helps people recognize the company or person that the domain name represents. For example, Google's domain name is google.com. The prefix *google* lets you know that it is very likely that this domain name will lead you to the Web site of Google. Domain names also have a suffix that indicates which **top-level domain** they belong to. For example, the ".com" suffix is reserved for commercial organizations. Some other popular suffixes are listed here:

- .edu—educational institutions
- .org—organizations (nonprofit)
- .gov—U.S. government entity
- .net—network organizations
- .de—Germany (there are over 240 two-letter "country code top-level domains")

Domain names ending with .com, .net, or .org can be registered through many different companies (known as registrars) that compete with one another. Given the proliferation of domain names, more of these top-level domain categories are being added, such as .aero for the air transport industry, .name for individuals, .coop for business industry cooperatives, and .museum for museums.

FIGURE 3.16

Dissecting a URL.

The host name is the particular Web server or group of Web servers (if it is a larger Web site) that will respond to the Web request. In most cases, the "www" host name refers to the default Web site or the home page of the particular domain. Other host names can be used. For example, spreadsheets.google.com will take you to the group of Web servers that are responsible for serving up Google's spreadsheet application. Larger companies have several host names for their different functions. Some examples used in Google are the following:

- mail.google.com (Google's free e-mail service)
- labs.google.com (Google's test applications)
- trends.google.com (see what other people are searching)
- maps.google.com (Google's mapping application)

All the domain names and the host names are associated with one or more IP addresses. For example, the domain name google.com represents about a dozen underlying IP addresses. IP addresses serve to identify all the computers or devices on the Internet (or on any TCP/IP network). The IP address serves as the destination address of that computer or device and enables the network to route messages to the proper destination. The format of an IP address is a 32-bit numeric address written as four numbers separated by periods. Each of the four numbers can be any number between 0 and 255. For example, 134.121.137.8 is an underlying IP address of www.wsu.edu, Washington State University's main Web page. You could set up a private network using the TCP/IP protocol and assign your own domain names and IP addresses for computers and other devices on that network. On the other hand, if you wish to connect to the Internet, you must use registered IP addresses.

IP addresses can also be used instead of URLs to navigate to particular Web addresses. This practice is not done regularly, as IP addresses are far more difficult to remember than domain names, and an organization may assign their domain name to a server with a different IP address; for example, whereas the IP address behind google.com may change, the domain name stays the same.

World Wide Web Architecture. The Web uses Web browsers, Web servers, and the TCP/IP networking protocol to facilitate the transmission of Web pages over the Internet. Figure 3.17 depicts the architecture of the Web. To access information on the Web, a Web browser, as well as

FIGURE 3.17

World Wide Web architecture.

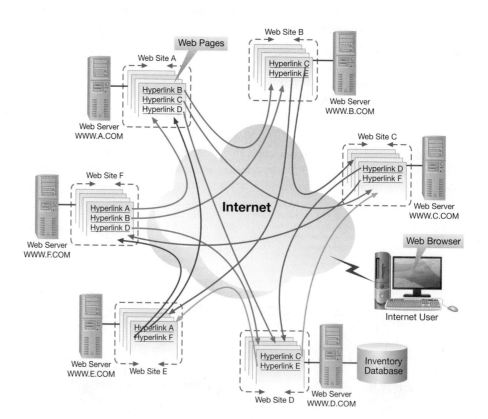

NET STATS

Broadband Access Increases

Reports show that broadband penetration in the United States is growing steadily, with 65 percent of U.S. adults having access to broadband connections at home in late 2009. Among all *active* Internet users, broadband penetration reached 95.2 percent in April 2010, up 5.9 percentage points from 89.3 percent in 2008. However, in terms of average connection speed, the United States is back in twenty-second place, behind South Korea and Hong Kong, but also behind countries like Romania and Latvia (see Figure 3.18).

Based on:

Anonymous. (2010, April 27). US drops to 22nd in broadband speed worldwide—Fastest broadband cities: College towns—US broadband penetration drops to 95.2% among active Internet users—April 2010 bandwidth report. *Websiteoptimization.com.* Retrieved June 4, 2010, from http://www.websiteoptimization.com/bw/1004.

Belson, D. (2010, April). The state of the Internet, 4th quarter, 2009. *Akamai.com.* Retrieved June 4, 2010, from http://www.akamai.com/dl/whitepapers/Akamai_State_Internet_Q4_2009.pdf.

Fox, S. (2010, February 23). FCC: Broadband adoption and use in America. *Pew Internet.* Retrieved June 4, 2010, from http://www.pewinternet.org/Commentary/2010/February/FCC-Broadband-Adoption-and-Use-in-America.aspx.

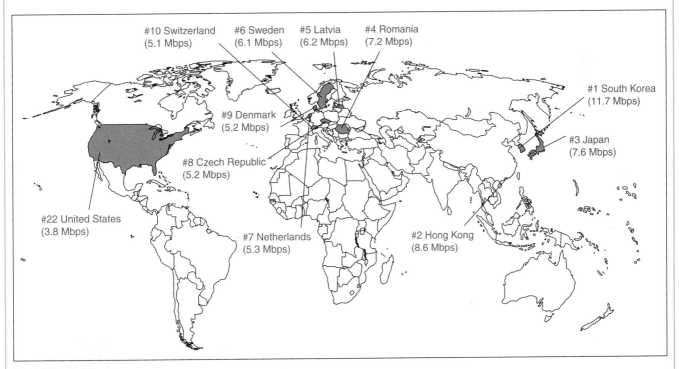

FIGURE 3.18

Average measured broadband connection speeds.

Source: Based on http://www.akamai.com/dl/whitepapers/Akamai_State_Internet_Q4_2009.pdf.

the TCP/IP protocol, must be installed on a user's computer. Users can access Web pages by entering the URL of the Web page into their Web browser. Once the user enters the URL in the Web browser, TCP/IP breaks the request into packets and routes them over the Internet to the Web server, where the requested Web page is stored. When the packets reach their destination, TCP/IP reassembles them and passes the request to the Web server. The Web server understands that the user is requesting a Web page (indicated by the http:// prefix in the URL) and retrieves the Web page, which is packetized by TCP/IP and transmitted over the Internet back to the Web browser.

TCP/IP reassembles the packets at the destination and delivers the Web page to the Web browser. In turn, the Web browser translates the HTML code contained in the Web page, formats its physical appearance, and displays the results. If the Web page contains a hyperlink, the user can click on it and the process repeats.

Issues Associated with Managing the IS Infrastructure

As you have undoubtedly noticed, computing technology has evolved rapidly and will most likely continue to evolve rapidly in the future. In general, because of the increasing pace of change with modern technologies, most organizations face accelerating obsolescence of their hardware and software investments as well as increasing storage and space constraints and increasing energy usage (see Figure 3.19). In the following section, we discuss how the interplay between the different infrastructure components both encourages and necessitates continuous upgrading of the infrastructure.

Obsolescence

Over the past 75 years, information systems have gone through many radical changes. Rapid advances in both hardware and software capabilities have enabled or facilitated many business processes, and organizations are continuously faced with the need to upgrade the IS infrastructure so as to gain or maintain competitive advantage. In this section, we discuss the history of computing, as well as the effects of rapid advances in technology.

Brief History of Computing   When the Zuse Z1 Computer (a mechanical computer using program punch cards) was introduced in 1936, almost all business and government information systems consisted of file folders, filing cabinets, and document repositories. Huge rooms were dedicated to the storage of these records. Information was often difficult to find, and corporate

FIGURE 3.19

IS infrastructure challenges
for modern organizations.

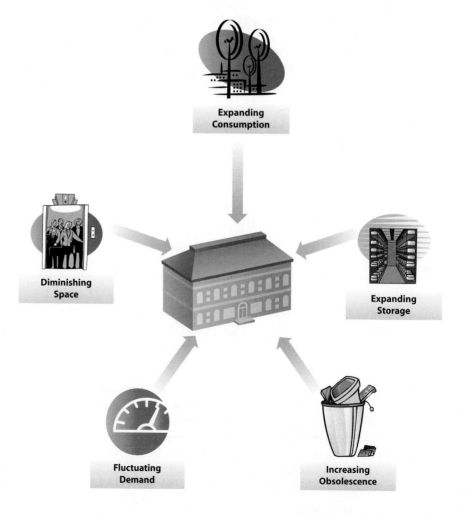

Expanding
Consumption

Diminishing
Space

Expanding
Storage

Fluctuating
Demand

Increasing
Obsolescence

TABLE 3.3 Five Generations of Computing

Generation	Time Line	Major Event	Characteristics
1	1946–1958	Vacuum tubes	• Mainframe era begins • ENIAC and UNIVAC were developed
2	1958–1964	Transistors	• Mainframe era expands • UNIVAC is updated with transistors
3	1964–1990s	Integrated circuits	• Mainframe era ends • Personal computer era begins • IBM 360 with general purpose operating system • Microprocessor revolution: Intel, Microsoft, Apple, IBM PC, MS-DOS
4	1990s–2000	Multimedia and low-cost PCs	• Personal computer era ends • Interpersonal computing era begins • High-speed microprocessor and networks • High-capacity storage • Low-cost, high-performance integrated video, audio, and data
5	2000–present	Widespread Internet accessibility	• Interpersonal computing era ends • Internetworking era begins • Ubiquitous access to Internet with a broad variety of devices • Prices continue to drop; performance continues to expand

knowledge and history were difficult to maintain. Only certain employees knew specific information. When these employees left the firm, so did all their knowledge about the organization. The computer provided the solution to the information storage and retrieval problems facing organizations up to the 1940s. Shifts in computing eras were facilitated by fundamental changes in the way computing technologies worked. Each of these fundamental changes is referred to as a distinct generation of computing. Table 3.3 highlights the technology that defined the five generations of computing.

Moore's Law In 1965, Intel cofounder Dr. Gordon Moore hypothesized that the number of transistors on a chip would double about every two years. When Moore made this bold prediction, he did not limit it to any specified period of time. This prediction became known as **Moore's Law.** Interestingly, whereas the first CPU had 2,200 transistors, the newest models have broken the 2-billion-transistor mark, so Dr. Moore's prediction has been fairly accurate so far (see www .intel.com/technology/mooreslaw). The number of transistors that can be packed into a modern CPU and the speed at which processing and other activities occur are remarkable. For example, the Intel Core i7 Extreme CPU can complete hundreds of millions of operations every second. To achieve these incredible speeds, the CPU must execute instructions very rapidly.

Software Obsolescence In addition to constant increases in hardware capabilities, companies such as Microsoft are continuously developing new and improved software that uses this power to help people be more productive. New operating systems such as Windows 7 can use new processor architectures and offer a richer set of features than older operating systems such as Windows XP. However, these new operating systems often require new hardware, and older-generation application software may not be compatible with the new operating system (see Figure 3.20). Further, new generations of application software promise better performance and more (or improved) features, enabling higher productivity. One example is Microsoft Office 2007 (and its most recent successor Office 2010); when developing Office 2007, Microsoft conducted many usability studies to improve the human–computer interface (see Chapter 9, "Developing and Acquiring Information Systems") so as to facilitate the execution of common tasks and, as a result, introduced the so-called Ribbon interface. Although people used to the "old" interface were initially reluctant to switch—because of the associated learning curve—many have now realized the benefits this new feature brings. Manufacturers of hardware and software often apply the concept of **planned obsolescence,** meaning that the product is designed to last only for a certain life span. For hardware, this can mean that certain components are not built to be serviceable, and the device has to be replaced once it breaks down; similarly, older versions of software may not be able to open newer file formats, or a company may cease support for a product (mainstream support for the Windows XP operating system ended in 2009, and

FIGURE 3.20

New hardware enables more
powerful software; more powerful
software often requires new
hardware.

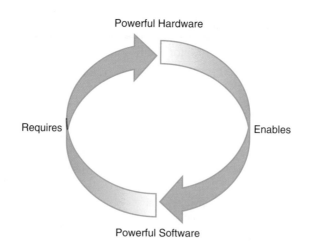

paid support as well as critical security updates will be offered only until 2014), effectively forcing
users to switch to newer versions. Hence, organizations are constantly faced with the decision of
when and how to upgrade their current hardware and software infrastructure. Although such upgrades
may increase productivity, often they do not but are still a large cost factor; at the same time, the rapid
obsolescence of computer hardware carries a high price tag for the environment in terms of resources
needed both to manufacture the new systems and to dispose of the old ones (see Figure 3.21).

Storage Needs

Another issue organizations face is the amount of data available and the amount of data needed to
stay ahead of the competition. Today, organizations can collect and analyze vast amounts of data
for *business intelligence* (see Chapter 6) and other purposes (such as compliance). For example,
organizations can analyze each visitor's actions on the company Web site in order to improve the
site's performance. Obviously, capturing this data requires ever more storage space and ever more
powerful computing hardware and database management systems for managing and analyzing this
data. Further, Internet bandwidth grew tremendously during the dot-com bubble, allowing organizations to provide their customers with richer (and more bandwidth-hungry) information. At the
same time, services such as YouTube or videos streamed by Netflix create a need for even more

FIGURE 3.21

The rapid obsolescence of
computer hardware carries a high
price tag for the environment.

Shutterstock

bandwidth. Hence, this is another example of a "vicious circle" where enhanced capabilities enable new applications, which in turn require a certain level of capabilities in terms of both data and communications infrastructure.

Space and Facility Requirements

To satisfy the increasing requirements for processing and storing the ever-growing volume of data, large organizations need hundreds or even thousands of servers. Organizations such as UPS need tremendous amounts of computing power to route and track packages, online stores such as Zappos need to provide Web content and track customer orders, and social networking game developers such as Zynga need to track each and every action users take on the popular game FarmVille (see Case 1 at the end of this chapter).

The IS hardware needed to provide these processing and storage resources has various requirements in terms of connectivity, floor space, provision of energy and cooling, and security; hence, organizations typically house this part of their IS infrastructure in large data centers that are equipped with different features to assure availability and reliability. The facilities for UPS in Atlanta, Georgia, and Mahwah, New Jersey, are prime examples for such high-availability facilities. To ensure uninterrupted service, the data centers are self-sufficient, and each can operate for up to two days on self-generated power. The power is needed not only for the computers but also for air-conditioning, as each facility needs air-conditioning capacity equaling that of or more than 2,000 homes. In case power fails, the cooling is provided using more than 600,000 gallons of chilled water, and the UPS facilities even have backup wells in case the municipal water supply should fail. Other protective measures include raised floors (to protect from floods) and buildings designed to withstand winds of 200 miles per hour. Alternatively, organizations can rent space for their servers in *collocation facilities,* which are data centers managed by a third party that rents out space to multiple organizational customers (see Chapter 10 for more on securing data centers and collocation facilities).

For organizations with an increasing customer (or user) base, this means that the facilities infrastructure has to grow along with any increase in computing resources (as Google grew, they eventually had to move their equipment out of their friend's garage; now Google is said to have more than 30 major data centers). Especially for fast-growing companies, this can be problematic, as renting (let alone building) additional facilities is expensive and takes time for locating the right facilities, contract negotiations, and setup; further, long-term contracts limit the companies' flexibility to scale the infrastructure down in times of lower demand.

Energy Consumption

The worldwide increase in demand for energy has become another concern for organizations. As computers process data, they consume electricity; further, various components (such as the CPU and the power supply) generate heat, and most computers have various fans to control the temperature. More powerful hardware thus needs more energy to enable the increase in computing power as well as more energy to cool the components. A typical desktop uses between 40 and 170 watts when idling and can use up to 300 watts or more under full load, generating between 400 and 1,000 BTUs (British Thermal Units) per hour in heat. Although you may not feel the impact of your personal computer usage on your home energy bill, for organizations having hundreds or thousands of computers, rising energy costs are becoming a major issue. Especially for companies such as Google or UPS, which need large data centers to support their operations, power and cooling can be a significant cost factor. Google has invested many resources into developing more efficient data centers. At its "Efficient Data Center Summit" in 2009, Google introduced modular data centers that use specially equipped shipping containers for housing servers so as to be able to maximize efficiency by optimizing airflow, cooling, and power transformation.

Demand Fluctuations

Taken together, managing the IS infrastructure can be a challenge for many organizations, because of the evolution of hardware and software, the demand for more storage and networking bandwidth, and the rising costs of energy. Further, organizations need dedicated staff to support their infrastructure, which incurs further costs; often, managing the IS infrastructure is not among the organization's core competencies, so others may be better at managing the infrastructure for them. An additional challenge for many organizations is that the demands for computing resources are often fluctuating, leading to either having too few resources at some times or having too many idle resources most of the time. Companies engaged in (or supporting) business-to-consumer electronic commerce (such as Amazon.com or FedEx; see Chapter 4, "Enabling Commerce Using the Internet"), for instance, face large spikes in demand during the pre-holiday season in December; consequently, increased capacity is needed to handle this demand. While it is relatively easy to hire temporary staff to handle an increase in orders, it is typically not that easy to make quick changes to the IS infrastructure based on changing needs. Just a few years ago, launching a start-up involved purchasing lots of hardware and installing Web servers in one's basement, with no real idea of how much demand would need to be met; fluctuation in demand for computing resources is especially difficult to cope with for new entrants who are not able to forecast demand and may not have the resources to quickly expand their IS infrastructure to meet increases in demand for their products or services.

Given these issues, organizations have been looking for ways to better manage their IS infrastructure so as to enhance flexibility and agility while reducing costs. In the following section, we introduce some solutions to these infrastructure-related challenges.

IS Infrastructure Trends

As information systems have become widespread, truly a ubiquitous part of modern organizations and society, knowledge workers have become adept at utilizing a broad range of applications to perform their jobs. Applications and technologies have also matured, allowing many organizations to abandon proprietary systems and infrastructure, using instead a variety of technology services to achieve their various needs and address the issues associated with managing an IS infrastructure. These trends are examined next.

Utility Computing

Over the past decades, there has been a shift away from thinking about the IS infrastructure toward thinking about what services the infrastructure should deliver. For example, people and organizations want to use e-mail rather than having to think about purchasing an e-mail server and dealing with associated issues such as administration, maintenance, storage, energy consumption, and so on. To satisfy the customers' desire to consume services, major IT services providers (such as IBM) started offering a **utility computing** model; under this model, organizations "rent" resources such as processing, data storage, or networking from an external provider on an as-needed basis; the organization only pays for the services used (see Figure 3.22).

FIGURE 3.22

Utility computing allows companies to pay for computing resources on an as-needed basis.

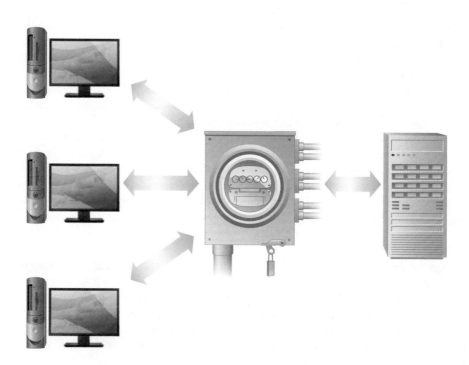

Utility computing is an effective way for managing fluctuating demand as well as controlling costs; in essence, all tasks associated with managing, maintaining, and upgrading the infrastructure are left to the external provider and are typically bundled into the "utility" bill—if you don't use, you don't pay. This offers tremendous benefits in terms of **scalability** (i.e., the ability to adapt to increases or decreases in demand for processing or data storage), which is especially important for companies just starting to operate in the digital world. Whereas some providers offered the option to rent time or space on specific physical resources (e.g., a dedicated Web server), others used *virtualization* to share resources among multiple customers. Using **virtualization,** multiple **virtual machines,** each with its own applications, can be configured to run on one single (but powerful) computer, enabling the IT service providers to better utilize their resources.

Cloud Computing

Technological advances such as increasing Internet bandwidth and advances in virtualization have given rise to cloud computing (the "cloud" is a metaphor for the Internet; see Figure 3.23). As defined by the National Institute of Standards and Technology (NIST), "Cloud computing is a model for enabling convenient, on-demand network access to a shared pool of configurable computing resources (e.g., networks, servers, storage, applications, and services) that can be rapidly provisioned and released with minimal management effort or service provider interaction." Using a utility computing model, cloud computing thus helps to transform IT infrastructure costs from a capital expenditure to an operational expenditure. One prime example of cloud computing is Amazon Web Services; having built an immense infrastructure (in terms of both information technology and logistics) for supporting its online store, Amazon.com has decided to use these resources to generate additional revenue streams. For example, individuals and organizations can rent storage space on Amazon's Simple Storage Service (S3) or computing time on Amazon's Elastic Compute Cloud (EC2), all on an as-needed basis. The ability to create an entire infrastructure by combining Amazon's various services has facilitated many successful start-up companies, such as Zynga, the makers of the Facebook application FarmVille, or Animoto, which offers a Web application that lets users create orchestrated videos from their own pictures and music. As Animoto became popular (it was featured on *CNN* and *BBC*, in the *New York Times,* and so on), it increased the number of EC2 server instances used from 50 to 3,500 within just three days; this would have been close to impossible were Animoto using their own data center because of both the time and the money needed to acquire this number of servers; and, at the time, who knew whether Animoto's business would actually take off? With a traditional in-house infrastructure, Animoto would have had to add capacity in "chunks," leading to either having too many unused resources or not being able to satisfy its users' demand;

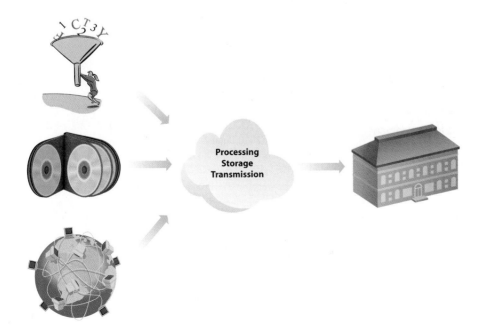

FIGURE 3.23

Processing, storing, and transmission of data taking place in the cloud.

WHEN THINGS GO WRONG

Google Buzz: A Privacy Fiasco

Google, the Internet giant based in Mountain View, California, is not just known for its search engine. People also know Google for the multiple Web tools and cloud computing services they provide. The products coming out of Google's "Labs" are used by millions of people all around the world on a daily basis. One of the most popular tools is Google's free e-mail service, Gmail. Gmail gives users over 7 GB (and counting) of free storage space, allows mobile access, and has fantastic spam-fighting capabilities. On February 9, 2010, Google added yet another new communication tool to their collection, Google Buzz.

Buzz is a social networking and messaging add-on to Gmail that many see as Google's response to Facebook. It allows users to share updates, photos, videos, and comments, organizing them all in the Gmail in-box. When Buzz went "live" on the Internet, every Gmail user was automatically enrolled.

Within hours of the launch of Buzz, cries of protest went up around the globe decrying Google's assault on user privacy. News outlets, blogs, message boards, and Twitter were inundated with negative stories about Buzz. At the heart of the privacy concern was Buzz's core functionality and integration with Gmail's address book. When Google activated Buzz, the program made links between the members of every Gmail user's address book. This linking instantly gave anyone in a user's address book visibility of all other names in the address book. Although Google allowed Gmail users to opt out of Buzz, users were unable to do so until after Buzz's initial activation.

The ramifications of such a peek into someone's address book can easily be imagined. For instance, you might not want your significant other to suddenly see all the names of your former partners in your address book. If a doctor's office used Gmail to communicate with patients, everyone in the address book would instantly know who other patients were of that doctor. A far more dangerous scenario can be imagined in authoritarian countries such as China, where dissenting citizens' address books could have been revealed to government Internet minders, allowing them to see who the dissidents had been communicating with.

In addition to just address books, Buzz also linked a user's Picasa Web Albums (Google's online photo service) and Google Reader shared items. This, too, gave everyone in the address book a direct look at the user's photos and items they were reading. Even though these items are technically already public, it is likely that most entries in a user's address book are unaware of them.

Google quickly responded to the public outcry. Google engineers slept at the Googleplex in Mountain View, working through the weekend to address privacy concerns with Buzz. Their first fix came two days after launch with options to make it easier to opt out of publicly displaying "followers" from the user address book. However, many online commentators still didn't like the fix, saying it was still too confusing to completely keep your private data out of Buzz's social stream. Two days later, Google completely replaced Buzz's opt-out feature with an opt-in feature instead. The move effectively turned off Buzz for Gmail users, requiring them to choose to activate Buzz and select how much data it shared with other users.

The aftermath of the Buzz debacle left Google rattled, as the Internet giant is frequently the target of conspiracy theories, accusations of copyright abuse, censorship debates, and other privacy concerns. However, once the initial privacy concerns were addressed and the initial outcries settled, Google Buzz took its place among the myriad other Google tools in use across the web.

Based on:

Bhat, A. (2010, February 19). Google Buzz: A recap of the controversy and the current legal issues. Retrieved April 26, 2010, from http://www.stlr.org/2010/02/google-buzz-a-recap-of-the-controversy-and-the-current-legal-issues.

Carlson, N. (2010, February 16). How Google went into "Code Red" and saved Google Buzz. Retrieved April 26, 2010, from http://www.businessinsider.com/how-google-went-into-code-red-and-saved-google-buzz-2010-2.

Google Buzz. (2010, June 7). In *Wikipedia, the free encyclopedia*. Retrieved June 8, 2010, from http://en.wikipedia.org/w/index.php?title=Google_Buzz&oldid=366642601.

using a cloud infrastructure, Animoto can elastically scale the resources to be just above what is needed to keep the users satisfied (see Figure 3.24).

Cloud Characteristics The cloud computing model has several unique and essential characteristics that distinguish cloud computing from an in-house infrastructure and provide various benefits to users (NIST, 2009). These characteristics are discussed next.

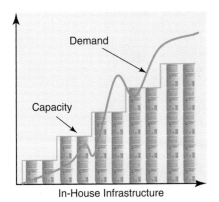 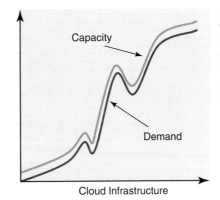

FIGURE 3.24

It is difficult to match demand using an in-house infrastructure; with a cloud infrastructure, resources can be added incrementally, on an as-needed basis.

On-Demand Self-Service. To allow for most flexibility, users can access cloud resources in a buffet-style fashion on an as-needed basis without the need for lengthy negotiations with the service provider; in many cases, resources in the cloud are accessible by the customer with no need for human interaction with the provider. In the case of Amazon Web Services, a customer needs only a credit card (for billing purposes) and can set up server instances or expand storage space via a control panel on a Web site.

Rapid Elasticity. Typically, servers and other elements of an IT infrastructure take several weeks to be delivered and days or weeks to be configured; in contrast, in a cloud environment, computing resources can be scaled up or down almost instantaneously and often automatically, based on user needs. Hence, there is no need to purchase expensive equipment to prepare for an anticipated surge in demand (which ultimately may not materialize) during the holiday season. If, however, the surge in demand does materialize, businesses can access the required resources instantaneously at almost any quantity.

Ubiquitous Network Access. As cloud services are accessed via the Internet, they are accessible from almost anywhere and from almost any Web-enabled device. For example, one can easily manage an EC2 computing instance from one's desktop or laptop; using an iPhone or Android smart phone application, one can even start or stop instances while on the road.

Resource Pooling. Rather than renting out space or time to each customer on one specific, physical machine, cloud providers manage multiple distributed resources that are dynamically assigned to multiple customers based on their needs. Hence, the customer only rents a resource, with no knowledge or control over how it is provided or where it is located. In some cases, however, service providers allow for specifying particular geographic areas of the resources; for example, a California company may want to rent time on servers located in California close to its customers so as to reduce response latency, or a European company may need to rent storage space on servers located in Europe so as to comply with data protection directives (see Chapter 1).

Measured Service. Service is typically provided using a utility computing model, where customers pay only for what they use, and the metering depends on type of resource. For example, customers are charged on an hourly basis for the use of server instances (the price typically depends on the instance's computing power, memory, and operating system) based on volume of data stored and/or on data transferred into or out of the cloud. For customers, the fixed costs associated with the IS infrastructure are thus transformed into variable costs, which are very easy to track and monitor.

Service Models As can be seen from the previously mentioned examples, various services are provided in the cloud. Whereas some users require access only to certain software, others want to have more control, being able to run the software of their choice on a server in the cloud (see Figure 3.25). Different cloud computing service models (NIST, 2009) are discussed next.

Software as a Service. In the **software as a service (SaaS)** model, the customer uses an application provided via a cloud infrastructure. Typically, such applications include Web-based e-mail services (e.g., Google's Gmail) and Web-based productivity suites (such as Zoho or Google Docs) but also advanced applications such as CRM systems, as provided by salesforce .com (see Chapter 8, "Improving Supply Chains and Strengthening Customer Relationships

FIGURE 3.25

Services provided by SaaS, PaaS, and IaaS providers.

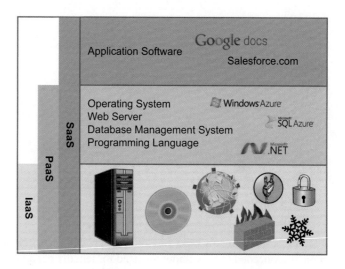

Using Enterprise Information Systems"). Typically, the consumer cares has only about the application, with no knowledge or control over the underlying infrastructure and typically has only limited ability to control or configure application-specific settings; further, the customer does not have to worry about maintaining or updating the software, the underlying platform, or the hardware infrastructure.

Platform as a Service. In the **platform as a service (PaaS)** model, the customer can run his or her own applications that are typically designed using tools provided by the service provider. In this model, the user has control over the applications but has limited or no control over the underlying infrastructure. One example is Microsoft's Windows Azure, which acts as a cloud services operating system that customers can use to deploy custom applications. For example, Outback Steakhouse launched a viral marketing campaign when it first introduced its Facebook Fan Page. To support the spikes in demand, Outback developed and deployed an e-mail marketing campaign using Windows Azure. As the underlying computing platform is provided, the customer does not have to worry about purchasing software licenses such as operating systems for Web servers or database management systems, and the service provider manages the functioning and updating of the platform provided.

Infrastructure as a Service. In the **infrastructure as a service (IaaS)** model, only the basic capabilities of processing, storage, and networking are provided. Hence, the customer has most control over the resources. Using Amazon Web Services, customers can choose computing power, memory, operating system, and storage based on individual needs and requirements, thus being able to build (almost) their entire infrastructure in the cloud; currently, Netflix is in the process of migrating its own IT infrastructure to Amazon Web Services using EC2 and S3 to transcode movies into various formats, powering its customer-focusing Web site and other mission-critical applications. The IaaS model provides the customer with the greatest flexibility; on the other hand, while the infrastructure is provided, managing licenses for operating systems and so on is still the responsibility of the customer.

Types of Clouds Cloud service providers such as Amazon offer what is referred to as a **public cloud.** Services in a public cloud can be used by any interested party on a pay-per-use basis; hence, they are often used for applications that need rapid scalability or in cases where the capital to build or expand an IT infrastructure is insufficient. In contrast, a **private cloud** (or internal cloud) is internal to an organization and can help the organization to balance demand and supply of computing resources within the organization. A private cloud does not free an organization from the issues associated with managing the cloud infrastructure but does give the organization a high degree of customizability and control over their data and applications (see Figure 3.26).

Management Issues

Because of its various benefits, cloud computing has gained much popularity, especially among executives who try to minimize IT infrastructure–related expenses. However, there are also

FIGURE 3.26

Private clouds versus public clouds.

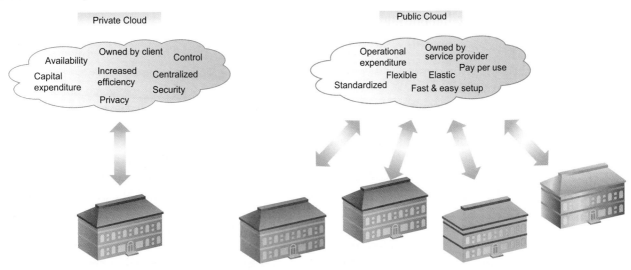

various issues management should consider when moving their infrastructure to the cloud. The first consideration is which applications, services, or data to move to the cloud. Increasing traffic on the Internet leads to bandwidth congestions and introduces latencies when accessing resources in the cloud; hence, organizations have to weigh the benefits and downsides of cloud computing in a differentiated way, as there is not one solution that fits all. You must also carefully consider which cloud services provider to choose. Some of the long-term, strategic issues that management should consider when evaluating different service providers include the following:

- *Scalability.* Will the provider be able to meet current and future business needs in terms of data storage, transaction volumes, and so on?
- *Viability.* Will the service provider survive in the long run? What is the provider's long-term stability?
- *Diversity of Offerings.* Will the service provider offer other services that may be needed in the future? (It is easier to manage fewer providers that can meet all your needs.)
- *Support Policies.* How will issues be resolved? Is there a way to quickly escalate severe problems?

Other issues to consider are of a more technical nature. The most important technical issues include the following:

- *Availability/Reliability.* What is the promised uptime of the application/system? What backups are made to the servers and storage? Will sufficient bandwidth be provided to access large amounts of data? What is the provider's track record of success?
- *Security.* How secure will the data be from outside intruders?
- *Compliance.* Does the data storage comply with regulations such as the Sarbanes-Oxley Act or standards such as the Payment Card Industry Data Security Standard?
- *Privacy.* Will the privacy of customer data be protected?
- *Openness.* How easy is it to move data and/or applications between service providers? Will the company be "locked in"?

Issues such as availability, reliability, or security are normally covered in **service-level agreements,** which are contracts specifying the level of service provided in terms of performance (e.g., as measured by uptime), warranties, disaster recovery, and so on.

Advanced Cloud Applications

Clearly, the "cloud" offers many ways for businesses to solve their IT infrastructure–related issues. In addition to the different cloud services models, the "cloud" has enabled other trends, such as

COMING ATTRACTIONS

Autonomic Computing

Have you ever wondered why you constantly have to upgrade your computer or download software patches for your application software or operating systems? As no system is without flaws, and users and developers periodically find programming errors or security holes, the need arises to fix these, especially if they compromise the security of the system. At other times, a system just breaks down. With increasing complexity of information systems, the time and money needed to manage these increase tremendously; however, the time and money needed doesn't add value to an organization. In fact, some people believe that for large organizations, the costs of managing their systems undermine the benefits these systems provide.

Why can't systems be designed that are easier and less resource intensive to manage? This question becomes increasingly important because of organizations' growing needs for complex information systems, paired with a shortage of skilled systems administrators. Recently, academic and industry researchers (e.g., at IBM) have begun working on autonomic computing systems designed to overcome these issues. Autonomic computing systems are self-managing and thus need only minimal human intervention to operate. In other words, in a traditional computing environment, system operators often have to fine-tune the computer's configuration in order to most efficiently solve a particular type of complex problem. In an autonomic computing environment, the ultimate goal is to allow the system to do everything else on its own, completely transparent to the user. In order to achieve this, an autonomic computing system must know itself and be self-configuring, self-optimizing, self-healing, and self-protecting.

How can a system be built to be autonomic, resembling a self-managing biological system? In organizational environments, conditions frequently change and are often unpredictable. In order to optimally perform under such conditions and swiftly react to any changes to the environment, an autonomic system must know itself; that is, it must know its configuration, capacity, and current status, but it must also know which resources it can draw on. Second, in order to be able to use different resources based on different needs, the system should be self-configuring so that the user does not have to take care of any configuration issues. Further, as any parts of a system can malfunction, an autonomic system

should be self-healing so that any potential problems are detected and the system is reconfigured so as to allow the user to continue performing the tasks, even if parts of the system are not operational. Finally, as almost any computer system can be the target of an attack (see Chapter 10), autonomic computing systems must be aware of any potential dangers and must be able to protect themselves from any malicious attacks (e.g., by automatically quarantining infected parts of the system). In sum, an autonomic computing system should be flexible in regard to changing conditions, always accessible to the user, and transparent, freeing the users from tasks associated with managing the system.

Clearly, these are some formidable tasks researchers have to address, but considering the time and money that is currently spent on managing and maintaining IT infrastructures, autonomic computing systems are promising for the future.

Although research on autonomic computing is still in its early stages and truly autonomic computing systems will still be a few years away, some of its premises are already being successfully employed. One recent example is 3PAR's autonomic storage tiering, primarily geared at cloud service providers. Typically, service providers have to balance service-level targets with the utilization of different technologies. In the case of storage, one trade-off is between performance (in terms of speed) and cost (as faster storage technologies, such as solid-state drives, are more expensive). Autonomic storage tiering allows high-end types of storage systems to efficiently distribute data over various storage technologies without human intervention. By intelligently monitoring performance at different levels of the system, the technology can dynamically shift data between different storage media, depending on the performance needed to meet the intended performance level with the least costly storage medium.

Based on:

Anonymous. (n.d.). Autonomic computing. Retrieved June 8, 2010, from http://www.research.ibm.com/autonomic/index.html.

Cooter, M. (2010, February 3). Autonomic computing: The route to systematic well-being? *IET.* Retrieved April 3, 2010, from http://kn .theiet.org/magazine/issues/1002/autonomic-computing.cfm.

Preimesberger, C. (2010, March 9). 3PAR launches autonomic storage tiering for high-end arrays. *eWeek.* Retrieved April 3, 2010, from http:// www.eweekeurope.co.uk/news/3par-launches-autonomic-storage -tiering-for-high-end-arrays-5733.

FIGURE 3.27

Jaguar, one of the world's fastest supercomputers, is used to simulate explosions of stars.

National Center for Computational Sciences

grid computing to help solving large-scale computing problems, *edge computing* for increasing Web application performance, and *IP convergence* for transmitting voice and video communication over the Internet. These applications are discussed next.

Grid Computing Businesses and public organizations heavily involved in research and development face an ever-increasing need for computing performance. For example, auto manufacturers, such as the GM German subsidiary Opel or Japanese Toyota, use large supercomputers to simulate automobile crashes and to evaluate design changes for vibrations and wind noise. Research facilities such as the U.S. National Center for Computational Science use supercomputers for simulating explosions of stars (see Figure 3.27), while others simulate earthquakes using supercomputers; such research sites have a tremendously complex hardware infrastructure.

Although today's supercomputers have tremendous computing power, some tasks are even beyond the capacity of a supercomputer. Indeed, some complex simulations can take a year or longer to calculate even on a supercomputer. Sometimes an organization or a research facility would have the need for a supercomputer but may not be able to afford one because of the extremely high cost. For example, the fastest supercomputers can cost more than $200 million, and this does not represent the "total cost of ownership," which also includes all the other related costs for making the system operational (e.g., personnel, facilities, storage, software, and so on; see Chapter 9). Additionally, the organization may not be able to justify the costs because the supercomputer may be needed only occasionally to solve a few complex problems. In these situations, organizations either have had to rent time on a supercomputer or decided simply not to solve the problem.

One way for overcoming cost or use limitations is to utilize **grid computing.** Grid computing refers to combining the computing power of a large number of smaller, independent, networked computers (often regular desktop PCs) into a cohesive system in order to solve problems that only supercomputers were previously capable of solving. Similar to cloud computing, grid computing makes use of distributed resources; however, in contrast to cloud computing, the resources in a grid are typically applied to a single large problem. To make grid computing work, large computing tasks are broken into small chunks, each of which can then be completed by individual computers (see Figure 3.28). However, as the individual computers are also in regular use, the individual calculations are performed during the computers' idle time so as to maximize the use of existing resources. For example, when writing this book, we used only minimal resources on our computers (i.e., we typically used only a word processor, the Internet, and e-mail); if our computers were part of a grid, the unused resources could be utilized to solve large-scale computing problems. This is especially useful for companies operating on a global scale. In each

FIGURE 3.28

Grid computing: Computers located around the world work on parts of a large, complex problem.

country, many of the resources are idle during the night hours, often more than 12 hours per day. Because of time zone differences, grid computing helps utilize those resources constructively. One way to put these resources into use would be to join the Berkeley Open Infrastructure for Network Computing (http://boinc.berkeley.edu/), which lets individuals "donate" computing time for various research projects, such as searching for extraterrestrial intelligence (SETI@home) or running climate change simulations.

However, as you can imagine, grid computing poses a number of demands in terms of the underlying network infrastructure or the software managing the distribution of the tasks. Further, the slowest computer often creates a bottleneck, thus slowing down the entire grid. A **dedicated grid,** consisting of a large number of homogeneous computers (and not relying on underutilized resources), can help overcome these problems. A dedicated grid is easier to set up and manage and, for many companies, much more cost effective than purchasing a supercomputer.

Edge Computing Another recent trend in IS hardware infrastructure management is **edge computing,** that is, moving processing and data storage away from a centralized location to the "edges" of a network. Many businesses use edge computing to improve performance of their online commerce sites. In such cases, customers interact with the servers of an edge computing service provider (such as Akamai). These edge servers, in turn, communicate with the business's computers (see Figure 3.29). This form of edge computing helps to reduce wait times for the consumers, as the sites (or media content, such as images or videos) are replicated on the provider's servers, while at the same time reducing the number of requests to the company's own infrastructure. This process not only saves valuable resources such as bandwidth but also offers superior performance that would otherwise be too expensive for organizations to offer. Akamai's services are utilized by organizations such as NBC, Fox Sports, BMW, and Victoria's Secret.

Convergence of Computing and Telecommunications Today, much of an organization's communication and collaboration needs are supported by Internet technologies; for example, e-mail has become the communications medium of choice for many people. However, for some topics, other forms of communication are more suited, so managers turn to the telephone, instant messaging, meetings, or videoconferences. One recent trend to satisfy such diverse communication and collaboration needs is the growing convergence of computing and telecommunications. The computing industry is experiencing an ever-increasing convergence of functionality of various devices. Whereas just a few years ago a cell phone was just a cell phone and people used personal digital assistants to support mobile computing needs, such devices are now converging such that the boundaries between devices are becoming increasingly blurred. Today, smart phones, such as the iPhone, BlackBerry, or HTC Droid, offer a variety of different functionalities—formerly often available only on separate dedicated devices—to address differing needs of knowledge workers and consumers alike (e.g., phone, e-mail, Web browser, navigation system, camera, music player, and so on).

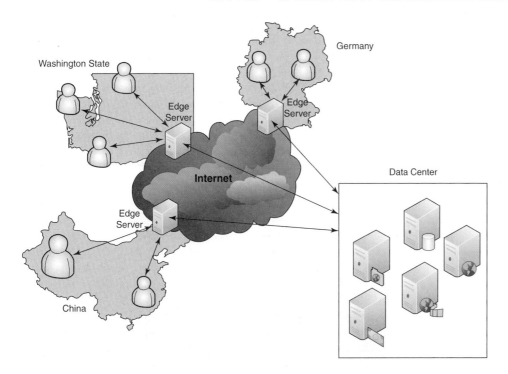

FIGURE 3.29

Edge computing brings computing resources closer to the end user.

In addition to a convergence of capabilities of devices, there is also increasing convergence within the underlying infrastructures. For example, in the past, the backbone networks for the telephone and Internet were distinct. Today, increasingly, most voice and data traffic share a common network infrastructure. To facilitate this convergence, also termed **IP convergence,** the use of IP for transporting voice, video, fax, and data traffic has allowed enterprises to make use of new forms of communication and collaboration (e.g., instant messaging and online whiteboard collaboration) as well as traditional forms of communication (such as phone and fax) at much lower costs (see Figure 3.30). In the following sections, we discuss two uses of IP for communication: voice over IP and videoconferencing over IP.

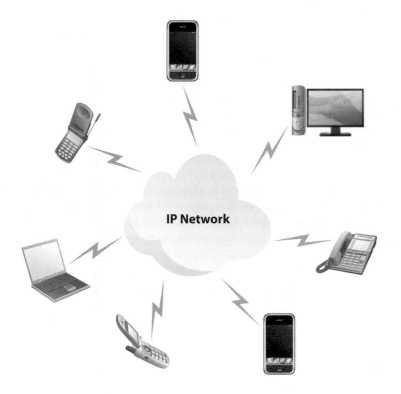

FIGURE 3.30

IP convergence allows various devices to communicate using IP technologies.

FIGURE 3.31

VoIP technology enables organizations and individuals to reduce their telecommunications costs.

Voice over IP. **Voice over IP (VoIP)** (or IP telephony) refers to the use of Internet technologies for placing telephone calls. Whereas just a few years ago the quality of VoIP calls was substandard, recent technological advances now allow the quality of calls to equal or even surpass the quality of traditional calls over (wired) telephone lines. In addition to the quality, VoIP offers a number of other benefits; for example, users can receive calls from almost anywhere they connect to the Internet. In other words, knowledge workers are not bound to their desk to receive VoIP calls; instead, using IP routing, their telephone number "follows" them to wherever they connect to the Internet. For example, Christoph, who lives in Hong Kong, has VoIP telephone numbers in the United States and Germany so that friends and family members living in these countries can call him at local rates. Organizations can also benefit from tremendous cost savings, as often there is little cost incurred over and above the costs for a broadband Internet connection (e.g., VoIP software such as Skype allows home users to make free PC-to-PC calls; see Figure 3.31).

Videoconferencing over IP. In addition to voice communications, IP can also be used to transmit video data. Traditionally, videoconferences were held either via traditional phone lines, which were not made to handle the transfer of data needed for high-quality videoconferencing, or via dedicated digital lines, which was a very costly option. Similar to VoIP, the Internet also helped to significantly reduce costs and enhance the versatility of videoconferences by enabling **videoconferencing over IP.**

For some videoconferences, desktop videoconferencing equipment (consisting of a webcam, a microphone, speakers, and software such as Microsoft Office Live Meeting or Skype) may be sufficient; for others, higher-end equipment may be needed. Such infrastructure can include specific videoconferencing hardware, or it can even be a $400,000 Hewlett-Packard (HP) HALO meeting room featuring life-sized images allowing people from across the globe to meet as if they were sitting in the same room (see Figure 3.32). In contrast to other applications,

FIGURE 3.32

The HP Halo meeting room features life-sized images.

Hewlett Packard Imaging &
Printing Group

with the HALO room, HP provides a videoconferencing service to its customers, offering features such as access to a dedicated network infrastructure and support services for a fixed monthly fee. We discuss videoconferencing in more detail in Chapter 4, "Enabling Commerce Using the Internet."

Green Computing

Fueled by the rapid advances of developing nations, the world has seen a tremendous increase in demand for and cost of energy. You may not feel the impact of your personal computer usage on your home energy bill; however, for organizations having hundreds or thousands of computers, rising energy costs are becoming a major issue. Further, organizations are being increasingly scrutinized for their contribution to societal issues such as global warming; more and more organizations are trying to portray a "greener" image when it comes to the use of energy and natural resources, as company executives have realized that they cannot afford the consequences of inaction on the company's reputation. As "green" efforts can save money on energy and water use, waste disposal, and carbon taxes, and can be subsidized by grants, rebates, or free technical advice, they can have positive impacts on a company's bottom line. Further, green efforts can improve the company's image and help to attract better employees and increase staff loyalty (Tebutt, 2010).

Green computing can contribute to these efforts by helping to use computers more efficiently, doing the same (or more) with less. For example, organizations can save large amounts of money for power and cooling by using virtualization to replace hundreds of individual servers with just a few powerful mainframe computers. As studies have shown, computing resources in organizations are often very much underutilized, and using virtualization can help lower an organization's energy bill and carbon footprint. Similarly, cloud computing has been argued to contribute to reduced energy consumption, as the service provider's infrastructure is shared by many users. Installing sophisticated power management software on individual desktops can save much energy that is wasted by leaving computers idling or on standby overnight; for instance, General Electric saved $6.5 million in electricity annually by simply changing the power saving settings for its computers (Wheeland, 2007). Further, discouraging employees from printing out e-mails or business documents can help to reduce the waste of paper—an average office worker prints more than a tree's worth of paper each year.

A related issue is the retiring of obsolete hardware. Today, companies cannot just send retired equipment to a landfill. Rather, companies as well as individuals have to evaluate how to best dispose of unwanted computers, monitors, and parts. Whereas the first step is to make the decision *when* to retire equipment, the next steps are equally important. Needless to say, it has to be ensured that old computers are wiped of all user data. Many third-party outsourcers ("IT asset disposition" vendors) offer services including wiping all computer hard drives, and either refurbishing and selling usable equipment, or dismantling the components to recycle valuable raw materials and properly dispose of hazardous waste (see Chapter 1 regarding ethical issues associated with disposing of e-waste).

INDUSTRY ANALYSIS

Movie Industry

Do you remember the original *Star Wars* movies or movies such as *King Kong* (1976) or *Godzilla*? Compare these to recent box office hits such as the *Lord of the Rings Trilogy* (2001–2003), *Star Wars Episode III: Revenge of the Sith* (2005), *King Kong* (2005), *2012* (2009), *Avatar* (2009), or *The Adventures of Tintin* (2011), or animated movies such as *Ice Age* (2002–2009), the *Shrek* series (2001–2010), *Bee Movie* (2007), *Madagascar: Escape 2 Africa* (2008), or *Cowboys & Aliens* (2011) The tremendous increase in computing power has enabled film studios such as Dreamworks or Universal Studios or special effects studios such as Weta Digital or Pixar to create animations and special effects of hitherto unimaginable quality using specialized powerful software and hardware for computer-generated imagery (CGI, also known as computer graphics).

As for major studios, rapidly evolving digital technology (specifically, recording hardware and sophisticated yet easy-to-use digital editing software) has opened vast opportunities for independent filmmakers who are producing studio-quality films without having to rely on expensive lighting, film development, and postproduction facilities. Thus, people who could never afford all the necessary equipment can now produce movies digitally. Further, digital cameras and projectors and advances in software have made the transition from celluloid to digital more attainable for filmmakers who until recently used traditional technology. In fact, over 30 percent of the submissions to the Sundance Film Festival (the primary film festival for independent movies, comparable to festivals in Cannes or Berlin for mainstream movies) are now in digital format.

However, the impact of technology on the movie industry does not stop with movie production. Many movie theaters across the world have shifted to digital projection technologies, reducing the need for duplicating and shipping large reels of film, reducing distribution costs by up to 90 percent, while speeding up the time from the studio to the theater. Rather than shipping reels of film (that are susceptible to out-of-focus projection, scratches, or "pops"), the movies are stored on central servers, from which they are accessed and downloaded via the Internet by individual theaters. Theater owners can much more swiftly react to fluctuating demand and easily show movies on more than one screen in case of high demand.

In addition, the extreme success of *Avatar* in 2010 accelerates the speed of the movie industry moving toward the 3D era. In fact, 3D movies have a pretty long history. The first commercially released 3D film can be traced back to 1922's *The Power of Love*. However, technology was a major limitation for early 3D films. As 3D projectors required two reels to be displayed in perfect synchronization, even very small errors in synchronization could result in eye strain and headache among viewers. Recently, the advances of information technology led to a resurrection of 3D films. James Cameron's *Avatar*, which broke several box office records during its release, was created using custom-built 3D cameras as well as specialized software, enabling the combined use of live action, miniature models, and computer-generated imagery; *Avatar* was nominated for nine Academy Awards and won three, including Best Cinematography, Best Visual Effects, and Best Art Direction. According to the National Association of Theater Owners, there were around 3,000 3D screens in 2009 in the United States, with about 90 to 100 screens being added every month. Following *Avatar's* success, many other films will be launched in 3D versions, including *Tron: Legacy*, *Harry Potter*, and *Kung Fu Panda*.

Despite recent advances in technology, 3D remains an imperfect and relatively expensive technology. For instance, 3D versions of films aren't as sharp or rich in color as their 2D counterparts. Polarized glasses also reduce peripheral vision and leave viewers focused on the center of the screen. It is hoped that newer 3D technologies will fix these flaws. In addition, 3D manufacturers are working to break through the next significant barrier in 3D display. A number of autostereoscopic displays are currently being designed. Like stereoscopic screens, autostereoscopic screens display two images that are merged into one to simulate a 3D effect, thereby eliminating the need for glasses entirely. Using lenticular screens, autostereoscopic displays produce a variable image depending on the angle at which a person views the screen. Movement of the head produces a distinct image in each eye—the familiar stereoscopic effect.

With the advances in information technology, it shouldn't be too long for viewers to be able to sit down in a theater and enjoy a true 3D experience without the need for glasses. Clearly, the use of information systems has tremendously changed the movie industry.

Questions

1. Can digital technologies help movie theaters compete with the increasing trend toward more sophisticated home theaters? How?
2. What are the ethical issues associated with special effects becoming more and more realistic with the help of digital technologies?
3. From the perspective of movie studios and theaters, list the pros and cons of using digital distribution technologies.

Based on:

Anonymous. (n.d.). U2 3D: The first live-action 3D concert movie, featuring U2. Retrieved April 24, 2010, from http://www.u23dmovie.com.

Avatar (2009 film). (2010, August 6). In *Wikipedia, the free encyclopedia*. Retrieved August 6, 2010, from http://en.wikipedia.org/w/index.php?title=Avatar_(2009_film)&oldid=377406015.

Cieply, M. (2010, January 12). For all its success, will "Avatar" change the industry? *New York Times*. Retrieved April 24, 2010, from http://www.nytimes.com/2010/01/13/movies/13avatar.html.

Hartvig, N. (2009, July 23). 3D projects new vision for the movie industry. *CNN.com*. Retrieved April 24, 2010, from http://www.cnn.com/2009/TECH/07/23/3D.cinema.business.

Jardin, X. (2005, July 28). Hollywood plots end of film reels. *Wired*. Retrieved April 24, 2010, from http://www.wired.com/entertainment/music/news/2005/07/68332.

Meyers, M. (2006, January 18). Tech plays supporting role at Sundance festival. *CNET News.com*. Retrieved April 24, 2010, from http://news.com.com/Tech+plays+supporting+role+at+Sundance+festival/2101-1025_3-6028354.html.

Schedeen, J. (2010, April 23). The history of 3D movie tech. *IGN*. Retrieved April 24, 2010, from http://gear.ign.com/articles/108/1085907p1.html.

Key Points Review

1. *List the essential IS infrastructure components and describe why they are necessary for satisfying an organization's informational needs.* Modern organizations heavily rely on IS infrastructure; its components include hardware, software, communications and collaboration, data and knowledge, and human resources. While the computing hardware is integral to an organization's IS infrastructure, as it is also needed to store and process organizational data, networking hardware is needed to connect the different systems to allow for collaboration and information sharing. IS hardware is classified into three types: input, processing, and output technologies. Input hardware consists of devices used to enter information into a computer. Processing hardware transforms inputs into outputs. The CPU is the device that performs this transformation, with the help of several other closely related devices that store and recall data. Finally, output-related hardware focuses on delivering information in a usable format to users. Software assists organizations in executing their business processes and competitive strategy. Consequently, with increased reliance on information systems for managing organizations, effectively utilizing software resources is becoming increasingly critical and complex. Systems software is the collection of programs that form the foundation for the basic operations of the computer hardware. The most prominent type of systems software, the operating system, coordinates the interaction between hardware devices (e.g., the CPU and the monitor), peripherals (e.g., printers), application software (e.g., office programs), and users. Application software allows the user to perform specific tasks, such as writing business letters, analyzing data, or processing payroll. Communication and collaboration is one of the reasons why information systems have become so powerful and important to modern organizations. As with human communication, a computer network needs senders, receivers, transmission media, and protocols. The most widely used network is the Internet, which is composed of networks that are developed and maintained by many different entities. The World Wide Web provides a graphical user interface to the Internet by using HTML documents called Web pages containing hyperlinks to other pages. Data and knowledge are probably among the most important assets an organization has, as data and knowledge are essential for both gaining business intelligence and executing business processes. Organizations store massive amounts of data for operational, backup, or archival purposes. A database is a collection of related data organized in a way that facilitates data searches and can be key to an organization's success.

2. *Discuss managerial issues associated with managing an organization's IS infrastructure.* Radical advances in information technology have opened many opportunities for organizations but have also brought about challenges. Advances in hardware have enabled advances in software. Hardware and software obsolescence presents issues such as when and how to upgrade the current infrastructure. Further, organization's storage needs are growing at an ever-increasing pace. The increasing need for both computing power and storage fuels an increasing demand for energy, which can affect a company's image as well as its bottom line. Increased technology use often requires additional and more sophisticated equipment that requires dedicated facilities for ensuring uninterrupted operation of the various infrastructure components. These facilities can be large and expensive to build and maintain, especially for fast-growing companies where predicting the right number of servers and other capabilities is often difficult. Finally, organizations have to deal with fluctuations in demand for computing power while often being unable to quickly scale the IS infrastructure accordingly.

3. *Describe current trends that can help an organization address IS infrastructure–related challenges.* To cope with the ever-increasing complexity of managing the IS infrastructure, organizations can draw on various new technologies and services. Major IT service providers have introduced utility computing as a business model to address fluctuating computing needs by

"renting" resources on an as-needed basis. Cloud computing uses a utility computing business model, where customers can draw on a variety of computing resources that can be accessed on demand, with minimal human interaction. Characteristics of cloud computing include on-demand self-service, rapid elasticity, ubiquitous network access, resource pooling, and measured service. Typical cloud computing service models are software as a service, platform as a service, and infrastructure as a service. Other applications in the cloud include grid computing for solving large-scale problems and edge computing for providing a more decentralized use of resources. The convergence of computing and telecommunications has helped organizations address their diverse communication needs, such as by enabling voice over IP or videoconferencing over IP. Finally, a recent trend is green computing, as companies realize potential cost savings and a positive effect on the company's image by implementing ways to reduce energy consumption and waste.

Key Terms

Advanced Research Projects Agency Network (ARPANET) 113
application software 105
bandwidth 110
campus area network 113
central processing unit (CPU) 102
client 112
computer networking 110
database 109
database management system 109
dedicated grid 130
Defense Advanced Research Projects Agency 113
digitize 102
domain name 115
edge computing 130
embedded system 107
flash drive 102
Gopher 115
green computing 133
grid computing 129
hard drive 102
hyperlink 115
hypertext 115
Hypertext Markup Language (HTML) 115
Hypertext Transfer Protocol (HTTP) 115
information systems infrastructure 100
infrastructure 99
infrastructure as a service (IaaS) 126
input technologies 102

Internet 113
IP address 114
IP convergence 131
IP datagram 114
local area network 113
mainframe 108
metropolitan area network 113
microcomputer 108
microprocessor 102
Moore's Law 119
National Science Foundation 113
National Science Foundation Network 113
network 112
nonvolatile memory 102
open source software 105
operating system 102
optical disk 102
output technologies 102
packet switching 113
peer 112
peer-to-peer networks 112
personal area network 113
planned obsolescence 119
platform as a service (PaaS) 126
primary storage 102
private branch exchange 113
private cloud 126
processing technologies 102
protocols 110
public cloud 126
random-access memory (RAM) 102
router 114

scalability 123
secondary storage 102
server 108
server-centric network 112
service-level agreement 127
software 102
software as a service (SaaS) 125
supercomputer 108
systems software 102
top-level domain 115
Transmission Control Protocol/Internet Protocol (TCP/IP) 114
transmission media 110
Uniform Resource Locator (URL) 115
utility computing 122
videoconferencing over IP 132
virtual machine 123
virtualization 123
voice over IP (VoIP) 132
volatile memory 102
Web browser 114
Web page 115
Web server 115
Web site 115
Wi-Fi network (wireless fidelity) 113
wide area network 113
wireless local area network (WLAN) 113
workstation 108
World Wide Web 114

Review Questions

1. IS hardware is classified into what major types?
2. In one paragraph, explain how a computer works.
3. Describe the difference between systems software and application software.
4. How is quality in open source software ensured?
5. Describe the different types of computers and their key distinguishing characteristics.
6. For which purposes are data stored in organizations?
7. How does computer networking work?
8. What are the major types of networks?
9. What is the World Wide Web, and what is its relationship to the Internet?
10. What are URLs, and why are they important to the World Wide Web?

11. What are the problems associated with software obsolescence?
12. Describe the characteristics of the cloud computing model.
13. What is the difference between SaaS, PaaS, and IaaS?
14. Define grid computing and describe its advantages and disadvantages.
15. Describe what is meant by the term "IP convergence."
16. Describe why green computing has become so important to modern organizations.

Self-Study Questions

1. All of the following are examples of nonvolatile memory except
   A. optical disks
   B. hard drives
   C. flash drives
   D. RAM

2. Which of the following is *not* an example of open source software?
   A. Windows 7
   B. OpenOffice
   C. Apache
   D. Linux

3. Engineering drawings are typically prepared using _____.
   A. mainframes
   B. servers
   C. microcomputers
   D. workstations

4. Tape drives are typically used for _____.
   A. storing operational data
   B. backing up critical data
   C. maintaining customer records
   D. archiving data

5. Which of the following is the protocol of the Internet?
   A. URL
   B HTML
   C. TCP/IP
   D. ARPA

6. All of the following are correct domain suffixes except
   A. edu—educational institutions
   B. gov—U.S. government
   C. neo—network organizations
   D. com—commercial businesses

7. The ability to adapt to increases or decreases in demand for processing or storage is referred to as _____.
   A. adaptability
   B. flexibility
   C. scalability
   D. agility

8. In cloud computing, services are typically offered using _____.
   A. private clouds
   B. heterogeneous grids
   C. a utility computing model
   D. edge computing

9. For most flexibility in the use of computing resources, companies choose a _____ provider.
   A. utility computing
   B. software as a service
   C. platform as a service
   D. infrastructure as a service

10. Large-scale computing problems can be solved using _____ computing.
    A. grid
    B. utility
    C. cloud
    D. edge

Answers are on page 139.

Problems and Exercises

1. Match the following terms with the appropriate definitions:
   i. Utility computing
   ii. Output technologies
   iii. Systems software
   iv. Software as a service
   v. Voice over IP
   vi. Cloud computing
   vii. Bandwidth
   viii. Server
   ix. Planned obsolescence
   x. Virtualization

   a. The incorporation of a life span into the design of a product
   b. The use of Internet technology for placing telephone calls
   c. A cloud computing model in which the customer uses an application provided via a cloud infrastructure
   d. A model for enabling convenient, on-demand network access to a shared pool of configurable computing resources
   e. Any computer on a network that makes access to files, printing, communications, and other services available to users of the network
   f. The transmission capacity of a computer or communications channel
   g. A business model where computing resources are rented on an as-needed basis
   h. Technology used to deliver information to the user in a usable format
   i. The collection of programs that control the basic operations of computer hardware
   j. The use of specialized software to allow multiple virtual machines to be run on one single computer

2. Go visit a computer shop or look on the Web for mice or touch pads. What is new about how these input devices look, or how they are used? What are some of the advantages and disadvantages of each device?

3. What happens when a computer runs out of RAM? Can more RAM be added? Is there a limit? Why is RAM so important in today's modern IS world? Search the Web for RAM retailers. Compare their prices and options.

4. How do software programs affect your life? Give examples of software from areas other than desktop computers. Are the uses for software increasing over time?

5. Interview an IS professional and ask him or her about open source software. Does he or she see all types of information systems to be candidates for open source software? Additionally, find out what systems are most likely and least likely to be open source.

6. Using the Web, find information about archiving your data. What options are available? What are the advantages and disadvantages of each option?

7. Scan the popular press and/or the Web for clues concerning emerging technologies for computer networking. This may include new uses for current technologies or new technologies altogether. Discuss as a group the "hot" issues. Do you feel they will become a reality in the near future? Why or why not? Prepare a 10-minute presentation of your findings to be given to the class.

8. Do you have your own Web site with a specific domain name? How did you decide on the domain name? If you don't have your own domain, research possibilities of obtaining one. Would your preferred name be available? Why might your preferred name not be available?

9. How does hardware and software obsolescence affect your life? Give examples of experiences with outdated hardware or software. How did you deal with these situations?

10. Using information on the Web, find (or try to estimate) your computer's energy consumption. What are ways to decrease your computer's energy consumption?

11. Research the Web for an example of a start-up using a cloud infrastructure. What were the main reasons for choosing a cloud infrastructure? What alternatives did the start-up have?

12. Are you using any services offered in the cloud? If so, what service model is offered by your provider? If not, what are your primary reasons for not using services offered in the cloud?

13. Interview an IS professional and ask him or her about cloud computing. Does he or she have a preference for public versus private clouds? Additionally, find out what data he or she would most likely entrust to a public cloud.

14. Research the Web for service-level agreements of two different providers of cloud services and compare these based on availability, security, and privacy. How do the agreements differ? Are the agreements reasonable? Which provider would you select for your cloud infrastructure if you were to start a company?

15. Using a search engine, enter the key phrase "voice over IP providers." Who are the large vendors in this industry? What type of solutions do they offer to their clients? Does any vendor suit your communication needs?

Application Exercises

Note: The existing data files referenced in these exercises are available on the Student Companion Web site: **www.pearsonhighered.com/valacich**.

Spreadsheet Application:
Tracking Frequent-Flier Mileage

You have recently landed a part-time job as a business analyst for Campus Travel. In your first meeting, the operations manager learned that you are taking an introductory MIS class. As the manager is not very proficient in using office software tools, he is doing all frequent-flier mileage in two separate Excel workbooks. One is the customer's contact information, and the second is the miles flown. Being familiar with the possibilities of spreadsheet applications, you suggest setting up one workbook to handle both functions. To complete this, you must do the following:

1. Open the spreadsheet frequentflier2.csv. You will see a tab for customers and a tab labeled "miles flown."

2. Use the vlookup function to enter the miles flown column by looking up the frequent-flier number (Hint: If

done correctly with absolute references, you should be able to enter the vlookup formula in the first cell in the "miles flown" column and copy it down for all the cells.)

3. Use conditional formatting to highlight all frequent fliers who have less than 4,000 total miles.

4. Finally, sort the frequent fliers by total miles in descending order and print out the spreadsheet.

Database Application:
Building a Knowledge Database

Campus Travel seems to be growing quite rapidly. Now they have franchises in three different states, totaling 16 locations. As the company has grown tremendously over the past few years, it has become increasingly difficult to keep track of the areas of expertise of each travel consultant; often, consultants waste valuable time trying to find out who in the company possesses the knowledge about a particular region. Impressed with your skills, the general manager of Campus Travel has asked you to add, modify, and delete the following records from its employee database:

1. Open employeedata.mdb.

2. Select the "employee" tab.

3. Add the following records:

    a. Eric Tang, Spokane Office, Expert in Southwest, Phone (509)555-2311

    b. Janna Connell, Spokane Office, Expert in Delta, Phone (509)555-1144

4. Delete the following record:

    a. Carl Looney from the Pullman office

5. Modify the following:

    a. Change Frank Herman from the Pullman office to the Spokane office

    b. Switch Ramon Sanchez's home number to (208)549-2544

Team Work Exercise: Your Personal Communication Infrastructure Assessment

Work in a team of four or five students and have each person list his or her number of wired telephone calls, cellular telephone calls, instant messages, e-mail messages, and so on. For each instance, also inventory the total time spent, who the call was to, and the purpose of the call. Have each person also document his or her demographic and relevant personal information (e.g., age, gender, relationship status, children, and so on). Combine the results of all team members and discuss patterns and anomalies.

Answers to the Self-Study Questions

1. D, p. 102
2. A, p. 105
3. D, p. 108
4. D, p. 109
5. C, p. 114
6. C, p. 115
7. C, p. 123
8. C, p. 123
9. D, p. 126
10. A, p. 129

Case 1

FarmVille, Mafia Wars, Etc.: The Infrastructure Behind Social Games

Since its initial launch in 2004, Facebook has become the world's largest social network, helping people to communicate with friends, family members, or coworkers. In addition to communication capabilities (such as a feature that allows posting "status updates," a chat system, or photo albums), users can access a variety of third-party applications developed using Facebook's own development platform. Interestingly, a category of applications that has become hugely popular is social network games, such as FarmVille, Mafia Wars, or Restaurant City. Social network games are typically asynchronous, multiplayer games, where users tend a farm, build up a mafia clan, or own and manage a virtual restaurant, all while interacting with their online social network.

San Francisco–based game developer Zynga has become one of the most important players in this market, having developed games such as Mafia Wars, FarmVille, FishVille, and Cafe World; in fact, six out of the seven most popular social games were developed by Zynga. Although joining the games is free, social network games are big business. Game developers make revenue through advertising or through the sale of relatively cheap game tokens (such as a special menu item for one's restaurant, sold for a few dollars or less) to large numbers of players. With 240 million users playing Zynga games every day, the company is estimated to be worth between $2.8 billion and $5 billion.

Zynga's flagship game, FarmVille, grew from 1 million daily users after four days to 10 million daily users after just 60 days; nine months after launch, 75 million people logged in to FarmVille each month. On FarmVille, users can grow crops and trees, raise animals, build barns and fences, and so on. Fields need to be plowed and crops sowed and harvested before they wither, forcing the user to log in to the game frequently. Successful farmers advance and receive "ribbons" that are announced in their Facebook news feed. Periodically, players receive game tokens (such as a mailbox, a flagpole, or a stray animal) that they can give away to their friends who also have a virtual farm; users can also buy game tokens if they want to add nicer features to their farms without having to wait for free tokens. In 2010, there were 30 million farms with 38 million horse stables (and many more horses) on FarmVille, compared with 2 million farms and 9 million horses in the entire United States. At times, Zynga sells limited edition game tokens for a good cause; in early 2010, Zynga raised more than $1.5 million for victims of the Haiti earthquake in just five days.

Comparable to other Web applications, response time is critical for social network games, as time lags in the game's response can quickly kill a player's gaming experience. Further, the introduction of new features (such as new game tokens being offered) often cause spikes in user activity. Hence, supporting a successful social network game requires an IS infrastructure that is solid, responsive, and highly scalable. In addition, social network games place further demands on an IS infrastructure; most Web sites primarily serve content to the user and are thus very "read intensive." In contrast, social network games are "write intensive"; that is, a large amount of data are written to the games' underlying databases. Whenever a player plants a new crop, builds a windmill, moves a fence, or milks a cow, an object changes its state or a new object is created; all these actions have to be properly stored so as to avoid objects colliding or other "illegal" maneuvers. Overall, FarmVille's read-to-write ratio is three to one, which is considered incredibly high.

To support this demand, Zynga uses a cloud computing architecture. Using Amazon EC2, Zynga deploys more than a thousand servers for FarmVille alone. To flexibly deal with changes in demand, Zynga uses a cloud management platform that automatically adds or removes servers based on predetermined parameters, such as when to start scaling or how fast to add or remove resources.

For Facebook, popular social games create synergies: These games entice people to log in to Facebook several times during the day, thus helping to drive advertising revenue; in addition, Facebook receives a share of the game developers' revenues from advertising or the sale of game tokens. However, this relationship is not always happy. Initially, social games could easily post notifications to a player's Facebook news feed, enticing the player to come back and advertising its presence to the player's friends. However, with an increasing number of games and players, many Facebook users have become increasingly annoyed with feeds about someone's lost duck or someone receiving yet another FarmVille ribbon. In 2010, Facebook has modified the way news feeds are presented, allowing users to easily block notices from unwanted applications. Whereas this was seen as a blessing for many users, this hampered an important marketing channel for social network game developers. As the relationship between Facebook and Zynga has deteriorated, inside sources have hinted at the possibility of Zynga launching its own platform dedicated only to social gaming. Relatedly, industry observers indicated that Zynga has leased space in a major data center in Virginia.

Questions

1. What will be the future of social networking and social gaming?
2. Can Facebook survive without Zynga and vice versa?
3. How does leasing a data center fit into a cloud infrastructure?

Based on:

Anonymous. (n.d.). Zynga press room: Numbers. Retrieved June 7, 2010, from http://www.zynga.com/about/numbers.php.

Anonymous. (2010, January 20). Zynga players raise over $1.5 million for Haiti in five days. Retrieved June 7, 2010, from http://www.zynga.com/about/article.php?a=20100120.

Gannes, L. (2010, May 7). Facebook vs. Zynga: The turf war. *Gigaom.* Retrieved June 7, 2010, from http://gigaom.com/2010/05/07/facebook-vs-zynga-the-turf-war.

Hoff, T. (2010, February 8). How FarmVille scales to harvest 75 million players a month. *Highscalability.com.* Retrieved June 7, 2010, from http://highscalability.com/blog/2010/2/8/how-farmville-scales-to-harvest-75-million-players-a-month.html.

Ingram, M. (2010, April 6). Say what? Yes, you heard right—Zynga could be worth $5 billion. *Gigaom.* Retrieved June 7, 2010, from http://gigaom.com/2010/04/06/what-is-zynga-worth.

Miller, R. (2010, May 12). Zynga leases data center in Virginia. *Data Center Knowledge.* Retrieved June 7, 2010, from http://www.datacenterknowledge.com/archives/2010/05/12/zynga-leases-data-center-in-virginia.

Case 2

Broadband Service on Airplanes: WiFi in the Sky

Broadband connectivity is fast becoming a competitive area in the airline industry. Since many passengers on long flights don't want to be deprived of their WiFi-enabled digital devices, the industry is rushing to comply.

Although many airlines just recently started advertising such services, the concept isn't new. Already between 2004 and 2006, Boeing tried offering broadband service to passengers through its service called Connexion by Boeing. The infrastructure for the system included phased array antennae or mechanically steered Ku-band antennae on the aircraft, leased satellite transponders, and ground stations located in Vancouver, British Columbia; Russia; Switzerland; the United States; and Japan. However, following the terrorist attacks of September 11, 2001, many U.S. domestic carriers faced severe financial difficulties and could not justify the costs associated with installing Connexion's systems. Thus, Connexion was launched internationally, and the first airline to use the service in 2004 was Lufthansa German Airlines. Signing up later in 2004 were ANA, Japan Airlines, and SAS. In 2005, airlines contracting for the service included China Airlines, Singapore Airlines, Asiana Airlines, Korean Air, El-Al Israel Airlines, and Etihad Airlines. In 2005, Connexion by Boeing added the first live streaming TV service on Singapore Airlines.

Costs to passengers using Connexion were $9.95 for one hour of access, $14.95 for less than three hours of access, $19.95 for three to six hours of access, and $29.95 for unlimited access. Despite indications supported by Boeing's market research, Boeing's broadband service was not as popular with passengers as anticipated, and Connexion was discontinued in 2006.

In 2008, broadband service was again positioned to take off, and Alaska, American, Southwest and Virgin America Airlines all announced that they would launch broadband access to flight passengers within a few months. Alaska and Southwest Airlines tested the use of satellite-based services via California-based Row 44. American and Virgin America Airlines would use a cell phone tower system from Illinois-based Aircell.

The two types of broadband service to be offered included the following:

- *Aircell Cell Phone Towers.* Ninety-two existing cell towers covering the entire continental United States relay data from tower to tower. Coverage is good, but as of 2010, the system only worked in the lower 48 states, with planned expansion to Canada, Mexico, and the Caribbean.

- *Row 44 Satellite Service.*
Geosynchronous satellites generate signals, and the system can work across international borders and over oceans but was offered at first only over North America. Passengers can expect to log on via lower-end DSL speeds.

As of 2010, Wi-Fi in the sky has become common among domestic carriers in the United States and is one of the key battlegrounds for attracting new passengers and keeping them loyal. Air Tran, Delta, JetBlue, US Airways, and Virgin America, as well as Southwest, Alaska, American, and United Airlines, all offer some form of wireless connectivity during flight. Some of the carriers provide Wi-Fi on all their planes, while others are in various stages of installation. Pricing for use of the service depends on the length of the flight, the type of device you are using (whether it is a laptop or a mobile device), and the carrier's Wi-Fi provider.

Aircell's cellular ground-based "Gogo" service has been installed on over 700 aircraft and is being used by most domestic airlines. It costs an airline company around $100,000 per plane to install the system. Customers using Gogo pay for the service in increments by flight hour. For instance, Internet access costs $5.95 for flights shorter than 1.5 hours, $9.95 for flights of 1.5 to 3 hours, and $12.95 for flights longer than 3 hours. Customers can also buy a single-airline 24-hour pass for $12.95, and frequent flyers can buy a single-airline monthly pass for $49.95. The costs also vary by device type being used. Users with

mobile and handheld devices will pay slightly less than those using laptops.

Row44's satellite service is currently being installed in Southwest's entire fleet of aircraft, with completion being scheduled for late 2010. Alaska Airlines announced after initial tests that it would not use Row 44's service; rather, Alaska is currently outfitting its aircraft with Gogo's technology because of lower costs, ease of installation, and the company's proven track record (Gogo agreed to install additional cell towers to provide service on Alaska's most important routes to and from Alaska). Current prices for connectivity on Southwest range from $5, $8, to $10 for laptops and $2, $4, to $6 for mobile devices, depending on the length of the flight.

JetBlue Airlines and several other airlines are bringing Wi-Fi connectivity to passengers through a satellite-based system offered by JetBlue's subsidiary LiveTV. Conventionally used to give passengers their choice of several television options, LiveTV is now offering a Wi-Fi option as well. JetBlue is already offering the service on many of their planes and at no additional charge to passengers.

Questions remain about if and how airlines will manage Internet content while in flight. Many airlines have chosen to block pornographic or other offensive sites, while other carriers have decided to leave the filtering to the user. One airline has gone as far to say that passengers are responsible for their surfing habits just as they are responsible for what books, magazines, and movies they bring on board.

Hoping to start using the plane's Wi-Fi connection to Skype with your friends and

get around that pesky "no cell phone use" while in the air? Not so fast—the Federal Communications Commission (FCC) has already banned the use of VoIP for in-flight communications. In the meantime, the European Commission has lifted the cell phone ban aboard aircraft in European airspace. Other areas of the world have followed suit. As of 2010, four continents allow cell phone use in flight. Ryanair, Qantas, Malaysia, Emirates, and Royal Jordanian Airlines all allow cell phone use on board. Other carriers, like Qatar Airways, Hong Kong Airlines, and British Airways, are planning on having cell service available by the end of 2010. Although it has been determined that cell phone signals don't interfere with a plane's instrumentation, their use is prohibited in the United States while planes are in flight because of possible annoyance of other passengers. The last time the FCC brought up the subject of allowing cell phone use on planes, they were met with fierce resistance from frequent fliers and the largest flight attendants' union. In fact, there is legislation working its way through Congress called the Halting Airplane Noise to Give Us Peace Act. The "Hang Up" Act would ban all voice communications on wireless devices during commercial flights.

After a few stumbles, it appears that Wi-Fi in the sky is here to stay. Airline Wi-Fi services will undoubtedly continue to improve as Wi-Fi devices become more ubiquitous. Whether voice services for airline passengers will come to North America remains to be seen.

Questions

1. How much would you be willing to pay for Wi-Fi access in the sky? Under which circumstances would you be willing to pay a higher price?
2. How do you feel about cell phone use during the flight? Would you switch to or abandon carriers if cell phone use were allowed on one but not the other? Why?
3. Do you think that using the Internet or cell phones creates any security problems on a flight? Why or why not?

Based on:

Anonymous. (n.d.). Lessons from the failure of Connexion-by-Boeing. Retrieved June 8, 2010, from http://www.tmfassociates.com/LessonsfromConnexion.pdf.

Anonymous. (2008, January 29). JetBlue providing WIFI/TV for other airlines? *Techdirt*. Retrieved June 8, 2010, from http://www.techdirt.com/articles/20080129/141951112.shtml.

Anonymous. (2008, April 7). Europe clears mobiles on aircraft. *BBC News*. Retrieved June 8, 2010, from http://news.bbc.co.uk/2/hi/technology/7334372.stm.

Anonymous. (2010, January 22). Gogo gets $176 million for in-flight Wi-Fi. *New York Times*. Retrieved June 8, 2010, from http://dealbook.blogs.nytimes.com/2010/01/22/gogo-lands-176-million-as-in-flight-wi-fi-takes-off.

Gammon, K. (2008, April 21). Coming this summer: Fly the Wi-Fi skies. *Wired*. Retrieved June 8, 2010, from http://www.wired.com/techbiz/it/magazine/16-05/st_wifi.

Gardner, W. D. (2010, February 1). Southwest Airlines to offer Wi-Fi. *InformationWeek*. Retrieved June 8, 2010, from http://www.informationweek.com/news/telecom/business/showArticle.jhtml?articleID=222600648.

Hamblen, M. (2008, January 23). Southwest, American test inflight Wi-Fi. *Macworld*. Retrieved June 8, 2010, from http://www.macworld.com/article/131781/2008/01/wifi.html.

Lawson, S. (2010, February 25). Alaska Airlines switches to Aircell for Wi-Fi. *PCWorld*. Retrieved June 8, 2010, from http://www.pcworld.com/businesscenter/article/190256/alaska_airlines_switches_to_aircell_for_wifi.html.

Mayerowitz, S. (2009, November 23). Airlines add Internet access: The definitive guide to navigating airplane Wi-Fi. *ABC News*. Retrieved June 8, 2010, from http://abcnews.go.com/Travel/BusinessTraveler/thanksgivng-travel-airline-wireless-internet-access-guide/story?id=8936104.

Sharkey, J. (2009, September 28). Foreign airlines ahead of U.S. on cellphone use. *New York Times*. Retrieved June 8, 2010, from http://www.nytimes.com/2009/09/29/technology/29phones.html.

four

Enabling Commerce Using the Internet

Preface

This chapter focuses on electronic commerce (e-commerce, or EC), explaining how companies conduct business with customers, business partners, and suppliers over the Internet. The Internet and World Wide Web are extremely well suited for conducting business electronically on a global basis. Web-based e-commerce has introduced unprecedented opportunities for the marketing of products and services, accompanied by features, functionality, and innovative methods to serve and support consumers, business partners, and suppliers. With e-commerce representing a growing proportion of overall retail sales and business-to-business exchanges, an understanding of e-commerce can be a powerful tool in your arsenal. People with e-commerce skills are in high demand in the marketplace; therefore, the more you know about e-commerce, the more valuable you will become.

Managing in the Digital World: Businesses Get Social

Social media sites have become regular destinations for many Web users. Catching the latest YouTube video, "friending" someone on Facebook, "following" someone on Twitter, or updating a professional profile on LinkedIn are typical activities for personal interaction with these and other social media outlets. People use social media for a variety of reasons, be it keeping up with friends and family in their social network, expressing themselves on a particular subject, scheduling events, or simply finding entertainment.

However, social media are no longer just being used by private individuals to tell the world about their new pet or show pictures from their graduation. From local coffee shops to global conglomerates, *businesses* are going social. By tapping into the powerful and far-reaching networks that social media sites can provide, companies are now armed with powerful tools to get their business name and brand out in front of the public quickly, at a much lower cost than traditional marketing methods. A successful social media presence can quickly build a business's reputation, increase trust with their customers, and grow their bottom line.

Businesses and companies of all shapes and sizes are racing to establish and promote themselves within social media networks. Those that already have a business presence continue to build and refine it as social media trends and sites evolve. Through a social media presence, both loyal and potential customers can get a more transparent and personal look at the company, interact with employees, and leave feedback about products and services. Businesses are able to leverage these platforms to attract new customers, build a following of loyal fans, generate potential contacts, build relationships, and create buzz about future events and products. Social media takes word of mouth and spreads it like wildfire through Internet and mobile connections. Traditional advertising and press releases are now being accompanied and sometimes replaced by social media posts bringing instantaneous information to customers and business watchers.

Although using social networking can save companies money on their traditional marketing and advertising budgets, it is not free. Keeping content fresh and updated takes time, and in business, time is money. Often, a business has to designate a dedicated person or team to work at keeping multiple social media outlets up to date. It's easier for large businesses with traditional marketing departments to dedicate staff to the task than it is for small businesses that may have only two or three employees. Another cost that businesses must consider is the damage that can be done to the company when a poor choice of words, an unpopular stance, or a rogue employee's rant is posted in a blog or disseminated through other outlets. Just as good word of

Shutterstock

FIGURE 4.1

Coca-Cola is using social media to connect with customers.

mouth can build up a company's reputation quickly, bad word of mouth can destroy it even quicker.

Nevertheless, many large companies are seeing the value of social media pay off and are investing heavily through their marketing departments across different social media platforms. According to a 2010 study of the top Fortune 100 companies, 65 percent were using Twitter to communicate with their customers with an average of 1,500 followers per account, with many companies having several different accounts. Fifty-four percent of the companies had a Facebook presence with nearly 41,000 "fans" per account. Fifty percent of them are actively using YouTube with an average of over 38,000 subscribers per channel. Corporate blogging is also actively used, with an average of four separate blogs per company averaging seven posts per month. Overall, 86 percent of the Fortune 100 companies were using some form of social media to interact with and promote business to their customers.

Another way big companies are using social media to connect with their customers is through contests and giveaways. For example, in 2010, the Coca-Cola Company began their "Expedition 206" campaign (see Figure 4.1). In the runup to the start of the campaign, visitors to Coca-Cola's social media outlets were able to vote for three people to travel to the 206 countries where Coca-Cola products are sold. Once chosen, the three "Happiness Ambassadors" set off to take photos, make videos, and connect with people around the world, using Facebook, Twitter, blogs, and other social media to chronicle the journey. Their journey's various stopping points were already decided for them, but how they get to the destinations and what they do while there is totally up to them. Coca-Cola fans who are following the trio are able to make suggestions about where to stay, how to get there, and places to avoid—all through the social media outlets in which Coca-Cola participates.

Small businesses are also leveraging social media sites to increase visibility and expand their customer base. According to the 2010 Small Business Success Index, social media use by small business has doubled in the last year. Seventy-five percent of small businesses have a company page on a social media platform, and 61 percent use social media to identify and attract new customers. One technique many small businesses use is a public wiki page where customers can post problems they are having with a particular product. A quick response and posted solution to the problem by the business typically builds trust with customers and engenders future sales. Public wikis also allow customers to assist other users if they've had similar problems. In addition, they can leave feedback or make suggestions to the company. The result is an interactive community of users that promotes information flow and produces positive word of mouth about the business.

Although the use of social media platforms by businesses is not without some drawbacks, the advantages of getting on the social bandwagon are clear. Through strategic use of social networking, companies large and small are reaping the benefits.

After reading this chapter, you will be able to answer the following:

1. What are the pros and cons of establishing a business presence in social media outlets?
2. In what ways could social media possibly help jump-start a small company's business in a competitive market?
3. How would you forecast the future of social media as an opportunity for business?

Based on:

Anonymous. (2010, February). Small businesses use social media to pursue customers. *Marketing Charts*. Retrieved June 21, 2010, from http://www.marketingcharts.com/interactive/small-businesses-use-social-media-to-pursue-customers-12010/small-biz-success- index-highlights-feb-2010jpg.

Balwani, S. (2009, July 28). 5 easy social media wins for your small business. *Mashable.com*. Retrieved June 21, 2010, from http://mashable.com/2009/07/28/social-media-small-business.

Bloch, E. (2010, March 7). How are companies leveraging social media? *Flowtown*. Retrieved June 21, 2010, from http://www.flowtown.com/blog/how-are-companies-leveraging-social-media.

Gordhammer, S. (2009, September 22). 4 ways social media is changing business. *Mashable.com*. Retrieved June 21, 2010, from http://mashable.com/2009/09/22/social-media-business.

Warren, C. (2009, November 17). Inside Coca-Cola's social media strategy and Happiness Ambassador Program. *Mashable.com*. Retrieved June 21, 2010, from http://mashable.com/2009/11/17/coke-expedition-206.

Electronic Commerce Defined

The Internet provides a set of interconnected networks for individuals and businesses to complete transactions electronically. We define **electronic commerce (EC)** very broadly as the exchange of goods, services, and money[1] among firms, between firms and their customers, and between customers, supported by communication technologies and, in particular, the Internet. The Census Bureau of the Department of Commerce reported that while total annual retail sales in 2009 decreased by 7 percent from 2008, online retail sales were up by 2 percent and that EC accounted for 3.7 percent of total retail sales, resulting in sales of more than $134.9 billion (see Figure 4.2). Surprisingly, these figures include only traditional online retail sales and do not account for

---

[1]EC can also include the distribution of digital products, such as software, music, movies, and digital images.

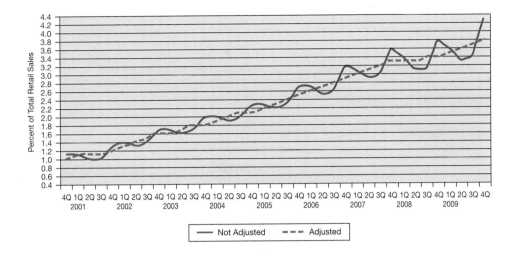

FIGURE 4.2

EC continues to grow rapidly.

Source: http://www.census.gov/mrts/www/data/html/09Q4.html.

auction sales (e.g., eBay), movie and music content rentals (e.g., iTunes or Netflix), or sales through online classifieds (e.g., Craigslist). Research firm eMarketer estimates steady growth, with online consumer sales exceeding $200 billion by 2013. Considering all online markets, it is clear that online transactions have become a major segment of the global economy. With this much money at stake, it is little wonder that no other information systems (IS) issue has captured as much attention as has EC. Although EC was being used as far back as 1948 during the Berlin Airlift (Zwass, 1996), the emergence of the Internet and Web has fueled a revolution in the manner in which products and services are marketed and sold. Their far-reaching effects have led to the creation of an electronic marketplace where a virtually limitless array of new services, features, and functionality can be offered. As a result, a presence on the Web has become a strategic necessity for most companies.

Contrary to popular belief, EC goes beyond consumers merely buying and selling products online. EC can involve the events leading up to the purchase of a product as well as customer service after the sale. Furthermore, EC is not limited to transactions between businesses and consumers, which is known as **business-to-consumer (B2C)** EC. EC is also used to conduct business with business partners such as suppliers and intermediaries. This form of EC is commonly referred to as **business-to-business (B2B)** EC. According to the U.S. Census Bureau, B2B EC is by far the largest form of EC in terms of revenues, and many firms concentrate solely on B2B EC. Further, almost all companies focusing on the B2C arena, such as the clothing and home furnishing retailer Eddie Bauer, also engage in B2B EC, such as for procurement of their inventory. Some forms of EC happen between businesses and their employees; these are referred to as **business-to-employee (B2E).** Some forms of EC do not even involve business firms, as would be the case with an online auction site such as eBay; these forms of EC are referred to as **consumer-to-consumer (C2C).** An emerging EC model that is referred to as **consumer-to-business (C2B)** is a complete reversal of the tradition B2C, where consumers offer products, labor, and services to companies. Finally, there are forms of EC that involve a country's government and its citizens (*government-to-citizen [G2C]*), businesses (*government-to-business [G2B]*), and other governments (*government-to-government [G2G]*). These basic types of EC are summarized in Table 4.1.

Furthermore, there is a wide variety of ways to conduct business in each arena. In the following section, we examine the reasons that Web-based EC is revolutionizing the way business is being done. This is followed by an in-depth analysis of how companies are utilizing EC in their daily operations.

Technological forces are driving business, and the Internet and Web have emerged as strong new agents of change. The resulting technological revolution has essentially broken down the barriers to entry, leveled the playing field, and propelled commerce into the electronic domain (Looney & Chatterjee, 2002). Companies are exploiting the capabilities of the Web to reach a wider customer base, offer a broader range of products, and develop closer relationships with customers by striving to meet their unique needs (Valacich, Parboteeah, & Wells, 2007). These wide-ranging capabilities include global information dissemination, integration, mass customization, interactive communication, collaboration, and transactional support (Chatterjee & Sambamurthy, 1999; Looney & Chatterjee, 2002; see Table 4.2).

TABLE 4.1 Types of EC

Types of EC	Description	Example
Business-to-consumer (B2C)	Transactions between businesses and their customers	A person buys a book from Amazon.com.
Business-to-business (B2B)	Transactions among businesses	A manufacturer conducts business over the Web with its suppliers.
Business-to-employee (B2E)	Transactions between businesses and their employees	An employee uses the Web to make a change to his or her health benefits.
Consumer-to-business (C2B)	Transactions between customers and businesses	A person offers his photography at shutterstock.com.
Consumer-to-consumer (C2C)	Transactions between people not necessarily working together	A person purchases some memorabilia from another person via eBay.com.
Government-to-citizen (G2C)	Transactions between a government and its citizens	A person files his or her income taxes online.
Government-to-business (G2B)	Transactions between a government and businesses	A government purchases supplies using an Internet-enabled procurement system.
Government-to-government (G2G)	Transactions among governments	A state agency reports birth and death information to the U.S. Social Security Administration using the Internet.

Internet and World Wide Web Capabilities

Information Dissemination The powerful combination of Internet and Web technologies has given rise to a global platform where firms from across the world can effectively compete for customers and gain access to new markets. EC has wide geographical potential given that many countries have at least some type of Internet access. The worldwide connectivity of the Internet enables **global information dissemination,** a relatively economical medium for firms to market their products and services over vast distances. This increased geographical reach has been facilitated by virtual storefronts that can be accessed from every Web-enabled computer in the world.

Integration Web technologies also allow for **integration** of information via Web sites that can be linked to corporate databases to provide real-time access to personalized information. No longer must customers rely on old information from printed catalogs or account statements that arrive in the mail once a month. For example, when Alaska Airlines (www.alaskaair.com) updates fare information in their corporate database, customers can access the most current fares simply by browsing the company's Web site. As with nearly every other major airline, the Web allows Alaska Airlines to disseminate real-time fare pricing. This is particularly important for

TABLE 4.2 Capabilities of the Web

Web Capability	Description	Example
Global information dissemination	Products and services can be marketed over vast distances.	Almost anyone can access Amazon.com.
Integration	Web sites can be linked to corporate databases to provide real-time access to personalized information.	Customers can check account balances at www.alaskaair.com.
Mass customization	Firms can tailor their products and services to meet a customer's particular needs.	Customers can build their own messenger bag on www.timbuk2.com.
Interactive communication	Companies can communicate with customers, improving their image of responsiveness.	Customers can receive real-time computer support from www.geeksquad.com.
Collaboration	Different departments of a company can use the Web to collaborate.	Virgin Megastores uses a collaboration site to improve managers' efficiency.
Transactional support	Clients and businesses can conduct business online without human support.	Customers can build and purchase their own PC online without human interaction on www.dell.com.

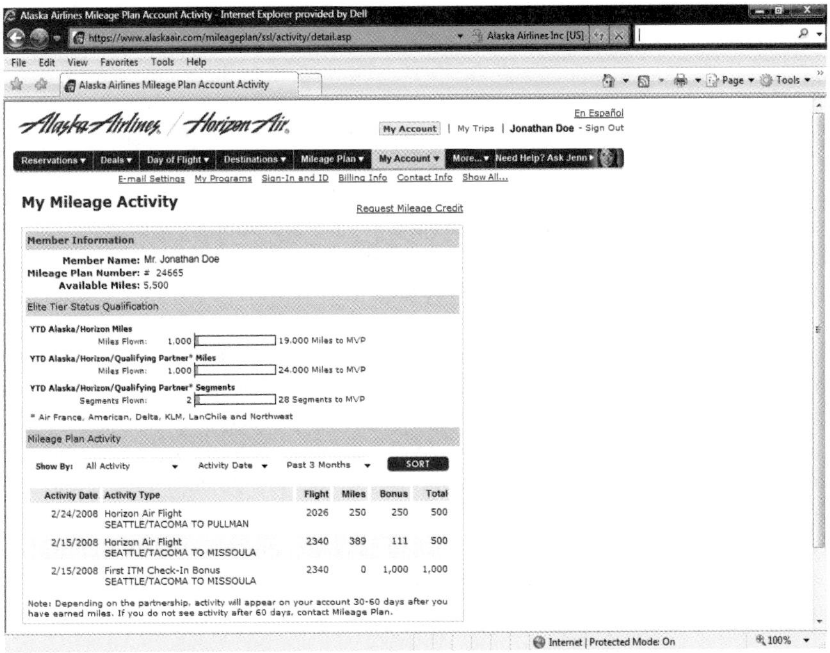

FIGURE 4.3

Alaska Airlines' mileage plan Web site.

Source: Used with permission of Alaska Airlines.

companies operating in highly competitive environments such as the air transport industry. Furthermore, Alaska Airlines offers their valued customers the ability to check the balances of their frequent-flier accounts, linking customers to information stored on the firm's corporate database (see Figure 4.3). Customers do not have to wait for monthly statements to see if they are eligible for travel benefits and awards.

Mass Customization Web technologies are also helping firms realize their goal of mass customization. **Mass customization** helps firms tailor their products and services to meet a customer's particular needs on a large scale. For instance, bag manufacturer Timbuk2 (www.Timbuk2.com) has developed an application called Custom Messenger Bag Builder, which allows customers to create a virtual bag that is modeled just for them (see Figure 4.4). Customers can configure the virtual bag

FIGURE 4.4

Timbuk2 bags can be customized in a variety of ways.

Butler Photography

based on a number of criteria, such as size, use (e.g., for carrying a laptop), colors, accessories, and even fabrics. The virtual model application also assists Timbuk2 in tracking customers' preferred styles and colors, allowing them to target marketing efforts to individual customers.

Interactive Communication   **Interactive communication** via the Web enables firms to build customer loyalty by providing immediate communication and feedback to and from customers, and this can dramatically improve the firm's image through demonstrated responsiveness. Many firms have augmented telephone-based ordering and customer support with Web-based applications and electronic mail. In many cases, online chat applications are provided to allow customers to communicate with a customer service representative in real time through the corporate Web site.

Best Buy, for example, has entered into the computer repair and support business with their Geek Squad brand (see Figure 4.5). Traditionally, customers having computer problems would have to take their computer to a Best Buy store for repair. Geek Squad online (www.geeksquad .com) has implemented a feature whereby customers can contact customer support representatives at any time of the day to receive real-time online support. Support options include operating system diagnostics, software installation issues, and computer optimization. Interactive communication agents aid the customers online in real time. This feature allows the customer service agent to walk the customer through the troubleshooting process step-by-step while the customer is at home. This customer-driven approach far outdistances traditional, nonelectronic means in terms of tailoring and timeliness.

Transaction Support   By providing ways for clients and firms to conduct business online without human assistance, the Internet and Web have greatly reduced transaction costs while enhancing operational efficiency. Many companies, such as Dell Computer Corporation, are utilizing the Web to provide automated **transaction support** (see Figure 4.6). Dell began selling computers on the Web in mid-1996. By early 1998, Dell was experiencing around $2 million in online sales per day. Dell derives about 90 percent of its overall revenues from sales to medium-sized and large businesses, yet more than half its Web-based sales have been from individuals and small businesses that typically buy one computer at a time. As a result, Dell is experiencing significant cost savings per sale by reducing the demand for phone representatives on the smaller purchases. Individual customers can access product information anytime from anywhere, benefiting not only the end consumer but also Dell. Customer service representatives can focus on lucrative corporate customers, reducing labor costs involved in servicing small-ticket items.

FIGURE 4.5

Geek Squad offers 24-hour computer support.

Joshua Lutz/Redux Pictures

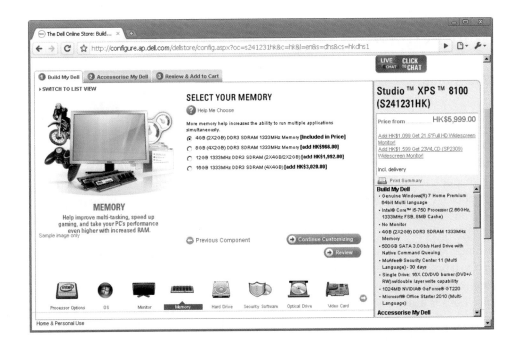

By streamlining operations and greatly increasing sales through both online and traditional channels, Dell has grown into one of the world's largest personal computer manufacturers, with revenue exceeding $61 billion for fiscal year 2009. This phenomenon of cutting out the "middleman" and reaching customers more directly and efficiently is known as **disintermediation.** Disintermediation creates both opportunities and challenges. While disintermediation allows producers or service providers to offer products at lower prices (or reap greater profits), they also have to take on those activities previously performed by the middleman. For example, when airlines started selling tickets online and dealing directly with customers, they disintermediated travel agents. To make up for this lost revenue, travel agents now charge booking fees when arranging a person's travel. In contrast, **reintermediation** refers to the design of business models that reintroduce middlemen in order to reduce the chaos brought on by disintermediation. For example, without middlemen like Travelocity.com, Orbitz.com, and other travel Web sites, a consumer would have to check all airline Web sites in order to find the flight with the best connection or lowest price.

EC Business Strategies

Given the vast capabilities of the Internet, the Web has transformed traditional business operations into a hypercompetitive electronic marketplace. Companies must strategically position themselves to compete in the new EC environment. At one extreme, companies following a **brick-and-mortar business strategy** choose to operate solely in the traditional physical markets. These companies approach business activities in a traditional manner by operating physical locations such as department stores, business offices, or manufacturing plants. In other words, the brick-and-mortar business strategy does not include EC. In contrast, companies following a **click-only business strategy** (i.e., **virtual companies**) conduct business electronically in cyberspace. These firms have no physical store locations, allowing them to focus purely on EC. An example of a click-only company might be the popular eBay.com trading and exchange Web site, which does not have a physical storefront in the classic sense. In e-business terminology, click-only companies are sometimes called "pure play companies," focusing on one very distinct way of doing business; other firms choose to straddle the two environments, operating in both physical and virtual arenas. These firms employ a **click-and-mortar business strategy** approach (also referred to as the **bricks-and-clicks business strategy**). The three general approaches are depicted in Figure 4.7 (Looney & Chatterjee, 2002).

WHEN THINGS GO WRONG

Apple Versus Adobe

The mobile Web is becoming more and more popular as the number of smart phones and handheld devices proliferates. Users can now have maps, music, and rich Internet content at their fingertips no matter where they happen to be. One of the champions in popularizing the mobile Web has been Apple, with their ubiquitous iPhones, iPods, and iPads taking a significant share of the market.

However, an important part of the Internet has been inaccessible to Apple's mobile customers. For proprietary reasons, Apple's mobile products have never been capable of displaying content developed using Adobe Flash. Flash is a multimedia platform that allows developers to add animation, video, and sound to Web pages, enabling many of the Web capabilities used by companies operating in the digital world. Popular video sites like YouTube and Hulu use flash to deliver their content. Many advertisements, games, and Web site "splash screens" also utilize Flash. Apple iPhone users, however, simply see a Lego-block icon where the flash content should be when accessing it through their mobile Safari browser.

Apple and Adobe have had a shaky relationship over the need for Flash support on Apple's products. Adobe has released Flash for mobile platforms for several of Apple's competitors in the mobile market but has not been able to develop a version of Flash that Apple would be happy with. Claiming that Flash software poses security and performance threats (such as shortened battery life) to its products, Apple has refused to integrate support for Flash into its mobile products. Apple's chief executive officer (CEO), Steve Jobs, was even reported to have said in a private meeting that Adobe developers were "lazy." In the meantime, Apple's customers have watched from the sidelines, frustrated with the software limitation that blocks them from a significant portion of the Web and hoping for a solution to the problem.

The hopes of a Flash-enabled product were shattered in the spring of 2010, when Jobs went public about his dissatisfaction with Adobe's product. Through a blog post, he related a list of philosophical and technical problems he had with Flash. Among them, Jobs stated that Flash was made for the PC and was not suited for the mobile Web and touch interfaces. He also accused Adobe of making Flash a "proprietary" product and encouraged the abandonment of Flash for open standards.

At about the same time as Jobs was publicly downplaying Flash, Adobe announced it would no longer be developing a Flash alternative for Apple's mobile devices. A few days after Job's post, Adobe also announced it would be distributing free Google Android–powered phones (that just happen to run the latest mobile version of Flash) to its employees to promote the use of Flash on the mobile Web. In May 2010, Adobe went into the offensive and started a "We Love Apple" campaign, arguing that Adobe would promote openness and choice. So far, there seems to be a stalemate between the two companies, and the users may be the ones ultimately losing out.

Based on:

Abell, J. (2010, April 29). Steve Jobs claims Flash will kill the mobile Web. *Wired*. Retrieved May 1, 2010, from http://www.wired.com/epicenter/2010/04/steve-jobs-blog-post-flash.

Adobe Flash. (2010, June 16). In *Wikipedia, the free encyclopedia.* Retrieved June 17, 2010, from http://en.wikipedia.org/w/index.php?title=Adobe_Flash&oldid=368356885.

Holwerda, T. (2010, May 13). Adobe launches "We Love Apple" campaign. *OSnews.com.* Retrieved June 22, 2010, from http://www.osnews.com/story/23291/Adobe_Launches_We_Love_Apple_Campaign.

Krazit, T. (2010, April 30). Free Android phones coming to Adobe employees. *CNET NEWS.com.* Retrieved May 1, 2010, from http://news.cnet.com/8301-1035_3-20003922-94.html.

The Click-and-Mortar Strategy The greatest impact of the Web-based EC revolution has occurred in companies adopting the click-and-mortar approach. Click-and-mortars continue to operate their physical locations and have added the EC component to their business activities. With transactions occurring in both physical and virtual environments, it is imperative that click-and-mortars learn how to fully maximize commercial opportunities in both domains. Conducting physical and virtual operations presents special challenges for these firms, as business activities must be tailored to each of these different environments in order for the firms to compete effectively.

Another challenge for click-and-mortars involves increasing IS complexity. Design and development of complex computing systems are required to support each aspect of the click-and-mortar approach. Furthermore, different skills are necessary to support Web-based computing, requiring

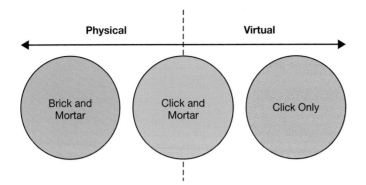

FIGURE 4.7

General approaches to EC.

substantial resource investments. Companies must design, develop, and deploy systems and applications to accommodate an open computing architecture that must be globally and persistently available. For instance, with total client assets of over $1 trillion, hundreds of thousands of daily trades by customers, a variety of ways that global customers use its Web site, and a dynamic, fast-changing set of online products and services, the click-and-mortar brokerage firm Charles Schwab has a large, diverse IS staff and a set of interrelated information systems (see Figure 4.8).

The Click-Only Strategy Click-only companies can often compete more effectively on price since they do not need to support the physical aspects of the click-and-mortar approach. Thus, these companies can reduce prices to rock-bottom levels (although a relatively small click-only firm may not sell enough products and/or may not order enough from suppliers to be able to realize economies of scale and thus reduce prices). Click-only firms, such as Amazon.com or eBay.com, also tend to be highly adept with technology and can innovate very rapidly as new technologies become available. This can enable them to stay one step ahead of their competition. However, conducting business in cyberspace has some problematic aspects. For example, it is more difficult for a customer to return a product to a purely online company than simply to return it to a local department store. In addition, some consumers may not be comfortable making purchases online. Individuals may be leery about the security of giving credit card numbers to a virtual company.

Business Models As is the case with any "traditional" business, you must develop a sound business model to be successful with EC. A **business model** or (business plan) is a summary of a business's strategic direction that outlines how the objectives will be achieved; a business model

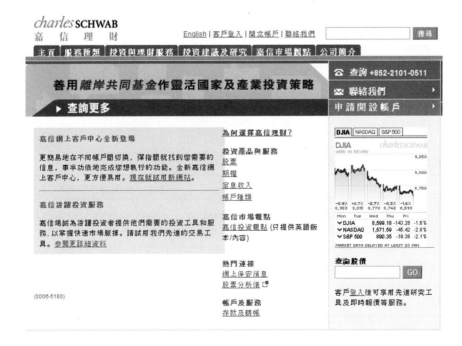

FIGURE 4.8

Brokerage firm Charles Schwab offers a variety of services online to meet the needs of its global customers.

TABLE 4.3 Components of a Business Model

Component	Description	Questions to Ask
Revenue model	The way a firm generates income (for more detail, see Table 4.4)	How do you generate income? What are you selling? How much are you selling it for?
Value proposition	The utility that the product/service has to offer to customers	Why do customers need your product/service?
Competitive environment	The existing players in the market and the nature of the competition	Who are your competitors? How fierce is the competition?
Marketing strategy	The promotion plan of your product/service	How do you plan to let your potential customers know about your product/service?
Management team	The background and experience of the company leadership	Can your leaders get the job done? How do they add value to the company?

includes how a company will generate revenue and identifies its product offerings, value-added services, revenue sources, and target customers. In other words, a business model reflects the following:

1. What does a company do?
2. How does a company uniquely do it?
3. In what way (or ways) does the company get paid for doing it?
4. How much gross margin does the company earn per average unit sale?

There are several components of a proper business model (see Table 4.3). Perhaps the most important ingredient for EC is a firm's revenue model. A **revenue model** describes how the firm will earn revenue, generate profits, and produce a superior return on invested capital. In addition to sales, transaction fee, or advertising-based business models common in the offline world, the Internet has enabled or enhanced other revenue models, such as affiliate marketing (see Table 4.4). Many companies (such as Amazon.com) use the Web as an economic medium to reach a large customer base; large numbers of customers allow these companies to turn over their inventory quickly, thus enabling the company to offer low prices while still making a profit. Other companies (such as Netflix.com or security software vendor Symantec) generate revenue using a subscription model where customers pay a monthly or annual fee for using the product or service. However, the Internet has provided large and small companies alike with the ability to generate revenues in various other ways. Traditionally, revenue models based on advertising, referrals, or transaction fees were difficult to sustain. For example, free newspapers have to set their rates for advertising space sufficiently high so as to offset the paper's production costs; in contrast, advertising on the Web is typically rather inexpensive, and the advertiser is charged on a pay-per-click basis (see our discussion of Web advertising later in this chapter). The Web site on which the ad is placed generates it revenue by serving cheap ads to large numbers of visitors. Using such revenue models, Web sites like Google or Facebook, as well as companies such as Zynga (the makers of FarmVille, a popular Facebook application), make millions of dollars in revenue.

As you can see, firms can conduct EC in a variety of ways. In the next section, we describe in greater detail how firms have evolved toward using the Internet and Web to support internal operations and to interact with each other.

TABLE 4.4 Typical Revenue Models for EC Businesses

Revenue Type	Description	Who Is Doing This?
Affiliate marketing	Paying businesses that bring or refer customers to another business. Revenue sharing is typically used.	Amazon.com's Associates program
Subscription based	Users pay a monthly or yearly recurring fee for the use of the product/service.	Netflix.com, World of Warcraft
Transaction fees	A commission is paid to the business for aiding in the transaction.	PayPal.com, eBay.com
Traditional sales	A consumer buys a product/service from the Web site.	Nordstrom.com, iTunes.com
Web advertising	A free service/product is supported by advertising displayed on the Web site.	Facebook.com, Digg.com

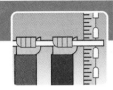

POWERFUL PARTNERSHIPS

YouTube's Steve Chen and Chad Hurley

Steve Chen (born in 1978) and Chad Hurley (born in 1977) met and became friends while both were PayPal employees. After taking video clips of a dinner party with friends, they found it difficult and time consuming to share these clips online. For instance, when they tried to send the videos in e-mail messages, services refused them because the files were too large; uploading the videos to Web sites that would accept them also proved difficult. Proving once again the adage, "Necessity is the mother of invention," Chen and Hurley then began work on a service that would allow anyone to upload a video and others to view the video at will.

YouTube went online in 2005 and within 11 months became one of the most popular sites on the Web, showing 30 million videos a day from 9.1 million people. Why was the site so quickly successful? Hurley and Chen designed the site exclusively for videos and for ease of use. When YouTube was launched, no one else had yet come up with an easy, fast method to electronically share videos that bypassed the usual process of attaching videos to e-mail messages. "From Day One we concentrated on building a service and community around video," Chen told *BusinessWeek* in April 2006. "That made us a lot different from the iTunes and the Googles out there."

Google Inc. bought YouTube in October 2006 for a reported $1.76 billion in stock. Consequently, Hurley, Chen, and Jawed Karim, a third PayPal employee who worked on the venture but left YouTube early on, joined the ranks of dot-com multimillionaires.

Hurley, YouTube's CEO, grew up in the Philadelphia suburbs and had a feel for business early on—at age five he sold his own paintings from his front yard. He studied design at Indiana University of Pennsylvania and applied for a job at PayPal after reading about it in *Wired* magazine. Hurley designed a logo for the company that is still in use today.

Chen, YouTube's chief technology officer, attended the Illinois Math and Science Academy and majored in computer science at the University of Illinois in Urbana-Champaign. PayPal recruited Chen during his last semester of college.

Despite legal problems over the posting of copyrighted videos on YouTube, the company has survived and continues to be high on the list of favorites for users. YouTube has consistently catered to the wishes of users, but spokespersons insist that the site has also attempted to work with the entertainment and music industries to discourage copyright violations. Now special software compares YouTube's content to video clips submitted for protection, and when copyrighted material that was not approved for submission is detected, it is removed.

Like many dot-com success stories, YouTube has provided a service that illustrates the recipe for success for future Web 2.0 entrepreneurs: to design sites that are easy to use and then let *users* create the content (see Chapter 5, "Enhancing Collaboration Using Web 2.0"). As of March 30, 2010, YouTube was rated by Alexa.com as the third most visited Web site in the world, behind Google and Facebook. YouTube is available in 14 different languages in 22 countries and receives 425 million unique visitors worldwide each month. In December 2009 alone, 134.4 million U.S. viewers watched more than 13 billion videos on YouTube, accounting for 84.1 percent of visits to video sites. Chen left YouTube in late 2008; in November 2010, Hurley stepped down as CEO of YouTube to focus on other projects, but continued serving in an advisory role.

Based on:

Anonymous. (n.d.). Agenda setters 2006. *Silicon.com.* Retrieved April 19, 2010, from http://www.silicon.com/research/specialreports/as2006/0,3800012300,39162381,00.htm.

Chad Hurley. (2010, May 27). In *Wikipedia, the free encyclopedia.* Retrieved June 11, 2010, from http://en.wikipedia.org/w/index.php?title=Chad_Hurley&oldid=364541855.

Green, H. (2006, April 10). YouTube: Way beyond home videos. *BusinessWeek.* Retrieved April 19, 2010, from http://www.businessweek.com/magazine/content/06_15/b3979093.htm.

Jarboe, G. (2010, February 6). YouTube was born five years ago and now it's the fifth largest website in the world. *SearchEngineWatch.* Retrieved April 19, 2010, from http://blog.searchenginewatch.com/100206-173401.

Steve Chen (YouTube). (2010, May 28). In *Wikipedia, the free encyclopedia.* Retrieved June 11, 2010, from http://en.wikipedia.org/w/index.php?title=Steve_Chen_(YouTube)&oldid=364582671.

YouTube. (2010, June 11). In *Wikipedia, the free encyclopedia.* Retrieved June 11, 2010, from http://en.wikipedia.org/w/index.php?title=YouTube&oldid=367369239.

FIGURE 4.9

YouTube's Steve Chen and Chad Hurley.

Noah Berger/AP Wide World Photos

Business-to-Business Electronic Commerce

As defined earlier, business-to-business EC refers to transactions conducted between different businesses, not involving the end consumer. In the process of producing goods and services, a business typically sources its raw materials from a variety of specialized suppliers. On the other hand, the business sells each finished product to a distributor or wholesaler (in a B2B transaction) or directly to the end consumer (in a B2C transaction). Thus, a collection of companies and processes are involved in moving a product from the suppliers of raw materials, to the suppliers of intermediate components, to final production, and ultimately, to the customer; these companies are collectively referred to as a *supply chain*. Typically, a company's suppliers work with their own suppliers to obtain goods; their suppliers work with additional suppliers, and so forth. The farther out in the supply chain one looks, the more suppliers are involved, forming a *supply network* (see Figure 4.10; we will discuss supply chains in more detail in Chapter 8, "Improving Supply Chains and Strengthening Customer Relationships Using Enterprise Information Systems"). Given the large number of suppliers needed for many products, it is no surprise that B2B EC accounts for 93 percent of all EC in the United States (U.S. Census Bureau).

The Need for Organizations to Exchange Data

B2B transactions require proprietary information (such as orders for parts) to be communicated to an organization's business partners. For many organizations, keeping such information private can be of strategic value; for example, Apple Computers tries to keep news about potential new product launches to a minimum, and any information about orders for key components (such as touch screens) could give away hints of what a new product may be. Prior to the introduction of the Internet and Web, the secure communication of proprietary information in B2B EC was facilitated using **Electronic Data Interchange (EDI).** EDI refers to computer–computer

FIGURE 4.10

A typical supply network.

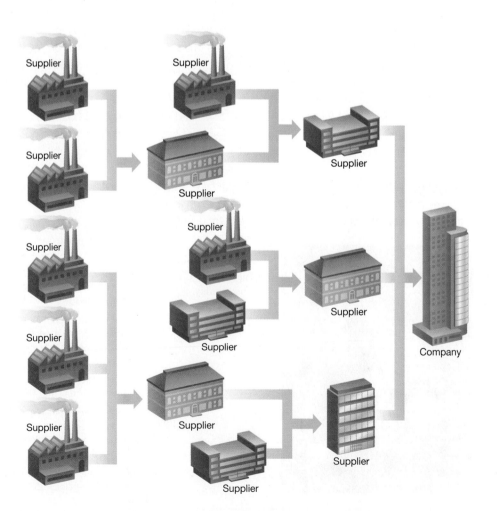

communication (without human intervention) following certain standards as set by the UN Economic Commission for Europe or the American National Standards Institute. Traditionally, using EDI, the exchange of business documents and other information took place via dedicated telecommunication networks between suppliers and customers, and thus the use of EDI was generally limited to large corporations that could afford the associated expenses. Today, the Internet and Web have become an economical medium over which this business-related information can be transmitted, enabling even small to midsized enterprises to use EDI; many large companies (such as the retail giant Walmart) require their suppliers to transmit information using Web-based EDI protocols. Further, companies have devised a number of innovative ways to facilitate B2B transactions using these technologies. We introduce these technologies in the following sections.

Exchanging Organizational Data Using Extranets

Web-based B2B systems range from simple extranet applications to complex trading exchanges where multiple buyers and sellers come together to conduct business. An **extranet,** which can be regarded as a private part of the Internet that is cordoned off from ordinary users, enables two or more firms to use the Internet to do business together. Although the content is "on the Web," only authorized users can access it after logging on to the company's extranet Web site.

Using the Internet to support B2B activities has become one of the best ways for organizations to gain a positive return on their technology-based investments. For example, U.S. aerospace giant The Boeing Company launched an extranet that can be accessed by over 1,000 authorized business partners. One of Boeing's business partners, aluminum supplier Alcoa, accesses the extranet to coordinate its shipments to Boeing as well as to check Boeing's raw materials supply to ensure appropriate inventory levels. Customers, such as the U.S. Department of Defense, log in to Boeing's extranet to receive status updates on the projects Boeing is working on for them. Overall, countless organizations are gaining benefits from B2B electronic commerce with nearly all Fortune 1000 companies deploying some type of B2B application.

Benefits of Extranets

Extranets, as well as *intranets* (discussion to follow), benefit corporations in a number of ways, so it is no surprise that firms have readily and rapidly adopted these technologies.

Information Timeliness and Accuracy First and foremost, extranets can dramatically improve the timeliness and accuracy of communications, reducing the number of misunderstandings within the organization as well as with business partners and customers. In the business world, very little information is static; therefore, information must be continually updated and disseminated as it changes. Extranets facilitate this process by providing a cost-effective, global medium over which proprietary information can be distributed. Furthermore, they allow central management of documents, thus reducing the number of versions and the amount of out-of-date information that may be stored throughout the organization. While security is still considered to be better on proprietary networks, the Internet can be made to be a relatively secure medium for business.

Technology Integration Web-based technologies are cross platform, meaning that disparate computing systems can communicate with each other provided that standard Web protocols have been implemented. For example, an Apple MacBook Air can request Web pages from a Linux Apache Web server. Even though the computers are running under different operating systems, they can communicate with each other over the Internet. The cross-platform nature of the Web makes implementing extranets extremely attractive as a way to connect disparate computing environments.

Low Cost–High Value In addition, extranets do not require large expenditures to train users on the technologies. Since many employees, customers, and business partners are familiar with the tools associated with the Web, they do not require special training to familiarize themselves with extranet interfaces. In other words, extranets look and act just like public Web sites. As long as users are familiar with a Web browser, they can utilize extranets with little difficulty.

Above all, extranets impact a company's bottom line. A company can use them to automate business transactions, reducing processing costs and achieving shortened cycle times. Extranets can also reduce errors by providing a single point of data entry from which the information can be updated on disparate corporate computing platforms without having to reenter the data. Management can then obtain real-time information to track and analyze business activities. Extranets are incredibly powerful and intensely popular. We describe in the following sections how they work and how they are being effectively utilized.

Extranet System Architecture

An extranet looks and acts just like a typical Internet-based application, using the same software, hardware, and networking technologies to communicate information (see Figure 4.11). However, an extranet uses the Internet infrastructure to connect two or more business partners and, thus, requires an additional component. Specifically, companies use *firewalls* to secure proprietary information stored within the corporate local area network and/or wide area network so that the information can be viewed only by authorized users. Firewalls with specialized software are placed between the organization's local or wide area network and the Internet, preventing unauthorized access to the companies' proprietary information. Organizations can connect their internal intranet infrastructures (see discussion of intranets to follow) together using a *virtual private network (VPN)* to facilitate the secured transmission of proprietary information between business partners. You will learn more about firewalls and VPNs in Chapter 10, "Securing Information Systems." To access information on an extranet, authorized business partners access their business partner's main extranet Web page using their Web browsers.

Extranet Applications

As the use of extranets has increased, a common set of applications has been found to be particularly beneficial to organizations. The primary use of extranets in organizations is for managing their supply chains; in other words, organizations exchange data and handle transactions with their suppliers or organizational customers, and extranets have evolved as a popular alternative to proprietary supply linkages.

Portals **Portals,** in the context of B2B supply chain management, can be defined as access points (or front doors) through which a business partner accesses secured, proprietary information from an organization (typically using extranets). Portals provide a single point of access to this type of information that may be dispersed throughout an organization. Thus, portals can provide substantial productivity gains and cost savings by creating a single point of access where the company can conduct business with any number of business partners.

Most companies are depending on a steady source of key supplies needed to produce their goods or services. For example, luxury restaurants require their produce to be consistently of

FIGURE 4.11

Typical extranet system architecture.

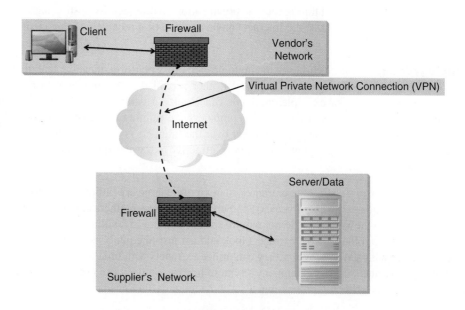

high quality; similarly, car manufacturers need steel, paint, or electronic components in the right quantities, at the right quality and price, and at the right time. Thus, most companies are seeking long-term B2B relationships with a limited number of carefully selected suppliers—rather than one-time deals—and invest considerable efforts in selecting their suppliers or business partners; often, suppliers are assessed not only on product features such as price or quality but also on supplier's characteristics, such as trustworthiness, commitment, or viability. As a result, in contrast to B2C EC, where anyone can set up a customer account with a retailer, the suppliers or customers in B2B transactions are typically known to the business, and access to the company's extranet will be given depending on the business relationship (typically, after a review of the supplier's or customer's application). To support different types of business relationships, portals come in two basic forms: supplier portals and customer portals. Supplier portals automate the business processes involved in purchasing or procuring products between a single buyer and multiple suppliers. On the other end of the spectrum, customer portals automate the business processes involved in selling or distributing products from a single supplier to multiple buyers. B2B marketplaces are typically run by separate entities and connect multiple buyers and multiple suppliers (see Figure 4.12).

Supplier Portals. Many companies that are dealing with large numbers of suppliers (e.g., The Boeing Company, Lilly, P&G, or Hewlett-Packard [HP]) set up **supplier portals** (sometimes referred to as sourcing portals or procurement portals). A supplier portal is a subset of an organization's extranet designed to automate the business processes that occur before, during, and after sales have been transacted between a single buyer and multiple suppliers. For example, on the HP Supplier Portal, companies can register their interest in becoming a supplier; access terms and conditions or guidelines (such as guidelines related to labeling, shipment, or packaging); and, once a business relationship is established with HP, manage ordering and payment activities.

Customer Portals. **Customer portals** are designed to automate the business processes that occur before, during, and after sales have been transacted between a supplier and multiple customers. In other words, customer portals provide efficient tools for business customers to manage all phases of the purchasing cycle, including reviewing product information, order entry, and customer service. For example, MyBoeingFleet, the customer portal of The Boeing Company, is part of Boeing's extranet and allows airplane owners, operators, and other parties to access information about their airplanes' configurations, maintenance documents, or spare parts. In other cases, customer portals are set up as B2B Web sites that provide custom-tailored offers or specific deals based on sales volume, as is the case with large office retailers such as OfficeMax (www .officemaxsolutions.com) or computer manufacturer Dell, which services business customers through its distribution portal Premier.Dell.com (see Figure 4.13).

B2B Marketplaces

The purpose of supplier portals and customer portals is to enable interaction between a single company and many suppliers or customers. Being owned/operated by a single organization, these portals can be considered a subset of the organization's extranet. However, setting up such portals tends to be beyond the reach of small to midsized businesses because of the costs

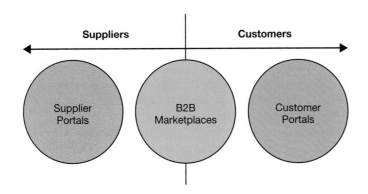

FIGURE 4.12

Supplier portals, B2B marketplaces, and customer portals.

FIGURE 4.13

Distribution portal Premier
.Dell.com.

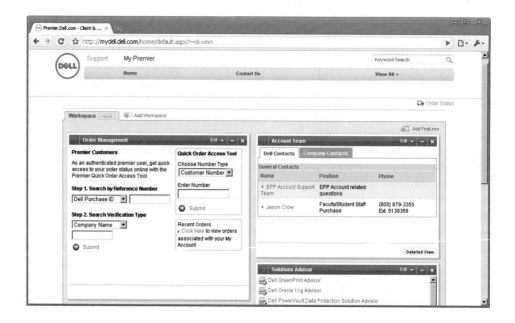

involved in designing, developing, and maintaining this type of system. Many of these firms do not have the necessary monetary resources or skilled personnel to develop large-scale supply chain management applications on their own, and the transaction volume does not justify the expenses. To service this market niche, a number of **business-to-business marketplaces** have sprung up. B2B marketplaces are operated by third-party vendors, meaning they are built and maintained by a separate entity rather than being associated with a particular buyer or supplier. These marketplaces generate revenue by taking a small commission for each transaction that occurs, by charging usage fees, by charging association fees, and/or by generating advertising revenues. Unlike customer and supplier portals, B2B marketplaces allow many buyers and many sellers to come together, offering firms access to real-time trading with other companies in their **vertical markets** (i.e., markets comprised of firms operating within a certain industry sector). Such B2B marketplaces can create tremendous efficiencies for companies since they bring together numerous participants along the supply network. Some popular B2B marketplaces include www.steellink.com (steel), www.paperindex.com (paper), and www.fibre2fashion.com (textile and fashion supplies).

In contrast to B2B marketplaces serving vertical markets, other B2B marketplaces are not focused on any particular industry. One of the most successful examples is the Chinese marketplace Alibaba.com. Alibaba.com brings together buyers and suppliers from around the globe, from almost every industry, selling almost any product, ranging from fresh ginger to manufacturing machinery. Alibaba.com offers various free services, such as posting item leads, displaying products, or contacting buyers or sellers. In addition to providing item listings, Alibaba.com offers features such as trading tips or price watch for raw materials. To generate revenue, Alibaba.com offers paid premium membership for sellers; the "Gold Supplier" premium membership entails a verified identity (signaling prospective buyers that the supplier is indeed a legitimate business entity) as well as unlimited product listings. Offering various trading tools including online storefronts, virtual factory tours, and real-time chat, such B2B marketplaces have enabled many small or little-known suppliers to engage in trade on a global basis.

Managing B2B Financial Transactions

In B2C EC, most transactions are settled using credit cards or electronic payment services such as PayPal; in contrast, B2B payments are lagging far behind. In fact, according to some estimates, about 75 percent of all noncash B2B business payments in the United States are made by check. While this may sound archaic, the time needed to process a check serves as a form of trade credit, which can amount to a significant part of an organizaton's working capital. For smaller purchases, organizations also often use puchasing cards. However, although productivity gains can be realized from using purchasing cards instead of checks, such cards are typically not used for large B2B transactions because of preset spending limits. In global B2B transactions, organizations often use letters of credit issued by a bank to make payments. While letters of credit help to reduce credit risk, these are often used only for relatively large amounts. Alternatively, businesses can make payments using providers such as Western Union. In any case, making B2B payments is far from being as simple as making a purchase at Amazon.com using your credit card, and making B2B payments easier can greatly enhance efficiency as well as reduce costs for organizations. Thus, it is no wonder that businesses have started asking for payment methods as simple as PayPal for B2B transactions.

When dealing with new, unknown suppliers, there is considerable fraud risk involved; this is especially of concern in global EC. This can become a limiting factor for B2B marketplaces such as Alibaba.com, which allow many smaller and lesser-known manufacturers to participate in global B2B EC. In 2004, the Alibaba Group (the parent company of Alibaba.com) founded Alipay, a third-party payment and escrow service. When businesses pay for orders using Alipay, payment is released only when the buyer has confirmed satisfactory delivery of the goods, reducing the risks for the buyer.

Business-to-Employee Electronic Commerce

In any business organization, much communication and interaction takes place between the organization and its employees or between its employees. As with the use of the Internet to support B2B activities, using the Internet to support internal organizational communication and processes—B2E—is also rapidly expanding. Especially for large organizations, communicating with and administering employees (e.g., sending out internal memos, enrolling employees in health care plans, changing benefits, and so on) can amount to large expenses.

As organizations have realized the advantage of using the Internet and Web to communicate public information outside corporate boundaries, they can also leverage Web-based technologies to support proprietary, internal communications through the implementation of an **intranet**[2] to support B2E EC. Organizations can use intranets for disseminating corporate information, employee training, project management, collaboration, or enabling employee self-service for administering benefits, managing retirement plans, or other human resources–based applications. For example, similar to their use of the Internet to support B2B activities, The Boeing Company also operates an intranet with more than 1 million pages registered with its internal search engine, serving nearly 200,000 employees. The intranet has become pervasive, impacting every department within the organization. Employees rely on the intranet to assist them in their daily business activities, ranging from tracking vacation benefits to monitoring aircraft production. In the remainder of this section, we examine the characteristics of an organizational intranet as well as the types of applications being deployed.

Supporting Internal Business Processes Using Intranets

Like an extranet, an intranet consists of a private network using Web technologies, but it is used to facilitate the secured transmission of proprietary information *within* an organization. Intranets take advantage of standard Internet and Web protocols to communicate information to and from authorized employees. As is the case with extranets, intranets provide many benefits to the organization, including improved information timeliness and accuracy, global reach, cross-platform integration, low-cost deployment, and a positive return on investment.

Intranet System Architecture

An intranet looks and acts just like a publicly accessible Web site and uses the same software, hardware, and networking technologies to communicate information. As with an extranet, users access their company's intranet using their Web browser. All intranet pages are behind the company's firewall, and in the simplest form of an intranet, communications take place only within

---

[2]It can be argued that, on a technological level, intranets and extranets are variants of the same thing in that both employ firewalls to cordon off ordinary users. However, given that intranets and extranets have very different purposes from a business point of view, we chose to distinguish between the two.

FIGURE 4.14

Typical intranet system
architecture.

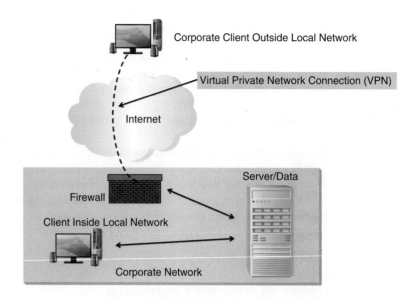

the confines of organizational boundaries and do not travel across the Internet. However, increases
in employees' mobility necessitate that an intranet be accessible from anywhere. Thus, most companies allow their employees to use VPNs to connect to the company's intranet while on the road
or working from home (i.e., telecommuting). Figure 4.14 depicts a typical intranet system architecture (see Chapter 10 for more on firewalls and VPNs).

Intranet Applications

Organizations are deploying a variety of common intranet applications to leverage their EC
investments. In this section, we briefly review a few of the most significant: training, application
integration, online entry of information, real-time access to information, and collaboration.

Training   Using its intranet, The Boeing Company offers training for nearly 200,000 of its
employees. In addition to intranet-based training about quality standards and procedures using a
system called "Quality eTraining," employees can choose from a wide range of multimedia
course offerings, including educational programs or supervisor training.

Personalized Intranet Pages   Many companies such as Boeing provide customized intranet
pages for each employee depending on job functions or even geographical location. Whereas
each employee's pages has the same look and feel and draws on the same underlying data, each
employee can access only the information he or she needs to perform his or her job function.
For example, if an employee from human resources logs on to the intranet Web site, he or she
would see only content that pertains to his or her job, such as payroll information or hiring
statistics.

Real-Time Access to Information   Unlike paper-based documents, which need to be continually updated and distributed to employees when changes occur, intranets make it less complicated
to manage, update, distribute, and access corporate information. For instance, Boeing disseminates
corporate news using multimedia files distributed over the company's intranet, allowing employees to view digital copies of company news releases as they occur, from the convenience of their
desktops. Boeing can now disseminate news in a more timely fashion while, in the process, saving
millions annually in distribution costs.

   With intranet-based solutions such as those deployed at Boeing, up-to-date, accurate information can be easily accessed on a company-wide basis from a single source that is both efficient and
user friendly. Companies can become more flexible with resources required to create, maintain,
and distribute corporate documents, while in the process employees become more knowledgeable
and current about the information that is important to them. Employees develop a sense of confidence and become self-reliant, reducing time spent dealing with employment-related issues and
allowing them to focus on their work responsibilities.

ETHICAL DILEMMA

Monitoring Productive Employees

"You have zero privacy; get over it," Scott McNeely, cofounder and longtime CEO of Sun Microsystems, once said. He was speaking about privacy expectations of Internet users in general, but the quote can also apply to privacy expectations of employees in the workplace.

If you work for a company where Internet connectivity is provided, it is legal for that company to track your computer use, including e-mails sent and received, Web sites visited, and downloads to your workstation computer. The question of whether such surveillance is ethical, however, is still under debate. The essence of the debate is this: Employers want employees to do a good job without abusing computer resources. Employees don't want their every keystroke and Web site visit tracked.

New technologies make it possible for employers to monitor employees' activities on the job, especially telephone use, electronic and voice mail, computer terminals, and Internet use. To date, such monitoring is unregulated; thus, your employer can listen to, watch, and read most of your on-the-job communications.

An American Management Association (AMA) survey in 2007 found that 66 percent of the employers surveyed monitor their employees' Internet use in order to prevent inappropriate surfing. Sixty-five percent use software to block employees' access to inappropriate Web sites. Forty-five percent track keyboard strokes and amount of time spent at the keyboard. Forty-three percent monitor employee e-mail messages, nearly 73 percent use technology to automatically monitor e-mail. Eighty-four percent of the companies surveyed disclose their monitoring practices to employees. In most cases, new employees are asked to sign the privacy practice disclosure and agree to abide by its provisions.

Increasingly, companies are vigorously enforcing technology policies. The survey reported that 30 percent of survey respondents had fired employees for misusing the Internet. Another 28 percent had fired employees for e-mail abuses.

While employee monitoring practices may be legal, are they ethical? On the employee side of the monitoring debate is the argument that when employers spy on employees, they are violating the individuals' privacy rights. Employers say they monitor to increase productivity but also to prevent liability. For instance, since employers are expected to maintain a workplace environment free of sexual harassment, shouldn't they be allowed to monitor e-mail messages that could implicate them in a sexual harassment suit?

Some legal experts argue that ethical questions about employee monitoring come down to the issue of contract. David D. Friedman, an economist and law professor at the University of Southern California, has said, "There isn't an agreement that is morally right for everybody. The important thing is what the parties agree to. If the employer gives a promise of privacy, then that should be respected." If, on the other hand, Friedman continues, the employer reserves the right to read e-mail or monitor Web browsing, the worker can either accept those terms or look elsewhere for employment. Friedman's comments do not address the issue of low-income employees who have no choice but to accept any job offered, regardless of employers' privacy policies.

In 2008, a federal government employee's right to e-mail privacy became an issue when members of Congress discovered that managers at the Small Business Administration had tracked a staff whistle-blower's e-mail. The worker had served as a confidential source for the Senate Committee on Small Business and Entrepreneurship, submitting anonymous testimony for a committee hearing. After Congress learned of the e-mail monitoring activities within the Small Business Administration, the agency took steps to limit the policy.

In any case, business law and ethics experts agree that employers who monitor should do so only if the surveillance serves a legitimate purpose, should follow clear procedures to protect a worker's personal life, and should inform workers about monitoring practices.

Based on:

AMA ePolicy Institute Research. (n.d.). 2007 Electronic monitoring and surveillance survey. *American Management Association.* Retrieved April 10, 2010, from http://press.amanet.org/press-releases/177/2007 -electronic-monitoring-surveillance-survey.

Anonymous. (2006, February). Employee monitoring: Is there privacy in the workplace? *Privacy Rights Clearinghouse.* Retrieved April 10, 2010, from http://www.privacyrights.org/fs/fs7-work.htm.

Loten, A. (2008, January 11). SBA whistleblower's email tracked. *New York Times.* Retrieved April 10,2010, from http://www.nytimes.com/ inc_com/inc1199710983718.html.

Schulman, M. (1998, Spring). Little brother is watching you. *Issues in Ethics.* Retrieved April 10, 2010, from http://www.scu.edu/ethics/ publications/iie/v9n2/brother.html.

Another component supporting employee productivity by providing real-time access to information is the integration of enterprise search functionality. As more and more content is accessible via a company's intranet, relevant information becomes increasingly more difficult to locate, especially if the information is in different languages and located on different servers or databases, as is the case in many large global organizations such as Nestlé. Hence, enterprise search engines have other requirements than Internet search engines such as Google or Bing: Enterprise search engines such as Microsoft's Enterprise Search or the Google Search Appliance are designed to retrieve content from various internal data sources, including documents, databases, or applications linked to the company's intranet. For example, prior to Kimberly-Clark's implementation of the Google Search Appliance, their search engine could search only about 500,000 internal documents, and the users' biggest complaint was that they were unable to find the information they were looking for; with the Google Search Appliance, the employees are now able to access more than 22 million documents located throughout the organization as well as external content. Thus, providing enterprise search functionality can be an important factor contributing to users' satisfaction with the company's intranet.

Online Entry of Information Companies can use intranets to streamline routine business processes because an intranet provides a Web browser interface to facilitate online entry of information. Especially for large companies, processing human resources–related forms can be a large cost factor. Depending on the complexity of the form, processing a paper-based form can cost U.S.\$20 to \$30, according to benefits administration solutions provider Workscape, Inc. Whereas interactive voice response–based applications can cut these costs to U.S.\$2 to \$4, using employee self-service applications can reduce this further, to a mere 5 to 10 cents per form (Wagner, 2002). Considering that employees, on average, conduct 15 human resources–related transactions per year, the savings can be significant. Using the intranet, report templates can be centrally managed, and modifications can be made instantaneously as conditions change; thus, employees can submit the appropriate template electronically with the assurance that they have used the correct version. Further, using online forms can help to significantly reduce error rates, as the entries can be checked for accuracy when the data are entered, thus preventing the user from inputting incorrect or illogical entries.

Collaboration One of the most common problems occurring in large corporations relates to the communication of business activities in a timely fashion across divisional areas of the organizations. For instance, Boeing uses its intranet to facilitate collaborative efforts, such as in the process of designing new aircraft components. In this process, three-dimensional digital models of aircraft designs frequently need to be shared between aerospace engineers. Using Boeing's intranet, an engineer can share a drawing with another engineer at a remote location; the second engineer revises the drawing as necessary and uploads the updated drawing to a shared folder on the intranet. The Boeing intranet provides the company with the capability of reducing product development cycles as well as the ability to stay abreast of current project, corporate, and market conditions.

Further, intranets are now being used to facilitate communication within organizations outside of traditional workflow. For example, Atomic Energy of Canada Labs (AECL), the manufacturer of the CANDU, one of the world's most popular nuclear reactors, has been using an intranet for employee blogs, to poll staff about current issues, and to communicate new executive initiatives. The company's intranet collaboration tools empower employees to communicate with each other and executives in a secure nonpublic forum. To be competitive, organizations constantly need to bring together the right combinations of people who have the appropriate set of knowledge, skills, information, and authority to solve problems quickly and easily. Traditionally, organizations have used task forces, which are temporary work groups with a finite task and life cycle, to solve problems that cannot be solved well by existing work groups. Unfortunately, traditional task forces, like traditional organizational structures, cannot always solve problems quickly. Structure and logistical problems often get in the way of people trying to get things done quickly.

Organizations routinely need flexible teams that can be assembled quickly and can solve problems effectively and efficiently. Time is of the essence. Membership on these virtual teams is fluid, with teams forming and disbanding as needed, with team size fluctuating as necessary, and with team members coming and going as they are needed. Employees may, at times, find themselves on multiple teams, and the life of a team may be very short. In addition, team members must have easy, flexible access to other team members, meeting contexts, and information. Think of these virtual teams as highly dynamic task forces.

Traditional office technologies, such as telephones or e-mail, are of some use to members of virtual teams but are not well suited to support the types of collaboration described previously. Telephones are not useful for rich, rapid, multiple-person team collaboration. This technology is best suited for person-to-person communication. E-mail is a useful technology for teams, but it does not provide the structure needed for effective multiperson, interactive problem solving. Companies need technologies that enable team members to interact through a set of media either at the same place and time or at different times and in different locations, with structure to aid in interactive problem solving and access to software tools and information. A number of technologies, described next, meet these requirements.

Groupware. The term **groupware** refers to a class of software that enables people to work together more effectively. Groupware and other collaboration technologies are often distinguished along two key dimensions:

1. Whether the system supports groups working together at the same time (synchronous groupware) or at different times (asynchronous groupware)
2. Whether the system supports groups working together face-to-face or distributed

Using these two dimensions, groupware systems can be categorized as being able to support four types of group interaction methods, as shown in Figure 4.15. With the increased use of group-based problem solving and virtual teams, there are many potential benefits of utilizing groupware systems. These benefits are summarized in Table 4.5

A large number of asynchronous groupware tools are becoming common in organizations, including e-mail, newsgroups and mailing lists, work flow automation systems, intranets, group calendars, and collaborative writing tools. One of the most popular groupware systems—and arguably the system that put groupware into the mainstream—appeared in 1989 when Lotus Development released its Notes software product (today, Lotus is owned by IBM). In recent years,

FIGURE 4.15

Groupware supports various modes of group interaction.

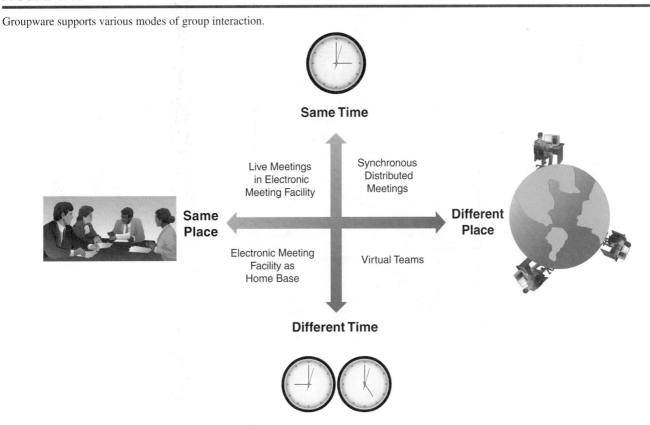

TABLE 4.5 Benefits of Groupware

Benefit	Example
Process structuring	Keeps the group on track and helps it avoid costly diversions (i.e., doesn't allow people to get off topic or off the agenda)
Parallelism	Enables many people to speak and listen at the same time (i.e., everyone has an equal opportunity to participate)
Group size	Enables larger groups to participate (i.e., brings together broader perspectives, expertise, and participation)
Group memory	Automatically records member ideas, comments, and votes (i.e., allows members to focus on content of discussions rather than on recording comments)
Access to external information	Can easily incorporate external electronic data and files (i.e., plans and proposal documents can be collected and easily distributed to all members)
Spanning time and space	Enables members to collaborate from different places at different times (i.e., reduces travel costs or allows people from remote locations to participate)
Anonymity	Member ideas, comments, and votes are not identified to others, if desired (i.e., can make it easier to discuss controversial or sensitive topics without fear of identification or retribution)

many new groupware products have emerged, most of which work through or with the Internet. Even with all these alternative groupware systems available, Notes continues to be an industry leader and is widely deployed throughout the world (see Figure 4.16).

Like asynchronous groupware, there are also many forms of synchronous groupware available to support a wide variety of activities, including shared whiteboards, online chat, electronic meeting support systems, and, of course, video communication systems (discussed in the following section). Although many forms of groupware can be used to help groups work more effectively, one category of groupware focuses on helping groups have better meetings. These systems are commonly referred to as **electronic meeting systems (EMSs).** An EMS is essentially a collection of personal computers networked together with sophisticated software tools to help group members solve problems and make decisions through interactive electronic idea generation, evaluation, and voting. EMSs have traditionally been housed within a dedicated meeting facility, as shown in Figure 4.17. Today, Web-based implementations support members around the globe.

Videoconferencing. In the 1960s, at Disneyland and other theme parks and special events, the picturephone was first being demonstrated to large audiences. The phone companies estimated

FIGURE 4.16

Lotus Notes is an award-winning groupware application with an installed base of millions of users worldwide.

Courtesy of Group Systems Corporation

FIGURE 4.17

A computer-supported meeting facility, complete with networked PCs and electronic meeting system software.

that we would be able to see a live picture with our phone calls in the near future. It took another 30 years, but that prediction has come true within many organizations. Many organizations are conducting videoconferencing to replace traditional meetings, using either desktop videoconferencing or dedicated videoconferencing systems that can cost from a few thousand dollars up to $500,000.

Desktop videoconferencing has been enabled by the growing power of processors powering personal computers and faster Internet connections. A desktop videoconferencing system usually comprises a fast personal computer, a **Web cam** (i.e., a small video camera that is connected directly to a PC), a speaker telephone or separate microphone, videoconferencing software (e.g., Skype, Gizmo, Yahoo! Messenger, or Windows Live Messenger), and a high-speed Internet connection.

Dedicated videoconferencing systems are typically located within organizational conference rooms, facilitating meetings with customers or project team members across town or around the world. These systems can be highly realistic—as if you are almost colocated with your colleagues—but high-end systems can be extremely expensive. No matter what type of videoconferencing system utilized by an organization, this collaboration technology has come a long way from the demonstration at Disneyland in the 1960s, becoming mainstream in most modern organizations.

Business-to-Consumer E-Commerce, Consumer-to-Consumer E-Commerce, and Internet Marketing

The Internet and Web have evolved with mind-boggling speed, achieving mass acceptance faster than any other technology in modern history. The widespread availability and adoption of the Internet and Web, which are based on an economical, open, ubiquitous computing platform, has made the emergence of B2C EC economically feasible. Unlike B2B, which concentrates on business relationships at the wholesale level, or B2E, which focuses on internal organizational communication and processes, B2C focuses on retail transactions between a company and end consumers. Table 4.6 provides a high-level comparison between these three approaches to utilizing Internet technologies.

TABLE 4.6 Characteristics of the Internet, Intranet, and Extranet

	Focus	Type of Information	Users	Access
Internet	External communications	General, public, and "advertorial" information	Any user with an Internet connection	Public and not restricted
Intranet	Internal communications	Specific, corporate, and proprietary information	Authorized employees	Private and restricted
Extranet	External communications	Communications between business partners	Authorized business partners	Private and restricted

Source: Based on Szuprowicz (1998) and Turban, Lee, King, Liang, and Turban (2008).

Stages of B2C EC

With millions of B2C-oriented Web sites in existence, Web sites range from passive to active. At one extreme are the relatively simple, passive Web sites that provide only product information and the company address and phone number, much like a traditional brochure would do. At the other extreme are the highly sophisticated, interactive Web sites that enable customers to see products, services, and related real-time information and to actually make purchases online. As shown in some early, pioneering research on EC (Kalakota, Olivia, & Donath, 1999; Quelch & Klein, 1996), companies usually start out with an electronic brochure and pass through a series of stages as depicted in Figure 4.18, adding additional capabilities as they become more comfortable with EC. These stages can be classified as **e-information** (i.e., providing electronic brochures and other types of information for customers), **e-integration** (i.e., providing customers with the ability to obtain personalized information by querying corporate databases and other information sources), and **e-transaction** (i.e., allowing customers to place orders and make payments).

Just a few years ago, integrating transactional capabilities into a company's Web site was very difficult, especially for smaller companies on a tight budget. Now, companies such as Yahoo! and Amazon.com offer small businesses the possibility to sell their goods and services online without having to invest large sums in an e-transaction infrastructure. Two major categories of e-transactions are the online sales of goods and services (or *e-tailing*) and financial transactions (such as *online banking*). These two categories are discussed next.

E-Tailing: Selling Goods and Services in the Digital World

The online sales of goods and services, or **e-tailing,** can take many forms. For example, using the Internet, bricks-and-clicks retailers such as Walmart.com or click-only companies such as Amazon.com sell products or services in ways similar to traditional retail channels. In contrast, virtual companies such as Priceline.com have developed innovative ways of generating revenue, such as offering consumers discounts on airline tickets, hotel rooms, rental cars, new cars, home financing, and long-distance telephone service. The revolutionary aspect of the Priceline.com Web site lies in its **reverse pricing system** called *Name Your Own Price* (see Figure 4.19). Customers specify the product they are looking for and how much they are willing to pay for it. This pricing scheme transcends traditional

FIGURE 4.18

Stages of B2C EC.

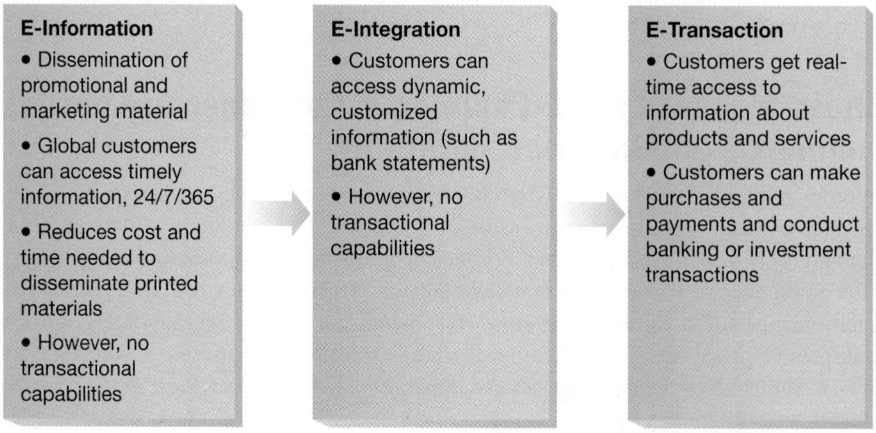

E-Information
- Dissemination of promotional and marketing material
- Global customers can access timely information, 24/7/365
- Reduces cost and time needed to disseminate printed materials
- However, no transactional capabilities

E-Integration
- Customers can access dynamic, customized information (such as bank statements)
- However, no transactional capabilities

E-Transaction
- Customers get real-time access to information about products and services
- Customers can make purchases and payments and conduct banking or investment transactions

David Young-Wolff/PhotoEdit Inc.

FIGURE 4.19

Priceline.com lets consumers name their own price for travel-related services.

menu-driven pricing, in which companies set the prices that consumers pay for products. After a user enters the product and price, the system routes the information to appropriate brandname companies, such as United Airlines and Avis Rent-a-Car, which either accept or reject the consumer's offer. In the first quarter of 2010, Priceline.com sold more than 20 million hotel room nights, 1.5 million airline tickets, and nearly 3 million rental car days for a gross booking of a little under $3 billion (Priceline, 2010). E-tailing has both benefits and drawbacks, which are examined next.

Benefits of E-Tailing   Using the marketing concepts of product, place, and price, e-tailing can provide many benefits over traditional brick-and-mortar retailing.

Product Benefits. Web sites can offer a virtually unlimited number and variety of products because e-tailing is not limited by physical store and shelf space restrictions. For instance, e-tailer Amazon.com offers millions of book titles on the Web, compared to a local brick-and-mortar–only book retailer, which can offer "only" a few thousand titles in a store because of the restricted physical space.

For online customers, comparison shopping is much easier on the Web. In particular, a number of comparison shopping services that focus on aggregating content are available to consumers. Some companies fulfilling this niche are AllBookstores (www.allbookstores.com), Biz-Rate (www.bizrate.com), and Google's Froogle (www.froogle.com). These comparison shopping sites can literally force sellers to focus on relatively low prices in order to be successful. If sellers do not have the lowest price, they must be able to offer better quality, better service, or some other advantage. These comparison shopping sites generate revenue by charging a small commission on transactions, by charging usage fees to sellers, and/or through advertising on their site.

Place Benefits. As company storefronts can (virtually) exist on every computer that is connected to the Web, e-tailers can compete more effectively for customers, giving e-tailers an advantage. Whereas traditional retailing can be accessed only at physical store locations during open hours, e-tailers can conduct business anywhere at anytime.

The ubiquity of the Internet has enabled companies to sell goods and services on a global scale. Consumers looking for a particular product are not limited to merchants from their own country; rather, they can search for the product where they are most likely to get it or where they may get the best quality. For example, if you're looking for fine wines from France, you can order directly from the French site Chateau Online (www.chateauonline.fr). This truly shows how the Internet has fueled globalization.

Price Benefits. E-tailers can also compete on price effectively since they can turn their inventory more often because of the sheer volume of products and customers who purchase them. Companies can sell more products, reducing prices for consumers while at the same time enhancing profits for the company. Further, virtual companies have no need to rent expensive retail space, allowing them to further reduce prices.

The Long Tail   Together, these benefits of e-tailing have enabled a form of business model centered on the "Long Tails." Coined by Chris Anderson (2004, 2006), the concept of the **Long Tail** refers to a focus on niche markets rather than purely on mainstream products. The distribution of consumers' needs and wants can be compared to a statistical normal distribution, where there are people with very diverse needs and wants on the tails (and very few of these people want the same products or services) and many people with "mainstream" needs and wants in the center of the distribution (see Figure 4.20). Because of high storage and distribution costs, most traditional brick-and-mortar retailers and service providers are forced to limit their product offerings to serving the needs and wants of the mainstream customers in the center of the distribution. For example, most independent movie productions are not shown at local cinemas, as they are unlikely to draw a large enough audience to cover the movie theater's costs to show the movie. Similarly, record stores carry only CDs of which a certain number of copies will be sold each year to cover the costs for shelf space, sales personnel, and so on. Given the limited local reach of brick-and-mortar stores, this ultimately limits the stores' product selection.

In contrast, enabled by their extended reach, many e-tailers can focus on the Long Tails, that is, on products outside the mainstream tastes. Whereas a local Blockbuster store is unlikely to have a large selection of documentaries (because of a lack of local demand), Netflix can afford to have a very large selection of rather unpopular movies and still make a profit with it. Rather than renting a few "blockbusters" to many people, many (often outside the mainstream) titles are rented to a large number of people spread out on the Long Tails. Similarly, online bookseller Amazon.com can carry a tremendous selection of (often obscure) titles, as the costs for storage are far less than those of their offline competitors. In fact, more than half of Amazon's book sales are titles that are *not* carried by the average physical bookstores, not even by megastores such as Barnes & Noble. In other words, focusing on those titles that are on the Long Tails of the distribution of consumers' wants can lead to a very successful business model in the digital world. A similar strategy is the mass-customization strategy pursued by Dell, which offers customized computers based on people's diverse needs and wants.

Drawbacks to E-Tailing   Despite all the recent hype associated with e-tailing, there are some downsides to this approach, in particular, issues associated with product delivery and the customer's inability to adequately experience the capabilities and characteristics of a product prior to purchase.

Product Delivery Drawbacks. Excepting products that you can download directly, such as music or an electronic magazine, e-tailing requires additional time for products to be delivered. If you have run out of ink for your printer and your research paper is due this afternoon, chances are that you will drive to your local office supply store to purchase a new ink cartridge rather than ordering it online. The ink cartridge purchased electronically needs to be packaged and shipped, delaying use of the product until it is delivered. Other issues can also arise. The credit card information that you provided online may not be approved, or the shipper may try to deliver the package when you are not home.

Direct Product Experience Drawbacks. Another problem associated with e-tailing relates to a lack of sensory information, such as taste, smell, and feel. When trying on clothes with your virtual model at Lands' End, how can you be sure that you will like the feel of the material? Or what if you discover that the pair of size 9 EE hockey skates you just purchased online fits you like an 8 D? Products such as

FIGURE 4.20

The Long Tails.

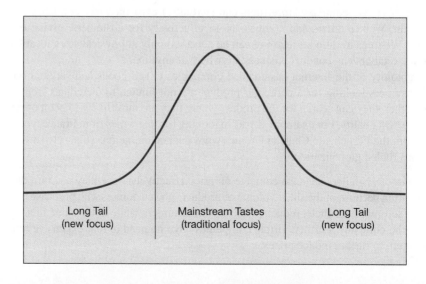

Long Tail
(new focus)

Mainstream Tastes
(traditional focus)

Long Tail
(new focus)

fragrances and foods can also be difficult for consumers to assess via the Web. Does the strawberry cheesecake offered online actually taste as good as it looks? How do you know if you will really like the smell of a perfume without actually sampling it? Finally, e-tailing eliminates the social aspects of the purchase. Although growing in popularity, e-tailers won't soon replace the local shopping mall because going to the mall with some friends is still an important social experience that cannot be replicated online.

EC Web Sites: Attracting and Retaining Online Customers

The basic rules of commerce are to offer valuable products and services at fair prices. These rules apply to EC as well as to any other business endeavor. However, having a good product at a fair price may not be enough to compete in the EC arena. Companies that were traditionally successful in the old markets will not necessarily dominate the new electronic markets. Successful companies are found to follow a basic set of principles, or rules, related to Web-based EC.[3] These rules are the following:

Rule 1—The Web site should offer something unique.
Rule 2—The Web site must be aesthetically pleasing.
Rule 3—The Web site must be easy to use and *fast*.
Rule 4—The Web site must motivate people to visit, to stay, and to return.
Rule 5—You must advertise your presence on the Web.
Rule 6—You should learn from your Web site.

Rule 1—The Web Site Should Offer Something Unique. Providing visitors with information or products that they can find nowhere else leads to EC profitability. Many small firms have found success on the Web by offering hard-to-find goods to a global audience at reasonable prices. Such niche markets can be in almost any category, be it diapers for birds (www.flightquarters.com), elk meat, art supplies, or hard-to-find auto parts.

Rule 2—The Web Site Must Be Aesthetically Pleasing. Successful firms on the Web have sites that are nice to look at. People are more likely to visit, stay at, and return to a Web site that looks good. Creating a unique look and feel can separate a Web site from its competition. Aesthetics can include the use of color schemes, backgrounds, and high-quality images. Furthermore, Web sites should have a clear, concise, and consistent layout, taking care to avoid unnecessary clutter.

Rule 3—The Web Site Must Be Easy to Use and Fast. As with nearly all software, Web sites that are easy to use are more popular. If Web surfers have trouble finding things at the site or navigating through the site's links or have to wait for screens to download, they are not apt to stay at the site long or to return. In fact, studies suggest that the average length of time that a Web surfer will wait for a Web page to download on his screen is only a couple of seconds. Rather than presenting a lot of information on a single page, successful Web sites present a brief summary of the information with hyperlinks, allowing users to "drill down" to locate the details they are interested in.

Rule 4—The Web Site Must Motivate People to Visit, to Stay, and to Return. Given the pervasiveness of e-tailing, online consumers can choose from a vast variety of vendors for any (mainstream) product they are looking for and are thus less likely to be loyal to a particular e-tailer. Rather, people go to the Web sites that offer the lowest prices, or they visit Web sites with which they have built a relationship, such as one that provides useful information, product ratings, and customer reviews or offers free goods and services that they value. These sites help to establish an online community where members can build relationships, help each other, and feel at home. Likewise, e-tailers such as Amazon.com try to "learn" about their customers' interests in order to provide customized recommendations and strengthen virtual relationships.

Rule 5—You Must Advertise Your Presence on the Web. Like any other business, a Web site cannot be successful without customers. Companies must attract visitors to their site and away from the thousands of other sites they could be visiting. One method of attracting visitors involves advertising the Web site. The first way to advertise your firm's presence on the Web is to include the Web site address on all company materials, from business cards and letterheads to advertising copy. It is now common to see a company's URL listed at the end of its television commercials. We discuss the topic of Internet marketing later in this chapter.

---

[3]Note that these rules apply mainly to how to make a Web site more successful. Realize that the underlying business model must be sound and that there are a host of similar rules that IS personnel must follow to ensure that (1) the Web site works well, (2) it interacts properly with back-end business information systems, and (3) the site is secure.

Rule 6—You Should Learn from Your Web Site. Smart companies learn from their Web sites. A firm can track the path that visitors take through the many pages of its Web site and record the length of the visits, page views, common entry and exit pages, and even the user's region or Internet service provider, among other statistics. The company can then use this information to improve its Web site. If 75 percent of the visitors leave the company's site after visiting a certain page, the company can then try to find out why this occurs and redesign the page to entice the users to stay. Similarly, pages that go unused can be eliminated from the site, reducing maintenance and upkeep. This process of analyzing Web surfers' behavior in order to improve Web site performance (and, ultimately, maximize sales) is known as **Web analytics** (for more on this topic, see Chapter 6, "Enhancing Business Intelligence Using Information Systems").

E-Banking

One special form of services frequently offered online is managing financial transactions. Whereas traditionally consumers had to visit their bank to conduct financial transactions, they can now manage credit card, checking, or savings accounts online using **online banking** or pay their bills using **electronic bill pay** services. However, concerns about security of online transactions have worried many online users.

In addition to online banking, **online investing** has seen steady growth over the past several years. The Internet has changed the investment landscape considerably; now, people use the Internet to get information about stock quotes or to manage their portfolios. For example, many consumers turn to sites such as MSN Money, Yahoo! Finance, or CNN Money to get the latest information about stock prices, firm performance, or mortgage rates. Then they can use online brokerage firms to buy or sell stocks.

C2C EC

C2C commerce has been with us since the start of commerce itself. Whether it was bartering, auctions, or tendering, commerce has always included C2C economics. According to the American Life Project, 17 percent of online American adults, or 25 million people, have used the Internet to sell things. Electronically facilitated interactions create unique opportunities (such as a large pool of potential buyers) and unique problems (such as the potential of being defrauded; see Table 4.7). This section discusses *e-auctions,* one of the most popular mechanisms consumers use to buy, sell, and trade with other consumers.

E-Auctions   As seen throughout this text, the Internet has provided the possibility to disseminate information and services that were previously unavailable in many locations. This dissemination can be seen clearly in the emergence of electronic auctions, or **e-auctions.** E-auctions provide a place where sellers can post goods and services for sale and buyers can bid on these items or vice versa. E-auctions can be categorized based on the number of sellers (one or many) and the number of buyers (one or many) involved, giving four distinct categories of e-auctions (see Figure 4.21). The most common form of e-auction is called **forward auction,** where the highest bid wins. A **reverse auction** is where buyers post a *request for quote,* which is similar to a request for proposal (for more on requests for proposal, see Chapter 9, "Developing and Acquiring Information Systems") in that the sellers respond with bids (and the seller with the lowest bid wins) rather than posting items or services for auction. Bartering typically takes place

TABLE 4.7 Opportunities and Threats of C2C EC

Opportunities	Threats
Consumers can buy and sell to broader markets	No quality control
Eliminates the middleman that increases the final price of products and services	Higher possibility of fraud
Always available for consumers, 24/7/365	Harder to use traditional methods to pay (checks, cash, ATM cards)
Market demand is an efficient mechanism for setting prices in the electronic environment	
Increases the numbers of buyers and sellers who can find each other	

FIGURE 4.21

Types of e-auctions.

Source: Based on Turban et al. (2010).

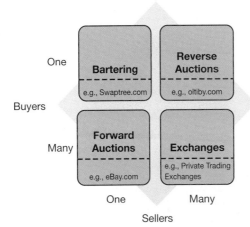

on a one-on-one basis, but Web sites such as swaptree.com bring together many people listing items to swap. Exchanges are typically taking place on a B2B level. Auctions are typically characterized as dynamic and competitive environments where market forces set the prices.

The largest e-auction site you probably know is eBay (www.ebay.com). eBay's revenue model is based on small fees that are associated with posting items, but these small fees quickly add up, so that in 2009 eBay's gross revenue exceeded $7.6 billion. Whereas eBay is hugely popular, there continue to be cases of fraud. According to the Internet Crime Complaint Center, e-auctions are marred with fraud (ic3.gov, 2010), with e-auction fraud being among the top 10 most common complaint categories filed with the center. There are several different types of e-auction fraud:

- *Bid Luring.* Luring bidders to leave a legitimate auction to buy the same item at a lower price outside the auction space, where return policies and buyer protection do not apply.
- *Reproductions.* Selling something that is said to be an original, but it turns out to be a reproduction.
- *Bid Shielding.* Sometimes called "shill bidding." Using two different accounts to place a low followed by a very high bid on a desired item, leading other bidders to drop out of the auction. The high bid is then retracted, and the item is won at the low bid.
- *Shipping Fraud.* Charging excessive shipping and handling fees, far above actual cost.
- *Payment Failure.* Buyers not paying for item after auction conclusion.
- *Nonshipment.* Sellers failing to ship item after payment has been received.
  E-auction providers such as eBay use sophisticated business intelligence applications (see Chapter 6) to detect and minimize e-auction fraud, attempting to make C2C EC a safer shopping experience.

Internet Marketing

One fundamental mistake companies can make when taking a current business online or creating an online business is assuming that if you build it, they will come. As with an offline business, marketing is a critical activity in any online endeavor.

Traditionally, companies' advertising budgets were mostly spent on noninteractive advertising campaigns, such as billboards, newspaper, radio, or television ads, and the distribution of ad spending has roughly matched people's media consumption habits. For example, in 2009, people spent 34 percent of their weekly "media time" watching TV; at the same time, companies spent about 31 percent of their advertising budget on TV ads. In contrast, while consumers spent about 34 percent of their media time on the Web, organizations spent only 12 percent of their advertising budget on Internet marketing (VanBoskirk, 2009). In light of shrinking advertising budgets and people's changing media consumption habits, companies are reevaluating the media mix of their advertising campaigns, and research firm Forrester estimates that by 2014, companies will spend 21 percent of their advertising budget on Internet marketing, including search marketing, display ads, e-mail marketing, social media, and mobile marketing. All of these are discussed next.

Search Marketing Whereas people would traditionally obtain information about products or companies from offline sources, many Web surfers now just enter the name of a product into a search engine such as Google or Bing and then visit the resulting pages. Given this trend, is not surprising

FIGURE 4.22

Search marketing will continue to have the largest share of interactive marketing spend.

Source: Based on VanBoskirk (2009).

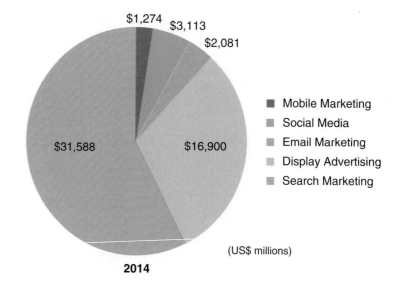

that search marketing is now big business. Research firm Forrester reports that by 2014, companies in the United States will spend $31.6 billion on search marketing (see Figure 4.22). Included in search marketing are paid search and search engine optimization, both of which are discussed next.

Paid Search. The results presented by search engines such as Google or Bing are typically separated into organic (i.e., based on the site's content) results and sponsored results. A way to ensure that your company's site is on the first page users see when searching for a specific term is using **search advertising** (or **sponsored search**). For example, using Google's "AdWords," a company can bid for being listed in the sponsored search results for the word "televisions" (see Figure 4.23). In order to present the most relevant ads to its users, Google then determines the relevance of the ad's content to the search term, and, depending on the amount of the bid, the company's Web site is listed in the sponsored results; the search engine receives revenue on a pay-per-click basis (see the following discussion of pricing models). As you can imagine, this can quickly become very expensive for advertisers, especially when the sponsored link is associated with a popular search term. On the other hand, a system such as Google's AdWords ensures high-quality leads, as the ads are presented only to users actually searching for a specific key word. As programs such as AdWords can be tweaked in myriad ways (such as by key words, negative key words, region, time of the day, and so on), many companies turn to professional consultants who help to optimize sponsored search campaigns. Alternatively, some search engines offer to elevate a company's position in the organic results after paying a fee **(paid inclusion).** Search engines (such as Google) that pride themselves on offering unbiased results,

FIGURE 4.23

Companies pay per click for being included in the sponsored listings.

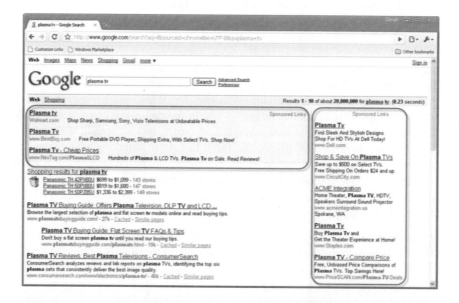

however, do not offer this option. Overall, Forrester Research estimates that spending on paid search will increase from $13 billion to $26 billion between 2009 and 2014.

Search Engine Optimization. Internet search engines such as Google, Yahoo!, and Bing order the organic results of a user's search according to complex, proprietary formulas, and the ranking (position of the link to a company's Web site) on a search results page is outside the control of a company (see Figure 4.24). Given the incredible numbers of results that are returned for common searches such as "apparel," "sportswear," or "digital camera," most surfers visit only the first few links that are presented and rarely go beyond the first results page; thus, companies use **search engine optimization (SEO)** in an attempt to move up in the organic search engine results. Although the exact formulas for a Web site's location in the organic results of a search engine are kept as trade secrets, the major search engines give tips on how to optimize a site's ranking, including having other pages link to one's site, keeping the content updated, and including key words for which a user might query. In other words, if a Web site is frequently updated, has content relevant to the search term, and is popular (as indicated by other pages linking to it), chances are that it will be positioned higher in the search results.

There are a multitude of companies promising to improve a page's ranking, but because search engines' algorithms are usually proprietary and are frequently changed, and there can be literally hundreds of factors influencing a site's rank, the success of using such services is often limited. Further, search engines such as Google try to figure out whether a site is using unethical "tricks" (such as "hidden" key words) to improve its ranking and ban such sites from the listing altogether. Nevertheless, even slight modifications to a company's Web site can have a large impact on the site's raking in search results, and investments in SEO are often worthwhile, especially in times of tight marketing budgets.

Display Ads In the early days of the Web, display advertising was the prevalent form of online advertising. Similar to traditional newspaper ads, companies would advertise their presence on other popular Web sites, such as that of the *New York Times* (www.nytimes.com), using static banner ads, video ads, or interactive banner ads, where users can interact with the advertisement. A recent trend in display advertising has been contextual advertising, where the ads placed on a page are in some way related to the content of that page. If, for example, you are reading tournament results from a PGA golf event at a popular sports Web site such as espn.com, you will also likely see an advertisement to buy new golf equipment or to visit a golf resort. Although display advertising has been regarded as being on the decline, more interactive features, as well as the ability to accurately measure an ad's impact, have contributed to display advertising's continued popularity.

E-mail Marketing E-mail marketing has been, and continues to be, very popular among advertisers, with over 95 percent of marketers using e-mail marketing in their overall interactive

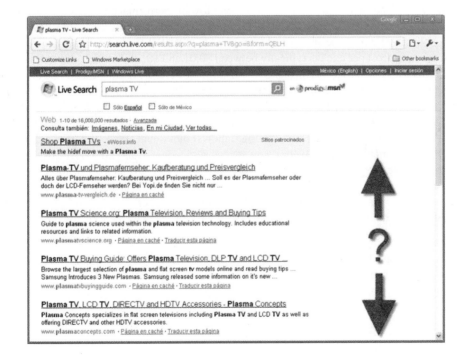

FIGURE 4.24

It is hard to influence the ranking of your company's page in the organic search results.

marketing mix (VanBoskirk, 2009). Given the low cost of less than U.S.$0.01 per e-mail, advertisers are increasingly trying to move away from direct-mail advertising and replace it with e-mail advertising. In addition to low cost, the effectiveness of e-mail advertising campaigns can be measured directly (such as by including special links or images in the e-mail that allow tracking which e-mails the customers have read or reacted to). Further, e-mail marketing saves tremendous amounts of paper over direct marketing, allowing a company to build a positive green image.

Social Media One relatively recent trend in Internet marketing is harnessing the power of social media, such as the social networking site Facebook. More and more people rely on social media to stay in contact with their friends or business associates, so including such sites in the interactive marketing mix is a natural move for companies. In addition to placing display ads on such sites, companies increasingly use social networking sites for interactive communication with their customers. For example, the Coca-Cola Company has created a page on Facebook, allowing it to interact with its over 5.3 million "fans" (i.e., Facebook users who "like" the page) in various ways; Coke's fans can download free virtual goodies, can upload pictures related to everything Coke, or can use interactive applications. By creating this page (which is free for Coke, except for the time needed to set it up and maintain it), Coke can build strong relationships with a large group of its target customers. Similarly, people can follow Coke on Twitter or visit Coke's channel on the video sharing site YouTube. We discuss social media in more detail in Chapter 5.

Mobile Marketing Finally, mobile marketing is another trend in Internet marketing. Increasing use of smart phones such as the iPhone or devices based on the Android mobile phone operating system has provided marketers with yet another channel. For example, the German car manufacturer Audi has built a game for the iPhone, where customers can drive an Audi around a racetrack. In early 2010, Apple announced the ability to place ads into iPhone applications. This will allow application developers to offer applications for lower prices (or free, under the freeconomics model; see Chapter 2, "Gaining Competitive Advantage Through Information Systems") and gives marketers the opportunity to reach their target audience through their favorite channels. This is likely to contribute to the growth of mobile marketing.

Pricing Models One common pricing model for online advertising is impression based, that is, based on the number of times the page containing an ad is viewed, typically expressed in cost per thousand impressions (i.e., cost per mille, or CPM). For example, for low-volume advertisers, the rates on the online edition of the *New York Times* are $8 to $10 per thousand impressions; on sites such as MSN or Yahoo, the CPM is around $20 and can be as high as $40 per thousand impressions on the online video site Hulu.com. Although large advertisers negotiate special rates with such sites, these online ads can quickly become quite expensive. Given the fact that many Web surfers do not even look at the online ads (and browsers such as Firefox offer the option to block online ads), the trend in Web advertising is moving toward performance-based pricing models whose return on investment is more direct, such as **pay-per-click** models. Under this type of pricing model, the firm running the advertisement pays only when a Web surfer actually clicks on the advertisement; the cost per click is typically between $0.01 and $0.50 per click, depending on the site, its viewers, and so on. The performance of this form of advertising can be assessed by metrics such as **click-through rate,** reflecting the ratio of surfers who click on an ad (i.e., clicks) divided by the number of times it was displayed (i.e., impressions), or **conversion rate,** reflecting the percentage of visitors who actually perform the marketer's desired action (such as making a purchase). Another option, **affiliate marketing,** allows individual Web site owners to post companies' ads on their pages; the Web site owner can earn money from referrals or ensuing sales. Today, sophisticated tools help to match advertisers and content providers, allowing for targeting a well-defined audience with relative ease and helping to increase the ad campaign's return on investment. For the content provider, having high-quality ads is beneficial, as it increases the site's perceived quality; in turn, the site can charge higher fees for the placement of ads.

Click Fraud. One drawback, however, of pay-per-click models is the possibility of abuse by repeatedly clicking on a link to inflate revenue to the host or increase the costs for the advertiser; this is known as **click fraud.** The first form of click fraud is called **network click fraud,** where a site hosting an advertisement creates fake clicks in order to get money from the advertiser. In other cases, a person—competitor, disgruntled employee, and so on—inflates an organization's online advertising costs by repeatedly clicking on an advertiser's link; this is called **competitive click fraud.**

NET STATS

Who Is Subsidizing Web Content?

When you subscribe to cable television, you typically have to decide between different packages, each offering various channels focusing on sports, movies, cartoons, and so on. In addition, you have the option of subscribing to other channels that interest you. Hence, the charges on your monthly cable bill are for your subscribed services. In contrast, the charges on your Internet bill are for connecting to the Internet rather than for the content on the Web. Hence, content providers on the Internet are dependent on other ways to generate revenue. Companies such as CNN, the Washington Post, Google, or Yahoo!, which provide content for free, subsidize their expenses by advertising revenue. One of the most common forms of advertising on the Web is display ads, which have moved from simple static images to rich, interactive advertisements. Although the CPM may be only between $5 and $20, display ads are big business.

Who are the biggest advertisers on the Web? Research firm Kantar Media regularly provides rankings of the Web's top advertisers, based on CPM estimates. In November 2009, the top 50 advertisers spent nearly $250 million on display

ads, with $84 million spent by brokerage and trading firms alone (see Figure 4.25). The top five advertisers in November 2009 were the following:

1. Scottrade: $30 million
2. Sprint Wireless: $21 million
3. TD Ameritrade $18 million
4. Scottrade Stock Brokerage: $17 million
5. Seroquel XR: $10 million

Based on:

Marshall, J. (2010, February 8). Scottrade Online leads top Internet advertisers by media value. *Clickz.com*. Retrieved June 17, 2010, from http://www.clickz.com/3636420.

Paparo, A. (2010, April 12). New frontiers in display advertising planning and measurement. *Google Blog*. Retrieved June 17, 2010, from http://googleblog.blogspot.com/2010/04/new-frontiers-in-display-advertising.html.

Wojcicki, S. (2010, March 15). The future of display advertising. *Google Blog*. Retrieved June 17, 2010, from http://googleblog.blogspot.com/2010/03/future-of-display-advertising.html.

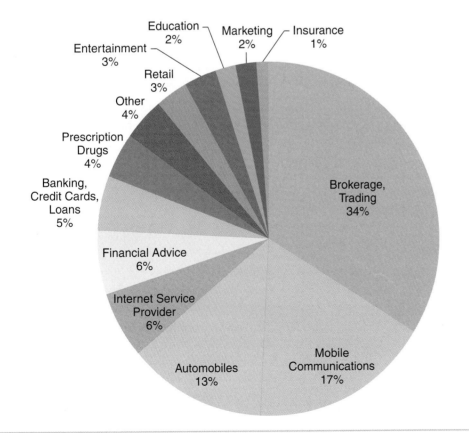

FIGURE 4.25

Top Internet advertisers by category.

Emerging Topics and Issues in EC

Although EC is only a little over a decade old, radical developments in technology and systems have brought EC from a fringe economic activity to one of the most prevalent in today's global economy. This innovation has not slowed down and has opened some promising new areas within EC. This section outlines some emerging topics within EC. This includes innovations in *C2B EC, mobile commerce* (or *m-commerce*), *location-based m-commerce,* and *mobile entertainment.* Also included in this section are descriptions of two issues related to EC, namely, how to secure payments in Web-based transactions and legal issues related EC transactions.

C2B EC

Just as the Web has enabled small businesses to participate in global EC, it has also enabled consumers to sell goods or services to businesses, reversing the more typical B2C model. As a relatively new phenomenon, **consumer-to-business (C2B)** EC has seen a few implementations. One prime example is stock photo sites such as www.shutterstock.com, which sells pictures, videos, or artwork to publishers, newspapers, Web designers, or advertising agencies; however, in contrast to traditional stock photo agencies, such as Getty Images, Shutterstock sources much of its content not from professionals but from amateur photographers. Similarly, companies use crowdsourcing (see Chapter 5) in order to have small, well-defined tasks (such as tagging pictures or describing products) performed by a scalable ad hoc workforce of everyday people. However, it can be argued that consumers who regularly engage in C2B transactions and make parts of their living with such transactions can be considered businesses; hence, the line between C2B and B2B transactions is somewhat blurry.

The Rise in M-Commerce

One exciting new form of EC is mobile electronic commerce, or **m-commerce.** M-commerce is defined as any electronic transaction or information interaction conducted using a wireless, mobile device and mobile networks (wireless or switched public network) that leads to the transfer of real or perceived value in exchange for information, services, or goods (MobileInfo, 2008).

The most common platform for m-commerce is the use of powerful smart phones like Apple's iPhone or RIM's BlackBerry, supporting high-speed data transfer and "always-on" connectivity over high-speed cellular networks (see the Technology Briefing for a detailed description of these and other handheld devices). These powerful devices provide a wide variety of services and capabilities in addition to voice communication, such as multimedia data transfer, video streaming, video telephony, and full Internet access. In Table 4.8, we list some sample m-commerce applications.

Location-Based M-Commerce One form of m-commerce is **location-based services,** which are highly personalized mobile services based on a user's location. Location-based services are

TABLE 4.8 Some M-Commerce Applications

Purchasing and Other Financially Related Transactions:
- Online purchasing of goods or services
- Instore purchases
- Directory/store-finder services
- M-wallets
- Vending machine purchases
- Stock trading and other investments
- Paying bills

Reserving and/or Booking:
- Reserving and/or purchasing tickets for airlines, movies, concerts, or sporting events
- Reservations for restaurants or hotels

Entertainment and Information:
- Downloading and playing games
- Streaming media for movies or music
- General information such as news and weather
- Accessing corporate extranets/intranets

implemented via the cellular network and Global Positioning System (GPS) functionality, now built into most modern cell phones.

One example of a very useful GPS-enabled location-based service is **e911,** or *enhanced 911* (which is part of a federal mandate to improve the effectiveness and reliability of the 911 emergency service). When someone in distress would dial 911 from an older cell phone, the call would most likely be routed to the wrong 911 dispatch center, and the dispatcher would have no way to find out the location of the caller. GPS-enabled location-based services enable correct routing of 911 calls and also provide dispatchers with location information on the wireless 911 calls. This includes information on the phone number used to call and GPS information that would indicate where the cell phone is located within 50 meters. Another popular GPS-enabled location-based service is the phone locator, which uses GPS phone tracking capabilities. This service, offered by major U.S. and European wireless providers, allows for users to log on to Web sites and view the location of family members' cell phones. Marketed as tracking capability built for family safety, phone locator applications can include everything from maps of a person's current location to messaging systems that alert parents when their child leaves a certain area (see Figure 4.26).

In addition to these location-based services, there is now a variety of consumer-oriented phone software that uses GPS and Bluetooth functionalities in cell phones. Table 4.9 lists a sample of GPS-enabled applications.

Social activities are another area that is supported by GPS technology in cell phones. With the success of social networking sites such as Facebook, many innovators are looking to social networks and cell phone technology to be the next big thing. Already several Web sites are providing mobile social networking services. For example, the Facebook application Gowalla allows people to "check in" at places like restaurants or attractions using their mobile devices, letting their friends know about their location or activities. Similarly, Google Buzz allows people to broadcast their location and other status updates to their friends or contacts using a mobile device. Many predict that within two years, 5 percent of all text messages will be cell phone social-networking related. Not bad considering that the current Short Message Service market is annually close to $3 billion.

FIGURE 4.26

Parents can track their children's movements using cell phones.

COMING ATTRACTIONS

Smart Phones of the Future

What can we expect from the smart phone of the future? We cannot predict exactly what it would be, but we may get some clues from what the industry leaders are doing.

Microsoft submitted a patent called *Smart Interface System for Mobile Communications Devices*, which can give us clues to what a future smart phone may look like. The idea behind Microsoft's patent is that you can turn a smart phone into a full-blown computer as long as you plug the smart phone into a docking station. The onboard memory and processor functions of the smart phone would still be used, but all peripherals, such as keyboards, monitors, printers, and network adapters, would be controlled by the docking station. In contrast to Microsoft, Apple is going a different route and integrates more functions into its iPhone so as to enable more applications to be used on the go. For example, the newest generation iPhone integrates a front-facing video camera that can be used for making video calls while on the go using Apple's "FaceTime" application. In addition, the iPhone 4 lets a user record and even edit high-definition videos.

Overall, the smart phone of the future will be more customized. It will have a touch screen, faster Bluetooth, more GPS-powered applications, more memory, and a higher data transmission rate; some predict that smart phones will act as full PC replacements, using powerful processors that allow even complex applications to run. Augmented reality will become more common so that mobile users can easily get additional information related to their current location. The smart phone of the future may even sport a 3D display, as recently presented by Texas Instruments, or it could be a "living" device. You may be able to change the shape of the smart phone (so as to more easily place it on your nightstand); you could interact with the phone by griping its sides or the phone may simulate a heartbeat, making it more "human."

Mobile phones of the future will definitely provide more than just person-to-person communication. They are poised to become artificial intelligence wonders that remind us of all the daily activities necessary to keep us living a healthy, goal-focused, stimulating lifestyle.

Based on:

Anonymous. (n.d.). iPhone 4. In so many ways, it's a first. *Apple.com*. Retrieved June 17, 2010, from http://www.apple.com/iphone/features.

Ayala, D. (2010, February 4). Will your next smartphone shape-shift? One researcher presents his ideas. *PC World*. Retrieved March 20, 2010, from http://www.pcworld.com/article/188543/will_your_next _smartphone_shapeshift_one_researcher_presents_his_ideas.html.

Ayala, D. (2010, February 19). Dreaming up the smartphone of the future. *PC World*. Retrieved June 17, 2010, from http://www.pcworld .com/article/189732/dreaming_up_the_smartphone_of_the_future .html.

Brandon, J. (2010, February 16). The future of smartphones: 2010–2015 and beyond. *Digitaltrends.com*. http://www.digitaltrends.com/features/ the-future-of-smartphones-2010-2015-and-beyond.

Kassner, M. (2009, February 4). Smartphone patents foretell the future. *Tech Republic*. Retrieved March 20, 2010, from http://blogs .techrepublic.com.com/networking/?p=904.

Key Drivers for M-Commerce Several factors have led to the rapid rise of m-commerce. First, there is exponential growth of consumer interest in and adoption of the Internet and EC in general. Second, there is now development and deployment of real-time transfer of data over 3G and soon 4G cellular networks that have enabled faster data transmission and "always-on" connectivity, resulting in tremendous growth in mobile telephony and availability of powerful wireless, handheld devices. We describe these types of cellular networks in detail in the Technology Briefing.

Through a convergence of Internet and wireless technologies, m-commerce promises to propel business by enabling the electronic exchange of capital, goods, and commercial information via mobile, untethered computing devices (Looney, Jessup, & Valacich, 2004). Indeed, the

TABLE 4.9 GPS-Enabled Location-Based Services

Service	Example
Location	Determining the basic geographic position of the cell phone
Mapping	Capturing specific locations to be viewed on the phone
Navigation	The ability to give route directions from one point to another
Tracking	The ability to see another person's location

Brief Case ⊙

HUMAN-POWERED SEARCH ENGINES: CHACHA

It's finally here: a free search service for mobile phones. Imagine you are in Chicago and you would like directions to the super new pizza restaurant you have seen advertised. Simply text your question to ChaCha, and within minutes the answer is texted back to you. It's handier than unwieldy maps and more accurate than asking directions from passersby, and it's free.

Scott Jones, inventor and entrepreneur, and Brad Bostic, chairman of Bostech Corporation, came up with the idea, and the service was launched first in alpha and then in beta versions in 2006. For people on the go, ChaCha is handier to use than most computer search engines because it is human powered. Human "guides" actually read the question you ask, find the answer, and get back to you.

ChaCha selects guides from applicants who pass a series of tests. These applicants then are trained via ChaCha's Search University and a simulation program to become certified live ChaCha guides. ChaCha's technology also "learns" from the answers guides provide, thus becoming more accurate over time. To test the ChaCha service for yourself, simply use your mobile phone to text your question to "242242" (spells "ChaCha") or call 1-800-2chacha to verbally ask a question. The answer to your question will be sent back to you via a text message. If your phone has a Web browser, you can access the link provided with the answer to see more information. The service itself is free, but standard mobile phone text messaging and voice rates apply.

ChaCha gained huge success in recent years. Having grown faster than NFL.com, NBC.com, FoxSports.com, and Time.com, ChaCha.com has become one of the fastest-growing Web sites. ChaCha has answered more than 500 million questions since its launch. Advertisers such as Coca-Cola, Ikea, and McDonald's can embed targeted ads within the text conversations between ChaCha and its over 10 million users per month.

In February 2010, ChaCha introduced its new Facebook application. A Facebook user who installs the application can pose questions to his or her wall; ChaCha searches its database to provide the best answer to the question. Individuals answering the question can get points for answers, helping ChaCha to further expand its database.

Questions

1. Describe a situation where you could have used ChaCha.
2. When do you think "old-fashioned" search engines would be more effective than ChaCha? When would ChaCha be preferred?

Based on:

Anonymous. (n.d.). About us. Retrieved April 3, 2010, from http://answers.chacha.com/about-chacha.

Barnard, P. (2010, February 09). ChaCha sets record with over a million mobile user questions on Super Bowl Sunday. *SportsTech*. Retrieved April 3, 2010, from http://sports.tmcnet.com/broadcasting/articles/74957-chacha-sets-record-with-over-million-mobile-user.htm.

ChaCha (search engine). (2010, August 4). In *Wikipedia, the free encyclopedia*. Retrieved August 9, 2010, from http://en.wikipedia.org/w/index.php?title=ChaCha_(search_engine)&oldid=377088219.

Iskold, A. (2006, December 14). ChaCha: A human-powered search engine. *ReadWriteWeb*. Retrieved April 3, 2010, from http://www.readwriteweb.com/archives/chacha_human-powered_search.php.

Mills, E. (2008, January 3). ChaCha gives you answers via text message. *CNET News.com*. Retrieved April 3, 2010, from http://www.news.com/8301-10784_3-9838019-7.html.

Rao, L. (2010, February 15). ChaCha turns to Facebook to socialize questions and answers; rolls out API. *TechCrunch*. Retrieved April 3, 2010, from http://techcrunch.com/2010/02/15/chacha-turns-to-facebook-to-socialize-questions-and-answers.

m-commerce market in the U.S. grew from $396 million to $1.2 billion from 2008 to 2009, and the worldwide market is predicted to grow to $119 billion by 2015 (ABI Research, 2010).

Mobile Entertainment

Another EC innovation in the entertainment industry involves media dissemination. With the advent of products such as Slingbox and TiVo, the entertainment industry, including the major U.S. network television stations and the major Hollywood studios, has no choice but to adopt the Internet as a viable dissemination medium. These industry players are now making their TV shows and movies available via Apple's iTunes and YouTube.com, responding to innovations such as Slingbox. A Slingbox, connected to a user's set-top box, acts as a personal media server and "placeshifts" television content to any Internet-enabled device. In other words, the television signal is received in the user's house and then relayed via the Internet so that the users can access TV shows or movies while traveling, being in the office, or sitting in the backyard.

Securing Payments in the Digital World

One of the biggest impediments to B2C EC, C2C EC, and m-commerce is how to ensure that consumers can make secure transactions on the Web site. Although the transfer of money is a critical factor in online shopping, online banking, and online investing, security researchers and software companies are lamenting that people are often reluctant to change their habits when surfing the Web and carelessly reveal sensitive information to unknown or fraudulent sites. In fact, more than 11 million consumers became victims of *identity theft* in 2009, up from nearly 10 million in 2008 (see Chapter 10). Security concerns and other factors (such as impatience, lengthy checkout procedures, or comparison shopping) lead shoppers to frequently abandon their shopping carts and to not follow through with a purchase—reports show that more than half of the online shopping carts are abandoned. Traditionally, paying for goods and services was limited to using credit and debit cards, but now different companies offer payment services for buying and selling goods or services online. These different forms of online payment are discussed next.

Credit and Debit Cards Credit and debit cards are still among the most accepted forms of payment in B2C EC. For customers, paying online using a credit card is easy; all the customer needs to do is to enter his or her name, billing address, credit card number, and expiration date to authorize a transaction. In many cases, the customer is also asked to provide the so-called **Customer Verification Value (CVV2),** a three-digit code located on the back of the card. This is one way to combat fraud in online purchases, as the code is used for authorization by the card-issuing bank. As the CVV2 is not included in the magnetic strip information, a person using a credit card for online transactions has to physically possess the actual credit card (see Table 4.10 for other guidelines on how to conduct safe transactions on the Internet).

For each transaction, an online customer has to transmit much personal information to a (sometimes unknown) merchant, and many Internet users (sometimes rightfully) fear being defrauded by an untrustworthy seller or falling victim to some other form of computer crime (see Chapter 10). Further, ordinary people can only *make* payments by using credit cards—to receive payments, one has to open up a merchant account to accept credit card payments. For people who sell things online only once in a while (such as on the online auction site eBay), this is not a good option. To combat these problems, online shoppers (and sellers) are increasingly using third-party payment services. These are discussed next.

Payment Services Concerns for security have led to the inception of independent payment services such as PayPal (owned by eBay) or Google Checkout. These services allow online customers to purchase goods online without having to give much private information to the actual sellers. Rather than paying a seller by providing credit card information, an online shopper can simply pay by using his or her account with the payment service. Thus, the customer has to provide the (sensitive) payment information only to the payment service, which keeps this

---

TABLE 4.10 Ways to Protect Yourself When Shopping Online

Tip	Example
Use a secure browser	Make sure that your browser has the latest encryption capabilities; also, always look for the padlock icon in your browser's status bar before transmitting sensitive information
Check the site's privacy policy	Make sure that the company you're about to do business with does not share any information you would prefer not to be shared
Read and understand the refund and shipping policies	Make sure that you can return unwanted/defective products for a refund
Keep your personal information private	Make sure that you don't give out information, such as your Social Security number, unless you know what the other entity is going to do with it
Give payment information only to businesses you know and trust	Make sure that you don't provide your payment information to fly-by-night operations
Keep records of your online transactions and check your e-mail	Make sure that you don't miss important information about your purchases
Review your monthly credit card and bank statements	Make sure to check for any erroneous or unauthorized transactions

Source: Based on Federal Trade Commission (2010).

information secure (along with other information such as e-mail address or purchase history) and does not share it with the online merchant. Google linked its payment service to the search results so that Internet users looking for a specific product can immediately see whether a merchant offers this payment option; this is intended to ease the online shopping experience for consumers, thus reducing the number of people abandoning their shopping carts. Another payment service, PayPal, goes a step further by allowing anyone with an e-mail address to send and receive money. In other words, using this service, you can send money to your friends or family members, or you can receive money for anything you're selling. This easy way to transfer money has been instrumental in the success of the online auction eBay, where anyone can sell or buy goods from other eBay users.

Legal Issues in EC

Although EC is now a viable and well-established business practice, there are issues that have changed the landscape for businesses and consumers and continue to do so. Two of the most important issues for EC businesses is taxation of online purchases and the protection of intellectual property, especially as if pertains to digital products, both of which are outlined next.

Taxation Although this issue is a relatively old one, it remains controversial within the American legal system. With EC global transactions increasing at an exponential rate, many governments are concerned that sales made via electronic sales channels have to be taxed in order to make up for the lost revenue in traditional sales methods. As people shop less in local retail stores, cities, states, and even countries are now seeing a decrease in their sales tax income because of EC. Table 4.11 highlights issues associated with taxation of EC transactions.

The Internet Tax Freedom Act. Starting in 1998, the **Internet Tax Freedom Act,** passed by the U.S. Senate, created a moratorium on EC taxation in the hopes of creating incentives for EC. The most recent version, called the Internet Tax Nondiscrimination Act, was signed into law in late 2004 by President George W. Bush. According to these tax laws (in addition to other provisions, such as a ban on Internet access or e-mail taxes), sales on the Internet were to be treated the same way as mail-order sales. As with mail-order sales, a company was required to collect sales tax only from customers residing in a state where the business had substantial presence. In other words, if an EC business had office facilities or a shipping warehouse in a certain state (say, California), it would have to collect sales tax only on sales to customers from that state (in that case, California). Many EC businesses thus strategically selected their home bases to offer "tax-free shopping" to most customers. For example, Jeff Bezos, the founder of Amazon.com, closely examined several states before choosing the state of Washington for Amazon.com's head office. This way, initially only the 6 million Washington State residents had to pay tax on Amazon.com purchases. As Amazon.com expands, it continues to be very selective in where it locates shipping facilities and warehouses. For example, Amazon.com selected Reno, Nevada, to serve the Californian market in order to allow its 36 million potential customers to avoid paying sales tax on purchases. Currently, Amazon.com collects sales tax only on purchases from customers located in Kansas, Kentucky, North Dakota, and Washington State. Walmart.com, on the other hand, charges taxes on all of their U.S. EC transactions, as they are physically present in every U.S. state.

On an international level, taxation is even more difficult. A customer ordering from a U.S. seller would not have to pay U.S. sales tax but may be liable for paying tax in his or her home country on the shipment's arrival. For digital products (such as software or music downloads),

TABLE 4.11 Arguments For and Against Taxation of EC Transactions

For	Against
Increases tax income of local, state, and federal governments	Slows EC growth and opportunity
	Creates additional compliance burden for e-tailers
Removes unfair advantage for e-tailers over brick-and-mortar stores	E-tailers located in one state would subsidize other states or jurisdictions
Increases accountability for e-tailers	Drives EC businesses to other countries

the movement of the product is difficult to track, and the tax revenue is easily lost. Obviously, e-businesses actively doing business in other countries have to comply with the various different tax laws in different countries.

Digital Rights Management With consumers increasingly using EC as viable alternatives for traditional commerce, the entertainment industry has no choice but to embrace the Internet as a distribution medium. At the same time, digital media are easily copied and shared by many people, as the entertainment industry has painfully learned after the introduction of the compact disc. Hence, the entertainment industry has turned to **digital rights management (DRM),** which is a technological solution that allows publishers to control their digital media (music, movies, and so on) to discourage, limit, or prevent illegal copying and distribution. DRM restrictions include which devices will play the media, how many devices the media will play on, and even how many times the media can be played.

The entertainment industry argues that DRM allows copyright holders to minimize sales losses by preventing unauthorized duplication. Critics refer to DRM as "digital restriction management," stating that publishers are arbitrary on how they enforce DRM. Further, critics argue that DRM enables publishers to infringe on existing consumer rights and to stifle innovation.

Before 2009, songs or videos purchased from Apple's iTunes could only be played on a limited number of devices, but Apple and other online music retailers, such as Amazon, are now offering DRM-free downloads. Many users want the ability to freely move their media, typically music or videos, from one device to another with ease. To prevent illegal sharing of DRM-free content, it is often watermarked so that any illegal copy can be traced to the original purchaser (e.g., content purchased on iTunes contains the email address used for the purchase, see Figure 4.27). A digital **watermark** is an electronic version of physical watermarks placed on paper currency to prevent counterfeiting. Likewise, to prevent counterfeiting of currency, most color laser printers print nearly invisible yellow dots uniquely identifying the originating printer on each page; privacy advocates argue that this could potentially be used to identify or persecute dissidents (EFF, 2010).

E-Government

E-government is the use of information systems to provide citizens, organizations, and other governmental agencies with information about public services and to allow for interaction with the government. E-government has become more widespread in the United States since the 1998 Government Paperwork Elimination Act. Similar to the EC business models, e-government involves three distinct relationships (see Figure 4.28).

FIGURE 4.27

Digital watermarks are used to trace illegal copies of digital media to the original purchaser.

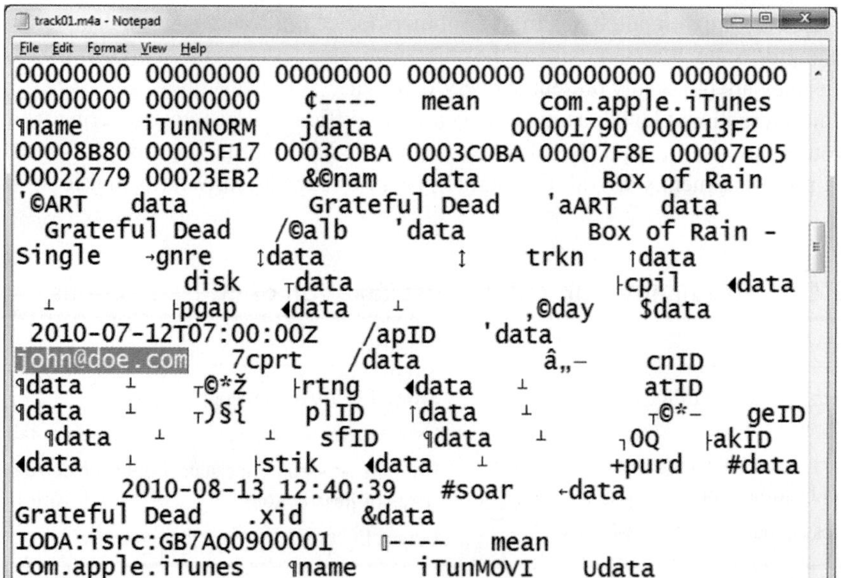

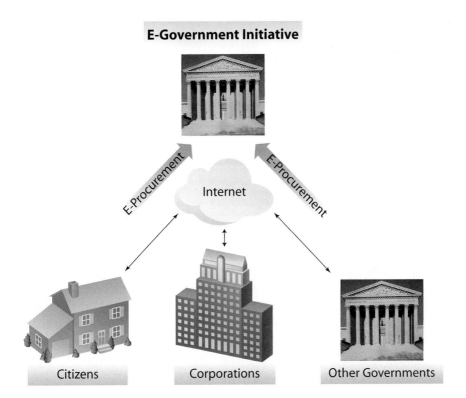

E-Government Initiative

FIGURE 4.28

E-government initiatives include interaction with citizens, corporations, and other governments.

Government-to-Citizens The first form of e-government is known as **government-to-citizen (G2C)** EC. This category allows for interactions between federal, state, and local governments and their constituents. The Internal Revenue Service's Internet tax filing, or *e-filing,* is one of the more recognizable G2C tools, saving resources in terms of time and paper. Another e-government tool in wide use today is grants.gov. Of the over 2,200 funding opportunities for federal discretion, 54 percent were available for online submission (www.whitehouse.gov). Some states have begun working on e-voting initiatives, allowing citizens to vote online. However, concerns over security and protection from manipulation have thus far slowed the adoption of e-voting. Whereas e-voting initiatives are still hotly debated in many countries, several countries have started to introduce "smart" ID cards; for example, in 2003, Hong Kong introduced smart ID cards that allow its residents to use automated channels for immigration clearance for arrival and departure. Moreover, the smart ID card can be used as library card in Hong Kong's public libraries or can be used as an electronic certificate to conduct secure transactions over the Internet.

Government-to-Business Government-to-business **(G2B)** is similar to G2C, but this form of EC involves businesses' relationships with all levels of government. This includes e-procurement, in which the government streamlines its supply chain by purchasing materials directly from suppliers using its proprietary Internet-enabled procurement system. Also included in G2B initiatives are forward auctions that allow businesses to buy seized and surplus government equipment. Similar to eBay.com, the government launched AuctionRP.com to provide a marketplace for real-time auctions for surplus and seized goods. Other G2B services include online application for export licenses, verification of employees' Social Security numbers, and online tax filing.

Government-to-Government Finally, **government-to-government (G2G)** EC is used for electronic interactions that take place between countries or between different levels of government within a country. Since 2002, the U.S. government has provided comprehensive e-government tools that allow foreign entities to find government-wide information related to business topics. This includes Regulations.gov and Export.gov; both allow information to be accessed regarding laws and regulations relevant to federal requirements. In addition, e-government has aligned its electronic capabilities with world issues. For example, the Consolidated Health Informatics Initiative has adopted electronic standards to allow worldwide health organizations to share information securely with government agencies. Other G2G transactions relate to the intergovernmental collaboration at the local, state, federal, and tribal levels.

INDUSTRY ANALYSIS

Retailing

You may make most of your large purchases online in order to benefit from greater convenience or lower prices, but most likely you will be setting your feet into a brick-and-mortar retail store at least once in a while, and you may have noticed some changes brought by technology. A few decades ago, large retail chains started introducing computerized point-of-sale inventory systems consisting of checkout computers and an inventory control system. A simple bar code scan captures a sale, and the item is automatically deducted from the store's inventory, allowing real-time tracking of purchases so that the retailer knows when to reorder merchandise or restock shelves. In addition to a speedier checkout process, such systems help to reduce stockouts, increasing customer satisfaction. In many grocery stores, this system has been taken a step further, allowing the customers to conduct the checkout process themselves, saving time and labor costs.

In the near future, many items will be equipped with radio frequency identification (RFID) tags (see Chapter 8) eliminating the need to scan every individual item so that the total price for a cart full of merchandise can be calculated within a second, saving even more time and adding convenience for the customer. Imagine the time you'll save when all you have to do is pass with your cart through an RFID reader and swipe your credit card. Similarly, a store's shelves will be equipped with RFID technology, tracking when an item is removed from the shelf or enabling the use of electronic shelf labels that can present much more than a product's price. With the capability to monitor stock levels and the best-before dates on all the items, RFID technology makes it possible to plan the in-house production of fresh vegetable and meat products extremely precisely, thereby optimizing the quality assurance processes. "Smart" dressing rooms, equipped with RFID technology, can help the customer find more information about a product, such as the availability of an item in additional sizes or different colors, or even suggest other matching items. Thus, the customer does not have to wait for a sales associate to go and look for items. A similar technology currently in use is handheld computers with bar code scanners. Linked to the store's inventory control system using wireless technologies,

these handheld computers allow the sales associates to inquire about stock levels at the same store or even inquire about the availability at other stores of the same chain. In addition, a new "Pay by Fingerprint" system allows customers to complete a purchase by placing their finger onto a fingerprint scanner, without the need to sign a sales slip or enter a PIN; this makes the checkout process extremely convenient and secure. Another innovative way to pay for a purchase is via mobile phone. Using a technology called Near Field Communication (NFC; similar to Bluetooth), the customer's mobile phone communicates with the retailer's payment terminal, and the payment amount is automatically debited from the customer's bank account. NFC-based payment systems have already begun to be implemented; major smart phone manufacturers such as Nokia actively support this new technology by integrating it into new handsets, and third-party manufacturers offer solutions that allow using NFC by inserting a special micro-SD card into a cell phone.

As you can see, information systems have had a huge impact on retailing, and many more changes are yet to hit the shelves.

Questions

1. How can technology help brick-and-mortar retailers compete against e-tailers?
2. Privacy advocates criticize the use of RFID, as it allows better tracking of purchasing habits. How can brick-and-mortar retailers alleviate these concerns?
3. As you have read, some of the "human element" in retailing is being replaced by technology. How can brick-and-mortar stores avoid becoming too "sterile" when using information systems to compete against e-tailers?

Based on:

Anonymous. (n.d.). METRO Group Future Store Initiative. Retrieved April 24, 2010, from http://www.future-store.org/fsi-internet/html/en/375/index.html.

Voerste, A., & von Truchsess, A. (2008, May 28). METRO Group and Real open the store of the future. Retrieved April 24, 2010, from http://www.future-store.org/fsi-internet/html/en/16668/index.html.

Key Points Review

1. *Describe EC, how it has evolved, and the strategies that companies are adopting to compete in cyberspace.* EC is the online exchange of goods, services, and money between firms and between firms and their customers. Although EC was being used as far back as 1948 during the Berlin Airlift, the emergence of the Internet and World Wide Web has fueled a revolution in the manner in which products and services are marketed and sold. Their far-reaching effects have led to the creation of a global electronic marketplace that offers a virtually limitless array of new services, features, and functionality. Unlike the situation with traditional storefronts, time limitations are not a factor, allowing firms to sell and service products seven days a week, 24 hours a day, 365 days a year to anyone, anywhere. Companies are exploiting one or more of the capabilities of the Web to reach a wider customer base, offer a broader range of product offerings, and develop closer relationships with customers by striving to meet their unique needs. These wide-ranging capabilities include global information dissemination, integration, mass customization, interactive communication, collaboration, and transactional support. The Web has transformed the traditional business operation into a hypercompetitive electronic marketplace. Companies must strategically position themselves to compete in the new EC environment. At one extreme, companies known as brick-and-mortars choose to operate solely in the traditional, physical markets. In contrast, click-only (or virtual) companies conduct business electronically in cyberspace. These firms have no physical locations, allowing them to focus purely on EC. Click-and-mortar (or bricks-and-clicks) companies straddle the two environments, operating in both physical and virtual arenas. Companies must also select a specific business model that defines how they will earn money, which markets they intend to serve, whom they will compete with, what competitive advantage they will have, how they will market themselves, and so on. Firms in cyberspace must also define a revenue model that can be based on advertising revenue, subscription revenue, transaction fee revenue, sales revenue, or some combination.

2. *Explain the differences between extranets and intranets and show how organizations utilize these environments.* Extranets enable two or more firms to use the Internet to engage in B2B electronic commerce. Extranets provide timely and accurate information, allow for technology integration, and provide high value at low cost. Also referred to as B2E EC, an intranet refers to the use of the Internet within an organization to support internal business processes and activities. Examples of the types of processes or activities that might be supported include things such as training, online entry of information, real-time access to information, and

employee collaboration. Both extranets and intranets provide significant benefits to organizations and are being very widely adopted by firms both big and small.

3. *Describe the stages of B2C EC and understand the keys to successful EC applications.* B2C EC focuses on retail transactions between a company and end consumers. Business Web sites can be relatively simple or very sophisticated and can be classified as e-information, e-integration, or e-transaction sites. E-information sites simply provide electronic brochures and other types of information for customers. E-integration sites provide customers with the ability to gain personalized information by querying corporate databases and other information sources. E-transaction sites allow customers to place orders and make payments. For successful EC applications, companies should follow several rules. The basic rules of commerce are to offer valuable products and services at fair prices. These rules apply to EC as well as to any business endeavor. In addition to having a sound business model and plan for generating revenue, successful companies are found to follow a basic set of principles, or rules, related to Web-based EC. These rules include having a Web site that offers something unique, is aesthetically pleasing, is easy to use, and is fast and that motivates people to visit, to stay, and to return. A company should also advertise its presence on the Web (e.g., using search engine marketing) and should try to learn from its Web site (using Web analytics).

4. *Describe how people can participate in C2C EC and explain the different forms of Internet marketing.* The Internet has fueled the development of a variety of ways people can trade goods, socialize, or voice their thoughts and opinions. Specifically, e-auctions allow private people to sell goods to large markets. Typical forms of e-auctions are forward auctions and reverse auctions. However, while e-auctions give people the availability to sell things to large markets, the potential of fraud is still considered a big problem. As with offline businesses, EC businesses have to market their product and services. Popular ways to advertise products or services on the Web are search marketing, display ads, e-mail marketing, social media, and mobile marketing. Advertisers pay for these types of Internet marketing on the basis of either the number of impressions or pay-per-click.

5. *Describe emerging issues and trends in EC.* One emerging topic in EC is C2B EC, where individuals offer products or services to businesses. Mobile EC, or m-commerce, enables people to take full advantage of the Internet on portable, wireless devices, such as smart phones. M-commerce is rapidly expanding with the continuing expansion of worldwide Internet adoption as well as the continued evolution of faster cellular networks, more powerful handheld devices, and more sophisticated applications. Location-based services, based on GPS

technology, are a key driver enabling even more creative m-commerce applications. Major issues and impediments to EC continue to be securing payments, protecting intellectual property, and taxation of EC transactions.

6. *Explain different forms of e-government.* E-government is a government's use of IS to provide a variety of services to citizens, businesses, and other governmental agencies. Depending on the services, e-government initiatives can be targeted at citizens (government-to-citizens), businesses (government-to-business), or other governmental agencies (either within a country or between countries; government-to-government).

Key Terms

affiliate marketing 174
brick-and-mortar business strategy 149
bricks-and-clicks business strategy 149
business model 151
business-to-business (B2B) 145
business-to-business marketplace 158
business-to-consumer (B2C) 145
business-to-employee (B2E) 145
click fraud 174
click-and-mortar business strategy 149
click-only business strategy 149
click-through rate 174
competitive click fraud 174
consumer-to-business (C2B) 145
consumer-to-business (C2B) 176
consumer-to-consumer (C2C) 145
conversion rate 174
customer portal 157
Customer Verification Value (CVV2) 180
desktop videoconferencing 165
digital rights management (DRM) 182
disintermediation 149

e911 177
e-auction 170
e-government 182
e-information 166
e-integration 166
electronic bill pay 170
electronic commerce (EC) 144
Electronic Data Interchange (EDI) 154
electronic meeting system (EMS) 164
e-tailing 166
e-transaction 166
extranet 155
forward auction 170
global information dissemination 146
government-to-business (G2B) 183
government-to-citizen (G2C) 183
government-to-government (G2G) 183
groupware 163
integration 146
interactive communication 148
Internet Tax Freedom Act 181
intranet 159
location-based services 176
Long Tail 168

mass customization 147
m-commerce 176
menu-driven pricing 167
network click fraud 174
online banking 170
online investing 170
paid inclusion 172
pay-per-click 174
portal 156
reintermediation 149
revenue model 152
reverse auction 170
reverse pricing system 166
search advertising 172
search engine optimization (SEO) 173
sponsored search 172
supplier portal 157
transaction support 148
vertical market 158
virtual company 149
watermark 182
Web analytics 170
Web cam 165

Review Questions

1. What is EC, and how has it evolved?
2. How have the Web and other technologies given rise to a global platform?
3. Compare and contrast two EC business strategies.
4. Explain the differences between the Internet, an intranet, and an extranet. What is the common bond among all three?
5. List and explain three benefits of using extranets.
6. What are the three stages of B2C EC?
7. Describe the differences between SEO, search marketing, and sponsored search.
8. List and describe six elements of or rules for a good Web site.
9. List and describe three emerging trends in C2C EC.
10. Explain the different forms of online auctions.
11. Describe m-commerce and explain how it is different from regular EC.
12. What are the primary forms of e-government? Provide examples for each.
13. How does taxation pose a threat to EC?

Self-Study Questions

1. EC is the online exchange of _____ among firms, between firms and their customers, and between customers, supported by communication technologies and, in particular, the Internet.
   A. goods
   B. services
   C. money
   D. all of the above

2. _____ are those companies that operate in the traditional, physical markets and do not conduct business electronically in cyberspace.
   A. Brick-and-mortars
   B. Click-onlys
   C. both A and B
   D. Dot-coms

3. A _____ describes how a firm will earn revenue, generate profits, and produce a superior return on invested capital.
   A. profit-and-loss statement
   B. revenue model
   C. business model
   D. annual report

4. According to the text, the three stages of Web sites include all of the following except _____.
   A. e-tailing
   B. e-integration
   C. e-transaction
   D. e-information

5. The revolutionary aspect of the Priceline.com Web site lies in its _____ system called Name Your Own Price. Customers specify the product they are looking for and how much they are willing to pay for it.
   A. immediate pricing
   B. menu-driven pricing
   C. forward pricing
   D. reverse pricing

6. _____ is a type of e-auction fraud where bidders are lured to leave a legitimate auction in order to buy the same item at a lower price.
   A. Bid luring
   B. Product luring
   C. Customer luring
   D. Low-price luring

7. A Web site should _____ .
   A. be easy to use and fast
   B. offer something unique and be aesthetically pleasing
   C. motivate people to visit, to stay, and to return
   D. all of the above

8. C2C EC can be categorized according to _____ .
   A. the number of goods sold
   B. the number of buyers and sellers
   C. the payment methods accepted
   D. all of the above

9. Trying to "outsmart" a search engine to improve a page's ranking is known as _____.
   A. rank enhancement
   B. SEO
   C. search engine hacking
   D. Google fooling

10. According to the Internet Tax Freedom Act, e-tailers _____.
   A. have to collect sales tax from all customers, regardless of their location
   B. have to collect sales tax based on the place of the customer's residence
   C. have to collect sales tax based on the prevalent tax rate at the e-tailer's headquarters
   D. have to collect sales tax only from customers residing in a state where the business has substantial presence

Answers are on page 189.

Problems and Exercises

1. Match the following terms with the appropriate definitions:
   i. Search marketing
   ii. Electronic data interchange
   iii. Web analytics
   iv. Paid inclusion
   v. E-transaction
   vi. Long Tails
   vii. Supplier portal
   viii. Search engine optimization
   ix. E-government
   x. E-integration

   a. The practice of trying to increase a company's visibility in search engine results
   b. The digital, or electronic, transmission of business documents and related data between organizations via dedicated telecommunications networks
   c. A business model focusing on niche markets, rather than purely on mainstream products
   d. A stage that takes the e-integration stage one step further by adding the ability for customers to enter orders and payments online
   e. A stage in which Web pages are created on the fly to produce tailored information that addresses the particular needs of a consumer
   f. The use of information systems to provide citizens and organizations with handy information about public services
   g. Methods used to improve a site's ranking
   h. The analysis of Web surfers' behavior in order to improve a site's performance
   i. The practice of paying a fee to be included in a search engine's listing
   j. A subset of an organization's extranet designed to automate the business processes that occur before, during, and after sales have been transacted between a single buyer and multiple suppliers

2. Visit Alaska Airlines' Web site (www.alaskaair.com) for real-time pricing and test the custom messenger bag builder at www.timbuk2.com. How have Internet technologies improved over the years?

3. Search the Web for a company that is purely Web based. Next, find the Web site of a company that is a hybrid (i.e., they have a traditional brick-and-mortar business plus a presence on the Web). What are the pros and cons of dealing with each type of company?

4. Have you purchased anything over the Internet? If so, how was it delivered? As compared to traditional shopping, how sustainable do you think EC is from an environmental perspective?

5. Do you receive advertisements through e-mail? Are they directed toward any specific audience or product category? Do you pay much attention or just delete them? How much work is it to get off an advertising list?

6. What is it about a company's Web site that draws you to it, keeps you there on the site longer, and keeps you coming back for more? If you could summarize these answers into a set of criteria for Web sites, what would those criteria be?

7. Visit the following services for comparison shopping: BestBookBuys (www.bestwebbuys.com/books), Bizrate (www.bizrate.com), and mySimon (www.mysimon.com). These companies focus on aggregating content for consumers. What are the advantages of these Web sites?

8. Compare three different search engines. What tips do they provide to improve a page's rankings? How much does it cost to advertise a page on their results pages? If you were a company, could you think of any situation where you would pay almost any amount to have the first listing on the first results page?

9. Describe your experiences in online shopping. How did you pay for your purchases? What information did you have to reveal to the merchant? Did you feel comfortable giving out that information?

10. Go to Amazon.com's affiliate site. How does affiliate marketing at Amazon.com work? How do Amazon.com business partners get paid? Who can sign up for this service?

11. Have you ever used a mobile, wireless device such as a smart phone? If so, what do you like or dislike about it? In what ways could your use of that device be made better? If you are not using one, what is preventing you from using one? What would have to happen before you would begin using such a device?

12. Visit www.firstgov.gov. What kind of services do you see that would help you? What services would you use? What areas are missing?

13. When you shop online, is sales tax a criterion for you? Do you try to purchase goods where you do not have to pay sales tax? If you would have to pay sales tax for everything you buy online, would that change your online shopping behavior?

Application Exercises

Note: The existing data files referenced in these exercises are available on the Student Companion Web site: **www.pearsonhighered.com/valacich**.

 Spreadsheet Application:
Analyzing Server Traffic

Campus Travel has recently found that its Internet connections between offices are becoming slow, especially during certain periods of the day. Since all the online traffic is maintained by another company, an increase in capacity requires a formal approval from the general manager. The IS manager has proposed to increase the capacity of the company's network; in a few days, he has to present the business case for this proposal at the weekly meeting of the department heads. You are asked to prepare graphs for the presentation to support the IS manager's business case. In the file ServerLogs.csv, you will find information about the network traffic for a one-week period. Prepare the following graphs:

1. Total bandwidth used for each day (line graph)
2. Bandwidth used per day, by time period (line graph)
3. Average bandwidth used in each two-hour period (line graph)

Format the graphs in a professional manner and print out each graph on a separate page (Hint: If you are using Microsoft Excel's Chart Wizard, select "Place chart: As New Sheet" in step 4).

 Database Application:
Tracking Network Hardware

As Campus Travel is new to EC, the management suggests following a stepwise approach for using the Internet to conduct business. Before using the Internet for conducting transactions, the managers recommend setting up a site that provides information to customers. Part of this informational site is an agency locator that shows the services each agency has. You have been asked to create a new database. This includes creating relationships in the current database. To create this new database, do the following:

1. Create a database called "agency."
2. Create a table called "agencies" and include fields for agency ID, street address, city, state, ZIP code, phone number, number of service agents, and working hours.
3. Create a table called "services" that includes service ID, name (i.e., type of service), and description.
4. Create a third table called "agencyservices" that includes the agency ID field from the agencies table and the service ID field from the services table.
5. Once these tables are created, go to the relationship view and connect the agencies (one side) and agencyservices (many side) tables and the services (one side) and agencyservices (many side) tables using two one-to-many relationships (i.e., each agency can offer many services; each service can be offered by many agencies).

Team Work Exercise: So Many Books, So Little Time

Have you ever bought books online? Compare and contrast your experiences with your classmates. What types of books have you purchased? Which Web sites did you use? How did you like your online purchase experience? Do you tend to stick with the same online bookstore, or do you shop around for the best bargains? Discuss strategies the different stores use to keep you from switching to another bookstore. If you have not yet bought books online, visit the Web sites of Amazon.com and Barnes & Noble as well as comparison sites, such as www.allbookstores.com, and evaluate their offerings. Summarize the benefits and drawbacks of purchasing books online.

Answers to the Self-Study Questions

1. D, p. 144
2. A, p. 149
3. C, p. 152
4. A, p. 166
5. D, p. 166
6. A, p. 171
7. D, p. 169
8. B, p. 171
9. B, p. 173
10. D, p. 181

Case 1

Global Picture Sharing: Flickr

Has there been a wedding, birth, confirmation, graduation, one-hundredth birthday celebration, or other commemorative event in your family lately? Would you like to see the photos your sister, Uncle Walt, and Grandma Mary took at the event? Invite everyone who attended to post their photos on Flickr.com—one of the easiest and most popular means of sharing photos online.

Flickr.com was developed by Ludicorp, a Vancouver, Canada–based company founded in 2002 and launched online in 2004. Yahoo! purchased Flickr in 2005. In just over a year after Flickr's launch, the site had over 350,000 members, who had collectively uploaded 31 million images.

Flickr didn't invent online photo sharing, but the tools members can use to navigate the photos on the site are unique. "Tags" let photo owners and viewers label photos to prescribe a category that makes them easier to find. For example, popular tags include summer, winter, cute, Europe, dog, cat, and so on. Flickr takes the tag concept further with clustering, a better way to explore photos through tags. Key in "summer beach vacations," for instance, and you can view a page of clustered photos with just those tags. Clustering has resulted in such far-out photo categories as confusing street signs, dogs' noses, Halloween costumes, margaritas, and mannequins.

Flickr sees photo sharing and the use of tags as a social process users call "folksonomy." That is, since viewers can add comments to photos, there is a level of involvement similar to a social gathering. For a person who is browsing through a set of photos, the notes on the photos tell little stories, as if that person were sitting by the photographer, who is explaining the photo.

Flickr photo viewers can also rate a photo according to "interestingness." Each calendar day, a few highly ranked photos are posted to a common page for easier viewer exploration.

Flickr also allows for basic photo manipulation, such as rotation, ordering prints, sending to a group of people, adding to a blog or even a map, and so on. Photos can be open for everyone everywhere to view, or viewing can be restricted to one's friends and family. In late 2009, Flickr also added the ability to "people tag" in photos uploaded to the site. The feature allows users to draw a small box around the subject they want to tag. You can add a note or the name of the person being tagged.

Users can get a free basic account that allows them to upload two videos and 100MB worth of photos each calendar month. For $25 a year, users can get a pro account that allows them an unlimited number of photo and video uploads per month, ad-free browsing, and a number of other advantages.

Since Flickr's basic photo-sharing service is free, revenue for the company is based on Yahoo!-placed ads on Flickr Web pages. Photographers who post images on the Flickr site, however, are free to sell their photos. The legal aspects of copyright are handled by a license called the "creative commons." This license has many different levels of copyright protection but is primarily for not-for-profit use of a user's photographs. Flickr offers a simple interface that allows photographers to choose a license for protecting copyright.

For programming enthusiasts, Flickr has released all application program interfaces for public use. For example, programmers have used the interfaces to develop uploading applications for the Mac, Windows, camera phones, and other devices.

Flickr is also one of the first Web sites to join the OpenID project. With OpenID, Internet users don't need multiple IDs and passwords; after registering once with the free service, the same login ID and password can be used to enter any site that participates in OpenID. The worldwide popularity of Flickr is another way in which information systems are fueling a flatter world.

Flickr continues to expand their services to users and grow in popularity. Pro members of the site can now upload high-definition video, viewable in a 16:9 HD player. Although the site is focused on still photos, users who have that great little video clip they caught with their camera can now upload and share. Another popular addition to the site came in 2010 when Facebook Connect was added. The connection to the popular social media site allows users to update their Facebook status from within the photo page.

Flickr has also joined forces with popular online mapping services. Both Microsoft's Bing Maps and Google Maps have now integrated Flickr photos into their services. Both services currently offer a "Street View" option (Bing Maps calls their view "street side"), allowing users to view a stitched panorama of photos of the area they are looking at on the map. These photos come from Microsoft or Google sources and are updated only periodically. With the new Flickr connection, users can now see alternative photos that Flickr users have geotagged and uploaded. This is a significant enhancement to the service because of the amount of geotagged photos in the Flickr library, which, as of 2010, stands at over 95.5 million photos. Some estimates put the number of geotagged photos uploaded to Flickr at over 2 million *a month*. This growing amount of data will give users a wealth of photographic data to utilize when planning a trip using online mapping services (especially when going to regions where no "Street Views" are provided). For example, when planning a vacation, users can look for clusters of user-generated pictures to identify interesting sites worth visiting.

Flickr's popularity has also reached the highest level of the U.S. government. In a historical move, the White House opened an official Flickr photo stream in April 2009. In its inaugural upload, the White House posted 293 photos of life surrounding President Obama and his first 100 days in office. Since the photo stream's inception, the Flickr page has chronicled most major events that surround the White House. For presidential history buffs and casual Web surfers alike, the photo stream has given an unprecedented look into the daily life of the president through Flickr's convenient and easy interface.

Questions

1. Why do you think Flickr has been so popular throughout the world?
2. What lessons could a Web site for a local business learn from Flickr?
3. How do Web sites like Flickr act to increase globalization?

Based on:

Anonymous. (2005, August 1). The new new things. *Flickr Blog*. Retrieved June 9, 2010, from http://blog.flickr.net/en/2005/08/01/the-new-new-things.

Axline, K. (2009, April 29). Presidential first: White House floods Flickr. *Wired*. Retrieved April 13, 2010, from http://www.wired.com/rawfile/2009/04/presidential-first-white-house-floods-flickr.

Chan, S. (2010, February 12). Bing maps now pulls in Flickr photos. *Seattle Times*. Retrieved April 13, 2010, from http://seattletimes.nwsource.com/html/microsoftpri0/2011056182_bingmapsnowsucksinflickrphotos.html.

Forrest, B. (2010, February 8). Flickr photos in Google Street View. *O'Reilly Radar.com*. Retrieved April 13, 2010, from, http://radar.oreilly.com/2010/02/flickr-photos-in-google-street.html.

Gilbertson, S. (2009, March 3). Flickr video goes HD and opens to everyone. *Wired*. Retrieved April 13, 2010, from http://www.wired.com/epicenter/2009/03/flickr-video-go.

Krazit, T. (2009, December 2). Yahoo brings Facebook Connect into its sites. *CNET News.com*. Retrieved April 13, 2010, from http://news.cnet.com/8301-30684_3-10407688-265.html.

Stone, B. (2004, March 11). Photos for the masses. *MSNBC-Newsweek*. Retrieved June 9, 2010, from http://www.newsweek.com/id/48941.

Terdiman, D. (2005, November 16). Tagging gives web a human meaning. *News.com*. Retrieved May 24, 2008, from http://news.com.com/Tagging+gives+Web+a+human+meaning/2009-1025_3-5944502.html.

Trenholm, R. (2009, October 22). Flickr adds face tagging. *CNET.co.uk*. Retrieved April 13, 2010, from, http://crave.cnet.co.uk/software/0,39029471,49304018,00.htm.

Case 2

YouTube

It's the Web site everyone visits at least once, and most surfers come back again and again. It's the ubiquitous YouTube. Where else can you watch a video of a cat swimming contentedly in a bathtub, a 12-year-old rendering a professional performance of the "The Star Spangled Banner" at a small-town basketball game, or a public political debate where candidates answer questions visitors to the site have submitted?

YouTube, a video-sharing Web site, went online in 2005. Two former PayPal employees, Steve Chen and Chad Hurley, created the site, and it was practically an overnight success. The San Bruno, California–based service uses Adobe Flash technology to display a wide variety of user-generated video content, including movie and TV clips, music videos, video blogging, and short original videos. In July 2006, YouTube reported that visitors to the site were viewing more than 100 million video clips a day—a fact that compelled Google Inc. to buy the site that year for $1.76 billion in stock. As of 2010, YouTube continues to be a successful video site and a top destination for Web surfers who watch an average of 15 minutes of video each day. According to the site, hundreds of millions of videos are watched daily, and 20 hours of video are uploaded every minute.

YouTube is free and registration is not necessary for visitors to view videos. To upload videos, however, registration is required. Videos with pornographic content and those showing nudity or that defame or harass are prohibited, as is advertising and anything encouraging criminal conduct. All of that video requires YouTube to have access to a lot of bandwidth. The bandwidth expenses for the service were estimated at $300 million for 2009. That same year, the viewing of videos on YouTube consumed an amount of bandwidth comparable to the entire Internet in the year 2000. In fact, in 2007 the British publication the *Telegraph* expressed fears that the Internet could "grind to a halt within two years" without massive upgrades to the Internet infrastructure. Fortunately for YouTube fans and Internet users in general, that didn't happen. Bandwidth issues aside,

YouTube continues to try and draw in more viewers. To that end, the site's user interface got a major overhaul in the spring of 2010. The main page was streamlined and redesigned to be more social-media friendly. In addition, the update made it easier to locate and watch a continuous stream of related video content.

As YouTube has gained in popularity, police forces around the country have used the service to help catch criminals. In April 2010, for example, homicide investigators in Vancouver, British Columbia, posted a video about a victim in an unsolved but high-profile murder case. Although the case was being actively investigated, the investigative team had exhausted their list of leads. The posted video included photos of the woman who had been killed and a recap of what the investigators had pieced together up to that point. Their hope was that by using social media and getting the story in front of viewers, it might help jog a memory of someone who might have seen something pertinent to the case. Some police departments, however, such as St. George County, Virginia, said they would not use YouTube for catching criminals because posting police videos next to those with "crazy" content would be "bad publicity" for the police.

Regardless of the propensity for catching criminals or lack thereof, YouTube has had its share of legal issues as well. After several lawsuits were filed alleging copyright violations over copyrighted material posted on YouTube, the company agreed to remove copyrighted material on request. In addition, YouTube installed software intended to automatically detect and remove copyrighted clips. In order to function correctly, however, the software needed to compare clips of copyrighted material to YouTube content, which meant that music, movie, and television companies would have to send decades of clips of copyrighted material to YouTube so that comparisons could be made.

In March 2010, the entertainment corporation Viacom entered into a $1 billion lawsuit against YouTube alleging that the video site knowingly made a financial gain from 62,637 Viacom video clips that were viewed over 507 million times. YouTube has countered by alleging that Viacom was covertly uploading clips of their content in an attempt to sabotage YouTube's efforts to remove copyrighted material. Although it remains to be seen how the lawsuit will be resolved, it is a sticky situation for the video site. Whatever YouTube's future, it's not likely that Internet users will soon lose interest in video sharing.

Questions

1. Do you use YouTube? If so, what is your favorite type of content? If not, why not?
2. How can businesses use YouTube to promote a good brand image? Have you seen any "good" campaigns on YouTube? If so, what made them appealing?
3. What potential dangers for a business' reputation can arise from user-generated content posted on sites such as YouTube? How can a business react to such dangers?

Based on:

Ahrens, F. (2007, March 14). Viacom sues YouTube over copyright. *Washington Post*. Retrieved June 10, 2010, from http://www.washingtonpost.com/wp-dyn/content/article/2007/03/13/AR2007031300595.html.

Anonymous. (2007, October 17). YouTube installs copyright-protection filters. *Fox News*. Retrieved June 10, 2010, from http://www.foxnews.com/story/0,2933,302376,00.html.

Bolan, K. (2010, April 1). Police enlist YouTube in hunt for a killer. *Vancouver Sun*. Retrieved June 10, 2010, from http://www.vancouversun.com/news/Police+enlist+YouTube+hunt+killer/2752334/story.html.

Carroll, J. (2008, January 16). The shrinking planet and YouTube. *ZDNet.com*. Retrieved June 10, 2010, from http://blogs.zdnet.com/carroll/?p=1789.

Carter, L. (2008, April 9). Web could collapse as video demand soars. *Telegraph.co.uk*. Retrieved June 10, 2010, from http://www.telegraph.co.uk/news/uknews/1584230/Web-could-collapse-as-video-demand-soars.html.

Claburn, T. (2010, February 10). YouTube offers filter for offensive content. *Informationweek*. Retrieved June 10, 2010, from http://www.informationweek.com/news/ security/management/showArticle.jhtml?articleID=22270078.

Delaney, K. (2006, June 27). With NBC pact, YouTube site tries to build a lasting business. *Wall Street Journal*. Retrieved June 10, 2010, from http://online.wsj.com/article/SB115137083424491406.html.

Delaney, K., & Smith, E. (2006, September 19). YouTube model is compromise over copyrights. *Wall Street Journal*. Retrieved June 10, 2010, from http://online.wsj.com/public/article/SB115862128600366836-HfXOBEjVMilRqWxOu6LMMFpVMKo_20061018.html.

Lane, T. (2010, April 2). YouTube's redesign focuses on social features & ease-of-use. *Sparxoo*. Retrieved June 10, 2010, from http://sparxoo.com/2010/04/02/youtubes-redesign-focuses-on-social-features-ease-of-use.

Reisinger, D. (2010, February 15). In just five years, YouTube became the go-to video site. *Los Angeles Times*. Retrieved June 10, 2010, from http://latimesblogs.latimes.com/technology/2010/02/youtube-fifth-birthday.html.

Sachoff, M. (2008, February 4). YouTube used by police for leads. *WebProNews*. Retrieved June 10, 2010, from http://www.webpronews.com/topnews/2008/02/04/youtube-used-by-police-for-leads.

Spangler, T. (2009, September 9). YouTube's bandwidth bill estimated at $300M for 2009. *Multichannel News*. Retrieved June 10, 2010, from http://www.multichannel.com/article/339947-YouTube_s_Bandwidth_Bill_Estimated_At_300M_For_2009.php.

Srinivasan, A. (2010, February 15). Average number of views on You-Tube videos. *Tech Crunchies*. Retrieved June 10, 2010, from http://techcrunchies.com/youtube-average-views.

Wagner, M. (2010, March 22). Viacom-YouTube lawsuit: Both sides look bad, YouTube looks worse. *Computerworld Blogs*. Retrieved June 10, 2010, from http://blogs.computerworld.com/15790/viacom_youtube.

YouTube. (2010, June 7). In *Wikipedia, the free encyclopedia*. Retrieved June 10, 2010, from http://en.wikipedia.org/w/index.php?title=YouTube&oldid=366639775.

five

Enhancing Collaboration Using Web 2.0

Preview

This chapter focuses on the revolution that is changing the World Wide Web, electronic commerce, and business in general. Web 2.0 is the term used to describe the wave of change in business models and in Web site functionality that has transformed the online landscape. Most likely, you are already familiar with popular Web 2.0 applications such as Facebook or Wikipedia, and you may ask, Why do we need to have a chapter on this? Web 2.0 introduces unprecedented ways to connect to friends, share knowledge with your colleagues, or collaborate with a team of engineers 5,000 miles away, and many of today's companies cannot afford to miss this trend. Most young people entering the workforce have grown accustomed to using Facebook or Twitter for their communication needs (and some even regard e-mail as an outmoded communication medium); if a company doesn't allow the use of those tools, they may leave and work for another company. Even more, you may have noticed your parents' generation joining sites such as Facebook, and those tools are more and more taken for granted by many.

With Web 2.0 providing a new set of capabilities for individuals and businesses, an understanding of how they can be applied can be very helpful. Being able to understand and apply these emerging capabilities and strategies that are associated with Web 2.0 is a highly marketable skill.

Managing in the Digital World: Facebook.com

Facebook.com calls itself "a social utility that helps people better understand the world around them . . . through social networks allowing people to share information online the same way they do in the real world." That it does. In early 2010, Facebook reported the following user statistics:

- More than 500 million active users—"active" meaning a user has visited the site in the past 30 days.
- More than 100 million active users accessing Facebook through their mobile devices.
- More than 1.5 million local businesses have pages on Facebook.
- In the United States, nearly half of all users are between the ages of 18 and 34.
- The average user spends more than 55 minutes a day on Facebook.
- Over 5 billion pieces of content are shared each week (photos, notes, blog posts, and so on).
- Nearly 70 percent of Facebook users are from outside the U.S.

Founded by a group of Harvard University students and launched in February 2004, Facebook was set to provide everything a college student needs to know about other students (see Figure 5.1). Users list their interests ("soccer" or "buying shoes"), friends, classes, and any other "tasteful" information about themselves. Anyone could form a subgroup within Facebook, such as "Cancer Corner" for smokers, "Collars Up!" for members who liked to wear their shirts with the collars turned up, and the self-described "Republican Princesses."

Initially, Facebook provided students with a private online directory that could be accessed only by people having an e-mail address ending in ".edu" (an ending that is usually reserved for educational institutions). This constraint was the major difference between Facebook and other online friendship and dating Web sites. Over time, Facebook realized that the restriction to just students alienated a large number of people. What was founded as a social networking site just for Harvard students was opened up to college students throughout the United States, to high school students,

and, in 2006, to anyone who wanted to join. To give its members the feeling of protection, the privacy controls were expanded, allowing people to prevent being included in search results and being contacted by people outside their networks. Further, Facebook's college and work networks require authenticated e-mail addresses to join.

Because of such restrictions, Facebook is also a good place for announcements—or not. For example, one student advertised a party in an off-campus apartment complex. As expected, fellow students who were on Facebook learned about the time and location of the party, but, unfortunately (for the host),

Adrian Wyld/AP Wide World Photos

FIGURE 5.1

Facebook is the most popular social network, with over 500 million active users.

a pair of roommates living next door to the party site also read about the party on Facebook. The pair of roommates dreaded the impending commotion and advised the police to be on alert that night. The party started mildly at 8:00 P.M. but got rowdy by 9:00 P.M. The police cars that were parked just outside the apartment complex stopped the party promptly at 10:00 P.M. to comply with the city's noise ordinance. The moral is, don't advertise an event on Facebook unless you want a crowd to show up.

Anyone belonging to the Facebook community can access other members' profiles and browse their interests as well as their friends' pages. Many active members post detailed profiles of themselves and admit to logging on to browse Facebook four or five times a day. A user's "wall" is another popular feature allowing anyone to post a message to the user on his or her wall. Other Facebook features include adding photo albums, listing coming activities, and "liking" others' posts or external Web sites. Facebook also provides rating scales for music, books, movies, television series, and other interests and activities. One of Facebook's most popular attractions is playing casual games such as FarmVille, a real-time farming simulation.

Over the past few years, Facebook has had a surge in popularity, replacing the once leading social site MySpace, to become a dominating force on the Web. Once squarely in the domain of students, Facebook use has spread across demographics. Mom, Dad, and Grandparents are now logging on as well to keep up with their social networks, find old classmates, or check out what their kids are up to. As a result, using social media is no longer just a "young" phenomenon. As Facebook has enlarged its audience across age-groups and the world, businesses and organizations alike have begun to see the value of having a presence on the social network. Organizations from churches to social clubs now use Facebook to spread announcements, coordinate activities, and create a public space for those looking for more information. Facebook's networking tools are especially helpful when coordination and feedback among lots of people is needed, making it the perfect tool for many groups.

Initially feared by many companies as a time waster for employees, Facebook has become prevalent on many corporate and small-business Web sites as a way to connect with customers and maintain relationships. Some companies are even beginning to use Facebook as a means of interoffice communication. For example, employees can post updates on what they're working on or request input on a project, giving coworkers and managers opportunities to view and respond simultaneously. One business in California has instituted "Facebook Fridays," when all office communication is completed using social media.

Not all businesses have completely embraced Facebook, however. A recent study found that 54 percent of U.S. companies have banned the use of Facebook and other social media sites while on the job. Nineteen percent of the companies allowed social networking use if it was company related, and 16 percent allowed their employees to have limited personal use time. While many worry about the productivity losses that may occur if employees are distracted updating their Facebook status, "time theft" is no longer the top concern in many cases. According to a recent poll of 500 firms by Sophos, network security is thought to be the biggest threat Facebook poses to companies. Since April 2009, the number of companies reporting malware attacks through social media sites has risen over 65 percent. Malware itself isn't the only problem, either. Many companies worry that their employees are not Web savvy enough to recognize malware when they encounter it and thus may respond to it, slowing corporate networks. Additionally, many companies fear their employees will accidentally (or, worse, maliciously) share important confidential data or trade secrets through their Facebook accounts, resulting in damaging repercussions.

A good example of this potentially disastrous problem happened in the summer of 2009 when the British Secret Intelligence Service (similar to the Central Intelligence Agency in the United States) was about to get a new director, John Sawers. As Sawers was due to take over the leadership position, it became known that his wife was on Facebook. On her page, she had posted family photos, vacation information, and information about where they lived, their friends, and social engagements. Unfortunately for Britain's newest top spy, she hadn't applied any security to her Facebook profile, making the details of her family and friends' lives open to Facebook's then 400 million users. Not only was this embarrassing to John Sawers, but it was potentially dangerous to him, his family, and his acquaintances, as hostile foreign powers or terrorists might use the information for nefarious purposes. Eventually, Sawers took the over as head of the agency. With Facebook's worldwide reach, however, one has to wonder if James Bond is still MI6's most famous spy.

To summarize, Facebook no longer provides a popular networking service just for college students. Its use has spread across demographic and usage groups and it has become an important and prevalent tool in many businesses and organizations.

After reading this chapter, you will be able to answer the following:

1. How can a social networking site such as Facebook become a part of everyday life?
2. Besides pure social interaction, what are some other ways Facebook can be used?
3. What are the pros and cons of using a social networking site in a business setting?

Based on:

Anonymous. (2009, October 9). Study: 54 percent of companies ban Facebook, Twitter at work. *Wired*. Retrieved June 26, 2010, from http://www.wired.com/epicenter/2009/10/study-54-of-companies-ban-facebook-twitter-at-work.

Anonymous. (2010). Facebook Statistics. Retrieved June 26, 2010, from http://www.facebook.com/press/info.php?statistics.

Doan, M. (2009, March 13). Businesses befriending Facebook. *The Kiplinger Letter*. Retrieved June 26, 2010, from http://www.kiplinger.com/businessresource/forecast/archive/more_firms_using_facebook_090313.html.

Lewis, J. (2009, July 5). MI6 chief blows his cover as wife's Facebook account reveals family holidays. *Mail Online*. Retrieved June 26, 2010, from http://www.dailymail.co.uk/news/article-1197562/MI6-chief-blows-cover-wifes-Facebook-account-reveals-family-holidays-showbiz-friends-links-David-Irving.html.

Perez, S. (2010, February 1). Why your boss hates Facebook. *ReadWriteWeb*. Retrieved June 26, 2010, from http://www.readwriteweb.com/archives/why_your_boss_hates_facebook.php.

Defining Web 2.0

Over the past few years, **Web 2.0** has received much attention from the popular press. Typically, the term refers to dynamic Web applications that allow people to collaborate and share information online. One of the basic concepts associated with Web 2.0 is a shift in the users' role from the passive consumer of content to its creator: in contrast to the TV network ABC's site, where content is provided by ABC, the Web 2.0 application YouTube depends on content created and uploaded by other users; similarly, whereas the *Encyclopaedia Britannica* invests large sums in professionally researched articles, the articles in the online encyclopedia Wikipedia are jointly written and edited by the online community. In addition to these applications, many organizations have successfully incorporated Web 2.0 concepts into their business models. For example, Amazon.com adds value to its site by incorporating book reviews from its customers. This way, they give customers a channel to voice their thoughts; at the same time, a larger number of reviews can help other customers make better decisions, thus attracting more visitors to Amazon.com's site (see Figure 5.2).

Social Software

Many successful Web 2.0 applications can be classified as **social software** (or **social media**), allowing people to communicate, interact, and collaborate in various ways. With the proliferation of Web 2.0, people's behaviors and societies have undergone rapid changes. For example, many people have changed the ways they search for information: Whereas in the past, people have turned to encyclopedias as sources of unbiased information, people now increasingly turn to Web sites such as Wikipedia, or ask their friends and acquaintances on Facebook for personalized information. Similarly, there has been a marked shift in the way people view privacy and share information; as criticized by privacy advocates, people are sharing more personal information than ever before. Repeatedly, you can read about people posting the most private information, without thinking about the consequences; as Facebook and other social Web sites have become pervasive in many people's lives, you have information about your friend's recent drinking escapades leading to a DUI, your coworker's breaking up with his girlfriend, and other things you may or may not want to know, all at your fingertips. Clearly, social software has strongly influenced the lives of many people. Table 5.1 highlights the shift in perspectives from the Web 1.0 to the Web 2.0 era.

Enterprise 2.0

Given these profound changes, many business organizations have looked for ways to control and/or utilize Web 2.0 and social software. Many organizations have built successful business models around Web 2.0, but most are trying to use Web 2.0 applications to support their existing business models. The use of Web 2.0 techniques and social software within a company's boundaries or between a company and its customers or stakeholders (often referred to as **Enterprise 2.0**) can help in sharing organizational knowledge, making businesses more innovative and productive, and helping them to effectively connect with their customers and the wider public (McAfee, 2006a).

FIGURE 5.2

Amazon.com lets readers provide feedback.

TABLE 5.1 Shifting Perspectives from Web 1.0 to Web 2.0

Web 1.0	Web 2.0
Me	Me and you
Read	Read and write
Connect ideas	Connect ideas and people
Search	Receive and give recommendations to friends and others
Find	Share
Techies rule	Users rule
Organizations	Individuals

Source: Based on Sessums (2009).

Collective Intelligence

One major benefit of social software is the ability to harness the "wisdom of crowds," or collective intelligence (Surowiecki, 2004). The concept of **collective intelligence** is based on the notion that distributed groups of people with a divergent range of information and expertise will be able to outperform the capabilities of individual experts, as demonstrated by the online encyclopedia Wikipedia, which is entirely based on its users' contributions (see Figure 5.3). Likewise, open source software is another example of the power of collective intelligence. High-quality software such as the Firefox Web browser, the Linux operating system, or the OpenOffice productivity suite are created by thousands of volunteers located all over the world. For organizations, making effective use of the collective intelligence of their employees, customers, and other stakeholders can prove extremely valuable. In addition to the benefits of harnessing the wisdom of crowds, societal changes, brought about by globalization, increasing wealth and consumerism, as well as the Web, are key drivers for Enterprise 2.0.

FIGURE 5.3

Distributed groups of people with a divergent range of information and expertise will be able to outperform the capabilities of individual experts.

Source: Anita Milivojevic\Shutterstock

The Facebook/LinkedIn/Twitter Workspace

In his book *The CEO: The Chief Engagement Officer: Turning Hierarchy Upside Down to Drive Performance*, John Smythe (2007) argues that there are some fundamental shifts taking place in employer/employee relationships. For example, employees are now looking for a portfolio career rather than a cradle-to-grave job, tend to view themselves as citizens rather than employees, and "loan their talent" to the employer rather than being a "human resource." The "millennials," or "Generation Y," who grew up being tied to MySpace, YouTube, or Facebook, are joining the workforce and are having much different expectations from their workplace than prior generations. A recent global study by Accenture revealed that for 37 percent of 18- to 27-year-olds, state-of-the-art technology is a vital consideration in the choice of workplace; of the working millennials, 55 percent use instant messaging; and 45 percent use social networking sites for work-related activities (Francis & Harrigan, 2010). The millennials bring with them many new and valuable skills but also attitudes that may be difficult to integrate with more traditional business environments. Although over 50 percent of businesses in the United States ban social networking sites at work (Gaudin, 2009), many millennials are skilled at finding creative work-arounds to circumvent such policies. As a result, companies are increasingly starting to embrace Web 2.0 techniques and social software to enhance communication, cooperation, collaboration, and connection (Cook, 2008). In the following sections, we will introduce various tools for the different purposes; needless to say, many Web 2.0 applications cannot be neatly categorized and fit into more than one category.

Enhancing Communication with Web 2.0

A prime application of Enterprise 2.0 is facilitating and enhancing the communication within an organization as well as between an organization and its stakeholders. For organizations, Web 2.0 tools have opened up a vast array of opportunities for presenting themselves to their (potential) customers; at the same time, Web 2.0 applications have opened up literally thousands of channels for customers to voice their opinions about an organization. In this section, we introduce various Web 2.0 tools used for communication.

One widely used tool for communication is discussion forums. Pre-dating the Web 2.0 era, **discussion forums** emulate traditional bulletin boards and allow for threaded discussions between participants. Typically, discussion forums are dedicated to specific topics, and users can start new threads. Depending on the owner or host of the forum, the discussion forum may be moderated so that new postings appear only after they have been vetted by a moderator; further, some discussion forums may only allow posts from registered users, whereas others allow anyone to contribute. As the purpose of such forums is to enable discussion, there are usually multiple participants exchanging (typically rather short) thoughts. In contrast, blogs allow individuals to express their thoughts in a one-to-many fashion.

Blogs

Blogging originally started out as a novice's way of expressing themselves using very simple Web pages. **Blogging** is the process of creating an online text diary (i.e., a **blog,** or Web log) made up of chronological entries that comment on everything from one's everyday life, to wine and food, or even computer problems (see Figure 5.4). Rather than trying to produce physical books to sell or use as gifts, bloggers (i.e., the people maintaining blogs) merely want to share stories about their lives or voice their opinions (although feedback is often encouraged through associated threaded discussions). Many bloggers use their blogs to hone their writing skills, often producing elaborate, thoughtful pieces of writing. Blogging has exploded into its own industry, and many companies and even the mainstream media embrace blogging (see Table 5.2). Engadget.com is one instance of a blogging business. Started in 2004 and later bought by America Online (AOL) in 2005, Engadget.com focuses on news and rumors from the customer electronics and gadgets areas. Engadget.com now employs several story editors and a multitude of reporters to cover the electronics industry. The influence of blogging has also hit the mainstream media. Many traditional media giants, such as CNN, now use blogs to paint a richer picture of the stories they produce. Anderson Cooper, one of CNN's anchors, currently edits and writes for CNN's flagship blog called Anderson Cooper 360.

FIGURE 5.4

Blogging is the process of creating an online text diary (i.e., a blog, or Web log) made up of chronological entries.

Blogs are being used by small, medium-sized, and large organizations and have become important voices that can sway public opinion. One famous example of the power of blogging is the 2004 election scandal known as "Rathergate." Dan Rather, appearing on *60 Minutes,* reported on some suspect findings concerning President George W. Bush's record of military service. Bloggers soon after (correctly) reported that the documents used in this news story were falsified. Without the bloggers' visibility, this misrepresentation could have gone unnoticed. Because of the bloggers' reports, Dan Rather resigned from *60 Minutes*, and some say that this eventually caused his dismissal from CBS News.

Blogs are not without controversy. Nicholas Carr, noted technology journalist (and active blogger himself), classifies blogging as the **"amateurization" of journalism.** Often the value of blogging is the ability to bring breaking news to the public in the fastest possible way. By doing so, some bloggers cut journalistic corners, rendering some of the posts on the blogs less than accurate. For example, in May 2007, Engadget.com reported that Apple's iPhone and OSX operating system were going to be delayed. This news spurred a 4 percent downturn in Apple's stock

TABLE 5.2 Examples of Prominent Blogs

Type of Blog	Example	Description
Technology	www.engadget.com	Consumer electronics blog
	news.cnet.com/tech-blogs	Various technology blogs
	www.roughtype.com	Blog of Nicholas Carr, author of the book *IT Doesn't Matter* and former executive editor of the *Harvard Business Review*
Financial	blogs.wsj.com/marketbeat	*Wall Street Journal*'s blog on stock market happenings
	www.dvorak.org/blog	John Dvorak from *Market Watch* reports on various news events
Entertainment	www.perezhilton.com	A gossip and news blog run by TV personality Mario Armando Lavandeira Jr.
	nymag.com/daily/fashion	*New York Magazine's* fashion blog
Political	corner.nationalreview.com	A blog run by *The National Review,* a magazine started in 1955 by William F. Buckley
	www.huffingtonpost.com	One of the most powerful political blogs; the *Huffington Post,* founded by Arianna Huffington, won the "Webby Award" as best political blog in 2006 and 2008.

price in less than 20 minutes. Soon after the story was released, users questioned the validity of the story, and Engadget.com retracted the story. Further, blogs have been criticized for frequently providing the biased opinions of the writers, particularly because many of the authors' sources cannot or have not been verified.

Nevertheless, blogs have massively influenced the way in which people gather and consume information. In fact, turning to free information from blogs and other online sources, many readers have cancelled newspaper subscriptions. In turn, diminishing readership in traditional newspapers has enticed advertisers to begin to withdraw from this traditional medium, leading to budget cuts and layoffs at reputable newspapers such as the *San Francisco Chronicle,* the *New York Times,* the *Washington Times,* and many others; in December 2008, newspaper giant Tribune Co., owner of the *Los Angeles Times,* the *Chicago Tribune,* and other newspapers, was forced to file for Chapter 11 bankruptcy protection, facing dwindling advertising revenues and a huge debt burden (as of 2010, Tribune was still under bankruptcy protection). Unfortunately—and ironically—this may erode the very sources that many bloggers base their information on. To show just how severe this problem is today, a Google Maps Web service has been created to visually show where layoffs are occurring at newspapers across the United States (http://papercuts .graphicdesignr.net). These examples show both the power of the blogs and some of the problems associated with them. The influence of blogs has also been called the power of the **blogosphere** (i.e., the community of all blogs).

In addition to blogs created by and/or for individual readers, companies increasingly use blogs for connecting with their employees or customers. For example, IBM's business-oriented social software suite Lotus Connection includes blogs, helping people to voice ideas and obtain feedback from others. Similarly, companies such as Google maintain official company blogs to inform their stakeholders about news, rumors, or current thoughts.

Social Presence

Social presence tools (sometimes called **microblogging** tools), similar to blogging, enable people to voice their thoughts; however, in contrast to blogs, which often contain lengthy posts, social presence tools are designed for relatively short "status updates." A popular social presence tool is Twitter, which allows users to post short (up to 140 characters of text) "tweets" that are delivered to the author's followers or subscribers via mobile phone or Twitter applications (see Figure 5.5). The recipient can "retweet" (i.e., re-broadcast) interesting tweets to his or her followers. Whereas Twitter's initial focus was on personal status updates, the focus has now shifted to users tweeting "what's happening." Hence, Twitter has become a source for breaking news; for example, messages about US Airways Flight 1549 crashing

FIGURE 5.5

Twitter allows posting short "tweets" that are delivered to the author's followers or subscribers via mobile phone or Twitter applications.

Brief Case ⊙

INSTANT MESSAGING AT WORK

You know the drill. You download the software necessary for instant messaging (IM) from a popular public IM service such as Microsoft's Windows Live Messenger, iChat, Jabber, Google Talk, Yahoo! Messenger, Skype, ICQ, or AOL Instant Messenger, and you're off. You can then invite your contacts to participate, and if they have downloaded IM software from a compatible service and they accept your invitation, they can contact you and vice versa—all in real time. It's a convenient and fast way to communicate directly with friends and family.

Companies have also found IM a great way to hold interactive conversations and share information with their customers and colleagues. In fact, the real-time communication environment created by IM has proven especially adaptable to organizations. The predominant business advantage to IM is that it saves time—an organizational IM user knows immediately if a contact is available as opposed to playing "telephone or e-mail tag" or, worse, waiting for snail mail deliveries. Furthermore, text and graphic files can be instantly transported for perusal during an IM conversation—a process that is more unwieldy and inconvenient via fax or e-mail.

Since the secure transport of information is vital to corporations, businesses prefer more secure alternatives over using public IM services. Organizations can establish their own IM network, using software designed specifically for that purpose. Organizations can choose among a variety of IM protocols for establishing an IM network, but any protocol selected should fit business-use requirements, which include the following:

1. The secure transfer of messages
2. The ability to handle hundreds or even thousands of employee accounts
3. Compatibility with operating systems used within the organization (e.g., Windows, Linux, and so on)
4. Access from outside the company's network
5. The ability to load existing user data to facilitate setup and ensure proper access rights

Alternatives to establishing one's own IM system within a corporation include (1) using one of the public IM services and (2) using an IM hosting service targeted at business needs. Disadvantages to using the public providers for business IM communication are clear:

1. Security cannot be enforced based on the corporation's needs.
2. Data resides on the provider's servers and in some cases becomes its property.

3. The corporation cannot block access to the network based on its own needs.
4. The corporation has no control over the stability and availability of the network. (Major public IM providers such as ICQ have blocked access to entire countries at times.)
5. The corporation cannot automate processes such as adding new employees to existing rosters.

The second alternative of the two listed here—using an IM hosting service—is better from security and availability standpoints than using the public Internet, but such services can be costly, and there are additional disadvantages:

- Data still resides on the provider's servers and is only as secure as the provider decides to make it.
- Privacy concerns may arise when the provider has access to all conversations.
- Although automation is possible, it will not be as flexible.

A face-to-face visit may still be the preferred method of doing business, but business IM is running a close second. In fact, communications in office workplaces have already started shifting from traditional communication channels such as e-mail and in-person meetings to new media communication, including IM. A recent survey by Directions Research Inc. found that although e-mail is still the primary choice for communication in office workplace, IM, text messaging, and social networking tools are increasingly used by white-collar workers under the age of 35, and increasingly, workers are exchanging instant messaging IDs with business contacts instead of or in addition to exchanging e-mail addresses and telephone numbers.

Questions

1. How can IM be used to better manage a distributed workforce?
2. If you were the owner of a small company, would you allow your employees to use IM while working? If so, what rules would you impose? If not, why?

Based on:

Altunergil, O. (2005, October 6). Company-wide instant messaging with Jabberd. *Onlamp*. Retrieved April 3, 2010, from http://www.onlamp .com/pub/a/onlamp/2005/10/06/jabberd.html.

Anonymous. (2009, May 13). New survey previews the 'future of work'. *EON*. Retrieved August 11, 2010, from http://eon.businesswire.com/portal/ site/eon/permalink/?ndmViewId=news_view&newsId=20090512006660.

Instant messaging. (2010, August 3). In *Wikipedia, the free encyclopedia*. Retrieved August 11, 2010, from http://en.wikipedia.org/w/index.php?title =Instant_messaging&oldid=376964873.

in the Hudson River were spreading on Twitter 15 minutes before traditional media outlets started to broadcast news about the incident. Many social networking sites (discussed later in this chapter) also have social presence functionality built in; for example, users can update their status on Facebook, letting their friends know about their current thoughts and allowing them to post replies.

Many organizations have used this trend and created accounts on Twitter. For example, Coca-Cola has an official Twitter account with over 36,000 followers and uses it to post news or interact with its followers; Coca-Cola follows 26,000 Twitter accounts and actively replies to and retweets Twitter messages. This way, Coca-Cola signals that it cares about its followers, and can increase its customers' brand loyalty.

Instant Messaging

In contrast to asynchronous discussion forums, blogs, and status updates, **instant messaging** (or online chat) emulates real-time written conversations. Using instant messaging, multiple participants can have conversations and enjoy immediate feedback from their conversation partners. Some social networking sites such as Facebook have integrated instant messaging functionality; however, instant messaging is often regarded as somewhat artificial, although most instant messaging environments also support both video and voice communication. Many organizations have adopted instant messaging for internal communications and also use live chat for sales and customer support functions. For example, the Chinese business-to-business marketplace Alibaba.com includes a chat interface so that interested buyers can immediately contact potential sellers.

Virtual Worlds

Virtual worlds take the concept of real-time communication a step further by allowing people to communicate using avatars. Popular virtual worlds such as Second Life, Meez, or IMVU consist of 3D environments where people can interact and build, buy, or sell virtual items, all using their personalized avatar (see Figure 5.6). However, while many individuals run successful small businesses in consumer-oriented virtual worlds, large companies have not been able to realize the potential of those environments beyond providing virtual showcases for their products. However, dedicated virtual worlds are increasingly used for rich communication, as is the case with the Cisco Live conference, which simultaneously takes place both in Las Vegas, Nevada, and in a virtual environment, allowing participants to attend sessions or interact with other attendees.

FIGURE 5.6

Virtual worlds consist of 3D environments where people can interact and build, buy, or sell virtual items, all using their personalized avatar.

ETHICAL DILEMMA

Virtual Reality People

Virtual reality is not limited just to a computer-generated environment where participants wear special headsets and other gear that allows them to interact with virtual situations. We experience virtual reality when we watch television or play computer games. Nature shows on television are enjoyed from the comfort of our living rooms—there are no biting mosquitoes and gnats, and we don't get hot and sweaty hiking for miles, or dunked in icy streams.

We all know by now that too much time spent watching television or using computers and game consoles is bad for our health since the sedentary lifestyle leads to obesity, diabetes, deteriorating muscles and social lives, and other unhealthy conditions. In fact, people who have a sedentary lifestyle had a 46 percent higher risk of death from all causes over people living a more active lifestyle. In addition to these critical health concerns, what happens when virtual reality becomes more desirable than experiencing nature in the wild?

Researchers Oliver Pergams and Patricia Zaradic reported in a February 2008 edition of the *Proceedings of the National Academy of Sciences* that camping, fishing, and visitors to national parks were all declining.

"Declining nature participation has crucial implications for current conservation efforts," Pergams and Zaradic wrote. "We think it probable that any major decline in the value placed on natural areas and experiences will greatly reduce the value people place on biodiversity conservation."

Pergams and Zaradic called the observed shift away from outdoor activities particularly damaging to children, and they refer to the preference for indoor, virtual reality activities as "videophilia."

By studying visits to national and state parks and the issuance of hunting and fishing licenses, the researchers documented declines of between 18 and 25 percent in various types of outdoor recreation:

- The decline, found in both the United States and Japan, apparently began in the 1980s and 1990s, the period of rapid growth of video games.
- The number of people fishing peaked in 1981 and had declined 25 percent by 2005. The number of hunters stayed relatively stable, possibly because deer populations across the United States exploded.
- Visits to U.S. national parks peaked in 1987 but had dropped 23 percent by 2006. Similarly, visits to Japan's national parks dropped by 18 percent between 1991 and 2005.
- Hiking on the Appalachian Trail peaked in 2000 and was down 18 percent by 2005.

Ethical implications of videophilia concern the fact that if people do, indeed, prefer virtual nature to reality, will nature conservation and concern for our natural environment deteriorate to the point that we no longer have an enjoyable and productive natural environment? It seems unlikely, with the growing trend of going "green" in the twenty-first century, but it may be worth studying as Web 2.0 assumes a more prominent place in our lives.

Based on:

American Heart Association. (2010, January 12). Sedentary TV time may cut life short. *ScienceDaily*. Retrieved June 22, 2010, from http://www.sciencedaily.com/releases/2010/01/100111161927 .htm.

Pergams, O. R. W., & Zaradic, P. A. (2008). Evidence for a fundamental and pervasive shift away from nature-based recreation. *Proceedings of the National Academy of Sciences* 105(7), 2295–2300.

Enhancing Cooperation with Web 2.0

In addition to communication, companies and individuals can benefit from Web 2.0 applications that enable cooperation. Cooperation between individuals or organizations creates win-win situations such that one participant's success improves the chances of success of other participants. Web 2.0 applications facilitating such cooperation rely on the **network effect** to provide the greatest benefits for users. The network effect refers to the notion that the value of a network (or tool or application based on a network) is dependent on the number of other users. In other words, if a network has few users, it has little or no value (e.g., how useful would e-mail be if none of your friends or family members had access to it?). For example, eBay would not be an effective auction Web site if only a few bidders were present. In order for eBay auctions to be

CHAPTER 5 • ENHANCING COLLABORATION USING WEB 2.0   **203**

valued, there must be a large number of users who are involved in the auctions. As more users hear about eBay and then become active buyers and sellers, the value of eBay continues to grow. These network effects also occur in various other applications, such as social networks or instant messaging applications.

Media Sharing

One example of cooperative Web 2.0 applications making use of the network effect is media sharing. The sharing of pictures, videos, audio, and even presentations has become immensely popular on the Web, using sites such as Flickr (images), YouTube (videos), or SlideShare (presentations). Typically, the shared content is hosted on media sharing sites; however, the content can also be embedded into other sites, creating a win-win situation for the content creator and the site embedding the content. For example, embedding an interesting and relevant YouTube video into a blog post helps to increase the attractiveness of the blog while at the same time increasing the viewership of the video, thus creating positive returns for both parties.

Similarly, netcasting is increasingly used for media sharing. **Netcasting** (or **podcasting**) is the distribution of digital media, such as audio or video files via *syndication feeds* for playback on digital media players. The term "podcasting," derived from combining the terms "broadcasting" and "iPod," is a misnomer, as **netcasts** (or **podcasts**) can be played on a variety of devices in addition to Apple's iPods. As with blogging, netcasting has grown substantially, with traditional media organizations now netcasting everything from shows on National Public Radio to Fox's *Family Guy* to the *Oprah Winfrey Show*. All of this is made possible using syndication feeds that allow netcast publishers (called **netcasters**) to publish and push current shows to the watchers/listeners. In addition to media organizations and independent netcasters, the educational sector uses netcasts for providing students access to lectures, lab demonstrations, or sports events; this allows students to review lectures or prepare for class during their morning and evening commutes. In 2007, Apple launched iTunes U, which offers free content provided by major U.S. universities, such as Stanford, Berkeley, and the Massachusetts Institute of Technology (see Figure 5.7).

Social Bookmarking

Another category of Web 2.0 applications relying on the network effect is social bookmarking. For many Web surfers, key challenges are finding information and finding it *again* at a later time; hence, people often keep long lists of bookmarks to sites they find interesting or visit frequently.

FIGURE 5.7

A student listens to a podcast on iTunes U.

Courtesy Christoph Schneider

FIGURE 5.8

delicious is a popular social bookmarking tool.

Although this is useful for an individual, he or she may miss a plethora of other, related, and potentially interesting Web sites. **Social bookmarking** helps to address this by allowing users to share Internet bookmarks and to create categorization systems (referred to as **folksonomies**). As more people participate in social bookmarking, the value for each user grows as the bookmarks become more complete and more relevant to each user. Widely used public social bookmarking tools include Digg.com and delicious (see Figure 5.8). For organizations, social bookmarking can be extremely valuable for knowledge management and harnessing the collective intelligence of employees. Using enterprise-oriented social bookmarking tools, it is easy to map "islands" of knowledge within an organization, thus helping to easily find experts on a given topic.

Social Cataloging

Similar to social bookmarking, **social cataloging** is the creation of a categorization system by users. Contributors build up catalogs regarding specific topics such as academic citations, wireless networks, books and music, and so on. For example, users can create virtual bookshelves with Google Books, organize their collections, and write reviews and then share this bookshelf with others on the Web. Similarly, students and researchers can use free tools such as Zotero (see Figure 5.9) to manage their citations, thus facilitating the creation of reference lists for research papers. Organizations are typically dealing with tremendous amounts of information, ranging from supplier information to frequent customer complaints, and can use social cataloging for structuring this information and making it more accessible and useful.

Tagging

Closely related to social cataloging is **tagging,** or manually adding metadata to media or other content. **Metadata** can be simply thought of as data about data. In essence, metadata describes data in terms of who, where, when, why, and so on. For example, metadata about a Word document includes the author, the time the document was created, and when it was last saved; metadata about a picture includes date and time, focal length, shutter speed, aperture value, and so on (see Figure 5.10).

Whereas certain metadata about documents or media files is captured automatically (e.g., when saving a document in a word processor, or when taking a picture with a digital camera),

FIGURE 5.9

Zotero helps in organizing citations and research resources.

Source: Zotero is a production of the center for History and New Media at George Mason University. It is generously funded by the United States Institute of Museum and Library Services, the Andrew W. Mellon Foundation, and the Alfred P. Sloan Foundation.

there are various other important pieces of information that are not automatically captured, such as the topic of a document or the names of people in a picture. Tagging is the process of adding such metadata to pieces of information. Tags are commonly added to pictures and videos in Web sites such as Flickr, a picture and video hosting Web site that allows users to upload their content. As of October 2009, Flickr, owned by Yahoo!, boasted millions of active users and over 4 billion pieces of media, making it all but impossible to find images related to a certain topic. However, because many of the images have been tagged by users, they can be easily searched by various descriptive tags. For example, by adding the key words "Washington State Basketball" to a picture on Flickr, we are adding metadata about the context of the picture. This metadata will help return this picture as one of the results whenever a user searches Flickr for basketball pictures.

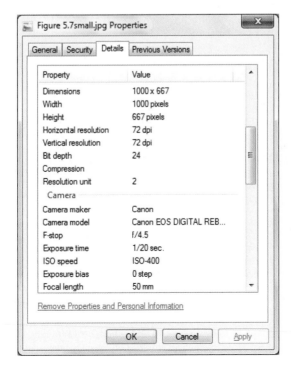

FIGURE 5.10

Metadata about a photo.

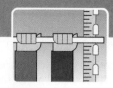

POWERFUL PARTNERSHIPS

Digg's Kevin Rose and Jay Adelson

Kevin Rose, born February 21, 1977, studied computers and animation in high school in Las Vegas, Nevada, and attended the University of Nevada, Las Vegas, studying computer science until he dropped out in 1999 to take part in the dot-com boom.

Rose was working in Los Angeles in 2003, hosting and contributing content to the TechTV show *The Screen Saver*, when he set up an interview with Jay Adelson, the founder and chief technology officer of data center company Equinix Inc. The two became friends, and in 2004, Rose came up with the idea of Digg, a social content Web site where users would post the content—news stories and links. Rose offered Adelson the position of chief executive officer (CEO) of Digg, and Adelson accepted. (Adelson corrects interviewers who write that he helped found Digg. Rose founded Digg.com, but Adelson serves as its CEO.) Rose was also involved in founding the Internet start-ups Revision3 and Pownce. Today, Rose spends much of his time podcasting, climbing, and inventing Digg's next-generation features.

Jay Adelson, born September 7, 1970, was enticed out of the world of film and broadcasting and into the Internet industry to found Equinix Inc. in 1998. When he accepted the job as Digg's CEO, it meant leaving his wife and three children in New York while he commuted to Digg's San Francisco headquarters. Adelson, seven years older than Rose, has commented that he is the "adult" of the pair, reminding Rose to pull up his jeans to cover his boxers on a number of occasions. (Advice that he claims Rose usually ignores.) Information about Adelson at the Digg Web site states, "Jay has testified before Congress and advised the government and other groups with his knowledge of the Internet's workings, and he habitually speaks at industry events and conferences."

Today, the Web site traffic of Digg ranks one-hundredth by Alexa.com. It has over 35 million unique users each month. Several reports surfaced that Digg has been trying to sell itself to a large company since early 2006. One most recent potential sale was with Google in July 2008 for about $200 million. However, on July 25, 2008, Google decided not to make the purchase. Since then, Rose and Adelson decided to keep Digg. On December 2008, Adelson said to *BusinessWeek* that Digg is no longer for sale. However, Digg is still struggling to build an independent business to reach profitability. On December 18, 2008, a report from *BusinessWeek* indicated that Digg lost $4 million on $6.4 million of revenue in the first three quarters of 2008.

Since the advent of Equinix and Digg, both Adelson and Rose continue to be involved in other successful Web 2.0 start-ups. On April 5, 2010, Rose assumed the CEO position as Adelson stepped down to incubate new business ideas.

FIGURE 5.11

Digg's Kevin Rose and Jay Adelson.

Jim Wilson/© The New York Times

Based on:

Adelson, J. (2010, April 4). Update from Jay. Retrieved August 11, 2010, from http://about.digg.com/blog/update-jay.

Anonymous (n.d.). About Kevin Rose. Retrieved August 11, 2010, from http://about.digg.com/kevin.

Arrington, M. (2010, April 5). Digg's Kevin Rose: "one of us has to leave." Retrieved August 11, 2010, from http://techcrunch.com/2010/04/05/kevin-rose-one-of-us-has-to-leave.

Beaumont, C. (2010, January 23). 'Drastic' Digg overhaul could 'shock' users, says Kevin Rose. *Telegraph.co.uk*. Retrieved September 24, 2010, from http://www.telegraph.co.uk/technology/news/7046519/Drastic-Digg-overhaul-could-shock-users-says-Kevin-Rose.html.

Digg. (2010, June 24). In *Wikipedia, the free encyclopedia*. Retrieved June 30, 2010, from http://en.wikipedia.org/w/index.php?title=Digg&oldid=369970137.

Grossman, L. (2008, May 5). Jay Adelson—The 2008 *Time* 100. *Time.com*. Retrieved April 19, 2010, from http://www.time.com/time/specials/2007/article/0,28804,1733748_1733758_1736343,00.html.

Lacy, S., & J. Hempel (2006, August 14). Valley boys. *BusinessWeek*. Retrieved April 19, 2010, from http://www.businessweek.com/magazine/content/06_33/b3997001.htm.

FIGURE 5.12

A tag cloud related to words and concepts that are key to Web 2.0 technologies.

Source: Shutterstock

A way to visualize user generated tags or content on a site is through **tag clouds** (see Figure 5.12). The size of a word in a tag cloud represents its importance or frequency so that it is easy to spot the most important or frequent words or tags.

Geotagging Another type of metadata about media such as photos, videos, or even blogs or tweets is of geospatial nature; knowing where exactly a photo was taken and in what direction the camera was pointing, or knowing the location of a person sending out a breaking news update on Twitter, can be extremely valuable. Adding geospatial metadata (such as latitude, longitude, or altitude) to media is referred to as **geotagging.** Once the location of an item is known, it can easily be visualized on a map. For example, Google maps can display various types of geotagged information, such as Wikipedia articles about places or landmarks, photos, webcams, or even Twitter posts. Thus, Google can offer a map experience containing pictures of attractions, reviews, and things to do without having to take a single picture or write a single review themselves.

Enhancing Collaboration with Web 2.0

Web 2.0 technologies such as those outlined previously also enable **collaboration** (i.e., two or more people working together to achieve a common goal). Web 2.0 exemplifies how people from different places can work together for a common goal using Web technologies. People frequently collaborate on many different tasks, whether it be writing software, preparing a business plan, or even writing a textbook. When collaborating on projects, communication can be either **synchronous** (i.e., at the same time) or **asynchronous** (i.e., not coordinated in time). For example, chatting online is an example of synchronous communication, whereas e-mail is an example of asynchronous communication; a student might send his professor an e-mail message at 7:00 A.M., and the professor might reply at 1:00 P.M. With increasing globalization and increasing use of the Internet, collaborators on projects do not have to be colocated, and meetings typically take the form of **virtual meetings** using an online environment. Virtual meetings can be done synchronously, like a teleconference, or asynchronously, using technologies such as online discussion boards.

Collaboration is often thought of as peers working together on a specific task. In addition, collaboration can also be a way for management and employees to interact. For example, the coffee giant Starbucks was dealing with problems stemming from its rapid growth and huge success (see Figure 5.13). Prior to implementing a Web portal to provide a centralized location for third-party vendor ordering, manifests and other resources were needed for managing inventory, training employees, and other communication and collaboration activities; and most correspondence between stores and corporate offices was very slow and inefficient using traditional paper-based mail and faxes. With over 100,000 employees, it was critical that Starbucks find a solution to improve its

FIGURE 5.13

Starbucks utilizes information systems to improve collaboration.

Brendon Howard\Shutterstock

communication and collaboration between headquarters and stores. To achieve this, a corporate Web portal was implemented in 2003. Today, this portal is the primary communication channel between the corporate office and stores, allowing managers to focus more time on increasing sales and providing superior customer service (Microsoft Corporation, 2007b).

Virtual Teams

In today's business environment, project teams comprise highly specialized members, many of whom may not be colocated (see Figure 5.14). Thus, rather than forming traditional teams, **virtual teams,** comprised of members from different geographic areas, are assembled to collaborate on a project (Sarker & Sahay, 2002). Virtual teams are commonly used for tasks such as developing systems and software; for example, the programmers are located in India, the project managers are in the United States, and the testers are in Europe. However, systems development is not the only place you will find virtual teams. For instance, the health care industry has embraced the idea of using technology to create superior care for patients. At the Rush University Medical Center in Chicago, team members may include dieticians, physicians, surgeons, pharmacists, and social workers from different cities, all of whom can coordinate care of the

FIGURE 5.14

Members of highly specialized virtual teams are often not colocated.

Toria\Shutterstock

TABLE 5.3 Categories of Collaborative Tools

Title	Description	Instances	Examples
Electronic communication tools	Tools allowing users to send files, documents, and pictures to each other and share information	Fax, e-mail, voice mail, blogs, wikis, static Web sites	MS Outlook, Blogger.com, Wikipedia.org
Electronic conferencing tools	Tools allowing information sharing and rich interactions between users	Internet forums, instant messaging, application sharing, videoconferencing	Apple FaceTime, Skype, Windows Live Messenger, WebEx
Collaboration management tools	Tools used to facilitate virtual or colocated meetings and manage group activities	Electronic calendars, knowledge management systems, intranets, online document systems	Google Docs, MS Office Live, MS SharePoint

patient using various Web technologies to collaborate. This allows the patients to get the best health care professionals regardless of where they reside. Rush University Hospital is finding that patients under "virtual team care" report fewer trips to the emergency room and gain a better understanding of the health care system.

Tools for Collaboration

If you have ever worked on a team project for your class (and you probably have), you have noticed that there are many different communication needs, such as talking, sharing documents, or making decisions. Just as there are many things to discuss within your team project, there are also many ways that you can communicate and collaborate. In fact, the Internet and various Web 2.0 technologies provide many capabilities that have forever transformed the way teams can work together. Here, we present the major categories of collaboration tools (see Table 5.3), followed by an examination of two popular collaboration environments.

Web-Based Collaboration Tools For organizations and individuals, **Web-based collaboration tools** can offer a number of benefits. For example, Web-based collaboration tools allow for easy access and easy transferability from one person to another, as the tools can run on any computer with a Web browser and Internet connectivity. Further, users don't have to e-mail documents back and forth or worry about having the latest version of the software installed. On the other hand, using Web-based collaboration tools requires a live Internet connection to work on shared documents, and thus users may not be able to work when traveling or when having Internet connectivity problems. Also, the applications are limited in what they can do. For example, an online spreadsheet can do only basic formulas. Table 5.4 outlines various benefits and risks of Web-based collaboration tools.

Organizations and individuals can choose from different options for using Web 2.0 collaboration tools. In the following sections, we discuss collaboration tools offered by Google and Microsoft, the major applications in use today.

TABLE 5.4 Benefits and Risks of Web-Based Collaboration Tools

Domain	Benefit	Risk
Information technology	Reduced costs and risks when using preexisting, easily deployed, and low-cost Web-based tools (versus in-house developed tools).	Loss of control regarding data and service quality (data and tools will likely reside on the provider's server).
Organization	Tools are easy to use, facilitating widespread adoption throughout an organization.	Little or no documentation, training, or support for system complexities or problems.
Competition	More efficient and effective than e-mail, FTP, or legacy collaboration tools, potentially speeding up product development cycles and enabling quick responses to competitors' actions.	Security and compliance policies are nearly impossible to enforce, which may increase the possibility of exposing sensitive corporate data; increased threat of industrial espionage.
Upgrade cycles	No need to purchase software upgrades.	Tools and features in the collaboration environment can change without notice, potentially causing problems with users and corporate IT strategy.

Google Apps. Google Apps is a family of Web-based collaboration tools designed to function similar to an offline office software suite while also allowing for easy collaboration. The following outlines various Google Apps tools:

1. *Gmail.* A Web-based e-mail client allowing users to send large attachments and offering large storage space and superior filing and search capabilities; users can select a custom domain name for an additional fee (e.g., joe@outfitter.com).
2. *Google Calendar.* A Web-based collaborative calendar that allows users to share events, send invitations to events, subscribe to public calendars for new events (e.g., Netflix's calendar for new DVD releases), and so on.
3. *Google Talk.* An instant messaging client.
4. *Google Docs.* An online office suite comprised of a spreadsheet application, a word processor, and a presentation application. The documents, spreadsheet, and presentations can be created in the Web application or imported from other tools (e.g., Microsoft Office).
5. *Google Sites.* An enterprise-level collaboration tool that allows users to create group Web sites and share team information.

A variety of other providers offer similar Web-based collaboration tools (see Table 5.5).

Although there are several Web-based office suites available, Google Apps has been adopted by many users. Backed by Google, one of the world's most recognized companies, Google Apps are free for individual users and educational institutions and are provided on a per-user fee for commercial and governmental organizations. In fact, in October 2006, Lakehead University in Thunder Bay, Canada, adopted Google Apps for all its 38,000 users. Similarly, in 2008, Boise State University in Boise, Idaho, migrated from the Novell Groupwise e-mail system to Gmail for all faculty, staff, and students, and rolled out Google Apps for document sharing and collaboration.

Microsoft SharePoint. Microsoft has also integrated collaboration capabilities into several of its current business tools, with Microsoft SharePoint being the most popular tool. In contrast to stand-alone Web collaboration tools such as Google Docs, Microsoft SharePoint is a document management platform that can be used to host Web sites that enable shared workspaces and integrate other collaborative applications such as wikis and blogs. SharePoint also includes workflow functionality such as to-do lists, discussion boards, and messaging alerts. Because SharePoint has been designed to be easily customizable, it has been installed in a variety of businesses, which can personalize the collaborative SharePoint Web sites to meet their needs. For example, Mary Kay Cosmetics uses SharePoint to distribute product and company information to its over 30,000 Canadian consultants. Microsoft also deploys its various Office products to support Web-based collaboration, where users can store, share, and collaborate on any type of Office document.

Content Management Systems

A **content management system** allows users to publish, edit, version track, and retrieve digital information (i.e., *content,* such as documents, images, audio files, videos, or anything that can be digitized). A content management system allows the assignment of different roles for different users; some users can create and edit content, others can edit but not create, and yet others can only view content contained in the system. Typical roles in a content management system include the following:

- *Creator.* Responsible for publishing new information
- *Editor.* Responsible for editing the content into a final form

TABLE 5.5 Web-Based Collaboration Tools

Type	Names
Spreadsheets	Bad Blue, EditGrid, Google Spreadsheets, Zoho Sheet
Word processors	Adobe Buzzword, Think Free, Zoho Writer, Google Docs, ZCubes
Presentation	PresenterNet, Slide, Adobe Connect, Google Docs, Zoho Show
Office suites	eDesk Online, Zoho, Google Docs
Project	Trac, Redmine, eGroupWare, Collabtive

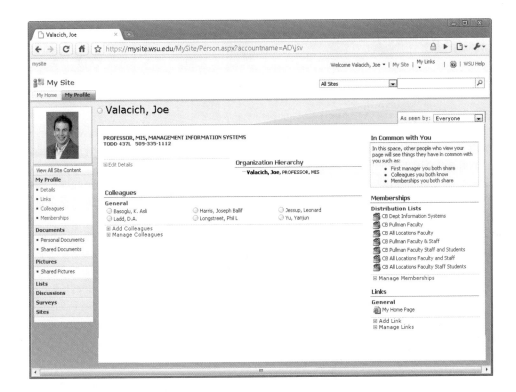

FIGURE 5.15

Washington State University uses the Microsoft SharePoint content management system to provide students and faculty with access to important information.

Source: Courtesy Washington State University.

- *Administrator.* Responsible for managing account access levels to the digital information
- *Guest.* A person who can only view the digital information

Content management systems are also known by several other names, including digital asset management systems, document management systems, and enterprise content systems. In addition to Microsoft SharePoint, which offers extensive content management capabilities (see Figure 5.15), IBM and Adobe are major players in this market space. For example, the All England Lawn Tennis and Croquet Club, the host of the annual Wimbledon tennis tournament, selected IBM's content management system to help distribute interactive digital content (such as videos) to fans worldwide. Similarly, as more and more content in the health care industry is stored in digital format, content management systems are becoming very valuable. CIGNA Healthcare, one of the first health management organizations to use Adobe's content management system to publish, edit, share, and secure health information, estimates that changing to a content management system saves millions, which can ultimately help improve patients' quality of care.

Peer Production

Another widely used Web 2.0 phenomenon is peer production. **Peer production** is the creation of goods or services by self-organizing communities. In peer production, the creation of the goods or services is dependent on the incremental contributions of the participants such that anyone can help in producing or improving the final outcome. Prime examples of peer production are open source projects (see Chapter 3, "Managing the Information Systems Infrastructure and Services") and wikis.

Wikis Ever since the inception of the online encyclopedia Wikipedia, wikis have become mainstream and are used for a variety of collaboration tasks. As discussed in Chapter 2, "Gaining Competitive Advantage Through Information Systems," a wiki is a Web site allowing people to post, add, edit, comment, and access information. In contrast to a regular Web site, a wiki is linked to a database keeping a history of all prior versions and changes, and thus a wiki allows viewing prior versions of the site as well as reverting any changes made to the content. The idea behind wikis is that they allow anyone to contribute information or edit others' contributions. Whereas some wikis can be public and open to anyone who wishes to contribute, others are private so that only certain registered users can contribute. The most

COMING ATTRACTIONS

The Future of TV

Imagine a day when you sit on a couch, push a button, and call up any video-related entertainment you desire on your TV. That day might not be so far away. In an age when nearly all forms of media are digital, the Internet will change the way we watch TV slowly but steadily. TV in the future will allow multiple layers of video, pictures, and text to be mixed with video feeds in ways that viewers can control with their remotes. It will integrate the best of the Internet while preserving the essence of the traditional TV medium. You will use remote controls to surf channels and explore electronic program guides, then use digital video recorders to record and time shift favorite programs. You can even use remote controls to search video, check ratings, and press the "buy me" button to watch the content.

Technology has been developed to ensure the quality of video distributed over the Internet. What is required is a user interface that is powerful enough to find and organize the near-infinite content available online but easy enough to use with a simple remote control. Apple TV is an early deployment of this vision, where a small digital media receiver (basically a small computer that connects to your home Internet router) is connected to your TV, allowing you to view photos, play music, and watch videos from various Internet media services, including iTunes, YouTube, Flickr, and MobileMe. Google TV was announced in 2010 to be integrated into future TVs and set-top boxes in order to provide similar capabilites as those from Apple TV, yet they argue that their system will provide fewer restrictions on where

Internet video and other content can originate. Likewise, in mid-2010, Sony announced it would release *Sony Internet TV*, which would be integrated into various Sony television and Blu-ray devices. In sum, various key vendors from the computer, software, and consumer electronics industries are actively pursuing a new vision of the home television experience.

While solving the technological part of this new vision may be not a big issue, the real obstacle comes from the traditional entertainment industry. Ditigal distribution empowered by the Internet poses a tremendous threat to that industry's business model. Although digital distribution is a trend, the industry is trying to slow it down and control the process to reduce its negative impact on them. Stay tuned!

Based on:

Anonymous. (n.d). The changing TV experience. *Intel*. Retrieved March 19, 2010, from http://www.intelconsumerelectronics.com/Consumer-Electronics-3.0/The-Changing-TV-Experience.aspx.

Anonymous. (2010). Apple TV. Retrieved August 11, 2010, from http://www.apple.com/appletv/what-is.html.

Anonymous. (2010). Google TV. Retrieved August 11, 2010, from http://www.google.com/tv.

Moyer, M. (November 2009). How the Internet is changing the way we will watch TV. *Scientific American*. Retrieved March 19, 2010, from http://www.scientificamerican.com/article.cfm?id=the-everything-tv.

Walker, L. (2006, January 12). Future of Internet TV is coming into view. *Washington Post*. Retrieved March 19, 2010, from http://www.washingtonpost.com/wp-dyn/content/article/2006/01/11/AR2006011102134.html.

popular wiki is the online encyclopedia **Wikipedia,** which has over 15 million articles in more than 270 languages (see Figure 5.16).[1] These articles have been created by Wikipedia users and almost any of these articles can be edited by either anonymous or registered users. By allowing easy access, Wikipedia has grown exponentially in a short amount of time. However, Wikipedia is not without its critics. Some argue that by allowing anyone to create and edit articles, a systematic bias in the content can occur. This includes the ability for users to add misinformation that is hard to verify. For example, in January 2006, it was revealed that staffers for several congresspeople deleted negative information about their particular bosses while adding negative information to articles about members of the other party. Sometimes, so-called wiki wars arise, where contributors continuously edit or delete each others' posts. Also, Wikipedia has been found to have a significant cultural bias, as most contributors are males from either North America or Europe. Since the information is often not backed by verifiable sources, Wikipedia is not considered a credible source, and many universities discourage students from citing Wikipedia. In fact, in some

---

[1]Wikipedia: About. (2010, June 14). In *Wikipedia, the free encyclopedia*. Retrieved June 14, 2010, from http://en.wikipedia.org/w/index.php?title=Wikipedia:About&oldid=367899366.

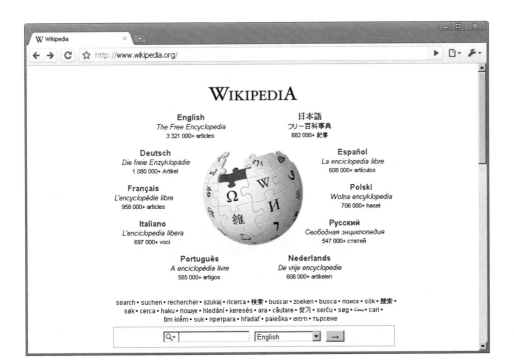

FIGURE 5.16

Wikipedia has over 15 million articles in more than 270 languages.

instances professors have been failing students for using Wikipedia as their primary (or only) source. While a Wikipedia article may be a good starting point for researching about a topic, it is good practice to evaluate the source used within the article, and to consult other sources as well. Wikipedia openly acknowledges this situation and encourages users to check the facts against multiple sources.

Wikis have been used for many more things than just an online encyclopedia. The ability for users to contribute and edit content has a wide variety of applications, such as designing software, helping people find media, and even helping people play video games. In fact, many organizations are using wiki technology to create internal knowledge repositories. Table 5.6 lists examples of several different uses of wikis.

Human-Based Computing (Crowdsourcing)

Another way individuals can collaborate with organizations is through crowdsourcing. When companies look for cheap labor, many immediately think about outsourcing work to *companies* in different countries, such as India, China, or Russia (see Chapter 1, "Managing in the Digital World"). However, companies have now found a way to use *everyday people* as a cheap labor force, a phenomenon called **crowdsourcing,** which ingeniously uses Web 2.0 technologies (see Figure 5.17).

TABLE 5.6 Examples of Wikis

Title	Description
Welker's Wikinomics (http://welkerswikinomics.wetpaint.com)	A learning wiki for understanding concepts in Advanced Placement Economics
Second Life Wiki (http://wiki.secondlife.com/wiki/Main_Page)	A wiki dedicated to the Massive Multiplayer game Second Life
Visual FoxPro Wiki (http://fox.wikis.com)	A wiki designed to help with questions on creating database applications using Microsoft's Visual FoxPro programming language
WikiDot (www.wikidot.com)	A site providing free wiki hosting to everyone (also known as wiki farm)
Lostpedia (www.lostpedia.com)	A wiki for the fans of the NBC TV show *Lost*
Oracle Wiki (http://wiki.oracle.com)	A public wiki about topics related to Oracle's software

FIGURE 5.17

Crowdsourcing uses everyday people from all over the world as a cheap labor force.

Source: Medioimages/Photodisc/ Thinkstock Royalty Free.

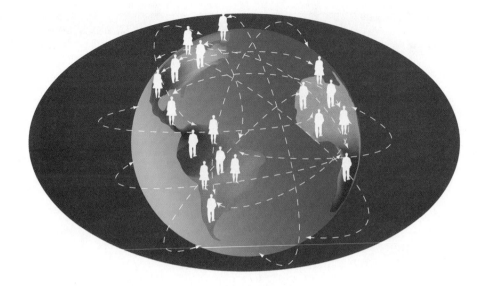

For example, up until a few years ago, book publishers such as Pearson Prentice Hall had to rely on so-called stock photography for many of a book's images; in other words, publishers had to pay large sums for pictures taken by professional photographers. Clearinghouses for stock photography had to charge high fees just to cover their expenses, as they had to purchase pictures from professional photographers. Today, high-quality digital cameras can be had for far less than $1,000, and, with the right editing software, amateur photographers can create images that almost match those of professional photographers. Amateur photographers can upload their pictures to image sharing sites such as iStockphoto.com, where interested parties can license and download the images for $1 to $5 per image, which is a fraction of the price of a regular stock photo. Given that overhead costs are almost negligible, iStockphoto can make a profit while still sharing part of the revenue with the pictures' creators.

Similarly, pharmaceutical giant Eli Lilly created a site called InnoCentive, where companies can post scientific problems, and everybody can take a shot at solving the problem. Usually, a reward is paid to a successful solver. This way, an ad hoc research-and-development network is created, and companies have to rely less on a dedicated research-and-development department or on hiring specialists to solve a certain problem. At the same time, people can use their spare time and expertise to solve problems and earn rewards for their contributions.

Amazon.com took crowdsourcing mainstream with its mturk (mechanical turk) application. Using the mechanical turk, requesters can crowdsource so-called human intelligence tasks (HITs), which are small, self-contained tasks that humans can solve easily but would be difficult for a computer to solve. Examples of HITs include tagging images, generating potential search key words for a product, fixing product titles on e-commerce sites, and so on. Users can find HITs that are of interest to them, solve the tasks, and earn money that is credited to their Amazon.com account.

As you can see, for companies, crowdsourcing is an innovative way to reduce costs by using the expertise of the crowds. Similar to grid computing (see Chapter 3), a person's "idle time" is used for a certain business task, and many people are willing to provide their resources in exchange for a relatively small amount of money. Just imagine that you could pay for your textbooks using the money you earned from the collection of digital pictures you've taken, all for almost no extra effort. Another emerging trend is **e-lancing.** Traditionally, companies have used self-employed freelancers to work on individual projects or provide content. E-lancing takes this concept a step further by enabling people to work in more flexible ways on a variety of Internet-related projects.

Enhancing Connection with Web 2.0

Social software also aids in connecting people with each other, companies with their customers or stakeholders, or people with content. Without a doubt, social networking has become the most popular type of application in this category; we explore social networking and other, lesser-known applications in the following sections.

TABLE 5.7 Top 10 Social Networking Sites

Social Network	Description	Market Share
Facebook	General social network	67%
MySpace	General social network	28%
Tagged	General social network focused on "social discovery" (i.e., facilitating meeting new people)	2%
myYearbook	General social network focusing on high school–based connections	1%
BlackPlanet	Niche social network targeted at African American users	0.3%
hi5	General social network popular among users located in Central America	0.25%
Bebo	General social network focused on self-expression and sharing digital content	0.2%
Orkut	General social network owned by Google	0.1%
Friendster	General social network popular in Southeast Asia	0.1%
Multiply	General social network focused on facilitating picture sharing; popular in Asia	0.05%

Source: Based on Prescott (2010).

Social Networking

In addition to direct collaboration, **social networking** has become one of the most popular uses of the Internet over the past few years. Social networking sites create **social online communities** where individuals with a broad and diverse set of interests meet and collaborate. Facebook.com exemplifies this trend, reaching 34 percent of global Internet users and accounting for nearly 5 percent of global page views (and being surpassed only by Google), according to Alexa.com (see Table 5.7). Facebook took the spot as the most frequented social network from MySpace.com, which originally was designed to be a social network based on musical interests but then changed to a general interest social network used primarily by teens and young adults. Initially, MySpace had been so successful that in 2005 it was purchased by Rupert Murdoch's NewsCorp for $580 million (see Figure 5.18). Although MySpace is still popular, with over 100 million users, it has lost momentum to Facebook. Some have blamed MySpace's management for focusing too much on revenue, thus alienating users. Because of the network effect, as Facebook grew, it became ever more attractive for other people to join. In July 2010, Facebook announced that it had 500 million users and is still growing.

Social networks were initially largely popular among preteens, teens, and young adults, but social networking demographics have slowly shifted. Although in 2010 about 50 percent of

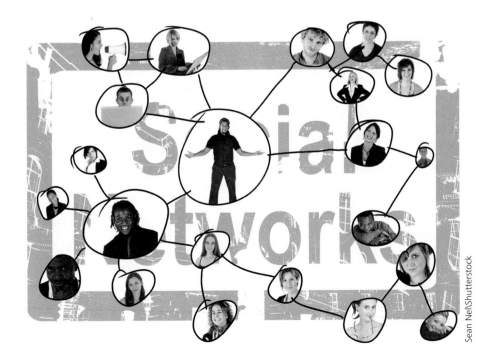

FIGURE 5.18

Individuals with a broad and diverse set of interests meet and communicate using social networks.

Sean Nel\Shutterstock

Facebook's users were between 18 and 34 years old, almost 40 percent of the users were 35 years or older (Gonzalez, 2010). In addition to general interest social networks, several social online communities are targeted at professional audiences, allowing users to meet business contacts, post career profiles, present themselves in a professional context, ask for expert advice, or be contacted regarding job opportunities. For example, LinkedIn has more than 70 million users, and Xing (which is widely popular in Europe) has more than 9 million users. Further, enterprise-oriented social software such as Lotus Connect features social networking tools, allowing people within organizations to connect to one another.

Organizations also increasingly use social networks to connect to their customers. Numerous companies have their own Facebook pages to interact with their customers, get feedback on new products or services, or in general portray a positive brand image (similar to mobile phone applications developed by companies; see Chapter 4, "Enabling Commerce Using the Internet").

Viral Marketing

In the offline world, marketing one's products or services is one of the most important aspects of successfully running a business. In an online context, marketing Web sites, products, and services is equally important, and business organizations use techniques such as search marketing, paid inclusion, and banner advertisements to promote their Web sites (see Chapter 4). Building on the foundations of social networking, advertisers have turned to **viral marketing** to promote their Web sites, products, or services. Viral marketing is using the network effect to increase brand awareness. The term *viral marketing* was coined by Harvard business professor Jeffrey Rayport to describe how good marketing techniques can be driven by word-of-mouth or person-to-person communication, similar to how real viruses are transmitted through offline social networks. Rather than creating traditional banner ads or sending out massive amounts of spam, businesses create advertisements in a way that entices the viewers to share the message with their friends through e-mail or social networks so that the message will spread like a virus. Viral marketing can take many forms such as video clips, e-books, flash games, and even text messages.

NET STATS

Most Popular Facebook Fan Pages

More and more organizations have discovered Facebook as a way to connect with their customers and drive word-of-mouth advertising. Any company can create a Facebook page containing basic information about the business, a "wall" to share content, a space for uploading photos or pictures (many organizations use this to show "behind-the-scenes" content), and so on. Further, businesses can add applications (such as an application that allows customers to make a reservation at a restaurant) to further engage with their customers.

Facebook users who "like" a page automatically receive the business's status updates in their news feeds. As the liking of a page is announced to others in the user's news feed and his or her profile, the liking of the page can spread throughout the user's network of friends. Further, each business's page has a listing of all Facebook users who like the page. What businesses are liked by most Facebook users? As of June 2010, 7 of the top 10 most-liked product pages were related to food and drinks:

Rank	Page	Fans
1	Starbucks	7,599,897
2	Coca-Cola	5,708,927
3	Skittles	4,746,496
4	Oreos	4,665,798
5	Red Bull	4,095,663
6	Nutella	3,833,237
7	Victoria's Secret	3,643,337
8	Converse All Star	3,427,888
9	Pringles	3,344,719
10	Adidas Originals	2,941,793

Based on:

Facebook: Browse all pages. Retrieved June 11, 2010, from http://www.facebook.com/pages/#!/pages/?browse.

Facebook: Pages.Retrieved June 29, 2010, from http://www.facebook.com/advertising/?pages.

The power of viral marketing can be a great tool, and there are several techniques that are critical to making a successful viral marketing campaign. Writer and interaction designer Thomas Baekdal (2006) has outlined some critical factors in viral marketing, including the following:

1. Do something unexpected
2. Make people feel something
3. Make sequels
4. Allow sharing and easy distribution
5. Never restrict access to the viral content

Following these principles entices users to view content, share it with their friends, and revisit the site to look for new content. For example, BMW created a series of short films directed by popular directors. Rather than being traditional car ads, these films told stories, presenting the vehicles in a certain context. Viewers would watch the films because of the content, would share the films, and come back to the BMW films Web site to watch the next film.

Another successful viral marketing campaign was used by Hotmail's founders during the launch of the free Hotmail e-mail service. One of the techniques involved adding a footer to every outbound message. This footer gave a short message about Hotmail.com's free e-mail service, and the message about the service was spread with every e-mail sent through the service (see Figure 5.19). This campaign proved very effective (Hotmail spent only $500,000 to get 12 million subscribers), and Microsoft later bought Hotmail.

In July 2006, a series of simple videos were posted to YouTube.com by a user called lonely-girl15. The supposed user was a teenage girl named Bree, who in short video blogs regularly talked about her friends and family. Lonelygirl15 gained worldwide attention, and her videos were watched by over 70 million viewers. A *New York Times* story eventually outed loneygirl15 as a paid actress who was hired by a small production company. This entertainment company, LG15, now produces several mock video blogs that remain popular.

Social Search

As the Web has grown explosively since its early days (in the first six years, the growth rate was 850 percent, and after only 15 years, the number of Web sites was larger than 100 million; Nielsen, 2006), finding relevant information has become increasingly difficult. Early search engines such as Altavista were based on key words embedded within pages and often tried to assemble "directories" of the Web (see http://dir.yahoo.com). In 1996, Sergey Brin and Larry Page came up with a new algorithm for Internet search. Called BackRub, the algorithm used the number of *other* pages linking to a Web page so as to return more relevant results to the users; in

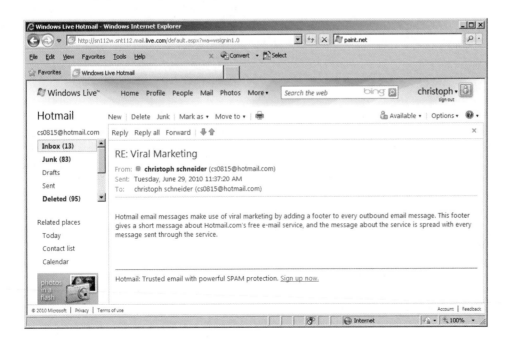

FIGURE 5.19

Hotmail uses viral marketing by adding a footer containing information about the e-mail service to each e-mail.

WHEN THINGS GO WRONG

Social Media Meltdown at Nestlé

In the past week, you've probably had something to eat that was made by Nestlé, the global producer of cereals, coffee, dairy, and other products. You probably know them best though for their wide range of confectionary treats like Kit Kat bars, Rolos, and anything from Willy Wonka. Life hasn't always been sweet for the company, however.

In early 2010, the environmental group Greenpeace began protesting Nestlé over their use of palm oil in some of their products. The group claimed that Nestlé was purchasing their oil from an Indonesian firm that was actively destroying vast swaths of rain forest in order to build palm oil plantations. The destruction of the rain forest, according to Greenpeace, was threatening Indonesia's orangutan population. Greenpeace's protest came in the form of a commercial (posted on YouTube) that showed an unsuspecting office worker opening a candy bar resembling a Kit Kat that had an orangutan finger inside. The shock parody got Nestlé's attention, and they quickly petitioned YouTube to remove the video.

The move by Nestlé to have the video taken down set off howls in the social media arena. Sites like Facebook were instantly abuzz about the orangutan story and the censorship Nestlé had imposed on the video. Although in the beginning, the parody had fewer than a 1,000 views on YouTube, it was picked up by other video sites and was linked to from multiple locations. Suddenly, the video was making the rounds on the Internet, and Nestlé's Facebook page was being overwhelmed with visitors decrying the company's censorship, their decision to buy palm oil from questionable suppliers, and the plight of the orangutan. Facebook posters were even changing their profile pictures to a modified Nestlé logo that read "Killer" in the Kit Kat font.

Surprisingly, instead of apologizing to their fans or explaining their position to try and control the growing controversy, Nestlé retaliated. On Facebook, the moderator of the page began deleting posts of protesters. A warning was posted that informed visitors to the site that although comments were welcome, any use of the company's logo would result in deleted posts. The moderator even began trading insults with users. The exchanges fueled the backlash even further, and the public relations nightmare began to snowball for Nestlé. By the time the company apologized for the online censorship and Facebook fighting, it was too late. The story had been picked up on Twitter, went viral, and quickly spread around the world.

The story is a lesson in the power of social media for all would-be public relations professionals and organizations. The global reach and lightning speed of these media allow messages, whether bitter or sweet, to spread like wildfire.

Based on:

Eccleston, P. (2007, November 8). Need for cheap palm oil drives deforestation. *Telegraph.co.uk*. Retrieved May 1, 2010, from http://www.telegraph.co.uk/earth/earthnews/3313623/Need-for-cheap-palm-oil-drives-deforestation.html.

Hargrave-Silk, A. (2010, April 12). Social media blunder: Nestlé censorship fuels firestorm on Twitter and Facebook. *Campaign Asia*. Retrieved May 1, 2010, from http://www.campaignasia.com/Article/213070, social-media-blunder-nestle-censorship-fuels-firestorm-on-twitter-and-facebook.aspx.

Titsworth, J. (2010, April 27). Nestlé, palm oil and social media, oh my! *Searchenginejournal.com*. Retrieved May 1, 2010, from http://www.searchenginejournal.com/nestle-palm-oil-and-social-media-oh-my/20400.

Toor, A. (2010, March 22). Nestlé's palm oil PR crisis pervades Facebook. *Switched.com*. Retrieved May 1, 2010, from, http://www.switched.com/2010/03/22/nestles-palm-oil-pr-crisis-pervades-facebook.

1998, Brin and Page founded Google (see Chapter 3). Although Google has become extremely successful, returning the most relevant results to each user is the holy grail for search engines. For Google, the optimum number of search results to be returned would be one—the single result that perfectly answers the user's question. In order to increase the relevance of search results, search engines such as Google or Bing now offer social search functionality. **Social search** attempts to provide relevant search results by including content from social networks, blogs, or microblogging services. For example, a search on Bing may return relevant status updates from Facebook or Twitter; Google goes a step further and narrows the results to content from one's online social circle, arguing that content posted by friends is typically more relevant than content posted by complete strangers. Other social search approaches let users annotate or tag search results, making it easier for others to find relevant information. This especially valuable for enterprise search applications, where other users within an organization can tag internal documents, making it easier to find information as well as to find people who have certain information within the organization.

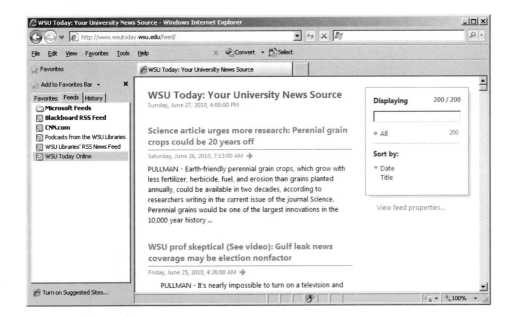

FIGURE 5.20

RSS feeds can be displayed by most Web browsers.

Source: Courtesy Washington State University.

Syndication

Real Simple Syndication (RSS) is a family of syndication feeds used to publish the most current blogs, podcasts, videos, and news stories. RSS feeds are offered by organizations so that the users can view the most current information, and users can subscribe to RSS feeds from different sources. Rather than users actively having to check multiple sources for the latest news, RSS readers automatically check the feeds for updated content. RSS feeds typically contain a synopsis of a document or the full text. For example, CNN.com publishes RSS feeds for each of its areas, such as world news, sports news, and entertainment news, and NBC uses RSS feeds to allow viewers to download the most current version of shows such as *Meet the Press* and the *Nightly News*.

RSS feeds can be read by most Web browsers (see Figure 5.20) and even e-mail clients such as Microsoft's Outlook, allowing users to browse different feeds as they would browse different bookmarks. Similarly, iGoogle, Google's personalized home page, allows users to add multiple RSS feeds to a single page. Finally, there are several stand-alone applications that can aggregate RSS feeds such as NewsBreak for Windows Mobile users, Liferea for Linux users, and Attensa for Mac users.

Web Services, Widgets, and Mashups

Web Services For companies operating in the digital world, online collaboration with suppliers, business partners, and customers is crucial to being successful. To enable seamless collaboration, organizations need to allow outsiders to connect to their data, typically using the Internet. However, the Internet was originally designed to enable human-to-computer interaction, with Web pages being a collection of text that hyperlinked to other Web pages. A computer could not use data from other computers without explicit knowledge of the physical location and the security configuration of the remote computer network. Today, **Web services** are one of the critical components of sharing data. Web services allow data to be accessed without intimate knowledge of other organizations' systems, enabling machine-to-machine interaction over the Internet. The central idea behind Web services is that *any device* can use *any network* to access *any service* (see Figure 5.21). A Web service can offer several benefits for organizations, including the following:

1. Utilizing the existing Internet infrastructure (i.e., no new technologies are needed)
2. Accessing remote or local data without having to know the complexities of this access
3. Creating unique and dynamic applications quickly and easily

Many organizations have recognized the power and benefits from offering free Web services to the public, with an increasing number of organizations offering free access to parts of their databases. Why are companies doing this? By providing access to useful Web services, organizations build and strengthen customer relationships, providing a base for revenue-generating

FIGURE 5.21

Web services allow any device to use any network to access any service.

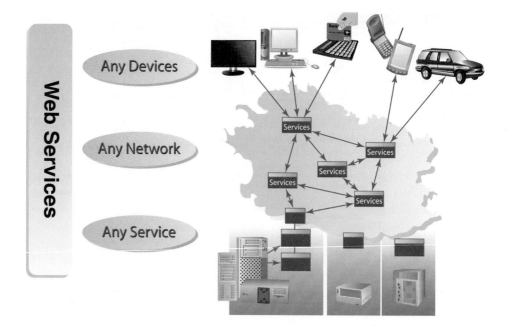

services. For example, Facebook.com has been using this idea to gain market share in the competitive social networking market space. Likewise, Google is offering a host of Web services to the public, including the following:

- *Android.* A Web service used for building mobile phone applications
- *Search.* A Web service allowing users to create customized search features in Google
- *Calendar.* A Web service for managing personal calendars
- *Maps.* A Web service used to integrate Google's mapping system into Web sites
- *OpenSocial.* A Web service designed to allow users to build applications that work with multiple social communities, such as Friendster and LinkedIn

Widgets Widgets provide a clear example of how Web 2.0 technology has changed the look and feel of Web pages. Specifically, **widgets** are small interactive tools used for a single purpose such as taking notes, viewing pictures, or simply displaying a clock. Widgets can either be placed on a desktop or be integrated into a Web page (see Figure 5.22). Apple pioneered the concept of

FIGURE 5.22

Users can choose among a variety of widgets performing different tasks.

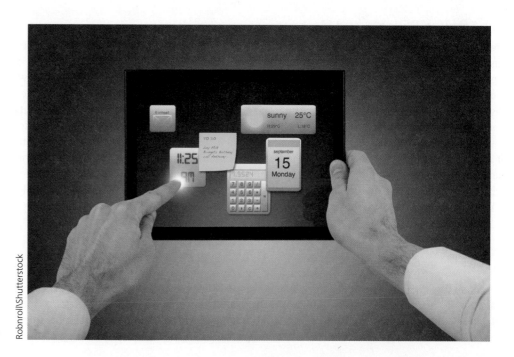

Robnroll\Shutterstock

widgets in its early version of the Mac operating system, and Microsoft followed by developing its active desktop environment. Widgets have now moved to the Web platform, where they can access data from Web sites to do more complicated things, such as translate languages, provide weather forecasts, display stock prices, and stream music. Often, widgets use Web services to pull their information from a remote source, such as Weather.com for weather information or Marketwatch.com for stock market information. Widgets currently have no standard format. For example, a Google-developed widget can run only on a Google Web page or a Google desktop widget engine; a Yahoo!-developed widget can run only on Yahoo!'s platforms. The World Wide Web Consortium is currently working toward a standard so that all widgets will run on any platform or Web page.

Together, Web services and widgets enable the creation of **mashups.** The idea of mashups came from popular music where many songs are produced by mixing two or more existing songs together; in Web 2.0 terminology, a mashup is a new application (or Web site) that integrates one or more Web services. One Web service frequently used to display geospatial information in mashups is Google Maps. For instance, Craigslist developed a dynamic map of all available apartments in the United States (www.housingmaps.com). Similarly, during the 2007 wildfires in southern California, KPBS, San Diego's local public television station, created a mashup displaying the locations of the fires, evacuation zones, and emergency shelters such that residents and friends and family members could easily get the latest information on the situation. Likewise, users and companies can create mashups using Microsoft's Bing maps. The mashup "what's nearby" aggregates content from various sources on the Web so as to display information, reviews, or driving directions about businesses, restaurants, or medical facilities near a given location (see Figure 5.23). For a list of useful mashups, visit www .programmableweb.com.

There are several large organizations that see value in end users creating unique applications using others' data. Yahoo! and Microsoft have specialized Web editors that allow users to create mashups from several data sources. Yahoo! was one of the first to offer this service (called "Yahoo! Pipes"), providing a graphical user interface that can aggregate RSS feeds, Web services, or Web pages. The software works by connecting "pipes" of information together to create a single Web page that fits the user's needs. The goal of this project is to allow a typical nonprogrammer Web user to create unique Web sites from existing Web content.

FIGURE 5.23

The mashup "what's nearby" aggregates content from various sources on the Web so as to display information, reviews, or driving directions about businesses, restaurants, or medical facilities near a given location.

Source: Bing.com

Future Web Capabilities

Web technologies and collaboration are ever-evolving topics, and many developments have yet to be fully realized. This section briefly forecasts future capabilities of the Web, in particular, focusing on efforts to create the semantic Web and characteristics of Web 3.0.

Semantic Web Since the Web opened up for public use, the number of Web pages and sites has grown exponentially. Although this increase in Web pages should mean that we have ever more information at our fingertips, it also means that the information is increasingly harder to find. What if the information on the Web was organized in a way that users could more easily find information or related media? At present, search engines cannot help to solve this formidable task, as Web pages can be understood by people but not by computers. For example, when you now go to Google.com and search for "what eats penguins," it returns Web sites that may have this information, but it is more likely that the sites just have the words or key terms "what" and "eats" and "penguins." For Larry Page, cofounder of Google, the perfect search engine would return only *one* result, namely, the one page that provides the best answer to the user's query. Currently, however, search engines are not sophisticated enough to be able to find, understand, and integrate information presented on Web pages. The **semantic Web,** originally envisioned by one of the founders of the Internet, Tim Berners-Lee, is a set of design principles that will allow computers to be able to better index Web sites, topics, and subjects. When Web pages are designed using semantic principles, computers will be able to read the pages, and search engines will be able to give richer and more accurate answers. Google Sets (http://labs.google.com/sets) provides an example of an attempt at using a search engine to categorize data using semantic Web principles. For example, when entering key words such as "Ford," "Audi," "GMC," and "Volvo" into the Google Sets engine, Google Sets predicts other items belonging to the set (in this case, this would be other car brands, such as Mercedes, Fiat, Honda, and so on). Although the semantic Web is largely unrealized, Google's efforts show that the semantic Web experience is getting closer.

Web 3.0 In many ways, Web 2.0 has already replaced Web 1.0, and the question is, What will replace Web 2.0? For some, Web 2.0 is just a short transitional period before the next wave of Internet technologies, which is predicted to last from 2010 to 2020. There are several ideas on what this next wave, Web 3.0, will entail. Eric Schmidt, CEO of Google, views **Web 3.0** as technologies providing for ubiquitous data access where all data is viewed as being in a "cloud," and applications that access this data can run on any device, PC, or mobile phone. Although there are different points of view on what will dominate Web 3.0, there are certain topics that are universally accepted as coming trends. These topics include the following:

1. *The World Wide Database.* The ability for databases to be distributed and accessed from anywhere
2. *Open Technologies.* The design of Web sites and other software so that they can be easily integrated
3. *Open ID.* The provision of an online identity that can easily be ported to mobile devices, PCs, and more, allowing for easy authentication across different Web sites
4. *Integration of Legacy Devices.* The ability to use current mobile devices, such as iPhones, laptops, and so on, as credit cards, tickets, and reservations
5. *Intelligent Applications.* The use of agents (discussed in Chapter 6, "Enhancing Business Intelligence Using Information Systems"), machine learning, and semantic Web concepts to complete intelligent tasks for users

Although you may have already seen some of these emerging technologies in practice, the coming trends involve true integration of the devices and connectivity to create powerful socially aware Internet appliances. Stay tuned to see what the future holds.

Managing the Enterprise 2.0 Strategy

As you have seen, there are various tools that organizations can use for communicating with external stakeholders as well as for enhancing collaboration and connection of employees within the enterprise. In the following sections, we discuss factors to be examined when considering the use of Enterprise 2.0 tools within an organization. Then we highlight potential pitfalls brought about by these tools, when used by people within and outside an organization.

Organizational Issues

In the previous chapters, you have learned that in many cases, technology can be an important enabler of strategic advantage. Similarly, with internal Enterprise 2.0 tools, the technology is a critical success factor, but it is not the only component. Given that Web 2.0 tools are based on close social interaction, information sharing, and network effects, corporate culture is key in successful Enterprise 2.0 implementations. Specifically, a corporate culture of knowledge sharing, trust, and honest feedback is conducive to Enterprise 2.0 implementations. In addition to culture, various other caveats have to be taken into consideration for any Enterprise 2.0 application (Khan, 2008) (see Figure 5.24).

Enterprise≠Web While reading this chapter, you have learned about many technologies you are familiar with from your daily life. Although many of those technologies are hugely successful in a consumer environment, this success does not always translate to success in a corporate environment. On the Web, sites such as YouTube, Wikipedia, or Facebook have evolved over years to become as successful as they are today, and examples such as MySpace show that success at one point in time is not guaranteed to continue. Further, what appears as seamless, "magic" collaboration is sometimes based on intricate processes. For example, good articles in Wikipedia are based on the contributions of many editors but also on many behind-the-scenes discussions over controversial issues or over how to improve an article. In contrast, many open source software projects closely guard changes to the software's programming code such that only a limited number of "committers" can actually implement suggested changes.

Culture As highlighted earlier, organizational culture is a critical Enterprise 2.0 success factor, and many proposed projects face strong cultural resistance. Enterprise 2.0 applications, based on the premise of open communication, do not always do well within traditional top-down organizational structures based on rigid hierarchies and control. Further, Web 2.0 sites base their success on user-driven self-expression (if no one were willing to update his or her status on Facebook, people would eventually stop visiting the site); on the Web, people participate by choice, but people in organizations cannot be forced to participate. Hence, organizations have to understand the multiple stakeholders, personalities, and perspectives of the future users and ensure that any Enterprise 2.0 initiative will appeal to the organizational members.

Organizational Context Any implementation of Enterprise 2.0 applications should be driven by a specific usage context. Just as users choose popular Web 2.0 applications such as YouTube or Wikipedia to fulfill a particular need, the work-related context should drive the choice of Enterprise 2.0 tools. In other words, organizations should always ask what objective is to be accomplished with

FIGURE 5.24

Various factors have to be taken into account for successful Enterprise 2.0 applications.

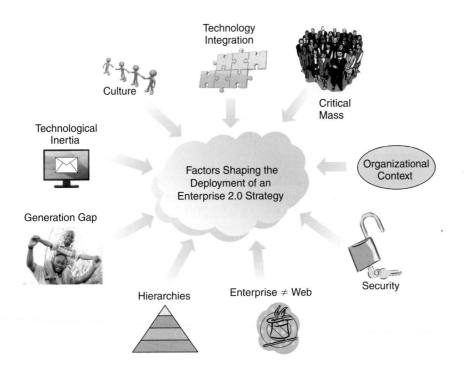

the tool and only then decide which type of tool to implement. Merely setting up a wiki site and hoping that the employees will use it for the "right" purpose most likely will not lead to the intended results.

Organizational Hierarchies Often, Enterprise 2.0 initiatives are driven by user departments, and small-scale pilot implementations appear to work quite well. However, organization-wide Enterprise 2.0 implementations typically need changes in terms of organizational culture and processes and often the flattening of organizational hierarchies. Therefore, to be successful, Enterprise 2.0 implementations need the support and active involvement of senior management so as to cope with the large magnitude of changes.

Network Effects and Critical Mass Successful Web 2.0 phenomena such as Wikipedia base their success on network effects and the Long Tail (see Chapter 4) and have needed some time to achieve a critical mass. For example, although Wikipedia enjoys millions of page views per day, there is only a small number of people who choose to actively participate in the creation of content. Within organizations, achieving the critical mass needed for an Enterprise 2.0 application is often difficult and takes considerable time and patience. Although for many smaller organizations collaborative Enterprise 2.0 tools can be beneficial, they will most likely not be able to harness the network effects that can be achieved with a larger user base.

Generation Gap The success of an Enterprise 2.0 initiative is also heavily dependent on the composition of the organization's workforce. In organizations with high numbers of millennials, who have grown accustomed to highly interactive and communicative online social environments, Enterprise 2.0 initiatives have a higher likelihood of success; in contrast, many baby boomers are used to rigid hierarchies and organizational structures and are less likely to fully embrace the capabilities of Enterprise 2.0 tools. Further, senior organizational members may not fully grasp the potential and implications of Web 2.0 applications in organizational settings.

Technological Inertia One factor hindering the adoption of many new technologies is technological inertia. In many cases, people are not willing to switch to new applications unless they see real, tangible benefits. This can be especially a hindrance with Web 2.0 applications, many of which incorporate a variety of other tools (such as chat or message interfaces within social networking sites).

Technological Integration Organizations will have to ensure that any Enterprise 2.0 applications are integrated well with the organization's existing information systems infrastructure so as to reap the greatest benefits from connecting people and connecting people with information. Typically, organizations choose systems provided by outside vendors such as Ning, which allows the organization to create its own social network. However, organizational users will use the tools they are used to as a benchmark, and public domain tools such as Facebook often create high expectations of usability for any internal tool.

Security A final issue is related to security and intellectual property. For organizations, securing their information systems infrastructure is of paramount concern (see Chapter 10, "Securing Information Systems"). Any application that allows closer collaboration by increasing data sharing will necessarily incur greater risks of security breaches. Companies thus have to balance their desire for enhancing collaboration with the need to protect intellectual property and comply with rules and regulations such as the Sarbanes-Oxley Act.

Pitfalls of Web 2.0 Marketing

Many organizations (and individuals) have learned painful lessons from public relations blunders and from not considering the fundamental rule: That the Internet never forgets. Another fundamental rule brought about by Web 2.0 applications is to constantly monitor social media and quickly and appropriately react to emerging issues. In this section, we highlight potential pitfalls of marketing using Web 2.0 applications.

Online Product Reviews Online as well as offline consumers increasingly consult the Web before making a purchase decision. When making a purchase on Amazon.com, many potential buyers first consult the user reviews; relatedly, people read other travelers' reviews of hotels or restaurants on Tripadvisor.com, or consult Websites dedicated to providing expert reviews. Unfortunately, such reviews are not always as unbiased as they seem; and sometimes, companies hire people to deliberately spread positive word-of-mouth across a variety of sites. Needless to say, the act of posting fake product reviews is unethical, to say the least. For companies operating globally, this is becoming even more problematic. For example, in China, where reviews are often posted by the millions, consulting the Web for advice is even more common, especially among online shoppers. As with other products, fakes are a problem with product reviews as well. In fact, Chinese Internet marketing companies employ legions of people who do nothing but post positive comments about a client—and negative comments about competitors. To make matters even worse, a number of Internet marketing companies specialize on removing negative posts about their clients, usually by bribing forum managers or administrators. Fees for removing a negative post can be as high as $1,500, depending on how urgent the request is or how popular the Web site or post is; for the companies paying for having negative posts removed, this is considered a regular advertising expense (Jiao, 2010). Companies operating globally should certainly be aware of such practices, and adjust their strategies accordingly.

Microblogging Whereas microblogging tools can be very valuable for corporate communications, they have to be used carefully and are not without controversy. For example, in mid-2010, Utah's attorney general announced an impending execution on Twitter with the post, "I just gave the go ahead to Corrections Director to proceed with Gardner's execution. May God grant him the mercy he denied his victims," which was seen as distasteful by many observers and quickly made worldwide news. In the aftermath of BP's Gulf of Mexico oil spill disaster, a person frustrated with the oil giant's response to the spill set up a satirical Twitter account named "BP Public Relations (BPGlobalPR)," posting tweets such as "Cleaning up oil spills is expensive. Buying judges so we can keep drilling? Relatively cheap." BPGlobalPR became immensely popular, with over 178,000 followers, dwarfing BP's official account with 16,000 followers. Needless to say, BP soon found out about this account and asked the account holder to modify the account so as to make it clearer that the account was satirical. However, by that time, the satirical site had already gained much attention from the press, and the oil giant's attempt to deal with the mock account further tarnished its image.

For individuals, posting the wrong "tweets" can also have serious consequences, as they are more likely than not to reach the wrong readers—sooner or later. A Chicago woman was recently sued by her landlord for posting a tweet complaining about the management company's reaction to mold in her apartment. The management company sued her for defamation, arguing that the tweet was published on a global scale. Whereas the lady had a mere 22 followers on Twitter, the landlord's lawsuit was covered in major news outlets, online and offline, including the *Chicago Tribune,* the Associated Press, and the *New York Times.*

Social Networks While free to host, having a page on a social network is not free for organizations—the company should take great care to monitor what is happening on the page and take appropriate action. For example, Starbucks lets its customers upload their favorite Starbucks-related pictures to its Facebook page. However, people frequently post unrelated pictures, play pranks with the company logo, or post otherwise inappropriate content. A company then has to walk the fine line of removing inappropriate content to preserve the company's image while not alienating its fans. Starbucks chooses to liberally allow unrelated content.

As with most social software, posting the "wrong" content can quickly get you in trouble. Companies routinely check social networking sites before making hiring decisions, and many applicants have lost a job offer they almost had secured. Similarly, your posts may make it farther than you think; in late 2009, a British woman got laid off after ranting about her job and her boss in a Facebook status update—unfortunately, her boss was in her contacts list and could immediately see the post. Further, many people never bother to adjust their accounts' privacy settings and inadvertently shout things out for the whole world to read. To see the extent of what people post on Facebook, try a search on http://openfacebooksearch.com; you'd be surprised by what you find out.

Viral Marketing As with other social media, viral marketing can be a blessing or a nightmare (see also "When Things go Wrong: Nestlé's Social Media Meltdown" earlier in this chapter). In 2008, a musician on a tour witnessed from his airplane window how baggage handlers mishandled—and broke—his $3,500 guitar. After not getting a satisfying response from the airline, the musician decided to write a song and post it on YouTube in 2009. The video quickly went viral, and the airline rushed to "make things right" for the musician. For the airline, however, the damage was done, and as of mid-2010, the video had over 8 million views. Domino's Pizza faced a similar disaster in 2009, when two employees played not-so-harmless pranks and filmed each other preparing sandwiches with disgusting ingredients. After the videos were posted on YouTube, they quickly went viral and attracted more than a million viewers in just a few days. Domino's was initially slow in responding and decided not to respond to the crisis, fearing that a reaction may draw even more interest. After 48 hours, however, Domino's changed its strategy, opened a Twitter account to interact with concerned customers, and posted a video response by the president of Domino's on YouTube assuring that the culprits had been found, that the entire store had been closed and sanitized, and that everything would be done to avoid hiring the "wrong" people in the future. A nationwide survey by a media research company has found the response to be fairly successful, with over 90 percent of the respondents indicating that the response video was effective in restoring trust in the brand.

Lessons Learned As you probably know from you own experience and have seen from these stories, news travel fast in social media. For the companies in question, this is an enormous threat, as negative publicity can quickly reach millions of people. At the same time, the company's reaction is equally critical, as it can reach people just as fast and thus has to be carefully crafted. Richard Levick, president of Levick Strategic Communications, has provided some tips on how prepare for and deal with such crisis:

1. Identify a crisis team including members from within your organization (e.g., public relations or executive team) and from the outside (e.g., lawyers).
2. Identify your worst social media nightmare (and make sure to know the signs to look for, such as search engine key words your opposition could use).
3. Monitor your social media environment (such as YouTube, Facebook, and Twitter) and be connected and responsive.
4. Act fast. The first 24 hours count.

As in the offline world, companies should try to avoid such crises in the first place, but being prepared for a public relations disaster is crucial in today's fast-paced world.

INDUSTRY ANALYSIS

Online Travel

Spring break is coming, and you've decided to go to Puerto Vallarta this year. Chances are that your first step will be to check the Web sites of Expedia, Travelocity, and Orbitz for flights to and hotels in your chosen destination. (Expedia's 2010 first-quarter report showed that it accounted for 38 percent of worldwide bookings.)

We all know the big three online travel agencies (OTAs). In today's digital world, they dominate the travel industry. They took the old brick-and-mortar travel industry and turned it into an online service where you can click to book flights and hotel reservations, change or cancel flights, reserve rental cars—even plan a vacation. In Internet terms, you can think of the big three as still being in Online Travel 1.0. But technology marches relentlessly on, and Online Travel 2.0 is in the works.

Travel service providers—airlines, hotels, and car rental companies—and travel customers pay fees to online travel agencies. And travel service providers selling through OTAs do not have the opportunity to build customer relationships. Therefore, some providers, including JetBlue and InterContinental Hotels, would rather have customers book directly from them. That way, they (and their customers) avoid OTA fees, and they are better

able to satisfy customers since they can provide up-to-the-minute information.

Enter Online Travel 2.0—the travel search engines. They don't book travel services for you, but they locate and list URLs for hundreds of suppliers, and when you choose one, you can then click the link to the supplier's Web site. Travel search engines becoming increasingly popular with online consumers include Kayak, Vayama, Mobissimo, and Yahoo!'s FareChase.

If you want to book a travel package, especially to an international destination, OTAs may be the best choice. But if you can navigate travel services yourself or want to deal directly with travel service providers, travel search engines can fill the bill.

More recently, a new trend is emerging. Following the retail industry, the travel sector is turning to mobile. Research firm The Nielsen Co. found that consumers increasingly choose mobile travel sites and applications so as to be able to book flights or hotel rooms, rent cars, or access information from anywhere at any time. According to Nielsen, the top five mobile sites and applications are Travelocity, Expedia, Priceline, Orbitz, and Delta Air Lines, with a combined total of 5.8 million unique visitors in October 2009.

Questions

1. Do you use online travel agencies for assisting you with travel plans? If so, which service provider do you use, and why did you make this choice? If not, why not?

2. Forecast the future of traditional travel agencies. How can travel agencies use social media to attract and retain customers?

Based on:

Anonymous. (2010, April 29). Expedia, Inc. reports first quarter 2010 results. Retrieved June 22, 2010, from http://phx.corporate-ir.net/External.File?item=UGFyZW50SUQ9NDM2NTJ8Q2hpbGRRJRD0tMXxUeXBlPTM=&t=1.

Smith, B. (2006, April 27). Yahoo's FareChase: The stealth disruptor? *SearchEngineWatch*. Retrieved April 24, 2010, from http://searchenginewatch.com/searchday/article.php/3601971.

Stambor, Z. (2010, January 11). Mobile flying high in the online travel industry. *Internet Retailer*. Retrieved April 24, 2010, from http://www.internetretailer.com/2010/01/11/mobile-is-flying-high-in-the-online-travel-industry.

Key Points Review

1. *Describe Web 2.0 and the key enablers of Enterprise 2.0.*   Web 2.0 refers to dynamic Web applications that allow people to collaborate and share information online. One of the basic concepts associated with Web 2.0 is a shift in the users' role from passive consumer of content to creator. Web 2.0 applications have spawned the emergence of social software that people widely use for communicating and socializing. Increasingly, organizations are using social software to connect with customers and internal or external stakeholders in order to become more innovative or productive. Social software can help to harness the wisdom of the crowd by leveraging the collective intelligence of large groups of people. For organizations, using Web 2.0 applications can be an important factor in being able to attract or retain employees as younger generations (who grew up using social software) are joining the workforce.

2. *Explain how organizations can enhance communication using Web 2.0 applications.*   Social software can enhance communication within organizations as well as between an organization and its stakeholders. Blogs, made up of chronological entries that comment on virtually any topic of interest to the author, are widely used by individuals and organizations to communicate with internal and external stakeholders. Social presence (or microblogging) tools allow sending relatively short status updates to one's followers. Instant messaging (or online chat) is used mainly for synchronous internal communication as well as for sales and customer support functions. Virtual worlds can be used to showcase products or hold rich interactive communication.

3. *Explain how organizations can enhance cooperation using Web 2.0 applications.*   Web 2.0 applications facilitating cooperation depend on the network effect to provide the greatest benefit to users. Media sharing applications allow people and organizations to share images, videos, slide shows, or podcasts with others. Social bookmarking allows users to share and categorize Internet bookmarks, which can be helpful in organizational knowledge management efforts. Similarly, social cataloging helps to categorize and share academic citations, information about books, music, and so on. Tagging refers to manually adding metadata to a piece of information such as a map, picture, or Web page, thus describing the piece of information for others and making it searchable.

4. *Explain how organizations can enhance collaboration using Web 2.0 applications.*   Web 2.0 technologies have enabled new forms of collaboration for organizations and individuals. With increasing globalization, virtual teams and virtual meetings have become more important for organizations. These and other technologies have enabled Web-based collaboration tools such as Google Apps or Microsoft SharePoint as well as content management systems. The users are central to the new Web environment and are no longer passive viewers of information. As the Web has evolved, individuals can now generate content using several methods, such as wikis, which are Web sites in which people can post, edit, comment, and access information. The idea behind wikis is that they allow anyone to contribute information or edit prior contributions. Another emerging topic in the Web 2.0 environment is crowdsourcing, or the use of everyday people as a cheap labor force.

5. *Explain how organizations can enhance connection using Web 2.0 applications.*   For individuals, social networking has become an important way to meet new friends, connect with family members, or meet new colleagues and business partners. Similarly, organizations use social networks for internal connection as well as to connect with their customers. The reach of social networks is also used by business organizations to market their products or services through viral marketing. Viral marketing resembles offline word-of-mouth communication, in which advertising messages are spread like viruses through

social networks. Social search incorporates blog posts, status updates, and other information from people within and outside a person's social network so as to supplement generic search results and enhance the quality. Syndication helps to connect people with the most current blog posts, podcasts, videos, and news stories. Further, Web 2.0 technologies enable a rich user experience through Web services, widgets, and mashups. However, many see Web 2.0 only as a transitional period and regard the semantic Web and Web 3.0 trends, such as the World Wide Database, open technologies, open ID, integration of legacy devices, and intelligent applications, as the future of the Web.

6. *Describe how companies can manage their Web 2.0 strategy and deal with potential pitfalls associated with Web 2.0.* Web 2.0 applications can be an important enabler for organizations. However, organizations have to take into account that success in a consumer environment does not necessarily translate into corporate environments. Further, organizations have to take into account issues associated with culture, organizational context, and organizational hierarchies; further, lack of critical mass, the generation gap, and technological inertia can hinder the success of Enterprise 2.0 initiatives. Finally, in organizational contexts, integration with existing technologies and security are of primary concern. As organizations can use social software for communicating with customers and viral marketing, an organization's opponents can use the same tools to spread damaging content or information to people all over the world within a very short time. Organizations should therefore plan for such incidents by identifying a crisis team, identifying crisis scenarios, monitoring the social media environment, and acting fast in case a crisis surfaces in the Web 2.0 environment.

Key Terms

"amateurization" of journalism 198
asynchronous 207
blog 197
blogging 197
blogosphere 199
collaboration 207
collective intelligence 196
content management system 210
crowdsourcing 213
discussion forum 197
e-lancing 214
Enterprise 2.0 195
folksonomy 204
geotagging 207
instant messaging 201
mashup 221

metadata 204
microblogging 199
netcast 203
netcaster 203
netcasting 203
network effect 202
peer production 211
podcast 203
podcasting 203
Real Simple Syndication (RSS) 219
semantic Web 222
social bookmarking 204
social cataloging 204
social media 195
social networking 215
social online community 215

social presence tool 199
social search 218
social software 195
synchronous 207
tag cloud 207
tagging 204
viral marketing 216
virtual meeting 207
virtual team 208
virtual world 201
Web 2.0 195
Web 3.0 222
Web service 219
Web-based collaboration tool 209
widget 220
Wikipedia 212

Review Questions

1. What is Web 2.0? Give some examples of Web 2.0 capabilities.
2. How can social software help harness the wisdom of the crowd?
3. Why is using Web 2.0 applications an important factor for attracting and retaining employees?
4. How can social software enhance communication?
5. What is blogging, and why are blogs sometimes controversial?
6. Explain the difference between blogging and microblogging tools
7. What is the network effect?
8. How can social bookmarking and social cataloging help in an organization's knowledge management efforts?
9. What is tagging, and how are organizations using it in their Web sites?
10. What are virtual teams, and how do they help to improve an organization's capabilities?
11. What is a wiki? Why would an organization want to implement a wiki?
12. Explain what is meant by crowdsourcing and how the Web is enabling this form of collaboration.
13. How can organizations use social networking to connect with their customers?
14. What is viral marketing? What capabilities of the Web help to spread the virus?

15. What capabilities will define the Web of the future?

16. Why is organizational culture an important factor in Enterprise 2.0 initiatives?

17. Why can social media be both a blessing and a threat for organizations?

18. How can organizations plan for social media disasters?

Self-Study Questions

1. Collective intelligence is based on the notion that distributed groups of people with a divergent range of information and expertise will be able to outperform the capabilities of _____.
   A. crowds
   B. customers
   C. individual experts
   D. virtual teams

2. Social presence tools are used for _____.
   A. creating an online text diary
   B. providing location information
   C. short status updates
   D. customer support functions

3. Tagging is adding _____ to a piece of information such as a map, picture, or Web page.
   A. metadata
   B. comments
   C. blogs
   D. knowledge

4. The process of adding information such as latitude and longitude to pictures, videos, or other information is called _____.
   A. flagging
   B. posting
   C. geotagging
   D. podcasting

5. Successful Enterprise 2.0 initiatives consider _____.
   A. organizational culture
   B. the organization's customers
   C. the latest social software applications
   D. all of the above

6. _____ is the process of creating an online diary made up of chronological entries.
   A. Wikiing
   B. Tagging
   C. Blogging
   D. None of the above

7. Netcasts are also known as _____.
   A. podcasts
   B. blogcasts
   C. radiocasts
   D. blogging

8. RSS allows you to do all of the following except _____.
   A. publish a video blog
   B. publish current news stories
   C. receive current news stories
   D. edit a netcast

9. Wikis are a type of Web site where people can _____.
   A. post information
   B. comment on information
   C. access information
   D. all of the above

10. _____ communication is when people are all meeting at the same time or in real time.
   A. Synchronous
   B. Asynchronous
   C. Collaboration
   D. None of the above

Answers are on page 231.

Problems and Exercises

1. Match the following terms with the appropriate definitions:

   i.   Social presence tools
   ii. Asynchronous
   iii. Metadata
   iv. Social networking
   v.   Peer production
   vi. Social software
   vii. Netcasts
   viii. Folksonomy
   ix. Network effect
   x.   Blogging

   a. Web 2.0 applications allowing people to communicate, interact, and collaborate in various ways
   b. Digital media streams that can be distributed to and played by digital audio players
   c. The creation of goods or services by self-organizing communities
   d. The notion that the value of a network (or tool or application based on a network) is dependent on the number of other users
   e. User-created categorization system
   f. The process of creating an online text diary made up of chronological entries
   g. Data about data
   h. Tools enabling people to voice their thoughts using relatively short "status updates"
   i. Using Web-based services to link friends or colleagues
   j. Not coordinated in time

2. Visit popular social online communities (such as Facebook or Bebo). What features would entice you to visit such sites over and over again? Do you have an account in an online community? If yes, why? If no, what is keeping you from having such account? Is there any content you definitely would or would not post on such page?

3. Go to the Web site Programmable Web (www .programmableweb.com). List some interesting mashups you find. What factors do you think make a good mashup Web site?

4. Go to Amazon's Mechanical Turk Web site (www.mturk.com). Which of the HITs do you think could be completed using a computer, and which could not? Why?

5. Search the Web for a social networking site that you have not heard about before. Describe the users of this social online community. Are the features of this site different from those you are familiar with? If so, describe those features. If not, describe common features.

6. Visit Google Page Creator (pages.google.com) and Microsoft Live Office (Officelive.com). Compare and contrast the features for each Web site. Which Web site would you choose to use, and why?

7. Have you ever blogged or read someone's blog? If so, what did you like or dislike about the experience? What do you see for the future in blogs?

8. Find an article you can contribute to on a wiki page. What do you like or dislike about this process? What would encourage you to contribute more to the wiki? Why?

9. Envision and describe general features of Web 3.0 applications. Describe a feature you would like to see in the next version of the Web.

10. Describe an application or service you would like to be able to use on the Web today that is not yet available. Describe the potential market for this application or service. Forecast how long you believe it will take before this will occur.

11. Search the Web for public relations blunders involving social software. How did the companies in question react? In your opinion, were the reactions effective? Why or why not?

12. Have you listened to or watched a netcast (or podcast)? If so, describe your experience. If not, why?

13. Describe the pros and cons of collaborating with colleagues over the Web. What is useful about this form of collaboration? What is difficult?

14. Describe an example of viral marketing that you have experienced.

Application Exercises

 Note: The existing data files referenced in these exercises are available on the Student Companion Web site: **www.pearsonhighered.com/valacich**.

Spreadsheet Application:
Online Versus Traditional Spreadsheets

Campus Travel is currently evaluating the possibility of using an online spreadsheet as opposed to the traditional locally installed spreadsheet. There are a variety of issues involved in this decision. The company wants you to investigate the possibilities that are currently available while also paying special attention to the company requirements. Campus Travel has the following requirements: (1) the ability to share spreadsheets easily, (2) the ability to secure this information, (3) the ability to save the spreadsheets into other forms (i.e., CSV files), and (4) the ability to do work from anywhere in the world. Prepare the following information:

1. On the Internet, find different options for online and traditional spreadsheets and list the available options.

2. Using the company requirements, list the pros and cons for each spreadsheet option.

3. Using an online spreadsheet, summarize the findings and provide a recommendation to the company. Present your findings with tables and/or graphs, if available.

Database Application:
Tracking Web Site Visits

As Campus Travel expands its Web presence, the importance of tracking what the competitors are doing has become very important. This includes making sure Campus Travel tracks the prices of packages and services that its closest competitor offers. To do so, a database must be created to track this information. Follow these steps to create the database:

1. Create a database called "tracking."

2. Create a table called "company_info." In this table, create fields for company_name and company_URL.

3. Create a table called "products." In this table, create fields for the company_name, product_name, product_description, product_price, and date_retrieved.

4. Create a table called "services." In this table, create fields for company_name, service_name, service description, service_price, and date_retrieved.

5. Once these tables are created, go to the relationship view (select "Relationships" under the "Database Tools" tab) and connect the company_info (one side) and products (many side) tables and the company_info (one side) and service (many side) tables.

6. Make sure that when you create the relationships, the referential integrity option is selected. (This will make sure that when you delete a company, the products associated with the company are also deleted.)

7. Test the referential integrity by adding data to the tables and make sure that when a company is deleted in the company table, the products table is updated too.

Team Work Exercise: Online Social Communities

Do you use social networks to communicate with your friends and family? Are you a member of multiple social networks? Compare and contrast your experiences in social networking with your classmates. Which Web sites do you use, and why do you use these Web sites? Can you see yourself changing to another social network Web site? What would make you change? Discuss strategies that these social networks are using to keep you active in the Web site. Visit LinkedIn (www.linkedin.com), Classmates (www.classmates.com), and Facebook (www.facebook.com). What are the similarities in these Web sites? What are the main differences in these three social networks?

Answers to the Self-Study Questions

1. C, p. 196
2. C, p. 199
3. A, p. 204
4. C, p. 207
5. A, p. 223
6. C, p. 197
7. A, p. 203
8. D, p. 219
9. D, p. 211
10. A, p. 207

Case 1

Digg.com: Changing How News Is Delivered

Submit a news story or link to Digg.com, and if site users like it (i.e., "dig" it), the story moves to the front page. If the story proves unpopular, site users vote to "bury" it, and it disappears.

In October 2004, Kevin Rose, a former regular on the TechTV show *The Screen Savers* and his friends Owen Byrne, Ron Gorodetzky, and Jay Adelson began playing around with the idea of a user-controlled, community-based news Web site. They launched the site on December 5, 2004, and it immediately began drawing visitors. The original design was advertisement free, but that has changed since Google AdSense was added to the site.

Digg has so many users that "digging" a news story or Web link posting can sometimes cause a phenomenon called the "Digg effect," whereby increased traffic to a linked Web site can cause it to either slow considerably or even crash. According to Compete.com, Digg's home page attracted over 500 million unique visitors in 2009.

While Digg remains popular, critics argue the following:

- The site gives users too much control over content, resulting in misinformation and sensationalism.
- Companies paying for submissions have skewed the site's original purpose.

- The site's operators, which are its founders, exert too much control over front-page and forum content.
- The "bury" option is undemocratic because those who vote to bury an item are allowed to remain anonymous.
- The site is too susceptible to "gaming"—to groups or Web site operators who deliberately try to dictate content.

In May 2007, when the Advanced Access Content System Consortium objected to Digg posts containing encryption-breaking code for HD-DVD and Blu-ray disks, management heeded advice from attorneys and took the offending articles and posts down. A user revolt followed that prompted Digg's Kevin Rose to post a comment that reversed direction: "We hear you, and effective immediately we won't delete stories or comments containing the code and will deal with whatever the consequences might be. If we lose, then what the hell, at least we died trying."

In 2009, Digg.com introduced the "DiggBar" to its Web site. The DiggBar was a toolbar that appeared at the top of the Digg home page that acted as a URL shortener. When a link was submitted to Digg, its URL was automatically shortened and prefixed with "www.digg.com." When a

link was clicked by a user, instead of going to the corresponding Web site, the page appeared inside a framed Digg.com window. Using the DiggBar, users had immediate access to features such as sharing Digg links via e-mail or social media sites like Facebook or Twitter. In addition, users could instantly see what other Digg users had commented about on the story, check out related stories, and see the analytics surrounding the number of people that visited the link.

However, not long after the DiggBar's introduction, backlash from the Web community began to make news. Criticism of the toolbar centered on the way shortened URLs started with a Digg domain prefix. Links that normally opened a page at another domain (thereby giving that Web site a "hit" to statistics counters) opened in a frame and stayed within the Digg environment. Since the use of DiggBar was not optional, millions of potential lost "hits" were at stake. Web site owners and operators made an outpouring of negative feedback to Digg. Within a month of launch, Digg changed the way the toolbar operated and made it an opt-in for all unregistered users, disabling the URL shortening and framing features.

The year 2009 also marked the year that cybercriminals used Digg to try to turn a profit. To set their trap, scammers loaded

Digg with headlines promising readers a view of leaked personal celebrity videos. Once the reader followed the headline link, they were presented with a software download for viewing the videos. What actually installed on the unknowing user's computer was a program that supposedly scanned for malicious software. The bogus program, a type of malware, reported back serious problems found on the computer and offered to fix the issues for a small fee. To make the deception more realistic, the malware prevented the user's computer from operating correctly. Although it was unknown how many people fell into this trap, at least 50 user accounts were determined to be participating in the scam. Digg has since terminated over 300 user accounts suspected of spreading malicious software.

With a major redesign and update of the Digg.com home page planned in late 2010, the company's future looks vibrant as it continues to exemplify the spirit of user-provided-content and community-based Web 2.0 start-ups.

Questions

1. What effect does the "Digg effect" have on Web sites that are featured on Digg.com?
2. What are the positives and negatives to a news site that organizes its stories using user input?
3. How do you think Digg.com generates revenue? How do you think Digg.com will do in the future? What are main threats to its current business?

Based on:

Anonymous. (2009, February 12). Crooks setting cyber traps on Digg. *Global Saskatoon*. Retrieved June 28, 2010, from http://www.globalsaskatoon.com/technology/Crooks+setting+cyber+traps+Digg/ 1277319/story.html.

Anonymous. (2009, April 4). Digg launches the DiggBar. *Techtree.com*. Retrieved June 28, 2010, from http://www.techtree.com/India/News/Digg_launches_the_DiggBar/551-100776-643.html.

Arrington, M. (2006, March 18). The power of Digg. *Techcrunch.com*. Retrieved June 28, 2010, from http://www.techcrunch.com/2006/03/18/the-power-of-digg.

Dhaliwal, A. (2010, January 23). Digg founder Kevin Rose: Digg's "drastic" overhaul could "shock" users. *Topnews.us*. Retrieved June 28, 2010, from http://topnews.us/content/210231-digg-founder-kevin-rose-digg-s-drastic-overhaul-could-shock-users.

Digg. (2010, June 24). In *Wikipedia, the free encyclopedia*. Retrieved June 28, 2010, from http://en.wikipedia.org/w/index.php?title=Digg&oldid=369970137.

Rose, K. (2007, May 1). Digg this: 09-f9-11-02-9d-74-e3-5b-d8-41-56-c5-63-56-88-c0. Retrieved June 28, 2010, from http://blog.digg.com/?p=74.

Case 2

Wikipedia: Who Is Editing?

Research almost any topic on the Web, and a URL for a Wikipedia entry will likely appear on the list of resources. Wikipedia is a free, online encyclopedia that gets its entries from users—be they amateurs, professionals, or pranksters with nothing better to do. ("Wiki wiki" is the Hawaiian term for "quick.") As of 2010, Wikipedia had over 15 million article pages in over 270 languages and 22 million registered users. It is the world's fifth most popular Web site, with over 320 million monthly visitors looking to read and edit its pages. Since Wikipedia's start in January 2001, there have been over 880 million edits of content entries. Users who are logged in are able to edit entries, but the Wikipedia site keeps detailed logs of the sources (IP addresses) of all changes. Users/editors are anonymous in that only their user names are known, but IP addresses can be traced back to the source.

Cal Tech computation and neural systems graduate student Virgil Griffith got curious about Wikipedia's anonymous editors in 2007 when he read that congressional aides had been editing entries about their employers—the senators and representatives of the U.S. Congress. Griffith wondered if other companies and organizations were doing the same thing, so he created a program to find out. Griffith created a database of all Wikipedia entries and changes, including the information logged each time an anonymous editor made a change. Griffith isolated the XML-based records of changes and IP addresses, then identified the owners of the IP addresses using public net-address lookup services, such as ARIN, as well as private domain name data obtained through http://IP2location.com.

Griffith's system revealed the following information about the editors:

- Someone on a computer at voting-machine maker Diebold Election Systems deleted 15 paragraphs from a Wikipedia article about electronic voting that were critical of Diebold's machines.
- Wal-Mart made changes to improve its image.
- Politicians are frequent editors. For instance, a former U.S. senator from Montana made changes to indicate that he was a voice for farmers in his state.
- Dave Winer, a famous blogger and developer of RSS, notes that his Wikipedia entry has been edited several times, removing all mention of his contributions to RSS, blogging, and podcasting.
- ExxonMobil deleted information about its nonpayment of damages to 32,000 Alaska fishermen after the *Exxon Valdez* oil spill.
- A computer registered to Disney deleted information critical of the company's digital rights management software.

Griffith emphasizes that his system, WikiScanner, cannot identify Wikipedia editors as agents of certain companies or organizations. It can only identify IP addresses that come from networks registered to a company or organization.

Since Wikipedia entries can be written and edited by any user registered at the site, its accuracy should obviously not be completely trusted. If one uses other reputable sources in addition to Wikipedia, however, it can often be a starting point for further research on a topic. Just don't depend on it exclusively when researching a topic, and be sure to verify content read there before quoting it as fact. Dave Winer, for instance, writes in March 2008 that he finds Wikipedia "a useful personal resource." He was "working his way" through all episodes of *Battlestar Galactica* and found it helpful to read a synopsis of each episode on Wikipedia after he had watched the episode.

Inaccuracies aside, the ability for anyone to contribute and edit entries has been seen as the main strength of Wikipedia, allowing knowledge to be built on, refined, and policed. By the end of 2009, however, there had been a steep dropoff in the number of volunteers editing Wikipedia's pages. According to Spanish researcher Felipe Ortega, who analyzed the site's editing activities, Wikipedia's English-language pages lost over 49,000 editors compared to around 5,000 only a year earlier.

What is causing the plunge in editor activity? Some observers think that the perception that most of the relevant information is now on the site, leaving little to be done but maintain what is there, is driving down the number of those willing to contribute and edit. Others point to the inaccuracies that plague the site and the amount of time it takes to police the information. Although editors try to maintain factual articles, anyone is free to go in and change the information. At times, a back-and-forth battle begins between two legitimate editors over what the article contains. At other times, mischievous pranksters revert legitimate edits to their original format, insert offensive content, or otherwise deface the article, forcing editors to go back in and make fixes. Still other explanations focus on the rules and protocols surrounding the actual editing of the content. Making changes to content requires navigating a complex interface and coding scheme.

Hoping to stop the exodus of volunteers from the site, Wikipedia got its first facelift in the spring of 2010. Besides some cosmetic and layout updates to the site, site navigation has been improved, making it easier for users to find essential functions more easily. In addition, the editing system has gotten a major overhaul. Users can now make changes to data in tables and information boxes through simple forms. The edit page has been "decluttered" and rewritten in simpler language. An outline tool has also been added, making it easy to navigate longer articles.

Clearly, Wikipedia has plenty to offer when you need some quick information on a subject. Although editors have been in decline, Wikipedia clearly is aware of the problem and has made strides to correct the issue.

Questions

1. Do you use Wikipedia for your research? Why or why not?
2. Have you ever made a change to a Wikipedia entry? If you were to see an obvious mistake (in your opinion), would you take the time to change it? Why or why not?
3. Anyone can edit entries on Wikipedia. Do you see this as a curse or as a blessing? Explain.

Based on:

Angwin, J., and Fowler, G. A. (2009, November 27). Volunteers log off as Wikipedia ages. *Wall Street Journal*. Retrieved June 28, 2010, from http://online.wsj.com/article/SB125893981183759969.html.

Blakely, R. (2007, August 16). Wal-Mart, CIA, and ExxonMobil changed Wikipedia entries. *Foxnews.com*. Retrieved June 28, 2010, from http://www.foxnews.com/story/0,2933,293389,00.html.

Borland, J. (2007, August 14). See who's editing Wikipedia—Diebold, the CIA, a campaign. *Wired.com*. Retrieved June 28, 2010, from http://www.wired.com/politics/onlinerights/news/2007/08/wiki_tracker.

Crum, C. (2010, March 29). Will Wikipedia's new changes boost editing? *WebProNews*. Retrieved June 28, 2010, from http://www.webpronews.com/topnews/2010/03/29/will-wikipedias-new-changes-boost-editing.

Jones, M. W. (2010, March 27). Wikipedia user interface getting first overhaul. *Tech.Blorge*. Retrieved June 28, 2010, from http://tech.blorge.com/Structure:%20/2010/03/27/wikipedia-user-interface-getting-first-overhaul.

List of Wikipedias. (2010, June 25). In *Wikipedia, the free encyclopedia*. Retrieved June 28, 2010, from http://en.wikipedia.org/w/index.php?title=List_of_Wikipedias&oldid=370160770.

Risley, D. (2008, March 21). Wikipedia accuracy: Dave Winer's criticism. *PCMech.com*. Retrieved June 28, 2010, from http://www.pcmech.com/article/wikipedia-accuracy-dave-winers-criticism.

Winer, D. (2008, March 10). What's wrong with Wikipedia. *Scripting News*. Retrieved June 8, 2008, from http://www.scripting.com/stories/2008/03/20/whatsWrongWithWikipedia.html.

Enhancing Business Intelligence Using Information Systems

After reading this chapter, you will be able to do the following:

1. Describe the concept of business intelligence and how databases serve as a foundation for gaining business intelligence.

2. Explain the three components of business intelligence: information and knowledge discovery, business analytics, and information visualization.

Preview

Today, organizations operate in a global, highly competitive, and rapidly changing environment. A key to effective management is high-quality and timely information to support decision making. This high-quality and timely information, or business intelligence, can be provided from a variety of information systems (IS). In this chapter, we first describe business intelligence, followed by a description of databases and data warehouses, two fundamental components for gaining business intelligence. Then we describe the primary IS components utilized by organizations to gain business intelligence. In Chapter 2, "Gaining Competitive Advantage Through Information Systems," you learned about general types of information systems supporting organizations' different decision-making levels and business functions that execute various business processes in order to realize the strategic goals of the organization. Here, we introduce different technologies utilized at various decision-making levels of modern organizations to gain business intelligence.

Managing in the Digital World: Providing Business Intelligence to eBay Customers

You are probably very familiar with the online auction Web site eBay (see Figure 6.1). Founded in 1995, it is the global online marketplace where practically anyone can trade practically anything, from baseball cards to rare vinyl records to a private jet. Today, nearly 89 million people from 39 countries have active eBay accounts, trading over $1,400 worth of goods, every second of every day. In 2008, total auction sales were over $60 billion, a considerable number, compared to the overall U.S. Internet retail sales of $135 billion in 2009.

With this amount of transactions, tremendous data is being processed on a daily basis, including seller and buyer data, current auction listings, and final sales. For eBay as well as its sellers, this massive amount of data can be a virtual gold mine. When is the best time to list a new item? What are the best strategies to respond to seasonal changes in demand? How can you learn from past auctions to adjust your strategies for future auctions? Which items are selling well, and which aren't worth listing? What is the best strategy for setting starting bids or reserve prices? These are questions that both private and commercial sellers are facing on a daily basis, hoping to improve the return on their auctions.

How can sellers gain this insight and benefit from the tremendous amounts of historical data? eBay offers a variety of tools and reports that help sellers analyze their past auctions; similarly, third-party providers offer different tools that help sellers get the most out of the data. However, it is not just the sellers that can benefit from the data that is being collected from everyday transactions; eBay itself is crunching the numbers on a daily basis. With growing auction volumes, eBay has to finetune its systems to offer maximum performance and minimize delays or system failures, as any technical problem will lead to customer dissatisfaction and lost revenues. Thus, it is critical for eBay to analyze bidding behavior over the life of an auction and how this behavior influences demand on its systems. In eBay's early days, performing such complex analyses had taken days or weeks. However, in 2000, a large data warehouse was implemented that allowed eBay to quickly perform complex analyses on its data. With the help of this data warehouse and sophisticated business intelligence software, eBay has managed to become the online auction site of choice for buyers and sellers alike.

Despite (or because of) its popularity and success, there are downsides to doing business on eBay, namely, account hijacking; counterfeit, doctored, or misrepresented merchandise; and payment fraud. Account hijacking, the biggest and most dangerous problem on eBay, refers to criminals taking over a legitimate eBay account with good feedback in order to buy merchandise with stolen credit cards or to sell expensive items that are never delivered to customers.

goldenangel/Shutterstock

FIGURE 6.1

eBay is the largest Internet auction site in the world.

Given the need to maintain customer and seller confidence, eBay is exerting a lot of effort and spending a lot of resources to maintain and improve the integrity of the site through the development of sophisticated business intelligence tools. Unfortunately, as with all forms of Internet crime, eBay cannot offer absolute protection for its customers.

For instance, in 2003, the Salt Lake City police arrested a 31-year-old man who was accused of perpetrating one of the biggest scams in eBay history. Hundreds of customers complained that they sent $1,000 to a company called Liquidation Universe for laptop computers they never received. Early in the investigation, police determined that the suspect scammed over 1,000 eBay customers to the tune of $1 million in just a few weeks. eBay worked with the victims of the scam to help them get their money back, but the company does not reimburse customers for items not received. In other cases, crooks were offering counterfeited products—anything from collectables to software—on eBay. By the time a buyer finds out, the seller's account is often closed. In fact, in 2005, over 16,000 entries offering pirated products were closed by the Business Software Alliance. In 2009, a phishing attack aimed at getting eBay users' financial data was launched. Users received a legitimate looking e-mail informing them that "inactive customers" would have their PayPal accounts (a popular form of payment on eBay) deleted if they did not confirm their personal data, including credit card number, expiration date, and PIN number. It is not known exactly how many people fell victim to the socially engineered attack.

Likewise, in 2010, a 46-year-old man was found guilty of perpetrating the "single largest counterfeiting conspiracy yet uncovered on eBay." The global operation centered on selling millions of dollars' worth of counterfeit golfing equipment and clothing. The bogus products were manufactured in China and then circulated for sale on eBay by conspirators in more than six countries.

eBay is dealing with other types of auction fraud, such as shill bidding, where sellers use multiple accounts to bid on their own items, thus driving up the highest bid. Although such behavior occurs in only a small percentage of all auctions, buyers are losing large amounts of money because of the high number of these transactions. For eBay, determining patterns of fraudulent behavior is in its own best interest, as such behavior ultimately drives away both buyers and legitimate sellers. Again, mining its massive data warehouse can help to find such patterns, helping eBay to detect fraudsters and close accounts that are engaging in these behaviors.

Needless to say, these examples represent only a small fraction of the criminal activities on eBay. Other problem areas include handling of stolen goods and obtaining property through deception. It should be clear that, because of eBay's success, criminals who prowl the Internet will continue to make it one of their biggest targets. The best hope for honest users is that technology designed to thwart scam artists can keep up and provide both buyers and sellers with needed intelligence to make good decisions. In response to the illegal activities, eBay has created a research group dedicated to trust and safety; this research group is actively involved in developing data mining systems that learn from historical data so as to be able to prevent and catch fraudulent transactions on eBay.

After reading this chapter, you will be able to answer the following:

1. How can eBay utilize its transactional data to help both buyers and sellers?
2. Given the speed and volume of transactions on eBay, what business analytics and visualization tools could be used to better track and reduce fraudulent transactions?
3. How could legitimate buyers and sellers help eBay improve its tools for fighting fraud?

Based on:

Anonymous. (n.d.). Analyzing your eBay data. *Allbusiness.com*. Retrieved July 9, 2010, from http://www.allbusiness.com/sales/internet-ebay/3236-1.html.

Anonymous. (2006, December 5). Online auction fraud: Data mining software fingers both perpetrators and accomplices. *Science Daily*. Retrieved July 9, 2010, from http://www.sciencedaily.com/releases/2006/12/061205143326.htm.

Colet, E. (n.d.). Using data mining to detect fraud in auctions. *DSStar*. Retrieved July 9, 2010, from http://www.taborcommunications.com/dsstar/00/0627/101834.html.

Deatsch, K. (2009, February 2). E-commerce sales grew 6% in 2008 despite holiday season drop, comScore says. *InternetRetailer*. Retrieved July 9, 2010, from http://www.internetretailer.com/dailyNews.asp?id=29288.

Fresco, A. (2010, March 5). eBay golf club conman Gary Bellchambers jailed for four years. *Times Online*. Retrieved July 9, 2010, from http://www.timesonline.co.uk/tol/news/uk/crime/article7049845.ece.

Shah, H., N. Joshi, and P. Wurman (2002, May 24). Mining for bidding strategies on eBay. Retrieved July 9, 2010, from http://www4.ncsu.edu/~wurman/Papers/Shah-WebKDD.pdf.

Skinner, C. (2009, November 2). eBay phishing scam scariest email blunder of 2009. *Networkworld*. Retrieved July 8, 2010, from http://www.networkworld.com/news/2009/110209-ebay-phishing-scam-scariest-email.html.

Sullivan, B. (2003, June 12). Man arrested in huge eBay fraud. *MSNBC*. Retrieved July 9, 2010, from http://msnbc.msn.com/id/3078461.

Business Intelligence

In Chapter 2, you learned about the importance of business planning for gaining and sustaining competitive advantage. To stay ahead of the competition, organizations have turned to **business intelligence,** or the use of information systems to gather and analyze information from internal and external sources in order to make better business decisions. To improve organizational performance, business executives are seeking answers to questions such as "How effective is this year's promotion as compared to last year's?" "Which customer segments should we focus on?" "Which customers are most likely to switch to a competitor if we raise prices by X percent?" or, even more important, "Do we care if those customers switch?" (Tapscott, 2008). Business intelligence also refers to the information gained from the use of such systems. Next, the need for business intelligence is examined.

Why Organizations Need Business Intelligence

Although a company's overall direction is decided on at the strategic level, business processes span all organizational levels and are highly interconnected. Recall from Chapter 2 that business processes refer to the activities that organizations perform in order to reach their business goals. Unfortunately, the business processes outlined within strategic plans are often not implemented as envisioned at the managerial and operational levels of the organization because the information needed to effectively monitor and control these processes is simply not available. This "missing" information, in fact, exists but often resides in disconnected spreadsheets, reports, or databases. A recent study surveying 154 senior executives from companies all around the world found that for almost 80 percent of the respondents, data is the single most important input when making strategic and operational decisions, and 56 percent of the respondents fear making poor decisions due to inaccurate, incomplete, or faulty data; while data quality was clearly the most important criterion, only about 10 percent indicated that they would have the necessary data when needed (Economist Intelligence Unit, 2007). Similarly, Gartner research predicted that "through 2012, more than 35 percent of the top 5,000 global companies will regularly fail to make insightful decisions about significant changes in their business and markets" (Pettey and Stevens, 2009). Consequently, to realize the goals of their strategic plans, organizations must have up-to-date, accurate, and *integrated* information to monitor and fine-tune a broad range of business processes. To make this possible, information systems that provide business intelligence—by collecting, analyzing, and delivering needed information to the right decision maker and at the right time—facilitate the effective management of modern organizations. Additionally, business intelligence allows organizations to better respond to ongoing threats and opportunities as well as to better plan for the future.

Responding to Threats and Opportunities External factors such as globalization, competitive pressures, consumer demands, and governmental regulations can create opportunities as well as threats for modern organizations. For example, increasing globalization provides opportunities to compete in new markets, but it also creates the challenge of gaining new types of information in order to effectively manage these opportunities. Globalization can also lead to the threat of increased competition from developing countries, forcing organizations to rethink strategies or to further improve business processes. Thus, as the world becomes increasingly flatter, market opportunities will expand, but, at the same time, markets will also become increasingly more competitive. Further, large corporate and banking failures have brought about increased regulations (such as the Sarbanes-Oxley Act; see Chapter 10, "Securing Information Systems"), and organizations have to comply with ever-increasing government reporting requirements. This means that today's business environment is characterized by factors such as unstable market conditions, fierce competition, shorter product life cycles, more stringent regulations, and wider choices for customers than ever before. Business intelligence can help organizations make better decisions in this increasingly complex, fast-changing, and competitive environment by more effectively collecting and analyzing both internal and external data (see Figure 6.2).

With increasing pressure to reduce costs, organizations have to focus on investing in systems that provide the greatest returns. Business intelligence solutions can provide quick returns, as they help to quickly react to problems by providing the right information at the right time. Further, business intelligence helps to leverage existing systems (such as enterprise-wide information systems; see Chapter 7) by enabling decision makers to extract and analyze data provided by those systems. Finally, quick returns can be provided by helping organizations to focus on customer satisfaction, helping to retain the most profitable customers.

Effective Planning Is Continuous In the past, organizations lacked the necessary information and tools to continuously plan for their future. Typically, organizations would first develop a strategic plan for some planning cycle (say, a year); then, once a strategic plan was agreed on, managers of various business units would prepare budgets for executing their portion of the plan. These budgets were often "backward looking" because they were typically based on historical data rather

FIGURE 6.2

Business intelligence helps organizations swiftly respond to external threats and opportunities.

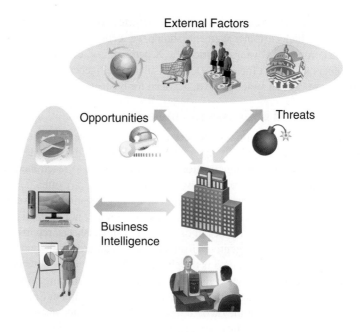

than being based on a clear understanding of current conditions and forecasts of future trends. Over time, managers would then execute their portion of the plan. For many organizations, this method of planning and managing was adequate given the relatively slow pace of change.

Today, however, given the need to swiftly respond to a highly competitive and rapidly changing environment, organizations must implement new ways of planning. In fact, successful organizations are utilizing a **continuous planning process** (see Figure 6.3). In a continuous planning process, organizations *continuously* monitor and analyze business processes; the results lead to ongoing adjustments to how the organization is managed, but these results are also reflected in ongoing updates to the organizational plans. It is only through timely and accurate business intelligence that continuous planning can be executed.

Responding to threats and opportunities and continuous planning is based on analyzing data from the operational level of the organization. In the next section, we describe how databases can be used to provide the necessary inputs to business intelligence applications.

FIGURE 6.3

Effective business planning is continuous.

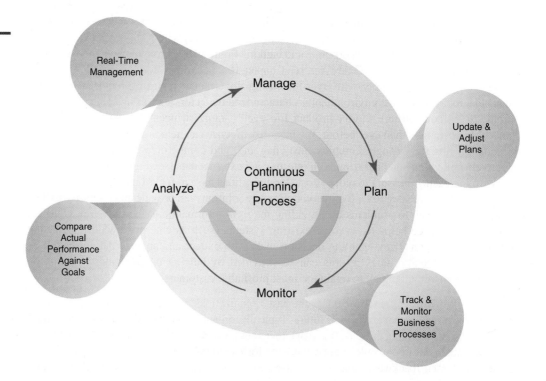

Databases: Providing Inputs into Business Intelligence Applications

Data and knowledge are probably among the most important assets an organization has, as data and knowledge are essential for both executing business processes and gaining business intelligence. **Databases,** which are collections of related data organized in a way that facilitates data searches, are vital to an organization's success.

For instance, organizations use databases to not only support sales transactions and track inventory, but to also identify potential customers in order to generate personalized communications when promoting a product or service for marketing purposes. The method of communication can be any addressable medium, including e-mail, customized web pages and catalogs, surface mail, and so on. Additionally, database technology fuels electronic commerce on the Web, from tracking available products for sale to providing customer service.

WHEN THINGS GO WRONG

Bad Intelligence—Misinformation Goes Viral Through Twitter

It seems everywhere you turn, Twitter is being used in different ways for a wide range of purposes. News sites put out tweets to cover live events, celebrities relate to fans their latest purchase, and politicians try to connect with their constituents. Twitter's ability to post thoughts in small snippets, referred to as microblogging, allows quick dissemination of information to a broad audience. Once tweets are published, they can be picked up and forwarded around, often gathering momentum as more and more users pick up the tweet and "retweet" it.

Twitter's viral momentum has been used in many ways, especially in the marketing arena. Perhaps its most famous use was in 2009 during the Iranian presidential election. As protests around the Persian nation erupted over the elections, the Iranian government censored much of the media outlets to block information flow to the rest of the world. However, Iranian citizens used Twitter to give real-time updates on what was happening, keeping the outside world informed. Details of events taking place were picked up, retweeted, and spread like wildfire to news rooms all around the globe. The information was then able to be put out through traditional media channels and news outlets.

Although Twitter has been used for good, its viral capabilities have also caused some problems and even spread lies about people. For instance, when a massive earthquake hit Haiti in early 2010, someone on the island nation tweeted that American Airlines was giving free flights to aid workers and provided the number to the Haitian consulate in New York. That post took on a viral nature when film critic Roger Ebert retweeted it to his more than 50,000 followers. Soon after that, the actor Rainn Wilson also retweeted the message to his 1.8 million followers. At this point, American Airlines was being deluged with phone calls from doctors, nurses, and other emergency aid workers wanting to get to Haiti. American fought back the tidal wave of misinformation by posting their own tweet and coordinating with news outlets. Fortunately, they were able to act quickly enough to mitigate the confusion the rumor was causing.

Another Twitter viral event was not so innocent. In early 2010, a fake CNN Web page screen capture claiming the actor Johnny Depp was dead was posted on a popular Internet hosting site. Fans of the site saw the fake Web page and began tweeting "RIP Johnny Depp," driving the tweet to the top of the trending topics. The phrase temporarily became the second most popular search phrase on Google. It didn't take very long before the news that Depp had been killed in a car wreck in France spread around the world. Hackers quickly took advantage of the viral news, creating Web sites claiming to have video footage of the crash that were embedded with malicious code to infect curious clickers with Trojan viruses. Weeks after the event, entertainment and news outlets were still posting stories refuting the claim that the actor was dead.

Although Twitter and other social media sites are powerful tools for connecting and sharing information, they can also have negative repercussions if bad information is put into the mix.

Based on:

Cluley, G. (2010, January 25). Johnny Depp is not dead, but hackers exploit false Twitter rumors. *Sophos.com*. Retrieved April 26, 2010, from http://www.sophos.com/pressoffice/news/articles/2010/01/johnny-depp.html.

Grossman, L. (2009, June 17). Iran protests: Twitter, the medium of the movement. *Time*. Retrieved April 26, 2010, from http://www.time.com/time/world/article/0,8599,1905125,00.html.

Kim, T. (2010, January 30). False American Airlines Twitter post offers fast lesson in social media. *Dallas Morning News*. Retrieved April 26, 2010, from http://www.dallasnews.com/sharedcontent/dws/bus/ptech/stories/013010dnmetsocialhaitiside.f4d307.html.

Enabling Interactive Web Sites Using Databases In today's highly dynamic, digital world, any organization engaged in e-commerce makes extensive use of databases to provide dynamic and customized rather than static information on their Web pages. For example, many companies are enabling users of their Web site to view product catalogs, check inventory, and place orders—all actions that ultimately read and write to organizations' databases. Similarly, information about products (name, description, dimensions, shipping weight, and so on) is stored in databases and dynamically inserted into a Web page, freeing the company from having to develop a separate Web site for each individual product. For example, companies such as Amazon.com need only a few page templates for different product categories. Depending on what the user is looking for, these templates are then populated dynamically with the relevant product information that is pulled from a database; similarly, whenever a registered user places an order, the customer's billing and shipping information is retrieved from a database and displayed to the user for confirmation.

Some Internet electronic commerce applications can receive and process millions of transactions per day. To ensure adequate system performance for customers as well as gain the greatest understanding of customer behavior, you must manage online data effectively. For example, Amazon.com is the world's largest bookstore, with more than 2.5 million titles, and is open 24 hours a day, 365 days a year, with customers from all over the world ordering books and a broad range of other products. Amazon's servers log millions of transactions per day. Amazon is a vast departure from a traditional physical bookstore. In fact, the largest physical bookstore carries "only" about 170,000 titles, and it would not be economically feasible to build a physical bookstore the size of Amazon; a physical bookstore that carried Amazon's 2.5 million titles would need to be the size of nearly 25 football fields. The key to effectively designing an online electronic commerce business is clearly the effective management of online data. Next we examine some basic concepts, advantages of the database approach, and database management.

Databases: Foundation Concepts The database approach now dominates nearly all the computer-based information systems used today. To understand databases, we must familiarize ourselves with some terminology. In Figure 6.4, we compare database terminology (middle column) with equivalents in a library (left column) and a business office (right column). We use database management systems (DBMSs) to interact with the data in databases. A DBMS is a software application with which you create, store, organize, and retrieve data from a single database or several databases. Microsoft Access is an example of a popular DBMS for personal computers. In

FIGURE 6.4

Computers make the process of storing and managing data much easier.

FIGURE 6.5

This sample data table for the entity Student includes eight attributes and 11 records.

ID Number	Last Name	First Name	Street Address	City	State	Zip Code	Major
209345	Judson	Jackie	216 Main	Pullman	WA	99164	Information Systems
213009	Schirmer	Birgit	233 Webb	Pullman	WA	99163	History
345987	Valacich	Jordan	1212 Valley View	Pullman	WA	99163	Computer Science
457838	Wright	Elizabeth	426 Main	Pullman	WA	99163	Nursing
459987	Schmidt	Lisa-Marie	1824 Lamont	Pullman	WA	99164	Pre-Medicine
466711	Ferrell	Lauren	412 C Street	Pullman	WA	99164	Business Management
512678	Gatewood	Lael	200 Hill	Pullman	WA	99163	Psychology
691112	Fuller	Grace	312 Mountain Drive	Pullman	WA	99164	Veterinary Medicine
910234	Hardin	Ethan	200 Sunset	Pullman	WA	99164	Sociology
979776	Valacich	James	1212 Valley View	Pullman	WA	99163	Computer Science
983445	Kabbe	Joshua	825 Skylark	Pullman	WA	99164	Human Resources

Attribute Types

Attribute

Record (One Row)

the DBMS, the individual database is a collection of related attributes about entities. An **entity** is something you collect data about, such as people or classes (see Figure 6.5). We often think of entities as **tables,** where each row is a **record** and each column is an **attribute** (also referred to as field). A record is a collection of related attributes about a single instance of an entity. Each record typically consists of many attributes, which are individual pieces of information. For example, a name and a Social Security number are attributes of a particular person.

Databases: Advantages Before there were DBMSs, organizations used the file processing approach to store and manipulate data electronically. Data were usually kept in a long, sequential computer file that was often stored on tape. Information about entities often appeared in several different places throughout the information system, and the data was often stored along with and sometimes embedded within the programming code that used the data. People had not yet envisioned the concept of separately storing information about entities in nonredundant databases, so different files often contained repetitive data about a customer, a supplier, or another entity. When someone's address changed, it had to be changed in every file where that information occurred, an often tedious process. Similarly, if programmers changed the code, they typically had to change the corresponding data along with it. Further, the programmer would have had to know *how* the data were stored in order to make any changes. This was often no better than the pen-and-paper approach to storing data.

It is possible for a database to consist of only a single file or table. However, most databases managed under a DBMS consist of multiple tables or entities, often organized in several files. A DBMS can manage hundreds or even thousands of tables simultaneously by linking the tables as part of a single system. The DBMS helps us manage the tremendous volume and complexity of interrelated data so that we can be sure that the right data is accessed, changed, or deleted. For example, if a student or customer address is changed, that change is made through all the parts of the system where that data might occur. Using the DBMS prevents unnecessary and problematic redundancies of the data, and the data are kept separate from the applications' programming code. This means that the database does not need to be changed if a change is made to an application. Consequently, there are numerous advantages to using a database approach to managing organizational data; these are summarized in Table 6.1. Of course, moving to the database approach comes with some costs and risks that must be recognized and managed (see Table 6.2). Nonetheless, most organizations have embraced the database approach because most feel that the advantages far exceed the risks or costs.

TABLE 6.1 Advantages of the Database Approach

Advantages	Description
Program–data independence	Much easier to evolve and alter software to changing business needs when data and programs are independent.
Minimal data redundancy	Single copy of data ensures that storage requirements are minimized.
Improved data consistency	Eliminating redundancy greatly reduces the possibilities of inconsistency.
Improved data sharing	Easier to deploy and control data access using a centralized system.
Increased productivity of application development	Data standards make it easier to build and modify applications.
Enforcement of standards	A centralized system makes it much easier to enforce standards and rules for data creation, modification, naming, and deletion.
Increased security	A centralized system makes it easier to enforce access restrictions.
Improved data quality	Centralized control, minimized redundancy, and improved data consistency help to enhance the quality of data.
Improved data accessibility	A centralized system makes it easier to provide access for personnel within or outside organizational boundaries.
Reduced program maintenance	Information changed in the central database is replicated seamlessly throughout all applications.

Databases: Effective Management Now that we have outlined why databases are important to organizations, we can talk about how organizational databases can be managed effectively. The best database in the world is no better than the data it holds. Conversely, all the data in the world will do you no good if they are not organized in a manner in which there are few or no redundancies and in which you can retrieve, analyze, and understand them. The two key elements of an organizational database are the data and the structure of that data. The structure of the data is typically captured in a **data model,** that is, a map or diagram that represents entities and their relationships. A common way to represent a data model is an **entity-relationship diagram.** Further, the structure of the data is documented to facilitate management of the database.

Each attribute in the database needs to be of a certain type. For example, an attribute may contain text, numbers, or dates. This **data type** helps the DBMS organize and sort the data, complete calculations, and allocate storage space. To finalize the data model in order to actually build the database, a process called **normalization** is used to make sure the database will operate efficiently. Normalization makes sure that each table contains only attributes that are *related* to the entity; hence, normalization helps to eliminate data duplication. If tables are designed correctly, they will be easier to update and it will be faster to extract vital information to improve an organization's business intelligence capabilities. We examine normalization more thoroughly in the Technology Briefing.

Once the data model is created, the format of the data is documented in a **data dictionary.** The data dictionary (or metadata repository) is a document explaining several pieces of information for each attribute, such as its name, whether it is a key or part of a key, the type of data expected (dates, alphanumeric, numbers, and so on), and valid values. Data dictionaries can include information such

TABLE 6.2 Costs and Risks of the Database Approach

Cost or Risk	Description
New, specialized personnel	Conversion to the database approach may require hiring additional personnel.
Installation and management cost and complexity	Database approach has higher up-front costs and complexity in order to gain long-term benefits.
Conversion costs	Extensive costs are common when converting existing systems, often referred to as *legacy systems,* to the database approach.
Need for explicit backup and recovery	A shared corporate data resource must be accurate and available at all times.
Organizational conflict	Ownership—creation, naming, modification, and deletion—of data can cause organizational conflict.

COMING ATTRACTIONS

The Future of Medical Records

The health care industry has been known for its slow pace of adopting information technology and integrating computer systems. However, in 2009, the U.S. government committed $19 billion to push electronic health records so as to speed up the information technology adoption process in the health care industry. Electronic health records (or electronic medical records) are digital records containing a patient's health information; hence, such records can easily be shared across different health care settings by being embedded in network-connected enterprise-wide information systems.

Implementing electronic health records promises benefits for health care providers, insurance companies, and patients; among other benefits, electronic health records help to do the following:

- Reduce costs
- Improve quality of care by helping doctors to make more informed decisions
- Speed up diagnosis and treatment
- Produce a more convenient data trail
- Simplify workflow and procedures, as all information is readily available electronically

Although electronic health records appear promising, there are many obstacles to overcome. One big obstacle is the resistance of doctors, staff, and other users. For example, doctors typically do not want to change the way they work, staff have to acquire new skills, and support has to be provided. As a result, the success of electronic health records is determined not only by the technology itself but also by how well the doctors are trained and use the technology.

Based on:

Browns, J., & Cox, L. (2009, March 10). Will electronic records really improve health care? *ABC News*. Retrieved March 19, 2010, from http://abcnews.go.com/Health/Technology/story?id=7042181.

Greenemeier, L. (2009, December 1). Will electronic medical records improve health care? *Scientific American*. Retrieved March 19, 2010, from http://www.scientificamerican.com/article.cfm?id=electronic-health-records.

MandaSpring. (2008, December 16). EMR advantages and disadvantages. *Bright Hub*. Retrieved March 19, 2010, from http://www.brighthub.com/health/technology/articles/7402.aspx.

---

as why the data item is needed, how often it should be updated, and on which forms and reports the data appears.

Data dictionaries can be used to enforce **business rules.** Business rules, such as who has authority to update a piece of data, are captured by the designers of the database and included in the data dictionary to prevent illegal or illogical entries from entering the database. For example, designers of a warehouse database could capture a rule in the data dictionary to prevent invalid ship dates from being entered into the database.

Entering and Querying Data At some point, data must be entered into the database. Traditionally, a clerk or other data entry professional would create records in the database by entering data. These data may come from telephone conversations, preprinted forms that must be filled out, historical records, or electronic files (see Figure 6.6a). Today, much organizational data are captured automatically, as is the case with transactional data from a point-of-sale terminal or a user's input in a Web form; whenever you place an order on the Web, sign up for a newsletter, or respond to an online survey, your input is directly stored in a database. A **form** (see Figure 6.6b) typically has blanks where the user can enter information or make choices, each of which represents an attribute within a database record (such as the user's first name, last name, gender, and so on). This form presents the information to the user in an intuitive way so that the user can easily see the required items and enter the data. Forms are often used to capture data to be added, modified, or deleted from the database (e.g., for modifying your password or closing your e-mail account).

In addition to transaction support, data stored in a database is extensively used for analysis and reporting. A **report** is a compilation of data from the database that is organized and produced in printed format (either electronic or on paper). Sophisticated **report generators** such as Crystal Reports can help users to quickly build interactive reports and visualizations to present the data in a useful format. To retrieve information from a database, we use a **query.** In fact, whenever a

FIGURE 6.6A

A preprinted form used for gathering information that could be stored in a database.

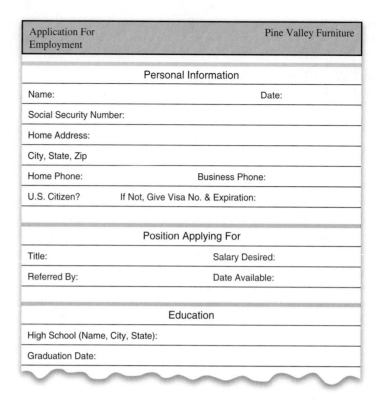

Web page is dynamically populated with content, a query is executed to retrieve the data from a database. **Structured Query Language (SQL)** is the most common language used to interface with databases. Figure 6.7 is an example of an SQL statement that an online bookstore would use to retrieve the information needed to populate a summary page containing all books written by the first author of this textbook, sorted by publishing date. Writing SQL statements requires time and practice, especially when you are dealing with complex databases with many entities or when

FIGURE 6.6B

A computer-based form used for gathering information that could be stored in a database.

Source: Courtesy Washington State University

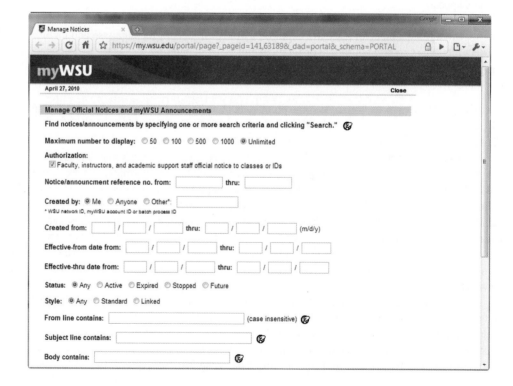

FIGURE 6.7

This sample SQL statement would be used to retrieve the information needed to populate a summary Web page containing all books written by the first author of this textbook, sorted by publication date.

```
SELECT AUTHOR, TITLE, PUBLICATION_DATE, PRICE
FROM BOOKS
WHERE AUTHOR="VALACICH"
ORDER BY PUBLICATION_DATE;
```

you are writing complex queries with multiple integrated criteria—such as adding numbers while sorting on two different attributes. Many desktop DBMS packages have a simpler way of interfacing with the databases—using a concept called **query by example (QBE).** QBE capabilities in a database enable us to fill out a grid, or template, in order to construct a sample or description of the data we would like to see, typically using the drag-and-drop features of a graphical user interface to create a query quickly and easily. In Figure 6.8, we provide an example of the QBE grid from Microsoft Access's desktop DBMS package.

Online Transaction Processing   The systems that are used to interact with customers and run a business in real time are called **operational systems.** Examples of operational systems are sales order processing and reservation systems, and fast customer response is fundamental to having a successful Internet-based business. **Online transaction processing (OLTP)** refers to immediate automated responses to the requests of users. OLTP systems are designed to handle multiple concurrent transactions from customers. Typically, these transactions have a fixed number of inputs, such as order items, payment data, and customer name and address, and a specified output, such as total order price or order tracking number. In other words, the primary use of OLTP systems is gathering new information, transforming that information, and updating information in the system. Common transactions include receiving user information, processing orders, and generating sales receipts. Consequently, OLTP is a big part of interactive electronic commerce applications on the Internet. Since customers can be located virtually anywhere in the world, it is critical that transactions be processed efficiently. The speed with which DBMSs can process transactions is, therefore, an important design decision when building Internet systems. In addition to which technology is chosen to process the transactions, how the data is organized is also a major factor in determining system performance.

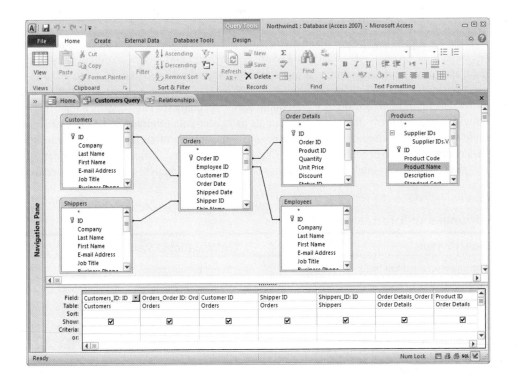

FIGURE 6.8

QBE provides a graphical interface to define what information you want to see.

Although the database operations behind most transactions are relatively simple, designers often spend considerable time making adjustments to the database design in order to "tune" processing for optimal system performance. Once an organization has all this data, it must design ways to gain the greatest value from its collection; each individual OLTP system could be queried individually, but the real power for an organization comes from analyzing the aggregation of data from different systems, or *data mining,* using methods such as *online analytical processing.*

Operational Systems and Business Intelligence Operational systems can generate a wealth of data that can serve as useful inputs into business intelligence applications. For example, a grocery checkout system processes a specific transaction (the purchase) that can be linked to an inventory system (for reordering purposes), but it can also capture valuable data such as time of the purchase, items purchased together, form of payment, or loyalty program details. Coupled with external data (such as store location, weather data, or competitor information), this data can be analyzed for spending patterns, effectiveness of sales promotions, or customer profiling.

The systems designed to support decision making based on stable point-in-time or historical data are called **informational systems.** The requirements for designing and supporting transactional and analytical systems are quite different (see Table 6.3 for the key differences between operational and informational systems). In a distributed online environment, performing real-time analytical processing diminishes the performance of transaction processing. For example, complex analytical queries require the locking of data resources for extended periods of execution time, whereas transactional events—data insertions and simple queries from customers—are fast and can often occur simultaneously. Thus, a well-tuned and responsive transaction system may have uneven performance for customers while analytical processing occurs. As a result, many organizations replicate all transactions on a second database server so that analytical processing does not slow customer transaction processing performance. This replication typically occurs in batches during off-peak hours, when site traffic volumes are at a minimum.

Master Data Management To make sound operational, tactical, and strategic business decisions, it is imperative that decisions made in different departments are based on the same underlying data, definitions, and assumptions; that is, there is a "single version of the truth." For example, do the marketing and accounting departments have the same definitions of a customer or a sale? Does a "customer" entail anyone who may be interested in the company's product or service (marketing view) or only those who actually made a purchase (accounting view)? Part of creating a single version of the truth is **master data management. Master data** is the data that is deemed most important in the operation of a business. Typically shared among multiple organizational units, master data includes data about customers, suppliers, inventory, employees, and the like. You can think of master data as the "actors" in an organization's transactions; for example, a *customer* purchases something, an *employee* is paid, and so on. Given the importance of an organization's master data, master data management is a management rather than a technology-focused issue, as different business units and different corporate levels have to come to consensus on the meaning of master data items or on how to deal with duplicates. Especially for large organizations, arriving at a single version of the truth can be a challenge, as master data often has to be integrated from multiple systems. Likewise, after mergers or acquisitions, organizations have to try to consolidate the master data from two or more companies. Once the meaning and format of the master data have been agreed on, business intelligence applications can base their analyses on the single version of

TABLE 6.3 Comparison of Operational and Informational Systems

Characteristic	Operational System	Informational System
Primary purpose	Run the business on a current basis	Support managerial decision making
Type of data	Current representation of state of the business	Historical or point-in-time (snapshot)
Primary users	Online customers, clerks, salespersons, administrators	Managers, business analysts, and customers (checking status and history)
Scope of usage	Narrow and simple updates and queries	Broad and complex queries and analyses
Design goal	Performance	Ease of access and use

the truth by accessing multiple databases or by using a *data warehouse* that integrates data from various operational systems.

Data Warehouses Large organizations, such as Walmart, UPS, and Alaska Airlines, have built **data warehouses** that integrate multiple large databases and other information sources into a single repository. This repository is suitable for direct querying, analysis, or processing. Much like a physical warehouse for products and components, a data warehouse stores and distributes data on computer-based information systems. A data warehouse is a company's virtual storehouse of valuable data from the organization's disparate information systems and external sources. It supports the online analysis of sales, inventory, and other vital business data that have been culled from operational systems. The purpose of a data warehouse is to put key business information into the hands of more decision makers, and an organization that successfully deploys a data warehouse has committed to pulling together, integrating, and sharing critical corporate data throughout the firm. Table 6.4 lists sample industry uses of data warehouses. Data warehouses can take up hundreds of gigabytes (even terabytes) of data. They usually run on fairly powerful mainframe computers and can cost millions of dollars.

TABLE 6.4 Sample Industry Uses of Data Warehousing

Uses of Data Warehousing	Representative Companies
Retail	
Analysis of scanner checkout data	Safeway
Tracking, analysis, and tuning of sales promotions and coupons	Costco, CVS Corporation
Inventory analysis and redeployment	Home Depot
Price reduction modeling to "move" the product	Office Depot
Negotiating leverage with suppliers	Sears
Frequent buyer program management	Target
Profitability analysis	Walgreen's
Product promotions for focused market segments	Walmart, Williams-Sonoma
Telecommunications	
Analysis of call volume, equipment sales, customer profitability, costs, inventory	Comcast Cable
Inventory analysis and redeployment	Hong Kong CSL
Purchasing leverage with suppliers	Telefonica SA
Frequent buyer program management	T-Mobile
Resource and network utilization	Verizon
Problem tracking and customer service	Qwest Communications
Banking and finance	
Relationship banking	Bank of America
Cross-segment marketing	Citigroup
Risk and credit analysis	HSBC
Merger and acquisition analysis	Goldman Sachs
Customer profiling	Morgan Stanley
Branch performance	UBS
Portfolio management	Wells Fargo
Automotive	
Inventory and supply chain management	Daimler AG
Resource utilization	Ford
Negotiating leverage with suppliers	General Motors
Warranty tracking and analysis	Honda
Profitability analysis and market segmentation	Toyota

FIGURE 6.9

Extraction, transformation, and loading are used to consolidate data from operational systems into a data warehouse.

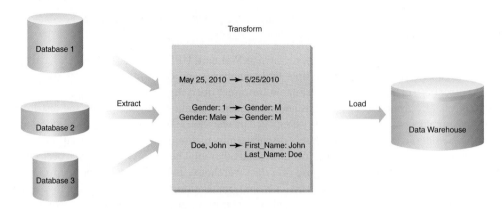

A crucial process for consolidating data from operational systems with other organizational data to facilitate the use of data mining techniques to gain the greatest and broadest understanding from the data is **extraction, transformation, and loading.** First, the data need to be extracted from various different systems. In the transformation stage, data are being cleansed and manipulated to fit the needs of the analysis (such as by creating new calculated fields or summary values). **Data cleansing** refers to the process of standardizing the format of data retrieved from different systems (such as differences in the way dates or ZIP codes are stored) and removing inaccurate records. Finally, the transformed data is loaded into the data warehouse and is ready for being used for complex analyses (see Figure 6.9).

NET STATS

The Demise of Broadcast TV

Recent studies of the TV industry indicate that it is in trouble. More and more people are choosing not to watch TV in the conventional "appointment" way. For example, in August 2009, Internet users in the United States consumed more than 11 billion video streams, averaging more than 81 streams (or 205 minutes) per viewer. This is a marked increase from the previous year: the total number of streams consumed increased by 41 percent (or by 20 percent per viewer). In 2009, almost a quarter of U.S. households watched online television, primarily for entertainment purposes. At the same time, 20 percent of U.S. consumers indicate that their TV viewing habits have changed, resulting in a decline in traditional TV consumption. In contrast to appointment TV, watching TV online offers the benefit of being able to watch programs anywhere at any time.

A survey conducted by Mediamark shows that consuming live TV on mobile devices is another growing trend: more than 20 percent of U.S. adults who own mobile phones are interested in being able to watch live TV on the go. However, only 13 percent would be willing to pay monthly subscription fees. Regardless of whether video content is accessed from mobile devices or on one's workplace computer, the "traditional" TV industry has to find ways to sustain its business model. Can

ads come to the rescue? Seventy percent of the respondents of Mediamark's survey find mobile ads annoying, but almost a quarter of the respondents are willing to view ads so as to lower the costs of live TV on their mobile devices. Further, a study by The Nielsen Company found that video ads embedded within streamed full-episode TV programs outperformed those in broadcast TV in terms of general recall, brand recall, message recall, and likability. Nielsen attributed this to the differences between rather passive traditional TV consumption and more interactive online TV consumption.

Based on:

Marshall, J. (2009, September 29). U.S. online video consumption grows considerably year-over-year. *Clickz.com*. Retrieved July 13, 2010, from http://www.clickz.com/3635128.

Marshall, J. (2010, April 27). Online video ads more effective than TV among U.S. viewers. *Clickz.com*. Retrieved July 13, 2010, from http://www.clickz.com/3640179.

MediaBuyerPlanner. (2009, September 8). Study: Two-thirds of households watch online TV. *MediaBuyerPlanner*. Retrieved March 3, 2010, from http://www.mediabuyerplanner.com/entry/45030/study-two-thirds-of-households-watch-online-tv.

Mediamark. (2009, August 27). Over 20% of adults are interested in TV on their phones. *Mediamark*. Retrieved March 3, 2010, from http://www.mediamark.com/PDF/MRIPR_082709_CellPhoneTV.pdf.

Data Marts Rather than storing all enterprise data in one data warehouse, many organizations have created multiple data marts, each containing a subset of the data for a single aspect of a company's business, such as finance, inventory, or personnel. A **data mart** is a data warehouse that is limited in scope. It contains selected information from the data warehouse such that each separate data mart is customized for the decision support applications of a particular end-user group. Data marts have been popular among small and medium-sized businesses and among departments within larger organizations, all of which were previously prohibited from developing their own data warehouses because of the high costs involved.

Williams-Sonoma, for example, known for its high-class home furnishing stores, is constantly looking to find new ways to increase sales and reach new target markets. Some of the most important data are coming from their catalog mailings, a database that contains 33 million active U.S. households. Using SAS data mining tools and different statistical models, Williams-Sonoma can segment customers into groups of 30,000 to 50,000 households and can predict the profitability of those segments based on the prior year's purchases. These models resulted in the creation of a new catalog for a market segment that had up to then not been served by Williams-Sonoma. Now, for example, Williams-Sonoma markets a variety of new products, such as fringed lamps, chic furniture, and cool accessories, to an identified market segment using its Pottery Barn Teen catalog.

Data marts typically contain tens of gigabytes of data as opposed to the hundreds of gigabytes in data warehouses. Therefore, data marts can be deployed on less powerful hardware. The differences in costs between different types of data marts and data warehouses can be significant. The cost to develop a data mart is typically less than $1 million, while the cost for a data warehouse can exceed $10 million. However, with the advent of cloud computing, several vendors are offering data warehousing as a service, which can help to significantly lower the company's initial investment (see Chapter 3, "Managing the Information Systems Infrastructure and Services"); similarly, companies such as SAP are offering on-demand business intelligence as a service.

Business Intelligence Components

Various different vendors offer a wide variety of tools as business intelligence applications. In general, however, there are three categories of business intelligence tools: tools for aiding information and knowledge discovery, tools for analyzing data to improve decision making, and tools for visualizing complex data relationships. Although each type of application by itself can be very valuable to an organization, it is their convergence that enables organizations to gain and sustain competitive advantage through enhanced business intelligence. In the following sections, we discuss each of these categories as well as the various systems and technologies that each encompasses.

Information and Knowledge Discovery

Information and knowledge discovery tools are used primarily to extract information from existing data. Sometimes, information and knowledge discovery is completely atheoretical, and companies use business intelligence tools to search for hidden relationships between data, akin to searching for the "needle in the haystack." In other cases, business users formulate hypotheses (such as "customers with a household income of $150,000 are twice as likely to respond to our marketing campaigns as customers with an income of $60,000 or less"), and these hypotheses are tested against existing data. In the following sections, we describe some of the applications used for discovering new and unexpected relationships and for testing hypotheses.

Ad Hoc Queries and Reports Business users across an organization need the right information at the right time. Such information is typically presented as reports based on data stored in organizational databases and can take the form of **scheduled reports, drill-down reports, exception reports,** and **key-indicator reports** (see Table 6.5). These reports are either produced at prespecified intervals or created whenever a prespecified event happens. However, decision makers frequently have information needs that are unforeseen and may never arise again. In such instances, the users need to run **ad hoc queries** (i.e., queries created because of unplanned information needs that are typically not saved for later use). Ad hoc query tools provide an easy-to-use

TABLE 6.5 Common Reports and Queries

Report/Query	Description
Scheduled reports	Reports produced at predefined intervals—daily, weekly, or monthly—to support routine decisions
Key-indicator reports	Reports that provide a summary of critical information on a recurring schedule
Exception reports	Reports that highlight situations that are out of the normal range
Drill-down reports	Reports that provide greater detail, so as to help analyze why a key indicator is not at an appropriate level or why an exception occurred
Ad hoc queries	Queries answering unplanned information requests to support a nonroutine decision; typically not saved to be run again

interface, allowing managers to run queries and reports themselves without having to know query languages or the structure of the underlying data. Installed on a person's desktop, notebook computer, or mobile device, these tools can be used to run queries and reports whenever an unplanned information need arises without having to resort to calling the IT department for help in creating a complex query or a special report.

Online Analytical Processing **Online analytical processing (OLAP)** refers to the process of quickly conducting complex, multidimensional analyses of data stored in a database that is optimized for retrieval, typically using graphical software tools. OLAP tools enable users to analyze different dimensions of data beyond simple data summaries and data aggregations of normal database queries. A typical question asked would be "What were the profits for each week in 2011 by sales region and customer type?" In contrast to relatively simple ad hoc queries, running such multidimensional queries requires a deeper understanding of the underlying data. Given the high volume of transactions within Internet-based systems and the potential business value in the data, analysts must provide extensive OLAP capabilities to managers. The chief component of an OLAP system is the **OLAP server,** which understands how data is organized in the database and has special functions for analyzing the data. The use of dedicated databases allows for tremendous increases in retrieval speed. In the past, multidimensional queries against large transactional databases could take hours to run; in contrast, OLAP systems preaggregate data so that only the subset of the data necessary for the queries is extracted, greatly improving performance.

Measures and Dimensions. Whenever a business transaction occurs, associated data can be stored and then analyzed from a variety of perspectives. To facilitate efficient processing of transactions, databases supporting online transaction processing systems treat all data in similar ways. In contrast, OLAP systems are designed for efficient retrieval of data and categorize data as measures and dimensions. **Measures** (or sometimes called **facts**) are the values or numbers the user wants to analyze, such as the sum of sales or the number of orders placed. **Dimensions** provide a way to summarize the data, such as region, time, or product line. Thus, sales (a measure) could be analyzed by product, time (year, quarter, or week), geographical region, or distributor (the dimensions). To enable the analysis of data at more or less detailed levels, the dimensions are organized as hierarchies (such as in year, quarter, month, or day). For example, when analyzing sales by geographical regions, a user can **drill down** from state, to county, to city, and to the individual store location or **roll up** from state to sales region (northwest, south, southeast, and so on), to country, or to continent.

Cubes, Slicing, and Dicing. To enable such multidimensional analyses, OLAP arranges the data as so-called cubes. An **OLAP cube** is a data structure allowing for multiple dimensions to be added to a traditional two-dimensional table (see Figure 6.10). Although the figure only shows three dimensions, data can be analyzed in more than three dimensions. Analyzing the data on subsets of the dimensions is referred to as **slicing and dicing.** For example, a slice may show sales by product type and region only for the second quarter of 2012. Another slice may only show sales for desktops in the western region (see Figure 6.11).

Data Mining **Data mining** complements OLAP in that it provides capabilities for discovering "hidden" predictive relationships in the data. Using powerful multiprocessor computers and complicated algorithms, data mining applications can analyze massive amounts of data to identify characteristics of profitable customers, purchasing patterns, or even fraudulent credit card

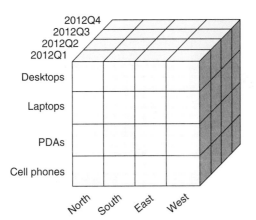

FIGURE 6.10

An OLAP cube allows for analyzing data by multiple dimensions.

transactions. Typically, data mining algorithms search for patterns, trends, or rules that are hidden in the data. Results from a data mining exercise (such as the characteristics of customers most likely to respond to a marketing campaign for a specific new product) can then be used in an ad hoc query (e.g., to identify customers sharing those characteristics so as to target them in the next campaign). It is important to note that any interesting predictive model derived from data mining should be tested against "fresh" data to determine if the model actually holds what it promises.

In order to increase predictive power, data mining algorithms are run against large data warehouses. Depending on the size of the data warehouse (large data warehouses often contain many terabytes of data), data mining algorithms can take a long time to run; thus, an important preparatory step to running data mining algorithms is **data reduction,** which reduces the complexity of the data to be analyzed. This can be achieved by rolling up a data cube to the smallest level of aggregation needed, reducing the dimensionality, or dividing continuous measures into discrete intervals.

Association Discovery. One frequently used application of data mining is association discovery. **Association discovery** is a technique used to find associations or correlations among sets of items. For example, a supermarket chain wants to find out which items are typically purchased together in order to redesign the store's layout and optimize the customers' "navigational path" through the store, or to launch a new promotion. Mining sales transactions over the past five years may reveal that 80 percent of the time, people who purchase coffee also purchase sugar (see Figure 6.12). Association rules typically contain two numbers: a percentage indicating support (e.g., the combination of coffee and sugar occurs in 20% of all transactions analyzed) and a confidence level indicating the reliability (e.g., 80 percent of all transactions that contain coffee also contain sugar). These numbers help managers decide if the association rule is meaningful and if any changes (e.g., to store layout or pricing) based on the findings are worthwhile. Similar to association discovery, **sequence discovery** is used to discover associations over time. For example, it may be

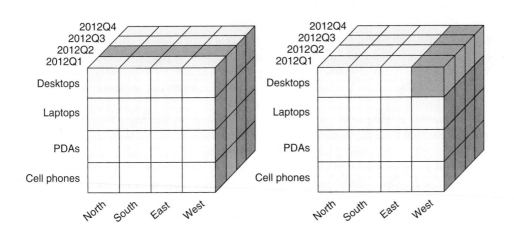

FIGURE 6.11

Slicing and dicing allows for analyzing subsets of the dimensions.

Coffee → Sugar [Support 20%, Confidence 80%]

discovered that 55 percent of all customers who purchase a new high-definition TV set also purchase a Blu-ray disc player within the next two months.

Clustering and Classification. Another useful application of data mining is clustering and classification. **Clustering** is the process of grouping related records together on the basis of having similar values for attributes. For example, an airline may cluster its frequent fliers based on miles flown or the number of flight segments. These results can then be used for targeting certain groups of customers in marketing campaigns. In contrast, **classification** is used when the groups ("classes") are known beforehand, and records are segmented into these classes. For example, a bank may have found that there are different classes of customers who differ in their likelihood of defaulting on a loan. As such, all customers can be classified into different (known) risk categories in order to ensure that the bank does not exceed a desired level of risk within its loan portfolio. Typically, classification would use a decision tree to classify the records.

Unstructured Data Analysis Although the quantitative methods described above can help decision makers get a better view of their organization's performance or their customer's behavior, they only provide a partial picture. By focusing purely on structured data (such as transactions, credit lines, and so on), a wealth of unstructured data (such as customer sentiments voiced in online forums, letters, or service-related call center records) is left untapped; in fact, studies show that between 50 and 80 percent of all enterprise information consists of unstructured or semistructured data (Swoyer, 2007), and with the tremendous increase of user-generated content on the Web, this figure may be even higher in the future. Making important business decisions purely based on structured data, thus, can be dangerous, as the massive amounts of unstructured data could either strengthen or contradict business decisions. Hence, organizations are trying not only to reach a single version of the truth but also to get the whole truth by analyzing unstructured data using *text mining, Web content mining,* or *Web usage mining.*

Text Mining and Web Content Mining. **Text mining** refers to the use of analytical techniques for extracting information from textual documents. For organizations, the analysis of textual documents can provide extremely valuable insights into business performance, competitors' activities, or regulatory compliance. Such textual documents can include internal data such as letters or e-mails from customers, customer calls, internal communications, or external data such as blog posts, wikis, and competitor's Web pages, marketing materials, patent filings, and so on. Text mining systems analyze a document's linguistic structures to extract data such as places, companies, concepts, or dates. Most systems can easily extract a wide range of content and can be customized to meet an organization's needs by adding specific key words related to competitors, product names, persons of interest, and the like.

Web content mining refers to extracting textual information from Web documents. To extract information from the overall Internet (or from some subset of Web sites), a document collection spider or *Web crawler* (discussed later in this chapter) would gather sites and documents that matched some prespecified criteria and place this information in a massive document warehouse. Once collected, the text mining system would apply a variety of analytical techniques to produce reports that can be used to gain additional insights beyond what is typically gained using data mining analytics alone (see Figure 6.13).

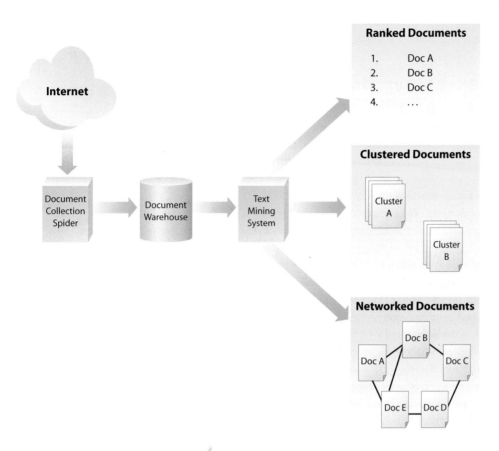

FIGURE 6.13

Text mining the Internet.

Analyzing textual documents can help organizations in various ways:

- The marketing department can learn about customers' thoughts, feelings, and emotions, by analyzing not only customer e-mails or letters but also blogs, wikis, or discussion forums.
- The operations department can learn about product performance by analyzing service records or customer calls.
- Strategic decision makers can gather **competitive intelligence** by analyzing press releases, news article, or customer-generated Web content about competitors' products.
- The sales department can learn about major accounts by analyzing news coverage.
- The human resources department can monitor employee satisfaction or compliance to company policies by analyzing internal communications (this is especially important in order to comply with regulations such as the Sarbanes-Oxley Act; see Chapter 10).

Many major companies, including Capital One, Marriott International, United Airlines, and Walmart, use text mining solutions to assess customer sentiments and increase customer satisfaction. Similarly, raveable.com provides hotel ratings by aggregating information from sources such as tripadvisor.com, expedia.com, or travelocity.com as well as individual travel blogs; in addition to aggregating numerical ratings given for aspects such as cleanliness, value, or location, raveable.com uses text mining to analyze review comments based on key words such as "earplugs," "noise," or "clean" and the associated sentiments so as to categorize the reviews and classify them as positive or negative.

Web Usage Mining. **Web usage mining** is used by organizations such as Amazon.com to determine patterns in customers' usage data, such as how users navigate through the site or how much time they spend on different pages. By analyzing users' **clickstream data** (i.e., a recording of a user's path through a Web site), a business such as Amazon can assess its pages' **stickiness** (i.e., the ability to attract and keep visitors) and how customers navigate through different item categories, ultimately helping Amazon to optimize the structure of its Web site.

The tools used for information and knowledge discovery can be embedded into a broad range of managerial, executive, and functional area information systems as well as into decision support and intelligent systems. Results from these analyses can be provided on digital dashboards,

Brief Case ⊙

THE INTERNET MOVIE DATABASE

If you love movies, there have probably been times when a film-related question drove you crazy. A friend bet you that the blond bombshell who played Irina Spalko in *Indiana Jones and the Kingdom of the Crystal Skull* was Nicole Kidman, and you knew he was wrong—but how to prove it? Which Native American actor played sidekick Tonto in Clayton Moore's *Lone Ranger?* Which television show made Robert Blake famous, and what animal was his costar on the show?

Of course, you could conduct a general Web search and find the answers to all of these questions, but it might take you a while. Instead, you can visit one Web site—the Internet Movie Database (IMDb)—and find all of the answers and more in minutes.

What began as a usenet list posted on the Internet in 1990 (the World Wide Web did not yet exist) has become the world's largest online accumulation of data about films, actors, film production and distribution crews and companies, television programs, direct-to-video productions, video games, movie trivia, plots, and quotes, and more to be found at one Web site. Amazon.com bought IMDb in 1998, allowing devoted IMDb volunteers to finally quit their day jobs and earn a living maintaining and expanding the site. In 2010, IMDb boasted information on more than 1.5 million movie and TV titles and 3.2 million celebrities, actors, directors, and even crew members.

Any computer user with a Web browser and an e-mail account can set up a free account that lets him or her submit information, leave comments for actors, and otherwise interact with the site, but setting up an account is not necessary to simply look up information about movies, television shows, and actors. In 2002, IMDb created a for-profit subscription service, IMDbPro, to provide additional information for business professionals. A résumé subscription service begun in 2006 lets actors

and production crew members post photos and additional information about themselves for an annual fee. IMDb gets most of its content from industry sources, filmmakers, and IMDb users but tries to ensure accuracy by manually scrutinizing the information before adding it to the database.

In April 2010, IMDb announced its IMDb Movies & TV App for iPad. With this new application, users can access IMDb's database using mobile devices. In addition to accessing information about film titles, actors, and film crew members, users can find localized movie show-times, browse TV listings, explore photo galleries, view movie trailers, and so on. IMDb founder and current managing director Col Needham says that "the IMDb didn't start as a dream to build a business or a Web site. It started as a dream to make a tool that we, as movie fans, would find really useful and fun. Over the years, millions of other movie fans have found it useful and fun too." IMDb has 57 million unique visitors each month.

So who was the blond in the Indiana Jones movie mentioned above? Who was the Native American actor who played Tonto? What show made Robert Blake famous, and what animal was his costar? Visit IMDb and find out.

Questions

1. How can IMDb use automated tools to ensure accuracy of the information submitted by users or other sources?
2. How could user-generated content be used to predict the success of future movie releases?

Based on:

Anonymous. (n.d.). IMDb App for iPhone™, iPad and iPod touch®. Retrieved July 12, 2010, from http://www.imdb.com/features/iphone.

IMDb history. (n.d.). Retrieved April 3, 2010, from http://www.imdb.com/help/show_leaf?history.

paper reports, Web portals, e-mail alerts (using monitoring or data mining agents), and mobile devices as well as a variety of information systems (see Figure 6.14).

Business Analytics to Support Decision Making

The second class of business intelligence applications comprises systems to support human and automated decision making. We first discuss applications designed to help predict future outcomes, followed by applications that support human decision makers in making unstructured decisions. Then we provide an overview of intelligent systems, which are designed to take some of these decisions out of the hands of the human decision makers, thus freeing up valuable resources. Finally, we examine various tools for enhancing organizational collaboration.

Business Analytics Traditional business intelligence applications for information and knowledge discovery are designed to focus on past and current performance, thus helping decision

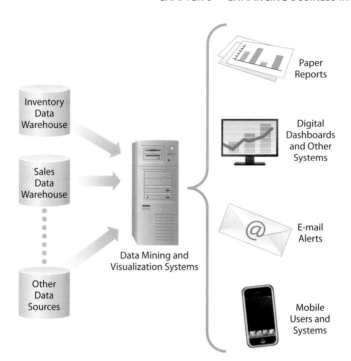

FIGURE 6.14

Data mining results can be delivered to users in a variety of ways.

makers to get a detailed picture about what *is*. **Business analytics** augments business intelligence by using **predictive analysis** to help identify trends or predict business outcomes; whereas business intelligence is good for knowing what is, predictive analysis helps in foreseeing what *will be*. For example, predictive analysis can help in understanding how a certain customer segment would respond to targeted promotions or help in determining measures to retain the most valuable customers (Business Objects, n.d.). However, predictive analysis is heavily dependent on statistical models and their underlying assumptions. Traditionally, such analyses were quite difficult for business users; in contrast, many of today's business analytics solutions offered by companies such as SAS or SAP guide the users through the process of conducting the desired analyses, selecting the right data, models, and so on, thus enabling "self-service business intelligence" and allowing business users to get self-service answers to the questions they have without relying on support staff.

Decision Support Systems A **decision support system (DSS)** is a special purpose information system designed to support organizational decision making related to a particular recurring problem. DSSs are typically used by managerial-level employees to help them solve semistructured problems such as sales and resource forecasting, yet a DSS can be used to support decisions at virtually all levels of the organization. A DSS augments human decision-making performance and problem solving by enabling managers to examine alternative solutions to a problem via "what-if" analyses. A **what-if analysis** allows you to make hypothetical changes to the data associated with a problem (e.g., loan duration or interest rate) and observe how these changes influence the results. For example, a cash manager for a bank could examine what-if scenarios of the effect of various interest rates on cash availability. With a DSS, the manager uses decision analysis tools such as Microsoft Excel—a widely used DSS environment—to either analyze or create meaningful information to support the decision making related to nonroutine problems. In contrast to systems that primarily present the outputs in a passive way, a DSS is designed to be an "interactive" decision aid. The results from any analysis are displayed in both textual and graphical formats.

Architecture of a DSS. Like the architecture of all systems, a DSS consists of input, process, and output components as illustrated in Figure 6.15 (Sprague, 1980). Within the process component, models and data are utilized. The DSS uses **models** to manipulate data. For example, if you have some historic sales data, you can use many different types of models to create a forecast of

FIGURE 6.15

Architecture of a DSS using the basic systems model.

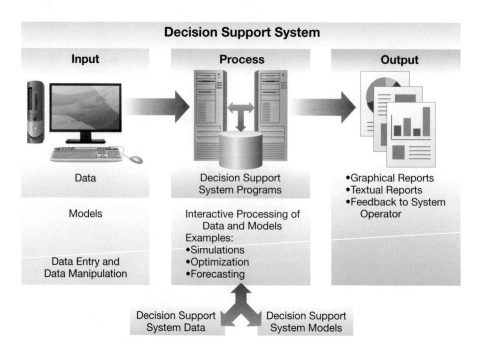

future sales. One technique is to take an average of the past sales. The formula you would use to calculate the average is the model. A more complicated forecasting model might use time-series analysis or linear regression. See Table 6.6 for a summary of the models used to support decision making in organizations. Data for the DSS primarily comes from TPSs, but can come from other sources as well. The user interface is the way in which the DSS interacts with the user by collecting inputs and displaying output and results.

Table 6.7 summarizes the characteristics of a DSS. Inputs are data and models. Processing supports the merging of data with models so that decision makers can examine alternative solution scenarios. Outputs are graphs and textual reports.

Intelligent Systems **Artificial intelligence (AI)** is the science of enabling information technologies—software, hardware, networks, and so on—to simulate human intelligence, such as reasoning and learning, as well as gaining sensing capabilities, such as seeing, hearing,

TABLE 6.6 Common DSS Models for Specific Organizational Areas

Area	Common DSS Models
Corporate level	Corporate planning, venture analysis, mergers and acquisitions
Accounting	Cost analysis, discriminant analysis, breakeven analysis, auditing, tax computation and analysis, depreciation methods, budgeting
Finance	Discounted cash flow analysis, return on investment, buy or lease, capital budgeting, bond refinancing, stock portfolio management, compound interest, after-tax yield, foreign exchange values
Marketing	Product demand forecast, advertising strategy analysis, pricing strategies, market share analysis, sales growth evaluation, sales performance
Human resources	Labor negotiations, labor market analysis, personnel skills assessment, employee business expenses, fringe benefit computations, payroll and deductions
Production	Product design, production scheduling, transportation analysis, product mix, inventory levels, quality control, plant location, material allocation, maintenance analysis, machine replacement, job assignment, material requirements planning
Management science	Linear programming, decision trees, simulation, project evaluation and planning, queuing, dynamic programming, network analysis
Statistics	Regression and correlation analysis, exponential smoothing, sampling, time-series analysis, hypothesis testing

TABLE 6.7 Characteristics of a DSS

Inputs	Data and models; data entry and data manipulation commands (via user interface)
Processing	Interactive processing of data and models; simulations, optimization, forecasts
Outputs	Graphs and textual reports; feedback to system operator (via user interface)
Typical users	Midlevel managers (although a DSS could be used at any level of the organization)

walking, talking, and feeling. AI has had a strong connection to science fiction writers where AI-enabled technologies aid humans (e.g., Mr. Data in *Star Trek: The Next Generation*) (Figure 6.16), attempt world domination (e.g., *The Matrix*), or enable humans to exist on an alien planet (e.g., *Avatar)*. The current reality of AI is that it is lagging far behind the imagination of most science fiction writers; but, nevertheless, great strides have been made. Most notably, the development of several types of intelligent systems is having great successes for a variety of applications. **Intelligent systems**—comprised of sensors, software, and computers embedded in machines and devices—emulate and enhance human capabilities. Intelligent systems are having a tremendous impact in a variety of areas, including banking and financial management, medicine, engineering, and the military. Three types of intelligent systems—expert systems, neural networks, and intelligent agents—are particularly relevant in business contexts and are discussed next.

Expert Systems. An **expert system (ES)** is a type of intelligent system that uses reasoning methods based on knowledge about a specific problem domain in order to provide advice, much like a human expert. ESs are used to mimic human expertise by manipulating knowledge (understanding acquired through experience and extensive learning) rather than simply manipulating information (for more information, see Turban, Sharda, & Delen, 2011). Human knowledge can be represented in an ES by facts and rules about a problem coded in a form that can be manipulated by a computer. When you use an ES, the system asks you a series of questions, much as a human expert would. It continues to ask questions, and each new question is determined by your response to the preceding question. The ES matches the responses with the defined facts and rules until the responses point the system to a solution. A **rule** is a way of encoding knowledge, such as a recommendation, after collecting information from a user. Rules are typically expressed using an "if–then" format. For example, a rule in an ES for assisting with decisions related to the approval of automobile loans for individuals could be represented as follows: *If* personal income is $50,000 or more, *then* approve the loan.

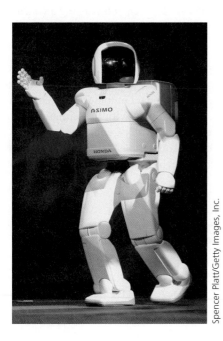

Spencer Platt/Getty Images, Inc.

© 2002 Paramount Pictures/Courtesy: Everett Collection.

FIGURE 6.16

AI in the real world lags behind the imagination of science-fiction writers.

FIGURE 6.17

Architecture of an ES using the basic systems model.

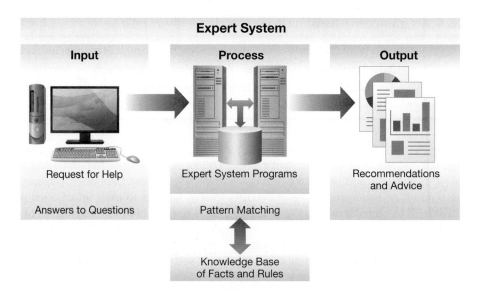

Given that most experts make decisions with limited information as well as use general categories of information when making judgments, researchers have developed **fuzzy logic** to broaden the capabilities of ESs and other intelligent systems. Specifically, fuzzy logic allows ES rules to be represented using approximations or subjective values in order to handle situations where information about a problem is incomplete. For example, a loan officer, when assessing a customer's loan application, may generally categorize some of the customer's financial information, such as income and debt level, as high, moderate, or low rather than using precise amounts. In addition to numerous business applications, fuzzy logic is used to better control antilock braking systems and household appliances as well as when making medical diagnoses or filtering offensive language in chat rooms.

The most difficult part of building an ES is acquiring the knowledge from the expert and gathering and compiling it into a consistent and complete form capable of making recommendations. ESs are used when expertise for a particular problem is rare or expensive, such as in the case of a complex machine repair or medical diagnosis. Using fuzzy logic, ESs are also utilized when knowledge about a problem is incomplete.

As with other information systems, the architecture of an ES (and other intelligent systems) can be described using the basic systems model (see Figure 6.17). Inputs to the system are questions and answers from the user. Processing is the matching of user questions and answers to information in the knowledge base. The processing in an ES is called **inferencing,** which consists of matching facts and rules, determining the sequence of questions presented to the user, and drawing a conclusion. The output from an ES is a recommendation. The general characteristics of an ES are summarized in Table 6.8.

Neural Networks. Whereas "conventional" computers are very adept at processing large amounts of data by rapidly executing a program's instructions, they cannot easily adapt to different circumstances or deal with noisy data. If a conventional computer is presented with a novel problem that it is not programmed to solve, it cannot deal with this situation. Neural networks are a novel approach to problem solving; **neural networks,** composed of a network of processing elements (neurons) that work in parallel to complete a task, attempt to approximate the functioning of the human brain and can learn by example. Typically, a neural

TABLE 6.8 Characteristics of an ES

Inputs	Request for help, answers to questions
Processing	Pattern matching and inferencing
Outputs	Recommendation or advice
Typical users	Midlevel managers (although an ES could be used at any level of the organization)

network is *trained* by having it categorize a large database of past information for common patterns. Once these patterns are established, new data can be compared to these learned patterns and conclusions drawn. For example, many financial institutions use neural network systems to analyze loan applications. These systems compare a person's loan application data with the neural network containing the *intelligence* of the success and failure of countless prior loans, ultimately making a loan acceptance (or rejection) recommendation (see Figure 6.18).

Intelligent Agent Systems. An **intelligent agent,** or simply an *agent* (also called a **bot**—short for "software robot"), is a program that works in the background to provide some service when a specific event occurs. There are several types of agents for use in a broad range of contexts, including the following:

1. **User Agents.** Agents that automatically perform a task for a user, such as automatically sending a report at the first of the month, assembling customized news, or filling out a Web form with routine information
2. **Buyer Agents (Shopping Bots).** Agents that search to find the best price for a particular product you wish to purchase
3. **Monitoring and Sensing Agents.** Agents that keep track of key information, such as inventory levels or competitors' prices, notifying the user when conditions change

FIGURE 6.18

Neural networks approximate the functioning of the brain by creating common patterns in data and then compare new data to learned patterns to make a recommendation.

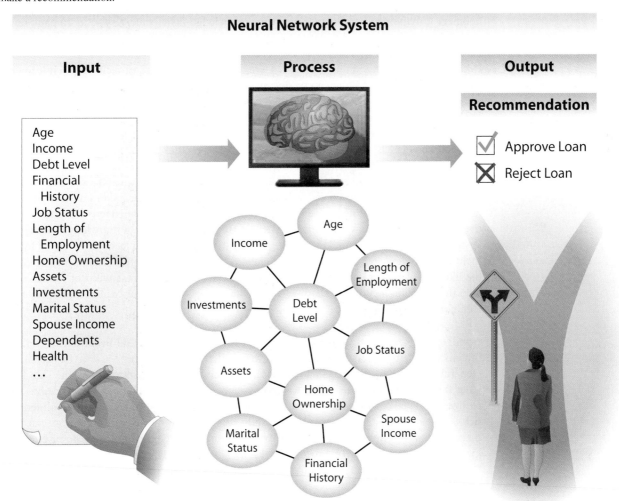

4. **Data Mining Agents.** Agents that continuously analyze large data warehouses to detect changes deemed important by a user, sending a notification when such changes occur
5. **Web Crawlers.** Agents that continuously browse the Web for specific information (e.g., used by search engines)—also known as **Web spiders**
6. **Destructive Agents.** Malicious agents designed by spammers and other Internet attackers to farm e-mail addresses off Web sites or deposit spyware on machines

In sum, there are ongoing developments to make information systems *smarter* so that organizational decision makers gain business intelligence. Although systems such as ESs, neural networks, and intelligent agents have yet to realize the imagination of science-fiction writers, they have taken great strides in helping information systems support business intelligence.

Knowledge Management Systems There is no universal agreement on what exactly is meant by the term "knowledge management." In general, however, **knowledge management** refers to the processes an organization uses to gain the greatest value from its knowledge assets. In Chapter 1 "Managing in the Digital World," we contrasted data, information, and knowledge. Recall that data are raw material—recorded, unformatted information, such as words or numbers. Information is data that have been formatted and organized in some way so that the result is useful to people. We need knowledge to understand relationships between different pieces of information. Consequently, what constitutes **knowledge assets** are all the underlying skills, routines, practices, principles, formulas, methods, heuristics, and intuitions, whether explicit or tacit. All databases, manuals, reference works, textbooks, diagrams, displays, computer files, proposals, plans, and any other artifacts in which both facts and procedures are recorded and stored are considered knowledge assets. From an organizational point of view, properly used knowledge assets enable an organization to improve its efficiency, effectiveness, and, of course, profitability. Additionally, as many companies are beginning to lose a large number of baby boomers to retirement, companies are using knowledge management systems to capture these crucial knowledge assets (Leonard, 2006). Clearly, effectively managing knowledge assets will enhance business intelligence.

Knowledge assets can be distinguished as being either explicit or tacit. **Explicit knowledge assets** reflect knowledge that can be documented, archived, and codified, often with the help of information systems. Explicit knowledge assets reflect much of what is typically stored in a DBMS. In contrast, **tacit knowledge assets** reflect the processes and procedures that are located in a person's mind on how to effectively perform a particular task (see Figure 6.19). Identifying key tacit knowledge assets and managing these assets so that they are accurate and available to people throughout the organization remains a significant challenge.

Tacit knowledge assets often reflect an organization's **best practices**—procedures and processes that are widely accepted as being among the most effective and/or efficient. Identifying how to recognize, generate, store, share, and manage this tacit knowledge is the primary objective for deploying a knowledge management system. Consequently, a **knowledge management system** is typically not a single technology but rather a collection of technology-based tools that include communication technologies—such as e-mail, groupware, instant messaging, and the like—as well as information storage and retrieval systems, such as wikis or DBMSs, to enable the generation, storage, sharing, and management of tacit and explicit knowledge assets (Malhotra, 2005).

Benefits of Knowledge Management Systems. Many potential benefits can come from organizations' effectively capturing and utilizing their tacit knowledge assets (Levinson, 2010) (see Table 6.9). For example, innovation and creativity may be enhanced by the free flow of ideas throughout the organization. Also, by widely sharing best practices, organizations should realize improved customer service, shorter product development times, and streamlined operations. Enhanced business operations not only will improve the overall organizational performance but also will enhance employee retention rates by recognizing the value of employees' knowledge and rewarding them for sharing it. Thus, organizations can realize many benefits from the successful deployment of a knowledge management system.

Although there are many potential benefits for organizations that effectively deploy knowledge management systems, to do so requires that several substantial challenges be overcome

Explicit Knowledge Assets   **Tacit Knowledge Assets**

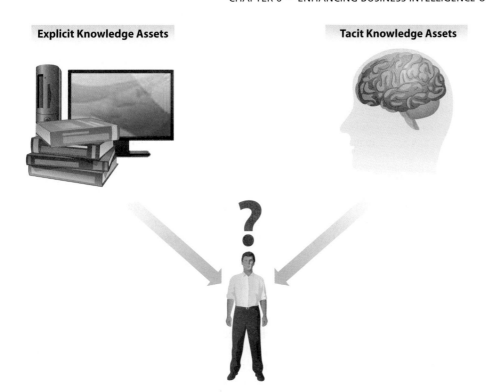

FIGURE 6.19

Explicit knowledge assets can easily be documented, archived, and codified, whereas tacit knowledge assets are located in a person's mind.

(Table 6.9). First, effective deployment requires employees to agree to share their personal tacit knowledge assets and to take extra steps to utilize the system for identifying best practices. Therefore, to encourage employee buy-in and also to enable the sharing of knowledge, organizations must create a culture that values and rewards widespread participation. Second, experience has shown that a successful deployment must first identify what knowledge is needed, why it is needed, and who is likely to have this knowledge. Once an organization understands "why, what, and who," identifying the best technologies for facilitating knowledge exchange is a much easier task. In other words, the best practices for deploying knowledge management systems suggest that organizations save the "how"—that is, what collaboration and storage technologies to use—for last.

Third, the successful deployment of a knowledge management system must be linked to a specific business objective. By linking the system to a specific business objective and coupling that with the use of an assessment technique, such as return on investment, an organization can identify costs and benefits and can also be sure that the system is providing value in an area that is indeed important to the organization. Fourth, the knowledge management system must be easy to use, not only for putting knowledge in but also for getting knowledge out. Similarly, the system cannot overload users with too much information or with information that is obsolete. Just as physical assets can erode over time, knowledge, too, can become stale and irrelevant. Therefore, an ongoing process of updating, amending, and removing obsolete or irrelevant knowledge must occur, or the system will fall into disarray and will not be used. In sum, to gain the greatest benefits from an investment in a knowledge management system, the organization must take care to overcome various challenges.

TABLE 6.9 Benefits and Challenges of Knowledge Management Systems

Benefits	Challenges
Enhanced innovation and creativity	Getting employee buy-in
Improved customer service, shorter product development, and streamlined operations	Focusing too much on technology
	Forgetting the goal
Enhanced employee retention	Dealing with knowledge overload and obsolescence
Improved organizational performance	

How Organizations Utilize Knowledge Management Systems. The people using a knowledge management system will be working in different departments within the organization, doing different functions, and will likely be located in different locations around the building, city, or even the world. Each person—or group of people—can be thought of as a separate island that is set apart from others by geography, job focus, expertise, age, and gender. Often, a person on one island is trying to solve a problem that has already been solved by another person located on some other island. Finding this "other" person is often a significant challenge. The goal of a successful knowledge management system is to facilitate the exchange of needed knowledge between these separate islands. To find and connect such separate islands, organizations use social network analysis. **Social network analysis** is a technique that attempts to find groups of people who work together, to find people who don't collaborate but should, or to find experts in particular subject areas. To do this, people's contacts are mapped so that connections or missing links within the organization can easily be discovered (see Figure 6.20). In addition to social network analysis, organizations use social bookmarking and social cataloging to capture and structure employees' knowledge and harness their collective intelligence (see Chapter 5, "Enhancing Collaboration Using Web 2.0").

Once organizations have collected their knowledge into a repository, they must find an easy way to share it with employees (often using an intranet), customers, suppliers (often with an extranet), or the general public (often using the Internet). These **knowledge portals** can be customized to meet the unique needs of their intended users. For example, the U.S. Food and Drug Administration (FDA) is responsible for keeping the public (e.g., citizens, researchers, and industry) informed on the most up-to-date information related to food (e.g., information on mad cow disease or product recalls) and drugs (e.g., the status of a drug trial). The FDA's Web site uses a Google *search appliance*—a special type of computer that analyzes and indexes information within a Web site—so that visitors can quickly search and find needed information within the FDA's more than 1 million documents (see Figure 6.21).

In addition to the FDA, countless other organizations, such as Ford Motor Company, Eli Lilly, Walmart, and Dell Computers, are also rapidly deploying knowledge management systems. We are learning from these deployments that all organizations, whether for-profit or nonprofit, struggle to get the right information to the right person at the right time. Through the use of a comprehensive strategy for managing knowledge assets, organizations are much more likely to gain a competitive advantage and a positive return on their IS investments.

Information Visualization

The third pillar of business intelligence applications is information visualization. **Visualization** refers to the display of complex data relationships using a variety of graphical methods, enabling managers to quickly grasp the results of the analysis. For example, Figure 6.22 shows the

FIGURE 6.20

Social network analysis can help to analyze collaboration patterns.

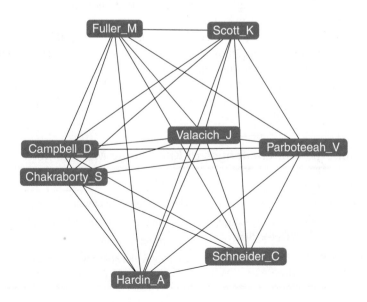

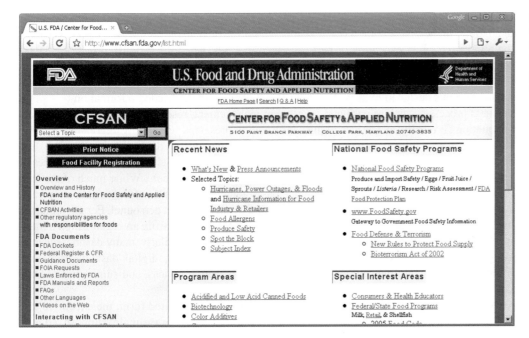

FIGURE 6.21

Countless organizations are using Web-based knowledge portals to provide information to employees, customers, and partners.

visualization of Hurricane Katrina in 2005 as the storm was gaining strength. The image shows towering thunderclouds (in red), called hot towers, that were spotted just before Katrina intensified to a Category 5 hurricane. Once represented visually, analysts can view changes over time and perform what-if analyses to better understand the behavior of hurricanes. In similar ways, organizations around the world are utilizing visualization technologies to enhance business intelligence.

Dashboards **Digital dashboards** are commonly used to present key performance indicators and other summary information used by managers and executives to make decisions. To provide the greatest benefits for decision makers, digital dashboards typically support three usage models: push reporting, exception reporting and alerts, and pull reporting. In other words, digital dashboards provide the decision makers with a quick overview of key performance indicators and

FIGURE 6.22

Visualization is the display of complex data relationships using a variety of graphical methods.

other key operational statistics and trends (i.e., push reporting) but also alert the user of any items that require immediate attention (i.e., exception reporting and alerts); if the user wants to analyze the root causes of an exception or perform other analyses, he or she can drill down or perform self-service ad hoc queries (i.e., pull reporting).

Digital dashboards (sometimes called executive dashboards) evolved from executive information systems designed to provide top-level managers with the needed information to support business processes, such as cash and investment management, resource allocation, and contract negotiation. Typically, executives require information presented in a highly aggregated form so that they can scan information quickly for trends and anomalies. Further, decisions made by executives typically require both "soft" and "hard" data. **Soft data** include textual news stories or other nonanalytical information. **Hard data** include facts and numbers. While much of the hard data can be gathered from organizational databases and other systems, soft information typically involves the use of text mining technologies or input from dedicated personnel. For example, the executive dashboard offered by Dow Jones integrates information from an organization's internal systems with external information provided by Dow Jones; similarly, many dashboards integrate RSS readers to display news feeds to the users. In sum, digital dashboards deliver information from multiple sources to provide warnings, action notices, and summaries of business conditions.

Although data are typically provided in a very highly aggregated form, the executive also has the capability to drill down and see the details if necessary. For example, suppose a digital dashboard summarizes employee absenteeism, and the system shows that today's numbers are significantly higher than normal. The executive can see this information in a running line chart, as illustrated in Figure 6.23. If the executive wants to understand why absenteeism is so high, a selection on the screen can provide the details behind the aggregate numbers, as shown in Figure 6.24. By drilling down into the data, the executive can see that the spike in absenteeism was centered in the manufacturing area. Also, the digital dashboard can connect the data in the system to the organization's internal communication systems (e.g., electronic or voice mail) so that the executive can quickly send a message to the appropriate managers to discuss solutions to the problem discovered in the drill-down.

Dashboards make use of a variety of design elements to present the data in the most user-friendly way. To highlight deviations that need to be addressed or to symbolize changes over time, dashboards use maps, charts, spark lines, or graphics symbolizing traffic lights, thermometers, or speedometers (see Figure 6.25); conditional formatting is often used to highlight exceptions and draw the user's attention to deviations from the normal course of business. Many dashboards now

FIGURE 6.23

A digital dashboard showing a total employee absenteeism line chart.

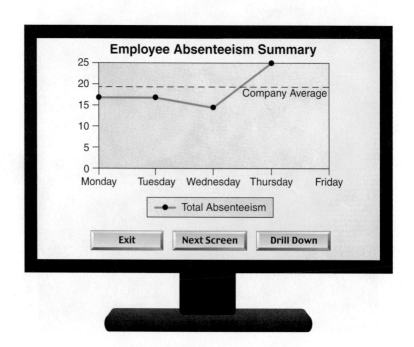

Absenteeism Drill Down

	Monday	Tuesday	Wednesday	Thursday
Manufacturing	10	11	6	19
Professional	2	2	0	1
Clerical	3	1	3	2
Sales	0	0	1	2
Support	2	3	5	1

Exit   Prior Screen   E-Mail

FIGURE 6.24

Drill-down numbers for employee absenteeism.

combine business intelligence with technologies typically used to deliver rich Internet applications (such as Adobe Flash) in order to provide the level of interactivity desired by users at different levels of an organization.

One recent trend influencing the design of dashboards is mobile business intelligence. With the advances in mobile communication technology, today's executives want to be in touch with their organizational performance anytime, anywhere. Further, most of today's knowledge workers are mobile in terms of the device they're using—during a workday, one may use a desktop computer, a laptop, a smart phone, or an iPad. Hence, dashboard vendors are offering solutions for multiple devices and screen sizes so that the user can get the same information regardless of location and device used to access the information.

Visual Analytics As discussed in previous sections, business intelligence systems can provide business decision makers with a wide variety of analyses to support decision making. However, in the end, it is still the humans who have to interpret the output from these systems. With growing complexity of the underlying data (such as multiple dimensions, including spatial dimensions), interpreting the

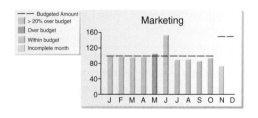

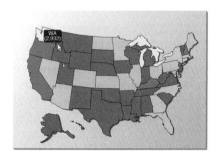

FIGURE 6.25

Dashboards use various graphical elements to highlight important information.

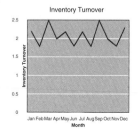

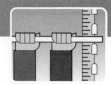

POWERFUL PARTNERSHIPS

Adobe's John Warnock and Chuck Geschke

John Warnock was born October 6, 1940, in Salt Lake City, Utah. He earned undergraduate and master's degrees in mathematics and a PhD in electrical engineering, all from the University of Utah. Chuck Geschke was born in Cleveland, Ohio, on September 11, 1939. He holds a PhD in computer science from Carnegie Mellon University in Pittsburgh. Warnock worked for Charles Geschke at Xerox Corporation's Palo Alto Research Center from 1978 to 1982, where they developed the foundation for PostScript, a technology aimed at simplifying the process of printing documents directly from a computer. Warnock and Geschke left Xerox in 1982 to start Adobe Systems Inc. to bring their technology to the market.

Being perceived as a wealthy Internet entrepreneur, Geschke was kidnapped from the Adobe parking lot in Mountain View, California, in 1992, 10 years after the company was founded. The abductors claimed to be members of a Middle Eastern organization and told Geschke they would kill him after they collected the ransom they were asking. The kidnappers also claimed to have planted explosives that would destroy Geschke's house and his neighbors' houses. Five days after his ordeal began, the FBI recovered Geschke unharmed. The kidnappers were arrested and sentenced to life in prison.

Today, Adobe is one of the biggest software companies, with over 8,300 employees. Its portfolio includes several industry-leading software products, including Acrobat (the PDF file format is the de facto standard for sharing documents on the Web), ColdFusion, Dreamweaver, Flash, Photoshop, and many others. Geschke retired as Adobe's president in 2000; Warnock retired in 2000 as the company's chief executive officer and in 2001 as chief technology officer. Warnock and Geschke continue to be cochairmen of Adobe's board, helping to guide the future for the $3 billion company they cofounded.

Based on:

Anonymous. (n.d.). Executive profiles. Retrieved April 18, 2010, from http://www.adobe.com/aboutadobe/pressroom/executivebios/charlesgeschke.html.

Belden, A. (1997, October 13). A dramatic kidnapping revisited. *Los Altos Town Crier*. Retrieved April 18, 2010, from http://www.losaltosonline.com/index.php?option=com_content&task=view&id=18583&Itemid=46.

Charles Geschke. (2010, June 5). In *Wikipedia, the free encyclopedia*. Retrieved July 12, 2010, from http://en.wikipedia.org/w/index.php?title =Charles_Geschke&oldid=366134919.

John Warnock. (2010, June 5). In *Wikipedia, the free encyclopedia*. Retrieved July 12, 2010, from http://en.wikipedia.org/w/index.php?title=John_Warnock&oldid=366134898.

outputs becomes extremely challenging. **Visual analytics** is the combination of various analysis techniques and interactive visualization to solve complex problems. By combining human intelligence and reasoning capabilities with technology's retrieval and analysis capabilities, visual analytics can help in decision making, as the strengths of both the human and the machine are merged. With the humans' ability to make sense of "noisy" data, unexpected patterns or relationships in the data can be discovered, and results of complex queries can be quickly interpreted. Visual analytics is used in a variety of settings, ranging from homeland security to disaster relief.

Geographic Information Systems One type of visualization system that is growing in popularity and is frequently incorporated into digital dashboards is called a **geographic information system (GIS)**. A GIS is a system for creating, storing, analyzing, and managing geographically referenced information. A GIS can visualize features and relationships between features drawn from an underlying geographic database that describes the data in geographic terms (such as a retail store's longitude, latitude, and altitude) and attribute data (additional data about a spatial item, such as a store's floor space or revenue) so as to enable querying and analysis. On a personal level, you probably frequently interact with GISs. For example, when you're accessing Google maps to search for a restaurant in your town, you can view geographic data (such as the map or the satellite image) as well as attribute data about restaurants, including name, address, and customer reviews.

Businesses typically face many decisions with a spatial dimension: Where are my customers located? Where is the best location to open a new store? Which areas should be included in the next mailing? How far are my customers willing to drive? The GIS can help to create models used to answer questions such as where a company such as Levi Strauss should add authorized resellers,

ETHICAL DILEMMA

Stealing WiFi

If your neighbor is watering his lawn and accidentally waters some of your grass, have you "stolen" your neighbor's water? When you tune in a station on your car radio, are you illegally using the "free" radio? Similarly, here is a question for the millions of laptop computer users: If you are sitting in your car in front of a business with in-house WiFi service and you are surfing the Internet by "piggybacking" on the businesses' Internet access, are you stealing Internet service? (Piggybacking refers to using someone else's WiFi service without their knowledge or consent.) Most Internet service providers would probably answer that question with a resounding "Yes." Why? Because piggybacking allows you to use, for free, a service that costs the business.

According to a 2007 survey by security firm Sophos, piggybacking is a popular activity. Fifty-four percent of the 560 Sophos survey respondents reported using someone else's bandwidth via piggybacking. But is it really theft? Great Britain says that it is and arrests bandwidth thieves when they can catch them. The WiFi "theft" issue is loosely defined under the U.S. Computer Fraud and Abuse Act—paragraph (a)(2) covers anyone who "intentionally accesses a computer without authorization or exceeds authorized access"—but when the 1986 law was passed, no one had anticipated 802.11x wireless links. WiFi mooching, however, has led to arrests in some states, where laws may differ somewhat from federal law. For example, in Alaska, a 21-year-old man was arrested while accessing a public library's WiFi service from his car, and a Wisconsin man was arrested for accessing a café's free WiFi service, as was a Florida man driving around a neighborhood looking for WiFi access.

Some people see the ethics of piggybacking differently. For example, one person posted a comment in response to an online article about piggybacking by Michael Santo: "My home router is intentionally left open, with some antispam restrictions. There are two to five connections weekly. I've no problem with people in need using it from time to time."

Just as hacking led to the 1986 Computer Fraud and Abuse Act, unauthorized WiFi use will eventually be conclusively addressed in federal legislation. Until then, the practice is largely an ethical issue that should be addressed by individual computer users. If an airport, Internet café, or public library advertises "take advantage of our free WiFi service," computer users can conclude that WiFi use in those facilities is legal and, therefore, worry free. If, on the other hand, a neighbor has not invited you to use his or her WiFi service, perhaps your conscience should tell you that using his or her broadband service uninvited and without their knowledge is not a good idea.

Based on:

Anonymous. (2007, August 22). Man arrested over wi-fi "theft." *BBC News*. Retrieved April 10, 2010, from http://news.bbc.co.uk/2/hi/uk_news/england/london/6958429.stm.

Bangemen, E. (2008, January 3). The ethics of "stealing" a WiFi connection. *ars technica*. Retrieved April 10, 2010, from http://arstechnica.com/news.ars/post/20080103-the-ethics-of-stealing-a-wifi-connection.html.

Cheng, J. (2007, May 22). Michigan man arrested for using cafe's free WiFi from his car. *ars technica*. Retrieved April 10, 2010, from http://arstechnica.com/news.ars/post/20070522-michigan-man-arrested-for-using-cafes-free-wifi-from-his-car.html.

McCullagh, D. (2005, July 8). FAQ: Wi-Fi mooching and the law. *CNET News.com*. Retrieved April 10, 2010, from http://www.news.com/FAQ-Wi-Fi-moaching-and-the-law/2100-7351_3-5778822.html.

Santo, M. (2007, November 17). Wi-Fi piggybacking widespread: Study. *Realtechnews*. Retrieved April 10, 2010, from http://www.realtechnews.com/2007/11/17/wi-fi-piggybacking-widespread-study.

or how, where, and what kinds of fertilizers farmers should apply, enabling precision farming (see Table 6.10 for various industry uses of GIS).

Using GIS, analysts can combine geographic, demographic, and other data for locating target customers, finding optimal site locations, or determining the right product mix at different locations; additionally, GIS can perform a variety of analyses, such as market share analysis and competitor analysis. Cities, counties, and states also use GIS for aiding in infrastructure design and zoning issues (e.g., where should the new elementary school be located?). For the various geospatial aspects you can map with GIS, refer to Table 6.11. How does a GIS help in analyzing geospatial and related data? Typically, a GIS provides a user with a blank map of an area. The user can then add information stored in different **layers,** each resembling a transparency containing different information about an area; for example, one layer may contain all roads, another layer may contain ZIP code boundaries, and yet another layer may contain floodplains, average

TABLE 6.10 Various Industry Uses of GIS

Industry	Sample Uses
Agriculture	Analyze crop yield by location, soil erosion, or differences in fertilizer needs (precision farming)
Banking	Identify lucrative areas for marketing campaigns
Disaster response	Analyze historical events, set up evacuation plans, and identify areas most likely to be affected by disasters
Insurance	Risk analysis (e.g., earthquake insurance)
Government	Urban planning, zoning, and census planning
Law enforcement	Analyze high-crime areas
Marine biology	Track movement of fish swarms
Media	Create maps to visualize locations of events and analyze circulation
Mining and drilling	Locate potential areas for extraction of natural resources
Real estate	Create maps to visualize locations of properties
Retail	Analyze sales, inventory, customers, and so on by location; identify new retail locations; and visualize and present business data
Transportation and logistics	Route planning

Source: Based on ESRI, http://www.gis.com/content/who-uses-gis.

household sizes, locations of coffee shops, or other information of interest (in Google Earth, you can view various layers, such as roads, traffic patterns, weather, earthquakes, golf courses, and so on; see Figure 6.26). Adding or removing those layers helps to view the relevant information needed to answer questions that have a spatial dimension.

One question that organizations often face is where the customers come from. In order to answer such question, organizations typically use data from survey respondents (or the cashier asks for customers' ZIP codes); this data is then geocoded (i.e., transformed into coordinates) to create a layer containing customer information that can then be added to a map. Comparing customers' locations with the location of one's business can help in deciding whether the store has the optimal location or whether opening a new store would be warranted. Relatedly, trade area analysis helps to assess where customers are coming from by combining location information with, for example, drive time information to determine if certain areas are underserved or if two stores' trade areas overlap. Another way to visualize geospatial data is by using thematic maps. Thematic maps color code data that is aggregated for specific geographic regions. For example, a thematic map could display the median household income in different blocks, or it could display average household sizes, helping a business to identify areas with the most promising target population; similarly, an insurance company could use GIS to determine where certain crimes (such as car theft) most frequently occur (see Figure 6.27).

In addition to helping in analysis, GISs are also increasingly used by government and organizations to effectively communicate with stakeholders. For example, many retail chains

TABLE 6.11 Various Ways of Representing Geospatial Data

Mapping	Example
Features and patterns (i.e., distribution of features)	Earthquake epicenters (features) and areas where the hazard may be highest (patterns).
Quantities	The number of young families with a high income in a census district.
Densities	Number of high-income family per square mile in a census district.
What's inside	Does a luxury real estate development fall within a 15-minute driving radius of a store?
What's nearby	How many Starbuck's stores are within 5 miles of my new coffee shop?
Change	How have store sales changed after a large ad campaign?

Source: Based on ESRI, http://www.gis.com/content/what-can-you-do-gis.

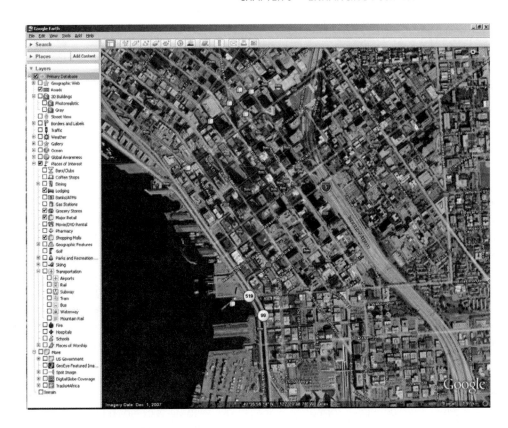

FIGURE 6.26

Google Earth uses layers to display information related to a specific geographical area.

such as Best Buy or Walmart incorporate map-based store locators into their Web sites. When searching for a store by city, state, or ZIP code, the Web site returns a map showing the store's location (geographic data), along with attribute information such as distance, street address, phone number, and opening hours. Similarly, organizations use output from GISs to communicate to their stockholders about expansion plans, retail store density, and the like.

Clearly, GIS, like all the systems described in this chapter, are providing organizations with business intelligence to better compete in the digital world.

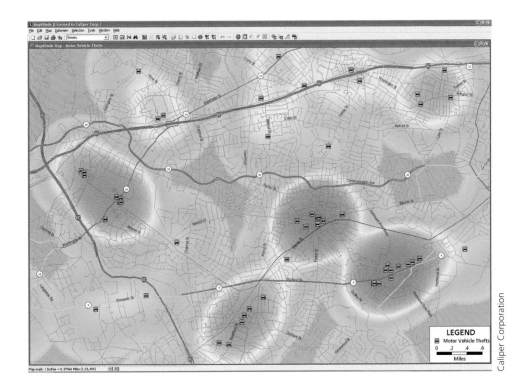

FIGURE 6.27

A thematic map showing car thefts in a town.

Caliper Corporation

INDUSTRY ANALYSIS

Health Care

Do you remember the times when your doctor wrote a prescription and the handwriting was worse than your professor's, making you wonder how the pharmacist could ever decipher it and dispense the correct drugs? If you recently went to a doctor, you may have noticed that information systems have had a huge impact on the health care field; indeed, health informatics has become a key focus of health care providers, insurance companies, and governments. Now, many doctors carry laptops or personal digital assistants (PDAs), allowing them to digitally store any diagnosis, facilitating the sharing of information between the physician, nurses, and even your medical insurance. In addition to providing access to electronic patient records, the laptop or PDA provides your physician access to medical and drug information, as offered by the *Physician's Desk Reference* Web site (www.pdr.net), where your physician can obtain the latest information about drugs and clinical guidelines or check interactions between different drugs. Electronic patient records are now even moving toward the Web. Pioneered by Microsoft's HealthVault and Google, Web-based electronic patient records free the patient from having to carry medical records from doctor to doctor.

Information systems have also tremendously changed the diagnosis and monitoring of patients. For example, modern EEG and EKG devices heavily depend on computer technology, and, as the name implies, computer tomography (used to produce images of internal organs) could not be performed without computer technology. Even diagnostic tests such as X-rays now use digital technology, allowing the doctor to digitally enhance the image for improved diagnosis or to electronically transmit the image to a remote specialist. Following the diagnosis of a serious condition, technology can even help in the operating room. For example, many modern clinics use surgical robots and endoscopes for delicate procedures such as neurosurgery or gastrointestinal surgery. Taken a step further, such systems can be used for what is referred to as telemedicine, including remote diagnosis and remote surgery. Whereas traditionally a patient had to travel thousands of miles to visit a specialized surgeon, many surgeries can now be performed remotely, reducing the strain on the patient and potentially saving precious time. Further, telemedicine applications can be used for remote locations, battlefields, or even prisons, reducing costs for transporting patients and improving care.

Although information technology can help to provide convenient health care to patients, privacy and data security may also be a concern for them. As vendors managing electronic health records have access to patient data, this can be an additional income stream; increasingly, such vendors are selling the "anonymized" patient data to pharmaceutical companies and other interested parties. These companies use data mining in order to detect disease patterns, cluster similar cases, or improve treatment. According to a *New York Times* report, however, often such data can be linked to other publicly available information so that is loses its anonymity. Currently, the overall market for health record systems is between $8 billion and $10 billion annually, and vendors generate about 5 percent of this income from selling patient data. With the increasing use of electronic health care systems, this number is likely to grow considerably.

As physicians, insurance companies, and health care providers are turning to information technology to improve business processes and better serve patients' needs, consumers are increasingly using the Internet for health information. For example, WebMD is one of the most popular Web sites providing health-related information, priding itself on having high-quality, timely, and unbiased information. In addition to objective information, people use social media to obtain information beyond what's published by the experts. Specifically, people seeking physician and hospital rankings or recommendations frequent blogs or health-related discussion forums. Further, major search engines such as Microsoft's Bing are constantly refining their search algorithms to provide the most relevant information to health-related queries. Regardless of whether you're visiting your doctor regarding a condition or just for a routine checkup, or if you need more information about what your doctor is telling you, various information systems are likely to play a major role.

Questions

1. Discuss the benefits and drawbacks of online medical records.
2. Computer-aided diagnosis can replace years of experience, providing opportunities for young, inexperienced physicians. Contrast the benefits and drawbacks for the patients and the physicians.
3. Will there be a place for physicians without computer skills in the future? Why or why not?

Based on:

Anonymous. (n.d.). Welcome to HealthVault. Retrieved April 24, 2010, from http://www.healthvault.com.

Anonymous. (n.d.). Welcome to PDR.net. Retrieved April 24, 2010, from http://www.pdr.net.

Anonymous. (2007, April 29). World's first image-guided surgical robot to enhance accuracy and safety of brain surgery. *Science Daily.* Retrieved April 24, 2010, from http://www.sciencedaily.com/releases/2007/04/070417114732.htm.

Anonymous. (2010, April 15). Consumers increasingly turning to Internet, social media for health care information. *iHealthBeat.* Retrieved

April 24, 2010, from http://www.ihealthbeat.org/special-reports/2010/consumers-increasingly-turning-to-internet-social-media-for-health-care-information.aspx.

Zetter, K. (2009, October 19). Medical records: Stored in the cloud, sold on the open market. *Wired.* Retrieved April 24, 2010, from http://www.wired.com/threatlevel/2009/10/medicalrecords.

Key Points Review

1. *Describe the concept of business intelligence and how databases serve as a foundation for gaining business intelligence.* Businesses need business intelligence to quickly respond to external threats and opportunities arising from unstable market conditions, fierce competition, short product life cycles, government regulation, and fickle customers. Business intelligence supports this by enabling a closed-loop approach to planning at all levels of the organization. Organizations use databases to capture and manage the data that can later be used as input to business intelligence applications. A database is a collection of related data organized in a way that facilitates data searches; databases are underlying all interactive Web sites. A database contains entities, attributes, records, and tables. Entities are things about which we collect data, such as people, courses, customers, or products. Attributes are the individual pieces of information about an entity, such as a person's last name or Social Security number, that are stored in a database record. A record is the collection of related attributes about an entity; usually, a record is displayed as a database row. A table is a collection of related records about an entity type; each row in the table is a record, and each column is an attribute. A DBMS is a software application with which you create, store, organize, and retrieve data from a single database or several databases. The data within a database must be adequately organized so that it is possible to store and retrieve information effectively. To support more effective business processes, businesses use online transaction processing. Data from operational systems serves as an input to analytical systems. Master data management helps organizations to arrive at a "single version of the truth" to gather business intelligence; data warehouses and data marts support the integration and analysis of large data sets.

2. *Explain the three components of business intelligence: information and knowledge discovery, business analytics, and information visualization.* Information and knowledge discovery tools are used to discover "hidden" relationships in data. Ad hoc query tools allow decision makers to run queries whenever needed. OLAP tools extend this capability by offering the ability to perform complex multidimensional queries. Data mining is used for association discovery and clustering and classification. Unstructured data analysis is used to extract information from textual documents. Business analytics augments business intelligence by using predictive analysis to identify trends or predict business outcomes. Decision support and intelligent systems are used to support human and automated decision making. DSSs support organizational decision making and are typically designed to solve a particular recurring problem in the organization. DSSs are most commonly used to support semistructured problems that are addressed by managerial-level employees. A DSS is designed to be an interactive decision aid. Intelligent systems such as ESs, neural networks, and intelligent agents work to emulate and enhance human capabilities. ESs apply knowledge within some topic area to provide advice by mimicking human expertise (understanding acquired through experience and extensive learning). ESs are used when expertise for a particular problem is rare or expensive. Neural networks attempt to approximate the functioning and decision making of the human brain by comparing patterns in new data versus complex patterns learned from prior data. Intelligent agents are programs that can be applied to a broad variety of situations, typically operating in the background to provide some service when a special event occurs or when a request is made. Knowledge management systems are a collection of technology-based tools that enable the generation, storage, sharing, and management of knowledge assets. Visualization refers to the display of complex data relationships using a variety of graphical methods, enabling managers to quickly grasp the results of the analysis. Results of complex analysis as well as key performance indicators are displayed on digital dashboards, which are often used to provide decision makers with the right information in an easy-to-understand way. Visual analytics combines the human visual system and analysis techniques to aid in the analysis of complex relationships and make sense of "noisy" data. GISs aid in storing, analyzing, and managing geographically referenced information, such as for locating target customers or finding optimal store locations.

Key Terms

ad hoc query 249
artificial intelligence (AI) 256
association discovery 251
attribute 241
best practices 260
bot 259
business analytics 255
business intelligence 236
business rules 243
buyer agent 259
classification 252
clickstream data 253
clustering 252
competitive intelligence 253
continuous planning process 238
data cleansing 248
data dictionary 242
data mart 249
data mining 250
data mining agent 260
data model 242
data reduction 251
data type 242
data warehouse 247
database 239
decision support system (DSS) 255
destructive agent 260
digital dashboard 263
dimension 250
drill down 250
drill-down report 249
entity 241
entity-relationship diagram 242

exception report 249
expert system (ES) 257
explicit knowledge asset 260
extraction, transformation, and loading 248
fact 250
form 243
fuzzy logic 258
geographic information system (GIS) 266
hard data 264
inferencing 258
informational system 246
intelligent agent 259
intelligent system 257
key-indicator report 249
knowledge assets 260
knowledge management 260
knowledge management system 260
knowledge portal 262
layer 267
master data 246
master data management 246
measure 250
model 255
monitoring and sensing agent 259
neural network 258
normalization 242
OLAP cube 250
OLAP server 250
online analytical processing (OLAP) 250

online transaction processing (OLTP) 245
operational systems 245
predictive analysis 255
query 243
query by example (QBE) 245
record 241
report 243
report generator 243
roll up 250
rule 257
scheduled report 249
sequence discovery 251
shopping bot 259
slicing and dicing 250
social network analysis 262
soft data 264
stickiness 253
Structured Query Language (SQL) 244
table 241
tacit knowledge asset 260
text mining 252
user agent 259
visual analytics 266
visualization 262
Web content mining 252
Web crawler 260
Web spider 260
Web usage mining 253
what-if analysis 255

Review Questions

1. How can a continuous planning process help businesses respond to external threats and opportunities?
2. Describe the differences between entities, tables, rows, and attributes in a database.
3. What is the importance of master data management?
4. What are the advantages of a DBMS?
5. Explain the differences between OLAP and OLTP.
6. Describe how OLAP enables a user to conduct multi-dimensional queries.
7. What is the meaning of support and confidence in the context of data mining?
8. Explain the difference between clustering and classification.

9. What is the relationship between measures and dimensions?
10. Describe and give examples of two types of Web mining.
11. What is a Web site's stickiness, and why is it important?
12. Explain the purpose of a model within a DSS.
13. Explain the difference between explicit and tacit knowledge.
14. Describe four types of intelligent agents. How can they be used to benefit organizations?
15. What is a knowledge management system, and what types of technologies make up a comprehensive system?
16. How can visual analytics be used to gain business intelligence and improve decision making?
17. What is the purpose of using layers in GIS applications?

Self-Study Questions

1. In a DBMS, an entity is represented as a(n) _____.
   A. attribute
   B. table
   C. row
   D. association

2. A(n) _____ report provides a summary of critical information on a recurring schedule.
   A. scheduled
   B. exception
   C. key indicator
   D. drill-down

3. In order to swiftly respond to a highly competitive and rapidly changing environment, organizations utilize a _____.
   A. continuous planning process
   B. structured decision making process
   C. decision support process
   D. decision making process

4. _____ is used to determine the likelihood of new customers to default on a loan.
   A. Association discovery
   B. Sequence discovery
   C. Classification
   D. Clustering

5. Web usage mining entails analyzing _____.
   A. clickstream data
   B. page content
   C. associations among sets of items
   D. unstructured data

6. Market share analysis is a type of model typically used by the _____ function of an organization.
   A. marketing
   B. accounting
   C. production
   D. management science

7. Examples of the types of activities that can be supported by ESs include all of the following except _____.
   A. payroll calculations
   B. financial planning
   C. machine configuration
   D. medical diagnosis

8. _____ agents keep track of key information such as inventory levels, notifying the users when conditions change.
   A. User
   B. Buyer
   C. Monitoring and sensing
   D. Data mining

9. What is true about knowledge management?
   A. As baby boomers retire at an increasing rate, knowledge management is helping organizations capture their knowledge.
   B. A knowledge management system is not a single technology but a collection of technology-based tools.
   C. Finding the right technology to manage knowledge assets is much easier than identifying what knowledge is needed, why it is needed, and who has this knowledge.
   D. All of the above are true.

10. Which of the following is an example of attribute data commonly used in GIS applications?
    A. structured data
    B. longitude
    C. trade area
    D. annual sales

Answers are on page 275.

Problems and Exercises

1. Match the following terms with the appropriate definitions:

   i. Social network analysis
   ii. Measures
   iii. Master data
   iv. Web content mining
   v. Online processing
   vi. Data mining
   vii. Expert system
   viii. Digital dashboard
   ix. Geographic information system
   x. DSS

   a. An information system designed to analyze and store spatially referenced data

   b. A special-purpose information system designed to mimic human expertise by manipulating knowledge (understanding acquired through experience and extensive learning) rather than simply information

   c. A technique that attempts to find groups of people who work together, to find people who don't collaborate but should, or to find experts in particular subject areas

   d. A set of applications used to find hidden predictive relationships in a data set

   e. Processing of information immediately as it occurs

   f. The values or numbers a user wants to analyze

   g. A special-purpose information system designed to support organizational decision making primarily at the managerial level of an organization

   h. Extracting textual information from Web documents

   i. A user interface visually representing summary information about a business's health, often from multiple sources

   j. The data that is deemed most important in the operation of a business

2. Interview a top-level executive within an organization with which you are familiar and find out their most important external threats. Can business intelligence help to respond to these threats? If so, how; if not, why not?

3. Visit www.amazon.com and search for a product of interest to you. What attributes are likely stored in Amazon's database?

4. Using a search engine, enter the key word "data warehousing." Who are the large vendors in this industry? What type of solutions do they offer to their clients? Do you see any common trend in data warehousing?

5. Visit MSN Money (www.moneycentral.msn.com/investor/calcs/n_expect/main.asp) on the Web to determine your life expectancy using a DSS. What did you learn? Is there a difference between life expectancies for different genders? If you browse through MSN Money, what other interesting stuff do you find? Also check out www.bigcharts.com.

6. Interview a top-level executive within an organization with which you are familiar and determine the extent to which the organization utilizes tools for information visualization or digital dashboards. Does this individual utilize these tools in any way? Why or why not? Which executives do utilize such tools?

7. Think about the junk mail you receive every day in your postal mail. Which mailings do you believe to be a result of data mining? How have the companies chosen you for their targeted mailings?

8. Using any program you choose or using the Web site www.moneycentral.com, find or create a template that you could use in the future to determine monthly payments on car or home loans. Compare your template with the one at www.bankrate.com/brm/auto-loan-calculator.asp. Would you have categorized the program you used to create this template as a DSS before doing this exercise?

9. Describe your experiences with ESs or go to www.exsys.com or www.easydiagnosis.com on the Web and spend some time interacting with their demonstration systems.

Now choose a problem that you know a lot about and would like to build your own ES for. Describe the problem and list the questions you would need to ask someone in order to make a recommendation.

10. Go out onto the Web and compare three shopping bots for a product you are interested in (e.g., www.mysimon.com, www.bottom dollar.com, www.shopzilla.com, www.shopping.com, or www.pricegrabber.com). Did the different agents find the same information, or were there any differences? Did you prefer one over the others? Why?

11. Have you seen or used ad hoc, exception, key-indicator, and/or drill-down reports? What is the purpose of each report? Who produces and who uses the reports? Do any of these reports look or sound familiar from your work experience?

12. Interview an IS manager within an organization. What types of information and knowledge discovery tools does the organization use? Was there an increase or decrease in the past few years? What predictions does this manager have regarding the future of these systems? Do you agree? Prepare a 10-minute presentation to the class on your findings.

13. For your university, identify several examples of various knowledge assets and rate these assets on their value to the university on a 10-point scale (1 = low value to 10 = high value).

14. Examine your university Web site to identify examples where a knowledge management system could be used or is being used to help provide improved services to students.

15. How do you prefer your desired information to be presented? Do you use any type of visualization tools? If so, which ones?

16. Visit Google maps (http://maps.google.com) and try out different layers provided under "More . . ." Which other information would you like to see? Are there any publicly available mashups that offer this information as layers on top of Google maps?

Application Exercises

Note: The existing data files referenced in these exercises are available on the Student Companion Web site: **www.pearsonhighered.com/valacich**.

Spreadsheet Application:
Travel Loan Facility

A new aspect of the business has been added to Campus Travel. Students can apply for a loan to help pay for their travels. However, loans for travel are available only to students who are traveling outside the country for at least two weeks. Since the costs for this type of international travel differ depending on how you travel, where you stay,

and what you do at the destination, different loan packages are available. For a month in Europe, you have decided to take out a loan. You have already taken a look at several offers but are unsure whether you can afford it. Set up a spreadsheet to calculate the payments per month for the following situations:

1. Two weeks in Eastern Europe; Price: $2,000; Percentage Rate: 5.5%; Time: one year

2. Two weeks in Western Europe; Price: $3,000; Percentage Rate: 6.0%; Time: one year

3. Three weeks in Eastern Europe; Price: $3,000; Percentage Rate: 6.5%; Time: two years

4. Three weeks in Western Europe; Price: $3,500; Percentage Rate: 5.5%; Time: two years

5. Four weeks in Eastern Europe; Price: $4,000; Percentage Rate: 6.0%; Time: two years

6. Four weeks in Western Europe; Price: $5,000; Percentage Rate: 6.5%; Time: three years

Once you have calculated the payments, calculate the total amount to be paid for each option as well as the total interest you would pay over the course of the loan. Make sure to use formulas for all calculations and print out a professionally formatted page displaying the results and a page displaying the formulas (Hint: In Microsoft Excel, use the "PMT" function in the category "Financial" to calculate the payments. Use Ctrl+´ [grave accent] to switch between formula and data views; calculate the number of payments before using the formula.)

 Database Application: Tracking Regional Office Performance at Campus Travel

The general manager wants to know which offices were most profitable during the previous year and asks you to prepare several reports. In the file FY2012.mdb, you find information about the offices, sales agents, and destinations. Use the report wizard to generate the following reports:

1. List of all sales agents grouped by office (including total number of agents per office)

2. List of sales agents for each destination (grouped by destination, including total number of agents)

3. Destinations sold by each sales agent (including total number of destinations)

Hint: You will need to generate the necessary queries before creating the reports.

Team Work Exercise: What's the Hot Topic in Business Intelligence?

Visit a Web site of an IS-related content provider, such as *InformationWeek*, *Computerworld*, *CIO*, or *NewsFactor*, and search for articles on business intelligence. You can find these online resources at www.informationweek.com, www.computerworld.com, www.cio.com, and www.newsfactor.com.

After having scanned the articles, get together with your team and discuss your findings. What is the focus of the different sites? What are the hot technologies and related issues? Which seem to be most important to business managers? Prepare a brief presentation for your classmates.

Answers to the Self-Study Questions

1. B, p.241
2. C, p.249
3. A, p.238
4. C, p.252
5. A, p.253
6. A, p.256
7. A, p.257
8. C, p.259
9. D, p.260
10. D, p.266

Case 1

The Netflix Prize

Netflix is the world's largest online movie provider. For a flat monthly fee, subscribers have access to thousands of movies and television shows through mail delivery or by download. For DVDs coming in the mail, the subscriber maintains a title queue on Netflix's site that he or she wants to watch, listed in order of viewing preference. Netflix chooses which movies or shows to mail next from the queue, and when one disc is returned, another is mailed. Customers are never charged late fees and after viewing the DVD simply drop it in a mailbox using the prepaid envelope Netflix provides.

Netflix has consistently ranked high in customer satisfaction surveys. In fact, the service has proved so successful that in April 2009, the company reported that it had shipped its two-billionth DVD. It's streaming "instant watch" service has proven extremely popular and for the first time in 2009 outperformed DVD shipments by 150 percent.

A key feature of the Netflix service is customers' ability to rate the movies they have seen on a five-point scale from "hated it" to "loved it." Based on customers' ratings, Netflix's movie recommendation system, Cinematch, then displays other movie titles customers might enjoy. While the system works well for Netflix's purpose, it admits that improvements are possible. With that in mind, Netflix started a contest in 2006 to improve their movie rating/recommendation system. The grand prize was $1 million, but to win the prize, contestants had to improve Cinematch's results by 10 percent—a difficult task. According to the contest rules published at the Netflix Prize Web site, "It's 'easy' really. We provide you with a lot of anonymous rating data and a prediction accuracy bar that is 10 percent better than what Cinematch can do on the same training data set. (Accuracy is a measurement of how closely predicted ratings of movies match subsequent actual ratings.) If you develop a system that we judge most beats that bar on the qualifying test set we provide, you get serious money and the bragging rights. But (and you knew there would be a catch, right?) only if you share your method with us and describe to the world how you did it and why it works."

Contestants registered for the contest as teams, and entries were limited to one per day. Any team whose members came up with an algorithm that improved Cinematch

performance by 1 percent would win $50,000. The $50,000 "progress prize" would be awarded once annually until someone reached the 10 percent increase or the contest ended. Entries would continue to be accepted in the Netflix Prize contest until the $1 million prize was awarded or until 2011, whichever came first. On September 21, 2009, a team led by AT&T researchers known as "BellKor's Pragmatic Chaos" took the grand prize by improving over the Cinematch score 10.06 percent. Immediately following the close of the contest, Netflix announced plans for a second contest in which they would release anonymous information on 100 million Neflix users. The contest would center around predicting the movie preferences of users based on key information like age, gender, and geographic location.

However, two and a half months after the first contest ended, a lawsuit filed against Netflix put the second contest in jeopardy. The lawsuit, *Doe v. Netflix*, was filed in California by an anonymous lesbian mother claiming that Netflix invaded her privacy. The logic behind her claim was that by making the movie

ratings available in the data set—along with the date of the rating, the movie information associated with the rating, and a unique identifier number for the subscriber that made the rating—anyone would be able to take that information and match it up against other publicly available data to determine someone's identity. In fact, that very scenario happened when two researchers working with the Neflix Prize data identified several users by comparing movie reviews on the Internet Movie Database (a popular movie information site) with the ratings in the "anonymous" data provided for the Netflix Prize contest. Information discovered about the identified users included political ideologies and sexual orientations.

In March 2010, the lawsuit was settled between the anonymous plaintiff and Netflix. Part of the settlement agreement was the cancellation of the second Netflix Prize contest. Netflix did not admit to any wrongdoing but said they will continue to collaborate with researchers in finding ways to improve their ratings system for customer use.

Questions

1. In what ways could Netflix visualize movie ratings, preferences, or trends to provide its subscribers with additional "movie intelligence"?

2. What are the pros and cons of having the winner of the Netflix Prize share the improved Cinematch method?

3. Describe another problem in business or society that could utilize an approach similar to that for winning the Netflix Prize (i.e., a contest that anyone can try to solve).

Based on:

Anonymous. (n.d.). The Netflix prize rules. Retrieved July 13, 2010, from http://www.netflixprize.com//rules.

Anonymous. (2009, September 18). Grand Prize awarded to team BellKor's Pragmatic Chaos. *Netflix Prize Forum*. Retrieved July 13, 2010, from http://www.netflixprize.com//community/viewtopic.php?id=1537.

Anonymous. (2010). Netflix DVD shipments vs Instant Watch. *FeedFlicks*. Retrieved July 13, 2010, from http://feedfliks.com/dvd-vs-instant.

Hunt, N. (2010, March 12). Netflix Prize update. *The Netflix Blog*. Retrieved July 13, 2010, from http://blog.netflix.com/2010/03/this-is-neil-hunt-chief-product-officer.html.

Lohr, S. (2009, September 22). A $1 million research bargain for Netflix, and maybe a model for others. *New York Times*. Retrieved July 13, 2010, from http://www.nytimes.com/2009/09/22/technology/internet/22netflix.html.

Singel, R. (2009, December 17). Netflix spilled your *Brokeback Mountain* secret, lawsuit claims. *Wired*. Retrieved July 13, 2010, from http://www.wired.com/threatlevel/2009/12/netflix-privacy-lawsuit.

Case 2

Are We There Yet?—Online Map Services

Everyone who drives a car and/or uses a computer is familiar with online map services. Three of the best and most frequently used are Google maps (http://maps.google.com), Microsoft's Bing Maps (www.bing.com/maps), and Yahoo! Maps (http://maps.yahoo.com). The services are

free for computer and mobile users who want to find the shortest route from point A to point B. Google has been especially popular for its satellite views and features such as real-time traffic information (in places like southern California) or the display of user generated content (e.g., landmarks or

restaurant reviews), although some of the overly inclusive satellite imagery of military bases has recently been taken down following a request by the U.S. military.

Although many online map services are free for consumers, the providers also offer fee-based enterprise versions. For example, all three of the above services provide a for-fee option for businesses wanting to add easy-to-use, interactive maps to their Web sites. With these applications, organizations can show customers how to reach stores or service centers in their areas, and employees on the road can more easily reach customers in various locations or find hotels and restaurants in their travel areas. Organizations can also track shipments or supply chains, manage employees and resources in the field, and insert relevant advertising into their customized maps when they are displayed on Web sites.

Online mapping has become a big component of the mobile phone experience as well. As more phones take advantage of location-based services and data networks, users can quickly find out what's around them through a simple Internet search. The search will return nearby businesses offering the products or services the user is looking for, and the user can choose a business to see a map and directions to the location.

In 2010, Google launched their latest advertising based revenue generator through their online mapping service. Dubbed "Sponsored Map Icons," businesses can now add their corporate or store logo to Google's map views. Currently in the testing phases, users will soon be able to see their favorite coffee shop's or restaurant's logo on Google map searches alongside directions or other map data instead of the generic grey category icon. Google believes that the logos will not only help people locate what they're looking for more easily on a map but also help them physically looking for the location by providing a logo to match up.

Google took online mapping to the next level when they introduced "Street View" to their mapping services. Touted as the "last zoom level" by Google, Street View allows the user to actually view a complete 360 degree photographic view from the street. Originally, Street View photography was available for only five U.S. cities. As of 2010, all 50 U.S. states and over 14 countries had extensive street view coverage. Nearly all of the United Kingdom's and Australia's highways and roads have coverage. Google has recently begun collecting photography of college campuses and surrounding paths and trails while continuing to add more streets in smaller cities and in other countries. Google's Street View has been criticized on fears of invasion of privacy and has come under increasing scrutiny in some countries, such as Germany. Many people have complained about having their home or license plate photographed. Although Google has gone through their photographic data and blurred faces, license plates, and other parts of photos, many are still troubled by Street View. Individuals who feel that their privacy is being violated can request imagery be blurred or removed from Google's data. Privacy fears aside, it appears that street-level imagery is here to stay and will continue to be updated. As of December 2009, Bing Maps started offering their own version of street-level photography with their "Streetside" feature.

Online mapping is now moving beyond the realm of the automobile alone and extending to bicycle riders. As of March 2010, a search on Google Maps can return biking directions and extensive bike trail data for many U.S. locations. Google map bike searches returns efficient routing, allows users to customize their trips, locate biking lanes, and find "rider-friendly" routes that avoid big hills.

Questions

1. Do you use Internet mapping sites? Why or why not?
2. As outlined in the case, there are many innovative mapping products and services; describe a new service that you want that doesn't yet exist.
3. Do you think that mapping software can be an invasion of privacy? Why or why not?

Based on:

Bass, S. (2005, June 29). Maps for fun and business. *PCWorld.* Retrieved July 13, 2010, from http://www.pcworld.com/article/121387/tips_and_tweaks_maps _for_fun_and_business.html.

Claburn, T. (2008, March 7). U.S. military restricts Google maps. *InformationWeek.* Retrieved July 13, 2010, from http://www.informationweek .com/news/security/government/howArticle.jhtml?articleID=206902500.

Fischman, J. (2009, June 22). Google's Street View eyeballs college campuses. *Chronicle of Higher Education.* Retrieved July 13, 2010, from http://chronicle .com/blogPost/Google-s-Street-View-/7231.

Guymon, S. (2010, March 10). Biking directions added to Google Maps. *The Official Google Blog.* Retrieved July 13, 2010, from http://googleblog.blogspot .com/2010/03/biking-directions-added-to-google-maps.html.

Spring, T. (2008, January 16). Google maps the key locations of popular TV shows. *PCWorld.* Retrieved July 13, 2010, from http://blogs.pcworld.com/ staffblog/archives/006311.html.

Vasquez, B. (2010, March 18). Google incorporates business logos into Google Maps in Australia. *Erictric.* Retrieved July 13, 2010, from http://erictric.com/ 2010/03/18/google-incorporates-business-logos-into-google-maps-in-australia.

Enhancing Business Processes Using Enterprise Information Systems

After reading this chapter, you will be able to do the following:

1. Explain core business processes that are common in organizations.

2. Describe what enterprise systems are and how they have evolved.

3. Describe enterprise resource planning systems and how they help to improve internal business processes.

4. Understand and utilize the keys to successfully implementing enterprise systems.

Preview

This chapter describes how companies are deploying enterprise-wide information systems to support and enable core business processes. Enterprise systems help to integrate various business activities, to increase coordination amongst various business departments and partners, to streamline and better manage interactions with customers, and to coordinate better with suppliers in order to more efficiently and effectively meet rapidly changing customer demands.

Large companies continue to find that they need systems that span their entire organization to tie everything together. As a result, an understanding of enterprise systems is critical to succeed in today's competitive and ever-changing digital world. This chapter focuses on how organizations are utilizing enterprise-wide information systems to best support internal business processes. In Chapter 8, "Improving Supply Chains and Strengthening Customer Relationships Using Enterprise Information Systems," we focus on systems that support business processes spanning multiple organizations, critical in today's competitive global environment.

Managing in the Digital World: Amazon.com

In the years since the company's inception in 1994, Amazon.com, founded and headed by Jeff Bezos, has grown from a garage-based online book reseller to one of the world's largest retailers for music, DVDs, videos, e-books, computer and video games, photography equipment, toys, software, tools and hardware, wireless products, electronics, and kitchen and housewares. In fact, Amazon is the top Internet retailer in the United States. In 2009, sales topped $24 billion, and nearly 836 million users visited the site—nearly double the number that visited Walmart.com during the same time period.

Amazon's commitment to be "customer-centric" has resulted in a satisfied, returning customer base unequaled in the dot-com marketplace. Among the innovations that make customers smile and return are the following:

- The Amazon.com Web site greets you by name each time you visit.
- The site remembers your recent purchases and recommends similar products you might like.
- At the top of Amazon.com's home page, a "gold box," custom-tailored for each returning customer, contains books, music, and DVDs he or she might want to buy—all at deep discounts.
- Amazon.com offers free shipping on most orders over $25 and offers "Amazon Prime," where customers pay a small monthly fee and receive complimentary upgrades on shipping.

To offer these features, Amazon not only needs a sophisticated information systems (IS) infrastructure but also needs to be able to excel at managing its supply chain. Included in this are not only efficiently shipping the physical goods from its warehouses to the customers but also acquiring and receiving the right goods at the right time (see Figure 7.1). On the "upstream" side of the supply chain, seasonality of products, short product cycles, and changes in consumer tastes make it very difficult to accurately forecast demand and thus control inventory levels. These problems are exacerbated by the broad selection and by product lines such as consumer electronics that tend to change frequently. On the "downstream" side, Amazon has to optimize the operation of their fulfillment centers to most efficiently ship the products to the customers. For example, insufficient inventory levels increase Amazon's shipping costs, as partial shipments or long-zone deliveries are needed. Further, Amazon's reliance on a few select shipping companies can have a negative impact on customer experience if any of these companies experience problems.

Over the years, Amazon has made tremendous efforts to address these issues and has built a network of 12 North American and seven international fulfillment centers, along with a sophisticated IS infrastructure. Recently, Amazon realized that it could gain additional revenue by utilizing this infrastructure in novel ways. "We have this beautiful, elegant, high-I.Q. part of our business that we have been working hard on for many years," Jeff Bezos told the *New York Times* in 2007. "We've gotten good at it. Why not make money off it another way?"

One step was managing the online store and fulfillment for large companies such as Target.com. For small Internet start-up companies, a solid and highly scalable infrastructure is also a prime need; however, such infrastructure can require huge investments and diverts the company's resources away from its primary tasks of attracting new customers and growing the business. Amazon Web Services allows companies to do just that. Based on Amazon's solid and reliable infrastructure, start-up companies can rent computing resources or storage space from Amazon on an as-needed basis. In addition to providing reliability and ease of use, it

© Jack Kurtz/ The Image Works

FIGURE 7.1

Companies can rent Amazon's warehouse infrastructure on an as-needed basis.

saves the start-up money, as they pay only for the resources used, which are scalable upward and downward, depending on demand. Fulfillment by Amazon extends Amazon Web Services from the computing infrastructure to the physical warehouse and fulfillment infrastructure. Fulfillment by Amazon lets independent retailers who list their goods on Amazon.com—or even elsewhere on the

Web—use its network of distribution centers to store products and ship orders. This frees smaller companies from the need to have a warehouse of their own and the need to deal with the myriad processes involved in getting a product to the customer, nearly creating a virtual business. As with Amazon Web Services, a seller pays only fulfillment fees for picking, packing, and shipping whenever an item is sold. Thus, the fixed cost of renting a warehouse is turned into a variable cost that depends on sales volume. As you can see, optimizing its supply chain has helped Amazon even beyond its own business.

Amazon continued making its customers smile in 2007 when they introduced the Kindle, a handheld e-book reading device. The Kindle had a six-inch diagonal screen, was less than an inch thick, and could hold up to 200 books. Getting e-books into the Kindle for reading could be accomplished through a USB hookup to a computer or books could be wirelessly downloaded directly into the device from Amazon's Kindle Store, an online e-book store. Wireless connectivity on the Kindle is achieved over Whispernet, Amazon's free cellular wireless service built into the device. Sold exclusively by Amazon, the Kindle was an instant hit and sold out initial stocks in the first six hours on sale. Those wanting a Kindle had to wait on back orders to catch up for the next five months.

In early 2009, Amazon released the Kindle 2, a major upgrade to the e-reader. The updated device measured in at less than half of an inch in thickness, had a 1,500-book capacity, and could speak text to read books aloud. Unlike the original Kindle, the updated model could travel internationally and utilize the free Whispernet service in over 100 countries. During the 2009 Christmas shopping season, Kindle e-books outsold paper books for the first time ever.

As of early 2010, the latest iteration of the device, the Kindle DX, continued to improve on the original. The DX sports such features as an accelerometer, allowing users to turn the Kindle on its side to read content in a landscape orientation. In addition, the DX is even thinner than its predecessor, holds up to 3,500 books, displays on a high-resolution screen, and has a battery life of up to two weeks on a single charge. Having realized that the Kindle is the "most gifted item ever in [Amazon's] history," according to Jeff Bezos, Amazon released its third generation of the Kindle in mid-2010.

Through the inventive use of technology infrastructure, solid supply chain management, and innovative product sales and development, Amazon.com continues to dominate the Internet retail landscape as the place to go to buy almost anything.

After reading this chapter, you will be able to answer the following:

1. How have enterprise-wide information systems enabled Amazon.com's strategy?
2. For Amazon.com, what are the pros and cons to providing Web services to assist smaller enterprises?
3. In what ways does Amazon differentiate itself from other online marketplaces such as eBay?

Based on:

Amazon Kindle. (2010, July 17). In *Wikipedia, the free encyclopedia*. Retrieved July 19, 2010, from http://en.wikipedia.org/w/index.php?title=Amazon_Kindle&oldid=374047587.

Anonymous. (n.d.). Amazon fulfillment Web service. Retrieved July 22, 2010, from http://www.amazon.com/b?ie=UTF8&node=402340011.

Anonymous. (n.d.). Fulfillment by Amazon. Retrieved July 22, 2010, from http://www.amazon.com/gp/seller/fba/fulfillment-by-amazon.html.

Anonymous. (n.d.). History of e-commerce. Retrieved July 22, 2010, from http://www.ecommerce-land.com/history_ecommerce.html.

Anonymous. (2010, January 28). Amazon.com 2009 Annual Report. Retrieved July 19, 2010, from http://phx.corporate-ir.net/phoenix.zhtml?c=97664&p=irol-newsarticle&id=1380452.

Anonymous. (2010). Trends and data. *Internet Retailer*. Retrieved July 19, 2010, from http://www.internetretailer.com/trends.

Ratcliffe, M. (2009, December 26). Updating Kindles sold estimate: 1.49 million. Retrieved July 19, 2010, from http://www.zdnet.com/blog/ratcliffe/updating-kindles-sold-estimate-149-million/486.

Stone, B. (2007, April 27). Sold on eBay, shipped by Amazon.com. *New York Times*. Retrieved July 22, 2010, from http://www.nytimes.com/2007/04/27/technology/27amazon.html.

Core Business Processes and Organizational Value Chains

Traditionally, companies are organized around four distinct functional areas, namely, marketing and sales, supply chain management, accounting and finance, and human resources. Each of these functional areas is responsible for several well-defined business functions, such as marketing a product; sales forecasting; manufacturing goods; planning and budgeting; or recruiting, hiring, and training. Although this model suggests that a company can be regarded as being comprised of distinct independent silos, the different functional areas are highly interrelated to perform

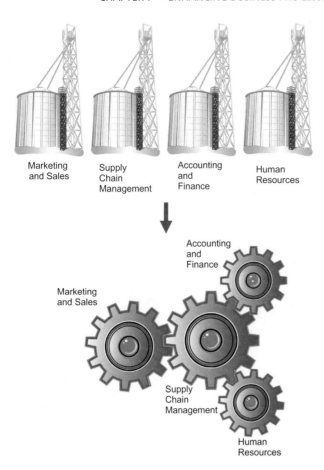

FIGURE 7.2

A company's functional areas should be interrelated.

value-added activities (see Figure 7.2). In fact, most business processes cross the boundaries of business functions, so it is helpful for managers to think in terms of business processes from a customer's (both internal and external) point of view.

Core Business Processes

In most cases, the customers do not care about how things are being done; they care only that things are being done to their satisfaction. When you buy a book at Amazon.com, you typically do not care which functional areas are involved in the transaction; you care only about quickly getting the right book for the right price. Buying a book at Amazon.com can help to illustrate one of the core business processes, namely, *order-to-cash;* other core business processes common to most business organizations are *procure-to-pay* and *make-to-stock.* Other important business processes are related to tracking a firm's revenues and expenses, managing employees, and so on. Next, we discuss the core business processes involved in generating revenue.

Order-to-Cash For business organizations, selling products or services are the main way of generating revenue. In the example of Amazon.com, you need to create an account and add items to your shopping cart. You then need to complete your order by entering shipping and billing information, and submitting the order. Amazon.com will then confirm that your address is valid and will check your credit card information. Many online retailers provide real-time stock information; however, in case an item is out of stock after placing an order, you will be notified. If the item is in stock, your order will be put together and shipped, and your credit card will be charged. Together, the processes associated with selling a product or service are referred to as the **order-to-cash process** (see Figure 7.3). As with all business processes, the order-to-cash process can be broken down into multiple subprocesses (most of which are common across organizations). For most businesses, the order-to-cash process entails subprocesses such as creating a customer record; checking the customer's creditworthiness; creating an order; checking and allocating stock; picking, packing, and shipping; invoicing; and collecting the payment. Depending on the

FIGURE 7.3

The order-to-cash process.

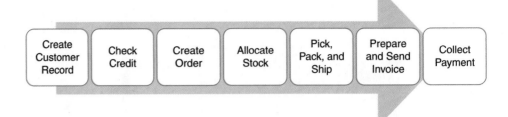

nature of the transaction, the individual subprocesses and the time in which these are completed can differ considerably. For example, a sale in a convenience store may take only several seconds, and many of the subprocesses mentioned are left out. In contrast, sales of many big-ticket items (such as commercial aircraft or specialized manufacturing machinery) may take months or years to complete and may involve many more steps. The subprocesses can be further broken down to a more granular level.

Obviously, an ineffective order-to-cash process can have various negative effects for organizations; for example, the manual input of order information often causes errors, as do suboptimal picking and shipping processes. Together, such errors can lead to a high rate of disputes that have to be resolved, ineffective collection processes, and, ultimately, defecting customers. In contrast, an effective order-to-cash process can create customer satisfaction, speed up the collection process, and serve to provide valuable inputs into business intelligence and customer relationship management applications (see Chapter 8, "Improving Supply Chains and Strengthening Customer Relationships Using Enterprise Information Systems").

Procure-to-Pay In order to be able to sell books and other products, Amazon.com needs to acquire these from its suppliers. Amazon.com needs to manage literally thousands of suppliers, place purchase orders, receive the products, allocate warehouse space, receive and pay invoices, and handle potential disputes. These processes associated with procuring goods from external vendors are together referred to as the **procure-to-pay process** (see Figure 7.4). Subprocesses of the procure-to-pay process include price and terms negotiations, issuing of the purchase order, receiving the goods, and receiving and paying the invoice.

An ineffective procure-to-pay process can increase error rates in purchase order and invoice processing; further, it inhibits a company from developing close relationships with preferred vendors. Together, this can increase the cost per transaction, lead to an increase in disputes to be resolved, and prohibit the company from obtaining the most favorable conditions from its vendors. In contrast, an effective procure-to-pay process can help to obtain favorable conditions, reduce transaction costs, and, ultimately, create customer goodwill as it helps to efficiently fulfill customer orders.

Make-to-Stock/Make-to-Order A third set of core business processes is associated with producing goods (such as Amazon's Kindle e-book reader), and entails make-to-stock and make-to order. In the **make-to-stock process,** goods are produced based on forecasts and are stocked in a warehouse (i.e., a push-based approach); sales orders are then fulfilled from inventory. In contrast, in the **make-to-order process,** raw materials, subcomponents, and accessories are procured based on forecasts, but actual manufacturing does not start until sales orders are received

FIGURE 7.4

The procure-to-pay process.

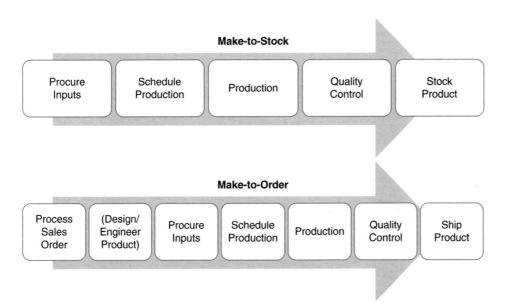

FIGURE 7.5

The make-to-stock versus the make-to-order process.

(a pull-based approach); in extreme cases, even design and engineering start only when an order is received. For example, mass-produced goods, such as television sets or home appliances, are typically produced under a make-to-stock approach. Here, the organization holds these stocked products, *pushing* the order out to customers after it is received. Alternatively, highly customizable or very expensive low-volume goods are often produced under a make-to-order approach, as is the case with Dell computers or with commercial aircraft, where the assembly starts only after you have placed your order. Here, the organization waits for an order, allowing it to initiate a *pulling* sequence to move the order through the production process. The processes associated with making products are comprised of processing sales orders, procuring the inputs to the manufacturing process, scheduling production, production, quality control, packaging, and stocking or shipping the product. Figure 7.5 illustrates the make-to-stock and make-to-order processes.

Together, these core business processes enable the creation of supply chains that are involved in transforming raw materials into products sold to the end consumer. A typical supply chain resembles a river, where the raw materials start out at the source and move downstream toward the end customer; at each step, the goods are transformed to make the end product. To meet the needs for various different inputs, each organization typically has multiple upstream suppliers; similarly, each organization typically sells to multiple downstream customers. Figure 7.6 shows the supply chain of a book. Within this supply chain, one company's sales-related processes overlap with the downstream company's procurement-related processes (supply chains are discussed in detail in Chapter 8).

Organizational Activities Along the Value Chain

To gain competitive advantage over their rivals, companies are trying to optimize the core business processes in different ways. One of the first challenges an organization must face is to understand how it can use information systems to support these and other business processes. For example, Amazon.com excels at using information systems to optimize both the procure-to-pay and the order-to-cash process. Generally, the set of business activities that add value to the end product is referred to as a *value chain* (Porter & Millar, 1985), in which information flows through functional areas that facilitate an organization's business processes. Figure 7.7 depicts the value chain framework. In Chapter 2, "Gaining Competitive Advantage Through Information Systems," we spoke of the strategic value of analyzing a value chain; now, we show you how the activities along the value chain support business processes.

Many business processes depend on activities performed by various functional areas within an organization; for example, Amazon's order-to-cash process involves activities performed by sales, shipping, accounting, and other functional areas. The functional areas directly involved in the process are responsible for the core activities, whereas other functional areas are performing support activities. In other words, *core activities* are performed by the functional areas that

FIGURE 7.6

Supply chain of a book.

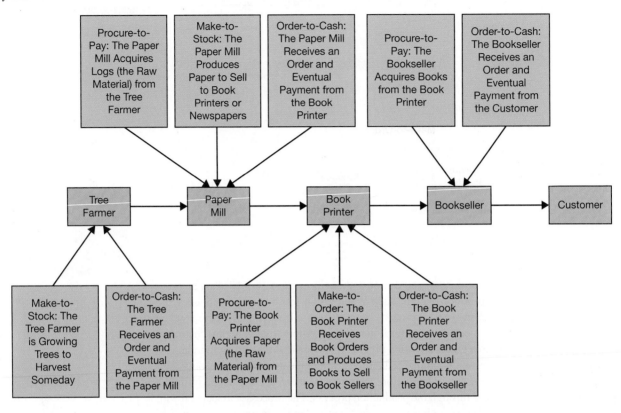

process inputs and produce outputs, and *support activities* are those activities that enable core activities to take place. In the following sections, we focus on core activities and then turn our attention to the support activities that make them possible.

Core Activities **Core activities** include inbound logistics (receiving), operations and manufacturing, outbound logistics (shipping), marketing and sales, and customer service. These activities may differ widely, depending on the unique requirements of the industry in which a company operates, although the basic concepts hold in most organizations.

Inbound Logistics Activities. Inbound logistics involves the business activities associated with receiving and stocking raw materials, parts, and products. For example, inbound logistics at Amazon.com involves not only the receipt of books, e-book readers, and various other products for

FIGURE 7.7

Value chain framework.

Source: Based on Porter and Millar (1985).

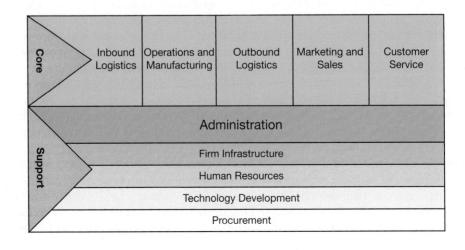

sale, but also the receipt of packaging materials and shipping labels. Shippers deliver these products to Amazon.com, where employees unwrap the packages and stock the products in the company's warehouse inventory or directly route the products to operations in order to fill open orders. Amazon.com can automatically update inventory levels at the point of delivery, allowing purchasing managers access to up-to-date information related to inventory levels and reorder points. Inbound logistics activities are a crucial part of the procure-to-pay business process, as these activities enable the company to efficiently and effectively fill customer orders.

Operations and Manufacturing Activities. Once the components have been stocked in inventory, operations and manufacturing activities transform the inputs into outputs. Operations and manufacturing can involve such activities as order processing (e.g., at Amazon.com) and/or manufacturing or assembly processes (e.g., at Dell) that transform raw materials and/or component parts into end products (i.e., the make-to-stock and make-to-order business processes). Companies such as Dell utilize Web-based information systems to allow customers to enter orders online. This information is used to coordinate the manufacturing of a customized personal computer in which the component parts are gathered and assembled to create the end product. During this process, inventory levels from inbound logistics are verified; if the appropriate inventory exists, workers pick the components from existing supplies and build the product to the customer's specifications. When components are picked, items are deducted from inventory; once the product is assembled, inventory levels for the final product are updated.

Outbound Logistics Activities. The activities associated with outbound logistics mirror those of inbound logistics. Instead of involving the receipt of raw materials, parts, and products, outbound logistics focuses on the distribution of end products within the order-to-cash business process. For example, outbound logistics at Amazon.com involves the delivery of books that customers have ordered. Orders that have been processed by operations are forwarded to outbound logistics, which picks the products from inventory and coordinates delivery to the customer. At that point, items are packaged and deducted from the company's inventory, and an invoice is created that will be sent to the customer. Amazon.com can automatically update sales information at the point of distribution, allowing managers to view inventory and revenue information in real time.

Marketing and Sales Activities. Marketing and sales activities are associated primarily with the presales (i.e., before the sale) activities of the company. These activities include the creation of marketing literature, communication with potential and existing customers, and pricing of goods and services. As discussed in Chapter 4, "Enabling Commerce Using the Internet," most companies support the business activity of marketing and sales by creating an e-brochure. Many companies, especially those focused on selling products or services to the end consumer (e.g., passenger airlines such as United or online retailers such as Amazon.com), use information systems to update pricing information and/or schedules. This information is entered directly into the pricing and scheduling systems, allowing the information to become immediately accessible throughout the organization and to end consumers through the organization's Web site.

Customer Service Activities. Whereas marketing and sales focus on presales activities, customer service focuses on the postsales (i.e., after the sale) activities. Customers may have questions and need help from a customer service representative. Many companies, such as Amazon .com, are utilizing information systems to provide customer service. These applications allow customers to search for and download information related to the products that they have purchased or the purchase itself. For example, on Amazon.com, customers can view their order status or can view and print invoices of current and past orders. Similarly, customers can find additional information and support about the Amazon Kindle or other digital products. Rather than calling a customer service representative, customers can easily find the needed information through a self-service customer support application.

Companies can use information systems to track service requests. When a customer calls in for repairs to a product, customer service representatives can access a bevy of information related to the customer. For instance, an agent can access technical information concerning the specific product as well as review any problems the customer has encountered in the past. This enables customer service representatives to react quickly to customer concerns, improving the customer service experience.

Brief Case ⊘

COMPLEXITY OF MODERN MANUFACTURING: TOYOTA AUTOMOBILES

The automobiles rolling off of factory floors today are a testament to modern ingenuity. The cars that ferry us to school, work, and play are often taken for granted but have come a long way from Ford's first Model-T and the original assembly line. The once relatively simple mechanical machines have been replaced with complex, technologically advanced vehicles. Today's automobiles are highly sophisticated and complex loaded with electronics, providing passengers with many cabin amenities, including advanced heads up displays, navigation systems, Internet access, and multimedia entertainment systems.

But the passenger interior isn't the only place you'll find advanced electronics. Virtually every system in modern cars is controlled by computers, from engine components such as fuel injection and safety features such as airbags to both the acceleration and braking systems. Computer control of these systems allows the components of the vehicle to operate more efficiently and, in many cases, in ways that a human operator couldn't control. For example, a car can get out of control if the brakes are applied hard enough to "lock up" the wheels—an occurrence that happened frequently before the advent of the antilock braking system (ABS). With ABS, a computer senses when a wheel is about to lock up from braking pressure. The ABS computer then "pulses" the braking pressure to that wheel, allowing it to spin momentarily, then reapplies the pressure. This process happens repeatedly within milliseconds of each pulse and on all four wheels at the same time, quickly and stably slowing the car. A human operator would be unable to initiate all these mini-braking motions, especially in an emergency situation. With this complexity also come challenges. For instance, in 2009–2010, it was a reported software bug in the ABS computer that caused some Toyota Prius owners a certain amount of frustration and fear. Toyota was forced to recall over 400,000 vehicles to fix the software bug. The recall was an embarrassment for Toyota, especially since they had previously had to recall 75,000 Prius vehicles in 2005 for another software glitch, this one affecting the hybrid's engine system. Even with these highly publicized problems, the Toyota Prius is one of the most popular cars in the world, with incredible customer loyalty and satisfaction.

Building modern automobiles is highly complex and would not be possible without information systems to schedule and procure components within vast supplier networks as well as to orchestrate the actual production of the vehicles. For instance, Toyota has over 200 direct suppliers not only from Japan but also from Canada, France, Sweden, and the United States. These suppliers provide around 150 thousand unique components, that equal nearly 2 billion items per year. And these are just the direct components sent to Toyota; many of these 150 thousand components consist of multiple parts and subassemblies, requiring a vast network of suppliers that must work together to produce the right number of the right components at the right time. Given this complexity, it is not surprising that occasional design defects occur, such as the software bugs in the Prius. Also, as vehicles of the future introduce more complex methods to provide safety, convenience, and fuel economy, it is likely that the value systems needed to orchestrate their production will become more complex.

Questions

1. What other consumer products likely require a complex value system in order to be produced? Can you think of any that do not?
2. Modern automobiles contain dozens of microprocessors, running over 100 million lines of software code. Have modern automobiles become too complex?

Based on:

Anonymous. (2005, October 13). Prius software problems? Is the Prius stopping or stalling on the highway? Retrieved April 25, 2010, from http://www.soultek.com/clean_energy/hybrid_cars/toyota_prius_hybrid _car_shut_down_or_stall_problems.htm.

Caruthers, B. (2010, February 18). Toyota software bugs unlike those in flaky PCs. *CNet News.com*. Retrieved April 25, 2010, from, http://news .cnet.com/8301-13924_3-10454331-64.html.

Toyota. (2010, July 27). In *Wikipedia, the free encyclopedia*. Retrieved July 27, 2010, from http://en.wikipedia.org/w/index.php?title=Toyota& oldid=375695252.

Williams, M. (2010, February 9). Toyota Prius software glitch forces global recall. *ComputerworldUK.com*. Retrieved April 25, 2010, from http://www.computerworlduk.com/toolbox/software-quality-testing/ quality-assurance/news/index.cfm?newsid=18732.

Support Activities **Support activities** are business activities that enable the primary activities to take place. Support activities include administrative activities, infrastructure, human resources, technology development, and procurement.

Administrative Activities. Administrative activities focus on the processes and decision making to orchestrate the day-to-day operations of an organization, particularly those processes that span organizational functions and levels. Administration includes systems and processes from virtually all functional areas—accounting, finance, marketing, operations, and so on—as well as both the executive and the managerial level.

Infrastructure Activities. Infrastructure refers to the hardware and software that must be implemented to support the applications that the primary activities use. An order entry application requires that employees who enter orders have a computer and the necessary software to accomplish their business objectives. In turn, the computer must be connected via the network to a database containing the order information so that the order can be saved and recalled later for processing. Infrastructure provides the necessary components to facilitate the order entry process (see Chapter 3, "Managing the Information Systems Infrastructure and Services").

Human Resource Activities. Human resources involves the business activities associated with employee management, such as hiring, interview scheduling, payroll, and benefits management. Human resources is classified as a support activity since the primary activities cannot be accomplished without the employees to perform them. In other words, all the primary activities use the human resource business activity. For example, if a company needs a new customer service representative to serve the growing volume of customers, the request is processed through the human resource function, which creates the job description and locates the appropriate person to fill the job.

Technology Development Activities. Technology development includes the design and development of applications that support the primary business activities. If you are planning on pursuing a career in the management information systems (MIS) field, you will frequently participate in activities related to the development or acquisition of new applications and systems. Technology can involve a wide array of responsibilities, such as the selection of packaged software or the design and development of custom software to meet a particular business need. Many companies are leveraging the technology business activity to build Internet, intranet, and extranet applications for these purposes. As seen in previous chapters, companies use these systems to support a wide variety of primary business activities.

Procurement Activities. Procurement refers to the purchasing of goods and services that are required as inputs to the primary activities. Allowing each functional area to send out purchase orders can create problems for companies, such as maintaining relationships with more suppliers than necessary and not taking advantage of volume discounts. The procurement business activity can leverage information systems by accumulating purchase orders from the different functional areas within the corporation. By having this information at their disposal, procurement personnel can combine multiple purchase orders containing the same item into a single purchase order. Ordering larger volumes from its suppliers means that the company can achieve dramatic cost savings through volume discounts. Procurement receives, approves, and processes requests for goods and services from the primary activities and coordinates the purchase of those items. This allows the primary activities to concentrate on running the business rather than adding to their workload.

Connecting Organizational Value Chains

The flow of information can be streamlined not only within a company but outside organizational boundaries as well. A company can create additional value by integrating internal applications with suppliers, business partners, and customers. Companies accomplish this by connecting their internal value chains to form a **value system** (Porter & Millar, 1985), in which information flows from one company's value chain to another company's value chain. Figure 7.8 depicts the value system framework. In this diagram, three companies are aligning their value chains to form a value system. First, company A processes information through its value chain and forwards the information along to its customer, company B, which processes the information through its value chain and sends the information along to its customer, company C, which processes the information through its value chain. Adding additional suppliers, business partners, and customers can create complex value systems. However, for our purposes, we simply view an organization's information systems as a value chain that interacts with the value chains of other organizations.

As information systems can be used to streamline an organization's internal value chain, information systems can also be used to coordinate a company's value chain with another company's value chain or with consumers (such as in business-to-consumer electronic commerce).

FIGURE 7.8

Three companies combine their value chains, forming a value system.

Source: Based on Christensen (1997) and Porter and Millar (1985).

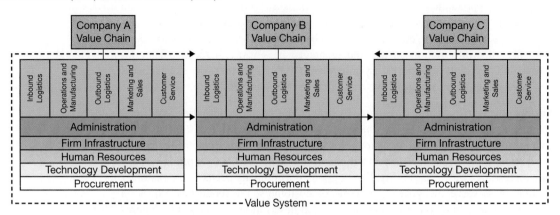

Any information that feeds into a company's value chain, whether its source is another company's value chain or an end consumer, is considered part of the value system.

As discussed previously, a supply chain can be viewed as a river, where physical goods "flow" from a source to an ultimate destination. Like a river, at any particular point there is a flow coming from upstream and progressing downstream. In a similar way, a value system can be viewed as a river of information, comprising upstream and downstream information flows. An **upstream information flow** consists of information that is received from another organization, whereas a **downstream information flow** relates to the information that is produced by a company and sent along to another organization. For instance, in the value system depicted in Figure 7.8, the upstream and downstream information flows for company B become quite evident. In this case, company B receives information from its upstream supplier, processes the information through its internal value chain, and subsequently passes information downstream to its distributors and/or customers. These flows of external information into and from a company can be leveraged to create additional value and competitive advantage.

Enterprise Systems

In order to efficiently conduct the core business processes (as well as other business processes), the different functional areas within a company need to share data. For example, data about your book order needs to be shared between accounting and finance (for billing purposes), marketing and sales (e.g., to feed into product recommendations for other customers), and supply chain management and operations (e.g., to fulfill the order and replenish the inventory). Businesses have leveraged information systems to support business processes for decades, beginning with the installation of applications to assist companies with specific business tasks, such as issuing paychecks.

The Rise of Enterprise Systems

As companies begin to leverage IS applications, they typically start out by fulfilling the needs of particular business activities in a particular department within the organization. Systems that focus on the specific needs of individual departments are typically not designed to communicate with other systems in the organization and are therefore referred to as **stand-alone applications.** Stand-alone applications usually run on a variety of computing hardware platforms, such as mainframes and midrange computers. However, although departmental systems enable departments to conduct their daily business activities efficiently and effectively, these systems often are not very helpful when people from one part of the firm need information from another part of the firm (e.g., people in manufacturing need forecasts from sales).

Organizations often purchased proprietary software systems from software vendors; these systems, however, were not designed to share data with other vendors' systems. Similarly, different employees or departments of a company develop or purchase a department-specific type of software (e.g., accounting) to meet their needs, and IS managers are then faced with the problem

ETHICAL DILEMMA

Too Much Intelligence? RFID and Privacy

Radio frequency identification (RFID) tags are the latest in technological tracking devices. Each tag contains unique identification information that can be accessed by an RFID reader. The identification is then sent to the information system that can identify the product that was tagged. For example, the pharmaceutical industry tags certain drugs in large quantities, such as 100-pill bottles of Viagra and Oxycontin, in order to track them as they move through the supply chain and thus prevent counterfeits from reaching the public.

As is true with all electronic tracking devices, privacy advocates are concerned about misuse. Since, theoretically, RFID tags can be read by anyone who has an RFID reader, the tags have the potential of revealing private consumer information. For example, if you buy a product that has an RFID tag, someone with an RFID reader can possibly identify where you bought the product and how much you paid for it. The amount of information imprinted on an RFID tag is limited, however, and since few retail businesses have purchased RFID writers, readers, or the erasers that can clear information from the tags before they leave the store, the likelihood of privacy abuse is currently slim. Although pharmaceutical companies use RFID tags to track certain products, drug company spokespersons say it is highly unlikely that consumers will take home tracking devices with their heart medications or birth control pills.

The state of Washington may be the first state that addresses RFID privacy issue. In April 2009, the state passed a law that prohibits anyone from scanning an RFID tag, except for the business owner or agency who issued the tag. Other states are also taking steps to protect privacy by limiting the use of RFID. As of mid-2010, similar bills were under review in Nevada, New York, and New Hampshire.

Based on:

Anonymous. (2010, Febrary 16). New Hampshire seeks to outlaw biometric IDs. *Infosecurity*. Retrieved April 10, 2010, from http://www.infosecurity-us.com/view/7360/new-hampshire-seeks-to-outlaw-biometric-ids.

Chartier, D. (2008, March 28). Washington State passes RFID privacy law: Where's Uncle Sam? *ArsTechnica*. Retrieved April 10, 2010, from http://arstechnica.com/news.ars/post/20080328-washington-state-passes-rfid-privacy-law-wheres-uncle-sam.html.

Jones, K. (2007, September 4). California passes bill to ban forced RFID tagging. *InformationWeek*. Retrieved April 10, 2010, from http://www.informationweek.com/news/security/showArticle.jhtml?articleID=201803861.

Long, M. (2005, December 29). Mind being tracked by a tiny chip? *Newsfactor*. Retrieved April 10, 2010, from http://www.newsfactor.com/story.xhtml?story_id=40435.

Swedberg, C. (2009, April 17). Washington State adopts second RFID privacy law. *RFIDJournal*. Retrieved April 10, 2010, from http://www.rfidjournal.com/article/view/4802.

---

of "knitting together" a hodgepodge portfolio of discordant proprietary applications into a system that shares information. This can be challenging, as applications running on different computing platforms are difficult to integrate; often, custom interfaces are required in order for one system to communicate with another, and such integration is typically very costly.

Given that old stand-alone systems (both software and hardware) were not necessarily designed to communicate with other applications beyond departmental boundaries (essentially "speaking different languages"), they are typically either fast approaching or beyond the end of their useful life within the organization and are referred to as **legacy systems.** Legacy systems can prove problematic when information from multiple departmental systems is required to support business processes and decision making (as is often the case). For example, if the applications for inbound logistics and operations are not integrated, companies will lose valuable time in accessing information related to inventory levels. When an order is placed through operations, personnel need to verify that the components are available in inventory before the order can be processed.

If the inventory and order-entry systems are not integrated, personnel may have to access two separate applications or use a custom interface that pulls information from both systems. Figure 7.9 provides an example of how information flows through legacy systems within an organization. As the diagram depicts, information is generated by the inbound logistics business activity, but it does not flow through to the next business activity, in this case operations; in other words, there are too many "rocks" in the river, impeding the flow of information. Since the inbound logistics and operations departments use different legacy systems, information cannot readily flow from one business activity to another. Understandably, this creates a highly inefficient process for operations personnel, who must

FIGURE 7.9

Information flows using legacy
systems.

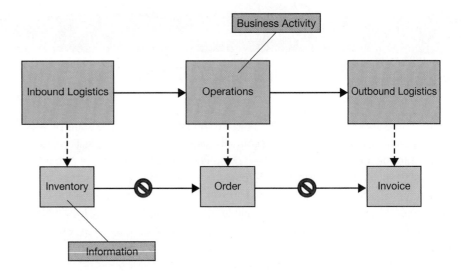

have access to two systems or a common interface that pulls information together in order to get both
the order entry and the inventory information. In some cases, inventory information may be stored on
both systems, creating the potential for inaccuracies. Should data be updated in one system but not
the other, the data becomes inaccurate. In addition, there are further, unnecessary costs associated with
entering, storing, and updating data redundantly.

To utilize data stored in separate applications to facilitate business processes and decision making, information must be reentered from one system to the next (by either manual typing, copying
and pasting, or even downloads to Excel) or be consolidated by a third system. Further, the same data
may also be stored in several (sometimes conflicting) versions throughout the organization, making
the information harder to consolidate, often causing the business to lose money because of inefficiencies or missed business opportunities. To address these challenges, organizations have turned to
enterprise-wide information systems. An **enterprise-wide information system** (or **enterprise system**) is an integrated suite of business applications for virtually every department, process, and industry, allowing companies to integrate information across operations on a company-wide basis
using one large database. Rather than storing information in separate places throughout the organization, enterprise systems provide a central repository common to all corporate users. This, along
with a common user interface, allows personnel to share information seamlessly, no matter where
the user is located or who is using the application (see Figure 7.10).

The emergence of the Internet and the Web has resulted in the globalization of customer and
supplier networks, opening up new opportunities and methods to conduct business. For example,
raw materials and component parts for a computer may come from China and be shipped to Europe for fabrication, and the final products are assembled and shipped to customers across the globe
(see Chapter 1, "Managing in the Digital World"). Customers have an increasing number of options available to them, so they are demanding more sophisticated products that are customized to
their unique needs. They also expect higher levels of customer service. If companies cannot keep
their customers satisfied, the customers will not hesitate to do business with a competitor. Companies need to provide quality customer service and develop products faster and more efficiently to
compete in global markets. Enterprise systems can be extended to streamline communications with
global customers and suppliers. For example, the enterprise systems of SAP, the German enterprise
systems pioneer, support over 30 different languages and currencies and perform translation and
currency exchange seamlessly. Rather than focusing only on internal operations, these systems can
also focus on business activities that occur outside organizational boundaries. Enterprise systems
can help companies find innovative ways to increase accurate on-time shipments, avoid (or at least
anticipate) surprises (such as shortages in raw materials or weather problems), minimize costs, and
ultimately increase customer satisfaction and the overall profitability of the company.

Enterprise systems come in a variety of shapes and sizes, each providing a unique set of features
and functionality. When deciding to implement enterprise solutions, managers need to be aware of a
number of issues. One of the most important involves selecting and implementing applications
that meet the requirements of the business as well as of its customers and suppliers. In the following

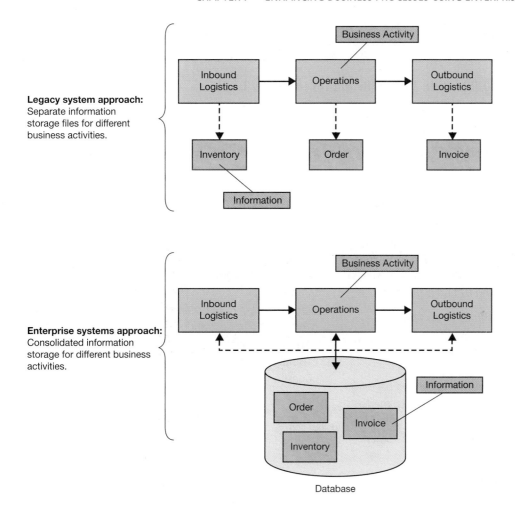

FIGURE 7.10

Enterprise systems allow companies to integrate information across operations on a company-wide basis.

sections, we examine the ways in which information systems can be leveraged to support business processes. This is followed by an in-depth analysis of how enterprise systems have evolved and how companies are using these systems to support their internal and external operations.

Supporting Business Processes

As discussed previously, information systems can be used to gain and sustain competitive advantage by supporting and/or streamlining activities along the value chain. For example, an information system could be used to support a billing process in such a way that it reduces the use of paper and, more important, the handling of paper, thus reducing material and labor costs. This system can help managers keep track of that same billing process more effectively because they will have more accurate, up-to-date information about the billing process, enabling them to make smart, timely business decisions.

Information systems can be used to support either internally or externally focused business processes. **Internally focused systems** support functional areas, business processes, and decision making *within* an organization. These activities can be viewed as a series of links in a chain along which information flows within the organization. At each stage (or link) in the process, value is added in the form of the work performed by people associated with that process, and new, useful information is generated. Information begins to accumulate at the point of entry and flows through the various links, or business processes, within the organization, progressing through the organization with new, useful information being added every step of the way (see Figure 7.11).

In contrast, **externally focused systems** coordinate business processes with customers, suppliers, business partners, and others who operate *outside* an organization's boundaries. A system that communicates across organizational boundaries is sometimes referred to as an **interorganizational system (IOS)** (Kumar & Crook, 1999). The key purpose of an IOS is to streamline the flow of information from one company's operations to another's (e.g., from a company to its potential or existing customers).

NET STATS

The Changing Value of Social Media in the Workplace

Not long ago, the idea of using Facebook at work was viewed by most as a non–work-related activity. However, today, as more organizations are working to have personal relationships with customers and suppliers, social media is no longer taboo in the office. Social media sites like Facebook, LinkedIn, and Twitter are increasingly being viewed as providing improved methods for connecting, sharing, and collaborating with customers and suppliers. A recent white paper by toolbox .com reports five trends that are shaping the way in which social media is viewed and being used by organizations:

- **Trend 1:** *Social media is increasingly being used to improve decision making.* Organizations are finding that important information can be obtained by actively participating in online communities.
- **Trend 2:** *The value of social media has expanded beyond networking.* Organizations are realizing that social media provides numerous benefits beyond networking of individuals, such as market intelligence, improved customer service, and loyalty.

- **Trend 3:** *Best practices communities are emerging, easing the search for key human resources.* Organizations are more easily finding individuals with unique and hard-to-find talents.
- **Trend 4:** *Talented personnel are attracted to organizations embracing social media as a part of their organizational strategy and tactics.* Organizations are finding that some of the best users of social media in their personal lives also want to work for companies who share these same values.
- **Trend 5:** *Talented personnel place strong value on organizations demonstrating transparency and responsiveness to the use of social media.* Individuals have greater trust and loyalty to organizations they believe to be honest and accessible.

Based on:

Toolbox.com. (2010). Top 5 trends in B2B social media usage. Retrieved July 27, 2010, from http://www.toolbox.com.

Competitive advantage can be accomplished here by integrating multiple business processes in ways that enable a firm to meet a wide range of unique customer needs. Sharing information between organizations helps companies to adapt more quickly to changing market conditions. For instance, should consumers demand that an additional component be added to a product, a company can gain this information from its information systems that support sales and instantaneously pass it along to its component suppliers. Information systems allow the company and its suppliers to satisfy the needs of customers efficiently since changes can be identified and managed immediately, creating a competitive advantage for companies that can respond quickly. We can view processes and information flows across organizations just as we previously viewed the processes and information flows within an organization. At each stage (or link) in the process,

FIGURE 7.11

Information flow
for a typical order.

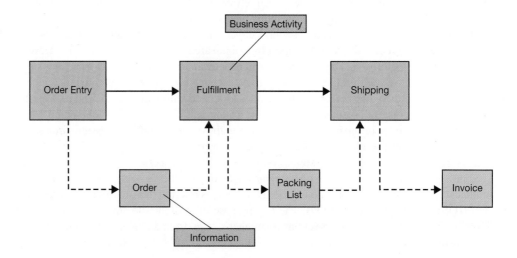

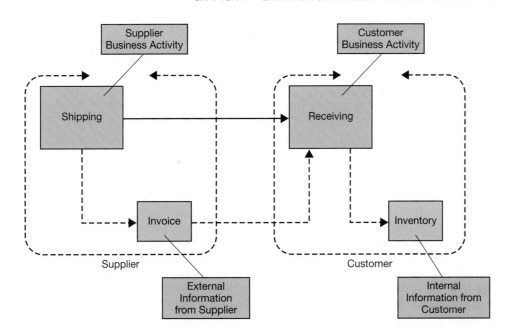

FIGURE 7.12

Information flow for a typical shipment across organizational boundaries.

value is added by the work performed, and new, useful information is generated and exchanged between organizations (see Figure 7.12). Using IOS, one company can create information and transmit it electronically to another company.

The Need for Integrated Enterprise Systems Companies can gain several advantages by integrating and converting legacy systems so that information stored on separate computing platforms can be consolidated to provide a centralized point of access, which typically comes in the form of *enterprise resource planning* applications (discussed later in this chapter). Although such applications do an excellent job of serving the needs of internal business operations on an

---

COMING ATTRACTIONS

Power of the Swarm

Social insects, such as ants, bees, termites, and wasps, have very powerful problem-solving skills with sophisticated collective intelligence. For instance, ants use pheromone trails to mark the routes they use to find food. The more traveled trails accumulate more pheromones, which attract new ants. Conversely, pheromones deposited on less traveled paths will evaporate eventually. The problems social insects solve—finding food, dividing labor among nestmates, building nests, responding to external challenges—have important counterparts in engineering and computer science. Swarm intelligence, inspired by the observation of these social insects, attempts to mimic the highly efficient behavior of social insects by combining hundreds or even thousands of relatively simple robots to generate behavior more complex than any individual device could achieve alone.

As a branch of artificial intelligence, swarm intelligence has many potential application areas, including the military,

surveillance and monitoring, health, micromanufacturing, and space exploration. For instance, maybe the only way we will truly explore the solar system and beyond is to build vast numbers of small robots that will be able to land on planetary bodies. Then they might build copies of themselves as well as new vehicles, eventually generating millions of robots spread throughout the galaxy.

Based on:

Bonabeau, E., Dorigo, M., & Theraulaz, G. (1999). *Swarm intelligence: From natural to artificial systems.* Oxford: Oxford University Press.

Boothroyd, D. (2010, August 3). By imitating insects, microrobots could open new avenues of research and application. *NewElectronics.* Retrieved March 20, 2010, from http://www.newelectronics.co.uk/article/22890/Hive-mentality-Microrobots.aspx.

Greenemeier, L. (2010, January 13). Group thinker: Researcher gets $2.9 million to further develop swarm intelligence. *Scientific American.* Retrieved March 20, 2010, from http://www.scientificamerican.com/article.cfm?id=swarm-intelligence-research.

TABLE 7.1 Core Applications of SAP's Business Suite

SAP customer relationship management	SAP supplier relationship management
SAP enterprise resource planning	SAP supply chain management
SAP product life cycle management	

organization-wide basis, they are not necessarily designed to completely accommodate the communication of information outside the organization's boundaries.

Systems that facilitate interorganizational communications focus on the upstream and downstream information flows. Since these systems coordinate business activities across organizational boundaries, they are classified as externally focused applications. *Customer relationship management* applications concentrate on the activities involved in promoting and selling products to the customers as well as providing customer service and nourishing long-term relationships. In contrast, *supply chain management* applications integrate the value chains of business partners within a supply chain, improving the coordination of suppliers, product or service production, and distribution (both types of applications are discussed in Chapter 8). Integrated enterprise systems can be extremely valuable for companies operating in global markets. For example, the enterprise systems offered by SAP have multilingual interfaces and automatically convert measurement units (e.g., kilograms versus pounds or centimeters versus inches) and currencies. This way, engineers in Germany, Spain, or Italy can input the bill of materials, manufacturing engineers and factory specialists can buy the parts and set up the production run, and marketing and sales staff in the United States can easily communicate with their clients. Most large enterprise systems vendors offer a suite of integrated core business applications that combine internally focused and externally focused applications (see Table 7.1 for the core applications available in SAP's Business Suite).

Improving Business Processes Through Enterprise Systems Software programs come in two forms—packaged and custom. **Packaged software** are applications written by third-party vendors for the needs of many different users and organizations, whereas **custom software** are applications that are designed and developed exclusively for a specific organization (see Chapter 9, "Developing and Acquiring Information Systems"). Packaged software that you are likely familiar with is Microsoft Office, which you can purchase off the shelf to help you with your personal documents and communications. Packaged software is highly useful for standardized, repetitive tasks, such as writing a report or preparing a presentation. They can be quite cost effective since the vendor that builds the application can spread out development costs through selling to a large number of users.

Yet packaged software may not be well suited for tasks that are unique to a particular business. In these cases, companies may prefer to develop (or have developed for them) custom software that can accommodate their particular business needs. The development costs of custom software are much higher than for packaged software because of the time, money, and resources that are required to design and develop them. Furthermore, applications need to be maintained internally when changes are required. With packaged software, the vendor makes the changes and distributes new versions to its customers. In all, there are trade-offs when choosing between the packaged and custom software routes. Managers must consider whether packaged software can meet the business requirements and, if not, conduct a cost–benefit analysis to ensure that taking the custom software approach will prove worthwhile to the company.

Because all companies are different, no packaged software application will exactly fit the unique requirements of a particular business. Thus, enterprise systems come in a variety of shapes and sizes, each designed to accommodate certain transaction volumes, industries, and business processes. Enterprise systems vendors such as SAP, Oracle, or Microsoft offer different **modules,** which are components that can be selected and implemented as needed. In essence, each module is designed to replace a legacy system, be it a finance, human resources, or manufacturing system; thus, after the conversion to an enterprise system, each business function has access to various modules that serve its needs, but the modules (and the underlying data) are tightly integrated and share the same look and feel (see Figure 7.13). For example, Oracle's JD Edwards EnterpriseOne offers more than 70 different modules to support a variety of business functions. Similarly, SAP offers a variety of modules related to four major groups of functions (see Table 7.2). The modules provided by different vendors may vary in the specific business processes they support as well as in what they are called.

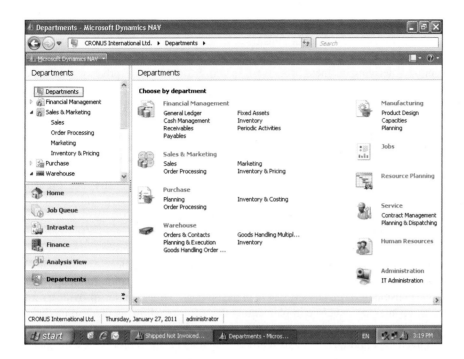

FIGURE 7.13

Each module in an enterprise system is designed to replace a stand-alone legacy system.

Vanilla versus Customized Software. As the naming and capabilities differ between the software vendors, it is critical for managers to understand the vendors' naming conventions and software modules to gain an understanding of how these features can be implemented to support the company's business processes. The features and modules that an enterprise system comes with out of the box are referred to as the **vanilla version.** If the vanilla version does not support a certain business process, the company may require a customized version. **Customization** provides either additional software that is integrated with the enterprise system or consists of direct changes to the vanilla application itself. SAP, for example, includes literally thousands of elements in its various enterprise systems that can be customized, and it also offers many industry-specific versions that have already been customized for a particular industry based on SAP's perceptions of the best way to do things (i.e., industry best practices). Companies must take special care when dealing with customization issues. Customizations can be extremely costly, and maintaining and upgrading customizations can be troublesome. For example, a customization made to the vanilla version will need to be reprogrammed when a new release of the system is implemented because subsequent releases of the software will not include the previous customizations. In other words, new vanilla versions must be continually upgraded to accommodate the company-specific customizations. This process can involve a substantial investment of time and resources, diverting attention away from other key business activities and reducing company profits.

TABLE 7.2 Key Capabilities of SAP's ERP System

Capability	Explanation
Financials	Allows organizations to manage corporate finance functions by automating financial supply chain management, financial accounting, and management accounting
Human capital management	Gives organizations the tools needed to maximize the profitability potential of the workforce, with functionality for employee transaction management and employee life cycle management
Operations	Empowers organizations to streamline operations with integrated functionality for managing end-to-end logistics processes while expanding collaborative capabilities in supply chain management, product life cycle management, and supplier relationship management
Corporate services	Allows organizations to optimize centralized and decentralized services for managing real estate, corporate travel, and incentives and commissions

Best Practices–Based Software. One of the major hurdles posed to companies that implement enterprise systems involves changing business processes to accommodate the manner in which the software works. Enterprise system implementations are often used as a catalyst for overall improvement of underlying business processes. As with SAP, most enterprise systems are designed to operate according to industry-standard business processes, or best practices. In fact, most enterprise system vendors build best practices into their applications to provide guidelines for management to identify business activities within their organizations that need to be streamlined. Implementations and future upgrades to the system will go more smoothly when companies change their business processes to fit the way the enterprise system operates.

Many organizations have spent many years developing business processes that provide them with a competitive advantage in the marketplace. Adopting their industry's best practices may force these companies to abandon their unique ways of doing business, putting them on par with their industry competitors. In other words, companies can potentially lose their competitive advantages by adopting the best practices within their industry. Best practices is an area that managers must carefully consider before selecting any type of enterprise system because some enterprise system vendors build their entire systems around best practices, and companies that reject best practices are in for a long and time-consuming implementation (although the vendors and external consultants typically offer help in the process). Other vendors provide a series of options that companies select before implementing the software, allowing them some (but not complete) flexibility in changing their business processes to accommodate the enterprise system modules. Given the importance and difficulty of changing business processes with enterprise and other systems implementations, we now briefly describe business process management.

Business Process Management. Since the first publishing of *The Principles of Scientific Management* by Fredrick Taylor in 1911 (and probably even before that), organizations have focused on improving business processes. Over the years, various approaches for improving business processes have been developed (see Table 7.3). Given the magnitude of change that an enterprise system can impose on an organization's business processes, understanding the role of business process management in the implementation of an enterprise system is necessary. **Business process management (BPM)** is a systematic, structured improvement approach by all or part of an organization whereby people critically examine, rethink, and redesign business processes in order to achieve dramatic improvements in one or more performance measures, such as quality, cycle time, or cost. BPM became very popular in the 1990s (and was then called **business process reengineering [BPR]**) when Michael Hammer and James Champy published their best-selling book *Reengineering the Corporation.*

Hammer and Champy and their proponents argued that radical redesign of an organization was sometimes necessary in order to lower costs and increase quality and that information systems were the key enabler for that radical change. The basic steps in BPM can be summarized as follows:

1. Develop a vision for the organization that specifies business objectives, such as reducing costs, shortening the time it takes to get products to market, improving quality of products and/or services, and so on
2. Identify the critical processes that are to be redesigned
3. Understand and measure the existing processes as a baseline for future improvements
4. Identify ways that information systems can be used to improve processes
5. Design and implement a prototype of the new processes

TABLE 7.3 Some Other Terms Closely Related to Business Process Management

Business activity modeling	Business process redesign
Business activity monitoring	Business process reengineering
Business architecture modernization	Functional process improvement
Business process improvement	Work flow management

At the heart of BPM initiatives are information systems that enable the streamlining of business processes. Given the importance of information systems in such endeavors, organizations are increasingly hiring information technology (IT) consultants and business analysts who have a sound understanding of the business but who are also well versed in technology. In fact, business analysts and business systems analysts are often listed among the hottest jobs because of good job prospects, high salaries, and the diversity of work. In enterprise systems projects, business analysts are deeply involved in analyzing and improving business processes and mapping the processes to the different enterprise systems modules.

BPM is similar to quality improvement approaches such as *total quality management* and *continuous process improvement* in that they are intended to be cross-functional approaches to improve an organization. BPM differs from these quality improvement approaches, however, in one fundamental way. These quality improvement approaches tend to focus on incremental change and gradual improvement of processes, while the intention behind BPM is radical redesign and drastic improvement of processes.

When BPR was introduced in the 1990s, many efforts were reported to have failed. These failures occurred for a variety of reasons, including the lack of sustained management commitment and leadership, unrealistic scope and expectations, and resistance to change. In fact, BPR gained the reputation of being a nice way of saying "downsizing."

Nevertheless, BPR (and its successors such as BPM) lives on today and is still a popular approach to improving organizations. No matter what it is called, the conditions that appear to lead to a successful business process improvement effort include the following:

- Support by senior management
- Shared vision by all organizational members
- Realistic expectations
- Participants empowered to make changes
- The right people participating
- Sound management practices
- Appropriate funding

In any event, it is clear that successful business process change, especially involving enterprise systems, requires a broad range of organizational factors to converge that are far beyond the technical implementation issues. Next, we examine the three most popular forms of enterprise systems.

Enterprise Resource Planning

When companies realize that legacy systems can create dramatic inefficiencies within their organizations, the next step is to integrate legacy information on a company-wide basis. As previously described, applications that integrate business activities across departmental boundaries are often referred to as **enterprise resource planning (ERP)** systems. In the 1990s, we witnessed companies' initial push to implement integrated applications, as exhibited by skyrocketing ERP sales at that time. Be aware that the terms "resource" and "planning" are somewhat misnomers, meaning that they only partially describe the purpose of ERP since these applications do much more than just planning or managing resources. The reason for the term "enterprise resource planning" is that these systems evolved in part during the 1990s from material requirements planning and manufacturing resource planning packages. Do not get hung up on the words "resource" and "planning." The key word to remember from the acronym ERP is "enterprise."

Integrating Data to Integrate Applications

ERP replaces stand-alone applications by providing various modules based on a common database and similar application interfaces that service the entire enterprise rather than portions of it. Information stored on legacy systems is converted into a large, centralized database that stores information related to the various business activities of an organization. The central database alleviates the problems associated with multiple computing platforms by providing

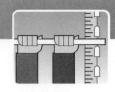

POWERFUL PARTNERSHIPS

SAP—Dietmar Hopp, Hans-Werner Hector, Hasso Plattner, Klaus Tschira, and Claus Wellenreuther

In what seems like the Dark Ages to today's computer users, five former IBM employees had a vision. The year was 1972, and Dietmar Hopp, Hans-Werner Hector, Hasso Plattner, Klaus Tschira, and Claus Wellenreuther founded a small company in Mannheim, Germany, to develop and sell business software for real-time processing (see Figure 7.14). They called the fledgling company Systems, Applications, and Products in Data Processing. After the first year, "R/1" was added to the product's name, "R" standing for "real-time" data processing.

The company continued to grow, and in the 1980s R/2 was born. During this decade, SAP expanded internationally with the opening of subsidiaries in Denmark, Sweden, Italy, and the United States. Client-server architecture had become the standard in business software, and SAP was poised to meet the need.

Today, SAP is the world's largest business software company, employing 47,578 people in over 50 countries. It is the largest software enterprise in Europe and the fourth-largest software enterprise in the world as of 2009. Currently, SAP has more than 75,000 customers in 120 countries, 140,000 installations, and 2,400 certified partners. Every day, more than 12 million users work with SAP solutions. Areas of concentration for SAP software developers include the following:

1. **ERP.** Helps integrate the various data sources and processes of an organization into a unified system
2. **Customer Relationship Management.** Helps companies win and retain customers, gain marketing and customer insight, and focus on customers
3. **Product Life Cycle Management.** Helps manufacturers set up a single source for all product-related information necessary for communicating closely with business partners and supporting product lines
4. **Supply Chain Management.** Helps companies enhance operational flexibility across global enterprises and provide real-time visibility for customers and suppliers
5. **Supplier Relationship Management.** Allows customers to collaborate closely with suppliers and organize sourcing processes that enhance transparency and lower costs

SAP's original founders have remained with the company and are often found in publications naming the world's wealthiest individuals. Plattner pledged large amounts of his personal fortune to fund higher education, such as the Hasso Plattner Institute at the University of Potsdam (Germany), the library at the University of Mannheim (Germany), and the Hasso Plattner Institute of Design at Stanford University. Klaus Tschira launched a foundation supporting research in informatics, mathematics, and the natural sciences.

Based on:

Anonymous. (n.d.). Geschichte der SAP. Retrieved July 29, 2010, from http://www.sap.com/germany/about/company/geschichte/geschichte_1.epx.

Anonymous. (n.d.). Das HPI. Retrieved July 29, 2010, from http://www.hpi.uni-potsdam.de/hpi.html?L=1.

Anonymous. (n.d.). KTS Foundation: Brief history. Retrieved July 29, 2010, from http://www.klaus-tschira-stiftung.de/english/about/foundation.html.

Anonymous. (n.d.). SAP history. Retrieved April 18, 2010, from http://www.sap.com/about/company/history/index.epx.

FIGURE 7.14

SAP, like many great technology companies, was built with a powerful partnership.

Vario Images/GmbH & Co. KG/Alamy Images

a single place where all information relevant to the company and particular departments can be stored and accessed, as depicted in Figure 7.15.

In contrast to legacy systems where it is difficult to share information between business activities, ERP applications make accessing information easier by providing a central information repository. For example, where an ERP solution is used, both inbound logistics and operations have access to current inventory data because both business activities have access to the same information.

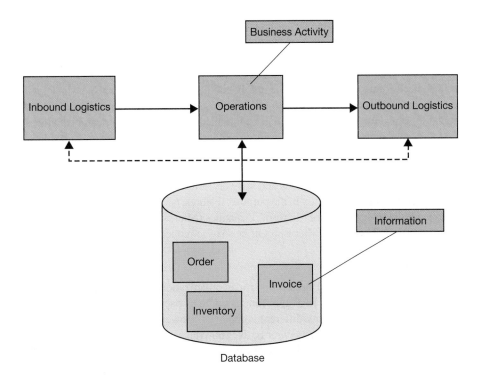

FIGURE 7.15

Information storage using an ERP solution.

Rather than information flowing from one department to the next, it can be accessed and updated at will, meaning that the next business activity can access information in the data warehouse whenever it needs to. This gives personnel access to accurate, up-to-date information. The beauty of ERP lies in the fact that information can be shared throughout the organization. For example, inventory information is accessible not only to inbound logistics and operations but also to accounting, sales, and customer service personnel. If a customer calls in wondering about the status of an order, customer service representatives can find out by accessing the database through the ERP application (see Figure 7.16). Prior to the emergence of ERP, customer service representatives may have had to retrieve information from two or more separate computing systems or, worse yet, call someone who would be able to access the information, making their job extremely difficult while

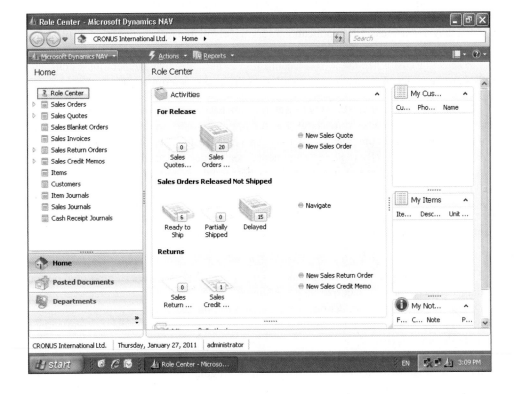

FIGURE 7.16

An ERP system can provide employees with relevant up-to-date information.

potentially resulting in dissatisfied customers. Storing data in a single place and making it available to everyone within the organization empowers everyone in the organization to be aware of the current state of business and to perform their jobs better.

ERP applications that access the database are designed to have the same look and feel regardless of the unique needs of a particular department. Inbound logistics and operations personnel will use a common user interface to access the same pieces of information from the shared database. Although the inbound logistics module and the operations module will have different features tailored to the unique needs of the business functions, the screens will look comparable, with similar designs, screen layouts, menu options, and so on. The Microsoft Office products provide a useful analogy. Microsoft Word and Microsoft Excel are designed to serve separate functions (word processing and spreadsheets, respectively), but overall the products look and feel very similar to one another. Word and Excel have similar user interfaces but differ vastly in the purpose, features, and functionality that each application offers. Likewise, the look and feel of Microsoft Dynamics (Microsoft's suite of enterprise-wide information systems) resembles that of Microsoft Office so as to reduce the learning curve for new users.

Choosing an ERP System

When selecting an appropriate ERP application for an organization, management needs to take many factors into careful consideration. ERP applications come as packaged software, which means that they are designed to appeal to many different companies. However, businesses have unique needs even within their own industries. In other words, like snowflakes, no two companies are exactly alike. Management must carefully select an ERP application that will meet the unique requirements of the particular company, and must consider a number of factors in the ERP selection. Among the most prevalent issues facing management are ERP control and ERP business requirements.

ERP Control ERP control refers to the locus of control over the computing systems and data contained in these systems, as well as decision making authority. Companies typically either opt for centralized control or allow particular business units to govern themselves. In the context of ERP, these decisions are based on the level of detail in the information that must be provided to management. Some corporations want to have as much detail as possible made available at the executive level, whereas other companies do not require such access. For instance, an accountant in one company may want the ability to view costs down to the level of individual transactions, while an accountant in another company may want only summary information. Another area related to control involves the consistency of policies and procedures. Some companies prefer that policies and procedures remain consistent throughout an organization. Other companies want to allow each business unit to develop its own policies and procedures to accommodate the unique ways that they do business. ERP applications vary widely in their allowance for control, typically assuming either a corporate or a business-unit locus of control. Some ERP applications allow users to select or customize the locus of control. In either case, management must consider the ERP's stance on control to ensure that it will meet the business requirements of the company.

ERP Business Requirements When selecting an ERP system, organizations must choose which modules to implement from a large menu of options—most organizations adopt only a subset of the available ERP components. There are two major categories of ERP components—ERP *core* components and ERP *extended* components (see Figure 7.17). Most ERP vendors provide components that are tailored to specific industry best practices and, of course, allow customization if desired by the customer.

ERP Core Components. **ERP core components** support the important *internal* activities of the organization for producing their products and services. These components support internal operations, such as the following:

1. *Financial Management.* Components to support accounting, financial reporting, performance management, and corporate governance
2. *Operations Management.* Components to simplify, standardize, and automate business processes related to inbound and outbound logistics, product development, manufacturing, and sales and service
3. *Human Resource Management.* Components to support employee recruitment, assignment tracking, performance reviews, payroll, and regulatory requirements

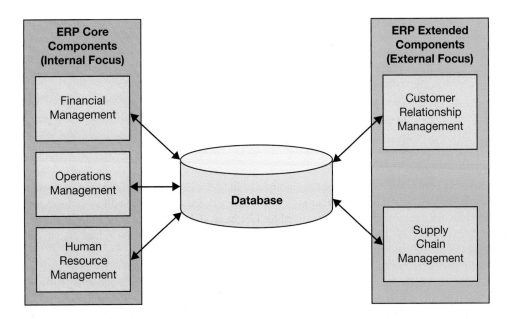

FIGURE 7.17

An ERP system consists of core and extended components.

Whereas the operations management component enable the core activities of the value chain, financial management and human resources management are associated with activities supporting the core activities (see Figure 7.18).

ERP Extended Components. **ERP extended components** support the primary *external* activities of the organization for dealing with suppliers and customers. Specifically, ERP extended components focus primarily on customer relationship management and supply chain management. Both are discussed in detail in Chapter 8.

Enabling Business Processes Using ERP Core Components

To fit the needs of various businesses in different industries, an ERP system's core components are typically implemented using a building-block approach through a series of modules. For example, SAP's ERP application is built around modules that are modeled after the best practices for 25 different industries. Depending on the industries, the modules are localized for different

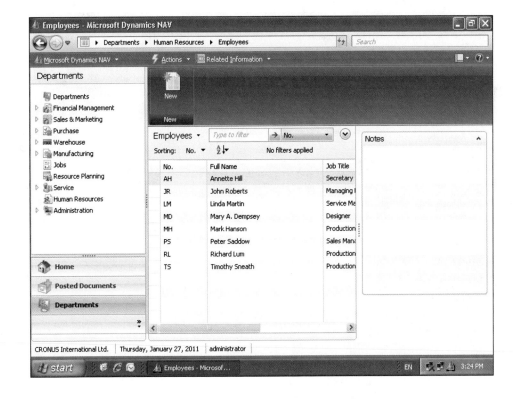

FIGURE 7.18

The human resources management component of an ERP enables core value chain activities to take place.

TABLE 7.4 Industry-Specific Versions of the Microsoft Dynamics ERP System

Construction	Distribution
Education	Financial services
Government	Health care
Manufacturing	Not-for-profit
Professional services	Retail

countries: Whereas the modules for the automotive industry are localized for Japan or Germany, the modules for apparel and footwear industries are localized for China and India, the modules for the pharmaceutical industry are localized for Germany and the United States, and so on. Similarly, Microsoft offers its Dynamics ERP system for various industries, including construction, health care, manufacturing, retail, and others (see Table 7.4). Depending on the way processes are typically performed in an industry, the modules within each industry-specific ERP package work together to enable the business processes needed to run a business efficiently and effectively. ERP vendors typically package the various modules that enable industry-specific processes and offer such systems as "industry solutions." This way, organizations have to spend less effort in selecting the needed modules and can more easily implement the ERP system.

Order-to-Cash As discussed above, the order-to-cash process entails the processes related to selling goods or services. Depending on the industry, the order-to-cash process can be very simple or extremely complex. In a retail environment, this process can be as simple as capturing product data, modifying the sale price (if needed), processing payment cards, and processing loyalty cards for customer profiling purposes. For a wholesale distributor, the order-to-cash process is more elaborate and consists of price quotation, stock allocation, credit limit check, picking, packing, shipping, billing, and receiving payment. For these processes to take place, different modules of the financial and operations management components work together. For example, the financial management component provides modules for checking credit limits, billing, and processing incoming payments. The operations management component provides modules related to sales and warehouse management operations, such as price quotation, stock allocation, picking, packing, and shipping (see Figure 7.19).

FIGURE 7.19

An ERP system can support all aspects of the order-to-cash process.

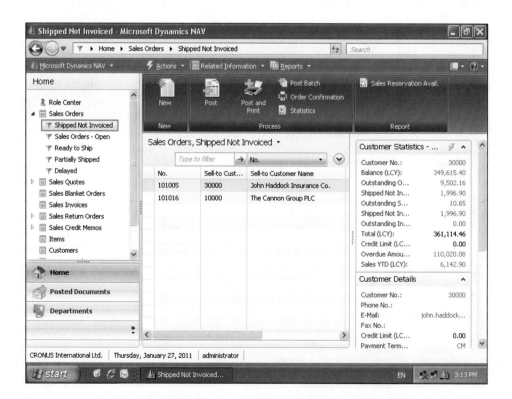

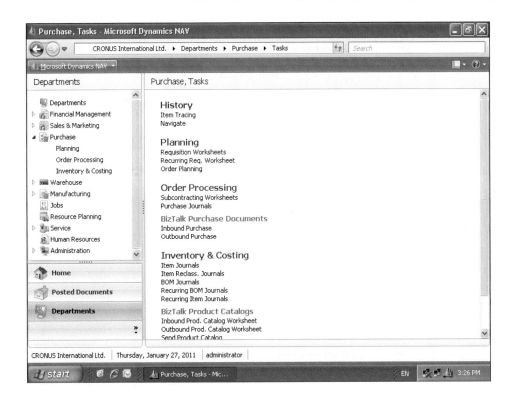

FIGURE 7.20

An ERP system can support all aspects of the procure-to-pay process.

Procure-to-Pay To recall, a generic procure-to-pay process entails negotiating price and terms, issuing purchase orders, receiving the goods, receiving the invoice, and settling the payment. As the order-to-cash process differs between industries, so does the procure-to-pay process. A grocery store, for example, typically orders a standard assortment of products but also faces additional constraints, such as having to optimize order quantities, taking into account demand and storage costs but also seasonality and perishability of products. In contrast, a construction company procures diverse materials, depending on the project at hand, and the procurement process could entail a lengthy sourcing process, including requests for quotations, a bidding process, reviewing of bids, awarding the contract, and thoroughly inspecting the delivered products or materials (see also Chapter 9 for the process of purchasing a new information system). Similar to the order-to-cash process, different modules of the financial management and operations management ERP components work together to enable the different activities related to the procure-to-pay process (see Figure 7.20).

Make-to-Stock/Make-to-Order The processes related to producing goods differ widely between different industries. The biggest distinction is between the make-to-stock and make-to-order processes. As indicated above, the make-to-stock process is typically used for commodities, whereas the make-to-order process is used for highly customizable goods or big-ticket items (such as aircraft or highway bridges). Many beverage companies, for instance, use a make-to-stock approach, involving production planning, manufacturing, and quality control. In contrast, an aerospace company has to start with planning the project and ordering subassemblies or raw materials with long lead times before planning and executing the production for each specific project and finally checking quality and shipping the product. Many of the activities associated with the production process are supported by the operations management component of an ERP (see Figure 7.21).

Other Business Processes In addition to these business processes, ERP systems typically enable a variety of other generic as well as industry-specific business processes. Any business needs to manage its workforce, including managing the hiring processes, scheduling the workforce, recording time and attendance, processing payroll, managing benefits, and so on. All these processes are supported by the human resources management component of an ERP. Similarly, the financial management component supports generic processes, such as financial and managerial accounting, corporate governance, and the like. Industry-specific process and the modules supporting these can vary widely. For example, the business of an aircraft manufacturer consists to a large

FIGURE 7.21

An ERP system can support all aspects of the production process.

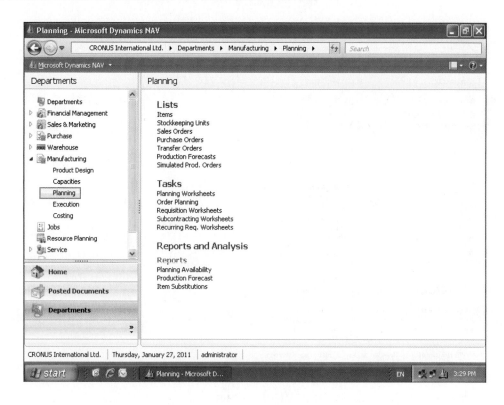

extent of aftermarket support; a retail chain, in contrast, needs modules supporting retail space planning and price and markdown management; a commercial real estate company needs modules for managing assets, leases, and common spaces; and a large part of an airline's operations is related to maintenance, repair, overhaul, flight operations, catering, and customer care.

ERP Installation

Previously, we discussed how organizations can benefit from the integration of stand-alone systems; further, you learned how business processes can differ between industries. Thus, any organization considering the implementation of an ERP system has to carefully evaluate the different options available not only in terms of the overall systems offered by different vendors but also in terms of the industry-specific solutions offered by the software vendors. An evaluation should entail the assessment of how far the different modules can support existing business processes, which modules may have to be added, and the extent to which existing business processes have to be modified in order to fit the modules offered by the ERP system.

An activity that is widely underestimated, however, is the *configuration* of the ERP systems. Whereas customization involves the programming of company-specific modules or changing how business processes are implemented within the system and is often discouraged, configuration is an activity to be performed during any ERP implementation. Specifically, the system must be configured to reflect the way an organization does business and the associated business rules. As one of the most important parts of an ERP system is the underlying company-wide database, setting up the database is key to a successful ERP implementation, and organizations have to make countless decisions on how to configure hundreds or thousands of database tables to fit the business's needs. Similarly, organizations have to make thousands of decisions related to the different business processes. For example, what should be the format of the unique identifier for a customer, when will a bill be considered overdue, what is considered the "standard" method of shipping, and so on? To make all these decisions, a good understanding of the way the company does its business is needed. Hence, many organizations hire experienced business analysts or outside consultants to assist with these configuration tasks.

ERP Limitations

While ERP helps companies to integrate systems across the organization, it falls short in communicating across organizational boundaries (Larson & Rogers, 1998). Since ERP core components are designed primarily to service internal business activities, they tend not to be well suited

WHEN THINGS GO WRONG

Air Traffic Control Systems

On average, there are over 38,000 commercial airline flights in the United States *per day*. That's a lot of information to track and organize. The Federal Aviation Administration (FAA) is the government organization that is responsible for keeping planes flying safely around the country. The FAA operates continuously to keep track of where planes are sitting, what their intended flight plans are, and where they are in the sky, using a computer system known as NADIN, the National Airspace Data Interchange Network. NADIN is linked across the United States and to international destinations and it transmits more than 1 million messages a day, including submitted flight plans, weather data, and advisory notices.

On the morning of November 19, 2009, just days before the start of the most heavily traveled time of Thanksgiving, the NADIN system went down. Immediately, hundreds of commercial flights were grounded because commercial airlines cannot take off without first filing a flight plan. As the NADIN outage continued to linger, flights started being delayed or outright canceled on the East Coast. This had the cascading effect of flight delays and cancellations all across the United States. If a commercial flight was going to move, pilots and airline employees had to submit the flight plans manually to the FAA through e-mail or via fax. Fortunately, the NADIN outage lasted for only four hours, and flight operations were restored to normal before the crushing Thanksgiving traffic arrived, but the outage caused stranded passengers lots of delay and frustration.

The problem was eventually tracked to one of NADIN's two main nodes in Salt Lake City, Utah. One of the system's communication routers encountered a software error that caused it to go offline. Unfortunately, the router's default restart function didn't activate, causing the entire Salt Lake City node to go down. For unknown reasons, the other key node of the NADIN system in Atlanta, Georgia, also went offline. Once both sites were down, NADIN was off-line, effectively halting air traffic across the United States.

As we rely more on automated and integrated systems to carry out crucial activities, ensuring their reliability becomes a key consideration. Fortunately, this mishap only kept planes from flying. If the failure had come in the radar and communications network that the FAA uses to direct planes, the results could have been disastrous.

Based on:

Anonymous. (n.d.). Air traffic control: By the numbers. Retrieved May 7, 2010, from http://www.natca.org/mediacenter/bythenumbers.msp#1.

Anonymous. (2005, March 14). FAA modernizing National Airspace Data Interchange Network with Stratus ftServer Systems. Retrieved May 7, 2010, from http://www.stratus.com/news/2005/20050314a.htm.

Claburn, T. (2009, November 19). FAA resolves flight plan system failure. *InformationWeek*. Retrieved May 8, 2010, from http://www.informationweek.com/news/government/security/showArticle.jhtml?articleID=221900332.

Preimesberger, C. (2009, November 19). FAA flight-plan system crashes again, delays hundreds of flights. *eWeek*. Retrieved May 8, 2010, from http://www.eweek.com/c/a/Data-Storage/FAAs-FlightPlan-System-Crashes-Again-Delays-Hundreds-of-US-Flights-199160.

Preimesberger, C. (2009, November 23). FAA issues post-mortem report on flight-plan systems failure. *eWeek*. Retrieved May 8, 2010, from http://www.eweek.com/c/a/Enterprise-Networking/FAA-Issues-Post-Mortem-Report-on-FlightPlan-System-Failure-260111.

for managing value system activities. Companies wanting to integrate their value chains with the business activities of their suppliers, business partners, and customers typically choose to implement systems other than (or in addition to) ERP to manage the upstream and/or downstream flows of information. These types of applications, designed to coordinate activities outside organizational boundaries, are discussed in Chapter 8.

The Formula for Enterprise System Success

To summarize, the main objective of enterprise systems is to create competitive advantage by streamlining business activities within and outside a company. However, many implementations turn out to be more costly and time consuming than originally envisioned. It is not uncommon to have projects that run over budget, meaning that identifying common problems and devising methods for dealing with these issues can prove invaluable to management. Surveys suggest that 40 to 60 percent of companies that undertake enterprise system implementations do not fully realize the results that they had hoped for (Langenwalter, 2000). On the other hand, more than 85 percent of IT executives of companies who have installed ERP systems regard the system as core to their business and indicated that they could not live without it, as shown by a survey of almost 400 IT executives (Wailgum, 2008). Companies that have successfully installed enterprise systems are found to follow a basic set of recommendations related to enterprise system implementations. Although the following list is not meant to be comprehensive, these recommendations will provide an understanding of some of the challenges involved in implementing enterprise systems:

Recommendation 1. Secure executive sponsorship
Recommendation 2. Get help from outside experts
Recommendation 3. Thoroughly train users
Recommendation 4. Take a multidisciplinary approach to implementations
Recommendation 5. Look beyond ERP

Secure Executive Sponsorship

The primary reason that enterprise system implementations fail is believed to be a direct result of lack of top-level management support. Although executives do not necessarily need to make decisions concerning the enterprise system, it is critical that they buy into the decisions made by project managers. Many problems can arise if projects fail to grab the attention of top-level management. In most companies, executives have the ultimate authority regarding the availability and distribution of resources within the organization. If executives do not understand the importance of the enterprise system, this will likely result in delays or stoppages because the necessary resources may not be available when they are needed.

A second problem that may arise deals with top-level management's ability to authorize changes in the way the company does business. When business processes need to be changed to incorporate best practices, these modifications need to be completed. Otherwise, the company will have a piece of software on its hands that does not fit the way people accomplish their business tasks. Lack of executive sponsorship can also have a trickle-down effect within the organization. If users and midlevel management perceive the enterprise system to be unimportant, they are not likely to view it as a priority. Enterprise systems require a concentrated effort, and executive sponsorship can propel or stifle the implementation. Executive management can obliterate any obstacles that arise.

Get Help from Outside Experts

Enterprise systems are complex. Even the most talented IS departments can struggle in coming to grips with ERP, customer relationship management, and supply chain management applications. Most vendors have trained project managers and experienced consultants to assist companies with installing enterprise systems. Using consultants tends to move companies through the implementation more quickly and tends to help companies train their personnel on the applications more effectively. However, companies should not rely too heavily on consultants and should plan for the consultants leaving once the implementation is complete. When consultants are physically present, company personnel tend to rely on them for assistance. Once the application goes live and the consultants are no longer there, users have to do the job themselves. A key focus should therefore be facilitating user learning.

Thoroughly Train Users

Training is often the most overlooked, underestimated, and poorly budgeted expense involved in planning enterprise system implementations. Enterprise systems are much more complicated to learn than stand-alone systems. Learning a single application requires users to become accustomed to a new software interface, but enterprise system users regularly need to learn a new set of business processes as well. Once enterprise systems go live, many companies experience a dramatic drop-off in productivity. This issue can potentially lead to heightened levels of dissatisfaction among users, as they prefer to accomplish their business activities in a familiar manner rather than doing things the new way. By training users before the system goes live and giving them sufficient opportunities to learn the new system, a company can allay fears and mitigate potential productivity issues.

Take a Multidisciplinary Approach to Implementations

Enterprise systems affect the entire organization; thus, companies should include personnel from different levels and departments in the implementation project (Kumar & Crook, 1999). In customer relationship management and supply chain management environments in which other organizations are participating in the implementation, it is critical to enlist the support of personnel in their organizations as well. During implementation, project managers need to include personnel from midlevel management, the IS department, external consultants, and, most important, end users.

Failing to include the appropriate people in the day-to-day activities of the project can prove problematic in many areas. From a needs-analysis standpoint, it is critical that all the business requirements be sufficiently captured before selection of an enterprise solution. Since end users are involved in every aspect of daily business activities, their insights can be invaluable. For instance, an end user might make salient a feature that no one on the project team had thought of. Having an application that does not meet all of the business's requirements can result in poorly fitting software or customizations. Another peril in leaving out key personnel is the threat of alienation. Departments and/or personnel that do not feel included may develop a sense of animosity toward the new system and view it in a negative light. In extreme cases, users will refuse to use the new application, resulting in conflicts and inefficiencies within the organization.

Evolving the ERP Architecture

As you can see, implementing ERP systems is a highly complex undertaking; although a successful implementation can have huge payoffs for an organization, some organizations fear losing the ability to quickly respond to changing business requirements, particularly since large ERP systems are difficult to install, maintain, and upgrade. A recent trend is to move away from such large, comprehensive systems to a **service-oriented architecture (SOA).** Using SOA, business processes are broken down into individual components (or **services**) that are designed to achieve the desired results for the service consumer (which can either be an application, another service, or a person). To illustrate this concept, think about the next oil change for your car. As you can't be expert in everything, it is probably more effective to have someone change the oil for you. You may take your car to the dealership, you may go to an independent garage or oil change service, or you may ask your friend to do it for you. In all cases, the desired service will be performed but at different levels of quality and cost.

By breaking down business processes into individual services, organizations can more swiftly react to changing business needs. For example, using an ERP approach, one application would handle all aspects of the customer order process; in contrast, using an SOA approach, multiple services (such as "check inventory" or "order supplies") would be orchestrated to handle the individual tasks associated with the order process and could be changed relatively easily if the business process changes. Web services, discussed in Chapter 5, "Enhancing Collaboration Using Web 2.0," are services that are invoked via a network and typically use standards such as XML. By using and reusing individual services as "building blocks," systems can be easily built and reconfigured as requirements change. To achieve these benefits, services have to follow three main principles:

1. *Reusability.* A service should be usable in many different applications.
2. *Interoperability.* A service should work with any other service.
3. *Componentization.* A service should be simple and modular.

Following these principles, multiple applications can invoke the same services. For example, both an organization's point-of-sale system and e-commerce Web site could invoke the service "process credit card," and the executive dashboard could invoke the services "display products," "display inventory," and "display sales" (see Figure 7.22). Using SOA can be very beneficial for an organization. For example, the Virgin Entertainment Group, which has 23 mega–record stores in North America and several more in Europe, implemented SOA to prevent employee theft and shrinkage in its stores. SOA was used to develop a real-time loss prevention system that could monitor point-of-sale activity, along with receiving systems. By breaking this complex business process into several small services, the theft prevention system could easily be integrated into the company's current enterprise system. The SOA approach was successful for Virgin, as losses and employee theft decreased 50 percent. Whereas an SOA approach appears to be appealing for many companies, it requires tremendous effort and expertise to plan the architecture and develop the services. Hence, while an SOA approach helps to increase flexibility, the integration of various services can be extremely complex and can be well beyond the means of small enterprises.

Recently, large ERP vendors such as Oracle and SAP introduced platforms enabling the transition to SOA. Such solutions allow incremental migration from an ERP system to SOA without having to immediately retire the ERP system. Further, these solutions allow the use of services from other systems or vendors, increasing an organization's flexibility.

FIGURE 7.22

Using SOA, multiple applications can invoke multiple services.

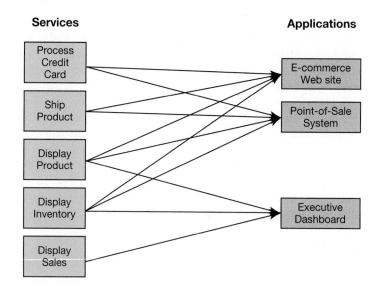

Although expansive enterprise system implementations, as well as SOA approaches, are often cumbersome and difficult, the potential payoff is huge. As a result, organizations are compelled to implement these systems. Further, given the popularity and necessity of integrating systems and processes on an organization-wide basis, you are likely to find yourself involved in the implementation and/or use of such a system. We are confident that after reading this chapter, you will be better able to understand and help with the development and use of such systems.

INDUSTRY ANALYSIS

The Automobile Industry

Recently, General Motors (GM) announced that its government bailout has been paid back in full to the U.S. and Canadian governments, five years ahead of original schedule. While reporting a $4.3 billion loss for the July–December 2009 time period, GM said it may turn a profit in 2010. Meanwhile, Chrysler reported a $197 million loss in the first quarter of 2010, far better than the $3.8 billion loss in the second half of 2009. It seems the "Big Three" automakers are making some progress toward recovery. Although most Americans think of the Big Three as "U.S. firms," all major automobile companies (both foreign and domestic) have global operations.

Auto industry experts have claimed for years that globalization—the flattening of the world—would result in a widespread consolidation of automakers. What is happening within the auto industry is indicative of globalization in general. A "flattened" world implies that the world is becoming more homogeneous. As the process continues, distinctions between national markets are fading and, for some products, may disappear entirely.

For instance, for decades manufacturers within the automobile industry have worked toward developing a "world car"—a basic car that with a few modifications can be sold all over the world. In the 1990s, three attempts were made to produce and market a world car: Honda's Accord, Ford's Mondeo/Contour, and GM's Cadillac Catera/Opel Omega. None of the models sold as well as hoped in North America, Europe, and Asia for several reasons:

- Consumers in different areas of the world have different tastes in automobiles. For example, small cab size has long been accepted in Europe, but American consumers prefer larger cabs.
- Europeans prefer steel construction over plastic, as in door panels, which are largely used in car manufacturing in the United States.
- Differences in infrastructure among countries lead to varying preferences in cars. Asians, for example, prefer smaller-sized cars that can maneuver well through narrow and crowded streets, while many Americans prefer sport-utility vehicles and pickups.
- The price of gasoline varies throughout the world. Europeans typically carefully consider fuel economy when buying a car, while, until recently because of sharp spikes

in gas prices, most Americans have not heavily weighed this criterion.

- Variations in regulations governing cars, such as emission standards, also vary with countries and affect car buyers' choices.

The development of a "world car" may yet be accomplished but probably not until cultural and economic conditions undergo even more globalization.

In the meantime, the automobile industry continues to move beyond geographic boundaries. Auto companies traditionally based in the United States are moving plants overseas, and foreign manufacturers are moving production facilities to the United States. The Japanese auto manufacturer Toyota operates production plants in many U.S. states, including Alabama, Texas, and West Virginia. The Ford Motor Company is based in the United States but operates satellite companies in Asia and Europe. A Chinese car manufacturer recently bought Volvo and planned to move production to China.

Another significant change in the auto industry involves sales channels. Traditionally, U.S. automakers maintain localized franchises that handle auto sales in a specific region. Now there are Internet franchises that have also created worldwide sales centers that did not previously exist.

Clearly, the global marketplace has changed the automobile industry profoundly by allowing the automakers to build global networks of suppliers (such as Bosch and Continental from Germany, Magna and Lear from the United States, or Yazaki from Japan) and selling to customers from all over the world. Although this has created new opportunities, the recent auto crisis has shown that in the age of Globalization 3.0, the success or failure of any major global firm has ripple effects far beyond its home country.

Questions

1. How is globalization changing in the auto industry?
2. Examine how cultural differences make it difficult to create a world car.

Based on:

Anonymous. (2010, April 20). Geely automobile picking sites for China-made Volvo. *TradingMarket*. Retrieved April 25, 2010, from http://www.tradingmarkets.com/news/stock-alert/volvy_geely-automobile-picking-sites-for-china-made-volvo-922498.html.

Anonymous. (2010, April 21). G.M. and Chrysler show progress after bankruptcy. *New York Times*. Retrieved April 25, 2010, from http://dealbook.blogs.nytimes.com/2010/04/21/automakers-show-progress-after-losses-in-bankruptcy.

Anonymous. (2010, April 21). Summary box: Chrysler posts 1st-quarter loss. *Bloomberg BusinessWeek*. Retrieved April 25, 2010, from http://www.businessweek.com/ap/financialnews/D9F7LPGG0.htm.

Chandler, C. (2000, May 22). Globalization: The automobile industry's quest for a "world car" strategy. Retrieved April 25, 2010, from http://globaledge.msu.edu/newsandviews/views/papers/globalization_automotive_industry_strategy.pdf.

Emmons, G. (2006, May 10). American auto's troubled road. *Working Knowledge*. Retrieved April 25, 2010, from http://hbswk.hbs.edu/item/5290.html.

Hyde, J. (2010, April 24). Obama hails auto industry turnaround in radio address. *Detroit Free Press*. Retrieved April 25, 2010, from http://www.freep.com/article/20100424/NEWS15/100424005/1320/Obama-hails-auto-industry-turnaround.

Langlois, S. (2010, April 21). GM announces full repayment of federal debt. *Market Watch*. Retrieved April 25, 2010, from http://www.marketwatch.com/story/gm-expected-to-announce-payback-of-fed-loans-2010-04-21.

Webster, S. (2006, July 2). Future of autos is global. *Detroit Free Press*. Retrieved July 25, 2010, from http://www.mema.org/publications/articledetail.php?articleId=3785.

Key Points Review

1. *Explain core business processes that are common in organizations.* Most organizations are organized around four distinct functional areas that are responsible for well-defined business functions: marketing and sales, supply chain management, accounting and finance, and human resources. These separate functional areas work together to execute core business processes. These core processes are order-to-cash, procure-to-pay, and make-to-stock/order. Order-to-cash refers to the various processes associated with selling a product or service to a customer. Procure-to-pay refers to the various processes associated with procuring goods from external vendors. The make-to-stock and make-to-order processes refer to those activities associated with producing goods to hold in inventory or after a customer order. Together, these core business processes enable the creation of supply chains that are involved in transforming raw materials into products sold to the end consumer. Supply chains are composed of both core and support activities. Core activities include inbound logistics (receiving), operations and manufacturing, outbound logistics (shipping), marketing and sales, and customer service. These activities may differ widely, depending on the unique requirements of the industry in which a company operates, although the basic concepts hold in most organizations. Support activities include administrative activities, infrastructure, human resources, technology development, and procurement. Companies connect their value chains with suppliers and customers, creating value systems such that information flows from one company's value chain to another company's value chain.

2. *Describe what enterprise systems are and how they have evolved.* Enterprise systems are information systems that span the entire organization and can be used to integrate business processes, activities, and information across all the functional areas of a firm. Enterprise systems can be either prepackaged software or custom-made applications. The implementation of enterprise systems often involves business process management, a systematic, structured improvement approach by all or part of an organization that critically examines, rethinks, and redesigns processes in order to achieve dramatic improvements in one or more performance measures, such as quality, cycle time, or cost. Enterprise systems evolved from legacy systems that supported distinct organizational activities by combining data and applications into a single comprehensive system.

3. *Describe ERP systems and how they help to improve internal business processes.* ERP systems evolved from "material requirements planning" systems during the 1990s and are, for the most part, used to support internal business processes. ERP systems allow information to be shared throughout the organization through the use of a large data warehouse, helping to streamline business processes and improve customer service. When selecting an ERP system, organizations must choose which modules to implement from a large menu of options—most organizations adopt only a subset of the available ERP components. ERP core components support the major internal activities of the organization for producing their products and services, while ERP extended components support the primary external activities of the organization for dealing with suppliers and customers.

4. *Understand and utilize the keys to successfully implementing enterprise systems.* Experience with enterprise system implementations suggests that there are some common problems that can be avoided and/or should be managed carefully. Organizations can avoid common implementation problems by (1) securing executive sponsorship, (2) getting necessary help from outside experts, (3) thoroughly training users, (4) taking a multidisciplinary approach to implementations, and (5) looking beyond ERP.

Key Terms

business process management (BPM) 296
business process reengineering (BPR) 296
core activities 284
custom software 294
customization 295
downstream information flow 288
enterprise resource planning (ERP) 297
enterprise system 290

enterprise-wide information system 290
ERP core components 300
ERP extended components 301
externally focused system 291
internally focused system 291
interorganizational system (IOS) 291
legacy system 289
make-to-order process 282
make-to-stock process 282
module 294

order-to-cash process 281
packaged software 294
procure-to-pay process 282
service 307
service-oriented architecture (SOA) 307
stand-alone application 288
support activities 286
upstream information flow 288
value system 287
vanilla version 295

Review Questions

1. What are core business processes?
2. Describe and contrast order-to-cash, procure-to-pay, make-to-stock, and make-to-order business processes.
3. What are the core and support activities of a value chain?
4. Give an example of upstream and downstream information flows in a value system
5. Describe what enterprise systems are and how they have evolved.

6. Contrast internally and externally focused systems.
7. Compare and contrast customized and packaged software as well as vanilla versions versus best practices–based software.
8. What are the core components of an ERP system?
9. What are the keys to successfully implementing an ERP system?

Self-Study Questions

1. _____ are information systems that allow companies to integrate information and support operations on a company-wide basis.
   A. Customer relationship management systems
   B. Enterprise systems
   C. Wide area networks
   D. Interorganizational systems

2. Which of the following is a core activity according to the value chain model?
   A. firm infrastructure
   B. customer service
   C. human resources
   D. procurement

3. According to the value chain model, which of the following is a support activity?
   A. technology development
   B. marketing and sales
   C. inbound logistics
   D. operations and manufacturing

4. All of the following are true about legacy systems except _____.
   A. they are stand-alone systems
   B. they are older software systems
   C. they are ERP systems
   D. they may be difficult to integrate into other systems

5. The processes associated with obtaining goods from external vendors are referred to as _____.
   A. make-to-order processes
   B. make-to-stock processes
   C. procure-to-pay processes
   D. order-to-cash processes

6. The processes associated with selling a product or service are referred to as _____.
   A. make-to-order processes
   B. make-to-stock processes
   C. procure-to-pay processes
   D. order-to-cash processes

7. Which processes are most often associated with pull-based manufacturing of products?
   A. make-to-order processes
   B. make-to-stock processes
   C. procure-to-pay processes
   D. order-to-cash processes

8. Information systems that focus on supporting functional areas, business processes, and decision making within an organization are referred to as _____.
   A. legacy systems
   B. enterprise-wide information systems
   C. interoganizational systems
   D. internally focused systems

9. An enterprise system that has not been customized is commonly referred to as _____.
   A. a vanilla version
   B. a root version
   C. a core version
   D. none of the above

10. _____ is a systematic, structured improvement approach by all or part of an organization that critically examines, rethinks, and redesigns processes in order to achieve dramatic improvements in one or more performance measures, such as quality, cycle time, or cost.
    A. Systems analysis
    B. Business process management
    C. Customer relationship management
    D. Total quality management

Answers are on page 313.

Problems and Exercises

1. Match the following terms with the appropriate definitions:
   i. Enterprise systems
   ii. Legacy systems
   iii. Value system
   iv. ERP extended components
   v. Stand-alone application
   vi. Vanilla version
   vii. Make-to-stock process
   viii. Business process management
   ix. Procure-to-pay process
   x. Internally focused systems

   a. Components that support the primary *external* activities of the organization for dealing with suppliers and customers
   b. Systems that focus on the specific needs of individual departments
   c. Goods are produced based on forecasted demand
   d. Older systems that are not designed to communicate with other applications beyond departmental boundaries
   e. Information systems that allow companies to integrate information on a company-wide basis
   f. The features and modules that a packaged software system comes with out of the box
   g. The processes involved with acquiring goods from suppliers
   h. A systematic, structured improvement approach by all or part of an organization whereby people critically examine, rethink, and redesign business processes in order to achieve dramatic improvements in one or more performance measures, such as quality, cycle time, or cost
   i. Information systems that support functional area, business processes, and decision making with an organization
   j. A collection of interlocking company value chains

2. Find an organization that you are familiar with and determine how many software applications it is utilizing concurrently. Is the company's information system cohesive, or does it need updating and streamlining?

3. What part does training users in an ERP system play, and how important is it in job satisfaction? What productivity problems can result from an ERP implementation?

4. What are the payoffs from taking a multidisciplinary approach to an ERP implementation? What departments are affected, and what is the typical time frame? Research an organization that has recently implemented an ERP system. What could the company have done better, and what did it do right?

5. Using Figure 7.6 as a guide, develop a supply chain diagram for some other product.

6. Based on your own experiences with applications, have you used customized or off-the-shelf applications? What is the difference, and how good was the system documentation?

7. Search the Web for the phrase "best practices," and you will find numerous sites that summarize the best practices for a variety of industries and professions. Choose one and summarize these best practices into a one-page report.

8. Examine and contrast the differences between packaged and custom software. When is one approach better or worse than the other?

9. Search the Web for recent articles on business process management and related approaches (e.g., business process reengineering) for improving organizations. What is the current state of the art for these approaches? To what extent are these "headlines" about IS implementations, especially regarding enterprise systems?

10. Search the Web for recent stories about the use of SOA. To what extent does it appear that SOA will be replacing ERP systems?

Application Exercises

 Note: The existing data files referenced in these exercises are available on the Student Companion Web site: **www.pearsonhighered.com/valacich**.

 Spreadsheet Application:
Choosing an ERP System at Campus Travel

Campus Travel is interested in integrating its business processes to streamline processes such as purchasing, sales, human resource management, and customer relationship management. Because of your success in implementing the e-commerce infrastructure, the general manager asks you for advice on what to do to streamline operations at Campus Travel. Use the data provided in the file ERPSystems.csv to make a recommendation about which ERP system to purchase. The file includes ratings of the different modules of the systems and the weights assigned to these ratings. You are asked to do the following:

1. Determine the product with the highest overall rating (Hint: Use the SUMPRODUCT formula to multiply each vendor's scores with the respective weights and add the weighted scores).

2. Prepare the necessary graphs to compare the products on the different dimensions and the overall score.

3. Be sure to professionally format the graphs before printing them out.

 Database Application:
Creating Forms at Campus Travel

After helping Campus Travel to a good start with its databases, you have decided that it should enter data using forms rather than doing it from tables. From your experience, you know that employees have an easier time being able to browse, modify, and add records from a form view. As this can be implemented using your existing database, you decide to set up a form. You can accomplish this by doing the following:

1. Open the employees' database (employeeData.mdb).

2. Select the employee table in the database window.

3. Create a form using the table (Hint: This can be done by selecting "More Forms >> Form Wizard" under "Forms" in the "Create" tab).

4. Save the form as "employees."

Team Work Exercise: Evaluating ERP Systems

Work in a small group with classmates and use a search engine such as Google to search the Web for sites with information on ERP systems. What types of Web sites are you finding? Choose a particular software package related to ERP and split up your group to research the company's site as well as related articles on the system at an online magazine such as *InformationWeek* or *Computerworld*. Get back together with your group and discuss your findings. How is the system portrayed by the company/vendors and by the magazines? Does the product seem to deliver what the company promises? Prepare a brief presentation of your findings.

Answers to the Self-Study Questions

1. B, p. 290
2. B, p. 284
3. A, p. 286
4. C, p. 289
5. C, p. 282
6. D, p. 281
7. A, p. 282
8. D, p. 291
9. A, p. 295
10. B, p. 296

Case 1

Software as a Service: ERP by the Hour

As you know by now, an organization's IT infrastructure is not simple to construct or maintain but is a complex infrastructure of servers and databases useful for managing large amounts of information. Although corporations can ask IT personnel to build an infrastructure to support an organization's goals, building such infrastructure generally proves to be time consuming and expensive. Alternatively, the IT department can design from scratch or purchase off-the-shelf software to meet the organization's data processing needs.

However, a new model of IT infrastructure and software has appeared and is rapidly changing the way many organizations do business. Software as a service, or SaaS, is a way for organizations to use cloud-based Internet services to accomplish the goals that traditional IT infrastructure and software models have in the past. Utilizing SaaS, organizations now have the opportunity to downsize their infrastructure, save money on software implementation, and move to a computing-by-the-hour frame of mind.

SaaS allows software application vendors to deploy their products over the Internet through Web-based services. SaaS customers pay to use applications on demand, giving them the freedom to access a software service only when needed. Applications and software are developed, hosted, and operated by SaaS vendors, although customers can host the software on their own hardware if they so choose. Once customers finish using the software, their "license" expires, and they no longer have to carry the cost of the software. If a future need for the software arises, the customer simply orders it again to have access. SaaS products can be licensed for single or multiple users within the organization, making them flexible and scalable.

Using the SaaS model has several advantages. Through SaaS applications, organizations can move their data storage into the cloud, reducing the cost of buying storage and diminishing the likelihood of catastrophic data loss. Software on demand allows for less resource expenditure on long-term software licensing because an organization can get what they need when they need it. Infrastructure operation costs are shifted to the SaaS vendor, freeing up IT resources for use in other areas. Implementation of SaaS products is also quick, increasing an organization's agility in responding to new challenges as they occur. In addition, it is in the vendor's financial interest to keep the services they provide running at peak performance, or they risk losing customers to other vendors. This incentive ensures that the IT vendor's infrastructure is regularly updated and modernized to minimize customer downtime. SaaS utilization also allows organizations to become more productive outside the physical confines of their buildings. Since SaaS services are in the cloud, employees can access services in remote offices, on the road, from their smart phone, or from their home PC.

One of the main disadvantages to SaaS is that customers must give up some autonomy over their applications and data. Not having the software in-house means organizations must use it "as is." This point leads to another issue in that some organizations require specialized software solutions and are used to customizing software in-house to meet their needs. Although some SaaS vendors are beginning to offer customizable solutions, the problem is still a roadblock for some. Computing off-site also means that security may be at issue. Organizational operations and data are effectively running on someone else's computer.

Security concerns are another roadblock that organizations must overcome in order to use SaaS products. It is impossible for some types of organizations to keep their data—and their secrets—in the cloud.

These disadvantages aside, organizations are reaping the benefits of SaaS, utilizing them for human resources activity, e-mail services, collaboration efforts, storage solutions, and financial tasks, such as billing, invoicing, and timekeeping. In addition to more general purpose applications, many organizations are deploying ERP capabilities via SaaS vendors. And the growth of the SaaS industry doesn't appear to be slowing. In fact, a recent study by Gartner found that by 2013, SaaS revenues should reach $16 billion.

Companies like Google, Amazon, and Microsoft have become well-known SaaS vendors offering a range of services to organizations. For instance, Google has a variety of cloud-based services available across their different platforms, including Internet shared-document management, communication services, cloud-based e-mail, calendaring, photo and video sharing, Web and intranet page management, and data storage services, just to name a few.

Likewise, while Amazon.com is known as a top e-commerce destination to most consumers, they also have SaaS solutions that many orgainizations employ. One of their offerings is SimpleDB—a service for organizations that can't afford in-house databases or simply want the convenience of letting a hosted service do most of the work. Database developers sign up for the service, which operates in conjunction with Amazon's Storage Service (S3), and pay only for time and storage space used. Amazon S3 customers are provided with a Web interface that allows them to store and retrieve any amount of data, any time they want, from anywhere there is an Internet connection available. S3 has redundant storage across several Amazon sites, ensuring data security, availability, and integrity.

Another household name in the computing industry, Microsoft, has also followed suit, offering their own cloud-based SaaS solution called Microsoft Azure. Although Microsoft came into the SaaS market later than others, they have the experience and resources to quickly become a formidable competitor to other already established vendors. Azure offers its customers a similar range of services as other SaaS vendors, from application data storage and hosted services to a framework for interconnecting resources and services. This linking framework, known as the AppFabric, allows developers to create "cloud-aware" services and applications for use within their organizations. Azure, like many other services, has a pay-as-you-go pricing structure. Alternatively, customers can take the "commitment" option and pay for a six-month obligation of use of service. The commitment option makes the customer eligible for discount pricing for purchasing six months of service.

Because of the issues associated with enterprise systems, ERP vendors are increasingly offering their software as a service as well. For example, SAP offers SAP Business ByDesign, an integrated on-demand ERP solution for small and medium-sized enterprises. Similarly, Microsoft offers its Dynamics customer relationship management system as as service, and Oracle offers the subscription-based Oracle On Demand customer relationship management solution.

Computing-by-the-hour has now become a viable and legitimate business model for many organizations. As more continue to adopt SaaS services as a way of carrying on their day-to-day activities, vendors will continue to upgrade and expand the available technologies for use. The question of whether organizations will adopt SaaS services has, for the most part, been answered. The question has now become how much of their business they will put in the cloud.

Questions

1. Would you trust an external provider with your organization's data? Why or why not? What would be needed to raise your trust in the reliability, security, and privacy of the data?
2. What are the potential drawbacks of using a relatively simple in-house database with limited capabilities versus a more robust, SaaS database solution? Do the benefits outweigh these limitations? Why or why not?
3. Are there any types of applications that should only be purchased rather than obtained through a SaaS relationship? If so, why or why not?

Based on:

Anonymous. (n.d.). Amazon SimpleDB—Limited beta. Retrieved July 27, 2010, from http://www.amazon.com/gp/browse.html?node=342335011.

Anonymous. (n.d.). What is SAAS? Retrieved April 18, 2010, from http://www.whatissaas.net.

Anonymous. (2009, July 1). Amazon's cloud: A SaaS solution. Retrieved April 18, 2010, from http://www.istockanalyst.com/article/viewarticle/articleid/3325300.

Biddick, M. (2010, January 16). Why you need a SaaS strategy. *InformationWeek*. Retrieved April 18, 2010, from http://www.informationweek.com/news/services/saas/showArticle.jhtml?articleID=222301002.

Foley, J. (2010, January 28). Microsoft to launch pennies-per-hour Azure cloud service Monday. *InformationWeek*. Retrieved April 18, 2010, from http://www.informationweek.com/news/services/saas/showArticle.jhtml?articleID=222600247.

Levine, B. (2007, December 17). Amazon launching database-as-a-service. *Newsfactor.com*. Retrieved July 29, 2010, from http://www.newsfactor.com/story.xhtml?story_id=110003L9MFM8.

Olsen, G. (2010, March 18). Microsoft Azure's place in the cloud. Retrieved April 18, 2010, from http://searchwinit.techtarget.com/tip/0,289483,sid1_gci1488526,00.html.

Software as a service. (2010, July 23). In *Wikipedia, the free encyclopedia*. Retrieved July 27, 2010, from http://en.wikipedia.org/w/index.php?title=Software_as_a_service&oldid=375069917.

Case 2

ERP Systems: Do They Satisfy?

ERP systems are the backbone of many business ventures and are found in organizations of all shapes and sizes around the globe. They are powerful systems designed to unify and economize operations across an organization's scope of operations. But these powerful systems also have drawbacks, and the mere utterance of the acronym ERP is enough to send some IT professionals reaching for the aspirin bottle.

ERPs systems sprang from manufacturers' requirements-planning software that was used to control inventory, manage manufacturing and delivery schedules, and handle purchasing activities. As these software platforms matured, they began appearing in organizations other than manufacturing. Modern ERP systems are designed to be an integrated computer system that stretches across every aspect of an organization, allowing users to access and build on information to meet task requirements and goals.

ERP systems are made up of modules that work together from a centralized database to form the enterprise system. With an ERP in place, each department within the organization will have a specialized module that allows them to accomplish their departmental tasks. Accounting, for instance, will have a module specialized with accounting software that handles all organization financial tasks. Since the modules are interconnected across the system through the central database, employees can call up information they need from outside their immediate department. If a shipping manager needs to know how many workers to schedule, he or she can call up information from the manufacturing module to see how many widgets are projected to come off the line and will need to be shipped that week. The scalability (the ability to handle organizational growth) of the module system is a key strength of ERP systems. If an organization adds new departments, new modules can be added to the ERP system to meet the needs of the expanded operation without interrupting the existing modules.

Although these powerful systems have the ability to aggregate huge amounts of data and manage organizational resources and activities, many users are unsatisfied with their ERP's performance and return on investment (ROI). This is partially due to the fact that organizations don't always consider the total cost of an ERP implementation. Buying new computer hardware and infrastructure upgrades to run the ERP system is not the only expense associated with project execution. Since the technology of ERP systems is either foreign or too complex for most "in-house" experts to handle, a consulting firm is usually hired to manage the implementation. Consultants help the organization map out how the new system will interact with business processes, customize the ERP software to meet task requirements, and train users on how to work with the new systems—all with a hefty price tag. Unfortunately for many organizations, the implementation stage can last much longer than expected, driving consultant fees and dissatisfaction with the project ever higher. Add to these costs software licensing fees and the

possibility of vendor "lock-in" on a range of services within the ERP system, and it becomes clear that organizations should consider a wide range of costs before undertaking an ERP project. According to a 2010 study by the Panorama Consulting Group, 57 percent of ERP implementations take longer than expected, and 54 percent exceed their budget.

Another cost that must be considered may not always have a price tag associated with it: that of organizational change. New ERP processes will likely involve members of the organization in learning how to do their daily tasks differently than they're used to doing them. ERP systems may also consolidate or eliminate the need for certain activities to be accomplished, leaving some to feel that their job or position is threatened. Additionally, since one of the ERP's main functions is to allow users across the organization to share data, it is more difficult to control the flow of information. For example, before an ERP implementation, departments can disseminate data as they see fit or even not at all. But after the ERP is in place, the power of the gatekeeper is diminished as data becomes more freely available to other users. Having open access to information can lead employees to having a sense of being watched or feeling that their positions are

threatened. Issues like these can make organizational change difficult and sometimes painful. Resistance to change is an expected human response, and ERP implementations typically do not escape this reality.

The Panorama study also found that more than half the organizations that implement ERP systems get less than 30 percent of the business benefit they expected after project completion. This statistic is not completely surprising, however. With ERP implementations historically running over on budget and time, organizations are often just happy to have the flow of organization money to consultants stopped and the project completed. Little thought is given as to whether the new system is an improvement over the old or if it is giving them as much return on investment as it can.

Traditional ERP implementations are challenging for organizations, so much so that many projects have outright failed, resulting in millions of dollars lost, organizational cohesiveness destroyed, and employees quitting. Today, tales of troublesome implementation projects are filling the pages of tech-industry magazines, and many others are having less than stellar track records.

Questions

1. What are the advantages to using an ERP system? What are the disadvantages?
2. If you were the chief information officer of a large company, would you recommend implementing an ERP system? Why or why not?
3. How can a small business avoid experiencing "just another ERP failure"?

Based on:

Enterprise resource planning. (2010, July 20). In *Wikipedia, the free encyclopedia*. Retrieved 03:02, July 25, 2010, from http://en.wikipedia.org/w/index.php?title=Enterprise_resource_planning&oldid=374480544.

Eresource. (2010). Why some people think ROI on ERP is low? *Eresource.com*. Retrieved April 12, 2010, from http://www.eresourceerp.com/Why-some-people-think-ROI-on-ERP-is-low.html.

Kanaracus, C. (2010, March 17). Widespread discontent persists with ERP projects. *PC World*. Retrieved April 12, 2010, from http://www.pcworld.com/businesscenter/article/191750/widespread_discontent_persists_with_erp_projects.html.

Kanaracus, C. (2010, March 31). Lawson puts its ERP on Amazon's cloud. *BusinessWeek*. Retrieved April 12, 2010, from http://www.businessweek.com/idg/2010-03-31/lawson-puts-its-erp-on-amazon-s-cloud.html.

Krigsman, M. (2010, February 3). ERP failure: New research and statistics. *Enterprise Irregulars*. Retrieved April 12, 2010, from http://www.enterpriseirregulars.com/11871/erp-failure-new-research-and-statistics.

Sootkoos, R. (2010, January 28). ERP and cloud computing trends. *ERP.com*. Retrieved April 12, 2010, from http://www.erp.com/section-layout/51-erp-success-stories/5674-erp-and-cloud-computing-trends.html.

eight

Improving Supply Chains and Strengthening Customer Relationships Using Enterprise Information Systems

After reading this chapter, you will be able to do the following:

1 Describe supply chain management systems and how they help to improve interorganizational business processes.

2 Describe customer relationship management systems and how they help to improve the activities involved in promoting and selling products to the customers as well as providing customer service and nourishing long-term relationships.

Preview

This chapter extends the prior discussion regarding how companies are deploying enterprise-wide information systems to build and strengthen organizational partnerships. Enterprise systems help integrate various business activities, streamline and better manage interactions with customers, and coordinate better with suppliers in order to meet changing customer demands more efficiently and effectively. In this chapter, two additional powerful business systems are introduced: supply chain management and customer relationship management. When added to enterprise resource planning (ERP) systems, both of these systems tie the customer to the supply chain that includes the manufacturer and suppliers all the way back to the raw materials that ultimately become the product no matter where in the world they originate.

More and more companies find that they need systems that span their entire organization to tie everything together. As a result, an understanding of supply chain management and customer relationship management is critical to succeed in today's competitive and ever-changing digital world.

Managing in the Digital World: Supply Chain Havoc

For centuries, people have been fascinated by geothermal activity, such as spewing geysers or active volcanoes. Every year, millions of tourists travel to Hawaii's Volcanoes National Park, Mount St. Helens, Yellowstone National Park, Spain's Canary Islands, Italy's Mount Etna, Iceland, or similar places. In March 2010, initial news reports of a volcano erupting in Iceland drew thousands of thrill seekers trying to get a good look at the volcano. However, the excitement dissipated when, within days of the initial minor eruptions, a major blast from the volcano named Eyjafjallajokull took place, melting parts of a glacier and forcing people to flee from flooding. The eruption also sent tons of volcanic ash into the jet stream, shutting down flights into and out of northern Europe for days (see Figure 8.1). As these flights were canceled, it was not only tourists and business travelers who were stranded or inconvenienced; the supply chains of numerous companies and industries were disrupted throughout the world as well. A supply chain is the global network of retailers, distributors, transporters, storage facilities, and suppliers that participate in the production, sale, and delivery of a particular product.

Many global organizations source various raw materials and components from countries where they can be obtained or produced at the best quality or lowest cost. For instance, one major source for European supplies of flowers and vegetables is Kenya, whereas North American wholesalers import tulips, peonies, and daffodils from the Netherlands. As most of the northern European airspace was closed, flowers and vegetables worth millions of dollars withered in African warehouses, waiting to be shipped to Europe. At the same time, the flower wholesale market in New York was awaiting shipments from the Netherlands that would never arrive, leaving tulips, peonies, daffodils, and hundreds of other varieties literally dying on the vine. Similarly, the distribution of unique but highly perishable goods, such as Italian mozzarella cheese and fresh fruits, was also disrupted, costing producers about $14 million per day. However, it was not only the supply chain for perishable goods that was disrupted. For example, time-critical consumer goods are flown from Southeast Asian countries to Europe. Similarly, lacking critical parts, auto giant

BMW had to halt production in several German plants, and parts that had already been produced in Germany could not be flown to its plant in South Carolina, causing work disruptions and delays at BMW's U.S. plant. Likewise, diamond cutters in India

iStockphoto.com

FIGURE 8.1

A major blast from the Icelandic volcano Eyjafjallajokull sent tons of volcanic ash into the jet stream.

could not ship gems to trading dealers in Belgium, and logistics companies such as UPS and DHL had to divert planes, cancel flights, and organize ground transport for shipments throughout Europe. Clearly, the disruptions of freight movements to and from Europe had global impacts on the supply chain of countless organizations.

While many organizations have designed highly efficient supply chains, they are also extremely fragile. A common strategy today for many organizations is to keep inventory levels to a minimum, relying on just-in-time delivery of materials in order to control costs. When disruptions in the supply chain occur because of weather, labor issues, or natural disasters, the operations of the business can be devastated and have ripple effects throughout the world.

Given the tremendous global impact of Iceland's volcano, many organizations are fine-tuning their supply chain strategy, looking at greater flexibility on sourcing (e.g., is having a single supplier of a critical component a sound business strategy?) and whether exclusive offshore production leaves a company too vulnerable to international transportation disruptions (e.g., should production be spread over multiple locations to minimize risk?). Needless to say, given the impact of Eyjafjallajokull on countless supply chains, organizations are fine-tuning their supply chain strategies, optimizing for both cost and risk considerations.

After reading this chapter, you will be able to answer the following:

1. How can organizations better manage their global supply chain?
2. What are the trade-offs when developing a supply chain strategy?
3. How are emerging technologies such as radio frequency identification improving the way in which organizations manage their supply chains?

Based on:

Anonymous. (2010, April 20). Flugverbote treffen Autoindustrie mit voller Wucht. *Die Welt*. Retrieved August 5, 2010, from http://www.welt.de/wirtschaft/article7258797/Flugverbote-treffen-Autoindustrie-mit-voller-Wucht.html.

Anonymous. (2010, June 10). Supply chain: What can supply chain executives learn from the Iceland volcano? Retrieved August 3, 2010, from http://www.scmr.com/article/supply_chain_what_can_supply_chain_executives_learn_from_the_iceland_volcan.

Bell, R. (2010, April 20). Volcano disrupts BMW supply chain to S.C. Retrieved August 3, 2010, from http://www.thestate.com/2010/04/20/1251405/volcano-disrupts-bmw-supply-chain.html.

Cooke, J. A. (2010, April 22). Commentary: Volcano's effects prove importance of managing supply chain risk. Retrieved August 3, 2010, from http://www.dcvelocity.com/print/article/20100422managing_supply_chain_risk.

Nicolai, B., & Siegmud, H. (2010, April 18). Vulkan macht iPhones und Papaya zur Mangelware. *Die Welt*. Retrieved August 5, 2010, from http://www.welt.de/wirtschaft/article7237211/Vulkan-macht-iPhones-und-Papaya-zur-Mangelware.html.

Sowinski, L. L. (2010, April 24). Iceland's volcano does a number on global supply chains. Retrieved August 3, 2010, from http://www.worldtrademag.com/Articles/Blog/BNP_GUID_9-5-2006_A_10000000000000809386.

Supply Chain Management

In the previous chapter, we discussed the need to share internal data in order to streamline business processes, improving coordination within the organization to improve efficiency and effectiveness. Now we turn our attention to collaborating with partners along the supply chain. Getting the raw materials and components that a company uses in its daily operations is an important key to business success. When deliveries from suppliers are accurate and timely, companies can convert them to finished products more efficiently. Coordinating this effort with suppliers has become a central part of many companies' overall business strategy, as it can help them reduce costs associated with inventory levels and get new products to market more quickly. Ultimately, this helps companies drive profitability and improve their customer service since they can react to changing market conditions swiftly. Collaborating, or sharing information, with suppliers has become a strategic necessity for business success. In other words, by developing and maintaining stronger, more integrated relationships with suppliers, companies can more effectively compete in their markets through cost reductions and responsiveness to market demands.

What Is a Supply Chain?

The term **supply chain** is commonly used to refer to a collection of companies and processes involved in moving a product from the suppliers of raw materials, to the suppliers of intermediate components, to final production, and, ultimately, to the customer. Companies often procure specific raw materials and components from many different "upstream" suppliers. These suppliers, in turn, work with their own suppliers to obtain raw materials and components; their suppliers work with additional suppliers, and so forth. The further out in the supply chain one looks, the more suppliers are involved. As a result, the term "chain" becomes somewhat of a misnomer since it implies one-to-one relationships facilitating a chain of events flowing from the first supplier to the second to the third and so on. Similarly, on the "downstream" side, the products move to many different customers. The flow of materials from suppliers to customers can thus be more accurately

FIGURE 8.2

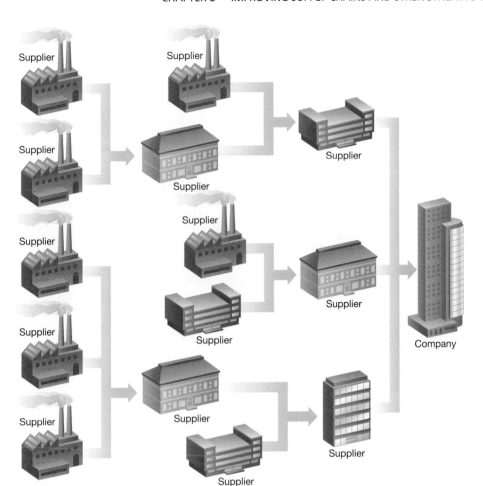

A typical supply network.

described as a **supply network** because of the various interrelated parties involved in moving raw materials, to intermediate components, and, finally, to the end product within the production process (see Figure 8.2).

A case in point is Apple and its latest extremely successful mobile devices, such as the iPhone 4 or the iPad. Apple sold 3 million iPads within the first 80 days of its release (or roughly 26 iPads per minute on average), and sold over 1.7 million iPhone 4s within the first three days of launching the product. In fact, the iPhone 4 has been so successful that several international product launch dates had to be delayed so as to meet the demand in the countries where the products were launched earlier. How does Apple manage to produce such an incredible amount of these products? If you take a close look at the devices, you will find a statement saying "Designed by Apple in California Assembled in China." Every time a new Apple device is launched, industry observers disassemble these devices to get a sneak peek into Apple's supply chain. The iPhone 4, like other Apple devices, is by no means *manufactured* by Apple. The components of the iPhone are sourced from dozens of companies located in various different countries. For example, according to market research firm iSuppli, the iPhone's flash memory and applications processor are produced by Korean Samsung; the display is sourced from Korean LG; the phone chips are made by German Infineon (manufactured in Germany or Southeast Asia); the Wi-Fi and Global Positioning System chips are produced by U.S.-based Broadcom (but possibly assembled in China, Korea, Singapore, or Taiwan); the touch-screen controller is made by Texas Instruments; many other parts, such as the camera, are possibly made in Taiwan; and so on. The final product is assembled in a factory owned by Taiwanese electronics giant Foxconn, located in Shenzhen, China (a city of almost 9 million people, located just north of Hong Kong), from where the finished iPhones are shipped by air to the different countries where the iPhone is on sale (see Figure 8.3). Although many have never heard of Foxconn, it is the largest electronics manufacturer in the world, producing components, cell phones, gaming consoles, and so on for various other companies, including Dell, HP, and Sony.

FIGURE 8.3

The iPhone is assembled in China from globally sourced components.

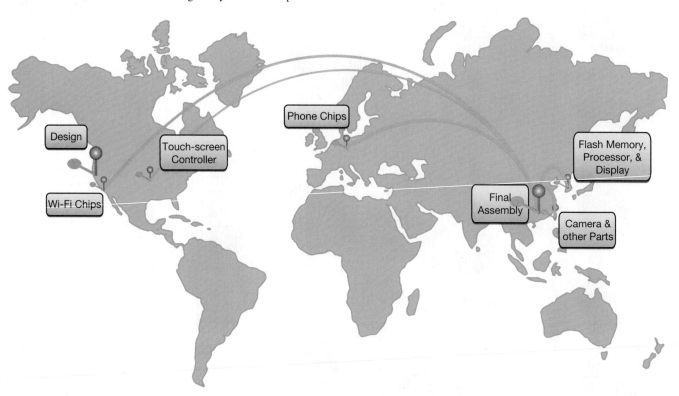

Coordinating such extensive supply network requires considerable expertise, especially when facing unexpected events such as shortages in touch-screen panels, other issues at suppliers' factories, or natural disasters. In 2010, for example, the eruption of a volcano in Iceland led to the closing of the northern European airspace for several days, causing delays in iPhone shipments to Europe; similarly, an earthquake in Taiwan in early 2010 severely affected the supply of large LCD panels used for monitors and televisions, as several manufacturers had to temporarily suspend production for safety reasons. A shrinking pool of suppliers for critical components exacerbates such problems, as companies have fewer options to switch suppliers if necessary. It is thus important not only to monitor one's own direct suppliers but also to constantly monitor the company's extended supply chain so as to anticipate any issues that may have an impact on one's direct suppliers.

Benefits of Effectively Managing Supply Chains

Whereas effectively managing the supply chain can create various opportunities, several problems can arise when firms within the network do not collaborate effectively. For example, collaboration within supply networks has enabled process innovations such as just-in-time manufacturing and vendor-managed inventory (discussed in the following sections). On the other hand, if firms do not collaborate effectively, information can easily become distorted as it moves from one company down through the supply network. Problems such as excessive inventories, inaccurate manufacturing capacity plans, and missed production schedules can run rampant, causing huge ripple effects that lead to degradations in profitability and poor customer service by everyone within the supply network. Further, effectively managing the supply chain is becoming increasingly important in terms of corporate social responsibility.

Just-in-Time Production One of the most significant advances to production has been the use of **just-in-time (JIT)** strategies. Based on the notion that keeping inventory is costly (in terms of both storage costs and the capital that is tied up) and does not add value, companies using a JIT method are trying to optimize their ordering quantities such that parts or raw material arrive just when they are needed for production. As the orders arrive in smaller quantities (but at higher frequency), the investment in storage space and inventory is minimized. Pioneered by Japanese automaker Toyota, many other businesses have now adopted a JIT approach. For example, computer maker Dell realized the problems with keeping large inventories, especially because of the fast rate of obsolescence of electronics components. To illustrate, recall our discussion of Moore's Law (see Chapter 3, "Managing the Information Systems Infrastructure and Services") where processor technology is doubling in performance approximately every 18 months. Because of this, successful computer manufacturers have learned that holding inventory that can quickly become obsolete or devalued is a poor strategy for success. In fact, Dell now only keeps about two hours of inventory in its factories. Obviously, using a JIT method is heavily dependent on tight cooperation between all partners in the supply network, including suppliers and other needed partners, such as shippers. In 2002, a labor lockout effectively shut down 29 U.S. West Coast ports for 10 days; events such as this can wreak havoc for companies depending on goods shipped from overseas for their business. For a computer maker such as Dell, which sources most of its components from Southeast Asia and depends on a steady stream of supplies for its JIT manufacturing processes, this could have potentially been devastating. However, foreseeing those potential problems in the supply network, Dell chartered 18 Boeing 747 freighter aircraft to shuttle parts from its Asian suppliers to the U.S. assembly facilities so as to keep business running. In the end, Dell successfully managed to weather this storm without having to delay any customer orders.

Vendor-Managed Inventory **Vendor-managed inventory (VMI)** is a business model in which the suppliers to a manufacturer (or retailer) manage the manufacturer's (or retailer's) inventory levels based on preestablished service levels. To make VMI possible, the manufacturer (or retailer) allows the supplier to monitor stock levels and ongoing sales data. Under a traditional inventory model, the manufacturer or retailer would manage these inventories themselves, sending out requests for additional items as needed. In contrast, under a VMI model, the manufacturer or retailer shares real-time sales data with their suppliers, who maintain inventory levels based on preestablished agreements. Such arrangement can help to reduce the manufacturer's (or retailer's) inventory, both saving costs and minimizing stockout situations (thus enhancing customer satisfaction); the supplier, in turn, benefits from the intense data sharing, which helps produce more accurate forecasts, reduces ordering errors, and helps prioritize the shipment of goods.

The Bullwhip Effect One major problem affecting supply chains are ripple effects referred to as the **bullwhip effect**. Each business forecasting demand typically includes a safety buffer in order to prevent possible stockouts. However, forecast errors and safety stocks multiply when moving up the supply chain such that a small fluctuation in demand for an end product can lead to tremendous fluctuation in demand for parts or raw materials farther up the supply chain. Like someone cracking a bullwhip, a tiny "flick of the wrists" will create a big movement at the other end of the whip. Likewise, a small forecasting error at the end of the supply chain can cause massive forecasting errors farther up the supply chain. Implementing integrated business processes allows a company to better coordinate the entire supply network and reduce the impact of the bullwhip.

Corporate Social Responsibility Effectively managing the supply chains has also become tremendously important for aspects related to corporate social responsibility. Specifically, transparency and accountability within the supply chain can help organizations save costs and/or create a good image. Two related issues are product recalls and sustainable business practices; both are discussed next.

Product Recalls. Given that a typical supply network comprises tens, hundreds, or sometimes thousands of players, many of which are dispersed across the globe, there are myriad possibilities where shortcuts are being taken or quality standards not being met. Often, such issues are caught somewhere along the supply chain, but sometimes such incidents go unnoticed until the product reaches the end consumer. For example, in mid-2010, it was detected that traces of cadmium were found in the decorative paint used for *Shrek*-themed glasses offered by McDonald's. Although the levels of cadmium were within the legal limits, McDonald's decided to recall the glasses. Similarly, in 2010, Johnson & Johnson had to recall 43 over-the-counter children's medicines produced by one of its subsidiaries after it was found that some of the medicine may contain foreign particles or substandard inactive ingredients or may exceed specified levels of the active ingredients; in total, more than 100,000 bottles of medicine were affected by the recall. The problems are exacerbated if companies are sourcing their products or raw materials globally, as this adds even more potential points of failure.

Hence, it is extremely important to have the necessary information to trace back the movement of the product through the supply chain so as to be able to quickly identify the problematic link. Being able to single out the source of the problem helps the company to perform an appropriate response, helping to save goodwill and limiting the costs of a recall. Further, in many cases, only some batches of a product may be problematic. If a company is not able to clearly identify the affected batches, the recall will have to be much broader, costing the company much more (in both goodwill and money) than just having to recall the affected batches. Hence, companies need to have a clear picture of their supply chain but also have to store this data in case of problems at a later point in time.

Sustainable Business Practices. Another aspect related to corporate social responsibility is a growing emphasis on sustainable business practices. Particularly, organizations come under increasing scrutiny for issues such as ethical treatment of workers (especially overseas) or environmental practices. For example, in early 2010, a number of employees at Foxconn's Shenzhen plant committed suicide. As the suicides happened at the plant manufacturing iPhones for Apple, many blamed Apple for the working conditions at the plant. Although Apple is certainly aware of the negative effects that a supplier's action can have on a company's reputation, it also faces a conundrum, as few (if any) companies besides Foxconn have sufficient production capacity to meet the demand for hugely popular products such as the iPhone.

Other companies are trying to portray a "green" image and attempt to minimize their carbon footprint. For example, HP takes a proactive approach, being the first major information technology company to publish its aggregate supply chain greenhouse gas emissions, restrict the use of hazardous materials, implement environmentally friendly packaging policies, and so on. In order to do that and to provide sound, convincing numbers to back their "green" image, a company such as HP needs to have a clear view of its entire supply chain.

Optimizing the Supply Chain Through Supply Chain Management

Information systems focusing on improving supply chains have two main objectives: to accelerate product development and innovation and to reduce costs. These systems, called **supply chain management (SCM),** improve the coordination of suppliers, product or service production, and distribution. When executed successfully, SCM helps in not only reducing inventory costs but also enhancing revenue through improved customer service. SCM is often integrated with ERP to leverage internal and external information in order to better collaborate with suppliers. Like ERP and customer relationship management applications, SCM packages are delivered in the form of modules (see Table 8.1) that companies select and implement according to their differing business requirements.

TABLE 8.1 Functions That Optimize the Supply Network

Module	Key Uses
Demand planning and forecasting	Forecast and plan anticipated demand for products
Safety stock planning	Assign optimal safety stock and target stock levels in all inventories in the supply network
Distribution planning	Optimize the allocation of available supply to meet demand
Supply network collaboration	Work with partners across the supply network to improve accuracy of demand forecasts, reduce inventory buffers, increase the velocity of materials, and improve customer service
Materials management	Ensure that the materials required for production are available where needed when needed
Manufacturing execution	Support production processes taking into account capacity and material constraints
Order promising	Provide answers to customer relationship management queries regarding product availability, costs, and delivery times
Transportation execution	Manage logistics between company locations or from company to customers, taking into account transportation modes and constraints
Warehouse management	Support receiving, storing, and picking of goods in a warehouse
Supply chain analytics	Monitor key performance indicators to assess performance across the supply chain

Source: Based on http://www.sap.com.

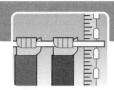

POWERFUL PARTNERSHIPS

Flickr's Caterina Fake and Stewart Butterfield

What's the tagline for a Web 2.0 company? Let them come, and *they* will build it. Following this motto, many successful Web 2.0 companies have turned large parts of their supply chains upside down—the consumers of content provided are also suppliers of content. Caterina Fake, marketing expert and art director, and Web designer Stewart Butterfield early on realized the business potential of this concept. Already operating a fledgling gaming company, Ludicorp, the pair was impressed when a coworker devised a photo sharing program for Web users. They added tools for users to add captions and key words to locate photos, and Flickr was born.

According to Fake, "Will you start a business with me?" came before "Will you marry me?" Two weeks after returning from their honeymoon, the couple started Game Neverending, a Vancouver, British Columbia–based business that designed a site for visitors to interact as they made virtual products which they traded, bought, and sold. Game Neverending morphed into Flickr, replacing objects of the game with photos, and now Ludicorp, based in Silicon Valley.

In the beginning, Fake said that she and a colleague greeted every single person who visited Flickr. "We introduced them to people, we chatted with them. This is a social product. People are putting things they love—photographs of their whole lives—into it. All of these people are your potential evangelists. You need to show those people love." The personal attention paid off. Since many Web-based businesses have proved cheaper to build, thanks to lower broadband and software costs, Fake and Butterfield started Flickr with no venture capital. They borrowed money from relatives, friends, and angel investors to start Flickr, and investors must have been pleased when Yahoo! bought the business for $30 million in 2005.

Today, Flickr is still growing with more than 30 million active accounts and over 4 billion photos uploaded. However, the Flickr cofounders are no longer involved in the business. After three years working for Yahoo!, both left to chase new dreams. In 2009, Caterina launched a new start-up, Hunch, while Butterfield launched his new start-up, Tiny Speck. On a personal partnership note, Butterfield and Fake are no longer together.

Based on:

Butterfield, S., & Fake, C. (2006, December 1). How we did it: Stewart Butterfield and Caterina Fake, co-founders, Flickr. *Inc.com.* Retrieved April 18, 2010, from http://www.inc.com/magazine/20061201/hidi-butterfield-fake.html.

Flickr. (2010, July 17). In *Wikipedia, the free encyclopedia.* Retrieved July 19, 2010, from http://en.wikipedia.org/w/index.php?title=Flickr&oldid=373913583.

Frommer, D. (2009, March 27). Flickr founder launches new startup, Hunch. *SAI.* Retrieved April 18, 2010, from http://www.businessinsider.com/flickr-co-founders-new-startup-hunch-launching-2009-3.

Ingram, M. (2010, February 9). Flickr co-founder proudly announces . . . Glitch. *BusinessWeek.* Retrieved April 18, 2010, from http://www.businessweek.com/technology/content/feb2010/tc2010029_657601.htm.

Quittner, J. (2006, April 30). The Flickr founders. *Times.* Retrieved April 18, 2010, from http://www.time.com/time/magazine/article/0,9171,1186931,00.html.

Thomas, O. (2009, March 27). Why Flickr's Caterina Fake is launching Hunch on her own. *GAWKER.* Retrieved April 18, 2010, from http://gawker.com/5186422/why-flickrs-caterina-fake-is-launching-hunch-on-her-own.

As discussed previously, ERP systems are primarily used to optimize business processes *within* the organization, whereas SCM is used to improve business processes that *span* organizational boundaries. Whereas some stand-alone SCM systems only automate the logistics aspects of the supply chain, organizations can reap the greatest benefits when the SCM system is tightly integrated with ERP and customer relationship management systems modules; this way, SCM systems can use data about customer orders (from the customer relationship management system), data about payments (from the ERP system), and so on. Given its scope, SCM is adopted primarily by large organizations with a large and/or complex supplier network. At the same time, many smaller suppliers are interacting with the systems of large companies. To obtain the greatest benefits from the SCM processes and systems, organizations need to extend the system to include all trading partners regardless of size, providing a central location for information integration and common processes so that all partners benefit.

For an effective SCM strategy, several challenges have to be overcome. First and foremost, as with any information system, an SCM system is only as good as the data that is entered into it. This means that to benefit most from an SCM system, the organization's employees have to actually use the system and move away from traditional ways of managing the supply chain, as an order placed by fax or telephone will most likely not find its way into the system. Another challenge to overcome is distrust among partners in the supply chain; for many companies, sales and supply chain data are strategic assets, and no one wants to show his or her cards to other members in the supply chain. Further, many organizations (such as Apple) tend to be very clandestine about their suppliers, as such information could reveal their pricing strategies or give clues about new product development. In addition, more and more organizations are reluctant to share data along the supply chain because of growing intellectual property theft, especially in China, a major source of supplies for many companies. A final challenge is to get all partners within the supply chain to adopt an SCM system. Several years ago, the retail giant Walmart began mandating its suppliers to use its RetailLink supply chain system, and refuses to engage in a business relationship with any supplier who is not willing to use the system. Whereas large companies can force their suppliers or partners to use a system, smaller companies do not have this power.

SCM Architecture

An SCM system includes more than simply hardware and software; it also integrates business processes and supply chain partners. As shown in Table 8.1, an SCM system consists of many modules or applications. Each of these modules supports either supply chain planning, supply chain execution, or supply chain visibility and analytics. All are described next.

Supply Chain Planning Supply chain planning (SCP) involves the development of various resource plans to support the efficient and effective production of goods and services (see Figure 8.4). Four key processes are generally supported by SCP modules:

1. *Demand Planning and Forecasting.* SCP begins with product demand planning and forecasting. To develop demand forecasts, SCM modules examine historical data to develop the most accurate forecasts possible. The accuracy of these forecasts will be influenced greatly by the stability of the data. When historic data is stable, plans can be longer in duration, whereas if historic data shows unpredictable fluctuations in demand, the forecasting time frame must be narrowed. SCM systems also support collaborative demand and supply planning such that a sales representative can work together with the demand planner, taking into account information provided by the organization's point-of-sale system, promotions entered in the customer relationship management system, and other factors influencing demand. Demand planning and forecasting leads to the development of the overall *demand forecast.*
2. *Distribution Planning.* Once final product planning forecasts are complete, plans for moving products to distributors can be developed. Specifically, distribution planning focuses on delivering products or services to consumers as well as warehousing, delivering, invoicing, and payment collection. Distribution planning leads to the development of the overall *transportation schedule.*
3. *Production Scheduling.* Production scheduling focuses on the coordination of all activities needed to create the product or service. When developing this plan, analytical tools are used to optimally utilize materials, equipment, and labor. Production also involves product testing, packaging, and delivery preparation. Production scheduling leads to the development of the *production plan.*

FIGURE 8.4

SCP includes demand planning and forecasting, distribution planning, production planning, and inventory and safety stock planning.

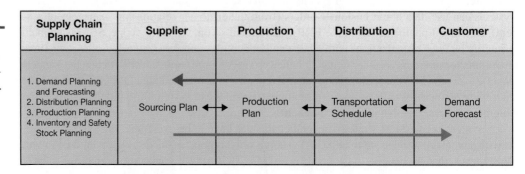

Supply Chain Planning	Supplier	Production	Distribution	Customer
1. Demand Planning and Forecasting 2. Distribution Planning 3. Production Planning 4. Inventory and Safety Stock Planning	Sourcing Plan	Production Plan	Transportation Schedule	Demand Forecast

4. ***Inventory and Safety Stock Planning.*** Inventory and safety stock planning focuses on the development of inventory estimates. Using inventory simulations and other analytical techniques, organizations can balance inventory costs and desired customer service levels to determine optimal inventory levels. Once inventory levels are estimated, suppliers are chosen who contractually agree to preestablished delivery and pricing terms. Inventory and safety stock planning leads to the development of a *sourcing plan.*

As suggested, various types of analytical tools—such as statistical analysis, simulation, and optimization—are used to forecast and visualize demand levels, distribution and warehouse locations, resource sequencing, and so on. Once these plans are developed, they are used to guide supply chain execution. Additionally, it is important to note that SCM planning is an ongoing process—as new data are obtained, plans are updated. For example, as shortages in the capacity for manufacturing touch-screen displays became evident in mid-2010, Apple had to dynamically adjust its plans so as to obtain the needed quantities to meet customer demand.

Supply Chain Execution Supply chain execution **(SCE)** is the execution of SCP. Essentially, SCE puts the SCM planning into motion and reflects the processes involved in improving the collaboration of all members of the supply chain—suppliers, producers, distributors, and customers. SCE involves the management of three key elements of the supply chain: product flow, information flow, and financial flow (see Figure 8.5). Each of these flows is discussed next.

Product Flow. **Product flow** refers to the movement of goods from the supplier to production, from production to distribution, and from distribution to the consumer. Although products primarily "flow" in one direction, an effective SCM system will also support the activities associated with product returns. Effectively processing returns and customer refunds is a critical part of SCE. Thus, an SCM system should support not only the physical product production process but also the necessary processes in place to efficiently receive excessive or defective products from customers (and ship replacements or credit accounts).

Information Flow. **Information flow** refers to the movement of information along the supply chain, such as order processing and delivery status updates. Like the product flow, information can also flow up or down the supply chain as needed. The key element to the information flow is the complete removal of paper documents. Specifically, all orders, fulfillment, billing, and consolidation information is shared electronically. These paperless information flows save not only paperwork but also time and money. Additionally, because SCM systems use a central database to store information, all supply chain partners have access to all the current information at all times.

Financial Flow. **Financial flow** refers primarily to the movement of financial assets throughout the supply chain. Financial flows also include information related to payment schedules, consignment and ownership of products and materials, and other relevant information. Linkages to electronic banking and financial institutions allow payments to automatically flow into the accounts of all members within the supply chain.

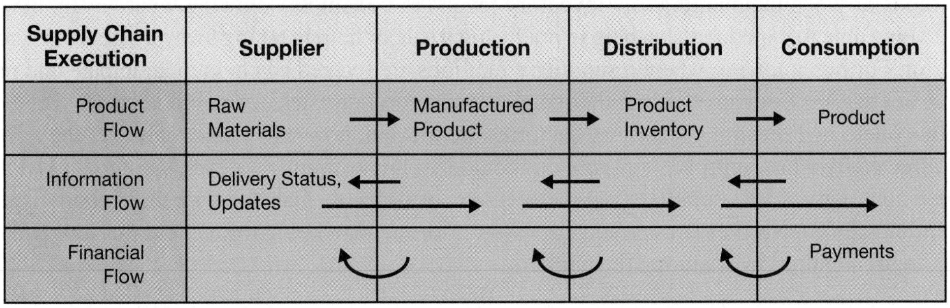

Supply Chain Execution	Supplier	Production	Distribution	Consumption
Product Flow	Raw Materials	Manufactured Product	Product Inventory	Product
Information Flow	Delivery Status, Updates			
Financial Flow				Payments

FIGURE 8.5

SCE focuses on the efficient and effective flow of products, information, and finances along the supply chain.

Brief Case ⟳

OUTSOURCING YOUR MCDONALD'S ORDER

Dial the customer service telephone number for countless companies, and chances are you will speak to a representative based in India, the Dominican Republic, Thailand, or another offshore location. The practice of outsourcing is becoming increasingly prominent in our lives: Customer service and catalog sales representatives are often located offshore. More than 50 percent of U.S. income tax returns are prepared outside the United States. And the latest major industry to outsource? Surprisingly, it's fast food. Since outsourcing lends itself to services and products not used or consumed where they are purchased, fast-food drive-through kiosks have proved the perfect opportunity for outsourcing.

McDonald's, one of America's largest success stories, is synonymous with fast food. Founded in 1948 in San Bernardino, California, the company has parlayed its original 15-cent hamburgers and 1-cent French fries into a worldwide, multi-billion-dollar business. The company strives for uniformity in its thousands of locations around the globe. That is, if a customer orders a quarter-pounder with fries in Miami, the meal should be of the same quality as the quarter-pounder with fries ordered in Moscow, Munich, or Melbourne.

As McDonald's became increasingly globalized, it made financial sense for the company to search for outsourcing possibilities. The drive-through service seemed especially well suited because of the repetitive nature of the service and the fact that it is difficult to retain staff in the low-paying drive-through positions.

McDonald's was not interested in investing millions of dollars in a new drive-through ordering system to facilitate outsourcing. Any changes made in technology had to be easy and cheap, and outsourcing fit the bill. McDonald's restaurants everywhere were already connected to the Internet since corporate offices downloaded daily sales from the restaurants and uploaded price changes to the outlets. Therefore, the software was updated to allow for orders to be processed overseas and be entered into McDonald's food management queue. It didn't matter if the order was taken 10 feet or 10,000 miles away; the process was the same—only the network was different.

Like most organizations, the Internet and information technology are vital in allowing McDonald's to improve its business processes. Now your McDonald's order might be going from router to router at light speed and arriving at a foreign destination, to be relayed back to the local McDonald's where your order will actually be served. For McDonald's, the end goal is the same as it was 60 years ago—customers will receive the same quality product at any McDonald's restaurant, but their orders may be routed to the Dominican Republic, India, or Thailand before they are filled and the food is served.

Questions

1. From the perspective of both McDonald's and its customers, what are the pros and cons of outsourcing drive-through ordering?
2. What risks to customer relationships does a local McDonald's restaurant assume when utilizing outsourced drive-through service? How can these risks be minimized?

Based on:

Anonymous. (2010, February 13). Local drive throughs outsource to call centers. *KITV.com*. Retrieved April 3, 2010, from http://www.kitv.com/news/22558921/detail.html.

Perry, L. (2010, February 15). A call from thousands of miles overseas for a hamburger served on a plate. *OfficialSpin*. Retrieved April 3, 2010, from http://www.officialwire.com/main.php?action=posted_news&rid=97520.

Richtel, M. (2006, April 11). The long-distance journey of a fast-food order. *New York Times*. Retrieved April 3, 2010, from http://www.nytimes.com/2006/04/11/technology/11fast.html.

Supply Chain Visibility and Analytics **Supply chain visibility** refers to the ability to track products as they move through the supply chain but also to foresee external events. Being able to see where a shipment is at any given time can be of tremendous help, especially when using JIT methods or when maintaining low inventory levels. For example, knowing where a shipment is and being able to expedite it can help in not losing a sale or help in taking away a sale from a competitor. Further, knowing where a supplier's facilities are located can help to anticipate and react to issues arising from adverse weather conditions, natural disasters, or political issues; if I don't know where in Taiwan my suppliers' factories are located, how will I know whether they might be affected by a fast-approaching typhoon? Similarly, some companies even want to know when labor contracts of key suppliers' workers expire in order to plan for potential labor disputes (Penfield, 2008). Needless to say, such levels of information sharing throughout the supply chain require tremendous trust among the partners.

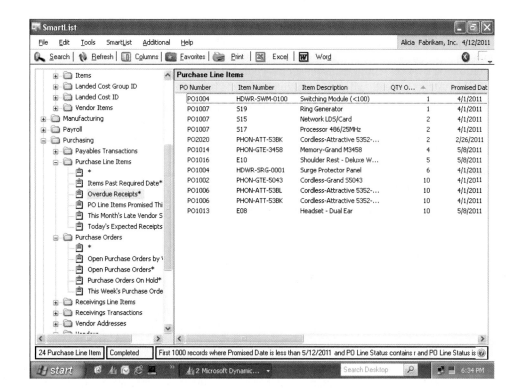

FIGURE 8.6

Supply chain analytics helps to monitor the performance of the supply chain.

Supply chain analytics refers to the use of key performance indicators to monitor performance of the entire supply chain, including sourcing, planning, production, and distribution. For example, a purchasing manager can identify the suppliers that are frequently unable to meet promised delivery dates (see Figure 8.6). Being able to access key performance metrics can help to identify and remove bottlenecks, such as by switching suppliers, spreading orders over multiple suppliers, expediting shipping for critical goods, and so on.

Developing an SCM Strategy

When developing an SCM strategy, an organization must consider a variety of factors that will affect the efficiency and effectiveness of the supply chain. **Supply chain efficiency** is the extent to which a company's supply chain is focusing on minimizing procurement, production, and transportation costs, sometimes by sacrificing excellent customer service. In contrast, **supply chain effectiveness** is the extent to which a company's supply chain is focusing on maximizing customer service regardless of procurement, production, and transportation costs (see Figure 8.7). In other words, the design of the supply chain must consider natural trade-offs between a variety

Supply Chain Strategy	Procurement	Production	Transportation
Effectiveness	More Inventory Multiple Inventory Sources ...	General Purpose Facilities More Facilities Higher Excess Capacity ...	Fast Delivery Times More Warehouses ...
↕	↕	↕	↕
Efficiency	... Single Inventory Source Less Inventory	... Less Excess Capacity Fewer Facilities Special Purpose Facilities	... Fewer Warehouses Longer Delivery Times

FIGURE 8.7

A supply chain strategy requires balancing supply chain efficiency and effectiveness.

of factors and should reflect the organization's competitive strategy to reap the greatest benefits. For example, an organization utilizing a low-cost provider competitive strategy would likely focus on supply chain efficiency. In contrast, an organization pursuing a superior customer service differentiation strategy would focus on supply chain effectiveness.

SCM systems typically allow for making trade-offs between efficiency and effectiveness for individual components or raw materials. For example, if a hurricane is likely to delay the arrival of a key component by sea, the company perform simulations to evaluate the effect of the delay on production and can assess the feasibility of temporarily switching suppliers, switching modes of transportation (e.g., expediting the shipment via air freight), or substituting the component altogether. In such cases, making changes to the original plans may be more costly but can help the organization to meet promised delivery deadlines, thus maintaining goodwill and avoiding possible contract penalties. On the other hand, companies can dynamically adjust schedules for non-critical components or raw materials so as to minimize costs while still meeting the targets set in the production schedule.

Emerging SCM Trends

As is the case with all technologies, SCM is evolving. One key trend is the development of supplier portals, customer portals, and business-to-business marketplaces, all of which provide an alternative to proprietary supply linkages, such as linkages using electronic data interchange. We have discussed these portals in Chapter 4, "Enabling Commerce Using the Internet." In addition, new technologies are helping to add greater value to SCM. These topics are briefly examined next.

Key Technologies for Enhancing SCM Several new technologies are helping organizations gain even more from their investments in SCM systems. In this section, we briefly review two that are providing significant benefits to managing supply chains.

Extensible Markup Language. **Extensible Markup Language (XML)** is a data presentation standard first specified by the World Wide Web Consortium, an international consortium of companies whose purpose is to develop open standards for the Web. XML allows designers of Web documents to create their own customized tags, enabling the definition, transmission, validation, and interpretation of data between applications and between organizations.

XML does not specify any particular formatting; rather, it specifies the rules for tagging elements. An **XML tag** is a command that is inserted into an XML document in order to specify how the document or a portion of the document should be interpreted and/or used. As described in the Technology Briefing, Hypertext Markup Language (HTML) uses HTML tags to instruct a Web browser how data on a Web page should be laid out cosmetically on a user's screen. Much like HTML, XML also uses tags, but they go well beyond HTML. XML instructs systems as to how information should be interpreted and used. For example, the tags <item_no>...</item_no> would instruct the application reading the XML file that the numbers enclosed in the tags should be interpreted as a product's item number (see Figure 8.8). The application could use this information when displaying a product on a Web page or when updating inventory records. As a result, XML is a powerful information tagging system that can be tailored to share similar data across applications over the Web. With these advanced data definition capabilities built into Web applications, organizations can then use the Web as the worldwide network for business-to-consumer electronic commerce and SCM.

Many people think that XML is on its way to becoming the standard for automating data exchange between business information systems and may well replace all other formats for electronic data interchange. Companies can, for example, use XML to create an application for doing Web-based ordering, for checking on and managing inventory, for signaling to a supplier that more parts are needed, for alerting a third-party logistics company that a delivery is needed, and so on. All these various applications can work together using the common language of XML.

XML is customizable, and a number of variations of XML have been developed. For example, **Extensible Business Reporting Language (XBRL)** is an XML-based specification for publishing financial information. XBRL makes it easier for public and private companies to share information with each other, with industry analysts, and with shareholders. XBRL includes tags for data such as annual and quarterly reports, Securities and Exchange Commission filings, general ledger information, and net revenue and accounting schedules (see Figure 8.9).

FIGURE 8.8

An XML file for transmitting a bill of materials for a bicycle.

XML is not, however, a panacea for SCM. Support for and use of XML is growing rapidly, and most necessary standards and agreements are in place to enable XML-based applications to work seamlessly with all other applications and systems. However, while nearly anyone can learn to use a text editor to create a basic HTML document, XML is far more complex and requires not only knowledge of XML but also expertise in distributed database design and management. Nevertheless, XML holds great promise for managing supply chains by its ability to inject more information into the process.

Radio Frequency Identification. Another exciting technology now being used within SCM systems is **radio frequency identification (RFID),** which is starting to replace the standard bar codes you find on almost every product. RFID is the use of the electromagnetic energy to transmit information between a reader (transceiver) and a processing device, or **RFID tag.**

RFID tags can be used just about anywhere a unique identification system might be needed, such as on clothing, pets, cars, keys, missiles, or manufactured parts. RFID tags can range in size from being a fraction of an inch, which can be inserted beneath an animal's skin, up to several

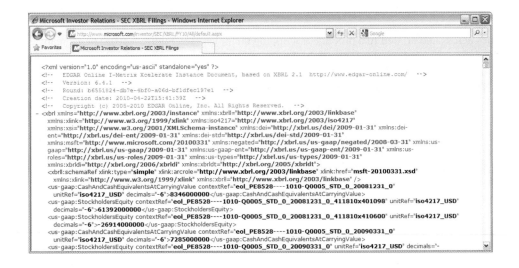

FIGURE 8.9

An XBRL file for sharing Securities and Exchange Commission filings.

COMING ATTRACTIONS

Simplifying the Recharging of Gadgets

Cell phones, MP3 players, digital cameras, and laptop computers are indispensable tools in today's world. They also have at least one downside—especially for travelers. Batteries run down and have to be recharged, which means carrying a charger for each device since one charger does *not* fit all—at least not yet.

Starting from 2011, cell phones sold in the European Union come with a standardized charging port, eliminating the need for multiple different chargers, thus minimizing the hassle for the consumer as well as the impact on the environment. However, this standard does not cover devices beyond cell phones, and several innovative technologies have been introduced as alternative solutions. In 2009, Qualcomm demonstrated a wireless charging technology called eZone that has two parts: a charging pad that houses the main transmitting power technology and a tiny receiver coil fitted inside portable gadgets. Using "near-field magnetic resonance" technology, there is no need to make direct electrical contact with the device it's charging. eZone can charge several gadgets at a time, and Wi-Fi and Bluetooth connections will still work while devices are charging, so it could be used while downloading photos from your camera or wirelessly adding music to your iPod. Qualcomm also notes that eZone is able to charge beefier items like cordless drills and is flexible enough to be integrated into furniture or even laptop lids.

In late 2009, Toshiba announced a direct-methanol fuel cell charger that produces electricity from a reaction of methanol, water, and air. The new charger has been successfully tested on gadgets like the PSP and iPod. Unfortunately, it currently won't charge every device that could be plugged into its USB socket, including the iPhone. Nevertheless, engineers feel that future versions of methanol-powered fuels cells have tremendous potential to allow you to charge your gadget without needing access to an electrical outlet. Similarly, in 2010, Nokia introduced a bicycle charger kit; using a special dynamo and charger, you can charge your cell phone enough for one hour of talk time by cycling for 20 minutes at a speed of only six miles per hour. Researchers at NTT Communications are currently working on a prototype of a walking power generator that, attached to your shoes, lets you recharge your gadgets simply by walking.

Over the next few years, expect many innovations that will help to free our gadgets from electrical outlets or to simplify the nest of cables for charging multiple phones, headsets, and cameras.

Based on:

Allen, D. (2009, October 27). The future of charging gadgets? Toshiba's methanol fuel cell is promising, flawed. *Gizmodo*. Retrieved March 18, 2010, from http://gizmodo.com/5390935/the-future-of-charging-gadgets-toshibas-methanol-fuel-cell-is-promising-flawed.

Anonymous. (2010). ICT for the future R&D forum. Retrieved August 3, 2010, from http://www.nttcomrdhk.com/exhibits.php.

Anonymous. (2010). Nokia bicycle charger kit. Retrieved August 3, 2010, from http://europe.nokia.com/find-products/accessories/all-accessories/power/chargers/nokia-bicycle-charger-kit.

Anonymous. (2010, July 30). Uniform cellphone chargers in EU in 2011. *CBC News*. Retrieved August 4, 2010, from http://www.cbc.ca/technology/story/2010/07/30/cell-phone-chargers.html.

Eaton, K. (2009, April 3). Qualcomm's vision of a wireless charging future. *Fast Company*. Retrieved March 18, 2010, from http://www.fastcompany.com/blog/kit-eaton/technomix/qualcomm-teases-vision-wireless-charging-future.

inches across and affixed to a product or shipping container (see Figure 8.10). The tag can carry information as simple as the name of the owner of a pet or as complex as how a product is to be manufactured on the shop floor.

RFID systems offer advantages over standard bar code technologies in that RFID eliminates the need for line-of-sight reading. RFID also does not require time-consuming hand scanning, and RFID information is readable regardless of the entity's position or whether the tag is plainly visible. RFID tags can also contain more information than bar codes. Further, a company can program any information that it wants or need onto an RFID tag, enabling a vast array of potential uses. Thus, it is possible to retrieve information about an entity's version, origin, location, maintenance history, and other important information and to manipulate that information on the tag. RFID scanning can also be done at greater distances than can bar code scanning. *Passive tags* are small and relatively inexpensive (starting from 10 cents) and typically have a range up to a few feet. *Active tags*, on the other hand, cost upward of $5, include a battery, and can transmit hundreds of feet.

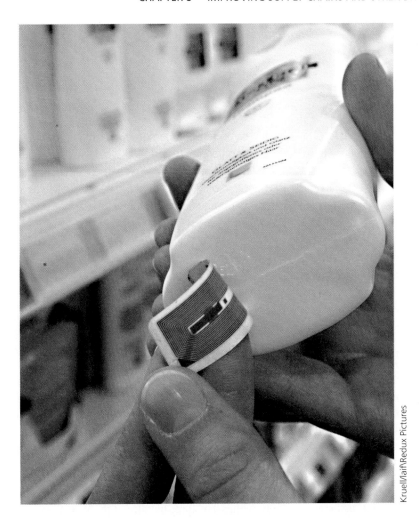

Kruell/laifRedux Pictures

FIGURE 8.10

An RFID tag is small but contains a lot of information.

Source: METRO AG.

RFID systems offer great opportunities for managing supply chains. For example, airlines are strapped for cash and think a lot about those metal, rolling serving carts that are used on airplanes and that can cost as much as $1,000 each. "We've heard horrific stories of airlines losing up to 1,500 of these things in three months," says Tony Naylor, vice president of in-flight solutions for eLSG.SkyChefs, a technology provider for the airline catering industry based in Irving, Texas (Edwards, 2003). To keep tabs on their vanishing carts, eLSG.SkyChefs now uses an RFID system with an RFID tag on each cart (LSG, 2010).

Additionally, virtually all major retailers are adopting RFID to better manage their supply chains, as are governments for tracking military supplies and weapons, drug shipments and ingredients (i.e., for eliminating counterfeit drugs), and citizens with RFID chips on passports. While RFID's deployment is growing rapidly, the systems are still relatively expensive, there isn't yet a clear set of data standards, and radio frequencies allocated to RFID differ between countries. Fortunately, these hurdles are being overcome by cooperation between vendors and regulating authorities. In any event, RFID is clearly a valuable new technology for managing supply chains.

Customer Relationship Management

With the changes introduced by the Web, in most industries a company's competition is simply a mouse click away. It is increasingly important for companies not only to generate new business but also to attract repeat business from existing customers (see Figure 8.11). This means that to remain competitive, companies must keep their customers satisfied. In today's highly competitive markets, customers hold the balance of power because, if they become dissatisfied with the levels of customer service they are receiving, they have many alternatives readily available. The global nature of the Web has affected companies worldwide in virtually all industries. An economic transformation is taking place, shifting the emphasis from conducting business transactions to

NET STATS

RFID on the Rise

The market for RFID tags, those high-tech devices that let businesses keep track of certain products via radio frequency transmitters and receivers, has been steadily for the past few years. According to a recent research report, the global RFID market is expected to grow at a compound annual rate of more than 28 percent between 2010 and 2013, generating approximately $11 billion in revenue by the end of 2013. As RFID become more mainstream in more industries, the software and services segment of this industry will play an increasingly larger role to help companies better utilize the data collected by these devices. The report also found that the adoption of RFID technology in health care, retail, automotive, consumer packaged goods, government, and transportation sectors has been quite impressive in light of the challenging global economic conditions. While the adoption of RFID technology may require a large start-up investment for organizations, it provides a strong long-term return on investment.

Based on:

Anonymous. (2010, February 23). Global RFID market to generate revenue of US$11 billion by 2013. Retrieved March 3, 2010, from http://www.prlog.org/10544167-global-rfid-market-to-generate-revenue-of-us-11-billion-by-2013.html.

managing relationships. If a company successfully manages the relationship with a customer—satisfying them and solving their problems—the customer is less price sensitive. Hence, leveraging and managing customer relationships is equally as important as product development. Indeed, customer relationship management systems often collect the data that can be mined to discover the next product line extension that consumers covet.

Many of the world's most successful corporations have realized the importance of developing and nurturing relationships with their customers. For example, Starbucks Coffee uses a variety of means to engage with their customers: Like many other businesses, Starbucks uses a loyalty card to entice people to return to its stores; further, Starbucks actively solicits feedback and new product ideas from its customers, not only within the stores but also at the Web site mystarbucksidea.com, and it has one of the most successful fan pages on Facebook. Computer manufacturer Dell,

FIGURE 8.11

Organizations must work harder than ever to attract and retain customers where comparison shopping is the norm and competitors are just a click away.

FIGURE 8.12

Companies search for ways to widen, lengthen, and deepen customer relationships.

Widen
Attract New Customers

Lengthen
Keep Current
Customers Satisfied

Deepen
Transform Minor
Customers into
Profitable Customers

in contrast, has various other needs when interacting with its customers. For instance, when Dell sales representatives are dealing with large corporate clients who routinely make large computer purchases, issues of quantity pricing and delivery are likely to be paramount; whereas when dealing with less computer-savvy individuals ordering a new notebook for personal use, questions about compatibility with an older printer or the ability to run a specific program may be asked. No matter the customer, Dell attempts to provide all customers with a positive experience during both the presale and the ongoing support phases. Large banks and insurance companies, in contrast, are trying to widen and deepen the relationships with customers so as to be able to sell more financial services and products, maximizing the lifetime value of each individual customer. Chase Card Services, for example, has more than 4,000 agents, handling 200 million customer calls a year. Being able to increase **first-call resolution,** that is, addressing the customers' issues during the first call, can help to save costs tremendously while increasing customer satisfaction.

Marketing researchers have found that the cost of trying to get back customers who have gone elsewhere can be up to 50 to 100 times as much as keeping a current one satisfied. Thus, companies are finding it imperative to develop and maintain customer satisfaction and widen (by attracting new customers), lengthen (by keeping existing profitable customers satisfied), and deepen (by transforming minor customers into profitable customers) the relationships with their customers in order to compete effectively in their markets (see Figure 8.12). To achieve this, companies need to not only understand who their customers are but also determine the lifetime value of each customer. With the increasing popularity of Web 2.0 phenomena such as social networks, blogs, and microblogs, companies have more ways than ever to learn about their customers.

In addition to the opportunities offered by Web 2.0, these phenomena have brought about tremendous challenges for organizations trying to present and maintain a positive public image. As these Web 2.0 technologies have exponentially increased the power and reach of word of mouth, companies have realized that unmonitored information can have huge negative impacts and that monitoring and participating in ongoing conversations can be an important part of shaping public opinion.

To assist in deploying an organization-wide strategy for managing these increasingly complex customer relationships, organizations are deploying **customer relationship management (CRM)** systems. CRM is not simply technology but also a corporate-level strategy to create and maintain, through the introduction of reliable systems, processes, and procedures, lasting relationships with customers by concentrating on the downstream information flows. Applications focusing on downstream information flows have three main objectives: to attract potential customers, to create customer loyalty, and to portray a positive corporate image. The appropriate CRM technology combined with the management of sales-related business processes can have tremendous benefits for an organization (see Table 8.2). To pursue customer satisfaction as a basis for achieving competitive advantage, organizations must be able to access information and

WHEN THINGS GO WRONG

Apple's "Antenna Gate" — *Mismanaging* Customer Relationships

Apple's customers are passionate about the company and its products; the release of the iPhone 4 in mid-2010 was no exception. Like many other product releases, it came with much fanfare, long lines of customers waiting to buy the product, and a media bonanza for Apple. Its stock price soared. Soon after the release, however, customers began complaining of a sharp increase in dropped calls over prior versions of the phone. It was soon revealed that customers who held the phone in a certain way blocked the antenna from operating; when this "death grip" occurred, calls were dropped and Web pages stopped downloading. Apple's initial reaction to the backlash was *not* customer relationship–friendly. After keeping silent for more than two weeks, Apple issued a statement advising that customers should "avoid gripping [the phone] in the lower left corner" when making or receiving a call. Soon after, class action lawsuits were initiated and *Consumer Reports,* the consumer watchdog group, could not recommend that consumers buy the iPhone 4. Like its initial release, these events too created a media bonanza for Apple, mostly negative.

Ultimately, Apple CEO Steven Jobs admitted that there was a problem with the iPhone 4's antenna, and offered consumers who had already purchased the phone a rubber bumper to fit around the phone, helping to keep fingers far enough away from the trouble spot on phone so that calls would be less-likely to drop. Apple did not effectively manage customer relationships in this instance. However, admitting that there was indeed a problem and offering a free solution to customers helped to rebuild Apple's reputation in the marketplace.

Based on:

Ionescu, D. (2010, June 25). Apple responds to iPhone 4 antenna problem. *PCWorld.com.* Retrieved on August 19, 2010, from http://www.pcworld.com/article/199853/apple_responds_to_iphone_4_antenna_problem.html.

iPhone 4. (2010, August 19). In *Wikipedia, the free encyclopedia.* Retrieved August 19, 2010, from http://en.wikipedia.org/w/index.php?title=IPhone_4&oldid=379756595.

Van Buskirk, E. (2010, July 21). Apple's antenna problem is different. *Wired.* Retrieved on August 19, 2010, from http://www.wired.com/epicenter/2010/07/apples-antenna-problem-is-different.

---

track customer interactions throughout the organization regardless of where, when, or how the interaction occurs. This means that companies need to have an integrated system that captures information from retail stores, Web sites, social networks, microblogs, call centers, and various other ways that organizations communicate downstream within their value chain. More important, managers need the capability to monitor and analyze factors that drive customer satisfaction (as well as dissatisfaction) as changes occur according to prevailing market conditions.

TABLE 8.2 Benefits of a CRM System

Benefit	Examples
Enables 24/7/365 operation	Web-based interfaces provide product information, sales status, support information, issue tracking, and so on.
Individualized service	Learn how each customer defines product and service quality so that customized product, pricing, and services can be designed or developed collaboratively.
Improved information	Integrate all information for all points of contact with the customers—marketing, sales, and service—so that all who interact with customers have the same view and understand current issues.
Speeds problem identification/resolution	Improved record keeping and efficient methods of capturing customer complaints help to identify and solve problems faster.
Speeds processes	Integrated information removes information handoffs, speeding both sales and support processes.
Improved integration	Information from the CRM can be integrated with other systems to streamline business processes and gain business intelligence as well as making other cross-functional systems more efficient and effective.
Improved product development	Tracking customer behavior over time helps to identify future opportunities for product and service offerings.
Improved planning	Provides mechanisms for managing and scheduling sales follow-ups to assess satisfaction, repurchase probabilities, time frames, and frequencies.

CRM applications come in the form of packaged software that is purchased from software vendors. CRM applications are commonly integrated with a comprehensive ERP implementation to leverage internal and external information to better serve customers. Thus, most large vendors of ERP packages, such as Oracle, SAP, and Microsoft, also offer CRM systems; further, specialized vendors, such as salesforce.com or Sugar CRM, offer CRM solutions on a software-as-a-service basis. Like ERP, CRM applications come with various features and modules. Management must carefully select a CRM application that will meet the unique requirements of their business processes.

Companies that have successfully implemented CRM can experience greater customer satisfaction and increased productivity of their sales and service personnel, which can translate into dramatic enhancements to the company's profitability. CRM allows organizations to focus on driving revenue as well as on reducing costs, as opposed to emphasizing only cost cutting. Cost cutting tends to have a lower limit because there are only so many costs that companies can reduce, whereas revenue generation strategies are bound only by the size of the market itself. The importance of focusing on customer satisfaction is emphasized by findings from the National Quality Research Center, which estimates that a one-percent increase in customer satisfaction can lead to a threefold increase in a company's market capitalization.

Developing a CRM Strategy

To develop a successful CRM strategy, organizations must do more than simply purchase and install CRM software. The first consideration is whether a comprehensive CRM system is even needed for a company; for example, the closer an organization is to the end customer, the more important CRM becomes. Further, companies have to realize that a successful CRM strategy must include enterprise-wide changes, including the following:

- *Policy and Business Process Changes.* Organizational policies and procedures need to reflect a customer-focused culture.
- *Customer Service Changes.* Key metrics for managing the business need to reflect customer-focused measures for quality and satisfaction as well as process changes to enhance the customer experience.
- *Employee Training Changes.* Employees from all areas—marketing, sales, and support—must have a consistent focus that values customer service and satisfaction.
- *Data Collection, Analysis, and Sharing Changes.* All aspects of the customer experience—prospecting, sales, support, and so on—must be tracked, analyzed, and shared to optimize the benefits of the CRM.

In sum, the organization must focus and organize its activities to provide the best customer service possible (see Figure 8.13). Additionally, a successful CRM strategy must carefully consider the ethical and privacy concerns of customers' data (discussed later in this chapter).

Architecture of a CRM System

A comprehensive CRM system comprises three primary components:

1. *Operational CRM.* Systems for automating the fundamental business processes—marketing, sales, and support—for interacting with the customer
2. *Analytical CRM.* Systems for analyzing customer behavior and perceptions (e.g., quality, price, and overall satisfaction) in order to provide business intelligence
3. *Collaborative CRM.* Systems for providing effective and efficient communication with the customer from the entire organization

Operational CRM enables direct interaction with customers; in contrast, analytical CRM provides the analysis necessary to more effectively manage the sales, service, and marketing activities. Whereas analytical CRM aids in the development of a company's CRM strategy, operational CRM helps in the execution of CRM strategy; thus, either component alone provides no real benefit for a business. Finally, collaborative CRM provides the communication capabilities of the CRM environment (see Figure 8.14). Next, we examine each of these components.

Operational CRM **Operational CRM** includes the systems used to enable customer interaction and service. For example, operational CRM systems help create the mass e-mail marketing campaigns wherein each consumer receives an individualized e-mail based on their prior purchase

FIGURE 8.13

A successful CRM strategy
requires enterprise-wide changes.

history (although many consumers just consider the unsolicited e-mails nothing but spam). With an effective operational CRM environment, organizations are able to provide personalized and highly efficient customer service. Customer-focused personnel are provided complete customer information—history, pending sales, and service requests—in order to optimize interaction and service. It is important to stress that the operational CRM environment provides *all* customer information regardless of the touch point (i.e., technical support, customer service, and in-store sales, as well as Web site interactions such as downloading content and e-commerce clickstream data). This means that marketing, sales, and support personnel see *all* prior and current interactions with the customer regardless of where it occurred within the organization. To facilitate the sharing of information and customer interaction, three separate modules are utilized (see Figure 8.15).

FIGURE 8.14

A comprehensive CRM environment includes operational, analytical, and collaborative components.

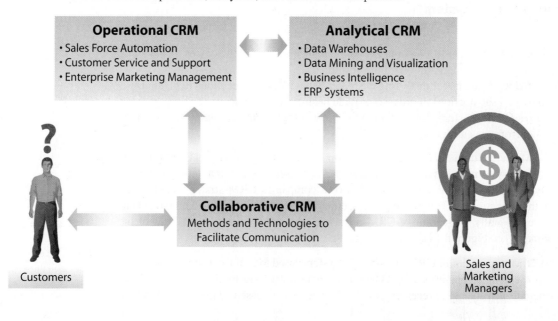

FIGURE 8.15

An operational CRM is used to enable customer interaction and service.

Sales Force Automation. The first component of an operational CRM is **sales force automation (SFA).** SFA refers to systems to support the day-to-day sales activities of an organization. For example, companies such as Dell have thousands of sales staff in various different countries, working with many different clients. Unless sales personnel and sales managers have an integrated view of Dell's entire sales pipeline, Dell sales staff may be competing with each other for the same contracts, unbeknownst to each other. SFA supports a broad range of sales-related business processes, including the following:

- Order processing and tracking
- Account and contact management
- Opportunity management
- Sales management
- Territory management
- Customer history and preferences (product and communication) management
- Sales forecasting and performance analyses

SFA systems provide advantages for sales personnel, sales managers, and marketing managers. For sales personnel, SFA helps them use their time more efficiently and ultimately focus more on selling than on paperwork and other nonselling tasks (see Table 8.3). Likewise, for sales managers, the SFA system provides improved information, allowing for better day-to-day management of the sales function and improved forecasting of future events (see Table 8.4). For example, SFA allows sales managers to track a plethora of sales performance measures, including the following:

- Sales pipeline for each salesperson, including rating and probability (see Figure 8.16)
- Revenue per salesperson, per territory, or as a percentage of sales quota
- Margins by product category, customer segment, or customer
- Number of calls per day, time spent per contact, revenue per call, cost per call, or ratio of orders to calls

TABLE 8.3 Advantages of Sales Force Management Systems for Sales Personnel

Advantages	Examples
Less paperwork	Customer contact information is recorded using e-forms that automatically provide known customer data; fill-in-the-blank forms are used to capture new information.
Fewer handoffs	Information is automatically routed to other team members and managers.
Fewer errors	E-forms ensure that customer data is automatically entered; forms can require necessary updates to be entered before saving and sharing.
Better information	Sales personnel have accurate, up-to-date, complete information on all interactions with customers as well as higher-quality sales leads.
Better training	Common systems ensure that sales personnel follow common processes and procedures.
Improved teamwork	Sharing of all sales-related information facilitates successful team selling and the sharing of best practices.
Improved morale	Improved training and less "busywork" allows a greater focus on selling and revenue generation.
Higher sales	Streamlined selling processes and improved communications allow sales personnel to focus more on selling than on nonselling activities.

- Number of lost customers per period or cost of customer acquisition
- Percentage of goods returned, number of customer complaints, or number of overdue accounts

Finally, SFA improves the effectiveness of the marketing function by providing an improved understanding of market conditions, competitors, and products. This enhanced information will provide numerous advantages for the management and execution of the marketing function. Specific advantages include the following:

- Improved understanding of markets, segments, and customers
- Improved understanding of competitors
- Enhanced understanding of the organization's strengths and weaknesses
- Better understanding of the economic structure of the industry
- Enhanced product development
- Improved strategy development and coordination with the sales function

In sum, the primary goals of SFA are to better identify potential customers, streamline selling processes, and improve managerial information. Next, we examine systems for improving customer service and support.

Customer Service and Support. The second component of an operational CRM system is **customer service and support (CSS).** CSS refers to systems that automate service requests, complaints, product returns, and information requests. In the past, organizations had *help desks* and *call centers* to provide customer service and support. Today, organizations are deploying a **customer interaction center (CIC),** using multiple communication channels to support the communication

TABLE 8.4 Advantages of Sales Force Management Systems for Sales Managers

Advantages	Examples
Improved information	Sales performance data is automatically tabulated and presented in easy-to-understand tables, charts, and graphs.
Improved time usage	Less time summarizing and tracking information allows greater time for advising and coaching sales personnel.
Better planning and forecasts	Improved accuracy and timeliness of information leads to better forecasts and plans.
Improved scheduling	Accurate and real-time data allow managers to more effectively deploy sales personnel.
Improved coordination	Accessible information allows better coordination with marketing, production, and finance.
Better sales force tracking	Systems allow managers to track a greater number of up-to-date measures, leading to improved management and faster response when problems arise.

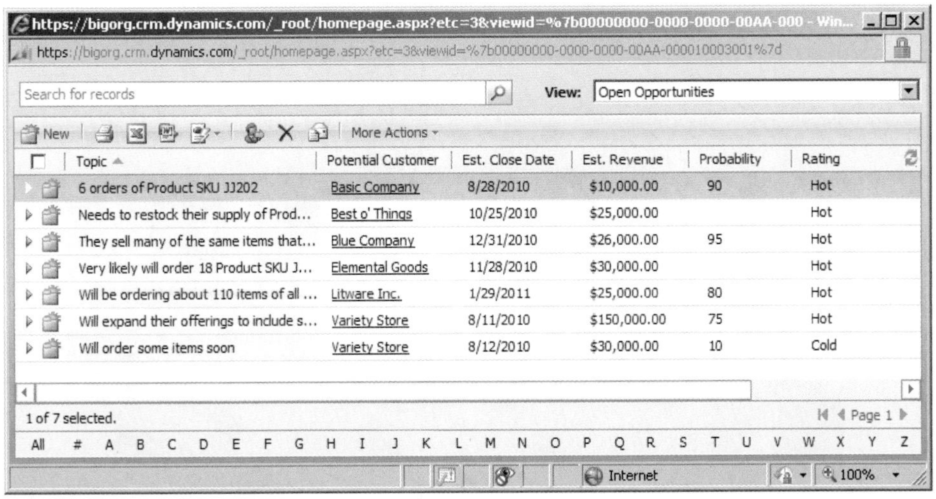

FIGURE 8.16

SFA allows sales managers to track sales performance.

preferences of customers, such as the Web, the company's Facebook page, industry blogs, face-to-face contact, telephone, and so on (see the section "Collaborative CRM" later in this chapter). The CIC utilizes a variety of communication technologies for optimizing customers' communications with the organization. For example, automatic call distribution systems forward calls to the next available person; while waiting to connect, customers can be given the option to use key or voice response technologies to check account status information. Southwest Airlines improves customer service by using "virtual hold technology," where customers can choose to stay on the line or to be called back when the next agent is available; this has helped to save almost 25 million toll minutes in 2009 and has reduced the number of abandoned calls, which provides additional opportunities for ticket sales and signals increased customer satisfaction. In essence, the goal of the CSS is to provide great customer service—anytime, anywhere, and through any channel—while keeping service and support costs low. For example, many CICs use powerful self-service diagnostic tools that guide consumers to their needed information. Customers can log service requests or gain updates to pending support requests using a variety of self-service or assisted technologies (see Figure 8.17). Successful CSS systems enable faster response times, increased first-contact resolution rates, and improved productivity of service and support personnel. Managers can utilize digital dashboards to monitor key metrics such as first-contact resolution and service personnel utilization, which allows for improved management of the service and support functions (see Chapter 6, "Enhancing Business Intelligence Using Information Systems").

Enterprise Marketing Management. The third component of an operational CRM system is **enterprise marketing management (EMM)**. EMM tools help a company in the execution of the CRM strategy by improving the management of promotional campaigns (see Figure 8.18). Today, many companies use a variety of channels (such as e-mail, telephone, direct mail, Facebook and Flickr pages, Twitter status updates, and so on; see Chapters 4 and 5) to reach potential customers and drive them back to Web sites customized for their target market (based on demographics and lifestyle). Using EMM tools can help integrate those campaigns such that the right messages are sent to the right people through the right channel. This necessitates that customer lists are managed carefully to avoid targeting people who have opted out of receiving marketing communication and to be able to personalize messages that can deliver individualized attention to each potential customer. At the same time, EMM tools provide extensive analytical capabilities that can help to analyze the effectiveness of marketing campaigns and can help to efficiently route sales leads to the right salespeople, leading to better conversion rates.

Analytical CRM **Analytical CRM** focuses on analyzing customer behavior and perceptions in order to provide the business intelligence necessary to identify new opportunities and to provide superior customer service. Organizations that effectively utilize analytical CRM can more easily customize marketing campaigns from the segment level to even the individual customer. Such customized campaigns help to increase cross- or up-selling (i.e., selling more or more profitable products or identifying popular bundles of products and services tailored to different market

FIGURE 8.17

A CIC allows customers to use a variety of self-service and assisted technologies to interact with the organization.

segments) as well as retaining customers by having accurate, timely, and personalized information. Analytical CRM systems also are used to spot sales trends by ZIP code, state, and region as well as specific target markets within those areas.

Key technologies within analytical CRM systems include data mining, decision support, and other business intelligence technologies that attempt to create predictive models of various customer attributes (see Chapter 6). These analyses can focus on enhancing a broad range of customer-focused business processes, including the following:

- Marketing campaign management and analysis
- Customer campaign customization
- Customer communication optimization
- Customer segmentation and sales coverage optimization
- Pricing optimization and risk assessment and management
- Price, quality, and satisfaction analysis of competitors
- Customer acquisition and retention analysis
- Customer satisfaction and complaint management
- Product usage, life cycle analysis, and product development
- Product and service quality tracking and management

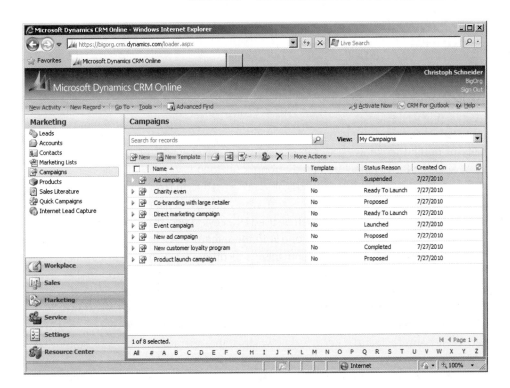

FIGURE 8.18

CRM systems allow for managing various types of promotional campaigns.

Once these predictive models are created, they can be delivered to marketing and sales managers using a variety of visualization methods, including digital dashboards and other reporting methods (see Figure 8.19). To gain the greatest value from analytical CRM applications, data collection and analysis must be continuous so that all decision making reflects the most accurate, comprehensive, and up-to-date information.

One goal that customer-focused organizations are constantly striving for is to get a 360-degree view of the customer so as to be able to maximize the outcomes of sales and marketing campaigns and to identify the most profitable customers. In order to get the most complete picture of a sales prospect or a customer, marketers have to tie together information from various sources, such as demographic information provided when signing up for a loyalty card program, the customer's

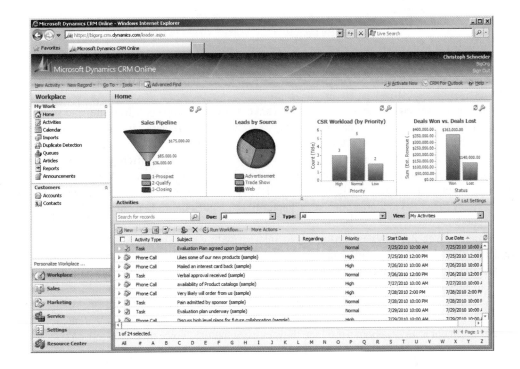

FIGURE 8.19

Digital dashboards help to visualize key CRM performance metrics.

ETHICAL DILEMMA

CRM: Targeting or Discriminating?

CRM systems could be called a marketer's dream because they promise companies the capability of getting to know their customers and at the same time maximizing the benefit gained from every customer. Through the use of sophisticated features, CRM software can let companies take a close look at customer behavior, drilling down to smaller and smaller market segments. Once so segmented, customers can be targeted with specific "special offers" or promotions. For the company, this process reaps the greatest returns from marketing efforts since only those customers are targeted who are likely to respond to the marketing campaign.

From a consumer's perspective, CRM systems seem like a great idea. Finally, you stop receiving advertisements for reams of stuff that doesn't interest you. But what if a company uses its CRM software in a more discriminating way? Where do companies draw the line between using CRM data to offer certain clients customized deals and unethically discriminating against other customers? For example, banks, which have the ability to segment their customers according to their creditworthiness, might use this credit risk data to target customers having a low credit rating. Although these customers are more risky for the banks, the higher fees and interest charged for credit make these customers especially lucrative.

A fine line exists between using CRM data for targeted marketing purposes and using such data to take advantage of certain groups. Some companies sell the customer data they have collected through CRM programs—without customer knowledge or consent. For example, a card found in the wallet of almost every person in Hong Kong is the "Octopus Card," an RFID-based stored value card that is accepted throughout Hong Kong's vast public transport network but can also be used to make payments at convenience and grocery stores, vending machines, or parking meters and can even be used as a keyless access card for residential buildings. Along with these features, Octopus Cards (the company managing this card) offers a reward program where users have to provide various personal details when signing up and can, in return, earn rewards at participating merchants; the merchants benefit from a widely accepted rewards program and can provide tailored offers to their clients. In 2010 it became known that the operator of the card system had, despite claims to the contrary, sold customer data to the insurance company CIGNA, resulting in a public relations nightmare for Octopus Cards. Such data sharing alliances benefit from the use of CRM programs, and they are legal—but are they ethical?

Based on:

Chan, S. (2010, July 27). Tentacle of lies. *The Standard.* Retrieved August 3, 2010, from http://www.thestandard.com.hk/news _detail.asp?pp_cat=30&art_id=101004&sid=29033262&con _type=3&d_str=20100727&sear_year=2010.

Jourdier, A. (2002, May 1). Privacy & ethics: Is CRM too close for comfort? *CIO.com.* Retrieved April 10, 2010, from http://www.cio.com/ article/31062/Privacy_Ethics_Is_CRM_Too_Close_for_Comfort_.

Shermach, K. (2006, August 25). Data mining: Where legality and ethics rarely meet. *CRMBuyer.com.* Retrieved April 10, 2010, from http://www.crmbuyer.com/story/52616.html.

address, purchase and contact history, clickstream data on the company's Web site, and so on. In addition to the data captured when interacting with a person, marketers can complete the picture with publicly available information posted on the person's Facebook or LinkedIn profile or the person's Twitter updates. Unfortunately, many people have various different online identities (e.g., for different social networks), use multiple e-mail addresses, and access Web sites from different computers (see Figure 8.20). Analytical CRM systems can help merge different identities by using fuzzy logic–based algorithms (see Chapter 6) to identify multiple records belonging to the same person.

Finally, Web 2.0 enables consumers to interact with each other in various ways, greatly facilitating the spreading of information as well as misinformation. Monitoring such conversations can help organizations to measure public perceptions, and participating can help organizations to keep customers satisfied and maintain a positive brand image. For example, monitoring online conversations can help to assess customer sentiments, find out what people really think about a product, and discover ways for improving a product: Whereas most customers do not bother to fill out a survey about a product, they are very likely to voice their thoughts on Facebook

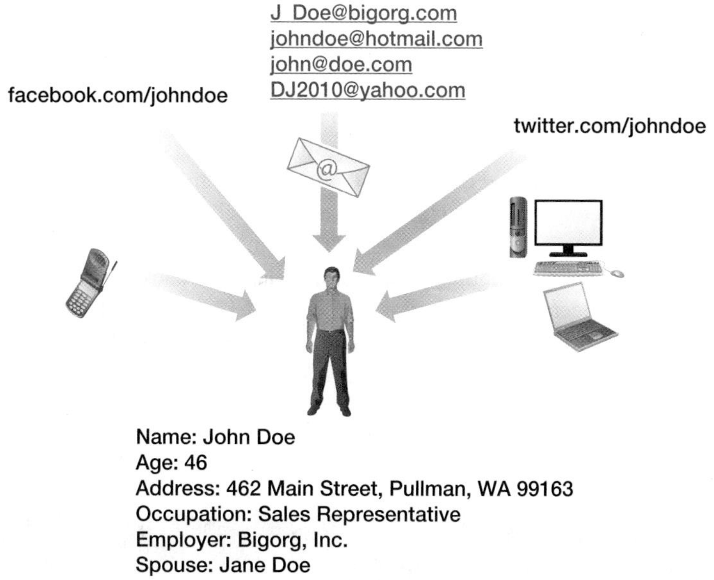

J_Doe@bigorg.com
johndoe@hotmail.com
john@doe.com
DJ2010@yahoo.com

facebook.com/johndoe

twitter.com/johndoe

Name: John Doe
Age: 46
Address: 462 Main Street, Pullman, WA 99163
Occupation: Sales Representative
Employer: Bigorg, Inc.
Spouse: Jane Doe

FIGURE 8.20

Many people interact with a company in many different ways using various online identities.

or Twitter if they are very satisfied or very dissatisfied with a product. Similarly, many people participate in online discussion forums related to a product or company, and the company should monitor the conversation and step in when needed (e.g., when customers have questions about a product, but no other customer answers within a certain time frame). Analytical CRM applications such as the Social Networking Accelerator add-on for Microsoft Dynamics CRM help in monitoring and analyzing ongoing conversations on social media sites, helping to spot potential perception issues or to discover trends in customer sentiment. Needless to say, an organization should have an appropriate social CRM strategy in place and should have clear policies, such as when to step into an online discussion, which (or how many) tweets to reply to, or how to strike a balance between grassroots marketing and deceiving people by posing as casual conversation partners.

Collaborative CRM **Collaborative CRM** refers to systems for providing effective and efficient communication with the customer from the entire organization. Collaborative CRM systems facilitate the sharing of information across the various departments of an organization in order to increase customer satisfaction and loyalty. Sharing useful customer information on a company-wide basis helps improve information quality and can be used to identify products or services a customer may be interested in. A collaborative CRM system supports customer communication and collaboration with the entire organization, thus providing more streamlined customer service with fewer handoffs. The CIC (as described previously) enables customers to utilize the communication method they prefer when interacting with the organization. In other words, collaborative CRM integrates the communication related to all aspects of the marketing, sales, and support processes in order to better serve and retain customers. Collaborative CRM enhances communication in the following ways:

- *Greater Customer Focus.* Understanding customer history and current needs helps to focus the communication on issues important to the customer.
- *Lower Communication Barriers.* Customers are more likely to communicate with the organization when personnel have complete information and when they utilize the communication methods and preferences of the customer.
- *Increased Information Integration.* All information about the customer as well as all prior and ongoing communication is given to all organizational personnel interacting with the customer; customers can get status updates from any organizational touch point.

In addition to these benefits, collaborative CRM environments are flexible such that they can support both routine and nonroutine events.

Ethical Concerns with CRM

Although CRM has become a strategic enabler for developing and maintaining customer relationships, it is not viewed positively by those who feel that it invades customer privacy and facilitates coercive sales practices. Proponents of CRM warn that relying too much on the "systems" profile of a customer, based on statistical analysis of past behavior, may categorize customers in a way that they will take exception to. Additionally, given that a goal of CRM is to better meet the needs of customers by providing highly *personalized* communication and service (such as Amazon.com's recommendations), at what point does the communication get *too* personal? It is intuitive to conclude that when customers feel that the system knows too much about them, personalization could backfire on a company. Clearly, CRM raises several ethical concerns in the digital world (see Chapter 1, "Managing in the Digital World," for a comprehensive discussion of information privacy). Nevertheless, as competition continues to increase in the digital world, CRM will be a key technology for attracting and retaining customers.

INDUSTRY ANALYSIS

Manufacturing

Regardless of whether you're thinking about a new computer, a TV, an automobile, or a toy for your baby brother, most of today's consumer products have undergone an elaborate design and manufacturing process, and few companies fail to make heavy use of information systems in the process. Traditionally, designers and engineers used large drawing boards to sketch detailed drawings of each component of a product. Today, designers use **computer-aided design (CAD)** software for this task, allowing them to create drawings faster and more accurately, thus cutting down cycle time (i.e., the time from inception to the shipment of the first product) tremendously. At the same time, CAD allows easier sharing of designs and can be used to produce three-dimensional (3-D) drawings of a new product. However, although you can create realistic 3-D drawings of a new product, people often still prefer holding a physical model in their hands to evaluate it. 3-D printing, sometimes known as "fabbing," can greatly speed up the creation of models. In essence, 3-D printers add successive layers of material onto a surface, thus building a 3-D model out of myriad individual slices. In fact, some 3-D printers even use materials such as titanium, allowing battleships to produce spare parts on an as-needed basis rather than carrying warehouses full of parts.

Engineers use **computer-aided engineering (CAE)** tools to test these designs. Whereas traditionally many features of a new product could be tested only after building prototypes, CAE allows for the testing and modification of features before the first prototypes are ever built, resulting in substantial savings of both time and money. For example, almost all automobile manufacturers now use CAE tools to perform tests for wind resistance, noise, vibrations, or simulating wear and tear. Rather than having to build prototype after prototype to test different design changes, these are tested on the computer, and the first working prototype is closer than ever to the final model.

Finally, **computer-aided manufacturing (CAM)** is the use of information systems to control the production of the final product. CAM systems take design input from a CAD system and then automatically control the manufacturing of a product's components, ranging from sheet metal presses to the spray painting of a car's exterior by "painting robots." This integration of design, engineering, and manufacturing has reduced manufacturing costs and at the same time improved product quality.

The use of technology doesn't stop there. Inventory planning, job scheduling, or warehouse management are all supported by information systems, often in the form of ERP and SCM systems. Once a product leaves the manufacturer, information systems are being used throughout the distribution of the product, from transportation scheduling to route optimization to improvement of a trucking company fleet's fuel efficiency. Clearly, information systems have changed and will continue to change the process of designing, manufacturing, and shipping products to you.

Based on:

Gardiner, B. (2007, November 21). 3-D printers redefine industrial design. *Wired*. Retrieved April 24, 2010, from http://www.wired.com/gadgets/miscellaneous/news/2007/11/3d_printers.

Groover, M. (2008). *Automation, production systems, and computer-integrated manufacturing* (3rd ed.). Upper Saddle River, NJ: Prentice Hall.

Leberecht, T. (2007, December 17). Trends 2008: Will 3-D printing finally go mainstream? *CNET News.com*. Retrieved April 24, 2010, from http://news.cnet.com/8301-13641_3-9835160-44.html.

Key Points Review

1. *Describe SCM systems and how they help to improve interorganizational business processes.* SCM focuses on improving interorganizational business processes and has two main objectives: to accelerate product development and to reduce costs associated with procuring raw materials, components, and services from suppliers. Advances in SCM have enabled concepts such as JIT strategies and VMI. At the same time, effectively managing the supply chain has become important to avoid the bullwhip effect, effectively manage quality problems, and pursue sustainable business practices. SCM systems consist of SCP, SCE, and supply chain visibility and analytics components. SCP involves the development of various resource plans to support the efficient and effective production of goods and services. SCE puts the SCP into motion and reflects the processes involved in improving the collaboration of all members of the supply chain—suppliers, producers, distributors, and customers. SCE involves the management of three key elements of the supply chain: product flow, information flow, and financial flow. Supply chain visibility and analytics help in foreseeing the impacts of external events and monitoring the performance of the supply chain to address performance issues. When developing an SCM strategy, an organization must consider a variety of factors that will affect the efficiency and effectiveness of the supply chain. Specifically, organizations must match their overall supply chain strategy to their overall competitive strategy to reap the greatest benefits. SCM is continuously advancing, using technologies such as XML and RFID.

2. *Describe CRM systems and how they help to improve the activities involved in promoting and selling products to the customers as well as providing customer service and nourishing long-term relationships.* CRM is a corporate-level strategy to create and maintain lasting relationships with customers by concentrating on the downstream information flows through the introduction of reliable systems, processes, and procedures. Applications focusing on downstream information flows have three main objectives: to attract potential customers, to create customer loyalty, and to portray a positive corporate image. Web 2.0 technologies have introduced various ways to communicate with customers but have also brought about challenges for companies trying to portray a positive brand image. To develop a successful CRM strategy, organizations must do more than simply purchase and install CRM software; they must also make changes to policy and business processes, customer service, employee training, and data utilization. A CRM consists of three primary components: operational CRM, analytical CRM, and collaborative CRM. Operational CRM focuses on activities that deal directly with customers and includes modules such as SFA, customer service and support, and EMM. Analytical CRM focuses on activities that aid managers in analyzing the sales and marketing functions as well as in monitoring ongoing conversations in social media. Finally, collaborative CRM provides effective communication capabilities within the organization and externally with customers. When implementing a CRM strategy, organizations have to be sure to carefully consider ethical concerns associated with profiling customers or treating them in ways they may object to.

Key Terms

analytical CRM 339
bullwhip effect 321
collaborative CRM 343
computer-aided design
    (CAD) 344
computer-aided engineering
    (CAE) 344
computer-aided manufacturing
    (CAM) 344
customer interaction center
    (CIC) 338
customer relationship management
    (CRM) 333
customer service and support
    (CSS) 338

enterprise marketing management
    (EMM) 339
Extensible Business Reporting
    Language (XBRL) 328
Extensible Markup Language
    (XML) 328
financial flow 325
first-call resolution 333
information flow 325
just-in-time (JIT) 320
operational CRM 335
product flow 325
radio frequency identification
    (RFID) 329
RFID tag 329

sales force automation (SFA) 337
supply chain 318
supply chain analytics 327
supply chain effectiveness 327
supply chain efficiency 327
supply chain execution (SCE) 325
supply chain management
    (SCM) 322
supply chain planning (SCP) 324
supply chain visibility 326
supply network 319
vendor-managed inventory
    (VMI) 321
XML tag 328

Review Questions

1. Describe supply chains and explain why "supply network" may be a more accurate term.
2. What are two process innovations enabled by effective collaboration within supply networks?
3. Explain how effectively managing the supply chain can help an organization be a responsible social citizen.
4. How does SCP differ from SCE?
5. How does supply chain visibility help an organization react to external events?
6. Contrast supply chain effectiveness and supply chain efficiency.
7. What is XML, and how does it impact SCM?
8. What is RFID, and how does it impact SCM?
9. How does CRM differ from SCM?
10. What is a CRM system, and what are its primary components?
11. Describe the enterprise-wide changes necessary for realizing a successful CRM strategy.
12. Contrast operational and analytical CRM.
13. How does analytical CRM help in monitoring social conversations?

Self-Study Questions

1. Which of the following is commonly used to refer to the producers of supplies that a company uses?
   A. procurement
   B. sales force
   C. supply network
   D. customers
2. Under a VMI model, _____ .
   A. a manufacturer has to signal restocking quantities to the supplier
   B. the suppliers to a manufacturer manage the manufacturer's inventory levels based on preestablished service levels
   C. the vendor has access only to stock levels
   D. stockout situations are more likely to occur
3. The bullwhip effect refers to _____ .
   A. contract penalties resulting from a supplier's inability to deliver raw materials on time
   B. small forecasting errors at the end of the supply chain causing massive forecasting errors farther up the supply chain
   C. pressure to use a specific SCM system by a company in a supply chain
   D. rising stock values due to effective SCM practices
4. Which type of flow does SCE not focus on?
   A. procurement flow
   B. product flow
   C. information flow
   D. financial flow
5. RFID tags can be used for _____ .
   A. tracking military weapons
   B. eliminating counterfeit drugs
   C. tracking passports
   D. all of the above
6. A comprehensive CRM system includes all but which of the following components?
   A. operational CRM
   B. analytical CRM
   C. diagnostic CRM
   D. collaborative CRM
7. SFA is most closely associated with what?
   A. operational CRM
   B. analytical CRM
   C. cooperative CRM
   D. collaborative CRM
8. All the following are channels used for promotional campaigns except _____ .
   A. Twitter
   B. telephone
   C. direct mail
   D. all of the above are used
9. A metric for being able to quickly resolve customers' issues is called _____ .
   A. customer satisfaction and complaint management
   B. customer communication optimization
   C. virtual-hold technology
   D. first-call resolution
10. Categorizing customers based on statistical analysis of past behavior is _____ .
    A. illegal
    B. unethical
    C. ethical and a common business practice
    D. technically impossible

Answers are on page 348.

Problems and Exercises

1. Match the following terms with the appropriate definitions:

   i. JIT
   ii. Supply chain efficiency
   iii. Supply chain
   iv. Supply chain visibility
   v. CRM
   vi. CIC
   vii. SCM
   viii. VMI
   ix. CAM
   x. RFID

   a. The ability to track products as they move through the supply chain but also to foresee external events
   b. The use of information systems to control production processes
   c. The use of electromagnetic energy to transmit information between a reader (transceiver) and a processing device, used to replace bar codes and bar code readers
   d. The extent to which a company's supply chain is focusing on minimizing procurement, production, and transportation costs
   e. An SCM innovation that optimizes ordering quantities such that parts or raw material arrive just when they are needed for production
   f. Applications that help to create and maintain lasting relationships with customers by concentrating on the downstream information flows
   g. Commonly used to refer to the network of producers of supplies that a company uses
   h. A business model in which the suppliers to a manufacturer (or retailer) manage the manufacturer's (or retailer's) inventory levels based on preestablished service levels
   i. The use of multiple communication channels to support the communication preferences of customers
   j. Applications that help to improve interorganizational business processes to accelerate product development and innovation and to reduce costs

2. Find an organization that you are familiar with and determine how it manages its supply chain. Is the company effective in managing the supply chain, or does it need closer integration and collaboration with its suppliers?

3. Search the Web for a recent product recall. How did the company affected handle the recall? Were the actions appropriate, or could increased supply chain visibility have helped?

4. Search the Web for companies using sustainable SCM practices. Are those attempts convincing? Why or why not? Under what circumstances would such practices influence your purchasing decisions?

5. Analyze the supply chain of your favorite electronic gadget and compare this with the supply chain of your favorite pair of jeans. How do the supply chains differ? What are potential reasons for this?

6. When purchasing a product on the Web, how important is the visibility of *your* supply chain for this product? Why? Does the importance differ for different products?

7. Choose a company you are familiar with and examine how efficiently or effectively it has designed the procurement, production, and transportation aspects of its business.

8. What applications other than those mentioned in the chapter are there for RFID tags? What must happen in order for the use of RFID to become more widespread?

9. Assume you are a sales manager. What sales performance measures would you want the CRM system to provide you in order to better manage your sales force? For each measure, describe how you would use it and at what interval you would need to update this information.

10. Find an organization that is utilizing CRM (visit vendor Web sites for case studies or industry journals such as *CIO Magazine* or *Computerworld*). Who within the organization is most involved in this process, and who benefits?

11. When you last contacted a company with a product or service request, which contact options did you have? Which option did you choose, and why?

12. Search the Web for recent articles on social CRM. What is the current state of the art for managing customer relationships in social media?

13. Use the Web to visit sites of three companies offering CRM systems. Do these companies sell only CRM systems? What do they have in common? What do they have that is unique?

14. Search on Facebook for your favorite company's page. How does this company present itself in the social media? How does it handle customer conversations? Is the organization's strategy effective?

15. Discuss the ethical trade-offs involved when using large databases that profile and categorize customers so that companies can more effectively market their products. Think about products that are "good" for the consumer versus those that are not.

Application Exercises

 Note: The existing data files referenced in these exercises are available on the Student Companion Web site: **www.pearsonhighered.com/valacich.**

 Spreadsheet Application:
Tracking Web Site Visits at Campus Travel

Campus Travel has recently started selling products on the Internet; the managers are eager to know how the company's Web site is accepted by the customers. The file CampusTravel.csv contains transaction information for the past three days, generated from the company's Web server, including IP addresses of the visitors, whether a transaction was completed, and the transaction amount. You are asked to present the current status of the e-commerce initiative. Use your spreadsheet program to prepare the following graphs:

1. A graph highlighting the total number of site visits and the total number of transactions per day
2. A graph highlighting the total sales per day

Make sure to format the graphs in a professional manner, including headers, footers, and the appropriate labels, and print each graph on a separate page (Hint: To calculate the total number of site visits and the total number of transactions, use the "countif" function to count the number

Database Application:
Managing Customer Relations at Campus Travel

Not all frequent fliers accumulate large amounts of miles. There are many who never travel for years but have frequent-flier accounts. As manager of sales and marketing, you want to find out how to target these individuals with promotions and special offers. To accomplish this task, you will need to create the following reports:

1. A report displaying all frequent fliers, sorted by distance traveled
2. A report displaying all frequent fliers, sorted by the total amount spent on air travel.

In the file InfrequentFliers.mdb, you find travel data of the members of a frequent-flier program for the year 2012. Prepare professionally formatted printouts of all reports, including headers, footers, dates, and so on. (Hint: Use the report wizard to create the reports; use queries to sum up the fares and distances for each traveler before creating the respective reports.)

Team Work Exercise: Your "Online Personas"

Work in a small group with classmates and analyze your "online personas." How many different e-mail addresses does each you have? How many different user names for social networks? Which e-mail addresses do you use when dealing with an online store, and which do you prefer to keep private? Would you give your social network user names to a company for CRM purposes? Do you see any ethical issues in a company trying to obtain this information? Prepare a brief presentation of your responses.

Answers to the Self-Study Questions

1. C, p. 319	2. B, p. 321	3. B, p. 321	4. A, p. 325	5. D, p. 329
6. C, p. 335	7. A, p. 337	8. D, p. 339	9. D, p. 333	10. B, p. 344

Case 1

The Battle for the Dashboard

Competition is stiff among electronics manufacturers as they battle for dominance of consumers' living rooms, desktops, and mobile devices. Now the battle extends to the automobile industry. It is clear that the tech industry sees the automobile industry as a key target for bringing new technologies to consumers. Many consumer tech-

nology shows and meetings are starting to look like car shows.

Nowhere is this more evident than at the International Consumer Electronics Show (CES), the granddaddy of all technology shows. For the third time in CES history, the 2010's opening keynote address was by an executive from the automobile manufactur-

ing industry. Ford Motor Corporation's president and chief executive officer Alan Mulally arrived onstage for the second time (he also gave the keynote at the 2009 CES) telling the audience how Ford had put over 1 million cars on the road equipped with "Sync" technology in the past year. The Sync system was codeveloped with

Microsoft and allows drivers to operate mobile phones and media players with voice controls. In addition, Sync can deliver traffic and direction services, provide auto-911 dialing in the event of an emergency, and give a vehicle health report; it will even read text messages aloud to drivers if they arrive on their mobile phone while driving.

Although Sync has become a popular option for most Ford vehicle buyers, Mulally said that the auto company wasn't resting on its laurels. He announced that Ford is moving forward with plans to further improve the system and connect their cars with the Internet. Through a connection with data-enabled smart phones, the new features will incorporate Twitter functions within the dashboard system. Drivers will be able to have their Twitter messages read aloud to them and then be able to compose and send replies—all through the voice-enabled, hands-free interface. In addition, users will be able to stream Internet radio from Pandora, a Web-based streaming music provider, through the car's sound system. In addition, the system will be Wi-Fi capable and have the option of USB ports and a place to plug in a keyboard.

The new system, called myFord Touch, will incorporate all of Sync's features, navigation, information, and data collected by the car and serve as a platform for adding other technologies as they are developed. One such planned development program is called American Journey 2.0. The program will allow university students to take data collected by the car's onboard computers and combine it with other Web information in a sort of "mashup" to create new applications. Mulally gave the example of everyone on a particular stretch of road turning on

their windshield wipers and fog lights and that information being shared by the car's computer through a social networking site to alert people to the weather conditions on a certain section of highway. Mulally sees future development of all types of new Web 2.0 applications being built that will interact with automobile data, giving drivers on and off the road access to information.

Ford is not the only automaker that has brought information and entertainment to the dashboard. Chrysler has a similar system called Uconnect that gives the driver access to navigation, music, television, and Internet. Audi has a system that allows drivers to bring up information about subjects while they drive. In fact, there has been an explosion of high-tech gadgetry appearing in car dashboards of all makes and models. These advances have brought plenty of new conveniences to drivers, but many question how safe they are. Studies have revealed that text-messaging drivers increase their time with eyes off the road by 400 percent, leading to a higher chance that they will not see something on the road that could lead to an accident. Drivers dialing on a cell phone are nearly three times as likely to be involved in an accident as those not dialing on a phone. So what will all these new gadgets, giving drivers a whole new set of possible distractions, mean for safety on the road? Safety advocates worry that increasing the amount of distraction for drivers will result in more crashes and injuries. In 2008, over half a million people were injured or killed from accidents resulting from distracted drivers.

With these fears in mind, some new dashboard technology has been designed to enhance driver safety. For example, Mercedes has a feature called "Attention-Assist,"

which monitors more than 70 streams of sensor data about the driver, looking for actions that might indicate that they are beginning to doze at the wheel. The system will warn these sleepy drivers that it's time to take a break with a flashing coffee cup and an audible warning.

Safety concerns aside, many cars already incorporate many of the electronics consumers have grown to love, such as the Global Positioning System, TV screens, touch-screen monitors, smart phone–enabled ports, and hands-free mobile dialing. Coming soon are headrests with computers in them (with monitors in the back of the headrest), cars that talk to each other, and cars that drive themselves.

Yes, drive themselves. Cars of the near future will contain electronic sensors to alert drivers to objects in the road ahead or behind if the vehicle is in reverse, and vehicle-to-vehicle transponder systems will let other cars know when conditions are changing, as when one car in a row of cars is braking. Electronics will also eventually keep cars spaced appropriately during highway driving, make cars obey all traffic signals, and allow cars to communicate with highway information centers along main routes.

As the electronics and auto industries merge, the technology-dominated home and workplace environments will no longer be separate from the automobile environment. According to Larry Burns, head of research and development at General Motors, "Consumers don't want to have a different experience when they're in their car versus when they're outside their car, so I think that tying in with consumer electronics is going to be really important for the future of our industry. Connectivity will be mainstream with the auto industry."

Questions

1. How can interorganizational systems help companies like General Motors better manage supplier and customer relationships, especially as the automobile industry is transformed?
2. Which capabilities of interorganizational systems will be most critical for manufacturing or selling the cars of the future?
3. What capabilities would you like to see in the car of the future?

Based on:

Abuelsamid, S. (2008, January 8). CES 2008: Live blogging the Rick Wagoner keynote on Electric Avenue. *Autoblog.com*. Retrieved July 24, 2010, from http://www.autoblog.com/2008/01/08/ces-2008-live-blogging-the-rick-wagoner-keynote.

Barrett, L. (2010, January 7). CES 2010: Ford promises a smarter digital dashboard. *InternetNews.com*. Retrieved July 24, 2010, from http://itmanagement.earthweb.com/entdev/article.php/3857151/CES-2010-Ford-Promises-a-Smarter-Digital-Dashboard.htm.

Ford Sync. (2010, June 7). In *Wikipedia, the free encyclopedia*. Retrieved July 25, 2010, from http://en.wikipedia.org/w/index.php?title=Ford _Sync&oldid=366496122.

Hartley, M. (2008, January 9). The battle for the dashboard. *The Globe and Mail*. Retrieved July 24, 2010, from http://www.theglobeandmail.com/news/technology/article658735.ece.

Massy, K. (2008, January 8). GM's Wagoner addresses CES, unveils Cadillac Provoq. *CNET.com*. Retrieved July 24, 2010, from http://ces.cnet.com/8301-1 _1-9846322-67.html.

Neate, R. (2010, January 8). CES 2010: Ford unveils Tweeting car. *Telegraph.co.uk*. Retrieved July 24, 2010, from http://www.telegraph.co.uk/technology/ces/6949335/CES-2010-Ford-unveils-Tweeting-car.html.

Vance, A., & Richtel, M. (2010, January 6). Despite risks, Internet creeps onto car dashboards. *New York Times*. Retrieved on July 24, 2010, from http://www.nytimes.com/2010/01/07/technology/07distracted.html.

Case 2

CRM 2.0

CRM is a process of learning more about customers' needs and how they behave in order to grow stronger relationships with them. It is a broadly recognized and implemented methodology for managing an organization's interactions with its customers and potential clients. It involves the use of technology for organizing and automating a number of organizational activities, such as marketing, customer service, tech support, and, most often, sales.

Visualizing CRM as just technology, however, is the wrong way to think about it; technology is merely one of the tools that enable CRM. CRM is a customer-centric business philosophy that helps organizations bring together information about their products, services, customers, and the market forces that are driving them. Data is gathered and aggregated from as many internal and external sources as possible to give an actual, real-time picture of the customer base. CRM allows an organization to provide better customer service, discover new customers, sell products more effectively, and simplify marketing and sales processes. Although there are many facets, the following are some core CRM components:

- CRM helps an organization enable its marketing departments to identify and target their best customers, manage marketing campaigns, and generate quality leads for the sales team.
- CRM assists an organization in improving its customer accounts and sales management by optimizing information shared across the employee base and streamlining existing processes.
- CRM allows the formation of individualized relationships with organization customers, with the aim of improving customer satisfaction and maximizing profits.
- CRM provides employees with the information and processes necessary to build relationships between the company, its customer base, and distribution partners.
- Once the best and most profitable customers are identified through CRM, organizations can ensure that they are providing them the highest level of service.

In addition to these features, CRM environments support collaboration and communication within the organization. Just as social media like Facebook, LinkedIn, Twitter, and other Web 2.0 technologies are becoming a preferred way to stay connected to friends and family members, CRM applications are also evolving to reflect the movement toward Web 2.0 capabilities. In fact, CRM pioneer Salesforce.com recently released a product called Salesforce Chatter, which provides a similar set of capabilities found on many of the popular social media sites, allowing individuals throughout an organization to collaborate more effectively using methods that have become extremely popular. For instance, with a Web-based interface that looks very similar to Facebook, Chatter allows individuals within the organizations to post profiles, provide real-time status updates about themselves or activities, organize groups, monitor feeds, share documents, and so on. Clarence So, senior vice president for Salesforce.com, when talking about how individuals within organizations are working together, states, "Increasingly, instead of using the Web for search, they're using platforms such as Facebook and YouTube. Instead of communicating by e-mail, they're using instant messaging and texts. And instead of accessing the Web from a desktop, they're turning to smartphones and other mobile devices." Chatter is designed to bring the best collaboration features found on the most popular Web sites into a single collaboration environment, allowing people within an organization to more effectively work together and collaborate. As So adds, "It's a Facebook-like feed interface that lets a user follow objects, which could be fellow employees, a customer record, a project, a document, anything that's an object within Salesforce.com. They can interact with and receive updates on the objects they follow in their Chatter feed." Chatter is also being targeted for mobile devices such as the iPad, supporting touch and gesture interfaces.

Interacting with customers via social media, however, still presents many challenges for most organizations that are increasingly finding themselves being left out of conversations that customers are having about them. Traditional CRM communication channels have been built on the telephone and e-mail, but many customers are moving to social media. Strategies for understanding which customers to connect with through social media are still developing, but organizations are moving to embrace the technology via products like Chatter in order to keep pace with ever-changing communication styles. Social media is actually very synergistic with CRM tools since social media is about interacting with someone on the other end. Organizations will do well to understand that social media is not just about pushing advertising or making announcements but also about connecting with their customers and building relationships. Expect CRM tools and the sophistication of their use to continue to evolve, transforming CRM into an Enterprise 2.0 technology.

Questions

1. What role does technology play in CRM? Is CRM mostly about technology or mostly about relationships?
2. What types of communication (e.g., e-mail, texting, Facebook, and so on) methods would you want to have with a company you do business with? Explain.
3. If you were the chief executive officer of a Fortune 500 company, would you be comfortable using social media sites like Facebook or LinkedIn as part of your CRM strategy? Why or why not?

Based on:

Anonymous. (2010, February 19). What is CRM? *DestinationCRM.com*. Retrieved April 24, 2010, from http://www.destinationcrm.com/Articles/CRM-News/Daily-News/What-Is-CRM-46033.aspx.

Jedras, J. (2010, July 19). Salesforce.com says stage set for cloud 2.0. *itbusiness.ca*. Retrieved August 3, 2010, from http://www.itbusiness.ca/it/client/en/home/News.asp?id=58434.

Lau, K. (2010, March 19). Social CRM's 18 use cases: Altimeter. *NetworkWorld*. Retrieved April 24, 2010, from http://www.networkworld.com/news/2010/031910-social-crms-18-use-cases.html.

Salesforce.com. (2010). Salesforce Chatter. Retrieved August 3, 2010, from http://www.salesforce.com/assets/pdf/datasheets/DS_Chatter.pdf.

Thompson, E. (2009, June 3). What's "hot" in CRM applications in 2009. *Gartner*. Retrieved April 24, 2010, from http://www.gartner.com/DisplayDocument?&id=1004212.

Vile, D. (2010, July 22). The significance of Salesforce.com's "Chatter." *Computing.co.uk*. Retrieved August 3, 2010, from http://freeform.computing.co.uk/2010/07/the-significance-of-salesforcecoms-chatter.html.

Williams, E. (2006, October 25). CRM. Retrieved April 24, 2010, from http://searchcrm.techtarget.com/definition/CRM.

After reading this chapter, you will be able to do the following:

1. Describe how to formulate and present the business case for technology investments.

2. Describe the systems development life cycle and its various phases.

3. Explain how organizations acquire systems via external acquisition and outsourcing.

Preview

As you have read throughout this book and have experienced in your own life, information systems and technologies are of many different types, including high-speed Web servers to rapidly process customer requests, decision support systems to aid managerial decision making, or customer relationship management systems to provide improved customer service. Given this variety, when we refer to "systems" in this chapter, we are talking about a broad range of technologies, including hardware, software, and services. Just as there are different types of systems, there are different approaches for developing and acquiring them. If you are a business student majoring in areas such as marketing, finance, accounting, or management, you might be wondering why we have a chapter on building and acquiring information systems. The answer is simple: No matter what area of an organization you are in, you will be involved in the systems development or technology acquisition process. In fact, research indicates that spending on systems in many organizations is controlled by the specific business functions rather than by the information systems (IS) department. What this means is that even if your career interests are in something other than information systems, it is very likely that you will be involved in the development and acquisition of systems, technologies, or services. Understanding this process is important to your future success.

Managing in the Digital World: Casual Gaming: You, Me, and Wii

Think of "gamers," and chances are that you visualize a portly, unkempt couch potato hunched over a game controller, fingers flying, for hours or maybe days at a time. Or maybe you see a hard-core nerd whose brain functions well only in virtual mode. In the past, the term "gamers" referred mostly to participants in role-playing or war games, but today it refers also to casual gamers who indulge occasionally for fun but also maintain a functioning life in the "real" world.

Until recently, the Microsoft Xbox and Sony PlayStation were the most popular game consoles for both hard-core and casual gamers. This all changed in 2006, when Nintendo introduced the Wii. Contrary to the Xbox and PlayStation, the Wii offered a level of *physical* gamer participation hitherto unknown (see Figure 9.1). Instead of exercising just the fingers to move around a game, the Wii's wireless, motion-sensing controllers let players get their entire bodies involved. Wii Sports, for example, gets players of all ages off the couch and swinging a baseball bat (with the help of a special interactivity-enabling device called the Wiimote), lobbing tennis balls, or driving golf balls. You can also *casually* try some extreme sports such as kite surfing or rock climbing or some wacky activities like "Tuna Tossing" or "Extreme Ironing."

The Wii also introduced a different way for players to interact with each other. Instead of going online to compete with players in distant locations, Wii gamers can participate with family members and friends in their own living rooms. Dance together (on a special dance pad), form bowling teams, or call friends together for a complete group workout using special mat-like controllers that detect distribution of weight.

The casual games developed for the Wii are not only being played in living rooms and college dorm rooms but have now found their way into hospital recovery and therapy wards. Stroke victims that have lost some of their motor skills are reaping the benefits of Wii-based physical therapy. Studies have found that patients undergoing Wii-based physical therapy, using casual games such as "Wii Tennis" or "Wii Cooking Mama," have shown a 30 percent better improvement than patients undergoing traditional recreational therapy measures.

Nintendo's gamble that consumers would enjoy playing games that require less time and less skill and that more closely parallel real-life activities paid off. For months after the Wii's introduction, Nintendo was unable to keep up with demand, and would-be buyers were lining up in front of stores such as Toys "R" Us and Best Buy, only to find that the latest shipment of the product had already sold out. The popularity of the Wii has continued to rise with consumers, as almost 4 million consoles were sold during the 2009 holiday season. To broaden the appeal of the Wii even further, Nintendo partnered with Netflix in 2010 to support movie downloads without the need of a DVR

iStockphoto.com

FIGURE 9.1

The Nintendo Wii puts the gamer into the game.

or computer. Today, the Wii is the best-selling game console in the world, with nearly 60% market share.

Clearly, a big reason why the Wii has become so popular is because Nintendo targeted casual gamers—those who did not play games at all or played them only occasionally because of the time required to master most games and the dexterity required. The multi-billion-dollar gaming industry had long been concerned that devoted gamers would eventually move on to other types of entertainment, but the casual gaming market has given the industry new life. The key to any successful product is volume, and the time has come for casual gaming. Game developers are working hard to provide shorter, less complicated, more interactive games for those who want to play occasionally but don't want games to be their one consuming passion. This system design strategy has clearly been a winner for Nintendo.

After reading this chapter, you will be able to answer the following:

1. What process would you use if you were designing a new computer game?
2. How would the process of determining system requirements differ if you were designing a new payroll system versus a new game?
3. How important is system testing for an online game versus a traditional type of software, such as a payroll system?

Based on:

Anonymous. (2007, July 2). Seven months later, Wii demand still outpaces supply. *FoxNews.com* Retrieved April 8, 2010, from http://www.foxnews.com/story/0,2933,287678,00.html.

Bishop, T. (2007, July 12). New Wii controller turns your video game into workout. *Seattlepi.com*. Retrieved April 8, 2010, from http://seattlepi.nwsource.com/business/323343_nintendosony12.html.

Gaudiosi, J. (2007, April 24). Games continue record pace. *Home Media Magazine*. Retrieved April 8, 2010, from http://www.homemediamagazine.com/news/html/breaking_article.cfm?article_id=10568.

Kohler, C. (2007, June 11). Triumph of the Wii: How fun won out in the console wars. *Wired*. Retrieved April 8, 2010, from http://www.wired.com:80/gaming/hardware/news/2007/06/wii.

Kohler, C. (2008, February 6). Game biz guns for mainstream by going casual. *Wired*. Retrieved April 8, 2010, from http://www.wired.com/gaming/gamingreviews/news/2008/02/dice_walkup.

Mozes, A. (2010, February 25). Wii-gaming could aid stroke rehab. *BusinessWeek*. Retrieved April 8, 2010, from http://www.businessweek.com/lifestyle/content/healthday/636395.html.

Rosmarin, R. (2007, November 16). Wii rules! *Forbes.com*. Retrieved April 8, 2010, from http://www.forbes.com/2007/11/15/wii-games-xbox-technology-personaltech-cx_rr_1116wii.html.

Simpson, O. (2010, February 1). Wii bestselling Nintendo console ever. *Digital Spy*. Retrieved July 20, 2010, from http://www.digitalspy.com/gaming/a200786/wii-bestselling-nintendo-console-ever.html.

Snider, M. (2009, July 27). Try your hand (and remote) at new casual games for Wii. *USA Today*. Retrieved April 8, 2010, from http://www.usatoday.com/life/lifestyle/2009-07-27-wii-casual-games_N.htm.

Stone, B. (2010, January 13). Nintendo Wii to add Netflix service for streaming video. *New York Times*. Retrieved April 8, 2010, from http://www.nytimes.com/2010/01/13/technology/companies/13netflix.html.

Making the Business Case

Before people are willing to spend money to build a new system or spend more money on an existing one, they want to be convinced that this will be a good investment. **Making the business case** refers to the process of identifying, quantifying, and presenting the value provided by a system.

Business Case Objectives

What does making the business case mean? Think for a moment about what defense lawyers do in court trials. They carefully build a strong, integrated set of arguments and evidence to prove that their clients are innocent to those who will pass judgment on their clients. In much the same way, people in business often have to build a strong, integrated set of arguments and evidence to prove that an information system is adding value to the organization or its constituents. This is, in business lingo, "making the business case" for a system.

As a business professional, you will be called on to make the business case for systems and other capital investments. As a finance, accounting, marketing, or management professional, you are likely to be involved in this process and will therefore need to know how to effectively make the business case for a system (or other capital expenditures) and need to understand the relevant organizational issues involved. It will be in the organization's best interest—and in your own—to ferret out systems that are not adding value. In these cases, you will need to either improve the systems or replace them.

Making the business case is as important for proposed systems as it is for the continued investment in an existing system. For a proposed system, the case will be used to determine whether the new system is a "go" or a "no-go." For an existing system, the case will be used to determine whether the company will continue to fund the system. Whether a new system or an existing one is being considered, your goal is to make sure that the investment adds value, that it helps the firm achieve its strategy and competitive advantage over its rivals, and that money is being spent wisely.

The Productivity Paradox

Unfortunately, while it is easy to quantify the costs associated with developing an information system, it is often difficult to quantify tangible productivity gains from its use. Over the past several years, the press has given a lot of attention to the impact of IS investments on worker productivity. In many cases, IS expenditures, salaries, and the number of people on the IS staff have all been rising, but results from these investments have often been disappointing. For instance, the information and technology research firm Gartner reports that worldwide spending on systems and technologies surpassed $3.3 trillion in 2010. American and Canadian companies are spending, on average, around 4 percent of company revenues on system-related investments. As a result, justifying the costs for IS investments has been a hot topic among senior managers at many firms. In particular, "white-collar" productivity, especially in the service sector, has not increased at the rate one might expect, given the trillions of dollars spent.

Why has it been difficult to show that these vast expenditures on technologies have led to productivity gains? Have information systems somehow failed us, promising increases in performance and productivity and then failing to deliver on that promise? Determining the answer is not easy. Information systems may have increased productivity, but other forces may have simultaneously worked to reduce it, the end results being difficult to identify. Factors such as government regulations, more complex tax codes and stricter financial reporting requirements (such as the Sarbanes-Oxley Act; see Chapter 10, "Securing Information Systems"), and more complex products can all have major impacts on a firm's productivity.

It is also true that information systems introduced with the best intentions may have had unintended consequences. A paramount example is giving employees access to e-mail and the Internet—now employees are spending excessive amounts of time surfing the Web to check sports scores on the ESPN Web site, to read volumes of electronic junk mail received from Internet marketing companies or from personal friends, or use company PCs to download and play software games (see Figure 9.2); recently, it was reported that visits to social networking sites such as Facebook and Twitter cost U.K. firms alone approximately $2.25 billion in lost productivity every year. In these situations, information systems can result in less efficient and less effective communication among employees and less productive uses of employee time than before the systems were implemented. Nevertheless, sound technology investments should increase organizational productivity. If this is so, why have organizations not been able to show larger productivity gains? A number of reasons have been given for the apparent **productivity paradox** of technology investments (Figure 9.3). This issue is examined next.

Measurement Problems In many cases, the benefits of information systems are difficult to pinpoint because firms may be measuring the wrong things. Often, the biggest increases in productivity result from increased **system effectiveness** (i.e., the extent to which a system enables

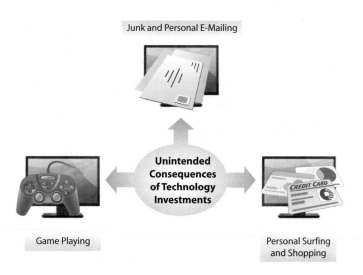

Junk and Personal E-Mailing

Unintended Consequences of Technology Investments

Game Playing

Personal Surfing and Shopping

FIGURE 9.2

Unintended consequences can limit the productivity gains from IS investments.

FIGURE 9.3

Factors leading to the IS
productivity paradox.

people and/or the firm to accomplish goals or tasks well). Unfortunately, many business metrics focus on **system efficiency** (i.e., the extent to which a system enables people and/or the firm to do things faster, at lower cost, or with relatively little time and effort).

A good example of measurement problems associated with a technology investment is the use of online banking. How much has online banking contributed to banking productivity? Traditional statistics might look at the adoption rate of the service and associated reductions in branch-based services and locations. While informative, such statistics may not work well for evaluating online banking, at least at this point in time. For instance, many older customers may not want to bank online, so a reduction in the number of traditional branches could threaten a potentially large number of very good customers while at the same time inflating the percentage of online banking users (i.e., if the number of traditional banking customers leave the bank because of a reduction of branches, the adoption rate of online customers as a percentage will be increased). So, investing in online banking may be unimportant for an important segment of customers while essential for others. Nevertheless, can you imagine a bank staying competitive without offering online services? Deploying technologies such as online banking has become a *strategic necessity*—something an organization must do in order to survive (see Chapter 2, "Gaining Competitve Advantage Through Information Systems"). The value of necessary benefits is often difficult to quantify.

Time Lags A second explanation for why productivity is sometimes difficult to demonstrate for some technology investments is that a significant time lag may occur from when a company makes the investment until that investment is translated into improvement in the bottom line. Let us return to our online banking example. In some markets, it may take years from the first implementation of this new system before the magnitude of benefits may be felt by the organization.

Redistribution A third possible explanation for why IS productivity figures are not always easy to define is that a new type of system may be beneficial for individual firms but not for a particular industry or the economy as a whole. Particularly in competitive situations, new innovations may be used to redistribute the pieces of the pie rather than making the whole pie bigger. The result for the industry or economy as a whole is a wash—that is, the same number of products is being sold, and the same number of dollars is being spread across all the firms.

Mismanagement A fourth explanation is that the new system has not been implemented and managed well. Some believe that people often simply build bad systems, implement them poorly, and rely on technology fixes when the organization has problems that require a joint

NET STATS

Moore's Law and the Laggards

The technology industry, laboring under Moore's Law, depends on technology users to regularly adopt new hardware and software. Millions of users, however, accustomed to the tried and true, would rather stick with those products they know—at least as long as possible. Sometimes the reason for not rushing to replace the old with the new is familiarity with and an acquired expertise in using the older version of a product or service:

- In mid-2010, more than 5 million people still used AOL's dial-up Internet access service, even when broadband was available at comparable prices.
- Although Yahoo! updated its e-mail interface in 2007, millions of subscribers still opt to use the older version today.
- More than a million Internet users continue to use Netscape, even though support and enhancements for this once popular browser have stopped years ago.

Other reasons why people may be slow to adopt new technologies are prohibitive costs or user views that the new product or service has yet to prove itself as superior to the old. Microsoft's Vista versus Windows 7 operating systems is a case in point. While Vista was viewed as an improvement over the prior Windows version, XP, most consumers did not adopt Vista, viewing its cost and high system requirements to be excessive. In mid-2010, just a few months after its release, the adoption rate for Windows 7 outpaced that of Vista over a similar period by more than two to one. It is forecasted to capture more than 50 percent of the market share by early 2011.

Individual computer users are free to opt to be tortoises or hares regarding the adoption of new technology. Information technology (IT) directors, however, must usually follow company culture and management preferences when opting whether to adopt new technology. If management is comfortable with risk and likes to be on the cutting edge, for example, IT directors can probably feel safe in adopting new technology early on. A staid, risk-averse management attitude, however, would probably not appreciate an IT director who rushes to adopt new technology.

In any event, whether to adopt new technology immediately as it becomes available is a decision that will always be with us.

Based on:

Helft, M. (2008, March 12). Tech's late adopters prefer the tried and true. *New York Times.* Retrieved April 9, 2010, from http://www.nytimes.com/2008/03/12/technology/12inertia.html.

Oiaga, M. (2010, February 22). Windows 7 crushes Vista. *Softpedia.* Retrieved April 9, 2010, from http://news.softpedia.com/news/Windows-7-Crushes-Vista-135712.shtml.

Warren, S. (2005, November 17). Adopting new tech: Conservative or Aggressive? *Earthweb.* Retrieved April 9, 2010, from http://itmanagement.earthweb.com/erp/article.php/3565056.

technology/process solution. Rather than increasing outputs or profits, IS investments might merely be a temporary bandage and may serve to mask or even increase organizational slack and inefficiency. Also, as we mentioned in Chapter 1, "Managing in the Digital World," an information system can be only as effective as the business model that it serves. Bad business models can't be overcome by good information systems.

If it is so difficult to quantify the benefits of information systems for individual firms and for entire industries, why do managers continue to invest in information systems? The answer is that competitive pressures force managers to invest in information systems whether they like it or not. You might ask, then, so why waste time making the business case for a system? Why not just build them? The answer: Given the vast number of potential systems and technologies that could be developed or acquired, a strong business case aids the decision-making process and helps direct resources in more strategic ways.

Making a Successful Business Case

People make a variety of arguments in their business cases for information systems. When managers make the business case for an information system, they typically base their arguments on faith, fear, and/or facts (Wheeler, 2002. Wheeler also adds a fourth "F," that being for "fiction," and notes that, unfortunately, managers sometimes base their arguments on pure fiction, which is not only bad for their careers but also not at all healthy for their firms.) Table 9.1 shows examples of these three types of arguments.

TABLE 9.1 Three Types of Arguments Commonly Made in the Business Case for an Information System

Type of Argument	Description	Example
Faith	Arguments based on beliefs about organizational strategy, competitive advantage, industry forces, customer perceptions, market share, and so on	"I know I don't have good data to back this up, but I'm convinced that having this customer relationship management system will enable us to serve our customers significantly better than our competitors do and, as a result, we'll beat the competition. . . . You just have to take it on faith."
Fear	Arguments based on the notion that if the system is not implemented, the firm will lose out to the competition or, worse, go out of business	"If we don't implement this enterprise resource planning system, we'll get killed by our competitors because they're all implementing these kinds of systems. . . . We either do this or we die."
Fact	Arguments based on data, quantitative analysis, and/or indisputable factors	"This analysis shows that implementing the inventory control system will help us reduce errors by 50 percent, reduce operating costs by 15 percent a year, increase production by 5 percent a year, and will pay for itself within eighteen months."

Do not assume that you must base your business case on facts only. It is entirely appropriate to base the business case on faith, fear, or facts (see Figure 9.4). Indeed, the strongest and most comprehensive business case will include a little of each type of argument. In the following sections, we talk about each of these types of arguments for the business case.

Business Case Arguments Based on Faith In some situations, arguments based on faith (or fear) can be the most compelling and can drive the decision to invest in an information system despite the lack of any hard data on system costs, or even in the face of some data that say that the dollar cost for the system will be high. Arguments based on faith often hold that an information system must be implemented in order to achieve the organization's strategy effectively and to gain or sustain a competitive advantage over rivals.

For example, a firm has set as its strategy that it will be the dominant, global force in its industry. As a result, this firm must adopt a variety of collaboration technologies, such as desktop videoconferencing and groupware tools, in order to enable employees from different parts of the globe to work together effectively and efficiently. Similarly, a firm that has set as its strategy that it will have a broad scope—producing products and services across a wide range of consumer needs—may need to adopt some form of an enterprise resource planning system to better coordinate business activities across its diverse product lines.

In short, successful business case arguments based on faith should clearly describe the firm's mission and objectives, the strategy for achieving them, and the types of information systems that are needed in order to enact the strategy. A word of caution is warranted here. In today's business

FIGURE 9.4

A successful business case will be based on faith, fear, and fact.

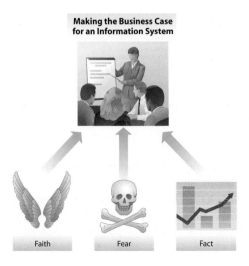

environment, cases based solely on strategic arguments, with no hard numbers demonstrating the value of the information system under consideration, are not likely to be funded.

Business Case Arguments Based on Fear There are several different factors to take into account when making a business case in which you will provide arguments based on fear. These include a number of factors involving competition and other elements of the industry in which the firm operates. For example, a mature industry, such as the automotive industry, may need systems simply to maintain the current pace of operations. While having the newest systems and technologies available may be nice, they may not be needed to stay in business. However, a company in a newer, expanding industry, such as the mobile phone industry, may find it more important to be on the leading edge of technology in order to compete effectively in the marketplace. Likewise, some industries are more highly regulated than others. In these cases, companies can use technology investments to better control processes and ensure compliance with appropriate regulations. The argument for the business case here would be something like "If we do not implement this system, we run the risk of being sued or, worse, being thrown in jail" (see Chapter 10).

Probably the most important industry factor that can affect technology investments is the nature of competition or rivalry in the industry. For example, when competition in an industry is high and use of the newest technologies is rampant, as it is in the mobile phone industry, strategic necessity, more than anything else, forces firms to adopt new systems. Given how tight profit margins are in this industry, Nokia and other manufacturers must use inventory control systems, Web-based purchasing and customer service, and a host of other systems that help them to be more effective and efficient. If they do not adopt these systems, they will likely go out of business. Introduced in Chapter 2, a common way for assessing the level of competition within an industry is the five forces model (Porter, 1979). By assessing the various competitive forces, you can determine which specific technologies may be more or less useful. For instance, in a highly price-competitive market, where buyers have strong bargaining power, investments to reduce production costs might be advantageous. Business case arguments formulated this way sound something like "If we do not implement this system, our competitors are going to beat us on price, we will lose market share, and we will go out of business."

Business Case Arguments Based on Fact Many people, including most chief financial officers, want to see the business case for an information system based on some convincing, quantitative analysis that proves beyond the shadow of a doubt that the benefits of the system will outweigh the costs. The most common way to prove this is to provide a detailed cost–benefit analysis of the information system. Although this step is critical, the manager must remember that there are inherent difficulties in, and limits to, cost–benefit, analyses for information systems. To illustrate how a cost–benefit analysis could be used to build a fact-based business case, let us consider the development of a Web-based order entry system for a relatively small firm.

Identifying Costs. One goal of a cost–benefit analysis is to accurately determine the **total cost of ownership (TCO)** for an investment. TCO is focused on understanding not only the total cost of *acquisition* but also all costs associated with ongoing *use and maintenance* of a system. Consequently, costs can usually be divided into two categories: **nonrecurring costs** and **recurring costs.** Nonrecurring costs are one-time costs that are not expected to continue after the system is implemented. These include costs for things such as site preparation and technology purchases. These one-time costs may also include the costs of attracting and training a Webmaster or renovating some office space for new personnel or for hosting the Web server.

Recurring costs are ongoing costs that occur throughout the life of the system. Recurring costs include the salary and benefits of the Webmaster and any other personnel assigned to maintain the system, upgrades and maintenance for the system components, monthly fees paid to a local Internet service provider, and the continuing costs for the space in which the Webmaster works or the *collocation facility* where the server resides (see Chapter 10). Personnel costs are usually the largest recurring costs, and the Web-based system is no exception in this regard. These recurring expenses can go well beyond the Webmaster to include expenses for customer support, content management, ongoing maintenance, and so on.

The sample costs described thus far are **tangible costs** that are relatively easy to quantify. Some **intangible costs** ought to be accounted for as well, even though they will not fit neatly into the quantitative analysis. These might include the costs of reduced traditional sales, losing some customers that are not "Web ready," or losing customers if the Web application is poorly designed

COMING ATTRACTIONS

Microsoft's Surface—Any Place, Any Time

If you have ever watched the television show *CSI Miami*, you have seen Surface in action (not the actual machine but a demonstration of the technology). A technician uses her fingers to manipulate images—photos, microscope slides, and documents—on a flat horizontal surface in front of her, and she can "throw" the images to a larger screen that displays them vertically. If you thought the concept was still science fiction, you were wrong. The technology exists, and Microsoft introduced it to the public commercially in April 2008 (see Figure 9.5).

With Surface, Microsoft reveals, "We can actually grab data with our hands and move information between objects with natural gestures and touch." No keyboards, no mice, just a thirty-inch tabletop display where fingers do the walking—and drawing and writing and tapping. And more than one user at once can manipulate data. Users can also place physical objects, like cell phones and even drinks, on the Surface to see additional information revealed, such as the features present in the cell phone or the ingredients in a drink.

Surface uses cameras to sense objects, hand gestures, and touch. User input is processed, and the results are projected on the tabletop surface.

According to Microsoft Chairman Bill Gates, surface computing will eventually become so pervasive that it won't be limited to tabletops and walls. He said, "Our view is that all surfaces—horizontal, vertical—will eventually have an inexpensive screen display capability, and software that sees what you're doing there, so it's completely interactive." Today, in addition to *CSI Miami*, Surface can be found in high-end restaurants and hotel lobbies; this technology has simply been too expensive for most households to afford. In addition to its high cost, current versions of Surface are also quite large and bulky, making it difficult to have in a cramped dorm room or apartment.

To overcome these constraints, Microsoft is spending a great deal on research and development to evolve the Surface to lower its cost and size. In fact, in 2010, Microsoft demonstrated a prototype called the Microsoft Mobile Surface, which links a camera-projector system that beams a touch-enabled interface onto any flat surface. This Mobile Surface can be powered by a laptop computer or even a smart phone. Although it is still just a prototype, it shows that cost and size constraints can be overcome. This technology has numerous potential applications that can transform how we interact with technology.

Based on:

Chen, J. (2008, May 8). Microsoft Surface + Xbox 360 = What? *Gizmodo*. Retrieved March 18, 2010, from http://gizmodo.com/388749/microsoft-surface-%252B-xbox-360-what.

Costa, D. (2007, May 30). Hands on with "Microsoft Surface": The coffee-table PC. *PC Magazine*. Retrieved March 18, 2010, from http://www.pcmag.com/article2/0,1759,2138251,00.asp.

Derene, G. (2007, July). Microsoft Surface: Behind-the-scenes first look. *Popular Mechanics*. Retrieved March 18, 2010, from http://www.popularmechanics.com/technology/industry/4217348.html.

McLaughlin, K. (2010, March 3). Microsoft working on mobile version of Surface. *ChannelWeb*. Retrieved March 18, 2010, from http://www.crn.com/software/223101445.

FIGURE 9.5

The Microsoft Surface.

Reprinted with permission from Microsoft Corporation.

or not on par with competitors' sites. You can choose to either quantify these in some way (i.e., determine the cost of losing a customer) or simply reserve these as important costs to consider outside of—but along with—the quantitative cost–benefit analysis.

Identifying Benefits. Next, you determine both **tangible benefits** and **intangible benefits.** Some tangible benefits are relatively easy to determine. For example, you can estimate that the increased customer reach of the new Web-based system will result in at least a modest increase in sales. Based on evidence from similar projects, you might estimate, say, a 5 percent increase in sales the first year, a 10 percent increase the second year, and a 15 percent increase the third year. In addition, you might also include as tangible benefits the reduction of order entry errors because orders will now be tracked electronically and shipped automatically. You could calculate the money previously lost on faulty and lost orders, along with the salaries and wages of personnel assigned to find and fix these orders, and then consider the reduction of these costs as a quantifiable benefit of the new system. Cost avoidance is a legitimate, quantifiable benefit of many systems. Similarly, the new system may enable the company to use fewer order entry clerks or redeploy these personnel to other, more important functions within the company. You could consider these cost reductions as benefits of the new system.

A Web-based system may have intangible benefits as well. Some intangible benefits of this new system might include faster turnaround on fulfilling orders and resulting improvements in customer service. These are real benefits, but they might be hard to quantify with confidence. Perhaps an even more intangible benefit would be the overall improved perception of the firm. Customers might consider it more progressive and customer service oriented than its rivals; in addition to attracting new customers, this might increase the value of the firm's stock if it is a publicly traded firm. Another intangible benefit might be simply that it was a strategic necessity to offer customers Web-based ordering to keep pace with rivals. While these intangibles are difficult to quantify, they must be considered along with the more quantitative analysis of benefits. In fact, the intangible benefits of this Web-based system might be so important that they could carry the day despite an inconclusive or even negative cost–benefit analysis.

Performing Cost–Benefit Analyses. An example of a simplified **cost–benefit analysis** that contrasts the total expected tangible costs versus the tangible benefits is presented in Figure 9.6.

		2010	2011	2012	2013	2014
Costs						
Nonrecurring						
Hardware		$ 20,000				
Software		$ 7,500				
Networking		$ 4,500				
Infrastructure		$ 7,500				
Personnel		$100,000				
Recurring						
Hardware			$ 500	$ 1,000	$ 2,500	$ 15,000
Software			$ 500	$ 500	$ 1,000	$ 2,500
Networking			$ 250	$ 250	$ 500	$ 1,000
Service fees			$ 250	$ 250	$ 250	$ 500
Infrastructure				$ 250	$ 500	$ 1,500
Personnel			$ 60,000	$ 62,500	$ 70,000	$ 90,000
Total costs		$139,500	$ 61,500	$ 64,750	$ 74,750	$110,500
Benefits						
Increased sales		$ 20,000	$ 50,000	$ 80,000	$115,000	$175,000
Error reduction		$ 15,000	$ 15,000	$ 15,000	$ 15,000	$ 15,000
Cost reduction		$100,000	$100,000	$100,000	$100,000	$100,000
Total benefits		$135,000	$165,000	$195,000	$230,000	$290,000
Net costs/benefits		$ (4,500)	$103,500	$130,250	$155,250	$179,500

FIGURE 9.6

Worksheet showing a simplified cost–benefit analysis for the Web-based order fulfillment system.

Notice the fairly large investment up front, with another significant outlay in the fifth year for a system upgrade. You could now use the net costs/benefits for each year as the basis of your conclusion about this system. Alternatively, you could perform a **break-even analysis**—a type of cost–benefit analysis to identify at what point (if ever) tangible benefits equal tangible costs (note that breakeven occurs early in the second year of the system's life in this example)—or a more formal **net-present-value analysis** of the relevant cash flow streams associated with the system at the organization's **discount rate** (i.e., the rate of return used by an organization to compute the present value of future cash flows). In any event, this cost–benefit analysis helps you make the business case for this proposed Web-based order fulfillment system. It clearly shows that the investment for this system is relatively small, and the company can fairly quickly recapture the investment. In addition, there appear to be intangible strategic benefits to deploying this system. This analysis—and the accompanying arguments and evidence—goes a long way toward convincing senior managers in the firm that this new system makes sense.

Comparing Competing Investments. One method for deciding among different IS investments or when considering alternative designs for a given system is **weighted multicriteria analysis,** as illustrated in Figure 9.7. For example, suppose that for a given system being considered, there are three alternative designs that could be pursued—A, B, or C. Let's also suppose that early planning meetings identified three key system requirements and four key constraints that could be used to help make a decision on which alternative to pursue. In the left column of Figure 9.7, three system requirements and four constraints are listed. Because not all requirements and constraints are of equal importance, they are weighted on the basis of their relative importance. In other words, you do not have to weight requirements and constraints equally; it is certainly possible to make requirements more or less important than constraints. Weights are arrived at in discussions among the analysis team, users, and managers. Weights tend to be fairly subjective and, for that reason, should be determined through a process of open discussion to reveal underlying assumptions, followed by an attempt to reach consensus among stakeholders. Notice that the total of the weights for both the requirements and constraints is 100 percent.

Next, each requirement and constraint is rated on a scale of 1 to 5. A rating of 1 indicates that the alternative does not meet the requirement very well or that the alternative violates the constraint. A rating of 5 indicates that the alternative meets or exceeds the requirement or clearly abides by the constraint. Ratings are even more subjective than weights and should also be determined through open discussion among users, analysts, and managers. For each requirement and constraint, a score is calculated by multiplying the rating for each requirement and each constraint by its weight. The final step is to add up the weighted scores for each alternative. Notice that we have included three sets of totals: for requirements, for constraints, and for overall totals. If you look at the totals for requirements, alternative B or C is the best choice because each meets or exceeds all requirements. However, if you look only at constraints, alternative A is the best

FIGURE 9.7

Alternative projects and system design decisions can be assisted using weighted multicriteria analysis.

Criteria	Weight	Alternative A		Alternative B		Alternative C	
		Rating	Score	Rating	Score	Rating	Score
Requirements							
Real-time data entry	18	5	90	5	90	5	90
Automatic reorder	18	1	18	5	90	5	90
Real-time data query	14	1	14	5	70	5	70
	50		122		250		250
Constraints							
Developer costs	15	4	60	5	75	3	45
Hardware costs	15	4	60	4	60	3	45
Operating costs	15	5	75	1	15	5	75
Ease of training	5	5	25	3	15	3	15
	50		220		165		180
Total	100		342		415		430

ETHICAL DILEMMA

Genetic Testing

The Human Genome Project has been big news since its beginning in 1990. Funded by the U.S. government, the project allowed scientists around the world to map the 20,000 to 25,000 genes within the 23 pairs of human chromosomes—groundbreaking science, for sure, but also a source of ethical dilemmas in a number of industries because of the personal information genetic testing can reveal. Do you carry genes for chronic diseases that may make you a bad risk for health insurance companies or for potential employers who provide health insurance for their employees? Would you want to know if you carry the gene or genes for a fatal disease for which there is currently no treatment or cure, such as Alzheimer's disease? How ethical are mail-order genetic testing laboratories that offer genetic analyses without counseling to help clients interpret results? Is genetic testing another example of technology outpacing legal and ethical issues?

As early as 1990, Lisa N. Geller and her Harvard Medical School colleagues were conducting a study of genetic discrimination in the United States. Out of 917 questionnaires sent out, 455 respondents in Geller's study said that they had experienced genetic discrimination. The often-quoted study revealed that a number of institutions were reported to have engaged in genetic discrimination, including health and life insurance companies, health care providers, blood banks, adoption agencies, the military, and schools. Some examples follow:

- A health maintenance organization refused to pay for occupational therapy for a child born with a disabling hereditary disease on grounds that the condition was "preexisting."
- Medical professionals reportedly pressured patients at risk for passing on defective genes to undergo prenatal diagnostic testing or to avoid having children.
- In one case, a 24-year-old respondent reported that she was denied life insurance because of her family history of Huntington's chorea (a hereditary, disabling, inevitably fatal disease). She had not been genetically tested for the gene causing Huntington's, and the insurance company did not want to risk issuing a policy to her in case she later developed the disease.

In May 2008, Congress passed the Genetic Information Nondiscrimination Act to bar discrimination based on genes. "People know we all have bad genes, and we are all potential victims of genetic discrimination," said Representative Louise M. Slaughter of New York, who proposed the legislation. The bill prohibited health insurance companies from using genetic information to deny benefits or raise premiums for individual policies. Furthermore, employers who use genetic information to make decisions about hiring, firing, or salaries could face hefty fines.

Technology has opened the door to the possibility of not only genetic discrimination but also new ways for unscrupulous doctors to take advantage of patients. Today, a plethora of genetic testing laboratories can be found online. "Paternity tests for $99," one lab advertised. A more extensive genetic profile could be obtained for $1,000 from a number of testing facilities. Companies will take a sample of your DNA from cheek cells (you spit into a vial), scan it, and send you information about your genetic future as well as your family tree. You and members of your family can track inherited traits, such as athletic endurance, heart disease, breast cancer, colorectal cancer, and lactose intolerance. Other companies focus on matching the genes you have discovered you have to current medical research, calculating your genetic risk for developing a wide range of diseases. Some doctors in several Third World countries are going a step further, promising miracle cures using untested stem cell therapies for people with devastating conditions and injuries.

The new genomics age comes with great promise and opportunity, but it also raises ethical questions that will be difficult to answer. How will knowing your genetic profile affect your life and your future? And how can we protect such information from those who would abuse it? Linda Avey and Anne Wojcicki (the wife of Google's cofounder Sergei Brin), cofounders of a genetic testing company called "23andMe," emphasize that one's genome is simply information. Information about our health or potential health to add to the information we're already collecting, such as blood pressure, cholesterol level, and height/weight comparisons. Using such information wisely and without prejudice is the challenge for the twenty-first century. As an "Alpha tester" for 23andMe, Sergei Brin discovered that he has a 50% chance of developing Parkinson's disease; Brin has donated $50 million to studying Parkinson's, hoping to contribute to finding a cure for the disease.

Based on:

Goetz, T. (2007, November 17). 23AndMe will decode your DNA for $1,000. Welcome to the age of genomics. *Wired*. Retrieved April 13, 2010, from http://www.wired.com:80/medtech/genetics/magazine/15-12/ff_genomics.

(continued)

Goetz, T. (2010, June). Sergey Brin's search for a Parkinson's cure. *Wired.* Retrieved August 1, 2010, from http://www.wired.com/magazine/2010/06/ff_sergeys_search.

Harmon, A. (2008, May 2). Congress passes bill to bar bias based on genes. *New York Times.* Retrieved April 13, 2010, from http://www.nytimes.com:80/2008/05/02/health/policy/02gene.html.

Human genome project information. (n.d.). Retrieved April 13, 2010, from http://www.ornl.gov/sci/techresources/Human_Genome/home.shtml.

Judson K., Harrison, C., & Hicks, S. (2006). *Law and ethics for medical careers.* Boston: McGraw-Hill.

Landau, M. (1996, April 12). Genetics testing leads to discrimination. Retrieved April 13, 2010, from http://focus.hms.harvard.edu/1996/Apr12_1996/Genetics.html.

Nolen, S. (2010, March 19). The stem-cell black market: Delhi doctor claims wonder cures. *The Globe and Mail.* Retrieved April 13, 2010, from http://www.theglobeandmail.com/news/technology/science/the-stem-cell-black-market-delhi-doctor-claims-wonder-cures/article1506296.

Pollack, A. (2009, March 11). Google Co-Founder Backs Vast Parkinson's Study. *New York Times.* Retrieved August 1, 2010, from http://www.nytimes.com/2009/03/12/business/12gene.html.

choice because it does not violate any constraints. When we combine the totals for requirements and constraints, we see that the best choice is alternative C. Whether alternative C is actually chosen for development, however, is another issue. The decision makers may choose alternative A, knowing that it does not meet two key requirements because it has the lowest cost. In short, what may appear to be the best choice for a systems development project may not always be the one that ends up being developed or acquired. By conducting a thorough analysis, organizations can greatly improve their decision-making performance.

Presenting the Business Case

Up to this point, we have discussed the key issues to consider as you prepare to make the business case for a system. We have also shown you some tools for determining the value that a system adds to an organization. Now you are actually ready to make the case—to present your arguments and evidence to the decision makers in the firm.

Know the Audience Depending on the firm, a number of people from various areas of the firm might be involved in the decision-making process. People from different areas of the firm typically hold very different perspectives about what investments should be made and how those investments should be managed (see Table 9.2). Consequently, presenting the business case for a new system investment can be quite challenging. Ultimately, a number of factors come into play in making investment decisions, and numerous outcomes can occur (see Figure 9.8). Understanding the audience and the issues important to them is a first step in making an effective presentation. Various ways to improve the development of a business case are examined next.

Convert Benefits to Monetary Terms When making the case for an IS investment, it is desirable to translate all potential benefits into monetary terms. For example, if a new system saves department managers an hour per day, try to quantify that savings in terms of dollars. Figure 9.9 shows how you might convert time savings into dollar figures. While merely explaining this benefit as "saving managers' time" makes it sound useful, managers may not consider it a significant enough inducement to warrant spending a significant amount of money. Justifying a

TABLE 9.2 Characteristics of Different Stakeholders Involved in Making IS Investment Decisions

Stakeholder	Perspective	Focus/Project Characteristics
Management	Representatives or managers from each of the functional areas within the firm	Greater strategic focus; largest project sizes; longest project durations
Steering committee	Representatives from various interest groups within the organization (they may have their own agendas at stake when making investment decisions)	Cross-functional focus; greater organizational change; formal cost–benefit analysis; larger and riskier projects
User department	Representatives of the intended users of the system	Narrow, nonstrategic focus; faster development
IS executive	Has overall responsibility for managing IS development, implementation, and maintenance of selected systems	Focus on integration with existing systems; fewer development delays; less concern with cost–benefit analysis

Source: Based on Hoffer et al. (2011) and McKeen, Guimaraes, and Wetherbe (1994).

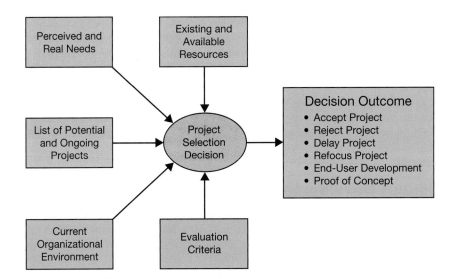

FIGURE 9.8

Investment selection decisions must consider numerous factors and can have numerous outcomes.

$50,000 system because it will "save time" may not be persuasive enough. However, an annual savings of $90,000 is more likely to capture the attention of decision makers and is more likely to result in project approval. Senior managers can easily rationalize a $50,000 expense for a $90,000 savings and can easily see why they should approve such a request. They can also more easily rationalize their decision later on if something goes wrong with the system.

Devise Proxy Variables The situation presented in Figure 9.9 is fairly straightforward. Anyone can see that a $50,000 investment is a good idea because the return on that investment is $90,000 the first year. Unfortunately, not all cases are this clear-cut. In cases in which it is not as easy to quantify the impact of an investment, you can come up with **proxy variables** (i.e., alternative measures of outcomes) to help clarify what the impact on the firm will be. Proxy variables can be used to measure changes in terms of their perceived value to the organization. For example, if mundane administrative tasks are seen as a low value (perhaps a 1 on a 5-point scale) but direct contact with customers is seen as a high value (a rating of 5), you can use these perceptions to indicate how new systems will add value to the organization. In this example, you can show that a new system will allow personnel to have more contact with customers while at the same time reducing the administrative workload. Senior managers can quickly see that individual workload is being shifted from low-value to high-value activities.

You can communicate these differences using percentages, increases or decreases, and so on—whatever best conveys the idea that the new system is creating changes in work, in performance, and in the way people think about their work. This gives decision makers some relatively solid data on which to base their decision.

Measure What Is Important to Management One of the most important things you can do to show the benefits of a system is one of the simplest: measure what senior managers think is important. You may think this is trivial advice, but you would be surprised how often people calculate impressive-looking statistics in terms of downtime, reliability, and so on, only to find that senior managers disregard or only briefly skim over those figures. You should concentrate on the

Benefit:	
New system saves at least one hour per day for 12 mid-level managers.	
Quantified as:	
Manager's salary (per hour)	$30.00
Number of managers affected	12
Daily savings (one hour saved × 12 managers)	$360.00
Weekly savings (daily savings × 5)	$1,800.00
Annual savings (weekly savings × 50)	$90,000.00

FIGURE 9.9

Converting time savings into dollar figures.

issues senior business managers care about. The "hot-button" issues with senior managers should be easy to discover, and they are not always financial reports. Hot issues with senior managers could include cycle time (how long it takes to process an order), regulatory or compliance issues, customer feedback, and employee morale. By focusing on what senior business managers believe to be important, you can make the business case for systems in a way that is more meaningful for those managers, which makes selling systems to decision makers much easier. Managers are more likely to buy in to the importance of systems if they can see the impact on areas that are important to them. Now that you understand how to make the business case for new information systems, we now examine the development process.

The Systems Development Process

No matter if a software company such as Microsoft is planning to build a new version of its popular Office software suite, or if a company such as Netflix is trying to build a system to improve its movie recommendations, companies follow a standardized approach. This process of designing, building, and maintaining information systems is often referred to as **systems analysis and design.** Likewise, the individual who performs this task is referred to as a **systems analyst.** Because few organizations can survive without effectively utilizing information and computing technology, the demand for skilled systems analysts is very strong. In fact, the *Wall Street Journal* named being a systems analyst the third-best job for 2010. Likewise, the U.S. Bureau of Labor Statistics ranks systems analysts near the top of all professions for job stability, income, and employment growth through 2016, with average growth exceeding 29 percent. Organizations want to hire systems analysts because they possess a unique blend of managerial and technical expertise—systems analysts are not just "techies." Systems analysts remain in demand precisely because of this unique blend of abilities.

Customized versus Off-the-Shelf Software

When deciding to deploy new systems to support their operations in order to gain or sustain a competitive advantage, organizations can typically choose between customized and off-the-shelf software. For example, many types of application software (such as word processors, spreadsheet, or accounting software) can be used by a variety of businesses within and across industries. These types of general purpose systems are typically purchased off the shelf. Often, however, organizations have very specific needs that cannot be met by generic technologies. This is especially true for companies trying to capitalize on a first-mover advantage and therefore may not be able to purchase a preexisting system to meet their specific needs. For example, pioneers in online retailing (such as Amazon.com) or budget air travel (such as Southwest Airlines) needed entirely new systems and technologies to support their revolutionary business models and had to develop (or have someone else develop) customized solutions. The approaches to developing or acquiring customized and off-the-shelf software are quite different but also have many similarities. Before going into the details of developing or acquiring such systems, we'll first contrast these two types of systems.

Customized Software

Customized software is developed to meet the specifications of an organization. These technologies may be developed (or configured) in-house by the company's own IS staff, or it may be contracted, or outsourced, to a specialized vendor charged with developing the system to the company's contractual specifications. Customized systems have two primary advantages over general purpose commercial technologies:

1. *Customizability.* The software can be tailored to meet unique organizational requirements. Such requirements, for example, can reflect a desire to achieve a competitive advantage through a specific type of system (e.g., Amazon's one-click ordering) or to better fit business operations, characteristics of the organizational culture, or proprietary security requirements, or to better interface with existing systems.
2. *Problem Specificity.* The company pays only for the features specifically required for its users. For example, company- or industry-specific terms or acronyms can be included in a new software application, as can unique types of required reports. Such specificity is not typically possible in off-the-shelf systems that are targeted to a more general audience.

TABLE 9.3 Examples of Off-the-Shelf Application Software

Category	Application	Description	Examples
Business information systems	Payroll	Automation of payroll services, from the optical reading of time sheets to generating paychecks	ZPAY Intuit Payroll
	Inventory	Automation of inventory tracking, order processing, billing, and shipping	Intuit QuickBooks InventoryPower 5
Office automation	Personal productivity	Support for a wide range of tasks from word processing to graphics to e-mail	OpenOffice Corel WordPerfect Microsoft Office

Today, building a complete system from scratch is quite rare; most information systems that are developed within an organization for its internal use typically include a large number of preprogrammed, reusable modules as well as off-the-shelf hardware technologies that are purchased from development organizations or consultants.

Off-the-Shelf Software

Although customized software has advantages, it is not automatically the best choice for an organization. Off-the-shelf software (or packaged software) is typically used to support common business processes that do not require any specific tailoring. In general, off-the-shelf systems, whether hardware or software, are less costly, faster to procure, of higher quality, and less risky than customized systems. Table 9.3 summarizes examples of off-the-shelf application software.

Combining Customized and Off-the-Shelf Systems

It is possible to combine the advantages of customized and off-the-shelf systems. Companies can purchase off-the-shelf technologies and then have these modified for their specific needs. For example, a retailer may want to purchase an off-the-shelf inventory management program and then modify it to account for the specific products, outlets, and reports it needs to conduct its day-to-day business. In some cases, the company selling the software makes these customized changes for a fee. Other vendors, however, may not allow their software to be modified.

Commercial, off-the-shelf systems are always acquired from an external vendor (unless you *are* the vendor, such as personnel within Microsoft using Word for their word processing tasks), whereas customized systems can be either developed in-house or developed by an outside vendor (see Figure 9.10). Regardless of the source of the new system, the primary role of managers and users in the organization is to make sure that it will meet the organization's business needs.

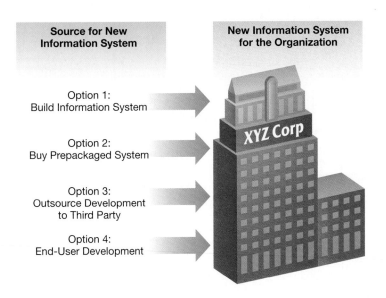

FIGURE 9.10

There are a variety of sources for information systems.

IS Development in Action

The tools and techniques used to develop information systems are continually evolving with the rapid changes in IS hardware and software. As you will see, the IS development approach is a fairly disciplined and structured process that moves from step to step. Systems analysts become adept at decomposing large, complex problems into many small, simple problems. The goal of the systems analyst is to design the final system by piecing together the many small programs and technologies into one comprehensive system (see Figure 9.11). For example, think about using LEGO blocks for building a model of a space station. Each individual block is a small, simple piece that is nothing without the others. When put together, the blocks can create a large and very complex design. When systems are built in this manner, they are much easier to design, build, and, most important, maintain.

Although many people in organizations, such as managers and users, are responsible and participate in a systems development project, the systems analyst has primary responsibility. Some projects may have one or several systems analysts working together, depending on the size and complexity of the project. The primary role of the systems analyst is to study the problems and needs of an organization in order to determine how people, methods, and information technology can best be combined to bring about improvements in the organization. A systems analyst helps systems users and other business managers define their requirements for new or enhanced information services.

A systems analyst typically also *manages* the development project. As the **project manager,** the systems analyst needs a diverse set of management, leadership, technical, conflict management, and customer relationships skills. The project manager is the person most responsible for ensuring that a project is a success. The project manager must deal with continual change and problem solving. Successful projects require effective resource and task management as well as effective communication as the project moves through its various steps. Project management is an important aspect of the system development or acquisition process and a critical skill for successful systems analysts. The focus of project management is to ensure that projects meet customer expectations and are delivered within budget and time constraints. Clearly, a systems analyst is an agent of change and innovation in modern organizations.

The Role of Users in the Systems Development Process

Many organizations have a huge investment in transaction processing and management information systems. These systems are most often designed, constructed, and maintained by systems analysts within the organization, using a variety of methods. When building and maintaining information systems, systems analysts rely on information provided by system users, who are involved in all phases of the system's development process. To effectively participate in the process, it is important for all members of the organization to understand what is meant by systems development and what activities occur. A close, mutually respectful working relationship between analysts and users is a key to project success.

FIGURE 9.11

Problem decomposition makes solving large, complex problems easier.

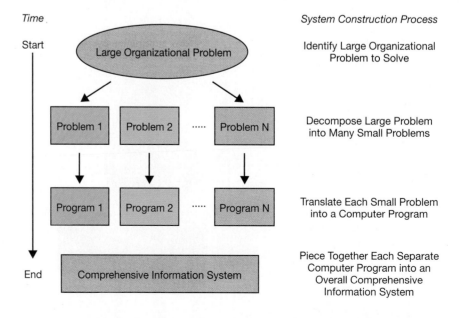

Steps in the Systems Development Process

Just as the products that a firm produces and sells follow a life cycle, so does an organizational information system. For example, a new type of tennis shoe follows a life cycle of being designed, introduced to the market, being accepted into the market, maturing, declining in popularity, and ultimately being retired. The term **systems development life cycle (SDLC)** describes the life of an information system from conception to retirement (Hoffer, George, & Valacich, 2011). The SDLC has five primary phases:

1. Systems planning and selection
2. Systems analysis
3. Systems design
4. Systems implementation and operation
5. Systems maintenance

Figure 9.12 is a graphical representation of the SDLC containing four boxes connected by arrows. Within the SDLC, arrows flow from systems planning and selection, to systems analysis, to systems design, and, finally, to systems implementation and operation. Once a system is in operation, it moves into an ongoing maintenance phase that parallels the initial development process. For example, when new features are added to an existing system, analysts must first plan and select which new features to add, then analyze the possible impact of adding these features to the existing system, then design how the new features will work, and, finally, implement these new features into the existing system. In this way, the SDLC becomes an ongoing *cycle*. During ongoing system maintenance, the entire SDLC is followed to implement system repairs and enhancements.

Phase 1: Systems Planning and Selection

The first phase of the SDLC is **systems planning and selection** (see Figure 9.12). Understanding that it can work on only a limited number of projects at a given time because of limited resources, an organization must take care that only those projects that are critical to enabling the organization's mission, goals, and objectives are undertaken. Consequently, the goal of systems planning and selection is simply to identify, plan, and select a development project from all possible projects that could be performed. Organizations differ in how they identify, plan, and select projects. Some organizations have a formal **information systems planning** process whereby a senior manager, a business group, an IS manager, or a steering committee identifies and assesses all possible systems development projects that an organization could undertake. Project managers present the business case for the new system and it is accepted or rejected. Others follow a more ad hoc process for identifying potential projects. Nonetheless, after all possible projects are identified, those deemed most likely to yield significant organizational benefits, given available resources, are selected for subsequent development activities.

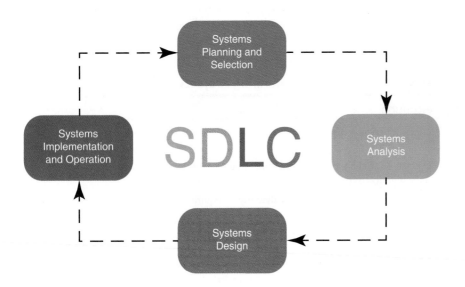

FIGURE 9.12

The SDLC defines the typical process for building systems.

Just as there are often differences in the source of systems projects within organizations, there are often different evaluation criteria used within organizations when classifying and ranking potential projects (Table 9.4). During project planning, the analyst works with the customers—the potential users of the system and their managers—to collect a broad range of information to gain an understanding of the project size, potential benefits and costs, and other relevant factors. After collecting and analyzing this information, the analyst builds the business case that can be reviewed and compared with other possible projects. Table 9.4 provides a sample of the criteria often used by organizations. If the organization accepts the project, systems analysis begins.

Phase 2: Systems Analysis

The second phase of the SDLC is called **systems analysis** (see Figure 9.12). One purpose of the systems analysis phase is for designers to gain a thorough understanding of an organization's current way of doing things in the area for which the new information system will be constructed. The process of conducting an analysis requires that many tasks, or subphases, be performed. The first subphase focuses on determining system requirements. To determine the requirements, an analyst works closely with users to determine what is needed from the proposed system. After collecting the requirements, analysts organize this information using data, process, and logic modeling tools.

Collecting Requirements The collection and structuring of requirements is arguably the most important activity in the systems development process because how well the IS requirements are defined influences all subsequent activities. The old saying "garbage in, garbage out" very much applies to the systems development process. **Requirements collection** is the process of gathering and organizing information from users, managers, customers, business processes, and documents to understand how a proposed information system should function. Systems analysts use a variety of techniques for collecting system requirements, including the following (Hoffer et al., 2011):

- *Interviews.* Analysts interview people informed about the operation and issues of the current or proposed system.
- *Questionnaires.* Analysts design and administer surveys to gather opinions from people informed about the operation and issues of the current or proposed system.
- *Observations.* Analysts observe workers at selected times to see how data are handled and what information people need to do their jobs.
- *Document Analysis.* Analysts study business documents to discover issues, policies, and rules as well as concrete examples of the use of data and information in the organization.
- *Joint Application Design.* **Joint application design (JAD)** is a group meeting–based process for requirements collection (see Figure 9.13). During this meeting, the users *jointly* define and agree on system requirements or designs. This process can result in dramatic reductions in the length of time needed to collect requirements or specify designs.

Modeling Data Data are facts that describe people, objects, or events. A lot of different facts can be used to describe a person: name, age, gender, race, and occupation, among others. To construct an information system, systems analysts must understand what data the information system

TABLE 9.4 Possible Evaluation Criteria for Classifying and Ranking Projects

Evaluation Criteria	Description
Strategic alignment	The extent to which the project is viewed as helping the organization achieve its strategic objectives and long-term goals
Potential benefits	The extent to which the project is viewed as improving profits, customer service, and so forth, and the duration of these benefits
Potential costs and resource availability	The number and types of resources the project requires and their availability
Project size and duration	The number of individuals and the length of time needed to complete the project
Technical difficulty and risks	The level of technical difficulty involved in successfully completing the project within a given time and resource constraint

Source: Hoffer, George, and Valacich (2011).

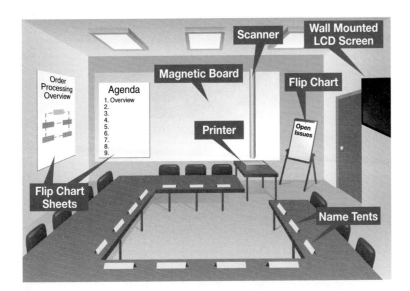

FIGURE 9.13

A JAD room.

Source: Based on Wood & Silver, 1989; Hoffer et al., 2011.

needs in order to accomplish the intended tasks. To do this, they use data modeling tools to collect and describe the data to users to confirm that all needed data are known and presented to users as useful information. Figure 9.14 shows an *entity-relationship diagram,* a type of data model describing students, classes, majors, and classrooms at a university. Each box in the diagram is referred to as a data entity. Each data entity may have one or more attributes that describe it. For example, a "student" entity may have attributes such as ID, name, and local address. Additionally, each data entity may be "related" to other data entities. For example, because students take classes, there is a relationship between students and classes: "Student Takes Class(es)" and "Class Has Student(s)." Relationships are represented in the diagram by lines drawn between related entities. Data modeling tools enable the systems analyst to represent data in a form that is easy for users to understand and critique. For more information on databases and data modeling, see the Technology Briefing, "Foundations of Information Systems Infrastructure".

Modeling Processes and Logic As the name implies, **data flows** represent the movement of data through an organization or within an information system. For example, your registration for a class may be captured in a registration form on paper or on an interactive form on the Web. After it is filled out, this form probably flows through several processes to validate and record the class registration, as shown as "Data Flows" in Figure 9.15. After all students have been registered, a repository of all

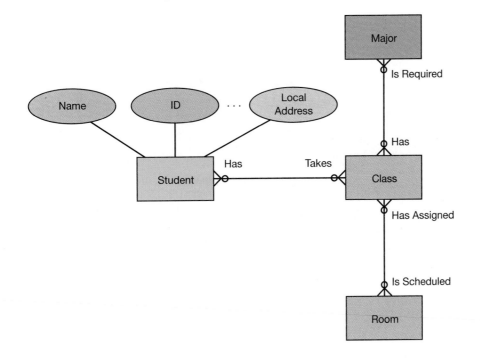

FIGURE 9.14

A sample *entity-relationship diagram* for students.

FIGURE 9.15

Four key elements to the
development of a system:
requirements, data, data flows,
and processing logic.

Requirements

Data

Name	Class	GPA
Patty Nicholls	Senior	3.7
Brett Williams	Grad	2.9
Mary Shide	Fresh	3.2

Data Flows

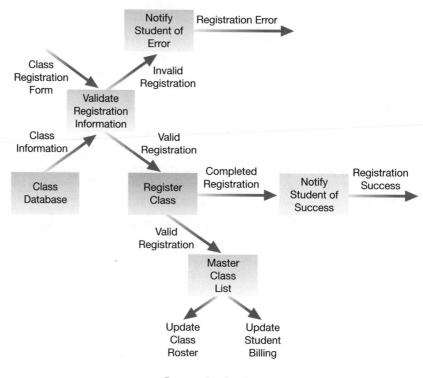

Processing Logic

```
i = read (number_of_classes)
total_hours = 0
total_grade = 0
total_gpa = 0
for j = 1 to i do
        begin
                read (course [ j ], hours [ j ], grade [ j ])
                total_hours = total_hours + hours [ j ]
                total_grade = total_grade + (hours [ j ] * grade [ j ])
        end
current_gpa = total_grade/total hours
```

registration information can be processed for developing class rosters or for generating student billing information, which is shown as "Data" in Figure 9.15. **Processing logic** represents the way in which data are transformed. Processing logic is often expressed in **pseudocode,** which is independent of the actual programming language being used. As there are no standards for pseudocode, the level of detail can vary. For example, pseudocode to calculate students' grade-point averages at the conclusion of a term is shown in the "Processing Logic" section in Figure 9.15.

After the data, data flow, and processing logic requirements for the proposed system have been identified, analysts develop one or many possible overall approaches—sometimes called designs—for the information system. For example, one approach for the system may possess only basic functionality but has the advantage of being relatively easy and inexpensive to build. An analyst might also propose a more elaborate approach for the system, but it may be more difficult and more costly to build. Analysts evaluate alternative system design approaches with the knowledge that different solutions yield different benefits and different costs. After a system approach is selected, details of that particular system approach can be defined.

Phase 3: Systems Design

The third phase of the SDLC is **systems design** (see Figure 9.12). As its name implies, it is during this phase that the proposed system is designed; that is, the details of the chosen approach are elaborated. As with analysis, many different activities must occur during systems design. The elements that must be designed when building an information system include the following:

- Human–computer interface
- Databases and files
- Processing and logic

Designing the Human–Computer Interface Just as people have different ways of interacting with other people, information systems can have different ways of interacting with people. A **human–computer interface (HCI)** is the point of contact between a system and users. Companies like Amazon.com or Microsoft spend considerable time and effort designing easy-to-use systems. In addition to the HCI, analysts take great care in designing data entry forms and management reports. A form is a business document containing some predefined data, often including some areas where additional data can be filled in (see Figure 9.16). Similarly, a report is a business document containing only predefined data for online viewing or printing (see Figure 9.17). For more on forms and reports, see Chapter 6, "Enhancing Business Intelligence Using Information Systems."

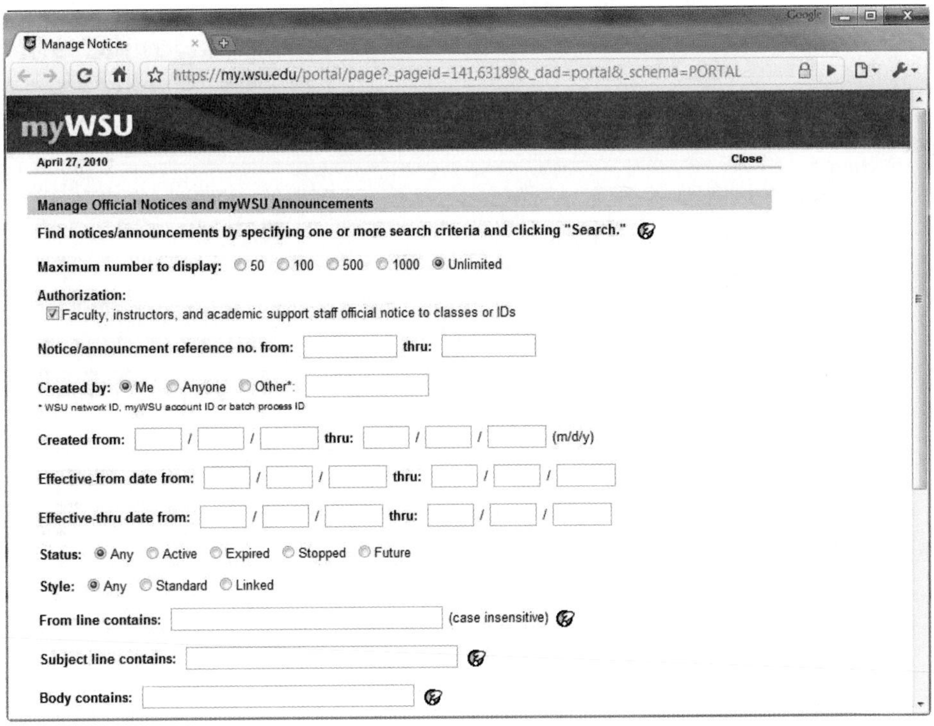

FIGURE 9.16

A form for managing official notices.

FIGURE 9.17

Sales summary report.

Ascend Systems Incorporated
SALESPERSON ANNUAL SUMMARY REPORT 2012

REGION	SALESPERSON	SSN	QUARTERLY ACTUAL SALES			
			FIRST	SECOND	THIRD	FOURTH
Northwest and Mountain						
	Wachter	999-99-0001	16,500	18,600	24,300	18,000
	Mennecke	999-99-0002	22,000	15,500	17,300	19,800
	Wheeler	999-99-0003	19,000	12,500	22,000	28,000
Midwest and Mid-Atlantic						
	Spurrier	999-99-0004	14,000	16,000	19,000	21,000
	Powell	999-99-0005	7,500	16,600	10,000	8,000
	Topi	999-99-0006	12,000	19,800	17,000	19,000
New England						
	Speier	999-99-0007	18,000	18,000	20,000	27,000
	Morris	999-99-0008	28,000	29,000	19,000	31,000

Designing Databases and Files To design databases and files, a systems analyst must have a thorough understanding of an organization's data and informational needs. For example, Figure 9.18 shows the database design to keep track of student information in a Microsoft Access database. The database design is more complete (shows each attribute of the student) and more detailed (shows how the information is formatted) than a conceptual data model built during systems analysis (see Figure 9.14).

Designing Processing and Logic The processing and logic operations of an information system are the steps and procedures that transform raw data inputs into new or modified information. For example, when calculating your grade-point average, your school needs to perform the following steps:

1. Obtain the prior grade-point average, credit hours earned, and list of prior courses
2. Obtain the list of each current course, final grade, and course credit hours

FIGURE 9.18

The database design for student information from an Access database.

C:\MSOFFICE\ACCESS\STUDENT.MDB   Saturday, June 23, 2012
Table: Students   Page: 1

Properties
Date Created: 6/23/12 10:35:41 PM   Def. Updatable: Yes
Last Updated: 6/23/12 10:35:43 PM   Record Count: 0

Columns

Name	Type	Size
StudentID	Number (Long)	4
FirstName	Text	50
MiddleName	Text	30
LastName	Text	50
Address	Text	255
City	Text	50
State	Text	50
Region	Text	50
PostalCode	Text	20
PhoneNumber	Text	30
EmailName	Text	50
Major	Text	50
Note	Memo	-

TABLE 9.5 General Testing Types, Their Focus, and Who Performs Them

Testing Type	Focus	Performed by
Developmental	Testing the correctness of individual modules and the integration of multiple modules	Programmer
Alpha	Testing of overall system to see whether it meets design requirements	Software tester
Beta	Testing of the capabilities of the system in the user environment with actual data	Actual system users

3. Combine the prior and current credit hours into aggregate sums
4. Calculate the new grade-point average

The logic and steps needed to make this calculation can be represented in many ways, including structure charts, decision trees, pseudocode, programming code, and so on (see Figure 9.15). Regardless of how the logic is represented, the process of converting pseudocode, structure charts, or decision trees into actual program code during system implementation is a relatively straightforward process.

Phase 4: Systems Implementation and Operation

Many separate activities occur during **systems implementation,** the fourth phase of the SDLC (see Figure 9.12). One group of activities focuses on transforming the system design into a working information system. These activities include software programming and testing. A second group of activities focuses on preparing the organization for using the new information system. These activities include system conversion, documentation, user training, and support. This section briefly describes what occurs during systems implementation.

Software Programming and Testing Programming is the process of transforming the system design into a working computer system. During this transformation, both processing and testing should occur in parallel. As you might expect, a broad range of tests are conducted before a system is complete, including **developmental testing, alpha testing,** and **beta testing** (see Table 9.5).

System Conversion, Documentation, Training, and Support **System conversion** is the process of decommissioning the current way of doing things (automated or manual) and installing the new system in the organization. Effective conversion of a system requires not only that the new software be installed but also that users be effectively trained and supported. System conversion can be performed in at least four ways, as shown in Figure 9.19.

Many types of documentation must be produced for an information system. Programmers develop system documentation that details the inner workings of the system to ease future maintenance. A second type of documentation is user-related documentation, which is typically

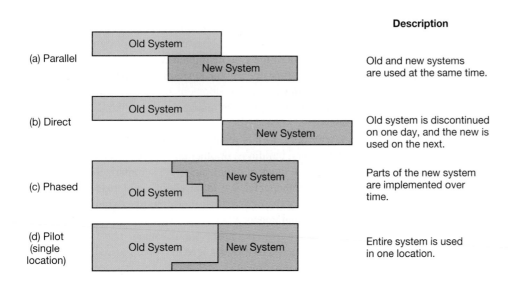

	Description
(a) Parallel	Old and new systems are used at the same time.
(b) Direct	Old system is discontinued on one day, and the new is used on the next.
(c) Phased	Parts of the new system are implemented over time.
(d) Pilot (single location)	Entire system is used in one location.

FIGURE 9.19

Software conversion strategies.

TABLE 9.6 User Training Options

Training Option	Description
Tutorial	One person taught at a time by a human or by paper-based exercises
Course	Several people taught at a time
Computer-aided instruction	One person taught at a time by the computer system
Interactive training manuals	Combination of tutorials and computer-aided instruction
Resident expert	Expert on call to assist users as needed
Software help components	Built-in system components designed to train users and troubleshoot problems
External sources	Vendors and training providers to provide tutorials, courses, and other training activities

written not by programmers or analysts but by users or professional technical writers. The range of documents can include the following:

- User and reference guides
- User training manuals and tutorials
- Installation procedures and troubleshooting suggestions

In addition to documentation, users may also need training and ongoing support to use a new system effectively. Different types of training and support require different levels of investment by the organization. Self-paced training and tutorials are the least expensive options, and one-on-one training is the most expensive. Table 9.6 summarizes various user training options.

Besides training, providing ongoing education and problem-solving assistance for users may also be necessary. This is commonly referred to as system support, which is often provided by a special group of people in the organization who make up an information center or help desk. Support personnel must have strong communication skills and be good problem solvers in addition to being expert users of the system. An alternative option for a system not developed internally is to outsource support activities to a vendor specializing in technical system support and training. Regardless of how support is provided, it is an ongoing issue that must be managed effectively for the company to realize the maximum benefits of a system.

Phase 5: Systems Maintenance

After an information system is installed, it is essentially in the maintenance phase of the SDLC, in which an information system is systematically repaired and/or improved. During maintenance, it is typical that one person within the systems development group is responsible for collecting maintenance requests from system users. Periodically, these requests are analyzed to evaluate how a proposed change might alter the system and what business benefits might result from such a change. If the change request is approved, a system change is designed and then implemented. As with the initial development of the system, implemented changes are formally reviewed and tested before being installed into operational systems. The **systems maintenance** process parallels the process used for the initial development of the information system, as shown in Figure 9.20. Interestingly, it is during system maintenance that the largest part of the system development effort occurs.

The question must be, then, why does all this maintenance occur? It is not as if software wears out in the physical manner that cars, buildings, or other physical objects do. Correct? Yes, but software must still be maintained. The types of maintenance are summarized in Table 9.7.

As with **adaptive maintenance,** both **perfective maintenance** and **preventive maintenance** are typically a much lower priority than **corrective maintenance,** which deals with repairing flaws in the system. Corrective maintenance is most likely to occur after initial system installation as well as over the life of a system after major system changes. This means that adaptive, perfective, and preventive maintenance activities can lead to corrective maintenance activities if they are not carefully designed and implemented.

Brief Case ⊘

HACKERS, PATCHES, AND REVERSE ENGINEERING

Microsoft dominates the market for operating systems, which is good news and bad news for the company. It's good news for Microsoft's bottom line but bad news in that its prominence has made its software a popular target for hackers (those who break into computer systems for the purpose of stealing or manipulating data) and other computer criminals. When security experts discover a breach, Microsoft releases a code "patch" to plug security holes. Downloading and installing these patches has become a regularly performed ritual for Windows users (this is often performed in the background).

You might reasonably expect that after an operating system, browser, or other application has been on the market for several years, all security holes will have been detected and closed. Not so. Unfortunately, there are invariably hackers who find new holes that have not yet been detected.

How do hackers find security holes? Smart hackers may study an application until they recognize an entrance hole, while not-so-smart hackers simply "free ride" on the efforts of others by following "recipes" posted on hacker Web sites.

Lately, the frequent release of patches has provided hackers another means of discovering security holes that require less time and effort than studying a program's code. When Microsoft, Mozilla, or other software producers release a security patch, hackers use special software tools to backtrack or reverse engineer the patch. Once they determine the location of the security hole for which the patch was issued, they work on ways to circumvent the patch and exploit the security hole in a new, unpatched way. (**Reverse engineering** is not always destructive and may be legally used to improve a program, but use of the term here implies using the process for gaining unauthorized access to a program's internal structure.)

Thus, the dilemma for software manufacturers and security companies is this: if they do not release patches, hackers can exploit security holes; if they do release patches, more people will know about the security holes and will attempt to exploit them. Yet consumers using software with security holes expect patches to be issued. The solution? Microsoft tries to deter hackers from reverse engineering by withholding detailed information about patches for security holes for three months after discovery of the hole, but that strategy does not usually deter hackers. There will always be hackers looking for security holes in software, but, fortunately, there will also always be software engineers, programmers, and security experts who can foil hackers' attempts to breach security. Solutions may come after the fact, but they do arrive.

Questions

1. Explain what type(s) of maintenance Microsoft is performing when fixing security holes and releasing patches to its customers.
2. Are there situations where it is justified for hackers to find and exploit security holes in software? If so or if not, explain.

Based on:

Espiner, T. (2008, May 6). Defend against patch-based exploits, warns Sans. *ZDNet*. Retrieved April 8, 2010, from http://news.zdnet.co.uk/security/0,1000000189,39411112,00.htm.

Lemos, R. (2008, April 23). Patches pose significant risk, say researchers. *SecurityFocus*. Retrieved April 8, 2010, from http://www.securityfocus.com/news/11514.

Mills, E. (2010, March 30). Microsoft issues emergency patch for 10 IE holes. *CNET news.com*. Retrieved April 8, 2010, from http://news.cnet.com/8301-27080_3-20001428-245.html.

Today, vendors of commercial off-the-shelf software packages incorporate **patch management systems** to facilitate the different forms of software maintenance for the user; patch management systems use the Internet to check the software vendor's Web site for available patches and/or updates. If the software vendor offers a new patch, the application will download and install the patch in order to fix the software flaw. An example of a patch management system in wide use is the Windows Update Service. The user's operating system automatically connects to a Microsoft Web service to download critical operating system patches for corrective maintenance (e.g., to fix bugs in the Windows operating system) or preventive maintenance (e.g., to fix security holes that could be exploited by malicious hackers).

As you can see, there is more to system maintenance than you might think. Lots of time, effort, and money are spent in this final phase of a system's development, and it is important to follow prescribed, structured steps. In fact, the approach to systems development described in this chapter—from the initial phase of identifying, selecting, and planning for systems to the final phase of system maintenance—is a very structured and systematic process. Each phase is fairly well prescribed and requires active involvement by systems people, users, and managers. It is likely that you will have numerous opportunities to participate in the acquisition or development

FIGURE 9.20

Mapping of systems maintenance activities to the SDLC.

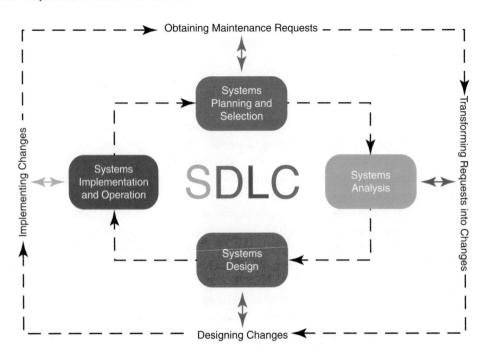

of a new system for an organization for which you currently work or will work in the future. Now that you have an understanding of the process, you should be better equipped to make a positive contribution to the success of any systems development project.

Other Approaches to Designing and Building Systems

The SDLC is one approach to managing the development process, and it is a very good approach to follow when the requirements for the information system are highly structured and straightforward— for example, for a payroll or inventory system. Today, in addition to "standard" systems such as payroll and inventory systems, organizations need a broad variety of company-specific information systems, for which requirements either are very hard to specify in advance or are constantly changing. For example, an organization's Web site is likely to evolve over time to keep pace with changing business requirements. How many Web sites have you visited in which the content or layout seemed to change almost every day? For this type of system, the SDLC might work as a development approach, but it would not be optimal.

A commonly used alternative to the SDLC is **prototyping,** which uses a trial-and-error approach for discovering how a system should operate. You may think that this does not sound like a process at all; however, you probably use prototyping all the time in many of your day-to-day activities, but you just do not know it. For example, when you buy new clothes, you likely use prototyping—that is, trial and error—by trying on several shirts before making a selection.

TABLE 9.7 Types of Software Maintenance

Maintenance Type	Description
Corrective maintenance	Making changes to an information system to repair flaws in the design, coding, or implementation
Adaptive maintenance	Making changes to an information system to evolve its functionality, to accommodate changing business needs, or to migrate it to a different operating environment
Perfective maintenance	Making enhancements to improve processing performance or interface usability, or adding desired but not necessarily required system features (in other words, "bells and whistles")
Preventive maintenance	Making changes to a system to reduce the chance of future system failure

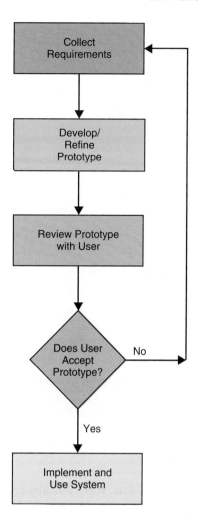

FIGURE 9.21

The prototyping process uses a trial-and-error approach to discovering how a system should operate.

Figure 9.21 diagrams the prototyping process when applied to identifying/determining system requirements. To begin the process, the system designer interviews one or several users of the system, either individually or as a group using a JAD session. After the designer gains a general understanding of what the users want, he or she develops a prototype of the new system as quickly as possible to share with the users. The users may like what they see or ask for changes. If the users request changes, the designer modifies the prototype and again shares it with them. This process of sharing and refinement continues until the users approve the functionality of the system.

Beyond the SDLC and prototyping, there are many more approaches for designing and constructing information systems (e.g., Agile Methodologies, Extreme Programming, RAD [Rapid Application Development], object-oriented analysis and design, and so on). Each alternative approach has its strengths and weaknesses, providing a skilled systems analyst with a variety of tools to best meet the needs of a situation (for more, see Hoffer et al., 2011).

Beyond systems development by trained professionals, some individuals within organizations build increasingly complex and useful applications. This approach to development is called **end-user development.** To illustrate this approach, envision a sales manager who builds a complex database of customer and sales data to improve her day-to-day decision making (see Figure 9.22). The drawback to end-user development is that nonprofessional developers are possibly being inefficient with their time building the system and, more critically, may not adhere to adequate quality standards for system security, reliability, and maintainability. Nevertheless, end-user development is a commonly used practice by tech-savvy managers who want to enhance their decision making and business intelligence.

FIGURE 9.22

Using tools such as Microsoft Access, a sales manager can develop an application to track sales.

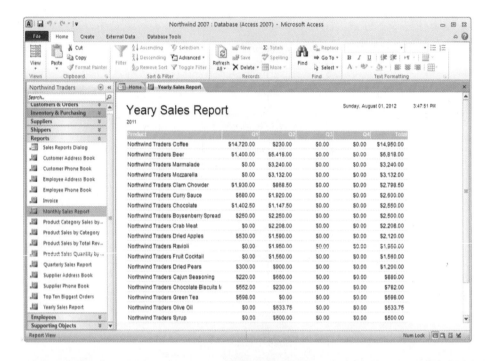

WHEN THINGS GO WRONG

Conquering Computer Contagion

Blue Security, an Israel-based Internet security company start-up, thought it had the answer to spammers. For every unwanted spam message that the half million clients of the company's service, Blue Frog, received, a message was returned to the advertiser. As a result, six of the top 10 spammers were inundated by the opt-out messages and were forced to eliminate Blue Frog's clients from their mailing list. One spamming company, however, decided to fight back. According to Blue Security, PharmaMaster responded by sending so many spam messages to Blue Frog's clients that several Internet service providers' servers crashed. Under PharmaMaster's threat of continuing and expanded attacks, on May 2, 2006, Blue Security folded. "We cannot take the responsibility for an ever-escalating cyberwar through our continued operations," said Eran Reshef, chief executive officer (CEO) and founder of Blue Security.

Like PharmaMaster, all authors of malware (destructive computer code such as viruses, Trojan horses and worms, and intrusive pop-up and spam ads) have continued to flout efforts to cleanse the Internet of their disruptive and exasperating wares. The top 10 malware reported to Sophos, an Internet security firm, in March 2010 are shown in Table 9.8.

Unfortunately, the battle against malware will probably rage as long as the Internet exists. On the plus side, however, the battle has given rise to new enterprises dedicated solely to protecting Internet users—the "white knights" who will continue to come to the rescue as long as the malware threat exists.

TABLE 9.8 Top 10 Malware Viruses Reported to Sophos in March 2010

Rank	Virus	Percentage of Reports
1	New Trojan/Invo-Zip	12.0
2	W32/Netsky	9.5
3	Malwarel/EncPk-EI	7.8
4	Trojan/Pushdo-Gen	6.3
5	Trojan/Agent-HFU	5.6
6	Malware/Iframe-E	5.5
7	Trojan/Mdrop-BTV	5.3
8	Trojan/Mdrop-BUF	4.5
9	Trojan/Agent-HFZ	4.4
10	Trojan/Agent-HGT	3.9

Source: Based on http://feeds.sophos.com/en/rss2_0-sophos-monthly-top-ten.xml.

Based on:

Lemos, R. (2006, May 17). Blue Security folds under spammer's wrath. *SecurityFocus*. Retrieved April 9, 2010, from http://www.securityfocus .com/news/11392.

Top 10 malware reported to Sophos in March 2010. (n.d.). Retrieved April 9, 2010, from http://feeds.sophos.com/en/rss2_0-sophos-monthly -top-ten.xml.

Acquiring Information Systems

We have now explained some of the general approaches that organizations follow when building systems in-house with their own IS staff. Many times, however, this is not a feasible solution. The following are four situations in which you might need to consider alternative development strategies.

- *Situation 1: Limited IS Staff.* Often, an organization does not have the capability to build a system itself. Perhaps its development staff is small or deployed on other activities and does not have the capability to take on an in-house development project.
- *Situation 2: IS Staff Has Limited Skill Set.* In other situations, the IS staff may not have the skills needed to develop a particular kind of system. This has been especially true with the explosive growth of the Web; many organizations are having outside groups develop and manage their sites.
- *Situation 3: IS Staff Is Overworked.* In some organizations, the IS staff may simply not have the time to work on all the systems that the organization requires or wants.
- *Situation 4: Problems with Performance of IS Staff.* Earlier in this book, we discussed how and why systems development projects could sometimes be risky. Often, the efforts of IS departments are derailed because of staff turnover, changing requirements, shifts in technology, or budget constraints. Regardless of the reason, the result is the same: another failed (or flawed) system.

When it isn't possible or advantageous to develop a system in-house, organizations are pursuing two popular options:

1. External acquisition of a prepackaged system
2. Outsourcing systems development

These options are examined next.

External Acquisition

Purchasing an existing system from an outside vendor such as IBM, HP Enterprise Services, or Accenture is referred to as **external acquisition.** How does external acquisition of an information system work? Think about the process that you might use when buying a car. Do you simply walk into the first dealership you see, tell them you need a car, and see what they try to sell you? You had better not. Probably you have done some up-front analysis and know how much money you can afford to spend and what your needs are. If you have done your homework, you probably have an idea of what you want and which dealership can provide the type of car you desire.

This up-front analysis of your needs can be extremely helpful in narrowing your options and can save you a lot of time. Understanding your needs can also help you sift through the salespeople's hype that you are likely to encounter from one dealer to the next as each tries to sell you on why his or her model is perfect for you. After getting some information, you may want to take a couple of promising models for a test drive, actually getting behind the wheel to see how well the car fits you and your driving habits. You might even talk to other people who have owned this type of car to see how they feel about it. Ultimately, you are the one who has to evaluate all the different cars to see which one is best for you. They may all be good cars; however, one may fit your needs just a little better than the others.

The external acquisition of an information system is very similar to the purchase of a car. When you acquire a new system, you should do some analysis of your specific needs. For example, how much can you afford to spend, what basic functionality is required, and approximately how many people will use the system? Next, you can begin to "shop" for the new system by asking potential vendors to provide information about the systems that they have to offer. After you evaluate this information, it may become clear that several vendors have systems that are worth considering. You may ask those vendors to come to your organization and set up their systems so that you and your colleagues are able to "test-drive" them (see Figure 9.23). Seeing how people react to the systems and seeing how each system performs in the organizational environment can help you "see" exactly what you are buying. By seeing the actual system and how it performs with real users, with real or simulated data, you can get a much clearer idea of whether that system fits your needs. When you take a car for a test-drive, you learn how the car meets your needs. By seeing how the system meets your needs before you buy, you can greatly reduce the risk associated with acquiring that system.

Steps in External Acquisition In many cases, your organization will use a competitive bid process for making an external acquisition. In the competitive bid process, vendors are given an

FIGURE 9.23

Taking software for a "test-drive" prior to purchase.

Thinkstock Royalty Free

opportunity to propose systems that meet the organization's needs. The goal of the competitive process is to help the organization ensure that it gets the best system at the lowest possible price. Most competitive external acquisition processes have at least five general steps:

1. Systems planning and selection
2. Systems analysis
3. Development of a request for proposal
4. Proposal evaluation
5. Vendor selection

You have already learned about the first two steps because they apply when you build a system yourself as well as when you purchase a system through an external vendor. Step 3, development of a request for proposal, is where the external acquisition process differs significantly from in-house development.

Development of a Request for Proposal A **request for proposal (RFP)** is simply a document that is used to tell vendors what your requirements are and to invite them to provide information about how they might be able to meet those requirements (see Figure 9.24). An RFP is sent to vendors who might potentially be interested in providing hardware and/or software for the system.

Among the areas that may be covered in an RFP are the following:

- A summary of existing systems and applications
- Requirements for system performance and features
- Reliability, backup, and service requirements
- The criteria that will be used to evaluate proposals
- Timetable and budget constraints (how much you can spend)

The RFP is then sent to prospective vendors along with an invitation to present their bids for the project. Eventually, you will likely receive a number of proposals to evaluate. If, on the other hand, you do not receive many proposals, it may be necessary to rethink the requirements—perhaps the requirements are greater than the budget limitations or the timetable is too short. In some situations, you may first need to send out a preliminary request for information simply to gather information from prospective vendors. This will help you determine whether, indeed, the

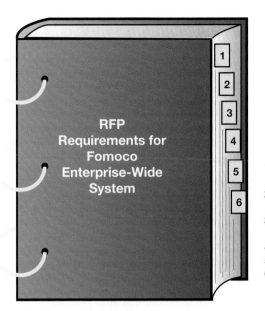

FIGURE 9.24

Sample RFP document for an information systems project.

1. Summary of existing systems and applications
2. System performance and features
3. Reliability, backup, and service requirements
4. Evaluation criteria
5. Timetable
6. Budget

desired system is feasible or even possible. If you determine that it is, you can then send out an RFP. Often, rather than trying to identify all potential vendors and sending out RFPs, companies set up a project Web site, allowing potential bidders to find out more about the organization and its current and planned information systems.

Proposal Evaluation The fourth step in external acquisition is to evaluate proposals received from vendors. This evaluation may include viewing system demonstrations, evaluating the performance of those systems, and examining criteria important to the organization and judging how the proposed systems "stack up" to those criteria. Demonstrations are a good way to get a feel for the different systems' capabilities. Just as you can go to the showroom to look over a new car and get a feel for whether it meets your needs, it is also possible to screen various systems through a demonstration from the vendor. During a demonstration, a sales team from the vendor gives an oral presentation about their system, its features and cost, followed by a demonstration of the actual system. Although such demonstrations are often useful in helping you understand the features of different systems being proposed, they are rarely enough in and of themselves to warrant purchasing the system without further evaluation.

One of the methods you can use to evaluate a proposed system is **systems benchmarking,** which is the use of standardized performance tests to facilitate comparison between systems. Benchmark programs are sample programs or jobs that simulate your computer workload. You can have benchmarks designed to test portions of the system that are most critical to your needs, based on your systems analysis. A benchmark might test how long it takes to calculate a set of numbers, how long it takes to access a set of records in a database, or how long it would take to access certain information given a certain number of concurrent users. Some common system benchmarks include the following:

- Response time given a specified number of users
- Time to sort records
- Time to retrieve a set of records
- Time to produce a given report
- Time to read in a set of data

In addition, vendors may also supply benchmarks that you can use, although you should not rely solely on vendor information. For popular systems, you may be able to rely on system benchmarks published in computer trade journals such as *PC Magazine* or on industry Web sites, such as www.cnet.com. However, in most cases, demos and benchmarks alone do not provide all the information you need to make a purchase. The systems analysis phase should have revealed some specific requirements for the new system. These requirements may be listed as criteria that the organization can use to further evaluate vendor proposals. Depending on what

TABLE 9.9 Commonly Used Evaluation Criteria

Hardware Criteria	Software Criteria	Other Criteria
Clock speed of CPU	Memory requirements	Installation
Memory availability	Help features	Testing
Secondary storage (including capacity, access time, and so on)	Usability	Price
	Learnability	
Video display size	Number of features supported	
Printer speed	Training and documentation	
	Maintenance and repair	

you are purchasing—hardware, software, or both—the criteria you use will change. Table 9.9 provides examples of commonly used evaluation criteria.

Vendor Selection In most cases, more than one system will meet your needs, just as more than one car will usually meet your needs. However, some probably "fit" better than others. In these cases, you should have a way of prioritizing or ranking competing proposals. One way of doing this is by devising a scoring system for each of the criteria and benchmarking results as described when making the business case.

Companies may use other, less formalized approaches to evaluate vendors. Sometimes they use simple checklists; other times they use a more subjective process. Regardless of the mechanism, eventually a company completes the evaluation stage and selects a vendor, ending the external acquisition process.

Managing Software Licensing When purchasing commercial, off-the-shelf software, companies usually have to agree to some license agreement. In general, software licenses can be classified based on their restrictiveness or the freedom they offer to use or modify the software. Software licensing has been a hot-button topic for software companies as they lose billions in piracy and mislicensed customers (see Chapter 10). Traditionally, software licensing is defined as the permission and rights that are imposed on applications; the use of software without a proper license is illegal in most countries.

Most software licenses differ in terms of restrictiveness, ranging from no restrictions at all to completely restricted. Note that although freeware or shareware is freely available, the copyright owners often retain their rights and do not provide access to the program's source code. For organizations using proprietary software, two types of licenses are of special importance. The first type includes the **shrink-wrap licenses** and **click-wrap licenses** that accompany the software and are used primarily for generic, off-the-shelf application and systems software. The shrink-wrapped contract has been named as such because the contract is activated when the shrink wrap on the packaging has been removed; similarly, a click-wrap license refers to a license primarily used for downloaded software that requires computer users to click on "I accept" before installing the software. The second type of license is an **enterprise license** (also known as a **volume license**). Enterprise licenses can vary greatly and are usually negotiated. In addition to rights and permissions, enterprise licenses usually contain limitations of liability and warranty disclaimers that protect the software vendor from being sued if their software does not operate as expected.

As shown in Table 9.10, there are a variety of software licenses. For different business needs, organizations often depend on a variety of software, each having different licenses, which can cause headaches for many organizations. Not knowing about the software an organization has can have a variety of consequences. For example, companies are not able to negotiate volume licensing options, unused licenses strain the organization's budget, or license violations can lead to fines or public embarrassment. **Software asset management** helps organizations to avoid such negative consequences. Usually, software asset management consists of a set of activities, such as performing a software inventory (either manually or using automated tools), matching the installed software with the licenses, reviewing software-related policies and procedures, and creating a software asset management plan. The results of these processes help organizations to better

TABLE 9.10 Different Types of Software Licenses

Restrictiveness	Software Types	Rights	Restrictions	Examples
Full rights	Public domain software	Full rights	No restrictions; owner forsakes copyright	Different programs for outdated IBM mainframes
	Nonprotective open source (e.g., Berkeley software development [BSD] license)	Freedom to copy, modify, and redistribute the software; can be incorporated into a commercial product	Creator retains copyright	Free BSD operating system; BSD components in (proprietary) Mac OS X operating system
	Protective open source (e.g., general public license [GPL])	Freedom to copy, modify, and redistribute the software	Modified or redistributed software must be made available under the same license; cannot be incorporated into commercial product	Linux operating system
	Proprietary software	Right to run the software (for licensed users)	Access to source code severely restricted; no rights to copy or modify software	Windows operating system
No rights	Trade secret	Software typically only used internally	Access to source code severely restricted; software is not distributed outside the organization	Google PageRank™ algorithm

manage their software infrastructure by being able to consolidate and standardize their software titles, decide to retire unused software, or decide when to upgrade or replace software.

External Acquisition Through Application Service Providers As introduced in Chapter 3, another way to acquire software externally is by the use of Software as a Service (SaaS). Undoubtedly, managing the software infrastructure is a complex task, often resulting in high operating costs for organizations; further, many systems are not scalable in response to large increases in demand. To deal with these issues, business organizations increasingly use Software as a Service—that is, clients access applications in the cloud on an as-needed basis using standard Web-enabled interfaces. For organizations, using SaaS provides a variety of benefits, such as a reduced need to maintain or upgrade software, a variable fee based on the actual use of the services (rather than fixed IT costs), and the ability to rely on a provider that has gained considerable expertise because of a large number of clients.

Outsourcing Systems Development

Outsourcing systems development is a way to acquire new systems that closely resembles the process of in-house development. However, in the case of outsourcing, the responsibility for some or all of an organization's information systems development (and potentially the day-to-day management of its operation) is turned over to an outside firm. Information systems outsourcing includes a variety of working relationships. The outside firm, or service provider, may develop your information systems applications and house them within their organization; they may run your applications on their computers; or they may develop systems to run on existing computers within your organization. Anything is fair game in an outsourcing arrangement. Today, outsourcing has become a big business and is a very popular option for many organizations (see Chapter 1 for more information on outsourcing).

Why Outsourcing? A firm might outsource some (or all) of its information systems services for many reasons. Some of these are old reasons, but some are new to today's environment (Applegate, Austin, & McFarlan, 2007):

■ ***Cost and Quality Concerns.*** In many cases it is possible to achieve higher-quality systems at a lower price through economies of scale, better management of hardware, lower labor costs, and better software licenses on the part of a service provider.

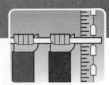

POWERFUL PARTNERSHIPS

Microsoft's Bill Gates and Paul Allen

Think of who's who in information technology, and the first names that come to mind are probably William (Bill) Henry Gates III and Paul Gardner Allen (see Figure 9.25). The two are almost cliché in the annals of technology: nerds as high school students at Lakeside School in Seattle who begged, borrowed, and stole computer usage time; college students with a brilliant idea; and entrants on the ground floor of computer technology when their programming skills paid off.

Both Gates and Allen were born in Seattle to upper-middle-class, educated parents, and both attended Lakeside High School in Seattle, where they formed a friendship based on their mutual interest and skills in computer technology. Gates went to Harvard after graduating from high school in 1973, but he dropped out in 1975 to run the business he and Allen cofounded called "Micro-Soft." The two worked out of company headquarters in Albuquerque, New Mexico, selling a language interpreter for BASIC.

Allen, born in 1953, is two years older than Gates and so was halfway through Washington State University in Pullman when Gates enrolled in Harvard. Both men dropped out of college in 1975 to devote all their time to their new project, now called Microsoft.

A partnership formed with IBM to install Microsoft's MS-DOS operating system on all IBM PCs was profitable early on and set the stage for Microsoft to become a major player in the PC operating system business. Windows. Enough said.

Allen stepped down from his position at Microsoft in 1983 after a bout with Hodgkin's disease. His cancer was successfully treated with radiation treatments and a bone marrow transplant, and Allen went on to found new profitable ventures on his own.

In 1998, Microsoft was prosecuted for violations of the Sherman Anti-Trust Law. In *United States v. Microsoft*, prosecutors alleged that Microsoft had committed monopoly violations in operating system and Web browser sales. In his trial testimony, Gates was described as arrogant, evasive, and uncooperative. Other Microsoft executives who testified were also labeled uncooperative, and the company was found guilty of monopolization under the Sherman Anti-Trust Law. Through a series of appeals, penalties against Microsoft have been modified, but the original verdict was allowed to stand. Microsoft agreed to settle the case in 2001. As of 2010, Microsoft continued to comply with the settlement terms.

Both Gates and Allen have withdrawn from active involvement with Microsoft's management. In 2006, Gates retired from Microsoft to focus his attention on the charitable foundation he and his wife, Melinda, formed in 2000. The Bill & Melinda Gates Foundation is the largest charitable organization in the world, with assets that have allowed the foundation to give away more than $1 billion annually to various charities since 2001. Warren Buffet, Gates's friend, who is rated number one on the *Forbes* list of wealthiest people in the world, matches Gates's foundation grants with his own.

Today Bill Gates is ranked by Fortune magazine as the second-richest person in the world, with a net worth exceeding $53 billion. Paul Allen, worth about $13.5 billion, is not within the top 20 on the world's billionaires list, but he has found satisfaction as owner of the Seattle Seahawks and Portland Trailblazers and as chairman of Vulcan Inc., his private asset management company. In late 2009, Allen was diagnosed with non-Hodgkin's lymphoma, a type of blood cancer. Today, Allen continues to work as a consultant to Microsoft, to donate to his favorite causes, and to aggressively fight to regain his health.

Regardless of Microsoft's future direction, Bill Gates and Paul Allen will always be at the top of the list of powerful partners in information technology.

FIGURE 9.25

Bill Gates and Paul Allen.

© UW/Mary Levin

Based on:

Anonymous. (n.d.). Paul Allen Bio, Founder of Microsoft. *Founderbios .com*. Retrieved August 1, 2010, from http://founderbios.com/paulallen .php.

Anonymous. (n.d.). Welcome to paulallen.com. Retrieved August 1, 2010, from http://www.paulallen.com.

Anonymous. (2000, September). Microsoft fast facts: 1975. *Microsoft .com*. Retrieved August 1, 2010, from http://www.microsoft.com/ presspass/features/2000/sept00/09-0525bookff75.mspx.

Anonymous. (2010, January 26). Bill Gates: Chairman. *Microsoft.com*. Retrieved August 1, 2010, from http://www.microsoft.com/presspass/ exec/billg/default.aspx?tab=biography.

U.S. vs. Microsoft: Current case. (n.d.). Retrieved April 9, 2010, from http://www.usdoj.gov/atr/cases/ms_index.htm.

United States Microsoft antitrust case. (2010, April 9). In *Wikipedia, the free encyclopedia*. Retrieved April 9, 2010, from http://en.wikipedia.org/ w/index.php?title=United_States_Microsoft_antitrust_case&oldid= 210317436.

- *Problems in IS Performance.* IS departments may have problems meeting acceptable service standards because of cost overruns, delayed systems, underutilized systems, or poorly performing systems. In such cases, organizational management may attempt to increase reliability through outsourcing.
- *Supplier Pressures.* Perhaps not surprisingly, some of the largest service providers are also the largest suppliers of computer equipment (e.g., IBM or Hewlett-Packard). In some cases, the aggressive sales forces of these suppliers are able to convince senior managers at other organizations to outsource their IS functions.
- *Simplifying, Downsizing, and Reengineering.* Organizations under competitive pressure often attempt to focus on only their "core competencies." In many cases, organizations simply decide that running information systems is not one of their core competencies and decide to outsource this function to companies such as IBM and HP Enterprise Services, whose primary competency is developing and maintaining information systems.
- *Financial Factors.* When firms turn over their information systems to a service provider, they can sometimes strengthen their balance sheets by liquidating their IT assets. Also, if users perceive that they are actually paying for their IT services rather than simply having them provided by an in-house staff, they may use those services more wisely and perceive them to be of greater value.
- *Organizational Culture.* Political or organizational problems are often difficult for an IS group to overcome. However, an external service provider often brings enough clout, devoid of any organizational or functional ties, to streamline IS operations as needed.
- *Internal Irritants.* Tension between end users and the IS staff is sometimes difficult to eliminate. At times this tension can intrude on the daily operations of the organization, and the idea of a remote, external, relatively neutral IS group can be appealing. Whether the tension between users and the IS staff (or service provider) is really eliminated is open to question; however, simply having the IS group external to the organization can remove a lingering thorn in management's side.

Managing the IS Outsourcing Relationship The ongoing management of an outsourcing alliance is the single most important aspect of the outsourcing project's success. Some advice includes the following:

1. A strong, active chief information officer (CIO) and staff should continually manage the legal and professional relationship with the outsourcing firm.
2. Clear, realistic performance measurements of the systems and of the outsourcing arrangement, such as tangible and intangible costs and benefits, should be developed.
3. The interface between the customer and the outsourcer should have multiple levels (e.g., links to deal with policy and relationship issues and links to deal with operational and tactical issues).

Managing outsourcing alliances in this way has important implications for the success of the relationship. For example, in addition to making sure a firm has a strong CIO and staff, McFarlan and Nolan (1995) recommend that firms assign full-time relationship managers and coordinating groups lower in the organization to "manage" the project. The structure and nature of the internal system activities change from exclusively building and managing systems to also including managing relationships with outside firms that build and manage systems under legal contract.

Not All Outsourcing Relationships Are the Same Most organizations no longer enter into a strictly legal contract with an outsourcing vendor but rather into a mutually beneficial relationship with a strategic partner. In such a relationship, both the firm and the vendor are concerned with—and perhaps have a direct stake in—the success of the other. Yet other types of relationships exist, meaning that not all outsourcing agreements need to be structured the same way. In fact, at least three different types of outsourcing relationships can be identified:

- Basic relationship
- Preferred relationship
- Strategic relationship

A basic relationship can best be thought of as a "cash-and-carry" relationship in which you buy products and services on the basis of price and convenience. Organizations should try to have a few preferred relationships in which the buyer and the supplier set preferences and prices to the benefit of each other. For example, a supplier can provide preferred pricing to customers that do a specified volume of business. Most organizations have just a few strategic relationships in which both sides share risks and rewards.

INDUSTRY ANALYSIS

Broadcasting

Only a few years ago, radio and television were among the primary sources for satisfying the desire for both entertainment and up-to-date news and information. Over the past few years, this situation has changed dramatically, with many people turning to the Internet for both information and entertainment. In fact, in 2010, for the first time, more American's would give up their TVs than the Internet. For traditional broadcasting media, this evolution in their consumers' habits has caused both tremendous opportunities and tremendous headaches.

For many television news companies, the Internet has opened opportunities, as news features can be easily transmitted over the Internet, allowing easier connection between the newsrooms and the "action" on the field. At the same time, viewing habits have changed, and many viewers prefer to obtain their latest news via the Internet. As a reaction, television stations (both focusing on news and entertainment) are increasingly using the Internet as a distribution medium for their content. Internet TV uses the Internet's TCP/IP protocol to transmit content, and viewers can watch parts of a provider's content at their home computers. Similarly, one of the local broadband providers in Hong Kong offers a multichannel IP TV station where subscribers

can watch the TV program on their televisions using a decoder hooked up to their broadband modem. The shift in people's viewing habits has also prompted television stations to change the format of their broadcasts—typically to include shorter segments to cater to ever-shortening attention spans. Some stations even started to produce limited-budget episodes of popular TV shows specifically for the Internet.

These changes force TV stations to adjust their revenue models. Whereas traditionally large revenues were derived from TV advertising, advertisers are now less willing to pay high advertising fees in light of dwindling viewership. On the other hand, TV stations can potentially charge more for advertising tied to online shows, as the Internet offers benefits such as advertising targeted at the individual viewer and provides detailed tracking metrics such as click-through rates, allowing the advertiser to directly evaluate the success of a campaign.

For radio stations, the situation is similar. With more and more people listening to various Internet radio stations or downloading music (legally or illegally), the number of listeners to traditional radio has dwindled and along with it advertising revenues. Online advertising now surpasses radio advertising spending. Facing competition from Internet radio, satellite radio, podcasting, and a plethora of other online diversions, many radio stations (as well as all forms of broadcasting) will have to find innovative ways to prosper in these times of profound change.

Questions

1. What is the effect of the Internet on television and radio content? With revenues from advertising in traditional channels diminishing, how can television and radio stations continue to produce high-quality content?

2. Today there are thousands of AM/FM stations competing with Internet radio stations and music downloading.

Forecast their future and provide a strategy for retaining and gaining market share.

Based on:

Edison Research. (2010, April 8). The infinite dial 2010: Digital platforms and the future of radio. Retrieved April 16, 2010, from http://www.edisonresearch.com/The_Infinite_Dial_2010.pdf.

Macklin, B. (2007, August). Radio trends: On air and online. *eMarketer*. Retrieved April 16, 2010, from http://www.emarketer.com/Report.aspx?code=emarketer_2000409.

TV networks looking for new eyeballs online. (2008, April 20). *Todayshow.com*. Retrieved April 16, 2010, from http://www.msnbc.msn.com/id/24096815.

Key Points Review

1. *Describe how to formulate and present the business case for technology investments.* Making the business case is the process of building and presenting the set of arguments that show that an information system investment is adding value to an organization. It is often difficult to quantify the value that a system provides because of measurement problems, time lags before benefits are realized, industry redistribution, and mismanagement. You must also understand your organization's particular business strategy in order to make an effective business case for systems. In short, technology investments should be closely linked to the organization's business strategy because these investments are becoming one of the major vehicles by which organizations can achieve their strategy. After you gain an understanding of your organization's position in the marketplace, its strategy for investing in systems that add value, and firm-level implementation factors, you can quantify the relative costs and benefits of the system. Considering all of these factors simultaneously will help you formulate an effective business case. In order to make a convincing presentation, you should be specific about the benefits this investment will provide for the organization. To do this, you must convert the benefits into monetary terms, such as the amount of money saved or revenue generated. If you have difficulty identifying specific monetary measures, you should devise some proxy measures to demonstrate the benefits of the system. Finally, make sure that you measure things that are important to the decision makers of the organizations. Choosing the wrong measures can yield a negative decision about a beneficial system.

2. *Describe the SDLC, its various phases, and alternatives to the SDLC.* The development of information systems follows a process called the SDLC. The SDLC is a process that first identifies the need for a system and then defines the processes for designing, developing, and maintaining an information system. The process is very structured and formal and requires the active involvement of managers and users. The SDLC has four phases: systems planning and selection, systems analysis, systems design, and systems implementation and operation. Systems identification, selection, and planning is the first phase of the SDLC, in which potential projects are identified, selected, and planned. Systems analysis is the second phase of the SDLC, in which the current ways of doing business are studied and alternative replacement systems are proposed. Systems design is the third phase of the SDLC, in which all features of the proposed system are described. Systems implementation and operation is the fourth phase of the SDLC, in which the information system is programmed, tested, installed, and supported. Systems maintenance, the fifth phase of the SDLC, is an ongoing process after initial system implementation that focuses on repairing and improving the system. Beyond the SDLC, there are many alternative systems development methods. One approach, prototyping, is an iterative systems development process in which requirements are converted into a working system that is continually revised through a close working relationship between analysts and users. A variety of other approaches are available to enhance the development process for different types of systems and contexts.

3. *Explain how organizations acquire systems via external acquisition and outsourcing.*   It is not feasible for an organization to build a system in-house in at least four situations. First, some organizations have limited IS staffing and, therefore, do not have the capability to build a system themselves. Second, an organization may have IS staff with a limited skill set. Existing IS staff may be highly skilled at producing traditional applications, but they may not have the skills to build new types of systems or systems that require emerging development tools. Third, in many organizations, the IS staff does not have the time to work on all the systems that the organization desires. Fourth, some organizations have performance problems with their IS staff whereby staff turnover, changing requirements, shifts in technology, or budget constraints have resulted in poor results. In any of these situations, it may be advantageous to an organization to consider an alternative to in-house systems development. External acquisition is the process of purchasing an existing information system from an external organization or vendor. External acquisition is a five-step process. Steps 1 and 2 mirror the first two steps of the SDLC. Step 3 is the development of a request for proposal (RFP). An RFP is a communication tool indicating an organization's requirements for a given system and requesting information from potential vendors on their ability to deliver such a system. Step 4 is proposal evaluation, which focuses on evaluating proposals received from vendors. This evaluation may include viewing system demonstrations, evaluating the performance of those systems, and examining criteria important to the organization and the ways the proposed systems meet those criteria. Step 5 is vendor selection, which focuses on choosing the vendor to provide the system. Outsourcing refers to the turning over of partial or entire responsibility for information systems development and management to an outside organization.

Key Terms

adaptive maintenance 376

alpha testing 375

beta testing 375

break-even analysis 362

click-wrap license 384

corrective maintenance 376

cost–benefit analysis 361

data flows 371

developmental testing 375

discount rate 362

end-user development 379

enterprise license 384

external acquisition 381

human–computer interface (HCI) 373

information systems planning 369

intangible benefit 360

intangible cost 359

joint application design (JAD) 370

making the business case 354

net-present value analysis 362

nonrecurring cost 359

patch management system 377

perfective maintenance 376

preventive maintenance 376

processing logic 373

productivity paradox 355

project manager 368

prototyping 378

proxy variable 365

pseudocode 373

recurring cost 359

request for proposal (RFP) 382

requirements collection 370

reverse engineering 377

shrink-wrap license 384

software asset management 384

system conversion 375

system effectiveness 355

system efficiency 356

systems analysis 370

systems analysis and design 366

systems analyst 366

systems benchmarking 383

systems design 373

systems development life cycle (SDLC) 369

systems implementation 375

systems maintenance 376

systems planning and selection 369

tangible benefit 360

tangible cost 359

total cost of ownership (TCO) 359

volume license 384

weighted multicriteria analysis 362

Review Questions

1. Describe the productivity paradox.
2. Describe how to make a successful business case, contrasting faith-, fear-, and fact-based arguments.
3. Compare and contrast tangible and intangible benefits and costs.
4. Contrast the perspectives of different stakeholders involved in making information systems investment decisions.
5. Define a proxy variable and give an example.
6. What are the five phases of the systems development life cycle (SDLC)?

7. List and describe five techniques used in requirements collection.
8. What are the three major components/tasks of the systems design phase of the SDLC?
9. What are the four options for system conversion? How do they differ from each other?
10. Compare and contrast the four types of systems maintenance.
11. What are the advantages and disadvantages of prototyping?
12. Define outsourcing and list three general types of outsourcing relationships.

13. What are some of the reasons outsourcing is more popular than ever?
14. What are the three recommendations made in this chapter for managing an IS outsourcing relationship?
15. List and describe two main types of software licenses.
16. What is software asset management, and why is it important for organizations?
17. What is system benchmarking, and what are some common benchmarks?

Self-Study Questions

1. Which of the following is not one of the five phases of the systems development life cycle?
   A. systems analysis
   B. systems implementation
   C. systems design
   D. systems resource acquisition
2. _____ is the process of gathering and organizing information from users, managers, business processes, and documents to understand how a proposed information system should function.
   A. Requirements collection
   B. Systems collection
   C. Systems analysis
   D. Records archiving
3. Which of the following is the correct order of phases in the systems development life cycle?
   A. analysis, planning, design, implementation, maintenance
   B. analysis, design, planning, maintenance, implementation
   C. planning, analysis, design, implementation, maintenance
   D. design, analysis, planning, maintenance, implementation
4. In the systems design phase, the elements that must be designed when building an information system include all of the following except _____.
   A. the human-computer interface
   B. questionnaires
   C. databases and files
   D. processing and logic
5. _____ maintenance involves making enhancements to improve processing performance or interface usability or adding desired (but not necessarily required) system features (in other words, "bells and whistles").
   A. Preventive
   B. Perfective
   C. Corrective
   D. Adaptive

6. Which of the following is not one of the three types of arguments commonly made in the business case for an information system?
   A. fear
   B. fact
   C. faith
   D. fun
7. A _____ is a report that an organization uses to tell vendors what its requirements are and to invite them to provide information about how they might be able to meet those requirements.
   A. request letter
   B. vendor request
   C. request for proposal
   D. requirements specification
8. Which of the following is not a type of outsourcing?
   A. basic
   B. elite
   C. strategic
   D. preferred
9. Which of the following factors is a good reason to outsource?
   A. problems in IS performance
   B. supplier pressures
   C. financial factors
   D. all of the above
10. Most competitive external acquisition processes have at least five general steps. Which of the following is not one of those steps?
    A. vendor selection
    B. proposal evaluation
    C. development of a request for proposal
    D. implementation

Answers are on page 394.

Problems and Exercises

1. Match the following terms with the appropriate definitions:
   - i. Request for proposal
   - ii. Systems benchmarking
   - iii. Alpha testing
   - iv. Systems development life cycle
   - v. Productivity paradox
   - vi. Prototyping
   - vii. Pilot conversion
   - viii. Systems analysis
   - ix. Outsourcing
   - x. External acquisition
   - xi. Data flows
   - xii. Requirements collection

   a. The movement of data through an organization or within an information system
   b. Term that describes the life of an information system from conception to retirement
   c. The second phase of the systems development life cycle
   d. The process of gathering and organizing information from users, managers, business processes, and documents to understand how a proposed information system should function
   e. Testing performed by the development organization to assess whether the entire system meets the design requirements of the users
   f. Using a new system in one location before rolling it out to the entire organization
   g. A systems development methodology that uses a trial-and-error approach for discovering how a system should operate
   h. The practice of turning over responsibility for some or all of an organization's information systems development and operations to an outside firm
   i. The observation that productivity increases at a rate that is lower than expected when new technologies are introduced
   j. The process of purchasing an existing system from an outside vendor
   k. A way to evaluate a proposed system by testing a portion of it with the system workload
   l. A report that is used to tell vendors what the requirements are and to invite them to provide information about how they might be able to meet those requirements

2. After reading this chapter, it should be fairly obvious why an IS professional should be able to make a business case for a given system. Why, however, is it just as important for non-IS professionals? How are they involved in this process? What is their role in making IS investment decisions?

3. Why is it important to look at industry factors when making a business case? What effect might strong competition have on IS investment and use? What effect might weak competition have on IS investment and use? Why?

4. Argue for or against the following statement: "When making the business case, you should concentrate on the decision makers' 'hot buttons' and gloss over some of the other details."

5. Why can it be difficult to develop an accurate cost–benefit analysis? What factors may be difficult to quantify? How can this be handled? Is this something that should just be avoided altogether? What are the consequences of that approach?

6. Within a small group of classmates, describe any involvement you have had with making the business case for buying something for yourself or within an organization. To whom were you making the case? Was it a difficult sell? Why? To what extent did you follow the guidelines set forth in this chapter? Were your arguments based on faith, fear, fact, or fiction? How did your business case differ from those of others in your group? Were you successful? Why or why not? Were they successful? Why or why not?

7. Discuss the following in a small group of classmates or with a friend. Describe a situation from your own experience in which something was purchased where a cost–benefit analysis showed it to have a negative return when based on tangible factors. Was the purchase decision based on intangible factors? Have these intangible factors proven themselves to be worth the investment? Was it harder to convince others of the purchase because of these intangible factors?

8. Contrast the total cost of acquisition versus the total cost of ownership for the purchase of a new car. Demonstrate how the type of car, year, make, model, and so on change the values of various types of costs and benefits.

9. Identify and describe three different situations where fear, faith, or fact arguments would be most compelling when making an information systems investment decision.

10. Talk to an information systems manager and have him or her describe a system that took some length of time to improve organizational productivity in some significant way. Specifically, find out how long and why it took this much time. Was the time frame longer than expected? Why or why not? Was this a typical situation or a unique one?

11. Contrast the differing perspectives of different stakeholders involved in making information systems investment decisions.

12. Explain the differences between data and data flows. How might systems analysts obtain the information they need to generate the data flows of a system? How are these data flows and the accompanying processing logic used in the system design phase of the life cycle? What happens when the data and data flows are modeled incorrectly?

13. When Microsoft posts a new version of Internet Explorer on its Web site and states that this is a beta version, what does it mean? Is this a final working version of the software, or is it still being tested? Who is doing the testing? Search the Web to find other companies that have beta versions of their products available to the public. You might try Corel (www.corel.com) or Adobe (www.adobe.com). What other companies did you find?

14. Why is the system documentation of a new information system so important? What information does it contain? For whom is this information intended? When will the system documentation most likely be used?

15. Conduct a search on the Web for "systems development life cycle." Check out some of the hits. Compare them with the SDLC outlined in this chapter. Do all these life cycles follow the same general path? How many phases do the ones you found on the Web contain? Is the terminology the same or different? Prepare a 10-minute presentation to the class on your findings.

16. Choose an organization with which you are familiar that develops its own information systems. Does this organization follow an SDLC? If not, why not? If so, how many phases does it have? Who developed this life cycle? Was it someone within the company, or was the life cycle adopted from somewhere else?

17. Describe your experiences with information systems that were undergoing changes or updates. What kind of conversion procedure was being used? How did this affect your interaction with the system as a user? Who else was affected? If the system was down altogether, for how long was it down? Do you or any of your classmates have horror stories, or were the situations not that bad?

18. Choose an organization with which you are familiar and determine whether it builds its applications in-house. How many IS staff members does the organization have, and how large is the organization they support?

19. Think about the requirements of a career in IS. Do IS positions generally require people to work 40 hours a week or more if a project has a deadline? Do positions in the IS department require people skills? To find these answers, visit the IS department at your university, a local business, or an online clearinghouse of jobs, such as hotjobs.yahoo.com or www.job-hunt.org.

20. Find an organization on the Internet (e.g., at www.computerworld.com or www.infoworld.com) or a company you may want to work for in the future that outsources work. What are the managerial challenges of outsourcing, and why is this a popular alternative to hiring additional staff?

21. Interview an IS professional about his or her company's use of software asset management processes. How does the company keep track of the different software installed? If anyone asked you about the software installed on your computer, would you know what you have installed? Would you be able to produce the licenses for all software installed?

Application Exercises

 Note: The existing data files referenced in these exercises are available on the Student Companion Web site: **www.pearsonhighered.com/valacich.**

 ### Spreadsheet Application: Outsourcing Information Systems at Campus Travel

Campus Travel wants to increase its customer focus and wants to be able to better serve its most valued customers. Many members of the frequent flier program have requested the ability to check on the status of their membership online; furthermore, the frequent fliers would welcome the opportunity to book reward flights online. As you know that there are a number of companies specializing in building such transactional systems, you have decided to outsource the development of such a system. The following weights are assigned to evaluate the different vendors' systems:

- Online booking capability: 20 percent
- User friendliness: 25 percent
- Maximum number of concurrent users: 20 percent
- Integration with current systems: 10 percent
- Vendor support: 10 percent
- Price: 15 percent

To evaluate the different offers, you need to calculate a weighted score for each vendor using the data provided in the

Outsourcing.csv spreadsheet. To calculate the total points for each vendor, do the following:

1. Open the file Outsourcing.csv.
2. Use the SUMPRODUCT formula to multiply each vendor's scores with the respective weights and add the weighted scores.
3. Use conditional formatting to highlight all vendors falling below a total of 60 percent and above a total of 85 percent to facilitate the vendor selection.

Database Application: Building a Special Needs Database for Campus Travel

In addition to international travel, travel reservations for people with special needs is an area of specialty of Campus Travel. However, to be able to recommend travel destinations and travel activities, you should know what facilities are available at each destination. Therefore, you have been asked to create a database of the destinations and the type of facilities that are available for people with special needs. In order to make the system as useful as possible for all, you need to design reports for the users to retrieve information about each destination. Your manager would like to have a system that contains the following information about the destinations:

- Location
- Availability of facilities for the physically handicapped
- Distance to medical facilities
- Pet friendliness

Each location may have one or more handicap facility (e.g., hearing, walking, sight, and so on). A type of handicap facility can be present at multiple locations. Also, each location has to have one pet-friendly accommodation/activity and may also have accommodation for different types of pets (dogs, cats, and so on). After designing the database, please design three professionally formatted reports that (1) list the locations in alphabetical order, (2) list all locations that have the handicap facilities for those that find it difficult to walk, and (3) list all locations that have a cat-friendly policy.

Hint: In Microsoft Access, you can create queries before preparing the reports. Enter a few sample data sets and print out the reports.

Team Work Exercise: Determining a Development Approach

You have just been hired by an organization, and you have been charged with purchasing 10 new standard desktop computers. Compile a list of criteria you will use to evaluate the vendor to choose. Having determined the different criteria, discuss the importance of these factors and rank them accordingly. Prepare a report explaining the criteria and rankings.

Answers to the Self-Study Questions

1. D, p. 369
2. A, p. 370
3. C, p. 369
4. B, p. 373
5. B, p. 376
6. D, p. 357
7. C, p. 382
8. B, p. 388
9. D, p. 387
10. D, p. 382

Case 1

FBI, ICE Databases Expand and Join Forces

As crime-solving aides, first there was fingerprinting; decades later came DNA analysis. Next, according to recent information from the FBI, is a $1 billion, 10-year plan to compile palm prints, iris eye patterns, photos of scars and tattoos, and distinctive facial characteristics for a far-reaching criminal identification database. In the past, fingerprints have been the most widely used means of uniquely identifying people, with the FBI keeping 55 million sets of fingerprints on file. The next step would be additional biometric characteristics. Unfortunately, taken alone, many of those have been proven to be rather unreliable (facial recognition accuracy in public places can be as low as 10 to 20 percent, depending on lighting conditions), such that a real increase in identification accuracy can come only from combining the results of multiple biometrics.

In defense of the FBI's extensive program, Kimberly Del Greco, the FBI's Biometric Services section chief, said that adding to the database is "important to protect the borders to keep the terrorists out, protect our citizens, our neighbors, our children so they can have good jobs and have a safe country to live in."

Some privacy experts disagreed. The American Civil Liberties Union saw the program as the beginning of super surveillance tactics that would allow the government to track individuals anywhere, anytime. In addition, privacy advocates fear the potential of widespread mistakes (as frequently happens with no-fly lists at airports). As more than half of all background checks involve people applying for certain jobs, any error in the system could prevent you from getting that job or even being fired from a job in case your record mistakenly changes. Others said the program may actually provide more personal privacy in that it could prevent identity theft and similar misuse of personal information.

The Immigration and Customs Enforcement Agency (ICE), part of the Department of Homeland Security (DHS), has developed a similar biometric database dubbed "Secure Communities" to aid in capturing criminal aliens. The Secure Communities program is a federal, state, and local government partnership that allows state and local law enforcement officials to quickly share information with ICE on captured suspects. The data forwarded to ICE is used to make immigration processing and removing more efficient if the suspect turns out to be a criminal alien. In 2009, when the database was in use in 14 states and 107 jurisdictions, it was

directly responsible for the removal of 11,000 such aliens from the United States. ICE's goal is to have Secure Communities operating in every state by 2011 and placed in each of the 3,100 state and local jails across the United Sates by 2013.

At the heart of the Secure Communities program is its utilization of biometric fingerprint matching. When someone is arrested, local law enforcement puts the suspect's fingerprints into the system. The fingerprints are checked against DHS immigration databases and FBI criminal biometric systems to see if the suspect is in the country legally. If the suspect isn't legal, ICE can immediately begin the deportation process. The system also prioritizes removal of criminal aliens based on their risk to national security and the local community. The prioritization helps ensure that serious criminals (aliens or otherwise) are not inadvertently released and cuts down on the time criminal aliens must be held in custody before being returned to their home country.

The Secure Communities program has been successful in slowing the practice of "catch and release" by local law enforcement.

Catch and release practices were driven by limited local resources to detain and investigate every suspect picked up. With ICE/DHS databases working in tandem with FBI databases, biometric data are helping to slash the time needed to determine a suspect's status and decide whether to release, put into local custody, or hold for federal authorities.

Not unlike the FBI's biometrics program, Secure Communities has gotten its share of criticism too. Critics say that Secure Communities can lead to unnecessary or prolonged detention, make accessing a lawyer difficult, and prevent release on bail. There is also a fear that there is no complaint mechanism associated with the system. Opponents of the system believe that victims of system error will have little redress if they are erroneously identified as a criminal or illegal alien.

While the FBI and ICE maintain that their programs are strictly limited to criminals and those in the country illegally, privacy and civil rights activists are watching the developments to ensure that the government respects the rights of its citizens.

Questions

1. Should the FBI expand its database to include palm prints, iris eye patterns, photos of scars and tattoos, and so on of suspected criminals and terrorists? Why or why not?
2. Who should verify that information in the FBI and ICE databases is true and accurate?
3. Some privacy advocates argue that biometric systems can become unreliable and single out innocent people, especially over time as these databases become less accurate because of a person's natural aging process, weight loss, weight gain, injury, or permanent disability. Discuss the problems associated with having these systems single out innocent people.

Based on:

American Immigration Council. (2009, November 23). Secure Communities: A fact sheet. *Immigrationpolicy.org*. Retrieved April 12, 2010, from http://www.immigrationpolicy.org/just-facts/secure-communities-fact-sheet.

Arena, K., & Cratty, C. (2008, February 4). FBI wants palm prints, eye scans, tattoo mapping. *CNN.com*. Retrieved April 16, 2010, from http://www.cnn.com/2008/TECH/02/04/fbi.biometrics/index.html.

McNeill, J. (2010, January 6). Secure Communities: A model for Obama's 2010 Immigration Enforcement Strategy. *Heritage.org*. Retrieved April 12, 2010, from http://www.heritage.org/Research/Reports/2010/01/Secure-Communities-A-Model-for-Obamas-2010-Immigration-Enforcement-Strategy.

Case 2

The Emergence of Open Source Software

You're probably well aware, by now, that some software, such as the Linux operating system and the Firefox browser, is *open source*. That is, creators of the programs made the source code available so that anyone could program changes to improve the application's performance.

Bruce Perens and Eric S. Raymond, two prominent proponents of open source software, formed the Open Source Initiative

(OSI) in 1998, a nonprofit organization dedicated to promoting open source software. The OSI formulated an *open source definition* to determine whether software can be considered for an open source license. An open source license is a copyright license for software that specifies that the source code is available for redistribution and modification without programmers having to pay the original author. OSI conditions for meeting

the open source definition include the following:

1. The software can be redistributed for free.
2. Source code is freely available.
3. Redistribution of modifications must be allowed.
4. Licenses may require that modifications be available only as patches.

5. Rights attached to the program must apply to all to whom the program is redistributed.
6. No one who wants to modify the code can be locked out.
7. Commercial software users cannot be excluded.
8. License may not be restricted to a specific product.
9. Licenses cannot specify that any other software distributed with the licensed software must also be open source.
10. No click-wrap acceptance of the license shall be required.

One category of open source software that meets these criteria and that has gained widespread acceptance is operating systems, including the following:

- Linux (www.linux.org). The most used Unix-like operating system on the planet. Versions have been run on anything from handheld computers and regular PCs to the world's most powerful supercomputers. For a list of popular Linux distributions, see www.linuxiso.org.
- FreeBSD (www.freebsd.org), OpenBSD (www.openbsd.org), and NetBSD (www.netbsd.org). The BSDs are all based on the Berkeley Software Distribution of the Unix operating system, developed at the University of California, Berkeley. Another BSD-based open source project is *Darwin* (developer.apple.com/opensource/index.html), which is the base of Apple's Mac OS X.

In addition, many of the router boxes and root DNS servers that keep the Internet working are based on one of the BSDs or on Linux. Microsoft also uses BSD to keep its Hotmail and MSN services working. Other open source software that keeps the Internet working includes the following:

- Apache (www.apache.org), which runs over 70 percent of the world's Web servers (see www.securityspace.com/s_survey/data/201003/index.html).
- BIND (www.isc.org/index.pl?/sw/bind), the software that provides the DNS (Domain Name Service) for the entire Internet.
- Sendmail (www.sendmail.org), the most important and widely used e-mail transport software on the Internet.

- Firefox (www.firefox.com), the open source redesign of the Netscape browser. With each new release, Firefox has added functionality, stability, cross-platform consistency, and features that are not available from any other browser; many of the popular features (such as tabbed browsing) have since been copied by its competitors.
- OpenSSL (www.openssl.org) is the standard for secure communication (strong encryption) over the Internet.

How did open source software manage to become so successful? Key to its success is using the inputs from a large user base to fix problems or improve the software; however, although the source code is freely available (and everyone can modify it as they see fit), with many open source projects, users can only *suggest* modifications for official releases. For example, users can program modifications to the Firefox browser, but only a small group of carefully selected "committers" can implement these modifications into the official releases of the software; this way, the quality and stability of the software is ensured. Some open source software is supported by commercial entities, as is the case with the popular MySQL database, which is used by Yahoo!, Facebook, the Associated Press, and many other companies. This software is provided under an open source license for personal use, but the company employs its own developers and offers commercial licenses (including dedicated 24/7 technical support, consulting, and indemnification clauses) to business users.

Open source software continues to make inroads into a broad range of commercial, personal, and governmental applications. In fact, in a recent survey by Talend, a provider of open source software, one in three respondents reported using a combination of open source and proprietary software. Those using open source pointed to the fact that proprietary software can become cost prohibitive or may no longer serve the purpose for which it was intended when originally deployed. When this happens, they turn to open source solutions. The overall survey paints a picture of open source software having an ever-expanding role in data warehousing and business intelligence solutions.

Open source software can also be found in many government applications, but advocates are pushing for more. For instance, several open source industry leaders sent a letter to President Obama asking him to consider the role that open source software could play in the government. In the letter, the authors point out that open source's transparency could help lead to more efficient government through its open platform. Since open source software gives the user access to everything from the user interface to the data level, the flexibility is there to deploy the software to a variety of contexts. Open source software's flexibility will also allow government to make changes as their needs change. The letter closed with a request to make open source a consideration in all government IT acquisition processes.

Microsoft, the proprietary software giant, is even lending a more supportive role to the open source community. Not surprisingly, Microsoft does not have the best reputation among open source enthusiasts. The Washington State–based company has threatened legal action against several open source companies in the past. Microsoft's concern centers on certain technologies found in many open source projects, including well-known applications like Linux. Microsoft claims that these technologies are patented and should therefore have licensing fees associated with their parent software. In September 2009, however, Microsoft started the CodePlex Foundation in an effort to "complement existing open source foundations and organizations, providing a forum in which best practices and shared understanding can be established by a broad group of participants, both software companies and open source communities." The board of directors is made up of mainly Microsoft employees but includes one popular open source guru. Time will tell if Microsoft's CodePlex Foundation can advance the cause of open source software and help smooth over some of the rough relations the company has had with the open source community.

Not only is open source software appearing in many organizations' server rooms and work station applications, but it has also moved into the cloud. In March 2010, the Free Cloud Alliance was formed, bringing together open source software publishers to build cloud-based, open source solutions for "high-performance, mission-critical applications." Its goal is to provide the same type of service that's currently delivered by SaaS providers like Amazon but in an open source format, giving users access to the source code and their data. "If you have access to the source code and your data in its native form you don't run the risk of being locked in to one vendor," says Jean-Paul Smets, CEO of Nexedi (one of the Free Cloud Alliance member companies). According to the Free Cloud Alliance Web site, all the products offered are "free as in beer and free as in freedom." Users have free use of the source code, but paid support is available if needed. The alliance hopes to gather more members in the future. All that is needed is a strong belief in open source and software freedom.

The Internet has clearly taken advantage of the open source concept and will undoubtedly continue to do so.

Questions

1. What are the pros and cons of having so much open source software enabling the Internet?
2. For what types of applications do you think open source is better than non–open source software? When is it worse?
3. Find a for-profit company that is distributing open source software. What is the software? How does the company make money? Is its revenue model sustainable?
4. Do you use any open source software on your personal computer, such as the Linux operating system or the Firefox browser? Why or why not?

Based on:

Coar, K. (2006, July 7). The open source definition. *Open Source Initiative.* Retrieved April 16, 2010, from http://www.opensource.org/docs/osd.

Free Cloud Alliance Press Release. (2010, March 29). Free Cloud Alliance formed: Open source IaaS, PaaS and SaaS for the Enterprise. *Freecloudalliance .org.* Retrieved April 12, 2010, from http://www.freecloudalliance.org/fca-Home/ news-free-cloud-alliance.

Kunkel, R. G. (2002, September). Recent developments in Shrinkwrap, Clickwrap and Browsewrap licenses in the United States. *E Law.* Retrieved April 16, 2010, from http://www.murdoch.edu.au/elaw/issues/v9n3/kunkel93_text.html #Shrinkwrap%20License%20Cases_T.

Montalbano, E. (2009, September 10). Microsoft forms, funds new open-source foundation. *PC World.* Retrieved April 12, 2010, from, http://www.pcworld .com/businesscenter/article/171756/microsoft_forms_funds_new_opensource _foundation.html.

Ricknäs, M. (2010, March 31). Companies create alliance to push open source clouds. *PC World.* Retrieved April 12, 2010, from http://www.pcworld.com/ businesscenter/article/193008/companies_create_alliance_to_push_open_source _clouds.html.

Scannell, E. (2009, March 13). 1 in 3 IT shops uses combo proprietary, open source software. *InformationWeek.* Retrieved April 12, 2010, from http:// www.informationweek.com/news/software/open_source/showArticle.jhtml ?articleID=215900159.

Tiemann, M. (2006, September 19). History of the OSI. *Open Source Initiative.* Retrieved April 16, 2010, from http://opensource.org/history.

ten

Securing Information Systems

Preview

As organizations become more dependent on information systems for enabling organizational strategy, they also become more vulnerable to catastrophic security disasters. Because of this, organizations are focusing more of their attention on information systems security. In this chapter, we first examine various threats to information systems security followed by a discussion of various approaches for securing information systems and the critical information they hold.

Managing in the digital world requires careful attention to IS security. Having thorough plans for dealing with IS security attacks and natural disasters is critical for effectively managing IS resources within organizations.

Managing in the Digital World: Drive-By Hacking

How did businesses and individuals make do without wireless networks before they became widely available? We can check e-mail messages while waiting in airports, access the Web using laptops in classrooms, keep a business running while attending conventions and meetings worldwide, and perform any number of additional tasks via wireless networks. A downside to the ease of communicating wirelessly, however, is that hackers have also migrated to wireless networks. Lax security on many wireless networks has allowed hackers to join networks and launch malicious attacks. Recent surveys show that between 60 and 80 percent of wireless corporate networks do not use adequate security (a shocking statistic, considering the prevalence of destructive hacker attacks).

Until recently, hackers were focused on discovering new ways to bypass firewalls and other security measures used to protect wired networks. Now, however, with the increasing availability of insecure wireless networks (Wi-Fi), hackers have found a new playground. With insecure wireless networks almost everywhere, hackers have instituted a new type of pursuit called "war driving," whereby they drive around densely populated areas looking for unsecured networks and usually find literally hundreds of potential unsuspecting victims. Antennas used for war driving can be easily built using a tin can and some electronics parts (see Figure 10.1); some companies sell ready-made war driving kits, some of which even incorporate the ability to crack Wi-Fi keys.

One common attack that war drivers perpetrate is called "war spamming," where hackers link into an e-mail server of an unsecured Wi-Fi network and send out millions of junk e-mails without the network administrators' knowledge. War spamming costs companies millions in bandwidth fees and is difficult to trace, so spammers are seldom caught. Some businesses are fighting back by using a technology that generates thousands of bogus wireless network access points, thus stymieing hackers trying to access personal or corporate Wi-Fi networks. Software tools called wireless camouflage, such as FakeAP, offer such protection by confusing war drivers so that they are not able to locate the "real" access point among the thousands of bogus ones. However, by using network scanners such as Netstumbler or Kismet and even some of Windows' built-in tools, one can distinguish between genuine access points and the thousands of bogus access

points. Most war drivers use these tools to find open networks, but organizations can also use network scanners to find holes in their protection. In 2010, Apple pulled all Wi-Fi sniffing applications (commonly known as "stumblers") from their popular App Store.

All wireless access points have built-in security in the form of Wired Equivalent Privacy (WEP). WEP uses a 64-bit key to encrypt the wireless signals, which, theoretically, allows only those network users with the 64-bit code to use the Wi-Fi signal. WEP, however, has documented security flaws. These flaws allow hackers to circumvent the secu-

Shutterstock

FIGURE 10.1

Accessories for "war driving" can be easily built using simple parts.

rity and easily access the Wi-Fi network. Recently, the engineering security community within the Institute of Electrical and Electronics Engineers has worked to fix WEP security flaws by adopting "Fast Packet Keying," which is designed to repair security flaws and to finally create a truly secure wireless network.

As with all new technologies, however, there are problems with Fast Packet Keying. For instance, it is difficult to administer and deploy. Network administrators must choose between allowing users easy access and thus compromising security or installing Fast Packet Keying, which tightens security but makes day-to-day network operations more difficult.

Currently, WEP is being abandoned for other, more secure forms of wireless encryption. The most current and popular format, Wi-Fi Protected Access 2 (WPA2), is being adopted by many users of Wi-Fi. WPA2 provides a new algorithm for encryption that is considered to be almost fully secure. For members of the Payment Card Industry Security Standards Council, a worldwide consortium of credit, debit, prepaid, and point-of-service businesses such as Visa and Mastercard, the WEP protocol was completely phased out of their wireless operations by the middle of 2010.

Since war driving, war spamming, and other forms of hacker theft cost companies millions in damages, some businesses are looking to cyberinsurance policies to help recoup losses. According to an article in *Economic Times*, back in 2007 there were only approximately 25 stand-alone cyberinsurance policies sold. By 2010, several global insurance companies were offering cyberpolicies, driving the value of the cyberinsurance market to over $500 million. The policies are expensive but may provide one more hedge for businesses suffering from the rising tide of cybercrime.

After reading this chapter, you will be able to answer the following:

1. How can organizations better secure their wireless networks to reduce security vulnerabilities?
2. Is using a wireless network without the owner's permission wrong? If so, why? If not, why not? Are there any ethical issues associated with "piggybacking" on your neighbor's unsecured wireless network?
3. Some believe that all wireless networks should be "open" to anyone. What are the pros and cons of this perspective?

Based on:

Anonymous. (2001, November 6). Welcome to the world of drive-by hacking. *BBC News*. Retrieved April 30, 2010, from http://news.bbc.co.uk/1/hi/sci/tech/1639661.stm.

Anonymous. (2009, May 27). Speakers at the Networkers conference discussed credit card security, video surveillance and how much money telework is saving them. *IDG Connect*. http://www.idgconnectglobal.com/index.cfm?event=showarticle&cid=116&pk=1460.

Dalrymple, J. (2010, March 4). Apple removes Wi-Fi finders from App Store. *CNET news.com*. Retrieved April 30, 2010, from http://news.cnet.com/8301-13579_3-10464021-37.html.

Fletcher, O. (2010, May 5). Wi-Fi key-cracking kits sold in China mean free Internet. *Networkworld.com*. Retrieved August 1, 2010, from http://www.networkworld.com/news/2010/050510-wi-fi-key-cracking-kits-sold-in.html.

Risen, T. (2010, February 10). Can insurers protect the U.S. from cyber-attack? *NationalJournal.com*. Retrieved April 30, 2010, from http://www.nationaljournal.com/njonline/no_20100208_9513.php.

Sengupta, D. (2008, January 31). IT cos seek insurance cover against virtual fraud. *Economic Times*. Retrieved April 30, 2010, from http://economictimes.indiatimes.com/infotech/it_cos_seek_insurance_cover_against_virtual_fraud/articleshow/2744918.cms.

Wearden, G. (2002, September 5). Heard of drive-by hacking? Meet drive-by spamming. *ZDNET*. Retrieved April 30, 2010, from http://news.zdnet.co.uk/internet/0,39020369,2121857,00.htm.

Computer Crime

Everyone who uses an information system (IS) knows that disasters can happen to stored information or to entire systems. Some disasters are accidents caused by power outages, inexperienced computer users, or mistakes, while others are caused on purpose by malicious hackers. The primary threats to the security of information systems include the following (see Figure 10.2):

- *Natural Disasters.* Power outages, hurricanes, floods, and so on.
- *Accidents.* Inexperienced or careless computer operators (or cats walking across keyboards!).
- *Employees and Consultants.* People within an organization who have access to electronic files.
- *Links to Outside Business Contacts.* Electronic information can be at risk when it travels between or among business affiliates as part of doing business.
- *Outsiders.* Hackers and crackers who penetrate networks and computer systems to snoop or to cause damage (viruses, perpetually rampant on the Internet, are included in this category).

For individuals as well as organizations, trying to recover from disasters can cost a lot in terms of time and money; in addition, organizations can lose much goodwill if their systems are unavailable (no matter what the reason is) or are compromised by malicious hackers. Hence, for organizations, it is essential to protect their systems from criminal activity and to ensure business continuity by securing their IS infrastructure. While you may not need the level of security or protection large organizations such as Amazon.com need, you will find many ways to protect your own information systems and data from disaster and computer criminals.

FIGURE 10.2

Threats to IS security.

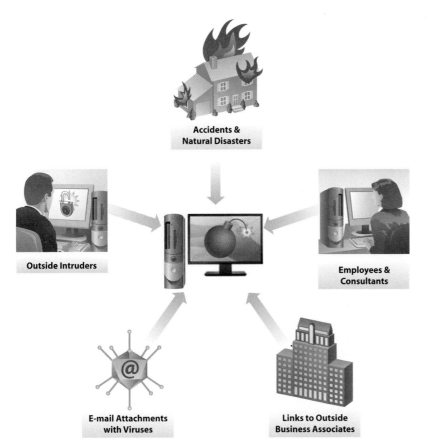

What Is Computer Crime?

Computer crime is defined as the act of using a computer to commit an illegal act. This broad definition of computer crime can include the following:

- Targeting a computer while committing an offense. For example, someone gains unauthorized entry to a computer system in order to cause damage to the computer system or to the data it contains.
- Using a computer to commit an offense. In such cases, computer criminals may steal credit card numbers from Web sites or a company's database, skim money from bank accounts, or make unauthorized electronic fund transfers from financial institutions.
- Using computers to support a criminal activity despite the fact that computers are not actually targeted. For example, drug dealers and other professional criminals may use computers to store records of their illegal transactions.

According to the 2009 Computer Security Institute (CSI) Computer Crime and Security Survey, the overall trend for computer crime has been declining over the past several years (CSI, 2009). Nevertheless, the reported losses for organizations due to computer crime have been tremendous. For example, the CSI survey of 443 organizations estimated that their average loss in 2008 related to computer crime exceeded $234,000. Likewise, worldwide losses for computer viruses alone were estimated to exceed $13.3 billion in 2006. The trends for losses in the future are unknown, as some experts believe that better security measures may be counteracted by increased sophistication of the criminals (see Figure 10.3). Many organizations do not report incidents of computer crime because of fear that negative publicity could hurt stock value or provide advantages to competitors. Thus, experts believe that many incidents are never reported and that real losses exceed these estimates. It is clear, however, that computer crime is a fact of life. In this section, we briefly introduce this topic of growing importance.

Federal and State Laws

In the United States, there are two main federal laws against computer crime: the Computer Fraud and Abuse Act of 1986 and the Electronic Communications Privacy Act of 1986. The Computer Fraud and Abuse Act of 1986 prohibits the following:

- Stealing or compromising data about national defense, foreign relations, atomic energy, or other restricted information

FIGURE 10.3

Financial impact of virus attacks, 1995–2006, and beyond.

Source: Based on: http://www .computereconomics.com.

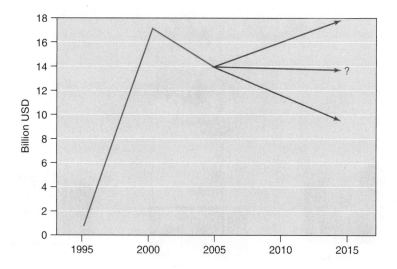

- Gaining unauthorized access to computers owned by any agency or department of the U.S. government
- Violating data belonging to banks or other financial institutions
- Intercepting or otherwise intruding on communications between states or foreign countries
- Threatening to damage computer systems in order to extort money or other valuables from persons, businesses, or institutions

In 1996, the Computer Abuse Amendments Act expanded the Computer Fraud and Abuse Act of 1986 to prohibit the dissemination of computer viruses and other harmful code.

The Electronic Communications Privacy Act of 1986 makes it a crime to break into any electronic communications service, including telephone services. It prohibits the interception of any type of electronic communications. Interception, as defined by the law, includes listening in on communications without authorization and recording or otherwise taking the contents of communications. In 2002, however, the U.S. Congress passed the USA PATRIOT Act (Patriot Act) to extend the Computer Fraud and Abuse Act. Under the prior law, investigators could not monitor voice communication—or stored voice communication—when investigating someone suspected of violating the Computer Fraud and Abuse Act. Under the Patriot Act, investigators can gain access to voice-related communications much more easily, and this makes it a very controversial law. Many civil libertarians feel that the Patriot Act greatly erodes many existing constitutional protections, and it is likely to be hotly debated long into the future.

In addition to the primary laws discussed here, other federal laws may apply to computer crime. Patent laws protect some software and computer hardware, and contract laws may protect trade secrets that are stored on computers. In 1980, the U.S. Copyright Act was amended to include computer software, making it a violation of this act to post online written compositions, photos, sound files, and software without the permission of the copyright holder.

The Federal Bureau of Investigation (FBI) and the U.S. Secret Service jointly enforce federal computer crime laws. The FBI is in charge when crimes involve espionage, terrorism, banking, organized crime, and threats to national security. The Secret Service investigates crimes against U.S. Treasury Department computers and against computers that contain information protected by the Right to Financial Privacy Act. Information protected by the Financial Privacy Act includes credit card information, credit reporting information, and data on bank loan applications. In some federal computer crime cases, the U.S. Customs Department, the Commerce Department, or the military may have jurisdiction. In addition to federal laws against computer crime, all 50 states have passed laws prohibiting computer crime. Many foreign countries also have similar laws.

Some violations of state and federal computer crime laws are charged as misdemeanors. These violations are punishable by fines and by not more than one year in prison. Other violations are classified as felonies and are punishable by fines and by more than one year in prison. The Patriot Act converted many misdemeanors into felony-level offenses. Nevertheless, intent can often determine whether crimes are prosecuted as misdemeanors or felonies. If intruders breach computer systems with intent to do harm, they may be charged with a felony. If a break-in is classified as reckless disregard but causes no damage, the offense may be classified as a misdemeanor.

Some critics argue that laws do not go far enough to prosecute computer crimes, while others believe that they should not be invoked when systems are breached but no damage is done. Even the definition of "damage" is debatable. For instance, has damage occurred if someone gains unauthorized access to a computer system but does not steal or change information?

There are additional difficulties in legislating and enforcing laws that affect global networks. Since many countries can be involved when break-ins and other crimes occur, who has jurisdiction? Should e-mail messages be monitored for libelous or other illegal content, and, if so, who should have monitoring responsibility? Is e-mail subject to the same laws as mail delivered by the U.S. Postal Service, or is it more akin to telephone conversations and the laws that apply to them?

Hacking and Cracking

Those individuals who are knowledgeable enough to gain access to computer systems without authorization have long been referred to as **hackers.** The name was first used in the 1960s to describe expert computer users and programmers who were students at the Massachusetts Institute of Technology. They wrote programs for the mainframes they used and freely exchanged information, but they followed unwritten rules against damaging or stealing information belonging to others. They claimed that their motives for roaming freely through computer systems were based entirely on curiosity and the desire to learn as much as possible about computers.

As computer crime became more prevalent and damaging, true hackers—those motivated by curiosity and not by a desire to do harm—objected to use of the term to describe computer criminals. Today, those who break into computer systems with the intention of doing damage or committing a crime are usually called **crackers.** Some computer criminals attempt to break into systems or deface Web sites to promote political or ideological goals (such as free speech, human rights, and antiwar campaigns); these Web vandals are referred to as **hacktivists.**

Types of Computer Criminals and Crimes

Computer crimes are almost as varied as the users who commit them. Some involve the use of a computer to steal money or other assets or to perpetrate a deception for money, such as advertising merchandise for sale on a Web auction site, collecting orders and payment, and then sending either inferior merchandise or no merchandise at all. Other computer crimes involve stealing or altering information. Some of those thieves who steal information or disrupt a computer system have demanded a ransom from victims in exchange for returning the information or repairing the damage. Cyberterrorists have planted destructive programs in computer systems, then threatened to activate them if a ransom is not paid (see more on cyberterrorism later in this chapter). Crimes in the form of electronic vandalism cause damage when offenders plant viruses, cause computer systems to crash, or deny service on a Web site.

Use of the Internet has fostered other types of criminal activity, such as the stalking of minors by sexual predators through newsgroups and chat rooms. Those who buy, sell, and distribute pornography have also found in the Internet a new medium for carrying out their activities.

Who Commits Computer Crimes? When you hear the term "cracker" or "computer criminal," you might imagine a techno-geek, someone who sits in front of his or her computer all day and night, attempting to break the ultra-super-secret security code of one of the most sophisticated computer systems in the world, perhaps a computer for the U.S. military, a Swiss bank, or the Central Intelligence Agency. While this fits the traditional profile for a computer criminal, there is no clear profile today. More and more people have the skills, the tools, and the motives to hack into a computer system. A modern-day computer criminal could be a disgruntled, middle-aged, white-collar worker sitting at a nice desk on the fourteenth floor of the headquarters building of a billion-dollar software manufacturer. Computer criminals have been around for decades. For the most part, we associate hackers and crackers with their pranks and crimes involving security systems and viruses. Nevertheless, hackers and crackers have caused the loss of billions of dollars' worth of stolen goods, repair bills, and lost goodwill with customers.

ETHICAL DILEMMA

Ethical Hacking

Some hackers who are skilled in "unauthorized computer access" have found that it makes more economic sense to be paid for their computer skills than to continue to operate outside the law. Marc Maiffret, cofounder of a computer security firm, is a case in point.

Maiffret has always been interested in figuring out how things work. When he was small, he took apart various household items to see how they worked, then "tried" to put them back together. He came relatively late to computers, however, but when he got his first machine at the age of 15, he immediately tried to figure out how the machine worked.

Maiffret soon discovered the online hacker culture and was intrigued by how they were thinking and approaching problems. To Maiffret, it seemed that hackers were among the greatest thinkers of society, particularly in regard to pushing the limits and understanding things. The progression for him was to go from just trying to understand how software and hardware worked to getting the hardware and software to do what he wanted it to do—beyond what the original manufacturer intended.

By the ripe old age of 17, Maiffret knew, through experience, that there were few, if any, computer systems that could keep him out. He had dropped out of high school and was looking for work when he was introduced to Jordanian businessman Firas Bushnaq, then the chief executive officer of eCompany, a software firm. Maiffret offered Bushnaq a deal—if he could break into Bushnaq's corporate network, Bushnaq would hire him as a security expert. Bushnaq agreed, and Maiffret cracked (broke into) eCompany's network in less than an hour. Bushnaq hired Maiffret and taught him how to write commercial software and, perhaps most important, how to run a business.

In 1997, Maiffret and Bushnaq started their own company, eEye Digital Security. The company finds holes in different types of software for its software-vendor clients. It then devises and sells software to prevent unauthorized visitors from breaching a client's system. In other words, eEye sells software that can find the ways a hacker could break into a computer system or network, then eEye offers information on how those security holes can be fixed. When asked to reveal some of the techniques he uses to discover software vulnerabilities, Maiffret's standard reply is, "I could tell you, but I would have to kill you."

Maiffret's insights into the hacker culture have contributed to his business success. To Maiffret, the "computer underground" is appealing, as differences are accepted far more often than in the "real" world. The hackers' way of thinking differs vastly from other people and especially businesspeople. This is partly because many of the best hackers don't have a formal education.

Maiffret's title at eEye was "Chief Hacking Officer." Check out the services offered on the company's Web site (www.eEye.com) to see how one "ethical hacker" has found success in the online business world. Today, Maiffret is the chief security architect at FireEye, a Silicon Valley–based company focusing on malware prevention systems.

While Maiffret has made a success of his security business, most hackers who dream of being recognized for their skills and hired by security firms will be disappointed. For example, the president of Rent-a-Hacker, a security troubleshooting firm headquartered in Boulder, Colorado, has said that he rejects job-seeking crackers every day. The company employs hackers, but not for illegal activities, and the chief executive officer of Rent-a-Hacker won't hire anyone with a criminal record. The hackers who haven't been arrested are the true experts, the man maintains, and he has employed nearly 100 of them.

Based on:

Higgins, K. J. (2007, December 12). Maiffret says bye to eEye. *DarkReading.* Retrieved April 10, 2010, from http://www.darkreading.com/document.asp?doc_id=141256.

Marc Maiffret. (2010, May 4). In *Wikipedia, the free encyclopedia.* Retrieved May 20, 2010, from http://en.wikipedia.org/w/index.php?title=Marc_Maiffret&oldid=360135625.

Rent-a-Hacker. (n.d.). Retrieved April 10, 2010, from http://www.rent-a-hacker.com.

Studies attempting to categorize computer criminals show that they generally fall into one of four groups. These groups are listed next, from those who commit most infractions to those who commit the fewest infractions:

1. Current or former employees who are in a position to steal or otherwise do damage to employers; most organizations report insider abuses as their most common crime (CSI, 2009).

2. People with technical knowledge who commit business or information sabotage for personal gain.
3. Career criminals who use computers to assist in crimes.
4. Outside crackers simply snooping or hoping to find information of value—crackers commit millions of intrusions per year, but most cause no harm. Estimates are that only around 12 percent of cracker attacks cause damage.

Some crackers probe others' computer systems, electronically stored data, or Web sites for fun, for curiosity, or just to prove they can. Others have malicious or financial motives and intend to steal for gain or do other harm. Whatever the motives, discovery, prosecution, fines, and jail terms can result.

Unauthorized Access **Unauthorized access** occurs whenever people who are not authorized to see, manipulate, or otherwise handle information look through electronically stored information files for interesting or useful data, peek at monitors displaying proprietary or confidential information, or intercept electronic information on the way to its destination. Here are a few additional examples from recent media reports:

- Employees steal time on company computers to do personal business.
- Intruders break into government Web sites and change the information displayed.
- Thieves steal credit card numbers and Social Security numbers from electronic databases, then use the stolen information to charge thousands of dollars in merchandise to victims.
- An employee at a Swiss bank steals data that could possibly help to charge the bank's customers for tax evasion, hoping to sell this data to other countries' governments for hefty sums of money.

When computer information is shared by several users, as in an organization, in-house system administrators can prevent casual snooping or theft of information by requiring correct permissions. Further, administrators can log attempts of unauthorized individuals trying to obtain access. Determined attackers, however, will try to gain access by giving themselves system administrator status or otherwise elevating their permission level—sometimes by stealing passwords and logging on to a system as authorized users (see Figure 10.4).

FIGURE 10.4

Unauthorized access can occur in many ways.

FIGURE 10.5

Information modification attack.

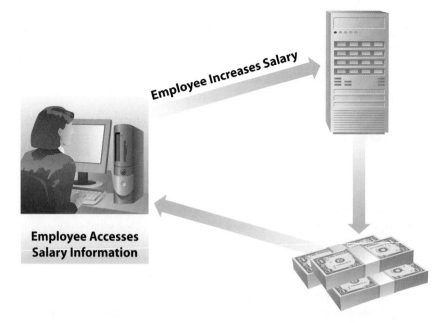

Information Modification Often related to unauthorized access, **information modification** occurs when someone accesses electronic information and then changes the information in some way, such as when crackers hack into government Web sites and change information or when employees give themselves electronic raises and bonuses (see Figure 10.5).

Other Threats to IS Security Many times, computer security is breached simply because organizations and individuals do not exercise proper care in safeguarding information. Some examples follow:

- Employees keep passwords or access codes on slips of paper in plain sight.
- Individuals have never bothered to install antivirus software, or they install the software but fail to keep it up to date.
- Computer users within an organization continue to use default network passwords after a network is set up instead of passwords that are more difficult to break.
- Employees are careless about letting outsiders view computer monitors, or they carelessly give out information over the telephone.
- Organizations fail to limit access to company files and system resources.
- Organizations fail to install effective firewalls or intrusion detection systems, or they install an intrusion detection system but fail to monitor it regularly.
- Proper background checks are not done on new hires.
- Employees are not properly monitored, and they steal company data or computer resources.
- Fired employees are resentful and install harmful code, such as computer viruses, when they leave the company.

While there are many threats to computer security, there are also ways to combat those threats. Later in this chapter, we discuss safeguards organizations can use to improve IS security.

Computer Viruses and Other Destructive Code

Malware—short for "malicious software" such as viruses, worms, and Trojan horses—continues to have a tremendous economic impact on the world, costing organizations more than $13 billion in 2006 (computereconomics.com, 2008). Antivirus Web vendors report thousands of new forms of malware each month.

Computer Viruses A **virus** is a destructive program that disrupt the normal functioning of computer systems. They differ from other types of malicious code in that they can reproduce themselves. Some viruses are intended to be harmless pranks, but more often they do damage to a computer system by erasing files on the hard drive or by slowing computer processing or otherwise compromising the system. Viruses are planted in host computers in a number of ways (Figure 10.6) but are most often spread through malicious e-mail attachments or file downloads from bogus Web sites.

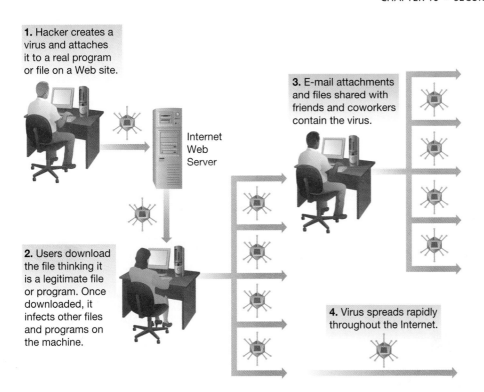

FIGURE 10.6

How a computer virus is spread.

1. Hacker creates a virus and attaches it to a real program or file on a Web site.

Internet Web Server

3. E-mail attachments and files shared with friends and coworkers contain the virus.

2. Users download the file thinking it is a legitimate file or program. Once downloaded, it infects other files and programs on the machine.

4. Virus spreads rapidly throughout the Internet.

Worms, Trojan Horses, and Other Sinister Programs Viruses are among the most virulent forms of computer infections, but other destructive code can also be damaging. A **worm,** a variation of a virus that is targeted at networks, takes advantage of security holes in operating systems and other software to replicate endlessly across the Internet, thus causing servers to crash, which denies service to Internet users.

Another destructive program is the **Trojan horse.** Unlike a virus, the Trojan horse does not copy itself, but, like viruses, it can do much damage. When a Trojan horse is planted in a computer, its instructions remain hidden. The computer appears to function normally, but in fact it is performing underlying functions dictated by the intrusive code. For example, under the pretext of playing chess with an unsuspecting systems operator, a cracker group installed a Trojan horse in a Canadian mainframe. While the game appeared to be proceeding normally, the Trojan horse program was sneakily establishing a powerful unauthorized account for the future use of the intruders.

Logic bombs or **time bombs** are variations of Trojan horses. They also do not reproduce themselves and are designed to operate without disrupting normal computer function. Instead, they lie in wait for unsuspecting computer users to perform a triggering operation. Time bombs are set off by specific dates, such as the birthday of a famous person. Logic bombs are set off by certain types of operations, such as entering a specific password or adding or deleting names and other information to and from certain computer files. Disgruntled employees have planted logic and time bombs on being fired, intending for the program to activate after they have left the company. In at least one instance in recent history, a former employee in Minnesota demanded money to deactivate the time bomb he had planted in company computers before it destroyed employee payroll records.

Denial of Service **Denial-of-service attacks** occur when electronic intruders deliberately attempt to prevent legitimate users of a service (e.g., customers accessing a Web site) from using that service, often by using up all of a system's resources. To execute such attacks, intruders often create armies of **zombie computers** by infecting with viruses or worms computers that are located in homes, schools, and businesses. Any computer connected to the Internet can be infected if it is not protected by firewalls and antivirus software and is, therefore, open to attacks and to being used as a zombie computer (in fact, some security experts believe that more than 10 percent of all computers connected to the Internet are used as zombies, unbeknownst to the owner). The zombie computers, without users' knowledge or consent, are used to spread the virus to other computers and to launch attacks on popular Web sites. The Web site servers under attack crash under the barrage of bogus computer-generated visitors, causing a denial of service to those Internet users who are legitimately trying to visit the sites

FIGURE 10.7

Denial-of-service attack.

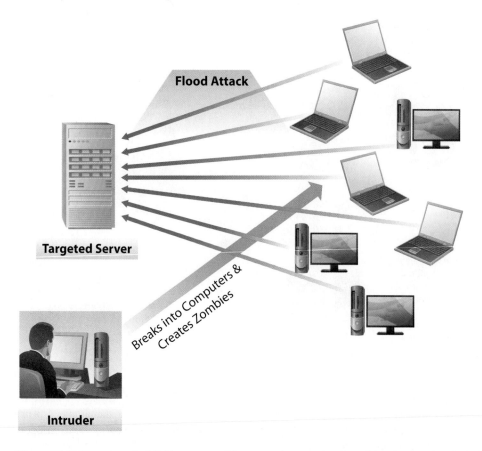

(see Figure 10.7). For example, MyDoom was able to recruit an army of zombies that bombarded Microsoft's Web site with traffic and literally locked out legitimate customers. (Microsoft is a popular target for virus writers, and the company must constantly provide downloadable patches to those using its software in order to prevent unauthorized intrusion.)

Spyware, Spam, and Cookies Three additional ways in which information systems can be threatened is by spyware, spam, and cookies.

Spyware. **Spyware** is any software that covertly gathers information about a user through an Internet connection without the user's knowledge. Spyware is sometimes hidden within freeware or shareware programs. In other instances, it is embedded within a Web site and is downloaded to the user's computer, without the user's knowledge, in order to track data about the user for marketing and advertisement purposes. Spyware can monitor your activity and secretly transmit that information to someone else. E-mail addresses, passwords, credit card numbers, and Web sites you have visited are among the various types of information that spyware can gather. Spyware presents problems because it uses your computer's memory resources; eats network bandwidth as it sends information back to the spyware's home base via your Internet connection; causes system instability or, worse, system crashes; and exposes users to identity theft, credit card fraud, and other types of crime. **Adware** (free software paid for by advertisements appearing during the use of the software) sometimes contains spyware that collects information about a person's Web surfing behavior in order to customize Web browser banner advertisements. It is important to note that spyware is not currently illegal, although there is ongoing legislative hype about regulating it in some way. Fortunately, firewalls and spyware protection software can be used to scan for and block spyware.

Spam. Another prevalent form of network traffic that invades our e-mail is spam. **Spam** is electronic junk mail or junk newsgroup postings, usually for the purpose of advertising for some product and/or service (see Figure 10.8). In addition to being a nuisance and wasting our time, spam also eats up huge amounts of storage space and network bandwidth. Today, according to websense.com, nearly 90 percent of all Internet e-mail is spam! Although there are federal, state, and international laws related to spam, most notably the CAN-SPAM Act of 2003, very little can be done to stop a motivated spammer (see www.spamlaws.com for more information). Spammers commonly use zombie

FIGURE 10.8

Spam is rampant and consumes an enormous amount of human and technology resources.

computers to send out millions of e-mail messages, unbeknownst to the computer users. Some spam consists of hoaxes, asking you to donate money to nonexistent causes or warning you of viruses and other Internet dangers that do not exist. Other times, spam includes attachments that carry destructive computer viruses. As a result, Internet service providers and those who manage e-mail within organizations often use **spam filters** to fight spam. Typical spam filters use multiple defense layers—and can utilize both hardware and software—to help reduce the amount of spam processed by the central e-mail servers and delivered to users' in-boxes. Spam filters fight not only spam but also other e-mail threats, such as directory harvest attacks (i.e., attempts to determine valid e-mail addresses for spam databases), phishing attacks, viruses, and more.

Some spam e-mail is used for **phishing** (or spoofing), which are attempts to trick financial account and credit card holders into giving away their authorization information, usually by sending spam messages to literally millions of e-mail accounts (i.e., attackers are "phishing" [fishing] for victims). These phony messages contain links to Web sites that duplicate legitimate sites to capture account information. For example, most e-mail users regularly receive phishing attempts from various spoofed banks, eBay, or PayPal (see Figure 10.9).

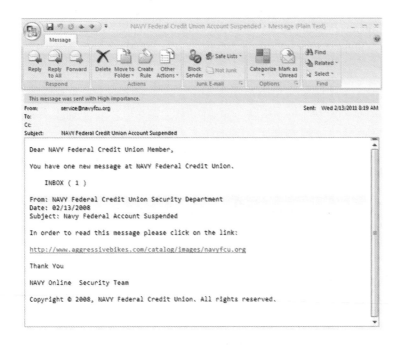

FIGURE 10.9

A phishing e-mail message.

In addition to e-mail–based spam, spam over text messaging and spam over instant messaging—called **spim**—are becoming increasingly used. Spim is particularly tricky because messages—typically a Web site link and some text saying how great the site is—are formatted to mimic communication chat sessions.

Often, spammers post their spam messages in online forums, blogs, or wikis, or create thousands of e-mail accounts at free providers such as Yahoo! or Hotmail to send out their messages. Rather than manually going through such tedious tasks to set up these accounts or post thousands of messages, spammers use bots (i.e., software robots that work in the background to provide services to their owners; see Chapter 6, "Enhancing Business Intelligence Using Information Systems") to do this. Faced with this problem, e-mail providers and managers of online forums are attempting to prevent spammers from using bots to automatically submit online forms. One commonly used approach for preventing bots from submitting forms is the use of CAPTCHAs. A **CAPTCHA** (Completely Automated Public Turing Test to Tell Computers and Humans Apart) typically consists of a distorted image displaying a combination of letters and/or numbers that a user has to input into a form (in addition to other required information) before submitting it. As the image is distorted, (currently) only humans can interpret the letters/numbers, preventing the use of automated bots for creating accounts or posting spam to forums, blogs, or wikis. CAPTCHAs are also used to prevent bots from trying to break passwords using a brute force approach (see Figure 10.10).

Unfortunately, in addition to posing challenges for the disabled, CAPTCHAs are becoming increasingly ineffective. Whereas some spammers try to break CAPTCHAs using sophisticated character recognition technology, others use cheap human labor; recently, inventive spammers created a striptease game, where the "players" had to solve CAPTCHAs for "Melissa" to expose herself. Unbeknownst to the users, the program would send the results to a remote server that would use the information for malicious purposes. Increasingly, Web masters are using a combination of multiple techniques to stop spammers, such as detecting mouse movements (as automated agents do not use a mouse), or detecting the rate at which text is entered into forms, or incorporating invisible fields (which would be "seen" and filled out by an automated agent but not a human user), together with CAPTCHAs in order to distinguish between malicious bots and legitimate users.

Cookies. Another nuisance in Internet usage are cookies. A **cookie** is a message passed to a Web browser on a user's computer by a Web server. The browser then stores the message in a text file, and the message is sent back to the server each time the user's browser requests a page from that server.

Cookies are normally used for legitimate purposes, such as identifying a user in order to present a customized Web page or for authentication purposes. Although you can choose to not accept the storage of cookies, you may not be able to visit the site, or it may not function properly. For example, to read the *New York Times* online, you must register by entering your name and other information. When you go through the registration process, cookies are stored on your machine. If you don't accept cookies or you delete the stored cookies, you are not allowed to

FIGURE 10.10

A CAPTCHA is used to prevent bots from submitting an online form.

access the online newspaper without reregistering. Similarly, you will have to accept cookies when purchasing from many e-tailers, as most online shopping carts require cookies to function properly. In such cases, cookies may contain sensitive information (such as credit card numbers) and thus pose a security risk in case unauthorized persons gain access to the computer.

Specific cookie management or cookie killer software can be used to manage cookies, but an even simpler way to manage cookies is through the settings in your Web browser. In the settings for the Firefox Web browser, for example, you can set levels of restrictions on the use of cookies, you can stop the use of them altogether, and, if you do allow them, you can go in periodically and delete them from your computer.

The Rise of Botnets and the Cyberattack Supply Chain Destructive software robots called bots (see Chapter 6), working together on a collection of zombie computers via the Internet, called **botnets,** have become the standard method of operation for professional cybercriminals. For example, about 85 percent of all e-mail spam is sent out by only six major botnets. Attacks using botnets are emerging into a global supply chain of highly specialized criminals. For instance, a phishing attack can involve the following:

1. A *programmer* writes a phishing attack template and makes this available for purchase.
2. A *phisher* who wants to run an attack purchases the template and designs an attack (e.g., ask recipients of a spam e-mail to update their banking information at the Wells Fargo Bank).
3. The *phisher* contracts with a *cracker* to provide hosting space for the phishing Web sites.
4. The *phisher* contacts a **bot herder**—a criminal who has a botnet residing on a collection of zombie computers—to send out the spam e-mail that carries the attack to unsuspecting people.
5. After launching the attack and collecting information from those who responded to the phishing attack, the *phisher* provides the stolen personal information to a *collector* who specializes in removing funds from the affected financial institutions.
6. The *collector* works with a criminal called a *mule herder* who has a network of people who carry out the withdrawals from affected banks.

Each member of the supply chain has very specialized skills and can be located anywhere in the world. In fact, one of the difficulties in stopping this global crime syndicate is the difficulty of not only tracking the locations of these villains but also prosecuting criminals across international borders. Today, a would-be cybercriminal does not need highly specialized computer skills to build a botnet; rather, the criminal can easily "rent" space on a botnet (including technical support from the bot herder, tremendous resources, and bandwidth) starting at $150, depending on the size of the botnet.

Identity Theft One of the fastest-growing "information" crimes in recent years has been **identity theft** (see Figure 10.11). Identity theft is the stealing of another person's Social Security number, credit card number, and other personal information for the purpose of using the victim's credit rating to borrow money, buy merchandise, and otherwise run up debts that are never repaid. In some cases, thieves even withdraw money directly from victims' bank accounts. Since many government and private organizations keep information about individuals in accessible databases, opportunities abound for thieves to retrieve it. Reclaiming one's identity and restoring a good credit rating can be frustrating and time consuming for victims.

The solution to identity theft lies in the government and private sector working together to change practices used to verify a person's identity. For example, a mother's maiden name and an individual's Social Security number are too easily obtained. Other methods of personal identification, such as biometrics and encryption, may need to be used if the problem is to be solved. Methods of information security, including biometrics and encryption, are discussed later in this chapter.

Internet Hoaxes

An **Internet hoax** is a false message circulated online about new viruses; funds for alleged victims of the January 12, 2010, Haiti earthquake; kids in trouble; cancer causes; or any other topic of public interest. In most cases, the consequences of passing on a hoax will be small, and your friends will just ridicule you; in other cases, spammers might "harvest" e-mail addresses from hoaxes, potentially causing your in-box to be flooded with junk mail. Several Web sites, such as Hoaxbusters (www.hoaxbusters.org), Symantec, or McAfee, publish lists of known hoaxes, and you should always check to see if a message is a hoax before you forward it to others.

FIGURE 10.11

Identity theft is one of the fastest-growing information crimes.

Getty Images - IStock Exclusive RF

Cybersquatting

Another information property issue relates to **cybersquatting**, the dubious practice of registering a domain name and then trying to sell the name for big bucks to the person, company, or organization most likely to want it. Domain names are one of the few scarce resources on the Internet, and victims of cybersquatting include Panasonic, Hertz, Avon, and numerous other companies and individuals. Fortunately, the U.S. government passed the Anti-Cybersquatting Consumer Protection Act in 1999, which made it a crime to register, traffic in, or use a domain name to profit from the goodwill of a trademark belonging to someone else. Fines for cybersquatting can reach as high as $100,000 in addition to the forfeiture of the disputed domain name. As a result, recent court cases have not been kind to cybersquatters. Many feel, however, that it is often much easier simply to pay the cybersquatter because that will likely be much faster and cheaper than to hire a lawyer and go through the lengthy legal process. Others, such as rapper Eminem, who won a case against a company that had registered the domain name eminemmobile.com, use a fast-track procedure of the World Intellectual Property Organization of the United Nations to stop others from using their names without permission. No matter how companies or individuals deal with this problem, valuable resources of time and money are wasted resolving these disputes.

Cyberharassment, Cyberstalking, and Cyberbullying

The Internet has become a place where people utilize its anonymity to harass, stalk, and bully others. **Cyberharassment,** a crime in many states and countries, broadly refers to the use of a computer to communicate obscene, vulgar, or threatening content that causes a reasonable person to endure distress. A single offensive message can be considered cyberharassment.

Repeated contacts with a victim are referred to as **cyberstalking.** Cyberstalking can take many forms, including the following:

- Making false accusations that damage the reputation of the victim on blogs, Web sites, chat rooms, or e-commerce sites (e.g., eBay)
- Gaining information on a victim by monitoring online activities, accessing databases, and so on
- Encouraging others to harass a victim by posting personal information about the victim on Web sites or in chat rooms
- Attacking data and equipment of the victim by sending e-mail viruses and other destructive code
- Using the Internet to place false orders for goods and services, such as magazines, pornography, and other embarrassing items, as well as having such items delivered to work addresses

NET STATS

Top Cyberthreats

Robert Morris's worm, a bug that crashed a record 6,000 computers (a statistic compiled from an estimate that there were 60,000 computers connected to the Internet at the time and the worm affected 10 percent of them), now seems as antiquated as the 1911 Stutz Bearcat automobile. Morris was a student at Cornell University in 1988 when he devised a program that he later insisted was intended simply to gauge how many computers were connected to the Internet. Errors in Morris's program turned it into a self-replicating monster that overloaded computers and threatened frightened Internet users. Dubbed simply the Internet Worm, Morris's program was the precursor for today's multitude of malevolent codes.

According to Kaspersky Lab, a leading developer of content management security solutions, 2009 was dominated by various malicious activities, including the Kido worm (also known as Conficker), Web attacks and botnets, SMS (short message service, the "formal" name for text messaging) fraud, and attacks on social networks. For 2010 and beyond, they expected to see an increase in the following:

1. File sharing network attacks: Cybercriminals will increasingly launch attacks from torrent portals and other peer-to-peer sites.
2. Use of botnet services: Cybercriminals trying to operate on the fringe of current law will increasingly provide botnet services to those wishing to send tons of spam, perform denial-of-service attacks, or distribute malware.
3. Fake antivirus programs: Cybercriminals will increasingly distribute fake antivirus programs so as to deploy malware to unsuspecting people.
4. More sophisticate malware: More sophisticated criminals are deploying malware that is increasingly difficult to detect and remove.
5. Web services: Attacks through Web services widely believed to be safe, such as collaboration platforms, will be on the rise.
6. Popular mobile handsets: Producers of malware will focus their efforts on the most popular devices such as the iPhone and Android platforms.
7. Social networking sites: Launching attacks through popular social networking sites such as Twitter and Facebook will again be on the rise.
8. Third-party software: Attacks through widely used applications like Adobe Acrobat will continue.

In addition to these various trends, an old favorite, the Windows operating system, will continue to be a popular target. Nevertheless, given some major security improvements within Windows 7, many experts believe that this is driving criminals to easier targets.

Based on:

Markoff, J. (1990, May 5). Computer intruder is put on probation and fined $10,000. *New York Times*. Retrieved October 12, 2008, from http://query.nytimes.com/gst/fullpage.html?res=9C0CE1D71038F936A 35756C0A966958260.

More, P. (2010, January 15). Kaspersky Lab issues 2010 cyberthreat forecast. Retrieved July 20, 2010, from http://www.prlog.org/10489945 -kaspersky-lab-issues-2010-cyber-threat-forecast.html.

Many states, the U.S. government, and many countries have anti-cyberstalking laws. Unfortunately, law enforcement has a difficult time catching most cyberstalkers. While cyberstalking can take many forms and can go undetected by the victim, the intent of **cyberbullying** is to *deliberately* cause emotional distress in the victim. Cyberharassment, cyberstalking, and cyberbullying are typically targeted at a particular person or group as a means of revenge or expressing hatred.

In contrast, **online predators** typically target vulnerable people, usually the young or old, for sexual or financial purposes. While typically online chat rooms and instant messaging systems have been the playground for online predators, these villains are also targeting many social networking sites like Facebook. To combat these online predators, parents must educate their children not to share personal information and possibly must use monitoring software to track online activity. Fortunately, most social networking and online chat sites also provide ways to report abuse by these predators.

Software Piracy

Software developers and marketers want you to buy as many copies of their products as you want, of course. But commercial software vendors do not want you or anyone else to buy one copy and then bootleg additional copies to sell or to give to others. Vendors also take a dim view of companies that buy one copy of a software application and then make many copies to distribute to employees. In fact, the practice is called **software piracy,** and it is illegal.

When you buy commercial software, it is typically legal for you to make one backup copy for your own use. It is also legal to offer shareware or public domain software for free on a Web site. But **warez** peddling—offering stolen proprietary software for free over the Internet—is a crime. ("Warez" is the slang term for such stolen software.)

Both patent and copyright laws can apply to software, which is a form of **intellectual property**—creations of the mind (e.g., music, software, and so on), inventions, names, images, designs, and other works used in commerce. Patents and copyrights are recognized and enforced by most countries, giving the creator exclusive rights to benefit from the creation for a limited period of time. **Patents** typically refer to process, machine, or material inventions. For example, Amazon.com's "one-click buying" process is protected by patent law, and Apple has patented its multitouch technology (including the "pinch" for shrinking and expanding items) used in the iPhone and iPad. **Copyrights** generally refer to creations of the mind such as music, literature, or software. Copyright laws covering software include the 1980 Computer Software Copyright Act, a 1992 act that made software piracy a felony, and the 1997 No Electronic Theft Act, which made copyright infringement a criminal act even when no profit was involved.

Software piracy has become a problem because it is so widespread, costing the commercial software industry and the entire economy billions of dollars a year. A 2008 study conducted by the Business Software Alliance (BSA) suggested that reducing software piracy by only 10 percent over the next four years could generate 32,000 new jobs, $41 billion in revenues for the software companies, and $7 billion in tax revenues. The crime is difficult to trace, but many individuals and even companies have been successfully prosecuted for pirating software. Many software vendors are trying to limit software piracy by requiring the users to enter license keys or verifying the key before allowing the customer to register or update the software.

Software Piracy Is a Global Business A major international issue that businesses deal with is the willingness (or unwillingness) of governments and individuals to recognize and enforce the ownership of intellectual property—in particular, software copyrights. Piracy of software and other technologies is widespread internationally (see Figure 10.12). The BSA (2010) points to countries such as Georgia (95 percent), Armenia (92 percent), and Bangladesh (92 percent) as those with the highest percentages of illegal software. Worldwide losses due to piracy exceeded $53 billion in 2008. Countries with the lowest piracy rates include the United States (20 percent), Japan (21 percent), Luxembourg (21 percent), and New Zealand (21 percent). Because technology usage varies significantly by region, average piracy levels and dollar losses

FIGURE 10.12

In many parts of the world, using pirated software is a common practice.

Courtesy Christoph Schneider

TABLE 10.1 Software Piracy Levels and Dollar Losses by Region

Region	Piracy Level	Dollar Loss (millions)
North America	21%	10,401
Western Europe	33%	13,023
Asia/Pacific	61%	15,261
Latin America	65%	4,311
Middle East/Africa	59%	2,999
Eastern Europe	65%	4,311
Worldwide	41%	52,998

Source: Based on Business Software Alliance (2010). Table 3, pages 14–15 from http://portal.bsa.org/globalpiracy2009/studies/globalpiracystudy2009.pdf.

greatly differ across regions (see Table 10.1). For instance, even though the United States has the lowest piracy rate, it also is where the greatest losses occur (more than $9 billion) because of its high level of computer usage.

In addition to being a crime, is software piracy also an ethical problem? Perhaps in part, but businesspeople must acknowledge and deal with other perspectives as well. In part, the problem stems from other countries' differing concepts of ownership. Many of the ideas about intellectual property ownership stem from long-standing cultural traditions. For example, the concept of individual ownership of knowledge is traditionally a strange one in many Middle Eastern countries, where knowledge is meant to be shared. Plagiarism does not exist in a country where words belong to everyone. By the same token, piracy does not exist either. This view is gradually changing; the Saudi Arabia Patent Office granted its first patents several years ago, and its piracy rates have plummeted from 79 percent in 1996 to 52 percent in 2008.

In other cases, there are political, social, and economic reasons for piracy. In many countries, software publishers are not catering to the needs of consumers, who often simply do not have the funds to purchase software legitimately. This is true in many areas of South America and other regions with low per capita income. It is particularly true of students and other members of university communities whose needs are critical in some areas.

Other factors leading to piracy or infringement of intellectual property agreements throughout the world include lack of public awareness about the issue, lack of an industrial infrastructure that can produce legitimate software, and the increasingly high demand for computers and other technology products. The United States has repeatedly pressured and threatened other countries accused of pirating. It is interesting to note, however, that despite the fact that few of these cultural and economic explanations are valid in the United States, the United States leads the world in the sheer volume of illegal software in use. Businesses that operate in glass offices should surely not throw stones.

Cyberwar and Cyberterrorism

Over the past several years, individual computer criminals have caused billions of dollars in losses through the use of viruses, worms, and unauthorized access to computers. In the future, many believe that coordinated efforts by national governments or terrorist groups have the potential to do hundreds of billions of dollars in damage as well as put the lives of countless people at stake (Panko, 2010). Most experts believe that cyberwar and cyberterrorism are imminent threats to the United States and other technologically advanced countries. A major attack that cripples a country's information infrastructure or power grid or even the global Internet could have devastating implications for a country's (or the world's) economic system and make transportation systems, medical capabilities, and other key infrastructure extremely vulnerable to disaster.

Cyberwar

Cyberwar refers to an organized attempt by a country's military to disrupt or destroy the information and communication systems of another country. Cyberwar is often executed simultaneously with traditional methods to quickly dissipate the capabilities of an enemy. Given that the

United States and the NATO alliance is the most technologically sophisticated war machine in the world—and also the most dependent on its networking and computing infrastructure—it is also the most vulnerable to cyberwar (or cyberterrorism) attacks.

Cyberwar Vulnerabilities The goal of cyberwar is to turn the balance of information and knowledge in one's favor in order to enhance one's capabilities while diminishing those of an opponent. Cyberwar will utilize a diverse range of technologies, including software, hardware, and networking technologies, to gain an information advantage over an opponent. These technologies will be used to electronically blind, jam, deceive, overload, and intrude into an enemy's computing and networking capabilities in order to diminish various capabilities, including the following:

- Command-and-control systems
- Intelligence collection, processing, and distribution systems
- Tactical communication systems and methods
- Troop and weapon positioning systems
- Friend-or-foe identification systems
- Smart weapons systems

Additionally, controlling the content and distribution of propaganda and information to an opponent's civilians, troops, and government is a key part of a cyberwar strategy. At the simplest level, **Web vandalism** can occur by simply defacing Web sites. Likewise, cyberpropaganda can be quickly and easily distributed through chat rooms, Web sites, and e-mail. Espionage—stealing of secrets or modifying information—can occur if data and systems are not adequately protected and secure.

The New Cold War According to the 2007 annual report of the Internet security company McAfee, a *cyber cold war* is an imminent threat for the world's computers. It reports that more than 120 nations are developing ways to use the Internet as a weapon to target financial markets, governmental computer systems, and key infrastructure. Reminiscent of the Cold War—a period of conflict, tension, and competition between the United States and the Soviet Union and their respective allies from the mid-1940s until the early 1990s (see Figure 10.13)—intelligence agencies from countries around the world are secretly testing networks and looking for weaknesses in their potential enemies' computer systems. There are several known attacks, although most governments deny involvement. Typically, governments accused of cyberwar activities blame uncontrolled **patriot hackers**—independent citizens or supporters of a country that perpetrate attacks on perceived or real enemies. Regardless of the source of these attacks, it is clear that one

FIGURE 10.13

The Cuban missile crisis was the height of the Cold War.

Shutterstock

of the big challenges for governments moving forward will be to fully integrate a cyberwar strategy into their overall plans and capabilities.

Cyberterrorism

Unlike cyberwar, **cyberterrorism** is launched not by governments but by individuals and organized groups. Cyberterrorism is the use of computer and networking technologies against persons or property to intimidate or coerce governments, civilians, or any segment of society in order to attain political, religious, or ideological goals. One of the great fears about cyberterrorism is that an attack can be launched from a computer anywhere in the world—no borders have to be crossed, no bombs smuggled and placed, and no lives lost in carrying out the attack. Because computers and networking systems control power plants, telephone systems, and transportation systems, as well as water and oil pipelines, any disruption in these systems could cause loss of life or widespread chaos (Volonino & Robinson, 2004). Just as physical terrorist attacks have physical and psychological effects, so also do cyberattacks. Dealing with the unknown—where, when, and how—of an indiscriminant terrorist attack is what leads to "terror."

What Kinds of Attacks Are Considered Cyberterrorism? Cyberterrorism could involve physical destruction of computer systems or acts that destroy economic stability or infrastructure. Cyberterrorist acts could likely damage the machines that control traffic lights, power plants, dams, or airline traffic in order to create fear and panic. Attacks launched in cyberspace could take many forms, such as viruses, denial of service, destruction of government computers, stealing classified files, altering Web page content, deleting or corrupting vital information, disrupting media broadcasts, and otherwise interrupting the flow of information. Table 10.2 summarizes several categories of attacks that experts believe cyberterrorists will try to deliver.

The goal of cyberterrorists is to cause fear, panic, and destruction. Through the power of computer technology and global networks, terrorists can gain access to critical parts of the world's infrastructure to produce both physical and virtual terror. Given the great potential for cyberterrorism, many experts believe that it will, unfortunately, become the weapon of choice for the world's most sophisticated terrorists.

How the Internet Is Changing the Business Processes of Terrorists Virtually all modern terrorist groups utilize the Internet (Weimann, 2006). Beyond using the Internet to wage cyberattacks, the Internet is a powerful tool for improving and streamlining the business processes of the modern terrorist (see Table 10.3). Just as the Internet has fueled globalization for organizations and societies, it too has fueled global terrorism. Clearly, the Internet is transforming the "business processes" of the modern terrorist.

Assessing the Cyberterrorism Threat Some experts claim that because of the general openness of access, the Internet infrastructure is extremely vulnerable to cyberterrorism. Each year, cyberattacks on critical infrastructure such as nuclear power plants, dams, and power grids are

TABLE 10.2 Categories of Potential Cyberterrorist Attacks

Category	Description
Coordinated bomb attacks	To distribute a number of devices—from small explosive devices to large weapons of mass destruction—that communicate with each other through the Internet or cellular phone networks and are made to simultaneously detonate if one device stops communicating with the others
Manipulation of financial and banking information	To disrupt the flow of financial information with the objective of causing fear and lack of confidence in the world's or a country's financial system
Manipulation of the pharmaceutical industry	To make hard-to-detect changes in the formulas of medications in order to cause fear and lack of confidence in this important industry
Manipulation of transportation control systems	To disrupt airline and railroad transportation systems, possibly leading to disastrous collisions
Manipulation of the broader civilian infrastructures	To compromise the communication, broadcast media, gas lines, water systems, and electrical grids in order to cause panic and fear within the population
Manipulation of nuclear power plants	To disrupt cooling systems in order to cause a meltdown that would disperse radiation

TABLE 10.3 How Terrorists Are Using the Internet

Use	Description
Information dissemination	The use of Web sites to disseminate propaganda to current and potential supporters, to influence international public opinion, and to notify potential enemies of pending plans.
Data mining	The use of the vast amount of information available on the Internet regarding virtually any topic for planning, recruitment, and numerous other endeavors.
Fund-raising	The use of Web sites for bogus charities and nongovernmental organizations to raise funds and transfer currencies around the world.
Recruiting and mobilization	The use of Web sites to provide information for recruiting new members as well as utilizing more interactive Internet technologies, such as roaming online chat rooms and cybercafés for receptive individuals.
Networking	The use of the Internet to enable a less hierarchical, cell-based organizational structure that is much more difficult to combat; networking capabilities also allow different groups, with common enemies, to better share and coordinate information.
Information sharing	The use of the Internet as a powerful tool for announcing events as well as sharing best practices; for example, the official Hamas Web site details how to make homemade poisons and gases.
Planning and coordinating	The use of communication and information dissemination capabilities to facilitate designing and executing plans.
Information gathering	The use of mapping software such as Google Earth to locate potential targets for terrorist attacks.
Location monitoring	The use of public Web cams to monitor and study potential attack sites (e.g., Times Square or public resources such as tunnels or power generation facilities).

increasing. While the majority of such attacks have not done damage at this point, a few have been alarmingly successful and concerning:

- During the Gulf War in 1991, a group of Dutch crackers stole electronic information about U.S. troop movements and offered it for sale to Iraq. The Iraqis turned down the offer, thinking it was a hoax.
- In 1998, a 20-year-old Israeli cracker, Ehud Tennebaum, also known as "The Analyzer," joined two crackers in California to disrupt U.S. troop movements by disabling computers at the Pentagon, the National Security Agency, and national labs.
- In 1999, crackers allegedly gained control of a British military communication satellite and held it for ransom. The British military denied that the satellite had ever been under the control of intruders.
- Also in 1999, during the Serbia/Kosovo war, Serb crackers allegedly gained access to NATO Web pages and flooded e-mail accounts with pro-Serb messages.
- During the 2000 presidential election in the United States, Web attacks were reported that involved intruders with various political motives. Information was changed on targeted Web sites, snooping on political sites was rampant, and many denial-of-service attacks were launched.
- In May 2003, Romanian crackers compromised systems that housed life support control for 58 scientists and contractors in Antarctica. FBI agents assisted in the arrest of the crackers who attempted to extort money from the research station.
- In May 2007, government networks and commercial banks within Estonia came under a very sophisticated cyberattack by cyberterrorists in retaliation for the removal of a Soviet-era memorial to fallen soldiers (see Figure 10.14).
- In early 2010, Chinese-based hackers attacked Google, prompting the search engine giant to threaten to no longer filter searches within China deemed objectionable by the Chinese government (e.g., democracy, pornography, Tibet, the Tiananmen Square protests, and so on).

While defense and security departments within the United States need to protect against cyberterrorism, the U.S. military has also researched methods of using information technology (IT) to its advantage in times of war. For example, the United States reportedly conducted its first cyberwar campaign during the 78-day Serbia/Kosovo war by establishing a team of information warriors to support its bombing campaign against Serbia. The U.S. information operation cell electronically attacked Serbia's critical networks and command-and-control systems.

FIGURE 10.14

The removal of a Soviet-era memorial motivated patriot hackers to attack networks in Estonia.

While cyberterrorism obviously remains a threat to computer and network security, some experts point out that there are disadvantages to using acts of cyberterrorism as a weapon, including the following:

1. Computer systems and networks are complex, so cyberattacks are difficult to control and may not achieve the desired destruction as effectively as physical weapons.
2. Computer systems and networks change and security measures improve, so it requires an ever-increasing level of knowledge and expertise on the part of intruders for cyberattacks to be effective. This means that perpetrators will be required to continuously study and hone their skills as older methods of attack no longer work.
3. Cyberattacks rarely cause physical harm to victims; therefore, there is less drama and emotional appeal for perpetrators than using conventional weapons.

While cyberterrorism and cyberwar may be methods of choice for future generations with advanced computer knowledge, experts are hopeful that the increasing sophistication of computer security measures will help reduce the number of such incidents.

The Globalization of Terrorism With the proliferation and dependence on technology increasing at an astronomical rate, the threat of cyberterrorism will continue to increase. As has been true with virtually all governments and business organizations, fueled by the digitization of information and the Internet, terrorism has become a global business. To be adequately prepared, national governments along with industry partners must design coordinated responses to various attack scenarios. In addition to greater cooperation and preparedness, governments must improve their intelligence-gathering capabilities so that potential attacks are thwarted before they begin. Industry must also be given incentives to secure their information resources so that losses and disruptions in operations are minimized. International laws and treaties must rapidly evolve to reflect the realities of cyberterrorism, where attacks can be launched from anywhere in the world to anywhere in the world. Fortunately, experts believe that the likelihood of a devastating attack that causes significant disruption in the major U.S. infrastructure systems is quite low because the attackers would need "$200 million, intelligence information, and years of preparation" to succeed (Volonino & Robinson, 2004). Nevertheless, small attacks have been occurring for years and are likely to increase in frequency and severity—even a "small" attack, like an individual suicide bomber, can cause tremendous chaos to a society. Clearly, there are great challenges ahead.

Brief Case ⊙

HACKING AN AIRPLANE

The fact that the latest generation of aircraft uses information technology as never before is undoubtedly beneficial for the pilots, ground control centers, and passengers, but, once again, hackers can become a problem.

For example, as Boeing's highly technical 787 Dreamliner passenger jet was under development, serious security vulnerabilities were voiced regarding its onboard computer networks that could potentially allow passengers to access the plane's control systems. A U.S. Federal Aviation Administration (FAA) report revealed that the computer network in the Dreamliner's passenger compartment, designed to give passengers in-flight Internet access, was also connected to the plane's control, navigation, and communication systems. This physical connection of the networks makes the plane's control system vulnerable to hackers. IT security experts said that a more secure system would physically separate the two systems. "This is serious," said Mark Loveless, a network security analyst with Autonomic Networks, a company that presented a conference talk in 2007, "Hacking the Friendly Skies." "This isn't a desktop computer. It's controlling the systems that are keeping people from plunging to their deaths. So I hope they are really thinking about how to get this right." As development of the Dreamliner progressed, Boeing made design modifications to its onboard networks to satisfy the concerns of the FAA.

More recently, the FAA had similar concerns with Boeing's forthcoming 747-8/-8F airplanes. In early 2010, the FAA issued a "special conditions alert" specifically aimed at Boeing 747-8/-8F airplanes and to make sure that the networking systems in the new plane was also hackproof.

Questions

1. If a passenger hacked into a plane's control system, even if no damage was done, how seriously do you think that passenger should be punished?
2. Given that air travel can never be perfectly safe, how safe should the networks be on modern aircraft?

Based on:

Terdiman, D. (December 15, 2009). 787 Dreamliner takes to the sky. *geek gestalt*. Retrieved April 3, 2010, from http://news.cnet.com/8301-13772_3-10415680-52.html.

Terdiman, D. (January 25, 2010). FAA wants to know Boeing 747-8 is hack-proof. *geek gestalt*. Retrieved April 3, 2010, from http://news.cnet.com/8301-13772_3-10440819-52.html.

Zetter, K. (2008, January 4). FAA: Boeing's new 787 may be vulnerable to hacker attack. *Wired*. Retrieved April 3, 2010, from http://www.wired.com/politics/security/news/2008/01/dreamliner_security.

Information Systems Security

How do you secure information systems from dangers such as natural disasters, criminal activity, cyberterrorism, and other threats? The rule of thumb for deciding whether an information system is at risk is simple: All systems connected to networks are vulnerable to security violations from outsiders as well as insiders as well as to virus infections and other forms of computer crime. Further, no information system is immune to intentional or unintentional physical harm. In short, threats to information systems can come from a variety of places inside and external to an organization. **Information systems security** refers to precautions taken to keep all aspects of information systems (e.g., all hardware, software, network equipment, and data) safe from destruction, manipulation, or unauthorized use or access. That means that you have to secure not only the personal computers on people's desks but also the notebook computers, the handhelds, and the servers: all levels of the network and any gateway between the network and the outside world.

As use of the Internet and related telecommunications technologies and systems has become pervasive, use of these networks now creates a new vulnerability for organizations. These networks can be infiltrated and/or subverted in a number of ways. As a result, the need for tight computer and network security has increased dramatically. Fortunately, there are a variety of managerial methods and security technologies that can be used to manage IS security effectively. In the remaining sections of this chapter, we address this new reality.

Safeguarding IS Resources

Any good approach to securing information systems begins first with a thorough audit of all aspects of those systems, including hardware, software, data, networks, and any business processes that involve them. By doing this, you can then decide which aspects of the various systems within the organization are most vulnerable to harm/destruction, break-ins by unauthorized users, and/or misuse by authorized users. After such an audit, you can then design and implement a security plan that makes the best use of the available resources in order to protect the systems and guard against (or at least minimize) any problems. People within the IS department are usually responsible for implementing the security measures chosen, though people from throughout the organization should participate in the systems security audit. Some organizations even go so far as to pay an external consulting firm to attempt to break in and breach their systems so that vulnerabilities will be uncovered and fixed.

It would not make sense to spend literally millions of dollars a year to protect an asset, the loss of which would cost the organization only a few thousand dollars. As a result, organizations frequently conduct IS audits (discussed later in this chapter). One critical component of a good IS audit is a thorough risk analysis. **Risk analysis** is a process in which you assess the value of the assets being protected, determine their likelihood of being compromised, and compare the probable costs of their being compromised with the estimated costs of whatever protections you might have to take. People in organizations often perform risk analyses for their systems to ensure that IS security programs make sense economically (Stallings & Brown, 2008).

Risk analysis then enables us to determine what steps, if any, to take to secure systems. There are three general ways to react:

1. ***Risk Reduction.*** Taking active countermeasures to protect your systems, such as installing firewalls like those described later in this chapter
2. ***Risk Acceptance.*** Implementing no countermeasures and simply absorbing any damages that occur
3. ***Risk Transference.*** Having someone else absorb the risk, such as by investing in insurance or by outsourcing certain functions to another organization with specific expertise

Large organizations typically use a balance of all three approaches, taking steps in **risk reduction** for some systems, accepting risk and living with it in other cases (i.e., **risk acceptance**), and also insuring all or most of their systems activities as well (i.e., **risk transference**). There are two broad categories of safeguards for reducing risk—technological- and human-based approaches— and any comprehensive security plan will include both.

COMING ATTRACTIONS

What Were You Thinking?

Every few months, a company will release and then often quickly withdraw a television advertisement that is viewed by many as being a bit over the top, too raunchy, or insensitive. Remember the 2007 Budweiser Super Bowl ad that had a horse with flatulence? Or how about the ad by People for the Ethical Treatment of Animals contrasting Tiger Wood's sex life and that of tigers in the wild? There are countless examples. In most cases, swift and decisive consumer backlash results in the advertiser pulling the ad shortly after its initial airing.

If only there were a product that could tell, before commercials are aired, how potential viewers would react. Ad designers could then adjust advertising content to appeal to the audience they are trying to reach and could avoid marketing faux pas such as the ones detailed here. It happens that research in this area is already in progress.

For example, Emsense, a San Francisco–based company, has developed a sensor-laden headset for tracking brain activity that occurs while wearers watch various commercials and other video material. The headset is wired with one electroencephalography sensor at the forehead and also has sensors for monitoring breathing and heart rate, head motion, blink rate, and skin temperature—all of which are intended to detect when the wearer is concentrating or excited. According to Hans Lee, chief technology officer at Emsense, the company has also devised algorithms that translate physiological data from the sensors into information about emotions that a marketer can use. "Our technology allows us to collect moment-by-moment metrics while avoiding the cognitive bias that can interfere with self-reporting and focus groups."

Another brain-sensor application, called the SmartCap by CRC Mining, is the first application of this kind to apply brain-monitoring technology to detect driver fatigue. Looking like a common baseball hat (it can also be embedded into any type of head gear, such as a helmet), it contains many sensors which

(continued)

measure brain wave information through the scalp. Miniature processors inside the hat use this information to identify when the wearer is experiencing symptoms of fatigue. If detected, the cap sends a warning message to an in-cab display that will alert the driver to stop, rest, and refresh. The SmartCap is currently being tested within mines of the Australian Coal Association.

Toshiba and NeuroSky also developed a new type of consumer headphone equipped with a brain-wave sensor. The device can scan brain response to virtually any kind of stimuli. This sensor also has Bluetooth capabilities so that its information can be sent to your computer, and with its *Brain-wave Visualizer* software, people can view their brain wave activity in real time.

Another breakthrough with brain sensor technology has occurred at the University of Maryland, where researchers are capturing brain waves through sensors placed on the scalp of participants to successfully reconstruct three-dimensional hand motions on a computer display. The study reveals that the electrical brain activity acquired through the scalp is sufficient to reconstruct unconstrained hand movements. The research has many applications, especially for people with paralysis and neuromuscular disorders. For instance, Jonathan Wolpaw of New York's Wadsworth Center in Albany says that "it may eventually be possible for people with severe neuromuscular disorders, such as amyotrophic lateral sclerosis (ALS), stroke, or spinal cord injury, to regain control of complex tasks without needing to have electrodes implanted in their brains."

Based on:

Anonymous. (n.d.). Brain sensor breakthrough "could change future spinal injury treatment." Retrieved May 2, 2010, from http://www .seriousinjurylaw.co.uk/news/Spinal-Injury-News/Brain-sensor -breakthrough-could-change-future-spinal-injury-treatment.php.

Anonymous. (2009, October 6). SmartCap invented that warns drivers they are about to nod off. *MailOnline.* Retrieved May 26, 2010, from http://www.dailymail.co.uk/sciencetech/article-1218545/SmartCap -invented-warns-drivers-nod-off.html.

EmSense Corporation. (n.d.). Retrieved May 2, 2010, from http://www .emsense.com.

Foo, J. (2010, March 2). Headphones that sense your brainwaves. *CNET Asia.* Retrieved May 2, 2010, from http://asia.cnet.com/crave/2010/03/ 02/headphones-that-sense-your-brainwaves.

Greene, K. (2007, December 7). Brain sensor for market research. *Technology Review.* Retrieved May 2, 2010, from http://www .technologyreview.com/Biztech/19833.

SAM Technology. (n.d.). Retrieved May 2, 2010, from http://www.eeg.com.

Technological Safeguards

There are six commonly used methods in which technology is employed to safeguard information systems:

- Physical access restrictions
- Firewalls
- Encryption
- Virus monitoring and prevention
- Audit-control software
- Secure data centers

Within any type of safeguard, there are a variety of ways in which it can be deployed. Next, we briefly review each of these methods.

Physical Access Restrictions Organizations can prevent unauthorized access to information systems by keeping stored information safe and allowing access only to those employees who need it to do their jobs. Of course, organizations can protect computers and data resources by physically securing computers to desks or requiring users to lock hard drives with keys when leaving a computer unattended. However, most organizations don't go to such lengths and control access only by requiring some form of **authentication.** The most common form of authentication is the use of passwords, which are effective only if chosen carefully and changed frequently (see Figure 10.15). Besides passwords, employees may be asked to provide an ID combination, a security code sequence, or personal data, such as a mother's maiden name. Employees authorized to use computer systems may also be issued keys to physically unlock a computer, photo ID cards, smart cards with digital ID, and other physical devices allowing computer access. In sum, access is usually limited by making it dependent on one of the following:

- *Something You Have.* Keys, picture identification cards, smart cards, or smart badges that contain memory chips with authorization data on them (see Figure 10.16)
- *Something You Know.* Passwords, code numbers, PIN numbers, lock combinations, or answers to secret questions (your pet's name, your mother's maiden name, and so on)
- *Something You Are.* Unique attributes, such as fingerprints, voice patterns, facial characteristics, or retinal patterns (collectively called *biometrics*)

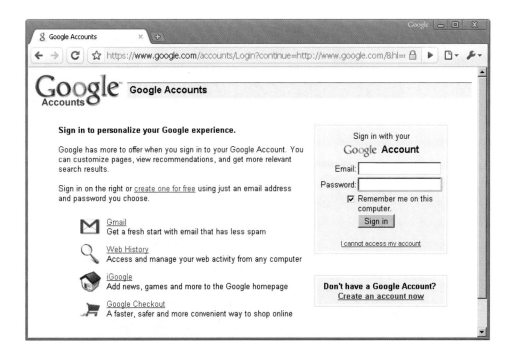

FIGURE 10.15

The most common form of authentication is through passwords.

Some measures that limit access to information are more secure than others. For example, smart cards and smart badges, passwords, lock combinations, and code numbers can be stolen. Biometric devices are difficult to fool, but determined intruders may sometimes devise ways to bypass them. Any of the previously mentioned single items can be used, but it is safer to use combinations of safeguards, such as a password *and* a smart card. Next, we examine various methods for implementing physical access control.

Biometrics. **Biometrics** is one of the most sophisticated forms of restricting computer user access. Biometrics is a form of authentication used to govern access to systems, data, and/or facilities. With biometrics, employees may be identified by fingerprints, retinal patterns in the eye, facial features, or other bodily characteristics before being granted access to use a computer

FIGURE 10.16

A smart card.

Fotolia, LLC-Royalty Free

FIGURE 10.17

Biometric devices are used to verify a person's identity.

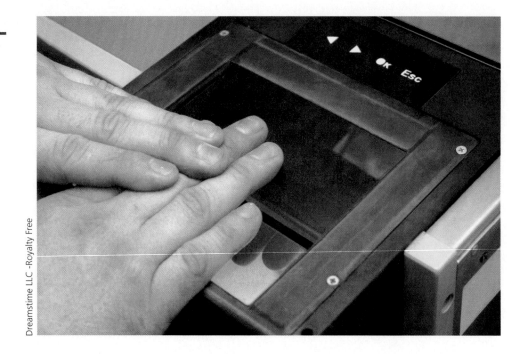

Dreamstime LLC –Royalty Free

or to enter a facility (see Figure 10.17). Biometrics has the promise of providing very high security while at the same time authenticating people extremely efficiently, so many governments and companies are investigating how best to use this technology. For example, many laptops and computer keyboards now incorporate fingerprint readers; similarly, residents of Hong Kong can quickly pass through immigration checkpoints by using a smart card and their thumbprints.

Access-Control Software. Special software can also be used to help keep stored information secure. **Access-control software,** for example, may allow computer users access only to those files related to their work. The user might even be restricted to these resources only at certain times or for specified periods of time, and, depending on the access level, the user can be restricted to being able to only read a file, to read and edit the file, to add to the file, and/or to delete the file. Many common business systems applications now build in these kinds of security features so that you do not have to have additional, separate access-control software running on top of your applications software.

Wireless LAN Control. Given how easy and inexpensive wireless local area networks (LANs) are to install and use, their use has skyrocketed, leaving many systems open to attack. On an unsecured network, for instance, unauthorized people can thus easily "steal" company resources (e.g., by surfing the Web for free, which is illegal in many countries) or do considerable damage to the network. A new form of attack known as **drive-by hacking** has arisen (see the chapter-opening case), where an attacker accesses the network, intercepts data from it, and even uses network services and/or sends attack instructions to it without entering the home, office, or organization that owns the network (see Figure 10.18). Wireless LAN control refers to methods of configuring the LAN so that only authorized users gain access.

Virtual Private Networks. A **virtual private network (VPN)** is a network connection that is constructed dynamically within an existing network—often called a secure tunnel—in order to connect users or nodes (see Figure 10.19). For example, a number of companies and software solutions enable you to create VPNs within the Internet as the medium for transporting data. These systems use authentication and encryption (discussed later) and other security mechanisms to ensure that only authorized users can access the VPN and that the data cannot be intercepted and compromised; this practice of creating an encrypted "tunnel" to send secure (private) data over the (public) Internet is known as **tunneling.** For example, Washington State University requires VPN software to be used when connecting remotely to the campus network or e-mail system or when using the on-campus wireless LAN.

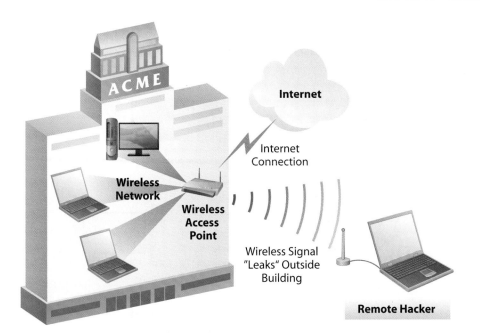

FIGURE 10.18

Drive-by hacking is on the rise given the proliferation of unsecured wireless LANs.

Firewalls A **firewall** is a part of a computer system designed to detect intrusion and prevent unauthorized access to or from a private network (see Figure 10.20). Think of a firewall essentially as a security fence around the perimeter of an organization that spots any intruders that try to penetrate the organization's outer defenses. Firewalls can be implemented in hardware, in software, or in a combination of both. Firewalls are frequently used to prevent unauthorized Internet users from accessing private networks connected to the Internet, especially private corporate intranets, described in Chapter 4, "Enabling Commerce Using the Internet." All messages entering or leaving the intranet pass through the firewall, which examines each message and blocks those that do not meet the specified security criteria.

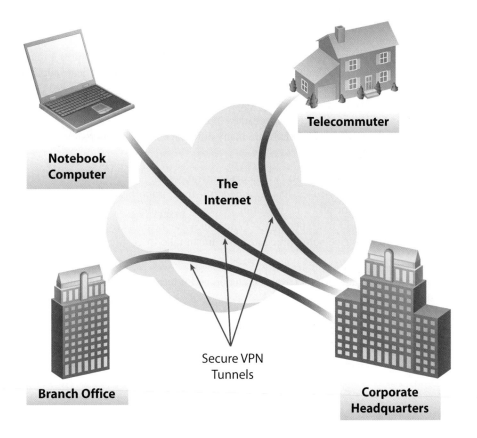

FIGURE 10.19

A virtual private network (VPN) allows remote sites and users to connect to organizational network resources using a secure tunnel.

FIGURE 10.20

A firewall blocks unauthorized access to organizational systems and data, while permitting authorized communication to flow in and out of the organization to the broader Internet.

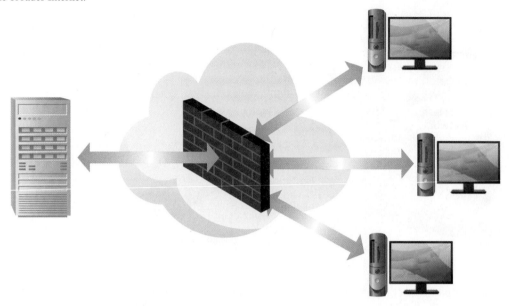

Encryption When you do not have access to a secure channel for sending information over a wired or wireless network, encryption is the best bet for keeping snoopers out. **Encryption** is the process of encoding messages before they enter the network or airwaves, then decoding them at the receiving end of the transfer so that the intended recipients can read or hear them (see Figure 10.21). The process works because if you scramble messages before you send them, eavesdroppers who might intercept them cannot decipher them without the decoding key. (The science of encryption is called *cryptography*.) All encryption methods use a key—the code that scrambles and then decodes messages. Encryption is used to protect data that is transmitted over the Internet (e.g., your new purchase at Amazon.com), your call on your mobile phone, or the information between your notebook and Bluetooth-connected printer.

Implementing encryption on a large scale, such as on a busy Web site, requires a third party, called a **certificate authority,** to help manage the distribution of keys. The certificate authority acts as a trusted middleman between computers and verifies that a Web site is a trusted site. The certificate authority knows that each computer is who it says it is and provides the encryption/decryption keys to each computer. **Secure Sockets Layer,** developed by Netscape, is a popular public key encryption method used on the Internet. There are many different encryption approaches for different types of data transmission.

Virus Monitoring and Prevention **Virus prevention,** which is a set of activities for detecting and preventing computer viruses, has become a full-time, important task for IS departments within organizations and for all of us with our personal computers. While viruses often have colorful names—Melissa, I Love You, Naked Wife—they can be catastrophic from a computing perspective. Here we describe some precautions you can take to ensure that your computer is protected:

- Purchase and install antivirus software, then update frequently to be sure you are protected against new viruses.

FIGURE 10.21

Encryption is used to encode information so that unauthorized people cannot understand it.

```
Ciphertext letters:
JOGPSNBUJPO TZTUFNT UPEBZ
Equivalent plaintext letters:
INFORMATION SYSTEMS TODAY
```

- Do not use flash drives, disks, or shareware from unknown or suspect sources and be equally careful when downloading material from the Internet, making sure that the source is reputable.
- Delete without opening any e-mail message received from an unknown source. Be especially wary of opening attachments. It is better to delete a legitimate message than to infect your computer system with a destructive germ.
- Do not blindly open e-mail attachments, even if they come from a known source (such as a friend or coworker). Many viruses are spread without the sender's knowledge, so it is better to check with the sender before opening a potentially unsafe attachment.
- If your computer system contracts a virus, report the infection to your school or company's IT department so that appropriate measures can be taken.

Audit-Control Software **Audit-control software** is used to keep track of computer activity so that auditors can spot suspicious activity and take action. Any user—authorized or unauthorized—leaves electronic footprints that auditors can trace. Audit-control software helps creating an audit trail, a record showing who has used a computer system and how it was used. For the software to effectively protect security, of course, auditors within an organization—most often someone in the IT department or information security department—must monitor and interpret results.

Secure Data Centers Specialized facilities are an important component of creating a reliable and secure IS infrastructure. Data and the ability to process the data are the lifeblood for many of today's large organizations, such as Amazon.com, Travelocity.com, or Facebook. Storing and processing massive amounts of data needs a lot of power as well as air-conditioning to keep the equipment running within the optimal temperature range (which helps to increase the life span of the equipment). In addition to these requirements, organizations need to protect important equipment from both outside intruders and the elements, such as water or fire. The most prominent threats to an organization's IS facilities come from floods, seismic activity, rolling blackouts, hurricanes, and the potential of criminal activities (see Figure 10.22). How can an organization reliably protect its facilities from such threats?

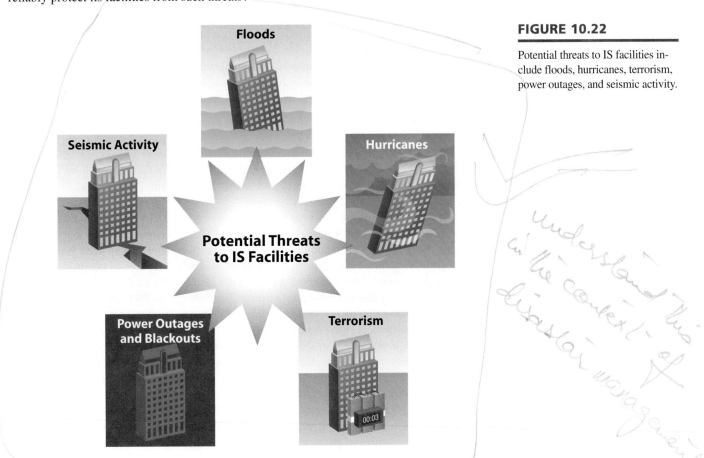

FIGURE 10.22

Potential threats to IS facilities include floods, hurricanes, terrorism, power outages, and seismic activity.

FIGURE 10.23

UPS's servers handle up to 20 million requests per day.

Shutterstock

Ensuring Availability. As many potential causes of disasters cannot be avoided (there's no way to stop a hurricane), organizations should attempt to plan for the worst and protect their infrastructure accordingly. For companies operating in the digital world, the IS infrastructure is often critical for most business processes, so special care has to be taken to secure it. Whereas some applications can tolerate some downtime in case something malfunctions or disaster strikes, other applications (such as UPS's package tracking databases) can't tolerate any downtime—these companies need 24/7/365 reliability (see Figure 10.23).

Securing the Facilities Infrastructure. An organization's IS infrastructure always needs to be secured to prevent it from outside intruders. Absolute protection against security breaches remains out of reach, but here are a few additional safeguards organizations can employ:

- ▪ *Backups.* Organizations and individual computer users should perform **backups** of important files to external hard drives, CDs, tapes, or online backup service providers at regular intervals. Some systems can be set to perform automatic backups at specified intervals, such as at the end of a working day. Information maintained in current databases and transferred to backup tapes should be encrypted so that if crackers enter databases or thieves steal tapes, the information is useless to them.
- ▪ *Backup Sites.* **Backup sites** are critical for business continuity in the event a disaster strikes; in other words, backup sites can be thought of as a company's office in a temporary location. Commonly, a distinction is made between cold and hot backup sites. A **cold backup site** is nothing more than an empty warehouse with all necessary connections for power and communication but nothing else. In the case of a disaster, a company has to first set up all necessary equipment, ranging from office furniture to Web servers. While this is the least expensive option, it also takes a relatively longer time before a company can resume working after a disaster. A **hot backup site,** in contrast, is a fully equipped backup facility, having everything from office chairs to a one-to-one replication of the most current data. In the event of a disaster, all that has to be done is to relocate the employees to the backup site to continue working. Obviously, this is a very expensive option, as the backup site has to be kept fully equipped and all the IS infrastructure duplicated. Further, hot backup sites also have a redundant backup of the data so that the business processes are interrupted as little as possible. To achieve this redundancy, all data are **mirrored** on separate servers (i.e., everything is stored synchronously on two independent systems). This might

seem expensive, but for a critical business application involving customers, it may be less expensive to run a redundant backup system in parallel than it would be to disrupt business or lose customers in the event of catastrophic system failure.

- ▪ ***Redundant Data Centers.*** Often, companies choose to replicate their data centers in multiple locations. Thinking about the location of redundant systems is an important aspect of disaster planning. If a company relies on redundant systems, all of which are located within the same building, a single event can incapacitate all the systems. Similarly, events such as a hurricane can damage systems that are located across town from each other. Thus, even if the primary infrastructure is located in-house, it pays to have a backup located in a different geographic area to minimize the risk of a disaster happening to both systems.

- ▪ ***Closed-Circuit Television.*** While installation and monitoring a closed-circuit television system is costly, the systems can monitor for physical intruders in data centers, server rooms, or collocation facilities. Video cameras display the physical interior and/or exterior of a facility and record all activity on tape. In-house security personnel or an outside security service can watch computer monitors and immediately report suspicious activity to the police. Digital video recording can be used to store this information digitally, even from remote cameras connected to the system via a company's intranet, wireless LANs, or the Internet.

- ▪ ***Uninterruptible Power Supply.*** An uninterruptible power supply does not protect against intruders, but it protects against power surges and temporary power failures that can cause information loss.

For reasons of business continuity, companies such as UPS maintain large data centers in different geographic areas. Many (especially smaller) organizations do not need facilities the size of one of the UPS data centers; instead, they may just need space for a few servers. For such needs, companies can turn to **collocation facilities.** Organizations can rent space (usually in the form of cabinets or shares of a cabinet; see Figure 10.24) for their servers in such collocation facilities, and the organizations managing collocation facilities provide the necessary infrastructure in terms of power, backups, connectivity, and security.

Clearly, there are a broad range of technology-based approaches for securing information systems, and no matter whether your server is located in a cabinet within your organization or you have rented space in a collocation facility, you should have physical safeguards in place to secure the equipment. A comprehensive security plan will include numerous technological methods. Next, we examine human-based methods.

FIGURE 10.24

Collocation facilities allow organizations to rent secure space for their infrastructure.

Shutterstock

FIGURE 10.25

Human safeguards for IS security.

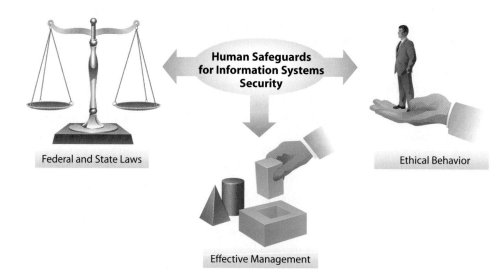

Human Safeguards

In addition to the technological safeguards, there are various human safeguards that can help to safeguard information systems, specifically ethics, laws, and effective management (see Figure 10.25). *IS ethics*, discussed in Chapter 1, relates to a broad range of standards of appropriate conduct by users. Educating potential users at an early age as to what constitutes appropriate behavior can help, but unethical users will undoubtedly always remain a problem for those wanting to maintain IS security. Additionally, there are numerous federal and state laws against unauthorized use of networks and computer systems. Unfortunately, individuals who want unauthorized access to networks and computer systems usually find a way to exploit them; often, after the fact, laws are enacted to prohibit that activity in the future.

Computer Forensics

As computer crime has gone mainstream, law enforcement has had to become much more sophisticated in their computer crime investigations. **Computer forensics** is the use of formal investigative techniques to evaluate digital information for judicial review. Most often, computer forensics experts evaluate various types of storage devices to find traces of illegal activity or to gain evidence in related but noncomputer crimes. In fact, in most missing-person or murder cases today, investigators immediately want to examine the victim's computer for clues or evidence.

Organizations and governments are increasingly utilizing *honeypots* to proactively gather intelligence to improve their defenses or to catch cybercriminals. A **honeypot** is a computer, data, or network site that is designed to be enticing to crackers so as to detect, deflect, or counteract illegal activity. For instance, the FBI operated a cybercrime clearinghouse called "DarkMarket" where unsuspecting hackers, credit card swindlers, and identity thieves bought and sold products and information (Poulsen, 2008). Products for sale included electronic banking logins, stolen personal data, and even specialized hardware for producing counterfeit credit cards. The FBI operated DarkMarket for more than two years to collect information on the global marketplace for cybercriminals. In late 2008, DarkMarket was shut down because it had become known to the criminals. It is without question that countless other honeypots are being operated by governments and computer forensics experts to track criminals and gather information.

Although computer forensics experts are extremely skilled in investigating prior and on-going computer crime, many computer criminals are also experts, making the forensics process extremely difficult in some cases. Some criminals, for example, have special "booby-trap" programs running on computers to destroy evidence if someone other than the criminal uses the machine. Using special software tools, computer forensics experts can often restore data that have been deleted from a computer's hard drive. Clearly, computer forensics will continue to evolve as criminals utilize more sophisticated computer-based methods for committing and aiding criminal activities.

Additionally, beyond human and technological safeguards, the quality of information security in any organization depends on *effective management*. Managers must continuously check for security problems, recognize that holes in security exist, and take appropriate action. We discuss methods for effectively managing IS security next.

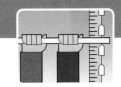

POWERFUL PARTNERSHIPS

Netscape's James H. Clark and Marc Andreessen

The World Wide Web came into existence in 1993, and a year later James H. Clark and Marc Andreessen (see Figure 10.26) founded the first company to take advantage of the Web, called Mosaic Communications Corporation. The company's first product, released in October 1994, was a Web browser (an application used to view and navigate the World Wide Web and other Internet resources) called Mosaic Netscape 0.9. The browser was subsequently renamed "Netscape" in November 1994.

James Clark was born in Plainview, Texas, in 1944. He dropped out of high school after being suspended and spent four years in the navy. After Clark's discharge from the military, he earned bachelor's and master's degrees in physics from the University of New Orleans and then went on to earn a PhD in computer science from the University of Utah in 1974. Clark's computer science research concerned geometry pipelines, specialized software or hardware that accelerates the display of three-dimensional images.

Marc Andreessen was born in Cedar Rapids, Iowa, in 1971. He earned a bachelor's degree in computer science at the University of Illinois in Urbana-Champaign in 1993. While still an undergraduate, he worked at the University's National Center for Supercomputing Applications (NCSA), where he and a salaried worker, Eric Bina, developed code

for a user-friendly browser with integrated graphics that could work on a wide range of computer platforms. They called the browser code Mosaic.

After college graduation, Andreessen took a job with Enterprise Integration Technologies in California, where he met James Clark, who had recently left Silicon Graphics, a successful company he founded with several others. Clark saw the potential in the browser code that Andreessen had helped develop, and the two founded Mosaic Communications Corporation. However, the University of Illinois owned exclusively the Mosaic browser code Andreessen had helped develop at NCSA and claimed that Clark and Andreessen had stolen it from them, so Clark and Andreessen changed the name of their company to Netscape Communications Corporation. Nevertheless, they continued to distribute the software they marketed as Netscape Navigator, and in December 1994, Netscape Communications settled with the University of Illinois. The settlement cost Netscape Communications $3 million, including legal fees, but the university dropped all claims to Netscape.

At first, Clark and Andreessen charged for the product, but there were a number of ways to receive the product free of charge, and most users did not pay. As the partners concentrated more on making their product ubiquitous, they

FIGURE 10.26

Netscapes's James H. Clark (left) and Marc Andreessen (below).

AP Wide World Photos

Loudcloud Inc.\AP Wide World Photos

(continued)

worried less about making money from sales of the browser and hoped to make money in other ways, such as selling advertising. Superior features of Netscape, such as new HTML tags that allowed Web designers more control and creativity, soon made Netscape the browser of choice. Despite competition from Microsoft's Internet Explorer, by 1996, 75 percent of Web surfers used Netscape.

Fierce competition with Microsoft began almost immediately after Netscape was released when Microsoft released Internet Explorer 1.0 in 1995 as part of a Windows 95 Plus-Pack add-on. For the next few years, the two browser companies worked to outdo each other (often termed the "browser wars"), adding features to their respective products so quickly that they often did not work correctly. Soon, Microsoft began bundling Internet Explorer with the Windows operating system, never charging extra for it, and by 1998, Netscape Communications was forced to offer its browser for free as well. Eventually, Netscape Communications could no longer compete with Microsoft's superior financing assets and effectively dropped out of the race.

Critics of Netscape Communications have argued that racing to the market before browser versions were fully operational and bad company management contributed to the company's decline. The company rested on its laurels, some said, and soon Internet Explorer had superior features and better performance as a browser.

America Online (AOL) acquired Netscape in 1999 for $10 billion in stock and hired Andreessen as chief technology officer. AOL has not promoted Netscape software and decided to retire the browser in 2008 after its share of the browser market dropped to 1 percent. Today, Andreessen is on the Board of Directors of both eBay and HP and is a frequent keynote speaker at many technology events and conferences. Clark, an avid sailor, owns several high-tech sailboats that he helped design. Both Clark and Andreessen have gone on to found several IT start-ups, and both are wealthy Web pioneers and philanthropists.

Based on:

Marc Andreessen. (2010, May 19). In *Wikipedia, the free encyclopedia*. Retrieved May 20, 2010, from http://en.wikipedia.org/w/index.php?title=Marc_Andreessen&oldid=363067407.

Anonymous. (n.d.). Internet pioneers. Retrieved April 19, 2010 from http://www.ibiblio.org/pioneers/andreesen.html.

Netscape. (2010, May 16). In *Wikipedia, the free encyclopedia*. Retrieved May 20, 2010, from http://en.wikipedia.org/w/index.php?title=Netscape&oldid=362499740.

Scott, M. (n.d.). Jim Clark 1944–. *Encyclopedia of Business*. Retrieved August 1, 2010, from http://www.referenceforbusiness.com/biography/A-E/Clark-Jim-1944.html.

Managing IS Security

Very often some of the best things that people can do to secure their information systems are not necessarily technical in nature. Instead, they may involve changes within the organization and/or better management of people's use of information systems. For example, one of the outcomes of the systems security risk analysis described here may well be a set of computer and/or Internet use policies (sometimes referred to as **acceptable use policies**) for people within the organization, with clearly spelled out penalties for noncompliance (see Figure 10.27). More fundamental to security than management techniques such as these is that you make every effort to hire trustworthy employees and treat them well. Trustworthy employees who are treated well are less likely to commit offenses affecting the organization's information systems.

Developing an IS Security Plan

All organizations should develop an IS security plan. An **information systems security plan** involves assessing risks, planning ways to reduce risk, implementing the plan, and ongoing monitoring. This planning process should be ongoing and include these five steps:

1. *Risk Analysis.* Organizations should do the following:
   a. Determine the value of electronic information
   b. Assess threats to confidentiality, integrity, and availability of information
   c. Determine which computer operations are most vulnerable to security breaches
   d. Assess current security policies
   e. Recommend changes to existing practices and/or policies that will improve computer security

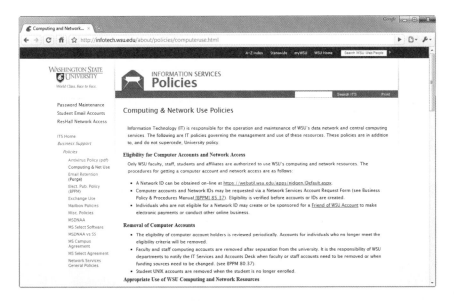

FIGURE 10.27

Most organizations provide employees or customers with an acceptable use policy.

Source: Courtesy Washington State University.

2. *Policies and Procedures.* Once risks are assessed, a plan should be formulated that details what action will be taken if security is breached. Policies and procedures related to computer security generally include the following:
   a. *Information Policy.* Outlines how sensitive information will be handled, stored, transmitted, and destroyed.
   b. *Security Policy.* Explains technical controls on all organizational computer systems, such as access limitations, audit-control software, firewalls, and so on.
   c. *Use Policy.* Outlines the organization's policy regarding appropriate use of in-house computer systems. May mandate no Internet surfing, use of company computer systems only for employment-related purposes, restricted use of social networking and e-mail, and so on.
   d. *Backup Policy.* Explains requirements for backing up information.
   e. *Account Management Policy.* Lists procedures for adding new users to systems and removing users who have left the organization.
   f. *Incident Handling Procedures.* Lists procedures to follow when handling a security breach.
   g. *Disaster Recovery Plan.* Lists all the steps an organization will take to restore computer operations in case of a natural or deliberate disaster. Each department within the organization generally has its own disaster recovery plan (see the following discussion).
3. *Implementation.* Once policies and plans are established, organizations can decide which security mechanisms to use and train personnel regarding security policies and measures. During this phase, network security mechanisms, such as firewalls, are put in place, as are intrusion detection systems, such as antivirus software, manual and automated log examination software, and host- and network-based intrusion detection software. Encryption information, passwords, and smart cards and smart badges are also disseminated and explained during this phase. The IT department is usually responsible for instituting security measures.
4. *Training.* Personnel within an organization should know the security policy and the plan for disaster recovery and be prepared to perform assigned tasks in that regard—both routinely on a daily basis and disaster related.
5. *Auditing.* Auditing is an ongoing process that assesses policy adherence, the security of new projects, and whether the organization's computer security can be penetrated. Penetration tests are conducted in-house and/or by an outside contractor to see how well the organization's computer security measures are working. Can the intrusion detection system detect attacks? Are incident response procedures effective? Can the network be penetrated? Is physical security adequate? Do employees know security policies and procedures?

Disaster Planning In some cases, all attempts to provide a reliable and secure IS infrastructure are in vain, and disasters cannot be avoided. Thus, organizations need to be prepared for when something catastrophic occurs. The most important aspect of preparing for disaster is creating a **business continuity plan,** which describes how a business resumes operation after a disaster. A subset of the business continuity plan is the **disaster recovery plan,** which spells out detailed procedures for recovering from systems-related disasters, such as virus infections and other disasters that might cripple the IS infrastructure. This way, even under the worst-case scenario, people will be able to replace or reconstruct critical files or data, or they will at least have a plan readily available to begin the recovery process. A typical disaster recovery plan includes information that answers the following questions:

- What events are considered a disaster?
- What should be done to prepare the backup site?
- What is the chain of command, and who can declare a disaster?
- What hardware and software are needed to recover from a disaster?
- Which personnel are needed for staffing the backup sites?
- What is the sequence for moving back to the original location after recovery?
- Which provider can be drawn on to aid in the disaster recovery process?

Designing the Recovery Plan When planning for disaster, two objectives should be considered by an organization: recovery time and recovery point objectives. **Recovery time objectives** specify the maximum time allowed to recover from a catastrophic event. For example, should the organization be able to resume operations in minutes, hours, or days after the disaster? Having completely redundant systems helps to minimize the recovery time and might be best suited for mission-critical applications, such as e-commerce transaction servers. For other applications, such as data mining, while important, the recovery time can be longer without disrupting primary business processes.

Additionally, **recovery point objectives** specify how current the backup data should be. Imagine that your computer's hard drive crashes while you are working on a term paper. Luckily, you recently backed up your data. Would you prefer the last backup to be a few days old, or would you rather have the last backup include your most recent changes to the term paper? Having completely redundant systems that mirror the data helps to minimize (or even avoid) data loss in the event of a catastrophic failure.

Responding to a Security Breach Organizations that have developed a comprehensive IS security plan, as outlined previously, will have the ability to rapidly respond to any type of security breach to their IS resources or to a natural disaster. In addition to restoring lost data using backups, common responses to a security breach include performing a new risk audit and implementing a combination of additional (more secure) safeguards (as described previously). Additionally, when intruders are discovered, organizations can contact local law enforcement agencies and the FBI for assistance in locating and prosecuting them. Several online organizations issue bulletins to alert organizations and individuals to possible software vulnerabilities or attacks based on reports from organizations when security breaches occur. The Computer Emergency Response Team Coordination Center, established by the U.S. federal government in 1988 as a major center of Internet security expertise, provides additional resources for organizations by publishing security alerts, conducting and publishing research, and providing training to incident response professionals (see www.cert.org).

The State of Systems Security Management

We continue to hear and read about cases where a breach of computer security was catastrophic and/or had potentially dire consequences. For example, a stolen laptop computer in May 2006 reportedly put 26.5 million U.S. military personnel at risk for identity theft because it contained a large database that included Social Security numbers, birth dates, and other personal information. Nevertheless, despite these highly publicized incidents, systems security measures are paying off for most organizations. According to the annual CSI Computer Crime and Security Survey (2009), the total financial losses resulting from cybercrime are decreasing. Key findings from their survey include the following:

- Financial fraud attacks result in the greatest financial losses for organizations; other significant costs were due to viruses, data theft, unauthorized access, and denial-of-service attacks.
- Relatively few organizations (about 29 percent) report computer intrusions to law enforcement because of various fears, such as how negative publicity would hurt stock values or how competitors might gain an advantage over news of a security incident.

- Most organizations do not outsource security activities.
- Nearly all organizations conduct routine and ongoing security audits.
- The majority of organizations believed security training of employees is important, but most respondents said their organization did not spend enough on security training.

In addition to these findings, organizations use a broad variety of security technologies, including the following:

- Activity logging and intrusion detection
- Antivirus and antispyware software
- Firewalls and VPNs
- Encryption for data in transit and at rest

Clearly, because malicious crackers won't become complacent anytime soon, it is encouraging that organizations appear to be gaining ground to guard against attacks. The lesson learned here is that we need to continue to implement vigilant approaches to better manage systems security in the digital world.

WHEN THINGS GO WRONG

Backhoe Cyberthreat

When you hear the word "cyberthreat," what comes to mind? Worms, viruses, and Trojan horses? These maladies are, indeed, serious cyberthreats. Take, for example, the notorious Kneber botnet, used to gain the log-in credentials of users from social networking sites, e-mail portals, and financial systems. A small cache of stolen data was retrieved by authorities showing over 68,000 corporate login credentials and user account data from Facebook, Yahoo!, and Hotmail. The recovered data represented a one-month snapshot of what the botnet has stolen over the course of its nearly two-year existence. Kneber infections started spreading in 2008, and as of February 2010, infections had been reported in over 196 countries and 75,000 different systems.

A less obvious type of cyberthreat, however—a threat usually considered only by security experts—is the threat to the "hard" infrastructure of the Internet. For instance, in early 2006, workers burying a TV cable in Arizona mistakenly dug up an unmarked fiber-optic cable. The workers had dutifully called the "call before you dig" number provided at the site and were given the go-ahead to bury the TV cable. This mishap had widespread consequences since the cable was part of the huge Internet backbone. Even though the cable was part of a self-healing ring, many Internet and cell phone users were immediately disconnected. Adding to the problem was the fact that other parts of the ring had been damaged earlier during a mudslide in California.

The fact that over 675,000 incidents have been reported in only one year, in which telephone lines, fiber-optic cables, water lines, or gas pipelines were accidentally damaged, illustrates how vulnerable the telecommunications infrastructure is. Even more worrisome, since information about the location of the infrastructure is publicly available, is the possibility for terrorists to exploit this vulnerability using nothing more than a backhoe.

In 2008, for example, underwater Internet cables serving certain sections of the Middle East were cut, disrupting service connecting Europe with the Middle East, North Africa, and the Indian subcontinent. Some suspicious Internet users were sure al-Qaeda was to blame, but telecommunications expert Stephan Beckert of TeleGeography Research said, "Cable cuts happen on average once every three days." In fact, 25 large ships do nothing but fix cable cuts and bends. Early reports blamed an errant ship's anchor for cutting the cable, but the cause was not confirmed.

While some cable cuts happen naturally or because of human error, the ease with which one could deliberately attack the telecommunications infrastructure was demonstrated by a graduate student who, for his dissertation, mapped the major fiber-optic cables across the United States. Interestingly, he found that most of the cables are buried along major interstate highways and railroads and that there are only two routes through which most of the Internet traffic flows. His dissertation soon got attention from the Department of Homeland Security, which realized that it would be disastrous if it fell into the

(continued)

wrong hands. (On the other hand, publicizing this type of information might have helped to sensitize the public as well as the authorities about how vulnerable the telecommunications infrastructure really is and what can be done to protect it.)

In April 2009, an actual cyberattack occurred on the hard infrastructure of Silicon Valley. From a manhole-covered service junction, a chainsaw-toting cybersaboteur cut critical fiber-optic cables in the middle of the night, knocking out Internet, landline communications, cell phone connectivity, and data networks across a large swath of California. The loss of these networks caused ATMs, credit and debit cards, and banking transactions to malfunction. People were unable to make telephone calls or send e-mails, and emergency services were seriously hampered. Despite a yearlong investigation by local, state, and federal authorities and a quarter-million-dollar reward by AT&T, no one has ever been arrested for the attack.

Although the investigation has ended, valuable lessons were learned. Telecommunication and power grids have since been hardened and security measures implemented. One thing the attack showed is how interconnected telecommunications and cybersystems are to everyday life—and how vulnerable they are to attack and disruption.

Based on:

Asimov, N. (2009, April 10). Sabotage attacks knock out phone service. *SFgate.com*. Retrieved April 26, 2010, from http://articles.sfgate.com/2009-04-10/news/17191717_1_cables-debit-cards-vandals.

Blumenfeld, L. (2003, July 8). Dissertation could be security threat. *Washington Post*. Retrieved May 12, 2010, from http://www.washingtonpost.com/ac2/wp-dyn/A23689-2003Jul7.

Newman, B. (2010, April 7). A year later, sabotage of key fiber optic cables remains a mystery. *Mercury News.com*. Retrieved April 26, 2010, from http://www.mercurynews.com/ci_14840101.

Poulsen, K. (2006, January 19). The backhoe: A real cyberthreat. *Wired*. Retrieved May 12, 2010, from http://www.wired.com/science/discoveries/news/2006/01/70040.

Singel, R. (2008, January 31). Fiber optic cable cuts insulate millions from Internet, future cuts likely. *Wired*. Retrieved May 12, 2010, from http://www.wired.com/threatlevel/2008/01/fiber-optic-cab.

Singel, R. (2008, February 6). Cable cut fever grips the web. *Wired*. Retrieved May 12, 2010, from http://www.wired.com/threatlevel/2008/02/who-cut-the-cab.

Top ten cyber security menaces for 2008. (n.d.). Retrieved May 12, 2010, from http://www.sans.org/2008menaces.

Vijayan, J. (2010, February 18). Over 75,000 systems compromised in cyberattack. *Computerworld*. Retrieved April 26, 2010, from http://www.computerworld.com/s/article/9158578/Over_75_000_systems_compromised_in_cyberattack.

Information Systems Controls, Auditing, and the Sarbanes-Oxley Act

As you have seen, there are a variety of issues to consider when managing IS security. To ensure security, control costs, gain and protect trust, remain competitive, and comply with internal or external governance (e.g., the Sarbanes-Oxley Act, discussed later in this section), **information systems controls** have to be put into place. Such controls, which help ensure the reliability of information, can consist of a variety of different measures, such as systems security policies and their physical implementation, access restrictions, or record keeping, to be able to trace actions and transactions and who is responsible for these. IS controls thus need to be applied throughout the entire IS infrastructure. To be most effective, controls should be a combination of three types of controls:

- Preventive controls (to prevent any potentially negative event from occurring, such as by preventing outside intruders from accessing a facility)
- Detective controls (to assess whether anything went wrong, such as unauthorized access attempts)
- Corrective controls (to mitigate the impact of any problem after it has arisen, such as restoring compromised data)

One way to conceptualize the different forms of controls is by a hierarchy ranging from high-level policies to the implementation at the application level (see Figure 10.28 for the hierarchy of controls); Table 10.4 gives a brief explanation of the different types of controls and presents examples for each. While reading this book, you have learned about a variety of IS controls, and you will continue to come across the different elements of control in the following sections when we will describe how companies use IS auditing to assess the IS controls in place and whether further IS controls need to be implemented or changed.

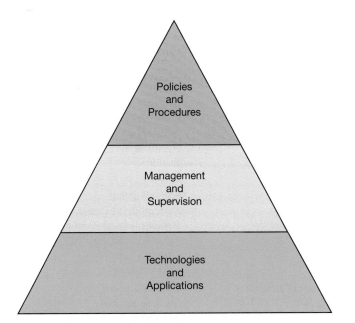

FIGURE 10.28

Hierarchy of IS controls.

Source: Based on http://infotech
.aicpa.org.

IS Auditing

Analyzing the IS controls should be an ongoing process for organizations. However, often it can be beneficial for organizations to periodically have an external entity review the controls so as to uncover any potential problems. An **information systems audit,** often performed by external auditors, can help organizations assess the state of their IS controls to determine necessary changes and to help ensure the information systems' availability, confidentiality, and integrity. The response to the strengths and weaknesses identified in the IS audit is often determined by the potential risks an organization faces. In other words, the IS audit has to assess whether the IS controls in place are sufficient to address the potential risks. Thus, a major component of the IS audit is a risk assessment (discussed in prior sections), which aims at determining what type of risks the organization's IS infrastructure faces, the criticality of those risks to the infrastructure, and the level of risks the organization is willing to tolerate.

Once the risk has been assessed, auditors have to evaluate the organization's internal controls. During such audits, the auditor tries to gather evidence regarding the effectiveness of the controls. However, testing all controls under all possible conditions is very inefficient and often infeasible. Thus, auditors frequently rely on **computer-assisted auditing tools,** or specific software that tests applications and data using test data or simulations. In addition to using specific auditing tools, auditors use audit sampling procedures to assess the controls, enabling the audit to be conducted in the most cost-effective manner. Once the audit has been performed and sufficient evidence has been gathered, reports are issued to the organization. Usually, such reports are followed up with a discussion of the results and potential courses of action.

The Sarbanes-Oxley Act

Performing an IS audit can help an organization reduce costs or remain competitive by identifying areas where IS controls are lacking and need improvement. Another major factor that has contributed to a high demand for IS auditors is the need to comply with government regulations, most notably the **Sarbanes-Oxley Act** of 2002 (hereafter S-OX). Formed as a reaction to large-scale accounting scandals that led to the downfall of corporations such as WorldCom and Enron, S-OX addresses primarily the accounting side of organizations. However, given the importance of an IS infrastructure and IS controls for an organization's financial applications, it is of major importance to include IS controls in compliance reviews.

According to S-OX, companies have to demonstrate that there are controls in place to prevent misuse or fraud, controls to detect any potential problems, and effective measures to correct any problems; S-OX goes so far that corporate executives face jail time and heavy fines if the appropriate controls are not in place or are ineffective. The IS architecture plays a key role

TABLE 10.4 Different Types of IS Controls

Type of Control	What Is It For?	Examples

Policies	Define aims and objectives of the organization	General policies about:
		    Security and privacy
		    Rights of access
		    Data and systems ownership
		    End-user development
		    Access to sensitive areas (e.g., high-availability facilities)
		    Disaster planning

Standards	Support the requirements of policies	Standards about:
		    Systems development process
		    Systems software configuration
		Application controls
		    Data structures
		    Documentation

Organization and management	Define lines of reporting to implement effective control and policy development	Policies about:
		    Security and use
		    Account authorization
		    Backup and recovery
		    Incident reporting

Physical and environmental controls	Protect the organization's IS assets	High-availability facilities Collocation facilities
Systems software controls	Enable applications and users to utilize the systems	Control access to applications Generate activity logs Prevent outside intrusion (e.g., by hackers)
Systems development and acquisition controls	Ensure that systems meet the organization's needs	Document user requirements Use formal processes for systems design, development, testing, and maintenance
Application-based controls	Ensure correct input, processing, storage, and output of data; maintain record of data as it moves through the system	Input controls (such as automated checking of the inputs into a Web form) Processing controls Output controls (comparing the outputs against intended results) Integrity controls (ensure that data remain correct) Audit trail (keep record of transactions to be able to locate sources of potential errors)

in S-OX compliance, given that many controls are IS based, providing capabilities to detect information exceptions and to provide a management trail for tracing exceptions. However, S-OX itself barely addresses IS controls specifically; rather, it addresses general processes and practices, leaving companies wondering how to comply with the guidelines put forth in the act. Further, it is often cumbersome and time consuming for organizations to identify the relevant systems to be audited for S-OX compliance. Thus, many organizations find it easier to review their entire IS infrastructure, following objectives set forth in guidelines such as the **control objectives for information and related technology (COBIT)**—a set of best practices that helps organizations both maximize the benefits from their IS infrastructure and establish appropriate controls.

Another issue faced by organizations because of S-OX is the requirement to preserve evidence to document compliance and for potential lawsuits. Since the inception of S-OX, e-mails and even instant messages have achieved the same status as regular business documents and thus need to be preserved for a period of time, typically up to seven years. Failure to present such documents in the case of litigious activity can lead to severe fines being imposed on companies and their executives, and courts usually will not accept the argument that a message could not be located. For example, the investment bank Morgan Stanley faced fines up to $15 million for failing to retain e-mail messages. On the surface, it seems easiest for an organization to simply archive all the e-mail messages sent and received. However, such a "digital landfill," where everything is stored, can quickly grow to an unmanageable size, and companies cannot comply with the mandate to present evidence in a timely manner. Thus, many organizations turn to e-mail management software that archives and categorizes all incoming and outgoing e-mails based on key words. Even using such specialized software, finding e-mails related to a certain topic within the archive can pose a tremendous task: Some analysts estimate that a business with 25,000 employees generates over 4 billion e-mail messages over the course of seven years (not counting any increase in e-mail activity), which would be hard to handle for even the most sophisticated programs.

INDUSTRY ANALYSIS

Cybercops Track Cybercriminals

The *CSI* (crime scene investigation) television shows have made "DNA testing" a household phrase. Virtually everyone knows that a criminal who leaves body cells or fluids—hair and skin cells, saliva, blood, semen, and so on—at the scene of a crime can be linked to the crime through DNA analysis. (DNA, or deoxyribonucleic acid, is present in all living tissue—plant or animal.) The *CSI* shows have helped to illustrate that just as crime laboratories have had to keep technologically current, so, too, have law enforcement officers at national, state, and local levels.

Because technological advancement has been rapid, law enforcement has lagged behind, but it is catching up. At the U.S. federal level, the Computer Crime and Intellectual Property Section within the Justice Department is devoted to combating cybercrime. In addition, the FBI has created computer crime squads in 16 metropolitan areas around the country specifically to investigate cybercrime. In Washington, D.C., the FBI's National Infrastructure Protection Center acts as a clearinghouse for information and expertise relating to cybercrime. And each federal judicial district has at least one assistant U.S. attorney, called a computer and telecommunications crime coordinator, who has received special training in how to investigate and prosecute cybercrime.

Furthermore, every state now has a computer crime investigation unit available as a resource to local law enforcement agencies, and many municipal police departments have their own computer crime investigative units.

Software tools available to law enforcement agencies have also improved. Programs such as the Software Forensic Tool Kit provide police with the ability to search and recreate deleted files on computers. Also digitized for law enforcement use are criminal identification systems, such as the Statewide Network of Agency Photos (SNAP). Law enforcement officers can search SNAP's digital database for mug shots that show a criminal's distinguishing marks, such as scars and tattoos, making criminal identification simpler. SNAP is connected to the Automatic Fingerprint Identification Systems, which electronically transmits fingerprints at the time a person is arrested.

Similarly, the Classification System for Serial Criminal Patterns, developed by the Chicago Police Department, allows detectives to look for possible patterns connecting crimes.

Like many of us who use social networking sites to stay connected to our family and friends, cybercops are also utilizing these valuable tools to reach out to their communities. In fact, Facebook, Twitter, and other social networking sites are being increasingly used to gather tips and solve crimes.

Radio communication has also been updated to provide a secure means of voice communication for law enforcement officers. No longer can any interested civilian buy a receiver and monitor police calls since digital voice communication can now be encrypted, allowing for a higher level of security.

It's an unfortunate fact that criminals have discovered how to use the Internet to their advantage. Clearly, however, law enforcement is gaining on them, as officers also use technological advancement to track, arrest, and prosecute online and offline criminals.

Questions
1. Today, is it harder or easier to be a criminal? Why?
2. Argue whether law enforcement can or cannot ever get ahead of criminals.

Based on:

Anonymous. (2010, April 27). Fighting crime on Facebook. *BBC News.* Retrieved April 30, 2010, from http://news.bbc.co.uk/2/hi/uk_news/northern_ireland/8646428.stm.

Ashcroft, J. (2001, May 22). Remarks of Attorney General John Ashcroft. Retrieved April 24, 2010, from http://www.usdoj.gov/criminal/cybercrime/AGCPPSI.htm.

Justice Technology Information Network. (n.d.). Retrieved April 24, 2010, from http://www.justnet.org/Pages/home.aspx.

Key Points Review

1. *Define computer crime and describe several types of computer crime.* Computer crime is defined as the act of using a computer to commit an illegal act, such as targeting a computer while committing an offense, using a computer to commit an offense, or using computers in the course of a criminal activity. A person who gains unauthorized access to a computer system has also committed a computer crime. Those individuals who are knowledgeable enough to gain access to computer systems without authorization have long been referred to as hackers. Today, those who break into computer systems with the intention of doing damage or committing a crime are usually called crackers. Hackers and crackers can commit a wide variety of computer crimes, including unauthorized access and information modification. Crackers are also associated with the making and distributing of computer viruses and other destructive codes. People are increasingly using information systems to aid in crimes against individuals, including identity theft, cyberharassment, cyberstalking, and cyberbullying. Finally, making illegal copies of software, a worldwide computer crime, is called software piracy.

2. *Describe and explain the differences between cyberwar and cyberterrorism.* Cyberwar refers to an organized attempt by a country's military to disrupt or destroy the information and communication systems of another country. The goal of cyberwar is to turn the balance of information and knowledge in one's favor in order to diminish an opponent's capabilities and also to enhance those of the attacker. Cyberterrorism is the use of computer and networking technologies by individuals and organized groups against persons or property to intimidate or coerce governments, civilians, or any segment of society to attain political, religious, or ideological goals. Now that terrorist groups are increasingly using the Internet for their purposes, one of the great fears about cyberterrorism is that an attack can be launched from a computer anywhere in the world.

3. *Explain what is meant by the term "information systems security" and describe both technology- and human-based safeguards for information systems.* "Information systems security" refers to precautions taken to keep all aspects of information systems (e.g., all hardware, software, network equipment, and data) safe from unauthorized use or access. There are five general categories of technological safeguards: physical access restrictions, firewalls, encryption, virus monitoring and protection, and audit-control software. Physical access restrictions prevent unauthorized access using authentication through something a person has (e.g., identification card), something a person knows (e.g., password), or something a person is (e.g., unique human attribute). Many organizations use some combination of methods to best control IS assets. A variety of technologies can be deployed to enhance system security, including firewalls, biometrics, virtual private networks, encryption, and virus protection tools. Firewalls are hardware or software used to detect intrusion and prevent unauthorized access to or from a private network. Biometrics is the use of technology to better authenticate users by matching fingerprints, retinal patterns in the eye, body weight, or other bodily characteristic before granting access to a computer. Virtual private networks use authentication and encryption to provide a secure tunnel within a public network such as the Internet so that information can pass securely between two computers. Encryption—the process of encoding messages before they enter the network or airwaves—is very useful for securing information when you do not have access to a secure telecommunications channel. Virus monitoring and protection utilizes a set of hardware and software to detect and prevent computer viruses. Audit-control software is used to keep track of computer activity so that auditors can spot suspicious activity and take action if necessary. Other technological safeguards include backups, closed-circuit television, and uninterruptible power supplies. Human safeguards include ethical standards, federal and state laws, and effective management. Organizations typically utilize a combination of both technological and human safeguards when protecting their IS resources.

4. *Discuss how to better manage IS security and explain the process of developing an IS security plan.* Because no system is 100 percent secure, organizations must utilize all available resources for implementing an effective IS security plan. The planning process includes a risk analysis, the development of policies and procedures, implementation, training, and ongoing auditing. Relatedly, organizations should develop a business continuity plan and a disaster recovery plan that specifies how to react to a disaster. After a security breach, organizations should perform new audits, implement new countermeasures, and possibly inform law enforcement agencies of the breach.

5. *Describe how organizations can establish IS controls to better ensure security.* IS controls can help ensure a secure and reliable infrastructure; such controls should be a mix of preventive, detective, and corrective controls. To assess the efficacy of these controls, organizations frequently conduct IS audits to determine the risks an organization faces and how far the IS controls can limit any potentially negative effects. Further, organizations perform IS audits to comply with government regulations, most notably the Sarbanes-Oxley Act of 2002. According to this act, companies have to demonstrate that there are controls in place to prevent misuse or fraud, controls to detect any potential problems, and effective measures to correct any problems; the act goes so far that a business executive could face heavy fines or substantial jail time if appropriate controls are not in place or are ineffective. Performing thorough IS audits on a regular basis can help assess compliance to these regulations.

Key Terms

acceptable use policy 432
access-control software 424
adware 408
audit-control software 427
authentication 422
backup 428
backup site 428
biometrics 423
bot herder 411
botnet 411
business continuity plan 434
CAPTCHA 410
certificate authority 426
cold backup site 428
collocation facility 429
computer-assisted auditing tool 437
computer crime 401
computer forensics 430
control objectives for information
    and related technology
    (COBIT) 438
cookie 410
copyright 414
cracker 403
cyberbullying 413
cyberharassment 412
cybersquatting 412

cyberstalking 412
cyberterrorism 417
cyberwar 415
denial-of-service attack 407
disaster recovery plan 434
drive-by hacking 424
encryption 426
firewall 425
hacker 403
hacktivist 403
honeypot 430
hot backup site 428
identity theft 411
information modification 406
information systems audit 437
information systems control 436
information systems
    security 420
information systems security
    plan 432
intellectual property 414
Internet hoax 411
logic bomb 407
malware 406
mirror 428
online predator 413
patent 414

patriot hacker 416
phishing 409
recovery point objective 434
recovery time objective 434
risk acceptance 421
risk analysis 421
risk reduction 421
risk transference 421
Sarbanes-Oxley Act 437
Secure Sockets Layer 426
software piracy 414
spam 408
spam filter 409
spim 410
spyware 408
time bomb 407
Trojan horse 407
tunneling 424
unauthorized access 405
virtual private network
    (VPN) 424
virus 406
virus prevention 426
warez 414
Web vandalism 416
worm 407
zombie computer 407

Review Questions

1. List and describe the primary threats to IS security.
2. Define computer crime and list several examples of computer crime.
3. Explain the purpose of the Computer Fraud and Abuse Act of 1986 and the Electronic Communications Privacy Act of 1986.
4. Contrast hackers versus crackers.
5. Define unauthorized access and give several examples from recent media reports.
6. Define malware and give several examples.
7. Define and contrast spyware, spam, and cookies.
8. Define and contrast cyberharassment, cyberstalking, and cyberbullying.

9. Define and contrast cyberwar and cyberterrorism.
10. Describe risk analysis as it relates to IS security and explain three ways to approach systems security risk.
11. What are physical access restrictions, and how do they make an information system more secure?
12. Describe several methods for preventing and/or managing the spread of computer viruses.
13. Describe three human-based approaches for safeguarding information systems.
14. What is an IS security plan, and what are the five steps for developing such a plan?
15. Describe how the Sarbanes-Oxley Act impacts the IS security of an organization.

Self-Study Questions

1. What is the common rule for deciding if an information system faces a security risk?
   A. Only desktop computers are at risk.
   B. Only network servers are at risk.
   C. All systems connected to networks are vulnerable to security violations.
   D. Networks have nothing to do with computer security.

2. Those individuals who break into computer systems with the intention of doing damage or committing a crime are usually called _____.
   A. hackers
   B. crackers
   C. computer geniuses
   D. computer operatives

3. Which of the following does *not* pose a threat to electronic information?
   A. unauthorized access
   B. lack of proper care and procedures
   C. unauthorized information modification
   D. all of the above can compromise information

4. Information modification attacks occur when _____.
   A. an authorized user changes a Web site address
   B. a Web site crashes
   C. the power is cut off
   D. someone who is not authorized to do so changes electronic information

5. Technological safeguards used to protect information include _____.
   A. laws
   B. effective management
   C. firewalls and physical access restrictions
   D. ethics

6. Limiting access to electronic information usually involves _____.
   A. something you have
   B. something you know
   C. something you are
   D. all of the above

7. Which of the following is the process of determining the true, accurate identity of a user of an information system?
   A. audit
   B. authentication
   C. firewall
   D. virtual private network

8. The use of computer and networking technologies by individuals and organized groups against persons or property to intimidate or coerce governments, civilians, or any segment of society in order to attain political, religious, or ideological goals is known as _____.
   A. cyberwar
   B. cybercrime
   C. cyberterrorism
   D. none of the above

9. A(n) _____ is a system composed of hardware, software, or both that is designed to detect intrusion and prevent unauthorized access to or from a private network.
   A encryption
   B firewall
   C alarm
   D logic bomb

10. _____ is the process of encoding messages before they enter the network or airwaves, then decoding them at the receiving end of the transfer so that recipients can read or hear them.
    A. Encryption
    B. Biometrics
    C. Authentication
    D. Disaster recovery

Answers are on page 444.

Problems and Exercises

1. Match the following terms to the appropriate definitions:
   i. Acceptable use policy
   ii. Authentication
   iii. Cyberwar
   iv. Biometrics
   v. Firewall
   vi. Phishing
   vii. Risk analysis
   viii. Spyware
   ix. Unauthorized access
   x. Zombie computer

   a. A type of security that grants or denies access to a computer system through the analysis of fingerprints, retinal patterns in the eye, or other bodily characteristics
   b. Specialized hardware and software that are used to keep unwanted users out of a system or to let users in with restricted access and privileges
   c. An organized attempt by a country's military to disrupt or destroy the information and communication systems of another country
   d. The process of identifying that the user is indeed who he or she claims to be, typically by requiring something that the user knows (e.g., a password) together with something that the user carries with him or her or has access to (e.g., an identification card or file)
   e. Computer and/or Internet use policy for people within an organization, with clearly spelled-out penalties for noncompliance
   f. A process in which the value of the assets being protected is assessed, the likelihood of their being compromised is determined, and the costs of their being compromised are compared with the costs of the protections to be taken
   g. An e-mail that attempts to trick financial account and credit card holders into giving away their private information
   h. A computer that has been infected with a virus allowing an attacker to control it without the knowledge of the owner
   i. Software that covertly gathers information about a user through an Internet connection without the knowledge of the owner
   j. An IS security breach where an unauthorized individual sees, manipulates, or otherwise handles electronically stored information

2. Take a poll of classmates to determine who has had personal experience with computer virus infections, identity theft, or other computer/information intrusions. How did victims handle the situation? What are classmates who have not been victimized doing to secure computers and personal information?

3. Research the statistics for the number of unauthorized intrusions into computer systems last year. Which type was most prevalent? Which groups committed the highest number of intrusions—hackers, employees, and so on?

4. Visit the Web site for the Computer Emergency Response Team at www.cert.org/tech_tips/denial_of_service.html and answer the following:
   a. What are the three basic types of denial-of-service attacks?
   b. What impact can denial-of-service attacks have on an organization?
   c. What other devices or activities within an organization might be impacted by denial-of-service attacks?
   d. Name three steps organizations might take to prevent denial-of-service attacks.

   If the previously given URL is no longer active, conduct a Web search for "denial-of-service attacks." Other active links can provide answers to the questions.

5. Do you feel the media generate too much hype regarding hackers and crackers? Since prominent companies such as Microsoft are often hacked into, are you concerned about your bank account or other sensitive information?

6. Identity theft is a new type of theft. Visit www.fraud.org to find ways to protect yourself. Search the Internet for additional sources that provide information on identity theft and make a list of other ways to safeguard against it. What are some of the losses in addition to stolen documents and additional bills to pay that may result from identity theft?

7. Search the Internet for information about the damaging effects of software piracy and/or look at the following Web sites: www.bsa.org and www.microsoft.com/piracy. Is software piracy a global problem? What can you do to mitigate the problem? Prepare a short presentation to present to the class.

8. Check one or more of the following Web sites to see which hoaxes are currently circulating online: www .hoax-slayer.com, www.truthorfiction.com, or www .snopes.com/info/top25uls.asp. What are five popular hoaxes now circulating online?

9. What laws should be enacted to combat cyberterrorism? How could such laws be enforced?

10. Contrast cyberharassment, cyberstalking, and cyberbullying using real-world examples found from recent news stories.

11. There are many brands of software firewalls, with ZoneAlarm, Norton 360, and Comodo Firewall Pro being three popular choices. Search for these products on the Web and learn more about how a firewall works and what it costs to give you this needed protection; prepare a one-page report that outlines what you have learned.

12. Search for further information on encryption. What is the difference between 128-bit and 40-bit encryption? What level of encryption is used in your Web browser? Why has the U.S. government been reluctant to release software with higher levels of encryption to other countries?

13. What levels of user authentication are used at your school and/or place of work? Do they seem to be effective? What if a higher level of authentication were necessary? Would it be worth it, or would the added steps cause you to be less productive?

14. Should the encryption issue be subject to ethical judgments? For instance, if an absolutely unbreakable code becomes feasible, should we use it with the knowledge that it may help terrorists and other criminals evade the law? Should governments regulate which encryption technology can be used so that government law enforcement agents can always read material generated by terrorists and other criminals? Explain your answer. Should the government continue to regulate the exportation of encryption technology to foreign countries, excluding those that support terrorism as it does now? Why or why not?

15. Assess and compare the security of the computers you use regularly at home, work, and/or school. What measures do you use at home to protect security? What measures are taken at work or school to protect security? (If possible, interview IT/IS personnel at work and/or at school to determine how security is protected in the workplace and in classrooms.) Describe any security vulnerabilities you find and explain how they might be corrected.

16. In some cases, individuals engage in cybersquatting in the hope of being able to sell the domain names to companies at a high price; in other cases, companies engage in cybersquatting by registering domain names that are very similar to their competitors' product names in order to generate traffic from people misspelling Web addresses. Would you differentiate between these practices? Why or why not? If so, where would you draw the boundaries?

17. Find your school's guidelines for ethical computer use on the Internet and answer the following questions: Are there limitations as to the type of Web sites and material that can be viewed (e.g., pornography)? Are students allowed to change the programs on the hard drives of the lab computers or download software for their own use? Are there rules governing personal use of computers and e-mail?

18. To learn more about protecting your privacy, visit www .cookiecentral.com and www.epubliceye.com. Did you learn something that will help protect your privacy? Why is privacy more important now than ever?

19. Should laws be passed to make spam a crime? If so, how should lawmakers deal with First Amendment rights? How would such laws be enforced?

Application Exercises

 Note: The existing data files referenced in these exercises are available on the Student Companion Web site: **www.pearsonhighered.com/valacich.**

 Spreadsheet Application:
Analyzing Ethical Concerns at Campus Travel

Because of the employees' increased use of IT resources for private purposes at Campus Travel, you have announced that a new IT use policy will be implemented. You have set up a Web site for the employees to provide feedback to the proposed changes; the results of this survey are stored in the file EthicsSurvey.csv. Your boss wants to use the survey results to find out what the greatest concerns in terms of ethical implications are for the employees, so you are asked to do the following:

1. Complete the spreadsheet to include descriptive statistics (mean, standard deviation, mode, minimum, maximum, and range) for each survey item. Use formulas to calculate all statistics for the responses to the individual questions

    (Hint: In Microsoft Excel, you can look up the necessary formulas in the category "Statistical"; you will have to calculate the ranges yourself.)

2. Format the means using color scales to highlight the items needing attention.

Make sure to professionally format the pages before printing them out.

 Database Application:
Tracking Software Licenses at Campus Travel

Recently, you have taken on the position of IS manager at Campus Travel. In your second week at work, you realize that many of the software licenses are about to expire or have already expired. As you know about the legal and ethical implications of unlicensed software, you have decided to set up a software asset management system that lets you keep track of the software licenses. You have already set up a database and stored some of the information, but you want to make the system more user friendly. Using the SWLicenses.mdb database, design a form to input the following information for new software products:

- Software title
- Installation location (office)
- License number
- Expiration date

Furthermore, design a report displaying all software licenses and expiration dates (sorted by expiration dates) (Hint: In Microsoft Access, use the form and report wizards to create the forms and reports; you will find the wizards under the "Create" tab.)

Team Work Exercise: Should Security Upgrades Be Made Available for Pirated Software?

Microsoft and other software producers make free upgrades available to legitimate buyers of applications when security risks are exposed. You probably have firsthand experience with updating Microsoft's products as new security risks are identified; only those who purchased and registered the software are eligible to receive these free downloads. Unfortunately, some people use pirated copies of Microsoft software and are, of course, not eligible to receive security downloads. An argument has been made that these security upgrades should be free to everyone because individuals using software with security vulnerabilities are a threat to everyone using the Internet since their computers are more easily converted to zombies that can spew spam in ever-increasing numbers, and they are more likely to

contract and spread viruses. Those who argue that security patches should be available to everyone say that there will always be pirated software in use—especially in those countries that have no laws against it or weak laws against it—so if we are ever to tighten security on the Internet, software manufacturers must provide security patches as a public service. Do you agree that security patches for popular software should be available free to everyone, no questions asked? Explain your answer. Do you agree that software vulnerable to security breaches threatens all computer users? Why or why not? In your opinion, is it possible for the Internet community to solve this problem without asking software developers to give away their product? Explain your answer.

Answers to the Self-Study Questions

1.	C, p. 420	**2.**	B, p. 403	**3.**	D, p. 405	**4.**	D, p. 405	**5.**	C, p. 422
6.	D, p. 422	**7.**	B, p. 422	**8.**	C, p. 417	**9.**	B, p. 425	**10.**	A, p. 426

Case 1

Under Attack

By now you know the scam. You receive an e-mail from eBay, PayPal, or your bank or credit card company that says they are "updating" your account information. The e-mail letterhead looks legitimate, so you read on. If you will just use the Web site address provided, the e-mail promises, the problem can be remedied, and your account won't be canceled. If you visit the URL provided, the site looks legitimate—that is, it's been "spoofed" to fool you—but the scam artists have posted it to steal your account information. By now you probably also know better than to respond to such a request. The scam is called "phishing"—meaning to "fish" for user information—and it's akin to identity theft. If you are conned into revealing account numbers, the scam artists will use that information to steal from you.

Phony e-mail is just one version of the phishing scam. Others include the following:

- Phishing via instant message, whereby users are sent a link to click on. Similar to the e-mail phishing, the user is directed to a fraudulent Web site that asks for sensitive information.
- Phishing via malware. Malware (short for "malicious software") is a malicious program that is installed on an unsuspecting user's computer via a virus or Trojan horse. This *malware*

then runs in the background waiting for the user to go to, for example, a financial site. As soon as the *malware* detects the user going to a prime site, a pop-up window appears asking for sensitive information. This pop-up cannot be blocked since it is generated from the infected PC, not the Web server.

Phishing con artists also like to take advantage of special times of the year, such as April 15, when tax returns are due. Taxpayers must now beware of bogus e-mails from the Internal Revenue Service that say something like this: "You are eligible to receive a tax refund of $285.67. To access the form for your tax refund, please click here." Clicking on the URL provided, of course, takes you to a counterfeit form, asking for personal information that the phishing thieves can use to steal from you. Fake IRS sites have also bilked taxpayers of personal information.

All types of phishing are a significant problem for Internet businesses and consumers. In 2009, according to the security company Trusteer, 45 percent of U.S. and European banking customers that were redirected to a phishing site disclosed their personal information. The Anti-Phishing Working Group's second half of 2009 report found the number of e-mail phishing attacks to be approximately 208,000. That

represents a 20 percent jump from the number of attacks during the same period in 2008. Although determining exact figures for how much financial damage is done due to phishing is difficult, the Gartner group reported that over 5 million people were affected by phishing scams in 2008 and lost an average of $351.

What is even more troublesome is the fact that in 2009, over 3,500 brands were hijacked or spoofed. As of February 2010, the top targets for phishing attacks were PayPal, eBay, HSBC bank, and Facebook. As social media sites become more popular, so are they becoming hotbeds of phishing activity. In fact, according to MarkMonitor Inc, phishing jumped 376 percent from 2008 to 2009 across popular social networking sites!

In an effort to defeat phishers, banks and other online entities are taking steps to protect their customers. PayPal, for instance, has stopped using e-mail to contact account holders. Instead, PayPal has its own proprietary messaging system that handles all transactions. If PayPal needs to contact you regarding your account, they will send a single e-mail message saying that there is a message waiting on the Web site messaging system. This procedure may further complicate access for an account holder, but it also adds a necessary layer of security.

Questions

1. What types of companies are most susceptible to phishing attacks?
2. Assume you have replied to a phishing e-mail; research on the Web what steps you should follow to limit any possible consequences.
3. Research on the Web for the telltale signs of a phishing message.

Based on:

About e-mail fraud. (n.d.). Retrieved April 30, 2010, from http://www10.americanexpress.com/sif/cda/page/0,1641,21372,00.asp.

Anonymous. (2007, December 17). Gartner survey shows phishing attacks escalated in 2007; more than $3 billion lost to these attacks. *Gartner.* Retrieved April 30, 2010, from http://www.gartner.com/it/page.jsp?id=565125.

Anonymous. (2009, December 2). Measuring the effectiveness of in-the-wild phishing attacks. *Trusteer.com.* Retrieved April 30, 2010, from http://www.trusteer.com/sites/default/files/Phishing-Statistics-Dec-2009-FIN.pdf.

Anonymous. (2010, March 24). Social network brands highly abused in phishing. *Spamfighter.com.* Retrieved April 30, 2010, from http://www

.spamfighter.com/News-14084-Social-Network-Brands-Highly-Abused-in-Phishing.htm.

Anti-Phishing Working Group. (2009). Phishing activity trends report. *apwg.org.* Retrieved April 30, 2010, from http://www.antiphishing.org/reports/apwg_report_Q4_2009.pdf.

Chickowski, E. (2007, December 19). Email phishing attacks still on the rise. *Baselinemag.* Retrieved April 30, 2010, from http://www.baselinemag.com/c/a/Projects-Security/Email-Phishing-Attacks-Still-on-the-Rise.

Crimeware double threat menaces Internet. (n.d.). Retrieved April 30, 2010, from http://www.antiphishing.org.

Dignan, L. (2008, January 14). Phishing for your tax return. *ZDNet.* Retrieved April 30, 2010, from http://blogs.zdnet.com/security/?p=805.

Seltzer, L. (2010, March 24). Twitter and email spam status reports. *PCMag.com Blogs.* Retrieved April 30, 2010, from http://blogs.pcmag.com/securitywatch/2010/03/twitter_and_email_spam_status.php.

Tetzlaff, R. (2010, April 2). A history of phishing. *BrightHub.com.* Retrieved April 30, 2010, from http://www.brighthub.com/internet/security-privacy/articles/67965.aspx.

Case 2

China's Great (Fire) Wall

When you were younger did your parents forbid you to socialize with certain kids? Was off-color reading material declared off limits? Was your computer use monitored and restricted? If so, you probably remember your absolute determination to circumvent the parental restrictions and censorship.

Similarly, as an adult, you would probably be insulted and outraged if the government attempted to assume the parental role and told you when and where you could travel, what types of literature you could purchase, which Web sites were off limits, and which e-mail and snail mail content was acceptable.

Welcome to modern-day China. The Chinese government blocks Web site access to the country's 360 million Internet users on such subjects as democracy, Tibet, Taiwan, health, education, news, entertainment, religion, or revolution. Chat rooms, blogs, photo and video sharing sites, gaming and podcasting sites, and bulletin boards are also forbidden stops on the Web. And, of course, if surfing from China, don't even think about googling "Tiananmen Square massacre" or anything remotely considered pornographic.

Building censorship into China's Internet infrastructure is the first step for the country's government in controlling access to politically sensitive material. To accomplish this, the Chinese government has prevented Internet service providers (ISPs)—many of them privately held businesses, some with foreign investments—from hosting any material the government calls politically objectionable. The government does this by holding the ISPs liable for content and imposing severe penalties for violations, including imprisonment.

The second step the Chinese government follows for censoring the Internet is to target Internet content providers (ICPs—organizations and individuals who post Web sites, both nonprofit and for profit). ICPs are required to register for and post a license to operate legally and like ISPs are held liable for politically incorrect content. To keep a license, ICPs must police sites for objectionable content and must take down those sites that violate regulations governing content. Yahoo!, Microsoft's MSN, and

Google all act as ICPs in China and have been criticized for complying with China's strict Internet censorship policy.

Managing ISPs and ICPs are not the only tool China has for controlling what content its citizens can see on the Internet. Beginning operations in 2003, China instituted the Golden Shield Project. It is now more popularly known as "The Great Firewall of China." The Golden Shield is a system that can automatically filter and block content that the government deems inappropriate for viewing. Through a system of Internet Protocol (IP) tracking, blocking, DNS/URL filtering, and redirection, the Golden Shield not only has served to block and filter content but acts as a surveillance system as well. An unfortunate side effect of the Great Firewall is that it creates a sluggish and congested network infrastructure, although some believe this is intentional to discourage Internet use. Interestingly, during the 2008 Olympics in Beijing, the Olympic Village, tourist hotels, resorts, and Internet cafés surrounding the Olympic grounds were ordered to be "unplugged" from the Golden Shield system, giving visitors from around the world access to fast and uncensored Internet access.

In addition to the Golden Shield, China introduced the Green Dam Youth Escort (GDYE) content-control software in 2009. It is designed to restrict online pornography sites in order to build "a green, healthy, and harmonious online environment." Initially mandated to be preinstalled on all new computers coming into the country, the requirement was delayed to an undetermined date. However, all computers in schools, Internet cafés, and other public use areas must run the software. According to reports, the GDYE also strengthens the blocking and tracking capabilities of the Golden Shield system. Through automatic updates, much like updates to the Windows operating system, the GDYE software maintains a list of banned sites maintained by the government. The updates are also able to collect the private user data on the machine and communicate it back to central servers.

As stated earlier, ICPs like MSN and Google have historically cooperated with

the Chinese government by self-censoring information in order to operate in the country. Yahoo!, the only non-Chinese company providing e-mail service to the People's Republic of China, has also turned over e-mail content to the authorities, resulting in the prosecution and conviction of at least four persons for criticizing the government. In 2010, however, Google took a different course with China.

In late 2009, Google was hit with a sophisticated attack on their Gmail servers and some of their other corporate networks. Google believed that "a primary goal of the attackers was accessing the Gmail accounts of Chinese human rights activists." Up until then, Google had been self-censoring content like other ICPs, tailoring results to remove topics deemed subversive or pornographic. However, after the network attack, tensions began to rise between Google and China. Although Google never directly accused China, they believed that the attacks came from the Chinese government or were at best sponsored by them in an effort to root out political dissidents. As a result, Google threatened to completely pull their business out of China or at the very least end its practice of censoring search results.

Early in 2010, Google made the decision to redirect all its search traffic in China to servers in Hong Kong, where greater civil liberties remain as part of the British handover. By doing so, Google ended its practice of censoring results and opened unrestricted searches to the Chinese public. Within days of the move, China began filtering and outright blocking searches directed to the Hong Kong servers using the Golden Shield system. Economic fallout from the controversy has already occurred. China quickly pulled out of lucrative agreements to use Google's Android operating system on a number of mobile platforms. In March 2010, Google's annual license to be an ICP in China expired. In summer 2010, China renewed Google's license, but it remains to be seen how this apparent standoff between the search giant and China will end.

As is true of most attempts to censor the Internet (you *will* continue to receive spam), tech-savvy users in China find ways to circumvent the government's firewall. Proxy servers have helped poke holes in the wall at Internet gateways and ISP levels. Users with the right knowledge can configure browsers to access the Internet through proxy servers located in other countries. The use of proxies slows the service but does allow surfers in China to visit "forbidden" Web sites. However, many Chinese Internet users have been unwilling or unable to use proxy servers. That has begun to change as sites like Facebook, Twitter, and YouTube were blocked after a Tibetan uprising in the summer of 2008. The loss of access to these popular sites has led to a greater number of Chinese Internet users finding ways to *fanqiang,* or "scale the wall." One Chinese Internet activist believes that the rise of social networking sites is causing the government censors to lose ground. He says that "China's censorship was built for Web 1.0, but everything now is Web 2.0."

While it's true that government surveillance is an ongoing activity for Internet users in China and dissidents are severely punished, those who want the freedom to peruse content at will are chipping away at the wall through circumvention methods, unstoppable blogs, and other Web content and through the objections of cyberprotestors around the world.

Questions

1. American companies like Yahoo! and Microsoft point out that European, Japanese, or other firms would quickly fill any gap left if American companies withheld their expertise. Nevertheless, should these companies provide their technologies to China, even if they are used to limit the individual freedom of Chinese citizens? Why or why not?

2. Given that China has the largest number of Internet users, do you think they can ultimately succeed in controlling information? Why or why not?

3. Should the rest of the world care if China limits information access within China? Why or why not? Now that Google has moved against censorship, do you think other companies will follow suit? Why or why not?

Based on:

Anonymous. (n.d.). Top 20 countries: Internet users. *InternetWorldStats.com.* Retrieved April 30, 2010, from http://www.internetworldstats.com/top20.htm.

Anonymous. (2002, December 3). China's Internet censorship. *CBS News.* Retrieved April 30, 2010, from http://www.cbsnews.com/stories/2002/12/03/tech/main531567.shtml.

Anonymous. (2006, August). Race to the bottom: Corporate complicity in Chinese Internet censorship. *Human Rights Watch.* Retrieved April 30, 2010, from http://www.hrw.org/reports/2006/china0806.

Arther, C. (2010, April 1). Google fails to renew licence in China. *Guardian.co.uk.* Retrieved April 30, 2010, from http://www.guardian.co.uk/technology/2010/apr/01/google-china-licence-expires.

August, O. (2007, October 23). The great firewall: China's misguided—and futile—attempt to control what happens online. *Wired.* Retrieved April 30, 2010, from http://www.wired.com/politics/security/magazine/15-11/ff_chinafirewall.

Fallows, J. (2008, March). The connection has been reset. *The Atlantic.* Retrieved April 30, 2010, from http://www.theatlantic.com/magazine/archive/2008/03/-ldquo-the-connection-has-been-reset-rdquo/6650.

Fang, Y. (2010, July 22). China confirms Google's operation license renewed. *Xinhua.* Retrieved August 1, 2010, from http://news.xinhuanet.com/english2010/china/2010-07/11/c_13394498.htm.

Helft, M., & Wines, M. (2010, March 23). Google faces fallout as China reacts to site shift. *New York Times.* Retrieved April 30, 2010, from http://www.nytimes.com/2010/03/24/technology/24google.html.

Markoff, J. (2008, October 1). Surveillance of Skype messages found in China. *New York Times.* Retrieved January 15, 2009, from http://www.nytimes.com/2008/10/02/technology/internet/02skype.htm.

Nakashima, E., Mufson, S., & Pomfret, J. (2010, January 13). Google threatens to leave China after attacks on activists' e-mail. *Washington Post.* Retrieved April 30, 2010, from http://www.washingtonpost.com/wp-dyn/content/article/2010/01/12/AR2010011203024.html.

Pierson, D. (2010, January 16). Despite censorship, cracks widen in China's Great Firewall. *Los Angeles Times.* Retrieved April 30, 2010, from http://articles.latimes.com/2010/jan/16/business/la-fi-china-firewall16-2010jan16/3.

Watts, J. (2009, June 8). China orders PC makers to install blocking software. *Guardian.co.uk.* Retrieved April 30, 2010, from http://www.guardian.co.uk/world/2009/jun/08/web-blocking-software-china.

Technology Briefing

Foundations of Information Systems Infrastructure

After reading this briefing, you will be able to do the following:

1. Discuss foundational information systems (IS) hardware concepts.

2. Describe foundational topics related to systems and application software as well as those of various types of programming languages and application development environments.

3. Describe network software and hardware, including media access control, network topologies, and protocols, as well as advanced Internet concepts.

4. Explain foundational database management concepts.

Preview

In Chapter 3, "Managing the Information Systems Infrastructure and Services," you learned about the primary hardware and software components of a computer as well as foundational concepts that include networking, the Internet, and databases. This Technology Briefing will expand this discussion, providing you with a deeper understanding of these topics. Each of these major sections within this briefing provides optional material that is stand-alone from the other sections as well as the entire book. Likewise, the end-of-chapter material is presented in separate sections to facilitate this independence.

Foundational Topics in IS Hardware

In this section, we will examine foundational topics related to IS hardware. Specifically, we will discuss additional topics related to input, processing, and output technologies, giving you a more thorough understanding of how computers work.

Input Technologies

In Chapter 3, we briefly discussed the typical input technologies used on today's computers, such as keyboards, scanners, or graphics tablets. Here, we delve deeper into current and emerging input technologies.

Entering Text and Numbers Historically, entering text and numbers had to be done using a **QWERTY keyboard.** QWERTY stands for how the letters are arranged on the keyboard, with Q-W-E-R-T-Y being the first six letters going from left to right on the keyboard. Additionally, there are several different flavors of keyboards that can be used. For example, **ergonomic keyboards** resemble a widened "V" shape that is designed to reduce the stress placed on the wrists, hands, and arms when typing. Of course, both the standard and the ergonomic keyboards can be wireless, using either RF (radio frequency) or Bluetooth technologies. Another type of keyboard gaining popularity is the laser keyboard. The laser keyboard, also known as the virtual laser keyboard, uses both laser and infrared technology to project a full-sized QWERTY keyboard onto any surface (see Figure TB1).

Selecting and Pointing The **mouse** is the most popular selecting and pointing device, primarily as it is easy to use and provides high precision. In addition to the mouse, various other pointing devices are used to select items from menus, to point, and to sketch or draw. Several of the most popular types of pointing devices are listed in Table TB1. Other, more specialized pointing devices include a **graphics tablet,** used to simulate the process of drawing or sketching on a sheet of paper, or an **eye-tracking device,** an innovative pointing device developed primarily for the disabled for help with computer pointing. The eye tracker is used in cases where voice and finger manipulation is not possible. This device is built around a monitor and tracks the eye movements of the user, moving the pointer to where the user is focusing on; a "click" is signaled by blinking for a set amount of time.

Entering Batch Data Large amounts of routine data, referred to as **batch data,** are often entered into the computer using scanners that convert printed text and images into digital data. Scanners range from small handheld devices that look like a mouse to large desktop boxes that

FIGURE TB1

The virtual laser keyboard.

iStockphoto.com

TABLE TB1 Selecting and Pointing Devices

Device	Description
Mouse	Pointing device that works by sliding a small box-like device on a flat surface; selections are made by pressing buttons on the mouse.
Trackball	Pointing device that works by rolling a ball that sits in a holder; selections are made by pressing buttons located near or on the holder.
Joystick	Pointing device that works by moving a small stick that sits in a holder; selections are made by pressing buttons located near or on the holder.
Touch screen	Pointing device using a touch-sensitive computer or mobile device display; selections are made by touching the display with a finger or a stylus.

resemble personal photocopiers (see Figure TB2). Rather than duplicating the image on another piece of paper, the computer translates the image into digital data that can be stored or manipulated by the computer. Insurance companies, universities, and other organizations that routinely process a large number of forms and documents are typically using scanner technology to increase employee productivity; entering a large number of separate forms or documents into a computer system and manipulating this data at a single time is referred to as **batch processing.**

Once a document is converted into digital format, **text recognition software** uses **optical character recognition** to convert typed, printed, or handwritten text into the computer-based characters that form the original letters and words.

Other special-purpose scanning technologies include **optical mark recognition** devices, **bar code readers,** and **magnetic ink character recognition,** as summarized in Table TB2. Also, RFID (radio frequency identification) scanners are a popular system input method for a variety of contexts (see Chapter 8, "Improving Supply Chains and Strengthening Customer Relationships Using Enterprise Information Systems").

Other Scanning Technologies. Used in many European and Asian countries, as well as at many colleges and universities, **smart cards** are special credit card–sized cards containing a microprocessor chip, memory circuits, and often a magnetic stripe. When issued by a school, smart

FIGURE TB2

Handheld scanners are a type of batch input device.

Grant Blakeman\Shutterstock

TABLE TB2 Specialized Scanners for Inputting Information

Scanner	Description
Optical mark recognition	Used to scan questionnaires and test answer forms ("bubble sheets") where answer choices are marked by filling in circles using pencil or pen
Optical character recognition	Used to read and digitize typewritten, computer-printed, and even handwritten characters such as on sales tags on department store merchandise, patient information in hospitals, or the address information on a piece of postal mail
Bar code reader	Used mostly in grocery stores and other retail businesses to read bar code data at the checkout counter; also used by libraries, banks, hospitals, utility companies, and so on
Magnetic ink character recognition	Used by the banking industry to read data, account numbers, bank codes, and check numbers on preprinted checks
Biometric scanner	Used to scan human body characteristics of users to enable everything from secure access to payment procurement

cards are photo-identification cards that can also be used to unlock dormitory doors, make telephone calls, do laundry, make purchases from vending machines or student cafeterias, and more. Some smart cards allow for contactless transmission of data using RFID technology (e.g., the Exxon Speedpass for purchasing gasoline). Biometric devices, discussed in more detail in Chapter 10, "Securing Information Systems," are being used primarily for identification and security purposes. These devices read certain features, including iris, fingerprints, and hand or face geometry, and compare them with stored profiles. Biometric devices are now also being included in consumer products, such as laptops, allowing users to log on to the laptop using a fingerprint scanner rather than the traditional keyboard entry of user name and password.

Entering Audio and Video When entering **audio** (i.e., sound) and **video** (i.e., still and moving images) data into a computer, it has to be digitized before it can be manipulated, stored, and played or displayed. In addition to the manipulation of music, audio input is helpful for operating a computer when a user's hands need to be free to do other tasks. Video has become popular for assisting in security-related applications, such as room monitoring and employee verification. It has also gained popularity for videoconferencing and chatting on the Internet, using your PC and a webcam.

Voice Input. Perhaps one of the easiest ways to enter data into a computer is simply to speak into a microphone. With the increased interest in such applications as Internet-based telephone calls and videoconferencing, microphones have become an important component of computer systems. A process called **speech recognition** also makes it possible for your computer to understand speech. For many disabled people, the use of the keyboard is not an option for entering in text and numbers. For this reason, researchers have developed a variety of options for disabled users, including voice-to-text translators. **Voice-to-text software** is an application that uses a microphone to monitor a person's speech and then converts the speech into text. There are consumer versions of voice-to-text software that are relatively cheap, but the professional software used by the disabled can be very expensive. Speech recognition technology can also be especially helpful for physicians and other medical professionals, airplane cockpit personnel, factory workers whose hands get too dirty to use keyboards, and computer users who cannot type and do not want to learn. Increasingly, **interactive voice response,** based on speech recognition technology, is used for telephone surveys or to guide you through the various menu options when calling a company's customer service line.

Other Forms of Audio Input. In addition to using a microphone, users can enter audio using electronic keyboards, or they can transfer audio from another device (such as an audio recorder). The users can then analyze and manipulate the sounds via sound editing software for output to MP3s, CDs, or other media.

Video Input. A final way in which data can be entered into a computer is through video input. Digital cameras record still images or short video clips in digital form on small, removable memory cards rather than on film. Storage capacity is influenced by the resolution and size you select for pictures or the length of the recording for video. At any time, you can connect the camera to a port on a PC for downloading to the computer's memory and then clear the memory card for later use. Digital camera technology has become so portable that it is used in a variety of products, including cell phones and laptops. High-quality digital cameras are generally more expensive than film-based cameras, ranging in price from $100 to $10,000 or more. However, they offer three main advantages. You can record digital images without using a scanner, you can take photographs without having film developed, and you can record video. Presently, photos taken with high-end digital cameras are suitable for professional-quality photos, but for video recordings, specialized digital video (DV) cameras are still the best choice. Since huge digital files are created when video clips are recorded, DV cameras use digital video tapes or DVDs rather than memory cards. Further, when the clips are downloaded to the computer, storage and processing requirements are demanding.

There are also lower-quality cameras that are priced from $30 to $200. These devices, often referred to as webcams, have become very popular with people wanting to use the Internet for chatting with friends and family, using programs like Skype, Google Talk, Windows Live Messenger, or Yahoo! Messenger. Using the input of a webcam, a PC can create **streaming video,** which is a sequence of moving images in a compressed format that can be sent over the Internet; the images are displayed on the receiver's screen as they arrive. **Streaming media** encompasses both streaming video and streaming audio. With streaming media, a Web user does not have to wait for the entire file to be downloaded before seeing the video or hearing the sound. Instead, the media are sent in a continuous stream that is played as it arrives. This is why streaming has become popular for real-time chatting, and it is how live broadcasts, like the news on CNN (www.cnn.com) or even baseball games (www.mlb.com), can be viewed on a computer over the Internet.

We have described numerous options for providing input to a computer. After data is entered into a computer, it can be processed, stored, and manipulated. In the next section, we describe the processing aspects of IS hardware.

Processing: Transforming Inputs into Outputs

In Chapter 3, we discussed how data and information are represented and processed within a computer. Next, we briefly describe different encoding standards and then highlight the different components of a desktop computer.

Binary Codes **Binary codes** are used to relay data and instructions to and from the central processing unit (CPU). Binary codes are represented as a series of binary numbers (i.e., zeros and ones), where each separate number is called a **bit** and the collection of bits for a single code is called a **byte.** There are several different types of binary codes that have been developed. Some are in wide use, such as the **American Standard Code for Information Interchange (ASCII),** and others are used for specialized equipment (see Table TB3).

System Unit The system unit contains the motherboard, power supply and fan, CPU(s), random access memory (RAM) and read-only memory (ROM), hard drive, optical drives, ports for plugging in peripherals, and add-in slots for sound, video, and network cards, Universal Serial Bus

TABLE TB3 Types of Encoding for Information Systems

Code	Name	Description	Variants
ASCII	American Standard Code for Information Interchange	Often pronounced "aski," a character encoding based on the English alphabet. ASCII codes represent symbols (letters and numbers) in binary form. Most character encodings have a historical basis in ASCII.	Extended US-ASCII IBM367
MIME	Multipurpose Internet Mail Extensions	This is the standard coding for the Internet. Virtually all e-mail is transmitted in MIME format.	RFC 2045 8BITMIM
MAC OS Roman		This encoding is used by Mac OS to represent text. It encodes 256 characters; this includes 128 characters that are identical to ASCII.	
Unicode		This encoding has become an industry standard that was designed to allow symbols from all languages, including Arabic, Chinese, and so on.	UTF-8 UTF-7 UCS-2

FIGURE TB3

A computer's motherboard holds or connects to all of the computer's electronic components.

Bretislav Horak\Shutterstock

(USB) devices, and other cards. In all types and models of computers, the main circuit board or system board, most often called the motherboard, is the heart of the system unit.

Motherboard. The **motherboard** is aptly named because it connects all the components that do the actual processing work of the computer (see Figure TB3). It is a large plastic or fiberglass circuit board that holds or connects to all of the computer's electronic components. Plugged into or otherwise connected to the motherboard are the CPU (often referred to as the computer's brain) as well as the other components mentioned previously. These devices are described next.

The computer's **power supply** converts electricity from the wall socket to a lower voltage. Whereas typically power supplied by the utility companies can vary from 110 to 240 volts AC, depending on where you are in the world, a PC's components use lower voltages—3.3 to 12 volts DC. The power supply converts the power accordingly and also regulates the voltage to eliminate spikes and surges common in most electrical systems. For added protection against external power surges, many PC owners opt to connect their systems to a separately purchased voltage surge suppressor. The power supply includes one or several fans for air cooling the electronic components inside the system unit—that low humming noise you hear while the computer is running is the fan.

Clock Speed. In Chapter 3, we discussed the influence of the number of transistors on the performance of the CPU. Other factors influencing performance are clock speed, registers, and cache memory. These are discussed next.

Within the computer, an electronic circuit generates pulses at a rapid rate, setting the pace for processing events to take place, rather like a metronome marks time for a musician. This circuit is called the **system clock.** A single pulse is a **clock tick,** and a fixed number of clock ticks is required to execute a single instruction. In microcomputers, the processor's **clock speed** is measured in hertz (Hz). One megahertz (MHz) is 1 million clock ticks, or instruction cycles, per second. Microprocessor speeds are measured in different units, depending on the type of computer. Personal computer speeds are most often measured in gigahertz (GHz, or 1 billion hertz). Microprocessor speeds improve so quickly that faster chips are on the market about every six months. Today, most new PCs operate at more than 3 GHz. To give you an idea of how things have changed, the original IBM PC had a clock speed of 4.77 MHz.

Storage. A computer has various different types of storage, each serving a specific purpose. The primary differences between different types of storage are capacity, volatility, and read/write speed (see Table TB4 for a description of computer speeds).

TABLE TB4 Elements of Computer Time

Name	Fraction of a Second	Description	Example
Millisecond	1/1000	One-thousandth of a second	Hard drives access data in about 3 to 10 milliseconds.
Microsecond	1/1,000,000	One-millionth of a second	A 3.2-GHz CPU executes approximately 3.2 billion operations in a second (i.e., about 3,200 operations every microsecond).
Nanosecond	1/1,000,000,000	One-billionth of a second	Most type of RAM used in PCs have access times (the time needed to read data from the RAM to the CPU) from 3 to 50 nanoseconds (lower is better). Most cache memory has access times less than 20 nanoseconds.
Picosecond	1/1,000,000,000,000	One-trillionth of a second	Inside a CPU, the time that it takes to switch a circuit from one state to another is in the range of 5 to 20 picoseconds.
Femtosecond	$1/10^{15}$, or 10^{-15}	One-quadrillionth of a second	Used in laser technology to measure the length of the laser pulse. Used for nanosurgery.
Attosecond	$1/10^{18}$, or 10^{-18}	One-quintillionth of a second	A term used in photon research. Currently, the shortest unit of time scientists are able to measure.

Primary Storage. RAM, also called main memory, is located on the motherboard and is used to store the data and programs currently in use (we discussed main memory in Chapter 3). Within the CPU itself, registers provide temporary storage locations where data must reside while it is being processed or manipulated. For example, if two numbers are to be added together, both must reside in registers, with the result placed in a register. Consequently, the number and size of the registers can also greatly influence the speed and power of a CPU.

A **cache** (pronounced "cash") is a small block of memory used by processors to store those instructions most recently or most often used. Just as you might keep file folders that you use most in a handy location on your desktop, cache memory is located within the CPU. Thanks to cache memory, before performing an operation, the processor does not have to go directly to main memory, which is farther away from the microprocessor and takes longer to reach. Instead, it can check first to see if needed data is contained in the cache. Cache memory is another way computer engineers have increased processing speed.

Cache memory is typically located inside the microprocessor. Modern CPUs have a hierarchy of cache memory (level 1, level 2, or even level 3); the lower levels of cache memory are faster but also smaller and more expensive. The more cache available to a CPU, the better the overall system performs because more data is readily available (although at a certain size, factors such as heat emission and power consumption become prohibitive to increasing the CPU cache).

Read-only memory (ROM) is used to store programs and instructions that are automatically loaded when the computer is turned on, such as the **basic input/output system (BIOS).**

Secondary Storage. Hard disk drives and tapes are secondary storage devices with **read/write heads** that inscribe data to or retrieve data from magnetic media. Hard disks and tape drives are usually installed internally but may be externally located and attached via cables to ports on the system unit. Tapes are removable secondary storage media. That is, they must be inserted into a tape reader to be read from or written to and are removed when these tasks are accomplished, just as a flash drive has to be plugged into a USB port on your computer.

Most of the software run on a computer, including the operating system, is stored on the hard drive (or hard disk). The hard drive is a secondary storage device usually located inside the system unit of a computer. It writes data and programs to a fixed disk. The storage capacity of the hard drives for today's microcomputers is now measured in gigabytes (GB), or billions of bytes. It is not unusual for PCs currently on the market to come equipped with hard drives with 100-GB to 500-GB storage capacities. Modern supercomputers can have millions of gigabytes of storage. Most microcomputers have one hard drive, but additional drives can usually be added either internally or externally. To make sure critical data is not lost, some computers employ **redundant array of independent disks (RAID)** technology to store redundant copies of data on two or more hard drives. RAID is not typically used on an individual's computer but is very common for Web

A hard drive consists of several disks that are stacked on top of one another and read/write heads to read and write data.

Studio Foxy\Shutterstock

servers and many business applications. RAID is sometimes called a "redundant array of *inexpensive* disks" because it is typically less expensive to have multiple redundant disks than fewer highly reliable and expensive ones.

Hard drives consist of several disks, or platters, stacked on top of one another so that they do not touch (see Figure TB4). Each disk within a disk pack has an access arm with two read/write heads—one positioned close to the top surface of the disk and another positioned close to the bottom surface of the disk. (Both surfaces of each disk are used for data storage.) When reading from or writing to the disks, the read/write heads are constantly repositioned to the desired storage location for the data while the disks are spinning at speeds of 5,400 to 15,000 revolutions per minute. The read/write heads do not actually touch either surface of the disks. In fact, a **head crash** occurs if the read/write head for some reason touches the disk, leading to a loss of data. Because of the mechanical action needed to position the read/write heads, hard drives are comparably slow; it takes a permanent storage device such as a hard disk about 3–10 milliseconds to access data. Within a CPU, however, a single transistor can be changed from a 0 to a 1 in about 10 picoseconds (10-trillionths of a second; see Table TB4). Changes inside the CPU occur about 1 billion times faster than they do in a fixed disk because the CPU operates only on electronic impulses, whereas the fixed disks perform both electronic and mechanical activities, such as spinning the disk and moving the read/write head. Mechanical activities are extremely slow relative to electronic activities; however, modern hard drives use cache memory to decrease the time needed to access frequently used data. A new secondary storage technology called *solid-state drive (SSD)* uses microchips to store information; as SSDs have no moving parts, they are typically faster (with access times of 0.1–0.5 milliseconds), quieter, and more reliable, but also more expensive than traditional hard disk-based drives. As prices come down on SSD-based hard drives, they will capture more of the secondary storage marketplace.

Removable Storage Media. Today, there are two primary types of removable storage: flash memory and optical disks. Flash memory drives are relatively inexpensive storage device typically having capacities of 16 to 128 GB; as of 2010, the highest-capacity flash drive could store 256 GB of data.

Optical disks (i.e., disks that are written/read using laser beam technology) are very inexpensive storage media used to store personal information (e.g., old photos and videos) and distribute software, video games, and movies. Optical disks store binary data in the form of pits and flat areas on the disk's surface; a laser beam can then read the data based on the reflection of the disk's surface. For many years, CD-ROMs (compact disc—read-only memory) were the standard for distributing data and software because of their low cost and their storage capacity of 700 MB. As CD-ROMs cannot be written to, most computers support another type of optical disk that data can be written to, the **CD-R (compact disc—recordable).** Whereas a CD-R can be written onto only once, a **CD-RW (compact disc—rewritable)** can be written onto multiple times using a CD-RW drive. However, many users desire higher storage capacity than CD-Rs or CD-RWs can offer for multimedia (such as video) or large data backups.

The **DVD-ROM (digital versatile disc—read-only memory)** has more storage space than a CD-ROM because DVD-ROM (or typically referred to as simply DVD) drives use a shorter-wavelength laser beam that allows more optical pits to be deposited on the disk. Like compact discs, there are recordable (DVD-R) and rewritable (DVD-RW) versions of this storage technology. DVDs used for the distribution of movies are also called **digital video disks.** The drive to offer high-definition video content led to the creation of Blu-ray, a new DVD format that provides up to 50 GB of storage.

Magnetic tapes used for data storage consist of narrow plastic tape coated with a magnetic substance. Storage tapes range from one-fourth inch wide, wound into a plastic cassette that looks much like a music cassette tape, to one-half inch wide, wound on a reel. As with other forms of magnetic storage, data are stored in tiny magnetic spots. The storage capacity of tapes is expressed as **density,** which equals the number of **characters per inch** or **bytes per inch** that can be stored on the tape.

Magnetic tape is still used for storing large amounts of computer data, but it is gradually being replaced by high-capacity disk storage since disk storage is equally reliable. In fact, data stored on disks is easier and faster to locate because using disks, computers do not have to scan an entire tape to find a specific data file.

Ports. To use the full functionality of a computer, you need to be able to connect various types of devices, such as mice, printers, and cameras, to the system unit. A **port** provides a hardware interface—plugs and sockets—for connecting devices to computers. The characteristics of various types of ports are summarized in Table TB5.

Now that you understand how data is input into a computer and how it can be processed and stored, we can turn our attention to the third category of hardware—output technologies.

Output Technologies

As you have learned in Chapter 3, computers can display information on a screen, print it, or emit sound. The following section provides further detail about various video output technologies.

TABLE TB5 Common Computer Ports, Their Applications, and Description

Port Name	Used to Connect	Description
Serial	Modem, mouse, keyboard, terminal display, MIDI	• Used to transfer one bit at a time • Slowest data transfer rates
Parallel	Printer	• Used to transfer several bits concurrently • Many times faster than serial
USB	Printer, scanner, mouse, keyboard, digital camera and camcorders, external disk drives	• A very high speed data transfer method • Up to 4.8 billion bytes per second using USB3.0 • Up to 127 devices simultaneously connected
IEEE 1394 ("Fire Wire")	Digital cameras and camcorders, external disk drives	• Extremely high speed data transfer method • Up to 800 million bytes per second • Up to 63 devices simultaneously connected
Ethernet	Network	• Most common standard for local area networks
VGA (Video Graphics Array), DVI (Digital Visual Interface)	Monitors	• VGA is designed for transmission of analog video signals • DVI allows for digital transmission of video signals
HDMI (High Definition Multimedia Interface)	Monitors, home theater	• HDMI allows for simultaneous transmission of digital audio and video signals

Monitors are used to display information from a computer and can be color, black and white, or monochrome (meaning all one color, usually green or amber). Today, monochrome monitors are used primarily in cash registers and other point-of-sale applications. Most monitors use **liquid crystal displays (LCDs)** because they are lighter and thinner than bulky **cathode ray tubes** used in old computer displays and televisions. Because display monitors are embedded into a broad range of products and devices, such as cell phones, digital cameras, or automobiles (e.g., to display route maps and other relevant information), they must be sturdy, reliable, lightweight, energy efficient, and low in cost. Recent developments in monitor technologies have thus focused on other display technologies, such as **organic light-emitting diodes,** which require far less power and are much thinner than traditional LCD panels. Finally, projectors are often used for presentation to an audience (and by many as a way to project a large video image in a home theater). Projectors have gone from large, very expensive equipment ($5,000 or more) to very small, relatively inexpensive equipment ($200). This is due primarily to the development of LCD technology, as previously discussed.

Especially for mobile computing, monitor technology is still a challenge. In addition to screen size and power requirements of commonly used display technologies, glare is often an issue, and many laptop screens are hard to read in bright sunlight. For years, many futurists have envisioned a day when computer displays would be lightweight, thin, and flexible like paper as well as be inexpensive and would not require external power to retain an image. Recently, devices using **electronic paper** (or **e-paper**) have been introduced into the market. E-paper uses microscopic beads that change color (and retain this image indefinitely) in response to small electrical charges. These beads are encased between very thin sheets of flexible material. The primary benefits of e-paper are that it needs no backlight (as LCD displays do) and reflects like ordinary paper. Current applications of e-paper include electronic signs (that can be automatically updated by a wireless network), infinitely reusable newspapers and magazines, improved displays for mobile phones, and e-book readers such as the Amazon Kindle. The Kindle DX can hold up to 3,500 titles that can be downloaded from Amazon.com via a wireless connection.

Now that you have learned more about IS hardware, we will focus on software, another key component of the IS infrastructure.

Foundational Topics in IS Software

Software directs the functions of all computer hardware. Without software, the biggest, fastest, most powerful computer in the world is nothing more than a fancy paperweight. Software is intertwined with all types of products and services—toys, music, appliances, health care, and countless other products. As a result, the term *software* can be confusing because it is used in many different ways. We unravel this confusion in the next section by describing the different types of software that are used in today's organizations.

Systems Software

In Chapter 3, you learned about one type of systems software, the operating system, and its many different tasks. More specifically, common tasks of an operating system include the following:

- Booting (or starting) your computer
- Reading programs into memory and managing memory allocation
- Managing where programs and files are located in secondary storage
- Maintaining the structure of directories and subdirectories
- Formatting disks
- Controlling the computer monitor
- Sending documents to the printer

Just as there are many kinds of computers, there are many different kinds of operating systems (see Table TB6). In general, operating systems—whether for large mainframe computers or for small notebook computers—perform similar operations. Obviously, large multiuser supercomputers are more complex than small desktop systems; therefore, the operating system must account for and manage that complexity. However, the basic purpose of all operating systems is the same.

TABLE TB6 Common Operating Systems

Operating System	Description
OS/390	A proprietary operating system developed specifically for large IBM mainframe systems.
Unix	A multiuser, multitasking operating system that is available for a wide variety of computer platforms. Commonly used because of its superior security.
Windows	Currently, the Windows desktop operating system is by far the most popular in the world. Variations are also used to operate large servers, small handhelds, and cell phones.
Mac OS	The first commercial graphical-based operating system, making its debut in 1984.
Linux	A freely distributed operating system designed in 1991 by a Finnish student. Known for providing a secure, low-cost, multiplatform operating system. Linux powers about one-third of all Web servers.
	Linux users can choose between different "flavors" (or distributions), depending on their needs (such as the novice-friendly Ubuntu).
Symbian OS	An operating system designed for mobile devices, jointly developed by Ericsson, Nokia, and Psion.
Android	Google's Linux-based operating system for mobile devices.
iOS	Apple's mobile operating system, previously named iPhone OS; also used on the iPod Touch and iPad.

The second type of systems software, **utilities** (or **utility programs**), are designed to manage computer resources and files. Some are included in operating systems software. Others must be purchased separately and installed on your computer. Table TB7 provides a sample of a few utility programs that are considered essential.

Application Software

With just the systems software alone, users can perform very few (if any) important business tasks. Application software can be generally categorized by its primary purpose, from large business systems (e.g., an enterprise resource planning system) to office automation and personal productivity tools. Throughout this book, we have examined many of these business systems. Applications in the "office automation and personal productivity" categories are used to support the daily work activities of individuals and small groups (see Table TB8).

TABLE TB7 Common Types of Computer Software Utilities

Utility	Description
Backup	Archives files from the hard disk to tapes, flash drives, or other storage devices
File defragmentation	Converts fragmented files (i.e., files not stored contiguously) on your hard disk into contiguous files that will load and be manipulated more rapidly
Disk and data recovery	Allows the recovery of damaged or erased data from hard disks and flash drives
Data compression	Compresses data by substituting a short code for frequently repeated patterns of data, much like the machine shorthand used by court reporters, allowing more data to be stored on a disk
File conversion	Translates a file from one format to another so that it can be used by an application other than the one used to create it
Antivirus	Scans files for viruses and removes or quarantines any virus found
Device drivers	Allows adding new hardware to your computer system, such as a game controller, printer, scanner, and so on, to function with your operating system
Spam blockers	Monitors your incoming e-mail messages and filters or blocks unwanted messages from arriving
Spyware detection and removal	Scans your computer for spyware and disables or removes any spyware found
Media players	Allows you to listen to music or watch video on a computer

TABLE TB8 Examples of Productivity Software

Tool	Examples
Word processor	Microsoft Word, Corel Word Perfect, OpenOffice Writer
Spreadsheet	Microsoft Excel, OpenOffice Calc, Google Spreadsheet, Simple Spreadsheets
Database management	OpenOffice Base, Microsoft Access, Borland Paradox, Microsoft SQL Server, IBM DB2, MySQL
Presentation software	Apple Keynote, OpenOffice Impress, Microsoft PowerPoint, Harvard Graphics
E-mail	Mozilla Thunderbird, Apple Mail, Opera M2, Microsoft Outlook and Outlook Express
Web browsers	Microsoft Internet Explorer, Mozilla Firefox, Opera Presto, Google Chrome
Chat	Microsoft Live Messenger, Yahoo! Messenger, Google GTalk, Trillian, Pidgin
Calendar and contact management	Lotus Notes, Microsoft Outlook and Outlook Express, ACT!

Programming Languages and Development Environments

Each piece of software is developed using some programming language. A programming language is the computer language the software vendor uses to write programs. For application software, such as spreadsheets or database management systems (DBMSs), the underlying programming language is invisible to the user. However, programmers in an organization's IS group and, in some instances, end users can use programming languages to develop their own specialized applications. The **source code** (i.e., the program written in a programming language) must be translated into object code—called assembly or machine language—that the hardware can understand. Most programming languages are translated into machine languages using programs called *compilers* and *interpreters*.

Compilers and Interpreters A **compiler** takes an entire program's source code written in a programming language and converts it into an **executable,** i.e., a program in machine language that can be read and executed directly by the computer (see Figure TB5). Although the compilation process can take quite some time (especially for large programs), the resulting executables run very fast; thus, programs are usually compiled before they are sold as executables to the customers. As in such cases, the customers purchase only the executable but do not have access to the program's source code; they can run the program but not make any modifications to it.

Some programming environments do not compile the entire program into machine language. Instead, each statement of the program is converted into machine language and executed "on the fly" (i.e., one statement at a time), as depicted in Figure TB6. The type of program that does the conversion and execution is called an **interpreter.** As the source code is translated each time the program is run, it is easy to quickly evaluate the effects of any changes made to the program's source code. However, this also causes interpreted programs to run much slower than compiled executables. Programming languages can be either compiled or interpreted.

Programming Languages Over the past few decades, software has evolved. In the early days of computing, programming languages were quite crude by today's standards. Initially used in the 1940s, the first generation of programming languages were called machine languages. Programmers wrote in binary code to indicate to the computer which circuits to turn on and which to turn off. As

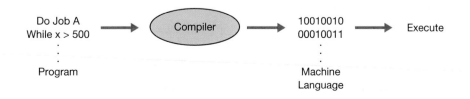

FIGURE TB5

A compiler translates the entire computer program into machine language, then the CPU executes the machine language program.

FIGURE TB6

Interpreters read, translate, and execute one line of source code at a time.

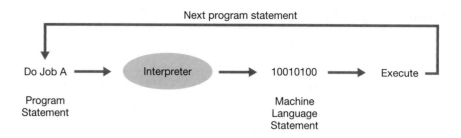

you might guess, machine language is very unsophisticated and therefore very difficult to write. Because it is so difficult, very few programs are actually written in machine language. Instead, programmers rely on higher-level languages. In the early 1950s, a more sophisticated method for programming was developed in which the binary codes used in machine language were replaced by symbols. These symbolic languages were a lot easier for humans to understand. Programs written in symbolic language or any higher-level language need to be converted into machine language in order to run. Many different types of programming languages exist, each with its own strengths and weaknesses. Popular languages used in businesses and industry today are summarized in Table TB9.

In the mid-1950s, the first high-level programming language, called FORTRAN, was developed by IBM. The big innovation of high-level languages was that they used English-like words to instruct the computer. Consequently, writing source code in high-level languages is much easier than in lower-level languages. Programmers must fully understand the tasks that are to be accomplished when writing a new application in order to choose the best programming language for those tasks.

In the 1970s, several user-oriented languages, called **fourth-generation languages (4GLs),** were created. These languages are more like English than third-generation languages in that they focus on the desired output instead of the procedures required to get that output. 4GLs, also called outcome-oriented languages, are commonly used to write and execute queries of a database. For example, the widely used database query language called Structured Query Language (SQL) is a 4GL. See Figure TB7 for several lines of SQL displayed in a sentence-like statement requesting information from a database.

TABLE TB9 Popular Programming Languages

Language	Application	Description
BASIC	General purpose	Beginner's All-Purpose Symbolic Interaction Code. An easy-to-learn language, BASIC works on almost all PCs.
C/C++	General purpose	C++ is a newer version of C. Developed at AT&T Bell Labs. Complex languages used for a wide range of applications.
COBOL	Business	COmmon Business-Oriented Language. Developed in the 1960s, it was the first language for developing business software. COBOL is used for most business transaction processing applications on mainframes.
FORTRAN	Scientific	FORmula TRANslator. The first commercial high-level language developed by IBM in the 1950s. Designed for scientific, mathematical, and engineering applications.
Pascal	Teaching structured programming	Named after the mathematician Blaise Pascal. Uses building block approach to programming. Useful in developing large programs.
HTML	World Wide Web	HyperText Markup Language. The most widely used language for developing Web pages. Markup languages simplify pages for transmission by using symbols that tell what document elements should look like when displayed.
Java	World Wide Web	An object-oriented programming language developed at Sun Microsystems in the early 1990s. It is a popular programming language for the Internet because it is highly transportable from one computer to another.
.NET Framework	World Wide Web	A variety of programming languages (e.g., ASP.NET and C#) offered by Microsoft that can easily be integrated into Web applications.
LISP	Artificial Intelligence	LISt Processor. Dates from the late 1950s. One of the main languages used to develop applications in artificial intelligence and high-speed arcade graphics.

FIGURE TB7

A fourth-generation language query using SQL that requests that the last and first names of those who have a credit limit equal to $100 be displayed from a database called "Customer."

```
SELECT LAST_NAME, FIRST_NAME
FROM CUSTOMER
WHERE CREDIT_LIMIT = 100

DIEHR GEORGE
JANKOWSKI DAVID
FERRELL LAUREN
HAGGARTY JOSEPH
SCHNEIDER BIRGIT
VALACICH JAMES
VALACICH JORDAN
```

More recently, **fifth-generation languages (5GLs)** have been developed for use within some expert system or artificial intelligence applications. 5GLs are called natural languages because they allow the user to communicate with the computer using true English sentences. For example, Hewlett-Packard and other software vendors have developed tools for document search and retrieval and database queries that let the user query the documents or databases using English-like sentences. These sentences are then automatically converted into the appropriate commands (in some cases SQL) needed to query the documents or databases and produce the result for the user. If the system does not understand exactly what the user wants, it can ask for clarification. The same code shown in Figure TB7 might appear as shown in Figure TB8 if a natural language were used. Although 5GL languages are not common and are still being further developed, they have been used to forecast the performance of financial portfolios, help diagnose medical problems, and estimate weather patterns.

Of course, programming languages continue to evolve, with object-oriented languages, visual programming languages, and Web development languages rapidly gaining popularity. We discuss these next.

Object-Oriented Languages. **Object-oriented languages** are the most recent in the progression of high-level programming languages and are extremely popular with application developers. Object-oriented languages use common modules (called objects), which combine properties and behaviors to define the relevant system components. An example of an object would be a specific student who has a name, an address, date of birth (i.e., the properties), but can also perform certain operations, such as register for a class (the behaviors). If an object-oriented

FIGURE TB8

A 5GL query using natural language to request the same information as the SQL query in Figure TB7.

```
BEGINNING WITH THE LAST NAME ON
THE FOLLOWING LIST OF
CUSTOMERS, FIND CUSTOMERS WHO
HAVE A CREDIT LIMIT OF $100

DIEHR GEORGE
JANKOWSKI DAVID
FERRELL LAUREN
HAGGARTY JOSEPH
SCHNEIDER BIRGIT
VALACICH JAMES
VALACICH JORDAN
```

TABLE TB10 Concepts Related to Object-Oriented Languages

Concept	Description	Examples
Class	Modules that allow programmers to group properties and behavior together. Classes can be reused for different programs.	A "student" has an address and a grade-point average (GPA) (properties) and can enroll in courses (behavior).
Encapsulation	Data and behavior of a class are hidden from other classes and are thus protected from unexpected changes.	The registrar doesn't need to know how the GPA is calculated within the "student" class; the registrar cares only that it is updated.
Inheritance	More specific classes include the properties and behaviors of the more general class.	Both "distance degree student" and "on-campus student" inherit properties (such as address and GPA) and behaviors (such as enroll in a course) from the general class "student."
Event-driven program execution	The programmer does not determine the sequence of execution for the program; the flow is determined by user input (e.g., mouse clicks) or messages from other applications.	A word processor reacts to your typing and clicking.

programming language is being used, it enables the design and implementation of the objects to happen quickly and simultaneously, as oftentimes, preexisting objects can be reused or adapted. For important concepts related to object-oriented languages, see Table TB10.

Visual Programming Languages. Just as you may have found it easier to use a computer operating system with a **graphical user interface (GUI),** such as Windows 7 or Mac OS X, programmers using **visual programming languages** may also take advantage of the GUI. For instance, programmers can easily add a command button to a screen with a few clicks of a mouse (see Figure TB9) instead of programming the button pixel by pixel and using many lines of code. Visual Basic.NET and Visual C# (pronounced as "C-sharp") are two popular examples of visual programming languages.

Web Development Languages. If you have been surfing the Web for a while, you may have thought of creating a personal Web page or already have one. In that event, you have some experience with using a programming language. The language you used to create your Web page is

FIGURE TB9

Visual Basic.NET, a visual programming language, is used to create standard business forms.

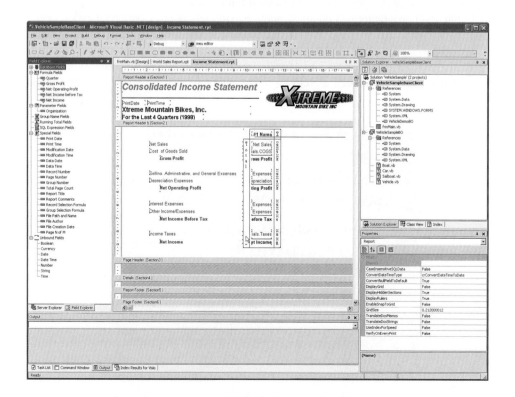

TABLE TB11 Common HTML Tags

Tag	Description
<html> . . . </html>	Creates an HTML document
<head> . . . </head>	Sets off the title and other information that is not displayed on the Web page itself
<body> . . . </body>	Sets off the visible portion of the document
<b> . . . </b>	Creates bold text
<a href="URL"> . . . </a>	Creates a hyperlink
<a href=mailto:EMAIL> . . . </a>	Creates a link creating a new e-mail message
<p> . . . </p>	Creates a new paragraph
<table> . . . </table>	Creates a table

called Hypertext Markup Language (HTML). HTML is a text-based file format that uses a series of codes (i.e., tags), to set up a document; **HTML tags** are used to instruct the Web browser on how a document should be formatted and presented to the user. Because HTML editing programs are visually oriented and easy to use, you do not need to memorize the language to set up a Web page. Programs for creating Web pages (such as Microsoft Expression Web and Adobe Dreamweaver) are called **Web page builders** or **HTML editors.**

In HTML, the tags used to identify different elements on a page and to format the page are set apart from the text with angle brackets (<>). Specific tags are used to mark the beginning and the ending of an element or a formatting command. For example, if you want text to appear in bold type, the tag to begin bolding is <b>. The tag to turn off bolding, at the end of the selected text, is </b>. The "a href" command sets up a hyperlink from a word or image on the page to another HTML document. Tags also denote document formatting commands, such as text to be used as a title, sizes of text in headings, the ends of paragraphs, underlining, italics, bolding, and places to insert pictures and sound (see Table TB11).

A good way to understand how HTML works is to find a Web page you like, then use the "View Source" command on your browser to see the hypertext that created the page (see Figure TB10). Once you have created your own Web page and saved it to a disk, you can upload it to an Internet account you have created through your Internet service provider.

FIGURE TB10

A Web page and the HTML source code used to create it.

Courtesy Washington State University.

Markup languages such as HTML are for laying out or formatting Web pages. If you want to add animated cartoons or other dynamic content or have users interact with your Web page other than by clicking on hypertext links, then you will need to use special purpose programming languages such as Java or use Web services, a scripting language, and so on.

Java is a programming language that was developed by Sun Microsystems in the early 1990s. It lets you spice up your Web page by adding active content such as circles that whirl and change colors, hamsters marching to a tune, forms to help users calculate car payments at various interest rates, or any other such dynamic content. You can do this in one of two ways: by learning Java or a similar language and programming the content you want, or by downloading free general purpose **applets** from the Web to provide the content you want on your Web page. Applets are small programs that are executed within another application, such as a Web page. When a user accesses your Web page, the applets you inserted are downloaded from the server along with your Web page to the user's browser, where they perform the desired action. Later, when the user leaves your Web page, the Web page and the applets disappear from his or her computer.

Microsoft.NET is a programming platform that is used to develop applications that are highly interoperable across a variety of platforms and devices. For example, .NET can create an application that runs on desktop computers, mobile computers, or Web-enabled phones. .NET applications can be constructed using a suite of visual programming languages including Visual C#, ASP.NET, and Visual Basic.NET. To gain its interoperability, .NET utilizes Web services.

Web services are Web-based software systems used to integrate data from different applications and databases over a network (see also Chapter 5, "Enhancing Collaboration Using Web 2.0"). To support the interoperability from machine to machine, Web services use XML. The *Extensible Markup Language (XML)* was designed (1) to be used as a Web page construction tool when users want to create their own markup tags and (2) to build database queries. One practical application of Web services is iGoogle, which lets users create personalized home pages by gathering data from several sources and aggregating the content (see Figure TB11).

The advantages of Web services include the following:

- Web services offer interoperability between a variety of software applications that are on different operating systems.
- Web services allow software and services from different companies and locations to be easily shared and combined to provide powerful integrated applications.
- Web services, similar to object-oriented languages, allow the reuse of components.
- Web services are easily distributed, thereby facilitating a distributed approach to application integration.

FIGURE TB11

Web services are enabling powerful applications.

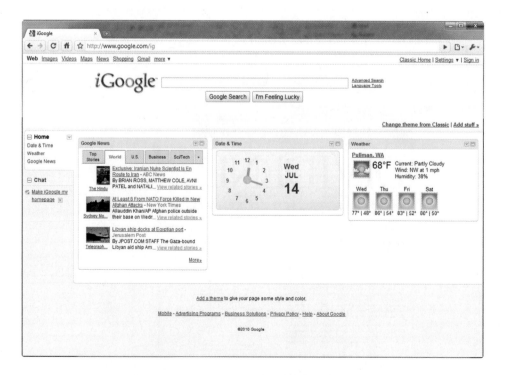

Scripting languages can also be used to supply interactive components to a Web page. These languages let you build programs or scripts directly into HTML page code. Web page designers frequently use them to check the accuracy of user-entered information, such as names, addresses, and credit card numbers. Two common scripting languages are Microsoft's VBScript and JavaScript.

JavaScript bears little resemblance to Java. The two are similar, however, in that both Java and JavaScript are useful component software tools for creating Web pages. That is, both allow users to add or create applets that lend dynamic content to Web pages. Both are also cross-platform programs, meaning that they can typically be used by computers running Windows, Linux, Mac OS, and other operating systems.

The development of programming languages is an ongoing process of change and innovation. These changes often result in more capable and complex systems for the user. The popularity of the Internet has spurred the creation of innovative and evolving software. From the pace of change that is occurring, it is clear that many more innovations are on the horizon.

Along with commercial products, there are several open source tools in wide use today. The most common is PHP, originally designed as a high-level tool for producing dynamic Web content. Another open source application used frequently is MySQL, a multiuser DBMS with over 6 million customers. This robust database can be used instead of commercial products, such as Oracle or Microsoft's SQL server.

Another common way to add dynamic content to Web sites is Flash. Using the application development suite Adobe Flash, developers can create animation and video that can be compressed small enough for fast download speeds. When you browse the Web and see animation or complex data streams, this is usually done in Flash. Flash animation is displayed on your screen using the Adobe Flash player. Flash can also include Web services to allow data-driven animation. Some examples of data-driven flash animation on Web sites are the bag builder at Timbuk2 (www.timbuk2.com) and the live Major League Baseball game update at Yahoo!'s sports site (http://sports.yahoo.com/mlb/gamechannel).

Automated Development Environments Over the years, the tools for developing information systems have increased both in variety and in power. In the early days of systems development, a developer was left to use a pencil and paper to sketch out design ideas and program code. Computers were cumbersome to use and slow to program, and most designers worked out on paper as much of the system design as they could before moving to the computer. Today, system developers have a vast array of powerful computer-based tools at their disposal. These tools have changed forever the ways in which systems are developed. **Computer-aided software engineering (CASE)** refers to automated software tools used by systems developers to design and implement information systems. Developers can use these tools to automate or support activities throughout the systems development process with the objective of increasing productivity and improving the overall quality of systems. The capabilities of CASE tools are continually evolving and being integrated into a variety of development environments. Next we briefly review some of the interesting characteristics of CASE.

Types of CASE Tools. Two of the primary activities in the development of large-scale information systems are the creation of design documents and the management of information. Over the life of a project, thousands of documents need to be created—from screen prototypes to database content and structure to layouts of sample forms and reports. At the heart of all CASE environments is a repository for managing information.

CASE also helps developers represent business processes and information flows by using graphical diagramming tools. By providing standard symbols to represent business processes, information flows between processes, data storage, and the organizational entities that interact with the business processes, CASE eases a very tedious and error-prone activity (see Figure TB12). The tools not only ease the drawing process but also ensure that the drawing conforms to development standards and is consistent with other design documents developed by other developers.

Another powerful capability of CASE is its ability to generate program source code automatically. CASE tools keep pace with contemporary programming languages and can automatically produce programming code directly from high-level designs in languages such as Java, Visual Basic.NET, and C#. In addition to diagramming tools and code generators, a broad range of other tools assists in the systems development process. The general types of CASE tools used throughout the development process are summarized in Table TB12.

FIGURE TB12

System design diagram from Microsoft Visio.

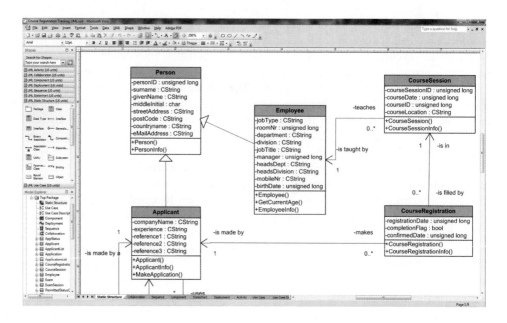

Open Source Software

Open source software refers to systems software, applications, and programming languages in which the source code (i.e., the program code written in a programming language) is freely available to the general public for use and/or modification. Many large mainstream software companies are actively involved in the open source community. For example, IBM is playing a leading role in evolving the Linux operating system. Likewise, Sun Microsystems is active in developing and extending the OpenOffice Productivity Suite. This is reflected in a variety of popular open source software, as presented in Table TB13.

TABLE TB12 General Types of CASE Tools

CASE Tool	Description
Diagramming tools	Tools that enable system process, data, and control structures to be represented graphically.
Screen and report generators	Tools that help model how systems look and feel to users. Screen and report generators also make it easier for the systems analyst to identify data requirements and relationships.
Analysis tools	Tools that automatically check for incomplete, inconsistent, or incorrect specifications in diagrams, screens, and reports.
Repositories	Tools that enable the integrated storage of specifications, diagrams, reports, and project management information.
Documentation generators	Tools that help produce both technical and user documentation in standard formats.
Code generators	Tools that enable the automatic generation of program and database definition code directly from the design documents, diagrams, screens, and reports.

Source: Hoffer, George, and Valacich (2011).

TABLE TB13 Examples of Open Source Software

Type of Software	Description	Examples
Operating systems	Software that operates the hardware on computers	Ubuntu Linux (www.ubuntu.com) openSuSE Linux (www.opensuse.org) FreeBSD (www.freebsd.org)
Business information systems	A wide variety of applications used in everyday businesses	Accounting: Turbo Cash (www.turbocashuk.com) GIS: GRASS GIS (www.osgeo.org/grass) Office Suite: OpenOffice (www.openoffice.org) Antivirus: Open Antivirus (www.openantivirus.org) Firewall: FWBuilder (www.fwbuilder.org) Web browser: Firefox (www.firefox.com) E-mail: Mozilla Thunderbird (www.mozillamessaging.com/thunderbird)
Developer tools	Application development suites	Languages: PERL (www.perl.org) PHP (www.php.net) Version control: Microsoft Codeplex (www.codeplex.com)
DBMSs	Software for accessing and maintaining data in a database	MySQL (www.mysql.com)
Web servers	Software providing access to Web sites	Apache (www.apache.org)

Foundational Topics in Networking

Telecommunications and networking technologies are taking on more and more importance as organizations rely more on computer-based information systems. Understanding how the underlying networking technologies work and where these technologies are heading will help you better understand the potential of information systems. The discussion begins with a description of the evolution of computer networking.

Evolution of Computer Networking

Over the past decades, computer networking underwent an evolution from centralized computing to distributed computing to collaborative computing. These eras of computer networking are discussed next.

Centralized Computing **Centralized computing,** depicted in Figure TB13, remained largely unchanged through the 1970s. In this model, large centralized computers, called mainframes, were used to process and store data. During the mainframe era (beginning in the 1940s), people entered data on mainframes through the use of local input devices called **terminals.** These devices were called "dumb" terminals because they did not conduct any processing, or "smart,"

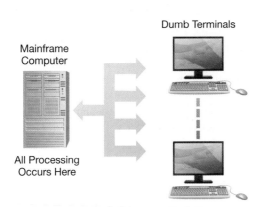

Dumb Terminals

Mainframe Computer

All Processing Occurs Here

FIGURE TB13

In the centralized computing model, all processing occurs in one central mainframe.

FIGURE TB14

In the distributed computing model, separate computers work on subsets of tasks and then pool their results by communicating over a network.

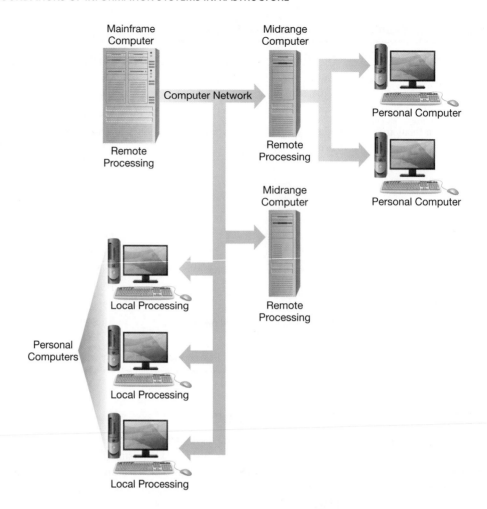

activities. The centralized computing model is not a true network because there is no sharing of data and capabilities. The mainframe provides all the capabilities, and the terminals are only input/output devices. Computer networks evolved in the 1980s when organizations needed separate, independent computers to communicate with each other.

Distributed Computing The introduction of personal computers in the late 1970s and early 1980s gave individuals control over their own computing. Organizations also realized that they could use multiple small computers to achieve many of the same processing goals of a single large computer. People could work on subsets of tasks on separate computers rather than using one mainframe to perform all the processing. To achieve this goal, computer networks were needed so that data and services could be easily shared between these distributed computers. The 1980s were characterized by an evolution to a computing model called **distributed computing,** shown in Figure TB14, in which multiple types of computers are networked together to share data and services.

Collaborative Computing In the 1990s, a new computing model, called **collaborative computing,** emerged. Collaborative computing is a synergistic form of distributed computing in which two or more networked computers are used to accomplish a common processing task. That is, in this model of computing, computers are not simply communicating data but are also sharing processing capabilities. For example, one computer may be used to store a large employee database. A second computer may be used to process and update individual employee records selected from this database. The two computers collaborate to keep the company's employee records current, as depicted in Figure TB15.

Types of Networks

Computing networks today include all three computing models: centralized, distributed, and collaborative. The emergence of new computing models did not mean that organizations completely discarded older technologies. Rather, a typical organizational computer network includes

1. Computer Requests Record to Change

2. Returns Requested Record

4. Returns Changed Record

3. Modifies Record

5. Stores Changed Record in Database

FIGURE TB15

In the collaborative computing model, two or more networked computers are used to accomplish a common processing task.

mainframes, servers, personal computers, and a variety of other devices. Computer networks are commonly classified by size, distance covered, and structure. The most common are described next.

Private Branch Exchange A private branch exchange (PBX) is a telephone system that serves a particular location, such as a business (see Figure TB16). It connects telephone extensions within the system and connects internal extensions to the outside telephone network. It can also connect computers within the system to other PBX systems, to an outside network, or to various office devices, such as fax machines or photocopiers. Since they use ordinary telephone lines, PBX systems have limited bandwidth, preventing them from transmitting such forms of data as interactive video, digital music, or high-resolution photos. Using PBX technology, a business requires few outside phone lines but has to purchase or lease the PBX equipment.

Local Area Network A local area network (LAN), shown in Figure TB17, is a computer network that spans a relatively small area, allowing all computer users to connect with each other to share data and peripheral devices, such as printers. LAN-based communications may involve the sharing of data, software applications, or other resources between several users. LANs typically do not exceed tens of kilometers in size and are typically contained within a single building or a limited geographical area. They typically use only one kind of transmission medium or cabling, such as twisted-pair wire or coaxial cable. There are also wireless local area network products available. These are very popular because they are relatively easy to set up, and they enable you to have a network without any network cables strewn around your home or office.

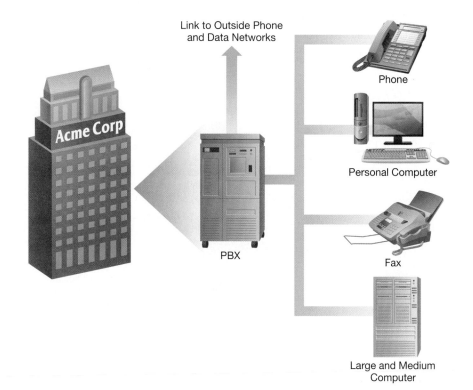

Link to Outside Phone and Data Networks

Phone

Personal Computer

Fax

PBX

Large and Medium Computer

Acme Corp

FIGURE TB16

A PBX supports local phone and data communications as well as links to outside phone and data networks.

FIGURE TB17

A LAN allows multiple computers located near each other to communicate directly with each other and to share peripheral devices, such as a printer.

Campus Area Network   A campus area network (CAN) is a computer network that is used by a single organization to connect multiple LANs. A CAN typically spans multiple buildings, such as at a corporate or university campus.

Wide Area Network   A wide area network (WAN) is a computer network that spans a relatively large geographical area. WANs are typically used to connect two or more LANs. Different hardware and transmission media are often used in WANs because they must cover large distances efficiently. Used by multinational companies, WANs transmit and receive data across cities and countries. A discussion follows of four specific types of WANs: metropolitan area networks, enterprise networks, value-added networks, and global networks.

Metropolitan Area Networks. A metropolitan area network is a computer network of limited geographic scope, typically a citywide area, that combines both LAN and high-speed fiber-optic technologies. Such networks are attractive to organizations that need high-speed data transmission within a limited geographic area.

Enterprise Networks. An **enterprise network** is a WAN connecting disparate networks of a single organization into a single network (see Figure TB18).

Value-Added Networks. **Value-added networks (VANs)** are private, third-party-managed medium-speed WANs that are shared by multiple organizations. VANs are economical because customers lease communication lines rather than investing in dedicated network equipment. The "added value" provided by VANs can include network management, e-mail, EDI, security, and

FIGURE TB18

An enterprise network allows an organization to connect distributed locations into a single network.

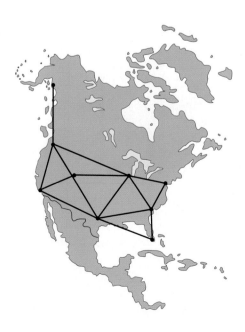

Getty Images—Thinkstock

other special capabilities. Consequently, VANs can be more expensive than generic communication lines leased from a common telecommunication company such as AT&T or Sprint, but they provide valuable services for customers.

Global Networks. A **global network** spans multiple countries and may include the networks of several organizations. The Internet is an example of a global network. The Internet is the world's largest computer network, consisting of thousands of individual networks supporting millions of computers and users in almost every country of the world.

Personal Area Networks A final type of computer network, called a personal area network (PAN), is an emerging technology that uses wireless communication to exchange data between computing devices using short-range radio communication, typically within an area of 10 meters (30 feet). The enabling technology for PAN is called **Bluetooth,** a specification for personal networking of desktop computers, peripheral devices, mobile phones, portable stereos, and other handheld devices. Bluetooth is integrated into a variety of personal devices to ease interoperability and information sharing (see Figure TB19).

Now that you have an understanding of the general types of networks, the next sections examine some of their fundamental components. This discussion is divided into two areas: networking fundamentals and network standards and technologies. Together, these sections provide a foundation for understanding various types of networks.

Networking Fundamentals

Telecommunications advances have enabled individual computer networks—constructed with a variety of hardware and software—to connect together in what appears to be a single network. Networks are increasingly being used to dynamically exchange relevant, value-added knowledge and information throughout global organizations and institutions. The following sections take a closer look at the fundamental building blocks of these complex networks and the services they provide.

Network Services Network **services** are the capabilities that networked computers share through the multiple combinations of hardware and software. The most common network services are file services, print services, message services, and application services. **File services** are used to store, retrieve, and move data files in an efficient manner, as shown in Figure TB20a. An individual can use the file services of the network to move a certain file electronically to multiple recipients across the network. **Print services** are used to control and manage users' access to network printers and fax equipment, as shown in Figure TB20b. Sharing printers on a network reduces the

FIGURE TB20

Networks can provide (a) file,
(b) print, (c) message, and
(d) application services.

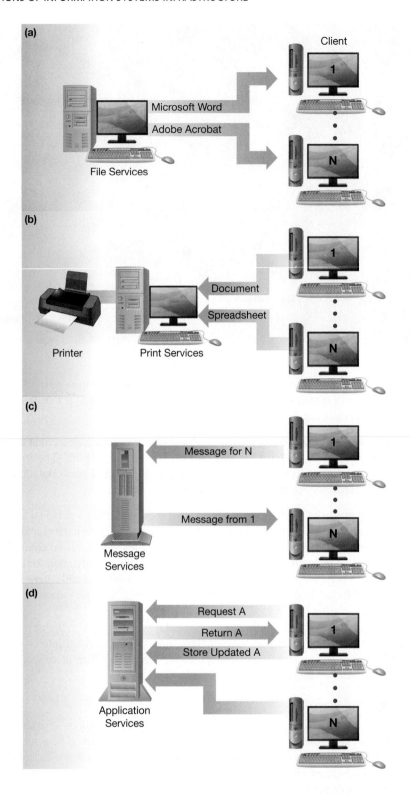

number of printers an organization needs. **Message services** include the storing, accessing, and delivering of text, binary, graphic, and digitized video and audio data across a network. These services are similar to file services, but they also deal with communication interactions between users and applications. Message services include electronic mail or the transfer of messages between two or more networked computers, as shown in Figure TB20c. **Application services** run software for network clients and enable computers to share processing power, as shown in Figure TB20d. Application services highlight the concept of client/server computing, in which processing is distributed between the client and server. Clients request data or services from the servers. The servers

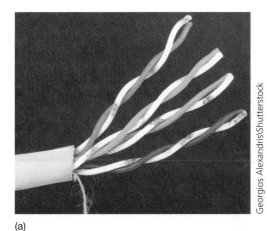

Georgios Alexandris\Shutterstock

Inara Prusakova\Shutterstock

(a)

(b)

FIGURE TB21

(a) A cable spliced open showing several twisted pairs; (b) a sample network installation that utilizes many TP cables at once.

store data and application programs. For example, the physical search of database records may take place on the server, while the user interacts with a much smaller database application that runs on the client.

When an organization decides to network its computers and devices, it must decide what services will be provided and whether these services will be centralized (a server-centric approach), distributed (a peer-to-peer approach), or some combination of both. These decisions ultimately affect the choice of the network operating system. The **network operating system (NOS)** is system software that controls the network and enables computers to communicate with each other. In other words, the NOS enables network services. In most LAN environments, the NOS consists of two parts. The first and most complex part is the system software that runs on the network server. The system software coordinates many functions, including user accounts, access information, security, and resource sharing. The second and much smaller part of the NOS runs on each workstation connected to the network. In peer-to-peer networks, usually a piece of the NOS is installed on each attached workstation and runs on top of the local operating system. Often, the second part of the NOS is integrated into the workstation operating system itself.

Cable Media Cable media physically link computers and other devices in a network. The most common forms of cable media are twisted pair, coaxial, and fiber-optic.

Twisted-Pair Cable. Twisted-pair (TP) cable is made of two or more pairs of insulated copper wires twisted together (see Figure TB21). TP cables are rated according to quality (in terms of the ability to transmit high frequency signals and the "crosstalk" between individual wires); category 3 (Cat 3), Cat 5, and Cat 6 cables are often used in network installations. Depending on the rating, TP cables have a capacity up to 10 gigabits per second (Gbps) at distances up to 100 meters (330 feet). The cable may be unshielded (UTP) or shielded (STP). Telephone wire installations as well as many local area networks use UTP cabling, as it is cheap and easy to install. However, like all copper wiring, it has rapid attenuation and is very sensitive to electromagnetic interference (EMI) and eavesdropping—the undetected capturing of data transmitted over a network. STP uses wires wrapped in an insulation, making it less prone to EMI and eavesdropping. STP cable is more expensive than unshielded TP cable, and it is more difficult to install because it requires special grounding connectors to drain EMI.

Coaxial Cable. Coaxial (or coax) cable contains a solid inner copper conductor surrounded by plastic insulation and an outer braided copper or foil shield (see Figure TB22). Coax cable comes in a variety of thicknesses—thinnet coax and thicknet coax—based on resistance to EMI. Although less costly than TP, thinnet coax is not commonly used in networks any more; thicknet coax is more expensive than TP. Coax cable is most commonly used for cable television installations and for networks operating at 10 to 100 megabits per second (Mbps). Its attenuation is lower than TP cable's, and it is moderately susceptible to EMI and eavesdropping.

Fiber-Optic Cable. Fiber-optic cable is made of a light-conducting glass or plastic core surrounded by more glass, called cladding, and a tough outer sheath (see Figure TB23). The sheath protects the fiber from changes in temperature as well as from bending or breaking. This technology uses pulses

FIGURE TB22

These coaxial cables are ready to be connected to a computer or other device.

of light sent along the optical cable to transmit data. Fiber-optic cable transmits clear and secure data because it is immune to EMI and eavesdropping. Transmission signals do not break up because fiber-optic cable has low attenuation. It can support bandwidths from 100 Mbps to greater than 2 Gbps and distances up to 25 kilometers (15 miles). It can transmit video and sound. Fiber-optic cable is more expensive than copper wire because the cost and difficulties of installation and repair are higher for fiber-optic. Fiber-optic cables are used for high-speed **backbones**—the high-speed central networks to which many smaller networks can be connected. A backbone may connect, for example, several different buildings in which other, smaller LANs reside. Submarine telecommunications cables (used for telephone and Internet traffic between continents) also use fiber-optic cable. In home environments, fiber-optic cable can be used to connect digital audio devices.

FIGURE TB23

Fiber-optic cable consists of a light-conducting glass or plastic core, surrounded by more glass, called cladding, and a tough outer sheath.

Wireless Media With the popularity of cellular phones, wireless media are rapidly gaining popularity. Wireless media transmit and receive electromagnetic signals using methods such as infrared line of sight, high-frequency radio, and microwave systems.

Infrared Line of Sight. Infrared line of sight uses high-frequency light waves to transmit data on an unobstructed path between nodes—computers or some other device such as a printer—on a network at a distance of up to 24.4 meters (80 feet). The remote controls for most audiovisual equipment, such as TVs, stereos, and other consumer electronics equipment, use infrared light. Infrared systems may be configured as either point-to-point or broadcast. For example, when you use your TV remote control, you have to be in front of the TV to have successful communication. This is an example of point-to-point infrared. Although many laptops and mobile phones were equipped with infrared interface in the 1990s, this technology has since been surpassed by Wi-Fi and Bluetooth, which do not require a line of sight.

High-Frequency Radio. High-frequency radio signals can transmit data at rates of up to several hundred Mbps to network nodes from 12.2 up to approximately 40 kilometers (7.5 to 25 miles) apart, depending on the nature of any obstructions between them. The flexibility of the signal path makes high-frequency radio ideal for mobile transmissions. For example, most police departments use high-frequency radio signals that enable police vehicles to communicate with each other as well as with the dispatch office. This medium is expensive because of the cost of antenna towers and high-output transceivers. Installation is complex and often dangerous because of the high voltages. Although attenuation is fairly low, this medium is very susceptible to EMI and eavesdropping.

   Two common applications of high-frequency radio communication are cellular phones and wireless networks. A **cellular phone** gets its name from how the signal is distributed. In a cellular system, a coverage area is divided into **cells** with a low-powered radio antenna/receiver in each cell; these cells are monitored and controlled by a central computer (see Figure TB24). Any given cellular network has a fixed number of radio frequencies. When a user initiates or receives a call, the mobile telephone switching office assigns the caller a unique frequency for the duration of the call. As a person travels within the network, the central computer at the switching office monitors the quality of the signal and automatically assigns the call to the closest cellular antenna. Cellular phones have gone through rapid changes since their first commercial use in the mid-1980s (see Table TB14). Cellular phones are now mostly digital in the United States except for a few rural areas. Digital transmission and reception offers many advantages over analog, some of which include wider reception range, less static, and the capability of data transmission. Because of the costs involved in setting up fixed telephone lines, cellular phones have become very popular in many African countries and are a key factor in bridging the digital divide.

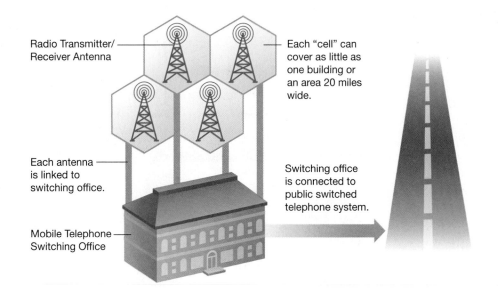

Radio Transmitter/Receiver Antenna

Each "cell" can cover as little as one building or an area 20 miles wide.

Each antenna is linked to switching office.

Switching office is connected to public switched telephone system.

Mobile Telephone Switching Office

FIGURE TB24

A cellular network divides a geographic region into cells.

TABLE TB14 Evolution of Cell Phone Technology

Generation	Description	Data Transfer	Advantages
0G	Preceded modern cellular mobile telephony and was usually mounted in cars or trucks; it was a closed circuit, so you could call only other radio telephone users.	Analog	Communicate on the go.
1G	This technology, introduced in the 1980s, used circuit switching with poor voice quality, unreliable handoffs between towers, and nonexistent security.	Analog	Can communicate with other cell phones and land lines.
2G	The first all-digital signal that was divided into TDMA and CDMA standards. Allowed for SMS (text) messaging and e-mails to be sent/received.	Digital (up to 9.6-Kbps transfer)	Lower-powered radio signals allow longer battery life. Digital format allows for clearer signal and reduced signal noise.
2.5G	Allows for faster data transmission via a packet-switched domain in addition to the circuit-switched domain.	Digital (up to 115-Kbps transfer)	Higher data speeds allow for more complex data to be transmitted (e.g., sports scores and news stories).
3G	Even faster. Requires a new cellular network, different from that already available in 2G systems.	Digital (minimum of 384 Kbps when moving and 2 Mbps when stationary)	Transfer full video and audio.
4G	Appears to be the future standard of wireless devices.	Digital (up to 100 Mbps when moving and 1 Gbps when stationary)	Data speeds similar to wired networks.

High-frequency radio-wave technology is increasingly being used to support wireless local area networks (WLANs). WLANs based on a family of standards called 802.11 are also referred to as Wi-Fi (wireless fidelity). The 802.11 family of standards has been universally adopted and has transmission speeds up to 300 Mbps (using the 802.11n standard). The ease of installation has made WLANs popular for business and home use. For example, some homes and many buildings have (or want) multiple computers and need to share Internet access, files, and peripheral devices. Unfortunately, many older buildings and homes do not have a wired infrastructure to easily connect computers and devices, making wireless networking particularly attractive. Through the use of wireless technologies, many organizations are transforming their work environments into better team collaboration environments.

FIGURE TB25

Terrestrial microwave requires a line-of-sight path between a sender and a receiver.

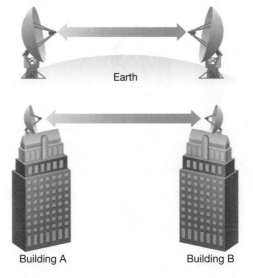

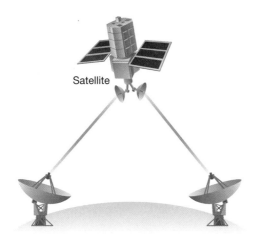

Satellite

FIGURE TB26

Communications satellites are relay stations that receive signals from one earth station and rebroadcast them to another.

Microwave. Microwave transmission is a high-frequency radio signal that is sent through the air using either terrestrial (earth-based) systems or satellite systems. Terrestrial microwave, shown in Figure TB25, uses antennae that require an unobstructed path or line of sight between nodes. The cost of a terrestrial microwave system depends on the distance to be covered. Typically, businesses lease access to these microwave systems from service providers rather than invest in antenna equipment. Data may be transmitted at up to 274 Mbps. Over short distances, attenuation is not a problem, but signals can be disrupted over longer distances by environmental conditions such as high winds and heavy rain. EMI and eavesdropping are significant problems with microwave communications.

Satellite microwave, shown in Figure TB26, uses satellites orbiting the earth as relay stations to transfer signals between ground stations located on earth. Satellites orbit from 400 to 22,300 miles above the earth and have different uses and characteristics (see Table TB15). Because of the distance signals must travel, satellite transmissions are delayed (also known as **propagation delay**). Satellite transmission has become very viable for media such as TV and radio, including the digital radio stations XM and Sirius, both of which have their own satellites that send out scrambled signals to proprietary receivers.

Another strength of satellite communication is that it can be used to access very remote and undeveloped locations on the earth. Such systems are extremely costly because their use and installation depends on space technology. Companies such as AT&T sell satellite services with typical transmission rates ranging from less than 1 to 10 Mbps, but the rates can be as high

TABLE TB15 Characteristics of Satellites with Different Orbits

Name	Distance from Earth	Characteristics/Common Application
Low Earth Orbit (LEO) Satellite	400–1,000 miles	• Not fixed in space in relation to the rotation of the earth; circles the earth several times per day. • Photography for mapping and locating mineral deposits; monitoring ice caps, coastlines, volcanoes, and rain forests; researching plant and crop changes; monitoring wildlife and animal habitat and animal changes; search and rescue for downed aircraft or ships that are in trouble; research projects in astronomy and physics.
Medium Earth Orbit (MEO)	1,000–22,300 miles	• Not fixed in space in relation to the rotation of the earth; circles the earth more than one time per day. • Primarily used in geographical positioning systems (such as the Global Positioning System) for navigation of ships at sea, spacecraft, airplanes, automobiles, and military weapons.
Geosynchronous Earth Orbit (GEO)	22,300 miles	• Fixed in space in relation to the rotation of the earth; circles the earth one time per day. • Because it is fixed in space, transmission is simplified. • Transmission of high-speed data for television, weather information, remote Internet connections, digital satellite radio, and telecommunications (satellite phones).

TABLE TB16 Relative Comparison of Wireless Media

Medium	Expense	Speed	Attenuation	EMI	Eavesdropping
Infrared line of sight	Low	Up to 16 Mbps	High	High	High
High-frequency radio	Moderate	Up to 300 Mbps	Low	High	High
Terrestrial microwave	Moderate	Up to 274 Mbps	Low	High	High
Satellite microwave	High	Up to 90 Mbps	Moderate	High	High

as 90 Mbps. Like terrestrial microwave, satellite systems are prone to attenuation and are susceptible to EMI and eavesdropping. Table TB16 compares wireless media across several criteria.

Network Standards and Technologies

Standards play a key role in creating networks. The physical elements of networks—adapters, cables, and connectors—are defined by a set of standards that have evolved since the early 1970s. Standards ensure the interoperability and compatibility of network devices. The Institute of Electrical and Electronics Engineers has established a number of telecommunications standards. Initially, the three major standards for LAN cabling and media access control were Ethernet, token ring, and ARCnet. Given its widespread acceptance and rapid advances in speed and capabilities, Ethernet has become the dominant standard; the competing standards have all but vanished. Each standard combined a media access control technique, network topology, and transmission media in different ways. Software interacts with hardware to implement protocols that allow different types of computers and networks to communicate successfully. Protocols are often implemented within a computer's operating system or within the network operating system. Each of these topics is described more thoroughly next.

Media Access Control **Media access control** is the set of rules that governs how a given node or workstation gains access to the network to send or receive data. Without access control, collisions are likely to happen if two or more workstations simultaneously transmit messages onto the network. There are two general types of access control: distributed and random access. With distributed control, only a single workstation at a time has authorization to transmit its data. This authorization is transferred sequentially from workstation to workstation, typically using a token. Under random control, any workstation can transmit its data by checking whether the medium is available. No specific permission is required. A commonly used method of random access control is called **carrier sense multiple access (CSMA).** In CSMA, (and its variants) each workstation "listens" to traffic on the transmission medium (either wired or wireless) to determine whether a message is being transmitted. If no traffic is detected, the workstation sends its message; otherwise, it waits. When a workstation gains access to the medium and sends data onto the network, messages are sent to all workstations on the network; however, only the destination with the proper address is able to "open" the message.

Network Topologies **Network topology** refers to the shape of a network. The four common network topologies are star, ring, bus, and mesh. A **star network** is configured, as you might expect, in the shape of a star, as shown in Figure TB27a. That is, all nodes or workstations are connected to a central hub, or concentrator, through which all messages pass. The workstations represent the points of the star. Star topologies are easy to lay out and modify. However, they are also the most costly because they require the largest amount of cabling. Although it is easy to diagnose problems at individual workstations, star networks are susceptible to a single point of failure at the hub that would result in all workstations losing network access. A **ring network** is configured in the shape of a closed loop or circle with each node connecting to the next node, as shown in Figure TB27b. In ring networks, messages move in one direction around the circle. As a message moves around the circle, each workstation examines it to see whether the message is for that workstation. If not, the message is regenerated and passed on to the next node. This regeneration process enables ring networks to cover much larger distances than star or bus networks can. Relatively little cabling is required, but a failure of any node on the ring network can cause complete network failure. Self-healing ring networks avoid this by having two rings with data

FIGURE TB27

(a) The star network has several workstations connected to a central hub. (b) The ring network is configured in a closed loop, with each workstation connected to another workstation. (c) The bus network is configured in the shape of an open-ended line where each workstation receives the same message simultaneously. (d) The mesh network consists of computers and other devices that are either fully or partially connected to each other.

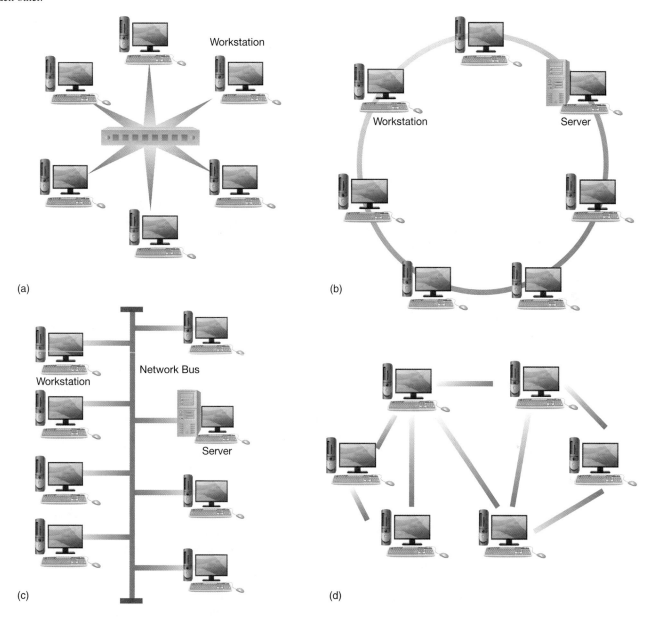

(a)

(b)

(c)

(d)

flowing in different directions; thus, the failure of a single node does not cause the network to fail. In either case, it is difficult to modify and reconfigure a ring network. Ring networks normally use some form of token-passing media access control method to regulate network traffic. A **bus network** is in the shape of an open-ended line, as shown in Figure TB27c; as a result, it is the easiest network to extend and has the simplest wiring layout. This topology enables all network nodes to receive the same message through the network cable at the same time. However, it is difficult to diagnose and isolate network faults. Bus networks use variants of CSMA for media access control. Finally, a **mesh network** consists of computers and other devices that are either fully or partially connected to each other. In a *full* mesh design, every computer and device is connected to every other computer and device. In a *partial* mesh design, many but not all computers and devices are connected (see Figure TB27d). Like a ring network, mesh networks provide relatively short routes from one node to another. Mesh networks also provide many possible routes through the

FIGURE TB28

The OSI model has seven layers and provides a framework for connecting different computers with different operating systems to a network.

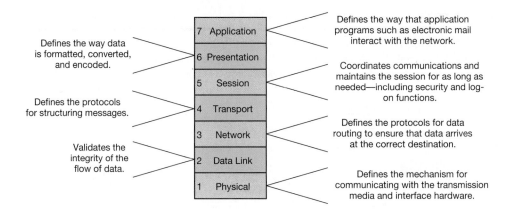

network—a design that prevents one circuit or computer from becoming overloaded when traffic is heavy. Given these benefits, most WANs, including the Internet, use a partial mesh design.

Protocols In addition to media access control and network topologies, all networks employ protocols to make sure communication between computers is successful. Protocols are agreed-on formats for transmitting data between connected computers. They specify how computers should be connected to the network, how errors will be checked, what data compression method will be used, how a sending computer will signal that it has finished sending a message, and how a receiving computer will signal that it has received a message. Protocols allow packets to be correctly routed to and from their destinations. There are literally thousands of protocols to choose from, but a few are a lot more important than the others. In this section, we will first review the worldwide standard, called the OSI model, for implementing protocols. Next, we briefly review two most widely used network protocols: Ethernet and TCP/IP.

The OSI Model. The need of organizations to interconnect computers and networks that use different protocols has driven the industry to an open system architecture in which different protocols can communicate with each other. The International Organization for Standardization defined a networking model called Open Systems Interconnection (OSI), which divides computer-to-computer communications into seven connected layers. The **Open Systems Interconnection (OSI) model** represents a group of specific tasks (represented in Figure TB28) as successive layers that enable computers to communicate data. Each successively higher layer builds on the functions of the layers below. For example, suppose you are using a PC running Windows and are connected to the Internet, and you want to send a message to a friend who is connected to the Internet through a large workstation computer running Unix—two different computers and two different operating systems. When you transmit your message, it is passed down from layer to layer in the Windows protocol environment of your system. At each layer, special bookkeeping information specific to the layer, called a header, is added to the data. Eventually, the data and headers are transferred from the Windows layer 1 to Unix's layer 1 over some physical pathway. On receipt, the message is passed up through the layers in the Unix application. At each layer, the corresponding header information is stripped away, the requested task is performed, and the remaining data package is passed on until your message arrives as you sent it, as shown in Figure TB29. In other words, protocols represent an agreement between different parts of the network about how data are to be transferred.

Ethernet. **Ethernet** is a LAN protocol developed by the Xerox Corporation in 1976. The original Ethernet protocol supports data transfer rates of 10 Mbps. A later version, called 100Base-T or Fast Ethernet, supports transfer rates of 100 Mbps; the latest version, called 10GB Ethernet, supports transfer rates of 10 gigabits, or 10,000 megabits, per second. Whereas older versions of Ethernet used random access control to send data, new Ethernet networks using routers or switches allow for full-duplex communication between nodes. Most new computers have an Ethernet card installed, allowing you to use this type of network connection.

TCP/IP. The Internet was based on the idea that individual networks could be separately designed and developed yet still connect their users to the Internet by using their own unique interfaces.

FIGURE TB29

Message passing between two different computers.

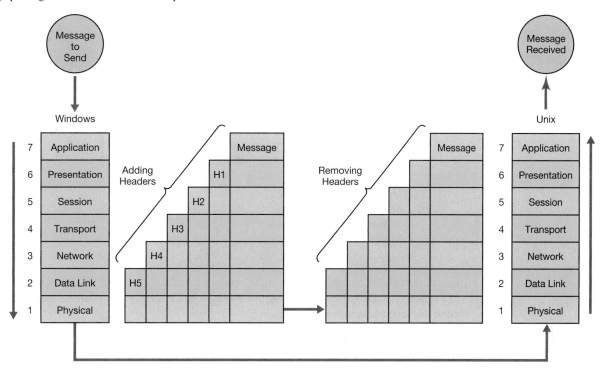

The Transmission Control Protocol/Internet Protocol (TCP/IP), the protocol of the Internet, allows different interconnected networks to communicate using the same language. For example, TCP/IP allows IBM, Macintosh, and Unix users to communicate despite any system differences. Computer scientist Vinton Cerf and engineer Robert Kahn defined the Internet Protocol (IP), by which packets are sent from one computer to another on their way to a destination, as part of the DARPA project (you learned about TCP/IP in Chapter 3).

Connectivity Hardware Stand-alone computers can be physically connected to create different types of networks. Most computers today are equipped with a **network interface card (NIC),** which is a PC expansion board that plugs into a computer so that it can be connected to a network. Each NIC has a unique identifier (called MAC address, assigned by the manufacturer) that is used to identify the computer on the network. The PC is then connected to other network components via transmission media, such as Ethernet cables. Transmission media connectors, or simply **connectors,** are used to terminate the cables so that they can be plugged into a NIC or into other network components. Connectors include T-connectors for coax cable and RJ-45 connectors (similar to a phone jack) for TP cable. Some computers connect to networks using (slower) telephone lines. Because the dial-up telephone system was designed to pass the sound of voices in the form of analog signals, it cannot pass the electrical pulses—**digital signals**—that computers use. The only way to pass digital data over conventional voice telephone lines is to convert it to audio tones—**analog signals**—that the telephone lines can carry. A **modem** (MOdulator/DEModulator) converts digital signals from a computer into analog signals so that telephone lines may be used as a transmission medium to send and receive electronic data, as shown in Figure TB30. After individual devices are connected to the network, multiple segments of transmission media can be connected to form one large network. In the next section, we describe networking hardware commonly used in business and home settings.

Networking Hardware Because of the complexity of current networks, there are several specialized pieces of equipment needed for computers to connect and transfer data. Not all pieces of equipment are necessary in order to connect computers together. The use of this equipment is dependent on the configuration of the network and the use of the network. As seen in Table TB17, businesses require various types of equipment to meet their networking needs. Some of these

FIGURE TB30

Modems convert digital signals into analog and analog signals into digital.

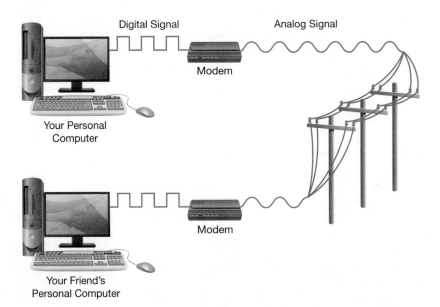

Digital Signal   Analog Signal

Your Personal Computer

Modem

Your Friend's Personal Computer

Modem

devices are also commonly used in home networks; for example, your DSL modem may also act as a wireless router. Other networking devices used by the telecommunications companies are beyond the scope of this discussion.

The Internet

The name "Internet" is derived from the concept of *internetworking,* which means connecting host computers and their networks to form even larger networks. The Internet is a large worldwide collection of networks that use a common protocol to communicate with each other. In Chapter 3, you learned that the Internet uses packet switching to transfer data from computer to computer. In the following sections, we discuss in more detail how independent networks are connected to form the Internet, who manages the Internet, and how home and business users can connect to the Internet.

Connecting Independent Networks   The Internet uses routers to interconnect independent networks. For example, Figure TB31 illustrates a router that connects networks 1, 2, and 3. A router, like a conventional computer, has a central processor, memory, and network interfaces. However, routers do not use conventional software, nor are they used to run applications. Their only job is to interconnect networks and forward data packets from one network to another. As illustrated in Figure TB31, computers A and F are connected to independent networks. If computer A generates a data packet destined for computer F, the packet is sent to the router that interconnects the two networks. The router forwards the packet onto network 2, where it is delivered to its destination at computer F.

TABLE TB17 Networking Hardware

Networking Hardware	Description
Switch	A **switch** is used to connect multiple computers, servers, or printers to create a network. Switches typically inspect data packets received and forward them to the correct addressee.
Router	A router is an intelligent device used to connect two or more individual networks. When a router receives a data packet, it looks at the network address and passes the packet on to the appropriate network. Routers are commonly used to connect a LAN to a WAN, such as the Internet.
Wireless access point	A **wireless access point** transmits and receives wireless (Wi-Fi) signals to allow wireless devices to connect to the network.
Wireless controller	A **wireless controller** manages multiple access points and can be used to manage transmission power and channel allocation to establish desired coverage throughout a building and minimize interference between individual access points. Further, wireless controllers can be used to manage authentication and other security features.

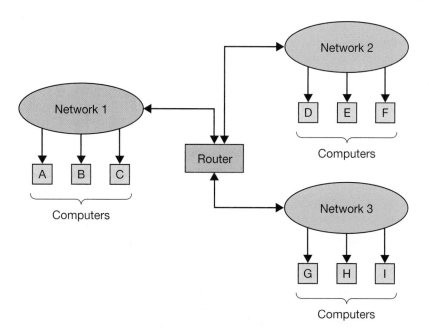

FIGURE TB31

Routers connect independent networks.

Routers are the fundamental building blocks of the Internet because they connect thousands of LANs and WANs. LANs are connected to backbone WANs, as depicted in Figure TB32. A backbone network manages the bulk of network traffic and typically uses a higher-speed connection than the individual LAN segments. For example, a backbone network might use fiber-optic cabling, which can transfer data at a rate of 2 Gbps, whereas a LAN connected to the backbone may use Ethernet with TP cabling, transferring data at a rate of 10 Mbps to 10 Gbps. To gain access to the Internet, an organization installs a router between one of its own networks and the closest Internet site. Business organizations typically connect to the Internet not only with personal computers but with Web servers as well.

Who Manages the Internet? As discussed in Chapter 3, individual computers on the Internet are identified by their IP addresses. So who keeps track of these IP addresses on the Internet? A number of national and international standing committees and task forces have been used to manage the development and use of the Internet. Most notably, the Internet Assigned Numbers Authority is responsible for managing global and country code top-level domains, as well as global IP number space assignments. Similarly, the Internet Assigned Numbers Authority also provides central maintenance of the **Domain Name System (DNS)** root database, which points to distributed DNS servers replicated throughout the Internet. This database is used to associate

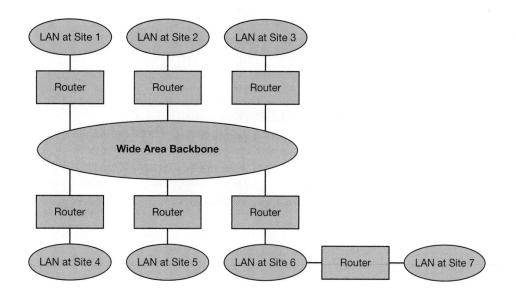

FIGURE TB32

LANs connect to wide area backbones.

Internet host names with their Internet IP addresses. As discussed in Chapter 3, users can access Web sites using domain name or IP addresses. The functionality of the DNS is to provide users easy-to-remember domain names to access Web sites. In other words, it is far easier to remember www.apple.com than it is to remember 17.149.160.10 (the IP address of a server mirroring Apple's content as of mid-2010), but both will work as a Uniform Resource Locator in any Web browser, as the DNS servers will translate the domain names into the accompanying IP address.

In 1993, the NSF created **InterNIC,** a government–industry collaboration, to manage directory and database services, domain registration services, and other information services on the Internet. In the late 1990s, this Internet oversight was transitioned more fully out into industry when InterNIC morphed into the **Internet Corporation for Assigned Names and Numbers,** a nonprofit corporation that assumed responsibility for managing IP addresses, domain names, and root server system management. The number of unassigned Internet addresses is running out, so new classes of addresses are being added as we adopt **IPv6,** the latest version of the IP.

How to Connect to the Internet   Now you can see how the Internet works and how it is managed. How do you connect to the Internet? For personal use (i.e., from home), we typically connect to the Internet through an **Internet service provider (ISP),** also called an Internet access provider. ISPs provide several different ways to access the Internet from home (see Table TB18).

ISPs connect to one another through **network access points (NAPs).** Much like railway stations, these NAPs serve as access points for ISPs and are an exchange point for Internet traffic. They determine how traffic is routed and are often the points of most Internet congestion. NAPs are a key component of the **Internet backbone,** which is the collection of main network connections and telecommunications lines that make up the Internet (see Figure TB33).

The Internet follows a hierarchical structure, similar to the interstate highway system. High-speed central network lines are like interstate highways, enabling traffic from midlevel networks to get on and off. Think of midlevel networks as city streets that, in turn, accept traffic from their neighborhood streets or member networks. However, you cannot get on an interstate or city street whenever you want to. You have to share the highway and follow traffic control signs to arrive safely at your destination. The same holds true for traffic on the Internet. People can connect to the Internet in a number of ways. The following outline how typical home users connect to the Internet.

Dial-Up.   Traditionally, most people connected to the Internet through a telephone line at home or work. The term we use for standard telephone lines is **plain old telephone service (POTS).** The speed, or bandwidth, of POTS is generally about 52 Kbps (52,000 bits per second). The

TABLE TB18 **Methods for Connecting to the Internet**

Service	Current Status and Future Outlook	Typical Bandwidth
Dial-up	Although still used in the United States, there are very few new dial-up customers. This market should dry up as broadband is moved to rural areas and developing nations.	52 Kbps
Integrated Services Digital Network	This technology has limited market share because of its expense. Typically, these connections are more expensive than broadband connections, although they offer less bandwidth.	128 Kbps
Cable	Coaxial cable used for cable TV provides much greater bandwidth than telephone lines and therefore is the market leader in broadband use for home users. Overselling of bandwidth that causes slower-than-average speeds tends to be a major problem for home users.	Upload: 2–10 Mbps Download: 12–50 Mbps
DSL	DSL technology has gained market share over cable. With many companies offering higher speeds at lower cost, DSL should continue to cut into cable's market share.	Upload: up to 10 Mbps Download: 1.5–50 Mbps
Satellite	Although satellite connectivity had a promising future, many users are moving away from this expensive technology in order to access faster and cheaper cable or DSL connections.	Upload: 50 Kbps Download: 5 Mbps
Wireless	Wireless offers the most promise of any of the current technologies, as the speeds are increasing while the coverage areas continue to grow.	Up to 54 Mbps
Fiber to the home	Fiber to the home has been adopted by several major players in the ISP industry. Although the technology typically can be placed only in new developments, the demand for fast connections is helping make this a significant technology for ISPs.	Up to 100 Mbps

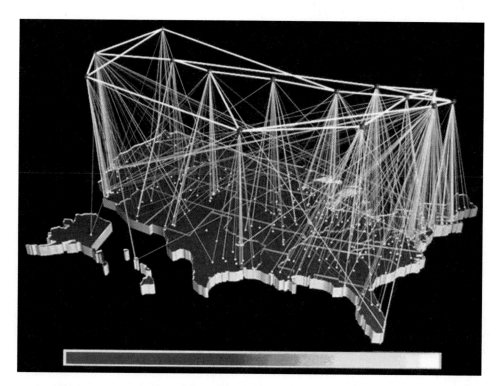

The Internet backbone.

POTS system is also called the **public switched telephone network.** Today, most people connect to the Internet using some form of digital, high-speed connection.

Integrated Services Digital Network. **Integrated services digital network (ISDN)** is a standard for worldwide digital communications. ISDN was designed in the 1980s to replace all analog systems, such as most telephone connections in the United States, with a completely digital transmission system. ISDN uses existing TP telephone wires to provide high-speed data service. ISDN systems can transmit voice, video, and data. Because ISDN is a purely digital network, you can connect your PC to the Internet without the use of a traditional modem. Removing the analog-to-digital conversion for sending data and the digital-to-analog conversion for receiving data and higher bandwidth greatly increase the data transfer rate. However, a small electronic box called an "ISDN modem" is typically required so that computers and older, analog-based devices such as telephones and fax machines can utilize and share the ISDN-based service. While ISDN has had moderate success in various parts of the world, it has largely been surpassed by DSL and cable modems.

Digital Subscriber Line. **Digital subscriber line (DSL)** is one of the more popular ways of connecting to the Internet. DSL is referred to as a "last-mile" solution because it is used only for connections from a telephone switching station to a home or office and generally is not used between telephone switching stations.

The abbreviation DSL is used to refer collectively to **asymmetric digital subscriber line (ADSL), symmetric digital subscriber line (SDSL),** and other forms of DSL. DSL enables more data to be sent over existing copper telephone lines by sending digital pulses in the high-frequency area of telephone wires. Because these high frequencies are not used by normal voice communications, DSL enables your computer to operate simultaneously with voice connections over the same wires. ADSL speeds range from 1.5 to 50 Mbps downstream and from 16 Kbps to 10 Mbps upstream. SDSL is said to be symmetric because it supports the same data rates for upstream and downstream traffic (up to 3 Mbps). Like ISDN, ADSL and SDSL require a special modem-like device. As most Internet users primarily download content, ADSL is most popular in consumer environments. SDSL is offered primarily to business customers.

Cable Modems. In most areas, the company that provides cable television service also provides Internet service. With this type of service, a special **cable modem** is designed to transmit data over cable TV lines. Coaxial cable used for cable TV provides much greater bandwidth than telephone lines, and millions of homes in the United States are already wired for cable TV, so cable modems are a fast, popular method for accessing the Internet. Cable modems offer download speeds up to 50 Mbps.

Satellite Connections. In many regions of the world, people can access the Internet via satellite, referred to as **Internet over satellite (IoS).** IoS technologies allow users to access the Internet via satellites that are placed in a geostationary orbit above the earth's surface. With these services, your PC is connected to a satellite dish hanging out on the side of your home or placed out on a pole (much like satellite services for your television), and it is able to maintain a reliable connection to the satellite in the sky because the satellite orbits the earth at the exact speed of the earth's rotation. Given the vast distance that signals must travel from the earth up to the satellite and back again, IoS is slower than high-speed terrestrial (i.e., land-based) connections to the Internet over copper or fiber-optic cables. In remote regions of the world, however, IoS is the only option available because installing the cables necessary for an Internet connection is not economically feasible or, in many cases, is just not physically possible.

Broadband Wireless. **Broadband wireless** is a technology that is becoming more prevalent with home users today. With speeds similar to DSL and cable, broadband wireless is usually found in rural areas where other connectivity options, such as DSL and cable, are not available. A common scenario is that the ISP will install an antenna at a high point, such as a large building or radio tower. The consumer will mount a small dish to the roof and point it at the antenna. Although broadband wireless can bridge a distance of up to 50 kilometers (30 miles), line of sight between the sender and receiver is necessary for wireless access to work.

Mobile Wireless Access. In addition to the fixed wireless approach, there are also many new **mobile wireless** approaches for connecting to the Internet. For example, there are Internet-enabled cellular phones that give you Internet access nearly anywhere. Also, special network adapter cards or USB "dongles" from a cellular service provider allow a notebook computer, tablet PC, or desktop computer to connect to cellular networks. The advantage of these systems is that as long as you are in the coverage area of that cell phone provider you have access to the Internet (much like coverage with cellular phones). One other option for wireless access to the Internet is to use a wireless network adapter card (typically built into most mobile computers) when you are within the range of a WLAN. Using a WLAN, you are free to roam around your office or building; with a cellular-based technology, you are able to connect anywhere within the cellular coverage area.

Fiber to the Home. **Fiber to the home (FTTH),** also known as **fiber to the premises,** refers to connectivity technology that provides a superspeed connection to people's homes. This is usually done by fiber-optic cabling running directly into new homes. FTTH is currently available only in major metropolitan areas. The growth in FTTH is dependent on new home building, as it is currently cost prohibitive to distribute the technology to existing structures.

Until now, we have talked about ways that individuals typically access the Internet. In the following section, we talk more about ways that organizations typically access the Internet.

Business Internet Connectivity Although home users have enjoyed a consistent increase in bandwidth availability, the demand for corporate use has increased at a greater pace; therefore, the need for faster speeds has become of great importance. In addition to the home connectivity options, business customers also have several high-speed options, described next.

T1 Lines. To gain adequate access to the Internet, organizations are turning to long-distance carriers to lease dedicated **T1 lines** for digital transmissions. The T1 line was developed by AT&T as a dedicated digital transmission line that can carry 1.544 Mbps of data. In the United States, companies such as MCI that sell long-distance services are called **interexchange carriers** because their circuits carry service between the major telephone exchanges. A T1 line usually traverses hundreds or thousands of miles over leased long-distance facilities.

AT&T and other carriers charge as little as $400 per month for a dedicated T1 circuit, and some providers will waive the installation fee if you sign up for some specified length of service. If you need an even faster link, you might choose a **T3 line.** T3 provides about 45 Mbps of service at about 10 times the cost of leasing a T1 line. Alternatively, organizations often choose to use two or more T1 lines simultaneously rather than jump to the more expensive T3 line. Higher speeds than the T3 are also available but are not typically used for normal business activity. For

TABLE TB19 Capacity of Telecommunication Lines

Type of Line	Data Rate
T1	1.544 Mbps
T3	44.736 Mbps
OC-1	51.85 Mbps
OC-3	155.52 Mbps
OC-12	622.08 Mbps
OC-24	1.244 Gbps
OC-48	2.488 Gbps

example, fiber-optic networks offer speeds considerably faster than T3 lines. See Table TB19 for a summary of telecommunication line capacities, including optical carrier (OC) lines that use the Synchronous Optical Network standard.

Asynchronous Transfer Mode. **Asynchronous transfer mode (ATM)** is a method of transmitting voice, video, and data. ATM has found wide acceptance in the LAN and WAN arenas as a solution to integrating disparate networks over large geographic distances. ATM uses a form of packet transmission in which data is sent over a packet-switched network in fixed-length, 53-byte cells. Although it is based on packet-switching technology, ATM has the potential to do away with routers, allocated bandwidth, and contention for communications media. Organizations in the movie and entertainment industries that need to deliver synchronized video and sound, for example, are particularly interested in ATM.

The Future of Connectivity Although there are many options for both business and home user alike, there are still many innovations yet to gain widespread acceptance. One such innovation is broadband over power lines. **Power line communication,** or broadband over power line, is a system that uses the existing power distribution wires for data transmission. Currently, the data rates are 5 Mbps and increasing every year. Although the technology is promising, as the infrastructure is currently available to virtually all consumers, it has not managed to compete with rapidly advancing DSL or cable offerings. Nevertheless, power line communication is increasingly used within individual households, where consumers can use their power lines to extend their home LANs without additional wiring. So-called HomePlug devices can operate at speeds between 85 and 200 Mbps.

WiMax is another promising innovation. WiMax, or Worldwide Interoperability for Microwave Access, is a standards-based technology that enables the delivery of the "last mile" in wireless form. WiMax is similar to broadband wireless in that it offers high-speed stationary wireless but is different in that it is not a line-of-sight technology. Further, WiMax can also be used for mobile applications. Currently, WiMax is being used primarily by corporate customers and ISPs because of the large investment needed in equipment. However, as equipment becomes less expensive, consumer versions of the technology will become available (see www.clearwire.com).

The Current State of Internet Usage The Internet is now the most prominent global network. Internet World Stats (www.internetworldstats.com) reports that, as of 2010, over 1.8 billion people worldwide use the Internet. This means that over 26 percent of the world's population has Internet access at home, an increase of almost 400 percent since 2000. Most Internet users are found in Asia, but North America has the largest percentage of users (76.2 percent of the North American population have access to the Internet). Africa, on the other hand, has the smallest percentage of its population using the Internet since 2000 (just 8.7 percent) but is experiencing rapid growth (1,810 percent).

One other way to measure the rapid growth of the Internet, in addition to the number of users, is to examine the growth in the number of **Internet hosts**—that is, computers working as servers on the Internet—as shown in Figure TB34.

FIGURE TB34

Growth in Internet servers (hosts).

Source: Based on Internet Systems Consortium. http://www.isc.org/solutions/survey.

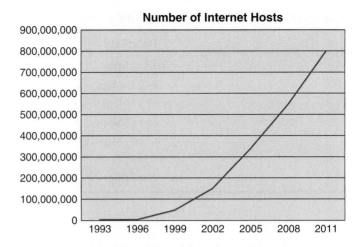

Number of Internet Hosts

Advanced Topics in Database Management

In Chapter 3, you were introduced to foundational database concepts, such as attributes, entities, and relationships. In the following sections, we delve deeper into the topic of database management to give you a better idea of the intricacies involved in designing a sound database.

Database Design

Much of the work of creating an effective organizational database is in the creation of the data model. If the model is not accurate, the database will not be effective. A poor data model will result in data that are inaccurate, redundant, or difficult to search. If the database is relatively small, the effects of a poor design might not be too severe. A corporate database, however, contains many entities, perhaps hundreds or thousands. In this case, the implications of a poor data model can be catastrophic. A poorly organized database is difficult to maintain and process—thus defeating the purpose of having a DBMS in the first place. Undoubtedly, your school maintains databases with a variety of entity types—for example, students and grades—with both of these entities having several attributes. Attributes of a Student entity might be Student ID, Name, Campus Address, Major, and Phone. Attributes of a Grades entity might include Student ID, Course ID, Section Number, Term, and Grade (see Figure TB35).

For the DBMS to distinguish between records correctly, each instance of an entity must have one unique identifier. For example, each student has a unique Student ID. Note that using the

FIGURE TB35

The attributes for and links between two entities—students and grades.

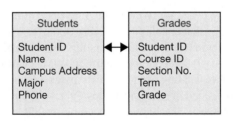

Students

Student ID	Name	Campus Address	Major	Phone
555-39-3232	Joe Jones	123 Any Avenue	Finance	335-2211
289-42-8776	Sally Carter	1200 Wolf Street #12	Marketing	335-8702

Grades

Student ID	Course ID	Section No.	Term	Grade
555-39-3232	MIS 250	2	F'05	D+
555-39-3232	MIS 250	1	F'06	A–
289-42-8776	MIS 250	3	S'07	B+

TABLE TB20 Rules for Expressing Relationships Among Entities and Their Corresponding Data Structures

Relationship	Examples	Instructions
One-to-one	Each team has only one home stadium, and each home stadium has only one team.	Place the primary key from one table (e.g., Stadium) into the other (e.g., Team) as a foreign key.
One-to-many	Each player is on only one team, but each team has many players.	Place the primary key from the table on the "one" side of the relationship (e.g., Team) as a foreign key in the table on the "many" side of the relationship (e.g., Player).
Many-to-Many	Each player participates in many games, and each game has many players.	Create a third table (e.g., Player Statistics) and place the primary keys from each of the original tables (e.g., Player and Team) together in the third as a combination primary key.

student name (or most other attributes) would not be adequate because students may have the exact same name, live at the same address, or have the same phone number. Consequently, when designing a database, we must always create and use a unique identifier, called a **primary key,** for each type of entity, in order to store and retrieve data accurately. In some instances, the primary key can also be a combination of two or more attributes, in which case it is called a **combination primary key.** An example of this is the Grades entity, shown in Figure TB35, where the combination of Student ID, Course ID, Section Number, and Term uniquely refers to the grade of an individual student in a particular class (section number) from a particular term. Attributes not used as the primary key can be referred to as **secondary keys** when they are used to identify one or more records within a table that share a common value. For example, a secondary key in the Student entity shown in Figure TB35 would be Major when used to find all students who share a particular major.

Associations To retrieve information from a database, it is necessary to associate or relate information from separate tables. The three types of **relationships** (or **associations**) among entities are one-to-one, one-to-many, and many-to-many. Table TB20 summarizes each of these three associations and shows how they should be handled in database design for a basketball league.

To understand how relationships work, consider Figure TB36, which shows four tables—Home Stadium, Team, Player, and Games—for keeping track of the information for a basketball league. The Home Stadium table lists the Stadium ID, Stadium Name, Capacity, and Location, with the primary key underlined. The Team table contains two attributes, Team ID and Team Name, but nothing about the stadium where the team plays. If we wanted to have such information, we could gain it only by creating a relationship between the Home Stadium and Team tables. For example, if each team has only one home stadium and each home stadium has only one team, we have a one-to-one relationship between the Team and the Home Stadium entities. In situations in which we have one-to-one relationships between entities, we place the primary key from one table in the table for the other entity and refer to this attribute as a **foreign key.** In other words, a foreign key refers to an attribute that appears as a nonprimary key attribute in one entity and as a primary key attribute (or part of a primary key) in another entity. By sharing this common—but unique—value, entities can be linked, or associated, together. We can choose in which of these

FIGURE TB36

Tables used for storing information about several basketball teams, with no foreign key attributes added; thus, associations cannot be made.

A. One-to-one relationship: Each team has only one home stadium, and each home stadium has only one team.

Team

Team ID	Team Name	Stadium ID

B. One-to-many relationship: Each player is on only one team, but each team has many players.

Player

Player ID	Player Name	Position	Team ID

C. Many-to-many relationship: Each player participates in many games, and each game has many players.

Player Statistics

Team 1	Team 2	Date	Player ID	Points	Minutes	Fouls

tables to place the foreign key of the other. After adding the primary key of the Home Stadium entity to the Team entity, we can identify which stadium is the home for a particular team and find all the details about that stadium (see section A in Figure TB37).

When we find a one-to-many relationship—for example, each player plays for only one team, but each team has many players—we place the primary key from the entity on the "one" side of the relationship, the Team entity, as a foreign key in the table for the entity on the "many" side of the relationship, the Player entity (see section B in Figure TB38). In essence, we take from the one and give to the many, a Robin Hood strategy.

When we find a many-to-many relationship (e.g., each player plays in many games, and each game has many players), we create a third (new) entity—in this case, the Player Statistics entity and corresponding table. We then place the primary keys from each of the original entities together into the third (new) table as a combination primary key (see section C in Figure TB38).

You may have noticed that by placing the primary key from one entity in the table of another entity, we are creating a bit of redundancy. We are repeating the data in different places. We are willing to live with this bit of redundancy, however, because it enables us to keep track of the interrelationships among the many pieces of important organizational data that are stored in different tables. By keeping track of these relationships, we can quickly answer questions such as "Which players on the SuperSonics played in the game on February 16 and scored more than 10 points?" In a business setting, the question might be "Which customers purchased a 2012 Toyota Prius from a salesperson named Jeff at the James Toyota dealership in Pullman, Washington, during the first quarter of 2012, and how much did each customer pay?" This kind of question would be useful in calculating the bonus money Jeff should receive for that quarter or in recalling those specific vehicles in the event of a recall by the manufacturer.

Entity-Relationship Diagramming A diagramming technique that creates an entity-relationship diagram (ERD) is commonly used when designing databases, especially when showing associations between entities. To create an ERD, you draw entities as boxes and draw lines between entities to show relationships. Each relationship can be labeled on the diagram to give it

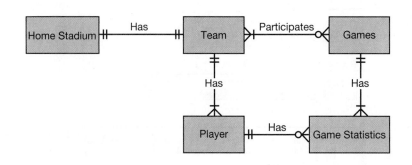

additional meaning. For example, Figure TB38 shows an ERD for the basketball league data previously discussed. From this diagram, you can see the following associations:

- Each Home Stadium has a Team.
- Each Team has Players.
- Each Team participates in Games.
- For each Player and Game, there are Game Statistics.

When you are designing a complex database, with numerous entities and relationships, ERDs are very useful. They allow the designer to talk with people throughout the organization to make sure that all entities and relationships have been found.

The Relational Model Now that we have discussed data, data models, and the storage of data, we need a mechanism for joining entities that have natural relationships with one another. For example, in the University database we described previously, there are several relationships among the four entities students, instructors, classes, and grades. Students are enrolled in multiple classes. Likewise, instructors teach multiple classes and have many students in their classes in a semester. At the end of the semester, instructors assign a grade to each student, and each student earns grades in multiple classes. It is important to keep track of these relationships. We might, for example, want to know which courses a student is enrolled in so that we can notify her instructors that she will miss courses because of an illness. The primary DBMS approach, or model, for keeping track of these relationships among data entities is the relational model. Other models—the hierarchical, network, and object-oriented models—are also used to join entities with commercial DBMSs, but this is beyond the scope of our discussion (see Hoffer, Ramesh, & Topi, 2011).

The most common DBMS approach in use today is the **relational database model.** A DBMS package using this approach is referred to as a relational DBMS. With this approach, the DBMS views and presents entities as two-dimensional tables, with records as rows and attributes as columns. Tables can be joined when there are common columns in the tables. The uniqueness of the primary key, as mentioned earlier, tells the DBMS which records should be joined with others in the corresponding tables. This structure supports very powerful data manipulation capabilities and linking of interrelated data. Database files in the relational model are three-dimensional: a table has rows (one dimension) and columns (a second dimension) and can contain rows of attributes in common with another table (a third dimension). This three-dimensional database is potentially much more powerful and useful than traditional, two-dimensional, "flat-file" databases (see Figure TB39).

A good relational database design eliminates unnecessary data duplications and is easy to maintain. To design a database with clear, nonredundant relationships, you perform a process called normalization.

Normalization To be effective, databases must be efficient. Developed in the 1970s, normalization is a technique to make complex databases more efficient and more easily handled by the DBMS (Hoffer et al., 2011). To understand the normalization process, let us return to the scenario

Department Records

Dept No	Dept Name	Location	Dean
Dept A			
Dept B			
Dept C			

Instructor Records

Instructor No	Inst Name	Title	Salary	Dept No
Inst 1				
Inst 2				
Inst 3				
Inst 4				

FIGURE TB39

With the relational model, we represent these two entities, department and instructor, as two separate tables and capture the relationship between them with a common column in each table.

FIGURE TB40

Database of students, courses, instructors, and grades with redundant data.

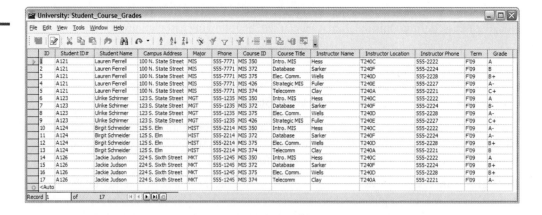

in the beginning of this section. Think about your report card. It looks like nearly any other form or invoice. Your personal information is usually at the top, and each of your classes is listed, along with an instructor, a class day and time, the number of credit hours, and a location. Now think about how this data is stored in a database. Imagine that this database is organized so that in each row of the database, the student's identification number is listed on the far left. To the right of the student ID are the student's name, local address, major, phone number, course and instructor information, and a final course grade (see Figure TB40). Notice that there is redundant data for students, courses, and instructors in each row of this database. This redundancy means that this database is not well organized. If, for example, we want to change the phone number of an instructor who has hundreds of students, we have to change this number hundreds of times. In addition, this redundancy wastes valuable storage space.

Elimination of data redundancy is a major goal and benefit of using data normalization techniques. After the normalization process, the student data is organized into five separate tables (see Figure TB41). This reorganization helps simplify the ongoing use and maintenance of the database and any associated analysis programs.

FIGURE TB41

Organization of information on students, courses, instructors, and grades after normalization.

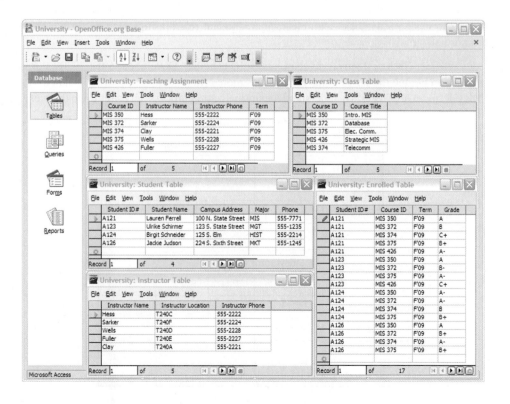

Key Points Review

1. *Discuss foundational IS hardware concepts.* IS hardware is classified into three types: input, processing, and output technologies. Input hardware consists of devices used to enter data into a computer. Processing hardware transforms inputs into outputs. The CPU is the device that performs this transformation, with the help of several other closely related devices that store and recall data. Data is stored on primary and secondary storage devices. Finally, output-related hardware focuses on delivering information in a usable format to users.

2. *Describe foundational topics related to systems and application software as well as the characteristics of various types of programming languages and application development environments.* Systems software, or the operating system, performs many different tasks. Some of these tasks include booting your computer, reading programs into memory, managing memory allocation to those programs, managing where programs and files are located in secondary storage, maintaining the structure of directories and subdirectories, and so on. Application software helps you to be productive with your computer. You can find a large number of computer software applications. For most personal productivity tools, you can find open source alternatives. A programming language is the computer language that programmers use to write application programs. In order to run on a computer, programs must be translated into binary machine language. Programming languages are translated into machine language through special types of programs, called compilers and interpreters. Over the past several decades, programming languages have evolved. Early programmers used machine language to tell the computer exactly which circuits to turn on and which to turn off. Next, symbolic languages used symbols to represent a series of binary statements. This was followed by the development of high-level languages, such as FORTRAN, COBOL, C, and Java. The difference between these high-level languages and earlier languages is that the high-level languages use English-like words and commands, making it easier to write programs. 4GLs are called outcome-oriented languages because they contain even more English-like commands and tend to focus on what output is desired instead of the procedures required to get that output. 5GLs are called natural languages because they allow the user to communicate with the computer using true English sentences. In addition to this generational evolution, object-oriented programming, visual programming, and Web development languages are relatively new enhancements to programming languages. Object-oriented languages group together data and their corresponding instructions into manipulable objects. Visual programming languages use a graphical interface to build graphical interfaces for other programs. Web development languages are a rapidly evolving set of tools designed for constructing Internet applications and Web content. Finally, CASE environments help systems developers construct large-scale systems more rapidly and with higher quality.

3. *Describe network software and hardware, including media access control, network topologies, and protocols, as well as advanced Internet concepts.* From the 1950s until the 1970s, the centralized computing model was dominant, where all processing occurs at a large central computer and users interact with the system through the use of terminals. From the late 1970s until the late 1980s, a distributed computing model was dominant. In this model, separate computers work on subsets of tasks and then pool their results by communicating via a network. In the 1990s, the collaborative computing model emerged, where two or more networked computers work together to accomplish a common processing task. There are several types of computer networks, classified according to their use and distance covered. These include a PAN, PBX, LAN, WLAN, CAN, and WAN. WANs can be further divided into metropolitan area networks, enterprise networks, VANs, and global networks. In networking, a distinction is made between servers, clients, and peers. Networks provide file, print, message, and application services that extend the capabilities of stand-alone computers. The NOS is the major piece of software that controls the network. Networks exchange data by using cable or wireless transmission media. Cable media include twisted pair, coaxial, and fiber-optic. Wireless media include infrared line of sight, high-frequency radio, and microwave. Network access control refers to the rules that govern how a given workstation gains access to the network. There are two general types: distributed and random access. With distributed access, only a single workstation at a time has authorization to transmit its data. Under random access control, any workstation can transmit its data by checking whether the medium is available. The shape of a network can vary; the four most common topologies are star, ring, bus, and mesh configurations. Protocols are agreed-on formats for transmitting data between connected computers. The International Organization for Standardization defined a networking model called the OSI model, which divides computer-to-computer communications into seven connected layers, allowing different networks to be more easily interconnected. Each successively higher layer builds on the functions of the layers below. Ethernet is an important protocol for LANs, whereas TCP/IP is most widely used for the world's largest WAN, the Internet. In a network, each

device or computer must be connected to the medium or cable segment using transmission media connectors, NICs, or modems. Multiple segments of transmission media can be connected to form one large network. A variety of different devices is used to extend the range and size of the network and to interconnect WANs. The Internet is composed of networks that are developed and maintained by many different entities; it follows a hierarchical structure, similar to the interstate highway system. High-speed central networks called backbones are like interstate highways, enabling traffic from midlevel networks to get on and off. Routers are used to interconnect independent networks. A collection of tools enables us to use the Internet in order to exchange messages, share data, or connect to remote computers. The most powerful application of the Internet is the World Wide Web, which binds together the various tools used on the Internet, providing users with a simple, consistent interface to a wide variety of information through the use of Web browsers.

4. *Explain foundational database management concepts.* In order to get the most of their data, organizations have to take care to create an accurate data model. A primary key is used to uniquely identify records in a database. A foreign key is used to link entities together. A useful diagramming technique is entity-relationship diagramming, displaying entities and the associations between them. Normalization is used to reduce redundancy in a database.

Key Terms

Foundational Hardware Key Terms

American Standard Code for Information Interchange (ASCII) 452
audio 451
bar code reader 450
basic input/output system (BIOS) 454
batch data 449
batch processing 450
binary code 452
biometric scanner 000
bit 452
byte 452
bytes per inch 456
cache 454
cathode ray tube 457
CD-R (compact disc—recordable) 456
CD-RW (compact disc—rewritable) 456
characters per inch 456
clock speed 453
clock tick 453
density 456
digital video disc 456
DVD-ROM (digital versatile disc—read-only memory) 456
electronic paper 457
e-paper 457
ergonomic keyboard 449
eye-tracking device 449
graphics tablet 449
head crash 455
interactive voice response 451
joystick 450

liquid crystal display (LCD) 457
magnetic ink character recognition 450
motherboard 453
mouse 449
optical character recognition 450
optical mark recognition 450
organic light-emitting diode 457
port 456
power supply 453
QWERTY keyboard 449
read-only memory (ROM) 454
read/write head 454
redundant array of independent disks (RAID) 454
smart card 450
speech recognition 451
streaming media 452
streaming video 452
system clock 453
text recognition software 450
touch screen 450
trackball 450
video 451
voice-to-text software 451

Foundational Software Key Terms

applet 464
compiler 459
computer-aided software engineering (CASE) 465
executable 459
fifth-generation language (5GL) 461
fourth-generation language (4GL) 460
graphical user interface (GUI) 462

HTML editor 463
HTML tag 463
interpreter 459
Java 464
JavaScript 465
Microsoft.NET 464
object-oriented language 461
scripting language 465
source code 459
utilities 458
utility program 458
visual programming language 462
Web page builder 463

Foundational Networking Key Terms

analog signal 481
application services 472
asymmetric digital subscriber line (ADSL) 485
asynchronous transfer mode (ATM) 487
backbone 474
Bluetooth 471
broadband wireless 486
bus network 479
cable modem 485
carrier sense multiple access (CSMA) 478
cell 475
cellular phone 475
centralized computing 467
collaborative computing 468
connector 481
digital signal 481
digital subscriber line (DSL) 485
distributed computing 468

**Foundational Database
Key Terms**

Review Questions

Foundational Hardware Review Questions

1. IS hardware is classified into what three major types?
2. Describe various methods for entering data into and interacting with a computer.
3. How do computers represent internal information?
4. Describe the system unit and its key components.
5. What determines the speed of a CPU?
6. Compare and contrast the different types of secondary data storage.
7. What are output devices? Describe various methods for providing computer output.

Foundational Software Review Questions

1. Define the term *software* and list several software packages and their uses.
2. Describe at least four different tasks performed by an operating system.
3. Describe the similarities and differences between at least two major operating systems in use today.
4. Name and describe four functions of utility programs.
5. What is HTML, and why is it important?
6. Describe various options for adding dynamic content to a Web page.
7. What is CASE, and how can it help in the development of information systems?
8. What is open source software? Why would business choose to implement open source software?

Foundational Networking Review Questions

1. Compare and contrast centralized, distributed, and collaborative computing.
2. How are LANs, WANs, enterprise networks, and global networks related to each other?
3. What are the major types of network services available?
4. What are three common types of transmission media that use cabling?
5. What are four common methods of wireless transmission media for networking, and how do they differ from each other?
6. What is a network topology? Describe the four common topologies that are used today.
7. What is the purpose of the OSI model?
8. What is the Internet, and why was it created?
9. Other than dial-up, what are three alternatives for connecting to the Internet at home?
10. What organization manages the registration for domain names?

Foundational Database Review Questions

1. Describe why databases have become so important to modern organizations.
2. Explain the difference between a database and a DBMS.
3. List some reasons that record keeping with physical filing systems is less efficient than using a database on a computer.

4. Describe how the following terms are related: entity, attribute, record, and table.

5. Compare and contrast the primary key, combination key, and foreign key within an entity.

6. What is the purpose of a secondary key?

7. What is the purpose of normalization?

8. Explain how organizations are getting the most from their investment in database technologies.

Self-Study Questions

Foundational Hardware Self-Study Questions

1. A system unit contains all the following except _____.

   A. optical drives
   B. CPU
   C. power supply
   D. monitor

2. Which of the following is not an input device?

   A. biometric scanner
   B. touch screen
   C. LCD screen
   D. stylus

3. Which of the following is an output device?

   A. cathode ray tube
   B. scanner
   C. video camera
   D. keyboard

4. _____ can convert handwritten text into computer-based characters.

   A. Scanners
   B. Bar code/optical character readers
   C. Text recognition software
   D. Audio/video

5. A _____ card is a special credit card with a microprocessor chip and memory circuits.

   A. smart
   B. master
   C. universal
   D. proprietary

   Answers are on page 499.

Foundational Software Self-Study Questions

1. An operating system performs which of the following tasks?

   A. booting the computer
   B. managing where programs and files are stored
   C. sending documents to the printer
   D. all of the above

2. What is the name of the programming language developed by Sun Microsystems in the 1990s?

   A. Latte
   B. Java
   C. Mocha
   D. none of the above

3. Which of the following programming languages would most likely *not* be used for building Web applications?

   A. HTML
   B. JavaScript
   C. XML
   D. Fortran

4. A utility program may provide _____.

   A. antivirus protection
   B. file conversion capability
   C. file compression and defragmentation
   D. all of the above

5. 5GLs are also referred to as _____ languages.

   A. assembly
   B. natural
   C. high-level
   D. low-level

   Answers are on page 499.

Foundational Networking Self-Study Questions

1. Which of the following is *not* a type of cable medium?

   A. twisted pair
   B. coaxial
   C. fiber-optic
   D. shielded pair

2. All of the following are common applications of high-frequency radio communication except _____.

   A. pagers
   B. cellular phones
   C. wireless networks
   D. facsimiles

3. Which of the following is the protocol of the Internet, allowing different interconnected networks to communicate using the same language?

   A. Ethernet
   B. C++
   C. TCP/IP
   D. router

4. Which is the fastest connection available for home users?

   A. dial-up
   B. DSL
   C. broadband wireless
   D. FTTH

5. Which of the following is a typical way large corporations connect to the Internet?

A. satellite

B. cable

C. T1 lines

D. all of the above

Answers are on page 499.

Foundational Database Self-Study Questions

1. A(n) _____ is a unique identifier that can be a combination of one or more attributes.

A. secondary key

B. primary key

C. tertiary key

D. elementary key

2. Which of the following is *not* true in regard to the relational database model?

A. Entities are viewed as tables, with records as rows and attributes as columns.

B. Databases use keys and redundant data in different tables in order to link interrelated data.

C. Entities are viewed as children of higher-level attributes.

D. A properly designed table has a unique identifier that may be one or more attributes.

3. Each team has only one home stadium, and each home stadium has only one team. This is an example of which of the following relationships?

A. one-to-one

B. one-to-many

C. many-to-many

D. many-to-one

4. A popular diagramming technique for designing databases is called _____.

A. flowcharting

B. database diagramming

C. entity-relationship diagramming

D. none of the above

5. _____ is a technique to make a complex database more efficient by eliminating redundancy.

A. Extraction, transformation, and loading

B. Associating

C. Normalization

D. Standardization

Answers are on page 499.

Problems and Exercises

Foundational Hardware Problems and Exercises

1. Match the following terms with the appropriate definitions:

i. Smart card

ii. Audio

iii. DVD-ROM

iv. Motherboard

v. Streaming video

a. Sound that has been digitized for storage and replay on the computer

b. A special type of credit card with a magnetic stripe that includes a microprocessor chip and memory circuits

c. An optical storage device that has more storage space than a diskette or CD-ROM disk and uses a shorter-wavelength laser beam, which allows more optical pits to be deposited on the disk

d. A sequence of moving images, sent in a compressed form over the Internet and displayed on the receiver's screen as the images arrive

e. A large printed plastic or fiberglass circuit board that contains all the components that do the actual processing work of the computer and holds or connects to all the computer's electronic components

2. Visit a computer shop or look on the Web for mice or touch pads. What is new about how these input devices look or how they are used? What are some of the advantages and disadvantages of each device?

3. What types of printers are most common today? What is the cost of a color printer versus a black-and-white one? Compare and contrast laser and ink-jet printers in terms of speed, cost, and quality of output. What kind of printer would you buy or have you bought?

4. Based on your experiences with different input devices, which do you like the best and least? Why? Are your preferences due to the devices' design or usability, or are they based on the integration of the device with the entire information system?

5. Choose a few of the computer hardware vendors that sell computers to the general public. These include Dell, HP, Lenovo, Gateway, Apple, and many lesser-known brands. Using each company's home page on the Web, determine what options these vendors provide for input devices, processing devices, and output devices. Does it seem that this company has a broad range of choices for its customers? Is there something that you did not find available from this company? Present your findings in a 10-minute presentation to the rest of the class.

Foundational Software Problems and Exercises

1. Match the following terms with the appropriate definitions:
    i. Applets
    ii. Visual programming languages
    iii. Scripting language
    iv. Interpreter
    v. Compiler
    a. A software program that translates an entire program's source code into machine language that can be read and executed directly by the computer
    b. Programming languages that provide a graphical user interface and are generally easier to use than non-GUI languages
    c. A program designed to be executed within another application (such as a Web page)
    d. A software program that translates a programming language into machine language one statement at a time
    e. Used to supply interactive components to a Web page by building programs or scripts directly into HTML page code

2. What are the implications for an organization of having more than one operating system? What might be the advantages? What are some of the disadvantages? Would you recommend such a situation? Prepare a 10-minute presentation to the rest of the class on your findings.

3. Imagine that you are in charge of procuring software applications for your division of a company. You are in need of a powerful business IS software application that will control most of the accounting and bookkeeping functions. Based on your current knowledge of the intricacies of the accounting profession and its practices, would you be more likely to purchase this application as a customized software application or an off-the-shelf software application? Why did you select this choice? What would make you choose the other option?

4. Based on your own experiences with computers and computer systems, what do you like and dislike about different operating systems that you have used? Were these uses on a professional or a personal level or both? Who made the decision to purchase that particular operating system? Did you have any say in the purchase decision?

5. Imagine that you and a friend are at a local ATM getting some cash from your account to pay for a movie. The ATM does not seem to be working. It is giving you an error message every time you press any button. Is this most likely a software-related problem, a hardware-related problem, or a network-related problem? Why? Use the information in this and other briefings to help you make your decision.

Foundational Networking Problems and Exercises

1. Match the following terms with the appropriate definitions:
    i. Protocols
    ii. Bus network
    iii. FTTH
    iv. T1
    v. Domain name
    a. A dedicated digital transmission line that can carry 1.544 Mbps of information
    b. Used in Uniform Resource Locators to identify a source or host entity on the Internet
    c. High-speed network connectivity to homes and offices that is implemented using fiber-optic cable
    d. A network topology in which all stations are connected to a single open-ended line
    e. The procedures that different computers follow when they transmit and receive data

2. Discuss the difference between PBX networks and LANs. What are the advantages of each? What are possible disadvantages of each? When would you recommend one over the other?

3. Personal area networks using Bluetooth are becoming increasingly popular. Visit www.bluetooth.com and investigate the types of products that this wireless technology is being used to enhance. Find three products that you find interesting and prepare a 10-minute presentation on what these products are and how Bluetooth is enhancing their operation and usage.

4. Describe one of your experiences with a computer network. What type of topology was being used? What was the network operating system? Was the network connected to any other networks? How?

5. Working in a group, have everyone describe what type of network would be most appropriate for a small office with about 10 computers, one printer, and one scanner, all within one floor in one building and relatively close to one another. Be sure to talk about transmission media, network topology, hardware, and software. Did all group members come up with the same option? Why or why not? What else would you need to know to make a good recommendation?

6. Investigate the options for high-speed, broadband Internet access into your home. What options are available to you, and how much do they cost?

7. You have probably experienced several different types of connection—from the university T1 connections to a home DSL or even dial-up connection. If you had to balance between cost and speed, which connection would you choose?

8. Explain in simple language how the Internet works. Be sure to talk about backbones, packet switching, networks, routers, TCP/IP, and Internet services. What technologies, hardware, and software do you utilize when using the Internet? What would you like to use that isn't available to you?

Foundational Database Problems and Exercises

1. Match the following terms with the appropriate definitions:
   i. Primary key
   ii. Foreign key
   iii. Relational database model
   iv. Relationship
   v. Secondary key
   a. Attributes not used as the primary key but can be used to identify one or more records within a table that share a common value
   b. An attribute that appears as a nonprimary key attribute in one entity and as a primary key in another
   c. A field included in a database that ensures that each instance of an entity is stored or retrieved accurately
   d. An association between entities in a database to enable data retrieval
   e. A data management approach in which entities are presented as two-dimensional tables that can be joined together with common columns

2. You see an announcement for a job as a database administrator for a large corporation but are unclear about what this title means. Research this on the Web and obtain a specific job announcement.

3. Why would it matter what data type is used for the attributes within a database? How does this relate to programming? How does this relate to queries and calculations? Does the size of the database matter?

4. Have several classmates interview database administrators within organizations with which they are familiar. To whom do these people report? How many employees report to these people? Is there a big variance in the responsibilities across organizations? Why or why not?

5. Based on your understanding of a primary key and the information in the following sample grades table, determine the best choice of attribute(s) for a primary key.

Student ID	Course	Grade
100013	Visual Programming	A
000117	Telesystems	A
000117	Introduction to MIS	A

6. Search the Web for an organization with a home page that utilizes a link between the home page and the organization's own database. Describe the data that the browser enters and the organization's possible uses for this data. Can you retrieve company information, or can you only send information to the company? How are the data displayed on the home page?

Answers to the Foundational Hardware Self-Study Questions

1. D, p. 452   **2.** C, p. 450   **3.** A, p. 457   **4.** C, p. 450   **5.** A, p. 450

Answers to the Foundational Software Self-Study Questions

1. D, p. 457   **2.** B, p. 464   **3.** D, p. 460   **4.** D, p. 458   **5.** B, p. 461

Answers to the Foundational Networking Self-Study Questions

1. D, p. 473   **2.** D, p. 475   **3.** C, p. 480   **4.** D, p. 486   **5.** C, p. 486

Answers to the Foundational Database Self-Study Questions

1. B, p. 489   **2.** C, p. 491   **3.** A, p. 489   **4.** C, p. 490   **5.** C, p. 491

Acronyms

ADSL: Asymmetric Digital Subscriber Line

AI: Artificial Intelligence

ARPANET: Advanced Research Projects Agency Network

ASCII: American Standard Code for Information Interchange

ATM: Asynchronous Transfer Mode

ATM: Automated Teller Machine

B2B: Business-to-Business

B2C: Business-to-Consumer

B2E: Business-to-Employee

BI: Business Intelligence

BIOS: Basic Input-Output System

BPI: Bytes per Inch

BPM: Business Process Management

BPR: Business Process Reengineering

C2B: Consumer-to-Business

C2C: Consumer-to-Consumer

CAAT: Computer-Assisted Auditing Tools

CAD: Computer-Aided Design

CAE: Computer-Aided Engineering

CAM: Computer-Aided Manufacturing

CAN: Campus Area Network

CAPTCHA: Completely Automated Public Turing Test to Tell Computers and Humans Apart

CASE: Computer-Aided Software Engineering

CD-R: Compact Disc–Recordable

CD-RW: Compact Disc–Rewritable

CIC: Customer Interaction Center

CIO: Chief Information Officer

COBIT: Control Objectives for Information and Related Technology

COPA: Child Online Protection Act

CPI: Characters per Inch

CPU: Central Processing Unit

CRM: Customer Relationship Management

CRT: Cathode Ray Tube

CSF: Critical Success Factor

CSMA: Carrier Sense Multiple Access

CSS: Customer Service and Support

CSU: Channel Service Unit

CVV2: Customer Verification Value

DARPA: Defense Advanced Research Projects Agency

DBA: Database Administrator

DBMS: Database Management System

DNS: Domain Name System

DoS: Denial of Service

DRM: Digital Rights Management

DSL: Digital Subscriber Line

DSS: Decision Support System

DVD-ROM: Digital Versatile Disc–Read-Only Memory

DVD: Digital Video Disc

EC: Electronic Commerce

EDI: Electronic Data Interchange

EEPROM: Electrically Erasable Programmable Read-Only Memory

EMI: Electromagnetic Interference

EMM: Enterprise Marketing Management

EMS: Electronic Meeting System

ERD: Entity-Relationship Diagram

ERP: Enterprise Resource Planning

ES: Expert System

ETL: Extraction, Transformation, and Loading

5GL: Fifth-Generation Language

FLOPS: Floating Point Operations per Second

4GL: Fourth-Generation Language

FTTH: Fiber to the Home

FTTP: Fiber to the Premises

G2B: Government-to-Business

G2C: Government-to-Citizens

G2G: Government-to-Government

GEO: Geosynchronous Earth Orbit

GIS: Geographic Information System

GPS: Global Positioning System

GUI: Graphical User Interface

HCI: Human–Computer Interface

HTML: Hypertext Markup Language

HTTP: Hypertext Transfer Protocol

IaaS: Infrastructure as a Service

ICANN: Internet Corporation for Assigned Names and Numbers

IoS: Internet over Satellite

IOS: Interorganizational System

IP: Internet Protocol

IS: Information System

ISDN: Integrated Services Digital Network

ISP: Internet Service Provider

IT: Information Technology

IVR: Interactive Voice Response

IXC: Interexchange Carrier

JAD: Joint Application Design

KPI: Key Performance Indicator

LAN: Local Area Network

LCD: Liquid Crystal Display

LEO: Low Earth Orbit

MAN: Metropolitan Area Network

MEO: Middle Earth Orbit

MICR: Magnetic Ink Character Recognition

MIS: Management Information System

NAP: Network Access Point

NAT: Network Address Translation

NIC: Network Interface Card

NOS: Network Operating System

NPV: Net Present Value

NSF: National Science Foundation

NSFNET: National Science Foundation Network

OAS: Office Automation System

OCR: Optical Character Recognition

OLAP: Online Analytical Processing

OLPC: One Laptop per Child

OLED: Organic Light-Emitting Diode

OLTP: Online Transaction Processing

OMR: Optical Mark Recognition

OOA&D: Object-Oriented Analysis and Design

OSI: Open Systems Interconnection

P2P: Peer-to-Peer

PaaS: Platform as a Service

PAN: Personal Area Network

PBX: Private Branch Exchange

PC: Personal Computer

PDA: Personal Digital Assistant

PIN: Personal Identification Number

PLC: Power Line Communication

POTS: Plain Old Telephone Service

PSTN: Public Switched Telephone Network

QBE: Query by Example

RAD: Rapid Application Development

RAID: Redundant Array of Independent Disks

RAM: Random Access Memory

RFID: Radio-Frequency Identification

RFP: Request for Proposal

ROM: Read-Only Memory

RSS: Real Simple Syndication

SaaS: Software as a Service

SAD: Systems Analysis and Design

SAM: Software Asset Management

SCE: Supply Chain Execution

SCM: Supply Chain Management

SCP: Supply Chain Planning

SDLC: Systems Development Life Cycle

SDSL: Symmetric Digital Subscriber Line

SEO: Search Engine Optimization

SFA: Sales Force Automation

SLA: Service-Level Agreement

SOA: Service-Oriented Architecture

SOX: Sarbanes-Oxley Act

SQL: Structured Query Language

SSL: Secure Sockets Layer

SSP: Storage Service Provider

TCO: Total Cost of Ownership

TCP/IP: Transmission Control Protocol/Internet Protocol

TP: Twisted Pair

TPS: Transaction Processing System

URL: Uniform Resource Locator

VAN: Value-Added Network

VMI: Vendor Managed Inventory

VoIP: Voice over IP

VPN: Virtual Private Network

Wi-Fi: Wireless Fidelity

WAN: Wide Area Network

WiMax: Worldwide Interoperability for Microwave Access

WLAN: Wireless Local Area Network

WWW: World Wide Web

XBRL: Extensible Business Reporting Language

XML: Extensible Markup Language

Acceptable use policies: Computer and/or Internet usage policies for people within an organization, with clearly spelled-out penalties for noncompliance.

Access-control software: Software for securing information systems that allows only specific users access to specific computers, applications, or data.

Ad hoc query: Request for information created due to unplanned information needs that is typically not saved for later use.

Adaptive maintenance: Making changes to an information system to make its functionality meet changing business needs or to migrate it to a different operating environment.

Advanced Research Projects Agency Network (ARPANET): A wide area network linking various universities and research centers; forerunner of the Internet.

Adware: Free software paid for by advertisements appearing during the use of the software; Adware sometimes contains spyware.

Affiliate marketing: A type of marketing that allows individual Web site owners to earn revenue by posting other companies' ads on their Web pages.

Alpha testing: Testing performed by the development organization to assess whether the entire system meets the design requirements of the users.

"Amateurization" of journalism: Replacement of professional journalism by amateur bloggers.

American Standard Code for Information Interchange (ASCII): Character encoding method based on the English alphabet that provides binary codes to represent symbols.

Analog signal: Audio tones used to transmit data over conventional voice telephone lines.

Analytical CRM: Systems for analyzing customer behavior and perceptions in order to provide business intelligence.

Applet: A program designed to be executed within another application (such as a Web page).

Application services: Provision of software for network clients, enabling computers to share the server's processing power.

Application software: Software used to perform a specific task that the user needs to accomplish.

Artificial intelligence (AI): The science of enabling information technologies to simulate human intelligence as well as gaining sensing capabilities.

Association: *See* Relationship.

Association discovery: A data mining technique used to find associations or correlations among sets of items.

Asymmetric digital subscriber line (ADSL): A variant of DSL offering faster download speeds than upload speeds.

Asynchronous: Not coordinated in time.

Asynchronous transfer mode (ATM): A technology for high-speed transmission of voice, video, and data.

Attribute: Individual piece of information about an entity in a database.

Audio: Analog or digital sound data.

Audit-control software: Software used to keep track of computer activity, enabling auditors to spot suspicious activity.

Authentication: The process of confirming the identity of a user who is attempting to access a restricted system or Web site.

Automating: Using information systems to do an activity faster, cheaper, and perhaps with more accuracy and/or consistency.

Backbone: High-speed central network to which many smaller networks can be connected.

Backup: Copy of critical data on a separate storage medium.

Backup site: A facility allowing businesses to continue functioning in the event a disaster strikes.

Bandwidth: The transmission capacity of a computer or communications channel.

Bar code reader: Specialized scanner used to read bar code data.

Basic input-output system (BIOS): Programs and instructions that are automatically loaded when the computer is turned on.

Batch data: Large amounts of routine data.

Batch processing: The processing of transactions after some quantity of transactions is collected; the transactions are processed together as a "batch" at some later time.

Best practices: Procedures and processes used by business organizations that are widely accepted as being among the most effective and/or efficient.

Best-cost provider strategy: Strategy to offer products or services of reasonably good quality at competitive prices.

Beta testing: Testing performed by actual system users with actual data in their work environment.

Binary code: Digital representation of data and information using sequences of zeros and ones.

Biometric scanner: Input technology used to scan a user's human body characteristics.

Biometrics: Body characteristics such as fingerprints, retinal patterns in the eye, or facial characteristics that allow the unique identification of a person.

Bit: Basic unit of data in computing. Short for "binary digit"; the individual ones and zeros that make up a byte.

Blog: Short for "Web log." Chronological online text diary that can focus on anything the user desires.

Blogging: The creation and maintenance of a blog. Also called "Weblogging."

Blogosphere: The community of all blogs.

Bluetooth: A wireless specification for personal area networking (PAN) of desktop computers, peripheral devices, mobile phones, pagers, portable stereos, and other handheld devices.

Bot: Short for "software robot"; a program that works in the background to provide some service when a specific event occurs.

Bot herder: Computer criminal "owning" a botnet.

Botnet: Collection of zombie computers used for destructive activities or spamming.

Breakeven analysis: A type of cost–benefit analysis to identify at what point (if ever) tangible benefits equal tangible costs.

Brick-and-mortar business strategy: A business approach exclusively utilizing physical locations, such as department stores, business offices, and manufacturing plants, without an online presence.

Bricks-and-clicks business strategy: *See* Click-and-mortar business strategy.

Broadband wireless: Wireless transmission technology with speeds similar to DSL and cable that requires line of sight between the sender and receiver.

Bullwhip effect: Large fluctuations in suppliers' forecasts caused by small fluctuations in demand for the end product and the need to create safety buffers.

Bus network: Network in the shape of an open-ended line.

Business analytics: Applications that augment business intelligence by using predictive analysis to help identify trends or predict business outcomes.

Business continuity plan: A plan describing how a business resumes operation after a disaster.

Business intelligence: The use of information systems to gather and analyze information from both external and internal sources to make better decisions, and the data derived from these processes.

Business model: Summary of a business's strategic direction, outlining how the objectives will be achieved.

Business process management (BPM): A systematic, structured improvement approach by all or part of an organization including a critical examination and redesign of business processes in order to achieve dramatic improvements in one or more performance measures such as quality, cycle time, or cost.

Business process reengineering (BPR): Legacy term for business process management (BPM).

Business processes: Activities organizations perform in order to reach their business goals, consisting of core processes and supporting processes.

Business rules: Policies by which a business runs.

Business/IT alignment: The alignment of information systems with a business's strategy.

Business-to-business (B2B): Electronic commerce between business partners, such as suppliers and intermediaries.

Business-to-business marketplace: A trading exchange operated by a third-party vendor, not associated with a particular buyer or supplier.

Business-to-consumer (B2C): Electronic commerce between businesses and consumers.

Business-to-employee (B2E): Electronic commerce between businesses and their employees.

Buyer agent: Intelligent agent used to find the best price for a particular product a consumer wishes to purchase. Also known as a "shopping bot."

Byte: Unit of data typically containing 8 bits, or about one typed character.

Bytes per inch (BPI): The numbers of bytes that can be stored on one inch of magnetic tape.

Cable modem: A specialized piece of equipment that enables a computer to access Internet service via cable TV lines.

Cache: A small block of special high-speed memory used by processors to store those instructions most recently or most often used (pronounced "cash").

Campus area network (CAN): Type of network spanning multiple buildings, such as a university or business campus.

CAPTCHA: Short for "Completely Automated Public Turing Test to Tell Computers and Humans Apart." A system designed to prevent automated mechanisms from repeatedly attempting to submit forms or gain access to a system. A CAPTCHA requires the user to enter letters or numbers that are presented in the form of a distorted image before submitting an online form.

Carrier sense multiple access (CSMA): A random access control method in which each workstation "listens" to the traffic on the transmission medium to determine whether a message is being transmitted. If no traffic is detected, the workstation sends its message; otherwise, it waits. When a workstation gains access to the medium and sends data onto the network, messages are sent to all workstations on the network; however, only the destination with the proper address is able to "open" the message.

Cathode ray tube (CRT): Display technology similar to a television monitor.

CD-R (compact disc–recordable): A type of optical disk that data can be written to.

CD-RW (compact disc–rewritable): A type of optical disk that be written onto multiple times.

Cell: A geographic area containing a low-powered radio antenna/receiver for transmitting telecommunications signals within that area; monitored and controlled by a central computer.

Cellular phone: Mobile phone technology using a communications system that divides a geographic region into sections called cells.

Central processing unit (CPU): Responsible for performing all the operations of the computer. Also called a microprocessor, processor, or chip.

Centralized computing: A computing model utilizing large centralized computers, called mainframes, to process and store data.

Certificate authority: A trusted middleman between computers that verifies that a Web site is a trusted site and that provides large-scale public-key encryption.

Characters per inch (CPI): The number of characters that can be stored on one inch of magnetic tape.

Classification: A data mining technique grouping instances into predefined categories.

Click fraud: Abuse of pay-per-click advertising models by repeatedly clicking on a link to inflate revenue to the host or increase the costs for the advertiser.

Click-and-mortar business strategy: A business approach utilizing both physical locations and virtual locations. Also referred to as "bricks-and-clicks."

Click-only business strategy: A business approach that exclusively utilizes an online presence. Companies using this strategy are also referred to as virtual companies.

Clickstream data: A recording of the users' path through a Web site.

Click-through rate: The ratio of surfers who click on an ad (i.e., clicks), divided by the number of times it was displayed (i.e., impressions).

Click-wrap license: A type of software license primarily used for downloaded software that requires computer users to click on "I accept" before installing the software.

Client: Any computer, such as a user's workstation or PC on a network, or any software application, such as a word processing application, that requests and uses the services provided by a server.

Clock speed: The speed of the system clock, typically measured in hertz (Hz).

Clock tick: A single pulse of the system clock.

Cloud computing: A computing model where not only the applications but also the data reside in the cloud (i.e., the Internet), to be accessed anytime from anywhere.

Clustering: Data mining technique grouping related records on the basis of having similar attributes.

Cold backup site: A backup facility consisting of an empty warehouse with all the necessary connections for power and communication but nothing else.

Collaboration: Two or more people working together to achieve a common goal.

Collaboration system: Software designed to enable people to communicate, collaborate, and coordinate with each other.

Collaborative computing: A synergistic form of distributed computing in which two or more networked computers are used to accomplish common processing tasks.

Collaborative CRM: Systems for providing effective and efficient communication with the customer from the entire organization.

Collective intelligence: A concept based on the notion that distributed groups of people with a divergent range of information and expertise will be able to outperform the capabilities of individual experts.

Collocation facility: Facility in which businesses can rent space for servers or other information systems equipment.

Combination primary key: A unique identifier consisting of two or more attributes.

Competitive advantage: A firm's ability to do something better, faster, cheaper, or uniquely when compared with rival firms in the market.

Competitive click fraud: A competitor's attempt to inflate an organization's online advertising costs by repeatedly clicking on an advertiser's link.

Competitive intelligence: Information about competitors, used to enhance a business's strategic position.

Compiler: A software program that translates an entire program's source code into machine language that can be read and executed directly by the computer.

Computer crime: The use of a computer to commit an illegal act.

Computer ethics: A broad range of issues and standards of conduct that have emerged through the use and proliferation of information systems.

Computer fluency: The ability to independently learn new technologies as they emerge and assess their impact on one's work and life.

Computer forensics: The use of formal investigative techniques to evaluate digital information for judicial review.

Computer literacy: The knowledge of how to operate a computer.

Computer networking: The sharing of information or services between computers using wireless or cable transmission media.

Computer-aided design (CAD): Software used to create design drawings and three-dimensional models during the product design process.

Computer-aided engineering (CAE): Software used to complement or replace the process of building prototypes during product development.

Computer-aided manufacturing (CAM): The use of information systems to control the production process of a product.

Computer-aided software engineering (CASE): The use of software tools that provide automated support for some portion of the systems development process.

Computer-assisted auditing tool (CAAT): Software used to test information systems controls.

Computer-based information system: A combination of hardware, software, and telecommunication networks that people build and use to collect, create, and distribute data.

Connector: Also called "transmission media connector"; used to terminate a cable in order to plug it into a network interface card or into other network components.

Consumer-to-business (C2B): Consumers selling goods or services to businesses.

Consumer-to-consumer (C2C): A form of electronic commerce that does not involve business firms but enables transactions between consumers.

Content management system: An information system enabling users to publish, edit, version track, and retrieve digital information (or content).

Continuous planning process: A strategic business planning process involving continuous monitoring and adjusting of business processes to enable rapid reaction to changing business conditions.

Control objectives for information and related technology (COBIT): A set of best practices that help organizations to both maximize the benefits from their information systems infrastructure and establish appropriate controls.

Conversion rate: The percentage of visitors to a Web site who perform the desired action.

Cookie: A message passed by a Web server to a Web browser to be stored on a user's computer; this message is then sent back to the server each time the user's browser requests a page from that server.

Copyright: A form of intellectual property, referring to creations of the mind such as music, literature, or software.

Core activities: The activities within a value chain that process inputs and produce outputs, including inbound logistics, operations and manufacturing, outbound logistics, marketing and sales, and customer service.

Corrective maintenance: Making changes to an information system to repair flaws in its design, coding, or implementation.

Cost–benefit analysis: Techniques that contrast the total expected tangible costs versus the tangible benefits for an investment.

Cracker: An individual who breaks into computer systems with the intention of doing damage or committing a crime.

Crowdsourcing: The use of everyday people as cheap labor force, enabled by information technology.

Custom software: Software programs that are designed and developed for a company's specific needs as opposed to being bought off the shelf.

Customer interaction center (CIC): A part of operational CRM that provides a central point of contact for an organization's customers, employing multiple communication channels to support the communication preferences of customers.

Customer portal: Enterprise portal designed to automate the business processes that occur before, during, and after sales have been transacted between a supplier and multiple customers.

Customer relationship management (CRM): A corporate-level strategy designed to create and maintain lasting relationships with customers by concentrating on the downstream information flows through the introduction of reliable systems, processes, and procedures.

Customer service and support (CSS): A part of operational CRM that automates service and information requests, complaints, and product returns.

Customer verification value (CVV2): A three-digit code located on the back of a credit card; used in transactions when the physical card is not present.

Customization: Modifying software so that it better suits user needs.

Cyberbullying: The use of a computer to intentionally cause emotional distress to a person.

Cyberharassment: The use of a computer to communicate obscene, vulgar, or threatening content that causes a reasonable person to endure distress.

Cybersquatting: The dubious practice of registering a domain name, then trying to sell the name to the person, company, or organization most likely to want it.

Cyberstalking: The use of a computer to repeatedly engage in threatening or harassing behavior.

Cyberterrorism: The use of computer and networking technologies against persons or property to intimidate or coerce governments, individuals, or any segment of society to attain political, religious, or ideological goals.

Cyberwar: An organized attempt by a country's military to disrupt or destroy the information and communications systems of another country.

Data: Recorded, unformatted information, such as words and numbers, that often has no meaning in and of itself.

Data cleansing: The process of standardizing the form of data retrieved from different systems and removing inaccurate records.

Data dictionary: A document prepared by database designers to describe the characteristics of all items in a database.

Data flows: Data moving through an organization or within an information system.

Data mart: A data warehouse that is limited in scope and customized for the decision support applications of a particular end-user group.

Data mining: A method used by companies to discover "hidden" predictive relationships in data to better understand their customers, products, markets, or any other phase of their business for which data has been captured.

Data mining agent: An intelligent agent that continuously analyzes large data warehouses to detect changes deemed important by a user, sending a notification when such changes occur.

Data model: A map or diagram that represents the entities of a database and their relationships.

Data reduction: A preparatory step to running data mining algorithms, performed by rolling up a data cube to the smallest level of aggregation needed, reducing the dimensionality, or dividing continuous measures into discrete intervals.

Data type: The type (e.g., text, number, or date) of an attribute in a database.

Data warehouse: An integration of multiple, large databases and other information sources into a single repository or access point that is suitable for direct querying, analysis, or processing.

Database: A collection of related data organized in a way to facilitate data searches.

Database management system (DBMS): A software application used to create, store, organize, and retrieve data from a single database or several databases.

Decision support system (DSS): A special-purpose information system designed to support organizational decision making.

Dedicated grid: A grid computing architecture consisting of homogeneous computers that are dedicated to performing the grid's computing tasks.

Defense Advanced Research Projects Agency (DARPA): The U.S. governmental agency that began to study ways to interconnect networks of various kinds, leading to the development of the ARPANET (Advanced Research Projects Agency Network).

Denial of service (DoS): Attack by crackers—often using zombie computers—that makes a network resource (e.g., Web site) unavailable to users or available with only a poor degree of service.

Density: The storage capacity of magnetic tape; typically expressed in characters per inch (CPI) or bytes per inch (BPI).

Desktop videoconferencing: The use of integrated computer, telephone, video recording, and playback technologies—typically by two people—to remotely interact with each other using their desktop computers.

Destructive agent: Malicious agent designed by spammers and other Internet attackers to farm e-mail addresses off Web sites or deposit spyware on machines.

Developmental testing: Testing performed by programmers to ensure that each module of a new program is error free.

Differentiation strategy: Strategy in which an organization differentiates itself by providing better products or services than its competitors.

Digital dashboard: A display delivering summary information to managers and executives to provide warnings, action notices, and summaries of business conditions.

Digital divide: The gap between those individuals in our society who are computer literate and have access to information resources such as the Internet and those who do not.

Digital rights management (DRM): A technological solution that allows publishers to control their digital media (music, movies, and so on) to discourage, limit, or prevent illegal copying and distribution.

Digital signals: The electrical pulses that computers use to send bits of information.

Digital subscriber line (DSL): A high-speed data transmission method that uses special modulation schemes to fit more data onto traditional copper telephone wires.

Digital video disk: A DVD used for storing movies.

Digitize: To convert analog into digital information, or bits, which can be used by computer-based information systems.

Dimension: A way to summarize data, such as region, time, or product line.

Disaster recovery plan: Organizational plan that spells out detailed procedures for recovering from systems-related disasters, such as virus infections and other disasters that might strike critical information systems.

Discount rate: The rate of return used by an organization to compute the present value of future cash flows.

Discussion forum: An electronic bulletin board that allows for threaded discussions between participants.

Disintermediation: The phenomenon of cutting out the "middleman" in transactions and reaching customers more directly and efficiently.

Disruptive innovation: A new technology, product, or service that eventually surpasses the existing dominant technology, product, or service in a market.

Distributed computing: Using separate computers to work on subsets of tasks and then pooling the results by communicating over a network.

Domain name: Used in Uniform Resource Locators (URLs) to identify a source or host entity on the Internet.

Domain Name System (DNS): A database used to associate Internet host names with their IP addresses.

Domestic company: A company operating solely in its domestic market.

Downsizing: The practice of slashing costs and streamlining operations by laying off employees.

Downstream information flow: Information flow that relates to the information that is produced by a company and sent along to another organization, such as a distributor.

Drill down: To analyze data at more detailed levels of a specific dimension.

Drill-down report: Report that provides details behind the summary values on a key-indicator or exception report.

Drive-by hacking: Computer attack in which an attacker accesses a wireless computer network, intercepts data, uses network services, and/or sends attack instructions without entering the office or organization that owns the network.

DVD-ROM (digital versatile disc—read-only memory): A DVD that can be read but not written to.

E911: Enhanced 911; a part of a federal mandate to improve the effectiveness and reliability of 911 service.

E-auction: Electronic auction.

E-business: Term used to refer to the use of a variety of types of information technologies and systems to support every part of the business.

E-business innovation cycle: A model suggesting that the extent to which modern organizations use information technologies and systems in timely, innovative ways is the key to success.

Economic opportunities: Opportunities that a firm finds for making more money and/or making money in new ways.

Edge computing: The location of relatively small servers close to the end users to save resources in terms of network bandwidth and provide improved access time.

E-government: The use of information systems to provide citizens, organizations, and other governmental agencies with information about and access to public services.

E-information: The use of the Internet to provide electronic brochures and other types of information for customers.

E-integration: The use of the Internet to provide customers with the ability to gain personalized information by querying corporate databases and other information sources.

E-lancing: Self-employed work, similar to freelancing, typically on Internet-related projects.

Electronic bill pay: The use of online banking for bill paying.

Electronic commerce (EC): Exchanges of goods and services via the Internet among and between customers, firms, employees, business partners, suppliers, and so on.

Electronic data interchange (EDI): The digital, or electronic, transmission of business documents and related data between organizations via dedicated telecommunications networks.

Electronic meeting system (EMS): A collection of personal computers networked together with sophisticated software tools to help group members solve problems and make decisions through interactive, electronic idea generation, evaluation, and voting.

Electronic paper: Flexible output medium using microscopic beads that change color in response to small electrical charges.

Embedded system: Microprocessor-based system (such as a digital video recorder [TiVo] or a network router) designed to perform only a specific, predefined task.

Enabling technology: Information technology that enables a firm to accomplish a task or goal or to gain or sustain a competitive advantage in some way.

Encryption: The process of encoding messages or files so that only intended recipients can decipher and understand them.

End-user development: The development, testing, and maintenance of applications by users in an organization.

Enterprise 2.0: The use of Web 2.0 techniques and social software within a company's boundaries or between a company and its customers or stakeholders.

Enterprise license: A type of software license that is usually negotiated and covers all users within an organization. Also known as "volume license."

Enterprise marketing management (EMM): CRM tools used to integrate and analyze marketing campaigns.

Enterprise network: A WAN connecting disparate networks of a single organization into a single network.

Enterprise resource planning (ERP): An information system that integrates business activities across departmental boundaries, including planning, manufacturing, sales, marketing, and so on.

Enterprise system: An information system that spans the entire organization and can be used to integrate business processes, activities, and information across all functional areas of a firm.

Enterprise-wide information systems: *See* Enterprise system.

Entity: Something data is collected about, such as people or classes.

Entity-relationship diagram (ERD): A diagram used to display the structure of data and show associations between entities.

E-paper: Electronic paper.

Ergonomic keyboard: Keyboard resembling a widened V shape that is designed to reduce the stress placed on the wrists, hands, and arms when typing.

ERP core components: The components of an ERP that support the internal activities of an organization for producing products and services.

ERP extended components: The components of an ERP that support the primary external activities of an organization for dealing with suppliers and customers.

E-tailing: Electronic retailing; the online sales of goods and services.

Ethernet: The most widely used local area network protocol, supporting data rates of up to 10 gigabits per second.

E-transaction: The use of the Internet to allow customers to place orders and make payments.

Exception report: Report providing users with information about situations that are out of the normal operating range.

Executable: A program in machine language that can be read and executed directly by the computer.

Executive level: The top level of the organization, where executives focus on long-term strategic issues facing the organization.

Expert system (ES): A special-purpose information system designed to mimic human expertise by manipulating knowledge—understanding acquired through experience and extensive learning—rather than simply information.

Explicit knowledge asset: Knowledge asset that can be documented, archived, and codified.

Extensible Business Reporting Language (XBRL): An XML-based specification for publishing financial information.

Extensible Markup Language (XML): A data presentation standard that allows designers to create customized features that enable data to be more easily shared between applications and organizations.

External acquisition: The process of purchasing an existing information system from an external organization or vendor.

Externally focused system: An information system that coordinates business activities with customers, suppliers, business partners, and others who operate outside an organization's boundaries.

Extraction, transformation, and loading (ETL): The process of consolidating, cleansing, and manipulating data before loading it into a data warehouse.

Extranet: A private Web site used by firms and companies for business-to-business interactions.

Eye-tracking device: A pointing device that uses the movement of someone's eyes to move the pointer.

Fact: *See* Measure.

Fiber to the home (FTTH): *See* Fiber to the premises.

Fiber to the premises (FTTP): High-speed network connectivity to homes and offices that is implemented using fiber-optic cable. Also known as "fiber to the home."

Fifth-generation language (5GL): Computer language using English sentences; developed for application within expert systems and artificial intelligence applications.

File services: Processes used to store, retrieve, and move data files in an efficient manner across a network.

Financial flow: The movement of financial assets throughout the supply chain.

Firewall: Hardware or software designed to keep unauthorized users out of network systems.

First-call resolution: Addressing the customers' issues during the first call.

Flash drive: Portable, removable data storage device using flash memory.

Folksonomy: Categorization system created by Internet users (as opposed to experts).

Foreign key: An attribute that appears as a nonprimary key attribute in one entity and as a primary key attribute (or part of a primary key) in another entity.

Form: A business document that contains some predefined data and may include some areas where additional data is to be filled in, typically for a single record.

Forward auction: A form of e-auctions that allows sellers to post goods and services for sale and buyers to bid on these items.

Fourth-generation language (4GL): Outcome-oriented programming language using English-like sentences.

Freeconomics: The leveraging of digital technologies to provide *free* goods and services to customers as a business strategy for gaining a competitive advantage.

Functional area information system: A cross-organizational-level information system designed to support a specific functional area.

Fuzzy logic: Type of logic used in intelligent systems that allows rules to be represented using approximations or subjective values in order to handle situations where information about a problem is incomplete.

Geographic information system (GIS): A system for creating, storing, analyzing, and managing geographically referenced information.

Geotagging: Adding geospatial metadata (such as latitude, longitude, or altitude) to digital media.

Global business strategy: An international business strategy employed to achieve economies of scale by producing identical products in large quantities for a variety of different markets.

Global information dissemination: The use of the Internet as an inexpensive means for distributing an organization's information.

Global network: Network spanning multiple countries that may include the networks of several organizations. The Internet is an example of a global network.

Globalization: The integration of economies throughout the world, enabled by innovation and technological progress.

Globalization 1.0: The first stage of globalization (fifteenth century through the 1800s), driven primarily by power from horses, wind, and steam. Countries (mainly European) were globalizing, shrinking the world from size large to size medium. Industries changed slowly and the effects of globalization on individuals was barely noticed.

Globalization 2.0: The second stage of globalization (1800–2000), driven by a reduction of transportation and telecommunication costs. Companies (mainly American and European) were globalizing, shrinking the world from size medium to size small. Changes were happening at a fairly slow pace.

Globalization 3.0: The third stage of globalization (starting around 2000), driven by the convergence of the 10 "flatteners." Individuals and small groups from virtually every nation were globalizing, shrinking the world from size small to size tiny. Changes are happening at a faster pace, making people readily feel the effects of industry changes.

Gopher: A text-based, menu-driven interface that enables users to access a large number of varied Internet resources as if they were in folders and menus on their own computers.

Government-to-business (G2B): Electronic commerce that involves a country's government and businesses.

Government-to-citizen (G2C): Online interactions between federal, state, and local governments and their constituents.

Government-to-government (G2G): Electronic interactions that take place between countries or between different levels of government within a country.

Graphical user interface (GUI): Computer interface that enables the user to select pictures, icons, and menus to send instructions to the computer.

Graphics tablet: An input device that simulates the process of drawing or sketching on a piece of paper.

Green computing: Attempts to use computing resources more efficiently, reducing energy needs.

Grid computing: A computing architecture that combines the computing power of a large number of smaller, independent, networked computers (often regular desktop PCs) into a cohesive system in order to solve large-scale computing problems.

Groupware: Software that enables people to work together more effectively.

Hacker: Individual who gains unauthorized access to computer systems.

Hacktivist: Cybercriminal pursuing political, religious, or ideological goals.

Hard data: Facts and numbers that are typically generated by transaction processing systems and management information systems.

Hard drive: A secondary storage device usually located inside the system unit of a computer for storing data. Also called "hard disk."

Hardware: Physical computer equipment, such as the computer monitor, central processing unit, or keyboard.

Head crash: A hard disk failure occurring when the read/write head touches the disk, resulting in the loss of the data and/or the operation of the hard disk.

Home-replication strategy: International business strategy that views the international business as an extension of the home business.

Honeypot: A computer, data, or network site that is designed to be enticing to crackers so as to detect, deflect, or counteract illegal activity.

Hot backup site: A fully equipped backup facility, having everything from hardware, software, and current data to office equipment.

HTML editor: *See* Web page builder.

HTML tag: A command that is inserted into a Web page to specify how the document is to be formatted or used.

Human–computer interface (HCI): The point of contact between an information system and its users.

Hyperlink: Reference or link on a Web page to another document that contains related information.

Hypertext: Text in a Web document that is linked to other text or files.

Hypertext Markup Language (HTML): The standard method of specifying the format of Web pages. Specific content within each Web page is enclosed within codes (called HTML tags) that stipulate how the content should appear to the user.

Hypertext Transfer Protocol (HTTP): The standard regulating how servers process user requests for Web pages.

Identity theft: Stealing another person's Social Security number, credit card number, and other personal information for the purpose of using the victim's credit rating to borrow money, buy merchandise, and run up debts that are never repaid.

Inferencing: The matching of user questions and answers to information in a knowledge base within an expert system in order to make a recommendation.

Informating: The ability of information technology to provide information about the operation within a firm and/or about the underlying work process that the system supports.

Information: Data that has been formatted and/or organized in some way as to be useful to people.

Information accessibility: An ethical issue that focuses on defining what information a person or organization has the right to obtain about others and how this information can be accessed and used.

Information accuracy: An ethical issue concerned with the authenticity and fidelity of information as well as identifying who is responsible for informational errors that harm people.

Information age: A period of time in society when information became a valuable or dominant currency.

Information flow: The movement of information along the supply chain.

Information modification: The intentional change of electronic information by unauthorized users.

Information privacy: An ethical issue that is concerned with what information an individual should have to reveal to others through the course of employment or through other transactions such as online shopping.

Information property: An ethical issue that focuses on who owns information about individuals and how information can be transferred, sold, and exchanged.

Information system (IS): Assumed to mean a computer-based information system; a combination of hardware, software, and telecommunications networks that people build and use to collect, create, and distribute useful data; this term is also used to represent the field in which people develop, use, manage, and study computer-based information systems in organizations.

Information systems audit: An assessment of the state of an organization's information systems controls to determine necessary changes and to help ensure the information systems' availability, confidentiality, and integrity.

Information systems controls: Controls helping to ensure the reliability of information, consisting of policies and their physical implementation, access restrictions, and record keeping of actions and transactions.

Information systems infrastructure: The hardware, software, networks, data, facilities, human resources, and services used by organizations to support their decision making, business processes, and competitive strategy.

Information systems planning: A formal organizational process for identifying and assessing all possible information systems development projects of an organization.

Information systems security: Precautions taken to keep all aspects of information systems safe from unauthorized use or access.

Information systems security plan: An ongoing planning process to secure information systems, involving risk assessment, risk-reduction planning, and plan implementation as well as ongoing monitoring.

Information technology (IT): Machine technology that is controlled by or uses information.

Informational system: System designed to support decision making based on stable point-in-time or historical data.

In-forming: Individuals' use of powerful search engines on the Internet to build their own personal supply chain of information, knowledge, and entertainment.

Infrastructure: The interconnection of various structural elements to support an overall entity, such as an organization, city, or country.

Infrastructure as a service (IaaS): A cloud computing model in which only the basic capabilities of processing, storage, and networking are provided.

Innovator's dilemma: The notion that disruptive innovations can cause established firms or industries to lose market dominance, often leading to failure.

Input technologies: Hardware that is used to enter information into a computer.

In-sourcing: The delegation of a company's logistics operations to a subcontractor that specializes in that operation, or to transferring a previously outsourced function to an in-house department.

Instant messaging: Online chat emulating real-time written conversations.

Intangible benefit: A benefit of using a particular system or technology that is difficult to quantify.

Intangible cost: The cost of using a particular system or technology that is difficult to quantify.

Integrated Services Digital Network (ISDN): A standard for worldwide digital telecommunications that uses existing twisted-pair telephone wires to provide high-speed data service.

Integration: The use of Web technologies to link Web sites to corporate databases to provide real-time access to personalized information.

Intellectual property (IP): Creations of the mind that have commercial value.

Intelligent agent: A program that works in the background to provide some service when a specific event occurs.

Intelligent system: System comprised of sensors, software, and computers embedded in machines and devices that emulate and enhance human capabilities.

Interactive communication: Immediate communication and feedback between a company and its customers using Web technologies.

Interactive voice response (IVR): System using speech recognition technology to guide callers through online surveys or menu options.

Interexchange carrier (IXC): Company selling long-distance services with circuits carrying service between the major telephone exchanges.

Internally focused system: Information system that supports functional areas, business processes, and decision making within an organization.

International business strategy: Set of strategies employed by organizations operating in different global markets.

Internet: A large worldwide collection of networks that use a common protocol to communicate with each other.

Internet backbone: The collection of primary network connections and telecommunications lines making up the Internet.

Internet Corporation for Assigned Names and Numbers (ICANN): A nonprofit corporation that is responsible for managing IP addresses, domain names, and the root server system.

Internet hoax: A false message circulated online about any topic of public interest, typically asking the recipient to perform a certain action.

Internet host: Computer working as a server on the Internet.

Internet over Satellite (IoS): Technology that allows users to access the Internet via satellites that are placed in a geostationary orbit.

Internet service provider (ISP): Individual or organization that enables other individuals and organizations to connect to the Internet.

Internet Tax Freedom Act: An act mandating a moratorium on electronic commerce taxation in order to stimulate electronic commerce.

Internetworking: Connecting host computers and their networks to form even larger networks.

InterNIC: A government–industry collaboration created by the NSF in 1993 to manage directory and database services, domain registration services, and other information services on the Internet.

Interorganizational system (IOS): An information system that communicates across organizational boundaries.

Interpreter: A software program that translates a programming language into machine language one statement at a time.

Intranet: An internal, private network using Web technologies to facilitate the secured transmission of proprietary information within an organization, thereby limiting access to authorized users within the organization.

IP address: A numerical address assigned to every computer and router connected to the Internet, serving as the destination address of that computer or device and enabling the network to route messages to the proper destination.

IP convergence: The use of the Internet protocol for transporting voice, video, fax, and data traffic.

IP datagram: A data packet that conforms to the Internet protocol specification.

IPv6: The latest version of the Internet protocol, also referred to as "IPng" (IP next generation).

Java: An object-oriented programming language developed by Sun Microsystems in the early 1990s that is used primarily for developing Web-based applications.

JavaScript: A scripting language, created by Netscape, that allows developers to add dynamic content to Web sites.

Joint application design (JAD): A special type of a group meeting in which all (or most) users meet with the analyst to jointly define and agree on system requirements or designs.

Joystick: Pointing device that works by moving a small stick that sits in a holder.

Just in time: A method to optimize ordering quantities such that parts or raw material arrive just when they are needed for production.

Key performance indicator (KPI): A metric deemed critical to assessing progress toward a certain organizational goal.

Key-indicator report: Report that provides a summary of critical information on a recurring schedule.

Knowledge: A body of governing procedures, such as guidelines or rules, that are used to organize or manipulate data to make it suitable for a given task.

Knowledge assets: The set of skills, routines, practices, principles, formulas, methods, heuristics, and intuitions (both explicit and tacit) used by organizations to improve efficiency, effectiveness, and profitability.

Knowledge management: The processes an organization uses to gain the greatest value from its knowledge assets.

Knowledge management system: A collection of technology-based tools that include communications technologies and information storage and retrieval systems to enable the generation, storage, sharing, and management of tacit knowledge assets.

Knowledge portal: Specific portal used to share knowledge collected into a repository with employees (often using an intranet), with customers and suppliers (often using an extranet), or the general public (often using the Internet).

Knowledge society: Term coined by Peter Drucker to refer to a society in which education is the cornerstone of society and there is an increase in importance of knowledge workers.

Knowledge worker: Term coined by Peter Drucker to refer to professionals who are relatively well educated and who create, modify, and/or synthesize knowledge as a fundamental part of their jobs.

Layer: In a GIS, related data can be made visible or invisible when viewing a map; each *layer* acts like a transparency that can be turned on or off and provides additional information, such as roads, utilities, ZIP code boundaries, floodplains, and so on.

Learning organization: An organization that is skilled at creating, acquiring, and transferring knowledge and at modifying its behavior to reflect new knowledge and insights.

Legacy system: Older stand-alone computer systems within an organization with older versions of applications that are either fast approaching or beyond the end of their useful life within the organization.

Liquid crystal display (LCD): A type of monitor used for most current notebook and desktop computers.

Local area network (LAN): A computer network that spans a relatively small area, allowing all computer users to connect with each other to share information and peripheral devices, such as printers.

Location-based services: Highly personalized mobile services based on a user's location.

Logic bomb: A type of computer virus that lies in wait for unsuspecting computer users to perform a triggering operation before executing its instructions.

Long tail: The parts of consumer demand that are outside the mainstream tastes (i.e., niche markets).

Low-cost leadership strategy: Strategy to offer the best prices in the industry on goods or services.

Luddite: Person feeling threatened by and protesting against or destroying technology.

Magnetic ink character recognition (MICR): Scanning technology used by the banking industry to read data, account numbers, bank codes, and check numbers on preprinted checks.

Mainframe: A very large computer that is used as the main, central computing system by major corporations and governmental agencies.

Make-to-order process: The processes associated with producing goods based on sales orders.

Make-to-stock process: The processes associated with producing goods based on demand forecasts.

Making the business case: The process of identifying, quantifying, and presenting the value provided by an information system.

Malware: Malicious software, such as viruses, worms, or Trojan horses.

Management information system (MIS): (1) A field of study that encompasses the development, use, management, and study of computer-based information systems in organizations. (2) An information system designed to support the management of organizational functions at the managerial level of the organization.

Managerial level: The middle level of the organization, where functional managers focus on monitoring and controlling operational-level activities and providing information to higher levels of the organization.

Mashup: A new application or Web site created by integrating one or more Web services.

Mass customization: Tailoring products and services to meet particular needs of individual customers on a large scale.

Master data: The data that is deemed most important in the operation of a business.

Master data management: Consolidating master data so as to facilitate arriving at a single version of the truth.

M-commerce: Any electronic transaction or information interaction conducted using a wireless, mobile device and mobile networks that leads to a transfer of real or perceived value in exchange for information, services, or goods.

Measure: The values and numbers a user wants to analyze.

Media access control: The rules that govern how a given node or workstation gains access to a network to send or receive information.

Menu-driven pricing: A pricing system in which companies set and present negotiable prices for products to consumers.

Mesh network: A network that consists of computers and other devices that are either fully or partially connected to each other.

Message services: The storing, accessing, and delivering of text, binary, graphic, digitized video, and audio data across a network.

Metadata: Data about data, describing data in terms of who, where, when, why, and so on.

Metropolitan area network (MAN): A computer network of limited geographic scope, typically a citywide area that combines both LAN and high-speed fiber-optic technologies.

Microblogging: Voicing thoughts through relatively short "status updates" using social presence tools.

Microcomputer: A category of computers that is generally used for personal computing, for small business computing, and as workstations attached to large computers or to other small computers on a network.

Microprocessor: *See* Central processing unit.

Microsoft.NET: A programming platform that is used to develop applications that are highly interoperable across a variety of platforms and devices.

Mirrored: Data stored synchronously on independent systems to achieve redundancy for purposes of reliability and/or performance.

Mobile wireless: Transfer of data to a moving computer or handheld device.

Model: Conceptual, mathematical, logical, and analytical formula used to represent or project business events or trends.

Modem: Short for "modulator-demodulator"; device or program that enables a computer to transmit data over telephone lines.

Module: Component of a software application that can be selected and implemented as needed.

Monitoring and sensing agent: Intelligent agent that keeps track of key information, notifying the user when conditions change.

Moore's Law: The prediction that computer processing performance would double every 18 months.

Motherboard: A large printed plastic or fiberglass circuit board that holds or connects to all the computer's electronic components.

Mouse: Pointing device used to select menu items and drag and drop items.

Multidomestic business strategy: A decentralized international business strategy using a federation of associated business units, employed to be flexible and responsive to needs and demands of heterogeneous local markets.

National Science Foundation (NSF): A United States government agency responsible for promoting science and engineering; the NSF initiated the development of the NSFNET (National Science Foundation Network), which became a major component of the Internet.

National Science Foundation Network (NSFNET): A network developed by the United States in 1986 that became a major component of the Internet.

Nearshoring: The reversal of offshoring; the use of locations closer to the home country in terms of geographical, political, linguistic, economic, or cultural distance.

Neo-Luddite: Person who opposes information systems, fearing negative impacts such as social decay, increased consumerism, or loss of privacy.

Netcast: A digital media stream that can be distributed to and played by digital audio players.

Netcaster: Person publishing a netcast.

Netcasting: The process of publishing netcasts.

Net-present-value analysis: A type of cost–benefit analysis of the cash flow streams associated with an investment.

Network: A group of computers and associated peripheral devices connected by a communication channel capable of sharing data and other resources (e.g., a printer) among users.

Network access point (NAP): Access points used by ISPs to connect to each other.

Network click fraud: A form of click fraud where a site hosting an advertisement creates fake clicks in order to get revenue from the advertiser.

Network effect: The notion that the value of a network (or tool or application based on a network) is dependent on the number of other users.

Network interface card (NIC): An expansion board that plugs into a computer so that it can be connected to a network.

Network operating system (NOS): System software that controls the network and enables computers to communicate with each other.

Network services: Capabilities of networked computers that enable them to share files, print, send and receive messages, and use shared software applications.

Network topology: The shape of a network; the four common network topologies are star, ring, bus, and mesh.

Neural network: An information system that attempts to approximate the functioning of a human brain.

Nonrecurring cost: One-time cost that is not expected to continue after a system is implemented.

Nonvolatile memory: Memory that does not lose its data after power is shut off.

Normalization: A technique for making complex databases more efficient and more easily handled by a database management system.

Object-oriented language: Programming language that groups together data and its corresponding instructions into manipulable objects.

Office automation system (OAS): A collection of software and hardware for developing documents, scheduling resources, and communicating.

Offshore outsourcing: Outsourcing of business processes on a global scale.

Offshoring: Having certain business functions performed by the same company but in a different country.

Off-the-shelf system: Software designed and used to support general business processes that does not require any specific tailoring to meet an organization's needs.

OLAP cube: A data structure allowing for multiple dimensions to be added to a traditional two-dimensional table for detailed analysis.

OLAP server: The chief component of an OLAP system that understands how data is organized in the database and has special functions for analyzing the data.

One Laptop per Child (OLPC): An initiative to distribute very low-cost laptop computers to children in developing countries around the world.

Online analytical processing (OLAP): The process of quickly conducting complex analyses of data stored in a database, typically using graphical software tools.

Online banking: The use of the Internet to conduct financial transactions.

Online investing: The use of the Internet to obtain information about stock quotes and manage financial portfolios.

Online predator: Cybercriminal using the Internet to target vulnerable people, usually the young or old, for sexual or financial purposes.

Online transaction processing (OLTP): Immediate automated responses to the requests from multiple concurrent transactions from customers.

Open source software: Software for which the source code is freely available for use and/or modification.

Open systems interconnection (OSI) model: A protocol that represents a group of specific communication tasks as successive layers.

Operating system: Software that coordinates the interaction between hardware devices, peripherals, application software, and users.

Operational CRM: Systems for automating the fundamental business processes—marketing, sales, and support—for interacting with the customer.

Operational level: The bottom level of an organization, where the routine, day-to-day business processes and interaction with customers occur.

Operational systems: The systems that are used to interact with customers and run a business in real time.

Optical character recognition (OCR): Scanning technology used to read and digitize typewritten, computer-printed, or hand-printed characters.

Optical disk: A storage disk coated with a metallic substance that is written to (or read from) when a laser beam passes over the surface of the disk.

Optical mark recognition (OMR): Scanning technology used to scan questionnaires and test answer forms ("bubble sheets") where answer choices are marked by filling in circles using pencil or pen.

Order-to-cash process: The processes associated with selling a product or service.

Organic light-emitting diode (OLED): Display technology using less power than LCD technology.

Organizational learning: The ability of an organization to learn from past behavior and information, improving as a result.

Organizational strategy: A firm's plan to accomplish its mission and goals as well as to gain or sustain competitive advantage over rivals.

Output technologies: Hardware devices that deliver information in a usable form.

Outsourcing: The moving of routine jobs and/or tasks to people in another firm to reduce costs.

Packaged application: Software program written by a third-party vendor for the needs of many different users and organizations.

Packet switching: The process of breaking information into small chunks called data packets and then managing the transfer of those packets from computer to computer via the Internet.

Paid inclusion: Inclusion of a Web site in a search engine's listing after payment of a fee.

Patch management system: An online system that utilizes Web services to automatically check for software updates, downloading and installing these "patches" as they are made available.

Patent: Type of intellectual property typically referring to process, machine, or material inventions.

Patriot hacker: Independent citizens or supporters of a country that perpetrate computer attacks on perceived or real enemies.

Pay-per-click: A payment model used in online advertising where the advertiser pays the Web site owner a fee for visitors visiting a certain link.

Peer: Any computer that may both request and provide services.

Peer production: The creation of goods or services by self-organizing communities.

Peer-to-peer networks: Networks that enable any computer or device on the network to provide and request services.

Perfective maintenance: Making enhancements to improve processing performance, to improve interface usability, or to add desired but not necessarily required system features.

Personal area network (PAN): A wireless network used to exchange data between computing devices using short-range radio communication, typically within an area of 10 meters.

Phishing: Attempts to trick financial account and credit card holders into giving away their authorization information, usually by sending spam messages to literally millions of e-mail accounts. Also known as "spoofing."

Plain old telephone service (POTS): Standard telephone lines with a speed, or bandwidth, that is generally about 52 Kbps (52,000 bits per second); also called "public switched telephone network (PSTN)."

Planned obsolescence: The design of a product so that it lasts for only a certain life span.

Platform as a service (PaaS): A cloud computing model in which the customer can run his or her own applications that are typically designed using tools provided by the service provider but has limited or no control over the underlying infrastructure.

Podcast: *See* Netcast.

Podcasting: *See* Netcasting.

Port: A hardware interface by which a computer communicates with another device or system.

Portal: Access point (or front door) through which a business partner accesses secured, proprietary information from an organization (typically using extranets).

Power line communication (PLC): A connectivity technology that uses existing power distribution wires for data transmission. Also referred to as "power line telecoms (PLTs)."

Power supply: A device that converts electricity from the wall socket to a lower voltage appropriate for computer components and regulates the voltage to eliminate surges common in most electrical systems.

Predictive analysis: Business analysis techniques focusing on identifying trends or predicting business outcomes.

Preventive maintenance: Making changes to a system to reduce the chance of future system failure.

Primary key: A field included in a database that contains a unique value for each instance of an entity to ensure that it is stored or retrieved accurately.

Primary storage: Temporary storage for current calculations.

Print services: Network applications used to control and manage users' access to network printers and fax equipment.

Private branch exchange (PBX): A telephone system that serves a particular location, such as a business, connecting one telephone extension to another within the system and connecting the internal extensions to the outside telephone network.

Private cloud: Cloud infrastructure that is internal to an organization.

Processing logic: The steps by which data is transformed or moved as well as a description of the events that trigger these steps.

Processing technologies: Computer hardware that transforms inputs into outputs.

Procure-to-pay process: The processes associated with procuring goods from external vendors.

Product flow: The movement of goods from the supplier to production, from production to distribution, and from distribution to the consumer.

Productivity paradox: The observation that productivity increases at a rate that is lower than expected when new technologies are introduced.

Project manager: The person most responsible for ensuring that a project is a success.

Propagation delay: The delay in the transmission of a satellite signal because of the distance the signal must travel.

Protocols: Procedures that different computers follow when they transmit and receive data.

Prototyping: An iterative systems development process in which requirements are converted into a working system that is continually revised through close work between analysts and users.

Proxy variable: Alternative measurement of outcomes, used when it is difficult to determine and measure direct effects.

Pseudocode: A way to express processing logic independent of the actual programming language being used.

Public cloud: Cloud infrastructure offered on a commercial basis by a cloud service provider.

Public switched telephone network (PSTN): *See* Plain old telephone service (POTS).

Query: Method used to retrieve information from a database.

Query by example (QBE): A capability of a DBMS that enables data to be requested by providing a sample or a description of the types of data the user would like to see.

QWERTY keyboard: The default keyboard layout for entering numbers and letters (QWERTY stands for how the letters are arranged on the keyboard, with Q-W-E-R-T-Y being the first six letters going from left to right on the keyboard).

Radio-frequency identification (RFID): The use of the electromagnetic energy to transmit information between a reader (transceiver) and a processing device, used to replace bar codes and bar code readers.

Random-access memory (RAM): A type of primary storage that is volatile and can be accessed randomly by the CPU.

Read-only memory (ROM): A type of nonvolatile primary storage that is used to store programs and instructions that are automatically loaded when the computer is turned on.

Read/write head: Components that inscribe data to or retrieve data from hard disks, diskettes, and tapes.

Real Simple Syndication (RSS): A set of standards for sharing updated Web content, such as news and sports scores, across sites.

Record: A collection of related attributes about a single entity.

Recovery point objective: Objective specifying how timely backup data should be preserved.

Recovery time objective: Objective specifying the maximum time allowed to recover from a catastrophic event.

Recurring cost: Ongoing cost that occurs throughout the life cycle of systems development, implementation, and maintenance.

Redundant array of independent disks (RAID): A secondary storage technology that makes redundant copies of data on two or more hard drives.

Reintermediation: The design of business models that reintroduce middlemen in order to reduce the chaos brought on by disintermediation.

Relational database model: The most common DBMS approach in which entities are presented as two-dimensional tables, with records as rows and attributes as columns.

Relationship: An association between entities in a database to enable data retrieval.

Report: A compilation of data from a database that is organized and produced in printed format.

Report generator: Software tool that helps users build reports quickly and describe the data in a useful format.

Request for proposal (RFP): A communication tool indicating buyer requirements for a given system and requesting information or soliciting bids from potential vendors.

Requirements collection: The process of gathering and organizing information from users, managers, customers, business processes, and documents to understand how a proposed information system should function.

Revenue model: Part of a business model that describes how the organization will earn revenue, generate profits, and produce a superior return on invested capital.

Reverse auction: A type of auction in which buyers post a request for proposal (RFP) and sellers respond with bids.

Reverse engineering: Disassembling a piece of software in order to understand its functioning.

Reverse pricing system: A pricing system in which customers specify the product they are looking for and how much they are willing to pay; this information is routed to appropriate companies who either accept or reject this offer.

RFID tag: The processing device used in an RFID system that uniquely identifies an object.

Ring network: A network that is configured in the shape of a closed loop or circle, with each node connecting to the next node.

Risk acceptance: A computer system security policy in which no countermeasures are adopted and any damages that occur are simply absorbed.

Risk analysis: The process in which the value of the assets being protected are assessed, the likelihood of their being compromised is determined, and the costs of their being compromised are compared with the costs of the protections to be taken.

Risk reduction: The process of taking active countermeasures to protect information systems.

Risk transference: A computer system security policy in which someone else absorbs the risk, as with insurance.

Roll up: To analyze data at less detailed levels of a certain dimension.

Router: An intelligent device used to connect and route data traffic across two or more individual networks.

Rule: A way of encoding knowledge, typically expressed using an "if–then" format, within an expert system.

Sales force automation (SFA): CRM systems to support the day-to-day sales activities of an organization.

Sarbanes-Oxley Act: Government regulation formed as a reaction to large-scale accounting scandals which led to the downfall of large corporations that includes the use of information systems controls in compliance reviews.

Scalability: The ability to adapt to increases or decreases in demand for processing or data storage.

Scheduled report: Report produced at predefined intervals—daily, weekly, or monthly—to support the routine informational needs of managerial-level decision making.

Scripting language: A programming technique for integrating interactive components into a Web page.

Search advertising: Attempting to ensure that a company's Web site is the first site a user sees when searching for a specific term.

Search engine optimization (SEO): Methods for improving a site's ranking in search engine results.

Secondary key: Attribute that can be used to identify one or more records within a table that share a common value.

Secondary storage: Methods for permanently storing data to a large-capacity storage component, such as a hard disk, diskette, CD-ROM disk, or tape.

Secure Sockets Layer (SSL): A popular public-key encryption method used on the Internet.

Semantic web: A set of design principles that will allow computers to be able to index Web sites, topics, and subjects, enabling computers to read Web pages and search engines to give richer and more accurate answers.

Semistructured decisions: Decisions where problems and solutions are not clear-cut and often require judgment and expertise.

Sequence discovery: Data mining technique used to discover associations over time.

Server: Any computer on the network that enables access to files, databases, communications, and other services available to users of the network; it typically has a more advanced microprocessor, more memory, a larger cache, and more disk storage than a single-user computer.

Server-centric network: Network in which servers and clients have defined roles.

Service: Individual software component designed to perform a specific task.

Service mentality: The belief among information systems personnel that their chief goal is satisfying their systems customers within the firm while fundamentally believing that the customers, not the systems personnel, own the technology and the information.

Service-level agreement: Contract specifying the level of service provided in terms of performance (e.g., as measured by uptime), warranties, disaster recovery, and so on.

Service-oriented architecture (SOA): A software architecture in which business processes are broken down into individual components (or services) that are designed to achieve the desired results for the service consumer (which can be either an application, another service, or a person).

Shopping bot: *See* Buyer agent.

Shrink-wrap license: A type of software license that is used primarily for consumer products; the contract is activated when the shrink wrap on the packaging has been removed.

Slicing and dicing: Analyzing data on subsets of certain dimensions.

Smart card: Special credit card–sized card containing a microprocessor chip, memory circuits, and often a magnetic stripe.

Social bookmarking: The sharing and categorization of Internet bookmarks by Internet users.

Social cataloging: The creation of categorizations by Internet users.

Social media: *See* Social software.

Social network analysis: A technique that attempts to find groups of people who work together, to find people who don't collaborate but should, or to find experts in particular subject areas.

Social networking: Connecting to colleagues, family members, or friends for business or entertainment purposes.

Social online community: A community within a social network.

Social presence tools: Tools enabling people to voice thoughts through relatively short "status updates."

Social search: Search functionality that attempts to provide relevant search results by including content from social networks, blogs, or microblogging services.

Social software: Web 2.0 applications allowing people to communicate, interact, and collaborate in various ways.

Soft data: Textual news stories or other nonanalytical information.

Software: A program or set of programs that tell the computer to perform certain processing functions.

Software as a service (SaaS): A cloud computing model in which a service provider offers applications via a cloud infrastructure.

Software asset management (SAM): A set of activities performed to better manage an organization's software infrastructure by helping to consolidate and standardize software titles, decide to retire unused software, or decide when to upgrade or replace software.

Software piracy: A type of computer crime where individuals make illegal copies of software protected by copyright laws.

Source code: A computer program's code written in a programming language.

Spam: Electronic junk mail.

Spam filter: Hardware or software device used to fight spam and other e-mail threats, such as directory harvest attacks, phishing attacks, viruses, and more.

Speech recognition: The process of converting spoken words into commands and data.

Spim: Spam sent via instant messaging.

Sponsored search: *See* Search advertising.

Spyware: Software that covertly gathers information about a user through an Internet connection without the user's knowledge.

Stand-alone application: A system that focuses on the specific needs of an individual department and is not designed to communicate with other systems in the organization.

Star network: A network with several workstations connected to a central hub.

Stickiness: A Web site's ability to attract and keep visitors.

Strategic: A way of thinking in which plans are made to accomplish specific goals.

Strategic necessity: Something an organization must do in order to survive.

Strategic planning: The process of forming a vision of where the organization needs to head, converting that vision into measurable objectives and performance targets, and crafting a plan to achieve the desired results.

Streaming media: Audio or video that can be sent over the Internet and is played/displayed as it arrives on the receiver's computer; developed so that Web users do not have to wait for an entire file to be downloaded before seeing a video or hearing sound.

Streaming video: A sequence of compressed moving images that can be sent over the Internet.

Structured decisions: Decisions where the procedures to follow for a given situation can be specified in advance.

Structured Query Language (SQL): The most common language used to interface with databases.

Supercomputer: The most expensive and most powerful category of computers. It is primarily used to assist in solving massive research and scientific problems.

Supplier portal: A subset of an organization's extranet designed to automate the business processes that occur before, during, and after sales have been transacted between a single buyer and multiple suppliers. Also referred to as a "sourcing portal" or "procurement portal."

Supply chain: The collection of companies and processes involved in moving a product from the suppliers of raw materials, to the suppliers of intermediate components, to final production, and, ultimately, to the customer.

Supply chain analytics: The use of key performance indicators to monitor performance of the entire supply chain, including sourcing, planning, production, and distribution.

Supply chain effectiveness: The extent to which a company's supply chain is focusing on maximizing customer service, regardless of procurement, production, and transportation costs.

Supply chain efficiency: The extent to which a company's supply chain is focusing on minimizing procurement, production, and transportation costs, sometimes by reducing customer service.

Supply chain execution (SCE): The execution of supply chain planning involving the management of product flows, information flows, and financial flows.

Supply chain management (SCM): Information systems focusing on improving upstream information flows with two main objectives—to accelerate product development and to reduce costs associated with procuring raw materials, components, and services from suppliers.

Supply chain planning (SCP): The process of developing various resource plans to support the efficient and effective production of goods and services.

Supply chain visibility: The ability to track products as they move through the supply chain and to foresee external events.

Supply network: The network of multiple (sometimes interrelated) producers of supplies that a company uses.

Support activities: Business activities that enable the primary activities to take place. Support activities include administrative activities, infrastructure, human resources, technology development, and procurement.

Switch: Device used to connect multiple computers, servers, or printers to create a network.

Symmetric digital subscriber line (SDSL): A variant of DSL that supports the same data rates for upstream and downstream traffic.

Synchronous: Coordinated in time.

System clock: An electronic circuit inside a computer that generates pulses at a rapid rate for setting the pace of processing events.

System conversion: The process of decommissioning the current system and installing a new system into the organization.

System effectiveness: The extent to which a system enables people and/or the firm to accomplish goals or tasks well.

System efficiency: The extent to which a system enables people and/or a firm to do things faster, at lower cost, or with relatively little time and effort.

Systems analysis: The second phase of the systems development life cycle in which the current ways of doing business are studied and alternative replacement systems are proposed.

Systems analysis and design: The process of designing, building, and maintaining information systems.

Systems analyst: The primary person responsible for performing systems analysis and design activities.

Systems benchmarking: A standardized set of performance tests designed to facilitate comparison between systems.

Systems design: The third phase of the systems development life cycle in which details of the chosen approach are developed.

Systems development life cycle (SDLC): A model describing the life of an information system from conception to retirement.

Systems implementation: The fourth phase of the systems development life cycle in which the information system is programmed, tested, installed, and supported.

Systems integration: Connecting separate information systems and data to improve business processes and decision making.

Systems maintenance: The process of systematically repairing and/or improving an information system.

Systems planning and selection: The first phase of the systems development life cycle in which potential projects are identified, selected, and planned.

Systems software: The collection of programs that controls the basic operations of computer hardware.

T1 line: A dedicated digital transmission line that can carry 1.544 Mbps of information.

T3 line: A digital transmission line that provides about 45 Mbps of information at about 10 times the cost of leasing a T1 line.

Table: A collection of related records in a database where each row is a record and each column is an attribute.

Tacit knowledge assets: Knowledge assets that reflect the processes and procedures located in employees' minds.

Tag cloud: A way to visualize user generated tags or content on a site, where the size of a word represents its importance or frequency.

Tagging: Adding metadata to media or other content.

Tangible benefit: A benefit of using a particular system or technology that is quantifiable.

Tangible cost: A cost of using a particular system of technology that is quantifiable.

Telecommunications network: A group of two or more computer systems linked together with communications equipment.

Terminal: Local input device used to enter data onto mainframes in centralized computing systems.

Text mining: Analytical techniques for extracting information from textual documents.

Text recognition software: Software designed to convert handwritten text into computer-based characters.

Time bomb: A type of computer virus that lies in wait for a specific date before executing its instructions.

Token passing: An access method that uses a constantly circulating electronic token (a small packet of data) to prevent collisions and give all workstations equal access to the network.

Top-level domains: The highest level of Internet domain names in the domain name system, as indicated by their suffix (i.e., .com, .edu, or .org).

Total cost of ownership (TCO): The cost of owning and operating a system, including the total cost of acquisition, as well as all costs associated with its ongoing use and maintenance.

Touch screen: Pointing device using a touch-sensitive computer display.

Trackball: Pointing device that works by rolling a ball that sits in a holder.

Transaction processing system (TPS): An information system designed to process day-to-day business-event data at the operational level of the organization.

Transaction support: Utilizing the Web to provide automatic support to clients and firms for conducting business online without human assistance.

Transmission Control Protocol/Internet Protocol (TCP/IP): The protocol of the Internet, which allows different interconnected networks to communicate using the same language.

Transmission media: The physical pathways to send data and information between two or more entities on a network.

Transnational business strategy: An international business strategy that allows companies to leverage the flexibility offered by a decentralized organization (to be more responsive to local conditions) while at the same time reaping economies of scale enjoyed by centralization; characterized by a balance between centralization and decentralization and interdependent resources.

Trojan horse: Destructive computer code whose instructions remain hidden to the user because the computer appears to function normally but, in fact, is performing underlying functions dictated by the intrusive code.

Tunneling: A technology used by VPNs to encapsulate, encrypt, and securely transmit data over the public Internet infrastructure, enabling business partners to exchange information in a secured, private manner between organizational networks.

Unauthorized access: An information systems security breach where an unauthorized individual sees, manipulates, or otherwise handles electronically stored information.

Uniform Resource Locator (URL): The unique Internet address for a Web site and specific Web pages within sites.

Unstructured decisions: Decisions where few or no procedures to follow for a given situation can be specified in advance.

Uploading: The ability of individuals and companies to actively participate in content generation on the Web.

Upstream information flow: An information flow consisting of information received from another organization, such as from a supplier.

User agent: Intelligent agent that automatically performs specific tasks for a user, such as automatically sending a report at the first of the month, assembling customized news, or filling out a Web form with routine information.

Utilities: *See* Utility programs.

Utility computing: A form of on-demand computing where resources in terms of processing, data storage, or networking are rented on an as-needed basis. The organization only pays for the services used.

Utility programs: Software designed to manage computer resources and files.

Value chain: The set of primary and support activities in an organization where value is added to a product or service.

Value chain analysis: The process of analyzing an organization's activities to determine where value is added to products and/or services and the costs that are incurred for doing so.

Value proposition: What a business provides to a customer and what that customer is willing to pay for that product or service.

Value system: A collection of interlocking company value chains.

Value-added networks (VANs): Private, third-party–managed WANs that are shared by multiple organizations and include leased communication lines, e-mail services, EDI, security, and other special capabilities.

Vanilla version: The features and modules that a packaged software system comes with out of the box.

Vendor-managed inventory (VMI): A business model in which the suppliers to a manufacturer (or retailer) manage the manufacturer's (or retailer's) inventory levels based on preestablished service levels.

Vertical market: A market comprised of firms within a specific industry sector.

Video: Still and moving images that can be recorded, manipulated, and displayed on a computer.

Videoconferencing over IP: The use of Internet technologies for videoconferences.

Viral marketing: Type of marketing that resembles offline word-of-mouth communication in which advertising messages are spread similar to how real viruses are transmitted through offline social networks.

Virtual company: *See* Click-only business strategy.

Virtual machine: A computer that does not exist as a physical machine but is implemented in software, allowing multiple computers to be run on a single server.

Virtual meeting: A meeting taking place using an online environment.

Virtual private network (VPN): A network connection that is constructed dynamically within an existing network—often called a "secure tunnel"—in order to securely connect remote users or nodes to an organization's network.

Virtual team: Work team that is composed of members that may be from different organizations and different locations that form and disband as needed.

Virtual world: Online environment allowing people to communicate synchronously using 3D avatars.

Virtualization: The use of multiple virtual machines (run on large servers) to reduce energy needs.

Virus: Destructive program that disrupts the normal functioning of computer systems.

Virus prevention: Set of activities designed to detect and prevent computer viruses.

Visual analytics: The combination of various analysis techniques and interactive visualizations to solve complex problems.

Visual programming language: Programming language that has a graphical user interface (GUI) for the programmer and is designed for programming applications that will have a GUI.

Visualization: The display of complex data relationships using a variety of graphical methods.

Voice over IP (VoIP): The use of Internet technologies for placing telephone calls.

Voice-to-text software: An application that uses a microphone to monitor a person's speech and then converts the speech into text.

Volatile memory: Memory that loses its contents when the power is turned off.

Warez: Slang term for stolen proprietary software that is sold or shared for free over the Internet.

Watermark: A digital or physical mark that is difficult to reproduce, used to prevent counterfeiting or to trace illegal copies to the original purchaser.

Web 2.0: Term used to describe dynamic Web applications that allow people to collaborate and share information online.

Web 3.0: The next wave of the Internet using technologies providing for ubiquitous data access where the data is viewed as being in a "cloud" and applications that access this data can be run on any device, PC, or mobile phone.

Web analytics: The analysis of Web surfers' behavior in order to improve a site's performance.

Web browser: A software application that can be used to locate and display Web pages including text, graphics, and multimedia content.

Webcam: A small camera that is used to transmit real-time video images within desktop videoconferencing systems.

Web content mining: Extracting textual information from Web documents.

Web crawler: Intelligent agent that continuously browses the Web for specific information (e.g., used by search engines). Also known as "Web spider."

Web page: A hypertext document stored on a Web server that contains not only information but also references or links to other documents that contain related information.

Web page builder: Program for assisting in the creation and maintenance of Web pages.

Web server: A computer used to host Web sites.

Web service: Component that allows data to be accessed without intimate knowledge of other organizations' systems, enabling machine-to-machine interaction over the Internet.

Web site: A collection of interlinked Web pages typically belonging to the same person or business organization.

Web spider: *See* Web crawler.

Web usage mining: Analysis of a Web site's usage patterns, such as navigational paths or time spent.

Web vandalism: The act of defacing Web sites.

Web-based collaboration tools: Tools enabling teams to collaborate on projects using the Internet.

Weighted multicriteria analysis: Method for deciding among different information systems investments or alternative designs for a given system in which requirements and constraints are weighted on the basis of their importance.

What-if analysis: An analysis of the effects hypothetical changes to data have on the results.

Wide area network (WAN): A computer network that spans a relatively large geographic area; typically used to connect two or more LANs.

Widget: Small interactive tool used for a single purpose such as taking notes, viewing pictures, or simply displaying a clock.

Wi-Fi network (wireless fidelity): Wireless LAN, based on the 802.11 family of standards.

Wiki: Web site allowing people to post, edit, comment, and access information. In contrast to a regular Web site, a wiki is linked to a database that keeps a history of all prior versions and changes; therefore, a wiki allows viewing prior versions of the site as well as reversing any changes made to the content.

Wikipedia: Online encyclopedia using wiki technology.

WiMax: Short for Worldwide Interoperability for Microwave Access (IEEE 802.16). High-speed wireless transmission technology that can be used for stationary and mobile applications and does not require a line of sight.

Wireless access point: Networking device that transmits and receives wireless (Wi-Fi) signals to allow wireless devices to connect to the network.

Wireless controller: Networking device that manages multiple access points and can be used to manage transmission power and channel allocation to establish desired coverage throughout a building and minimize interference between individual access points.

Wireless local area network (WLAN): Local area network using a wireless transmission protocol.

Work flow software: Software applications that allow people worldwide to communicate.

Workstation: Computers offering lower performance than mainframes but higher performance than microcomputers that are designed for medical, engineering, or animation and graphics design uses, and are optimized for visualization and rendering of three-dimensional models..

World Wide Web (WWW): A system of Internet servers that support documents formatted in HTML, which supports links to other documents, as well as graphics, audio, and video files.

Worm: Destructive computer code that is designed to copy and send itself throughout networked computers.

XML tag: A command that is inserted in a document in order to specify how information should be interpreted and used.

Zombie computer: Virus-infected computer that can be used to launch attacks on Web sites.

References

CHAPTER 1

Anonymous. (2010, July 1). Average information technology manager salary. *Salary.com.* Retrieved July 2, 2010, from http://swz.salary .com/salarywizard/layouthtmls/swzl _compresult_national_IT10000246.html

Brandel, M. (2009, December 29). 6 hottest IT skills for 2010. *Computerworld.* Retrieved July 1, 2010, from http://www.computerworld .com/s/article/345529/6_hottest_IT_skills _for_2010

Bureau of Labor Statistics. (2010, May 14). Occupational employment and wages, May 2009. *BLS.gov.* Retrieved July 1, 2010, from http://www.bls.gov/oes/current/oes113021.htm

Carr, N. (2003). IT doesn't matter. *Harvard Business Review, 81*(5), 41–49.

Carr, N. (2004). *Does IT matter? Information technology and the corrosion of competitive advantage.* Boston: Harvard Business School Press.

CIO.com. (2004). Metrics: Offshore spending swells. Retrieved June 30, 2010, from http:// www2.cio.com/metrics/2004/metric667.html

Collett, S. (2006). Hot skills, cold skills: The IT worker of 2010 won't be a technology guru but rather a "versatilist." *Computerworld.* Retrieved June 30, 2010, from http://www.computerworld .com/s/article/112360/Hot_Skills_Cold_Skills

Drucker, P. (1959). *Landmarks of tomorrow.* New York: Harper.

Elgan, M. (2010, February 20). Mike Elgan: How Buzz, Facebook and Twitter create "social insecurity." *Computerworld.* Retrieved July 1, 2010, from http://www.computerworld.com/s/ article/9159679/Mike_Elgan_How_Buzz _Facebook_and_Twitter_create_social _insecurity_

Farrell, D., Kaka, N., & Stürze, S. (2005). Ensuring India's offshoring future. *McKinsey Quarterly,* September. Retrieved June 30, 2010, from http://www.mckinsey.com/mgi/ publications/India_offshoring.asp

Friedman, T. L. (2007). *The world is flat 3.0: A brief history of the twenty-first century.* New York: Farrar, Straus and Giroux.

Galbraith, J. K. (1987). *The affluent society.* New York: Houghton Mifflin.

Heath, N. (2009, November 19). Outsourcers to fall victim to cloud computing rush? *Silicon.com.* Retrieved July 1, 2010, from http://www.silicon.com/technology/it-services/ 2009/11/19/outsourcers-to-fall-victim-to -cloud-computing-rush-39646338

International Monetary Fund. (2002). Globalization: Threat or opportunity? Retrieved June 30, 2010, from http://www.imf .org/external/np/exr/ib/2000/041200to.htm

King, J. (2003, September 15). IT's global itinerary: Offshore outsourcing is inevitable. *Computerworld.* Retrieved June 30, 2010, from http://www.computerworld.com/management topics/outsourcing/story/0,10801,84861,00 .html

Koncz, A., & Collins, M. (2010, February 4). Early report shows lower average salary for college class of 2010. *NACE.com.* Retrieved July 1, 2010, from http://www.naceweb.org/ Press/Releases/Early_Report_Shows_Lower _Average_Salary_for_College_Class_of_2010 _(2-4-10).aspx

Leung, L. (2009). 10 hot skills for 2009. *Global Knowledge.* Retrieved July 1, 2010, from http://www.globalknowledge.com/training/ generic.asp?pageid=2321

Lundberg, A. (2004, May 1). Interview with N. Carr. *CIO.com.* Retrieved June 30, 2010, from http://www.cio.com/article/32264/Interview _Nicholas_Carr_The_Argument_Over_IT

Mallaby, S. (2006, January 2). In India, engineering success. *Washington Post,* January 2. Retrieved July 9, 2010, from http://www.washingtonpost .com/wp-dyn/content/article/2006/01/02/ AR2006010200566.html.

Mason, R. O. (1986). Four ethical issues of the information age. *MIS Quarterly, 10*(1), 5–12.

Michaeli, R. (2009). *Competitive intelligence: Competitive advantage through analysis of competition, markets and technologies.* New York: Springer.

Overby, S. (2006, September 5). Global outsourc- ing guide 2006. *CIO.com.* Retrieved July 2, 2010, from http://www.cio.com.au/article/ 170687/global_outsourcing_guide_2006

Porter, M. E. (1985). *Competitive advantage: Creating and sustaining superior performance.* New York: Free Press.

Porter, M. E., & Millar, V. (1985). How information gives you competitive advantage. *Harvard Business Review, 63*(4), 149–161.

Rothfeder, J., & Driscoll, L. (1990, February 26). CIO is starting to stand for "career is over": Once deemed indispensable, the chief information officer has become an endangered species. *BusinessWeek,* 78–80.

Sipior, J. C., & Ward, B. T. (1995). The ethical and legal quandary of e-mail privacy. *Communications of the ACM, 38*(12), 48–54.

Stevens, D. (1994). Reinvent IS or Jane will. *Datamation, 40*(24), 84.

Tapscott, D. (2004, May 1). The engine that drives success: The best companies have the best business models because they have the best IT strategies. *CIO.com.* Retrieved June 30, 2010, from http://www.cio.com/article/32265/IT_The_Engine_That_Drives_Success

Todd, P., McKeen, J., & Gallupe, R. (1995). The evolution of IS job skills: A content analysis of IS jobs. *MIS Quarterly, 19*(1), 1–27.

Veritude (2009). 2009 IT hiring outlook. Retrieved September 1, 2010, from https://www.vtrenz.net/imaeds/ownerassets/1010/Ver_WP_2009 IT Outlook Report_FINAL.pdf

Weisband, S. P., & Reinig, B. A. (1995, December). Managing user perceptions of e-mail privacy. *Communications of the ACM, 38*(12), 40–47.

CHAPTER 2

Alavi, M., & Young, G. (1992). Information technologies in international enterprise: An organizing framework. In S. Palvia, P. Palvia, & R. Zigli (Eds.), *Global issues in information technology management* (pp. 495–516). Harrisburg, PA: Idea Group.

Anderson, C. (2009). *Free: The future of a radical price.* New York: Hyperion.

Applegate, L. M., Austin, R. D., & McFarlan, F. W. (2007). *Corporate information strategy and management* (7th ed.). Burr Ridge, IL: Richard D. Irwin.

Bakos, J. Y., & Treacy, M. E. (1986). Information technology and corporate strategy: A research perspective. *MIS Quarterly, 10*(2), 107–120.

Bartlett, C., & Ghoshal, S. (1998). *Managing across borders: The transnational solution.* Boston: Harvard Business School Press.

Christensen, C. M. (1997). *The innovator's dilemma.* Boston: Harvard Business School Press.

Christensen, C. M., & Raynor, M. E. (2003). *The innovator's solution: Creating and sustaining successful growth.* Boston: Harvard Business School Press.

Christensen, C. M., Roth, E. A., & Anthony, S. D. (2004). *Seeing what's next: Using theories of innovation to predict industry change.* Boston: Harvard Business School Press.

Garvin, D. A. (1993). Building a learning organization. *Harvard Business Review, 71*(4), 78–91.

Ghoshal, S. (1987). Global strategy: An organizing framework. *Strategic Management Journal, 8*(5), 425–440.

Hitt, M. A., Ireland, R. D., & Hoskisson, R. E. (2009). *Strategic management: Competitiveness and globalization* (8th ed.). Boston: South-Western.

Karami, J., & Konsynski, B. R. (1991). Globalization and information management strategies. *Journal of Management Information Systems, 7*(4), 7–26.

Maddox, J. (1999, December). The unexpected science to come. *Scientific American, 281,* 62–67.

McKeen, J. D., Guimaraes, T., & Wetherbe, J. C. (1994). A comparative analysis of MIS project selection mechanisms. *Database, 25*(2), 43–59.

Porter, M. E. (1979, March–April). How competitive forces shape strategy. *Harvard Business Review, 57,* 137–145.

Porter, M. E. (1985). *Competitive advantage: Creating and sustaining superior performance.* New York: Free Press.

Porter, M. E. (2001). Strategy and the internet. *Harvard Business Review, 79*(3), 62–78.

Prahalad, C. K., & Doz, Y. L. (1987). *The multinational mission: Balancing local demands and global vision.* New York: Free Press.

Ramarapu, N. K., & Lado, A. A. (1995). Linking information technology to global business strategy to gain competitive advantage: An integrative model. *Journal of Information Technology, 10,* 115–124.

Rogers, E. (2003). *Diffusion of innovations* (5th ed.). New York: Free Press.

Rubin, H. (2004, June 1). Practical counsel for capturing IT value: The elusive value of infrastructure. *CIO.com.* Retrieved June 30, 2010, from http://www.cio.com/article/32321/Real_Value_The_Elusive_Value_of_Infrastructure

Shank, J., & Govindarajan, V. (1993). *Strategic cost management: Three key themes for managing costs effectively.* New York: Free Press.

Wheeler, B. C. (2002). NeBIC: A dynamic capabilities theory for assessing net-enablement. *Information Systems Research, 13*(2), 125–146.

Zuboff, S. (1988). *In the age of the smart machine: The future of work and power.* New York: Basic Books.

CHAPTER 3

Amazon. (2010). Amazon Web services. *Amazon.com.* Retrieved July 2, 2010, from http://aws.amazon.com

Berghel, H. (1996). U.S. technology policy in the information age. *Communications of the ACM, 39*(6), 15–18.

Google. (2010). Google's green initiatives. *Google.com.* Retrieved July 2, 2010, from http://www.google.com/corporate/green

Hoffer, J. A., George, J. F., & Valacich, J. S. (2011). *Modern systems analysis and design* (6th ed.). Upper Saddle River, NJ: Prentice Hall.

Hoffer, J., Ramesh, V., & Topi, H. (2011). *Modern database management* (10th ed.). Upper Saddle River, NJ: Prentice Hall.

Laberta, C. (2011). *Computers are your future* (11th ed.). Upper Saddle River, NJ: Prentice Hall.

National Institute of Standards and Technology. (2009, October 7). The NIST definition of cloud computing, v. 15. Retrieved July 2, 2010, from http://csrc.nist.gov/groups/SNS/cloud-computing/cloud-def-v15.doc

Netcraft. (2010, May 14). May 2010 Web server survey. *Netcraft.com.* Retrieved July 2, 2010, from http://news.netcraft.com/archives/2010/05/14/may_2010_web_server_survey.html

Panko, R., & Panko, J. (2011). *Business data networks and telecommunications* (8th ed.). Upper Saddle River, NJ: Prentice Hall.

Stallings, W. (2011). *Network security essentials: Applications and standards* (4th ed.). Upper Saddle River, NJ: Prentice Hall.

Tebutt, D. (2010, February 9). Ten green issues for CIOs. *Techworld.* Retrieved July 2, 2010, from http://features.techworld.com/green-it/3212282/ten-green-issues-for-cios

Te'eni, D., Carey, J. M., & Zhang, P. (2007). *Human-computer interaction: Developing effective organizational information systems.* New York: Wiley.

Top 500. (2010). Retrieved July 2, 2010, from http://www.top500.org/lists/2010/06

Wheeland, M. (2007). Green computing at Google. Retrieved June 30, 2010, from http://www.climatebiz.com/feature/2007/05/03/green-computing-google

CHAPTER 4

ABI Research. (2010, February 19). Shopping by mobile will grow to $119 billion in 2015. Retrieved August 9, 2010, from http://www.abiresearch.com/press/1605-Shopping+by+Mobile+Will+Grow+to+$119+Billion+in+2015

Alipay. (2010). About Alipay. Retrieved June 30, 2010, from https://www.alipay.com/static/aboutalipay/englishabout.htm

Anderson, C. (2004). The long tail. *Wired.* Retrieved June 30, 2010, from http://www.wired.com/wired/archive/12.10/tail.html

Anderson, C. (2006). *The long tail: Why the future of business is selling less of more.* New York: Hyperion.

Anonymous. (2010, June 29). Industry adoption updates. *CheckImage Central.* Retrieved June 30, 2010, from http://www.checkimagecentral.org/industryAdoptionUpdates

Benson, C. (2009, April 2). The problem with B2B payments. *Paymentsviews.* Retrieved June 30, 2010, from http://paymentsviews.com/2009/04/02/the-problem-with-b2b-payments

Chatterjee, D., & Sambamurthy, V. (1999). Business implications of web technology: An insight into usage of the World Wide Web by U.S. companies. *Electronic Markets, 9*(2), 126–131.

EFF. (2010). Is your printer spying on you? *Electronic Frontier Foundation.* Retrieved August 14, 2010, from http://www.eff.org/issues/printers.

Evan, P., & Wurster, T. (1999). *Blown to bits: How the new economics of information transforms strategy.* Boston: Harvard Business School Press.

Federal Trade Commission. (2010, May 21). A consumer's guide to e-payments. *ftc.gov.* Retrieved August 9, 2010, from http://www.ftc.gov/bcp/edu/pubs/consumer/tech/tec01.shtm.

Firstdata. (2009, October 26). Why b2b payments need a "BizPal": An international perspective. Retrieved June 30, 2010, from http://www.firstdata.com/en_au/insights/b2b_payments_intl_marketinsights

Google. (2007). Marketing and advertising using Google. Retrieved June 30, 2010, from books.google.com/intl/en/googlebooks/pdf/MarketingAndAdvertisingUsingGoogle.pdf

Grau, J. (2009, June). Retail e-commerce forecast: Cautious optimism. *eMarketer.* Retrieved June 30, 2010, from http://www.emarketer.com/Reports/All/Emarketer_2000565.aspx

Internet Crime Complaint Center. (2010, March 12). 2009 IC3 annual report. Retrieved June 30, 2010, from http://www.ic3.gov/media/annualreport/2009_IC3Report.pdf

Javelin Strategy. (2010, February). 2010 identity fraud survey report: Consumer version. Retrieved June 30, 2010, from https://www.javelinstrategy.com/uploads/files/1004.R_2010IdentityFraudSurveyConsumer.pdf

Kalakota, R., Oliva, R. A., & Donath, E. (1999). Move over, e-commerce. *Marketing Management, 8*(3), 23–32.

Laudon, K., & Guercio Traver, C. (2010). *E-commerce 2010,* (6th ed.). New York: Pearson Addison Wesley.

Lee, M., & Lin, D. (2009, November 24). Alipay to become world's No 1 e-payment firm. *Reuters.* Retrieved June 30, 2010, from http://www.reuters.com/article/idUSSHA32192420091124

Looney, C., & Chatterjee, D. (2002). Web enabled transformation of the brokerage industry: An analysis of emerging business models. *Communications of the ACM, 45*(8), 75–81.

Looney, C., Jessup, L., & Valacich, J. (2004). Emerging business models for mobile brokerage services. *Communications of the ACM, 47*(6), 71–77.

MacMillan, D. (2009, August 31). Can Hulu's high prices hold? *BusinessWeek.* Retrieved June 30, 2010, from http://www.businessweek.com/the_thread/techbeat/archives/2009/08/can_hulus_high.html

MobileInfo. (2008). M-commerce. *MobileInfo.com.* Retrieved July 14, 2008, from http://www.mobileinfo.com/Mcommerce/index.htm

Nystedt, D. (2009, October 12). Researchers advise cyber self defense in the cloud. *PCWorld.* Retrieved June 30, 2010, from http://www.pcworld.com/businesscenter/article/173467/researchers_advise_cyber_self_defense_in_the_cloud.html

Priceline. (2010). 2009 annual report. Retrieved June 30, 2010, from http://phx.corporate-ir.net/External.File?item=UGFyZW50SUQ9NDM4ODh8Q2hpbGRJRD0tMXxUeXBlPTM=&t=1

Quelch, J. A., & Klein, L. R. (1996, Spring). The Internet and internal marketing. *Sloan Management Review, 63,* 60–75.

Szuprowicz, B.O. (1998). *Extranets and Intranets: E-Commerce Business Strategies for the Future.* Charleston, S.C.: Computer Technology Research.

Turban, E., Lee, J. K., King, D., Liang, T. P., & Turban, D. (2010). *Electronic commerce 2010: A managerial perspective* (6th ed.). Upper Saddle River, NJ: Pearson Education.

U.S. Census Bureau. (2010, May 27). E-stats 2008. Retrieved June 30, 2010, from http://www.census.gov/econ/estats/2008/2008reportfinal.pdf

U.S. Census Bureau News. (2010, May 18). Quarterly retail e-commerce sales 1st quarter 2010. Retrieved June 30, 2010, from http://www.census.gov/retail/mrts/www/data/html/10Q1.html.

Valacich, J. S., Parboteeah, D. V., & Wells, J. D. (2007). The online consumer's hierarchy of needs. *Communications of the ACM, 50*(9), 84–90.

VanBoskirk, S. (2009, July 30). *US interactive marketing forecast, 2009 to 2014.* Cambridge, MA: Forrester Research.

Wagner, M. (2002, May 23). Saving trees and serving up benefits. *Internet Retailer.* Retrieved June 30, 2010, from http://www.internetretailer.com/2002/05/23/saving-trees-and-serving-up-benefits

Wells, J., & Gobeli, D. (2003). The three R framework: Improving e-strategy across reach, richness and range. *Business Horizons, 46*(2), 5–14.

Yang, A., & Birge, J. (2010). How inventory is (should be) financed? Trade credit in supply chains with financial constraints and distress cost. Retrieved May 5, 2010, from http://faculty.chicagobooth.edu/workshops/omscience/pdf/YangBirge_trade%20credit.pdf

Zwass, V. (1996). Electronic commerce: Structures and issues. *International Journal of Electronic Commerce, 1*(1), 3–23.

CHAPTER 5

Adobe Corporation. (2010). Cigna Healthcare. Retrieved June 30, 2010, from http://www.adobe.com/products/contribute/customers

Anderson, C. (2004). The long tail. *Wired.* Retrieved June 30, 2010, from http://www.wired.com/wired/archive/12.10/tail.html

Anderson, C. (2006). *The long tail: Why the future of business is selling less of more.* New York: Hyperion.

Anonymous. (2010, June 30). Facebook.com site info. *Alexa.com.* Retrieved June 30, 2010, from http://www.alexa.com/siteinfo/facebook.com

Arrington, M. (2007). Engadget knocks $4 billion off Apple market cap on bogus iphone email. *Techcrunch.* Retrieved June 30, 2010, from http://www.techcrunch.com/2007/05/16/engadget-knocks-4-billion-of-apple-market-cap-on-bogus-iphone-email

Baekdal, T. (2006, November 23). 7 tricks to viral Web marketing. *Baekdal.com.* Retrieved June 25, 2010, from http://www.baekdal .com/media/viral-marketing-tricks

Brown, D. (2010, June 21). PR disaster aside, BP should leave satire alone. *CNN.com.* Retrieved June 25, 2010, from http://www.cnn .com/2010/TECH/web/06/21/bp.fake.twitter.norm/index.html

Carr, N. (2005). The amorality of Web 2.0. Retrieved June 30, 2010, from http://www.roughtype.com/archives/2005/10/the _amorality_o.php

CBS. (2005). CBA ousts 4 for Bush guard story. *CBS News.* Retrieved June 30, 2010, from http://www.cbsnews.com/stories/ 2005/01/10/national/main665727.shtml

Cook, N. (2008). *Enterprise 2.0: How social software will change the future of work.* Burlington, VT: Gower.

Flandez, R. (2009, April 20). Domino's response offers lesson in crisis management. *Wall Street Journal.* Retrieved June 30, 2010, from http://blogs.wsj.com/independentstreet/2009/04/20/ dominos-response-offers-lessons-in-crisis-management

Francis, J. A., & Harrigan, G. M. (2010). Jumping the boundaries of corporate IT: Accenture global research on Millennials' use of technology. Retrieved June 23, 2010, from http://nstore.accenture .com/technology/millennials/global_millennial_generation _research.pdf

Gaudin, S. (2009, October 6). Study: 54% of companies ban Facebook, Twitter at work. *Computerworld.* Retrieved June 23, 2010, from http://www.computerworld.com/s/article/9139020/ Study_54_of_companies_ban_Facebook_Twitter_at_work

Gonzalez, N. (2010, June 23). Facebook marketing statistics, demographics, reports, and news. Retrieved June 24, 2010, from http://www.checkfacebook.com

Google. (2010). Lakehead University success story. Retrieved June 30, 2010, from http://www.google.com/a/help/intl/en/ admins/case_studies/lakehead.html

Hinchcliffe, D. (2010, April 14). Enterprise 2.0 and improved business performance. *ZDNet.com.* Retrieved June 30, 2010, from http://www.zdnet.com/blog/hinchcliffe/enterprise-20-and -improved-business-performance/1355

Holahan, C. (2009, July 8). How Facebook is killing MySpace. *MSN Money.* Retrieved June 24, 2010, from http://articles.moneycentral .msn.com/Investing/Extra/How-Facebook-is%20killing -MySpace.aspx

IBM Corporation. (2008). Wimbledon delivers a previously unimag- ined tennis experience. Retrieved June 30, 2010, from http:// www-935.ibm.com/services/au/igs/pdf/wimbledon-case-study.pdf

Jiao, P. (2010, August 17). The traits that separate China's Net from rest. *South China Morning Post.* Retrieved August 17, 2010, from http://www.scmp.com

Keen, W. (2007). *The cult of the amateur: How today's Internet is killing our culture.* New York: Doubleday.

Khan, S. (2008, June 24). Enterprise 2.0—Giving the hype a second thought. *CIOUpdate.com.* Retrieved June 27, 2010, from http://www.cioupdate.com/reports/article.php/11050 _3755056_1/Enterprise-20—Giving-the-Hype-a-Second -Thought.htm

Kravets, D. (2010, June 18). Utah attorney general announces execution on Twitter. *Wired.com.* Retrieved June 25, 2010, from http://www.wired.com/threatlevel/2010/06/execution -announced-on-twitter

MacManus, R. (2007, August 7). Eric Schmidt defines Web 3.0. Retrieved June 30, 2010, from http://www.readwriteweb.com/ archives/eric_schmidt_defines_web_30.php

Mascarenhas, A. (2010, June 4). BP's global PR vs. BPGlobalPR. *Newsweek.* Retrieved June 20, 2010, from http://www.newsweek .com/2010/06/04/bp-s-global-pr-vs-bpglobalpr.html

McAfee, A. (2006a, April 1). Enterprise 2.0: The dawn of emergent collaboration. *MIT Sloan Management Review, 47*(3), 21–28.

McAfee, A. (2006b, May 27). Enterprise 2.0, version 2.0. Retrieved June 30, 2010, from http://andrewmcafee.org/2006/05/enterprise _20_version_20

Meyerson, B., & Wang, A. (2009, July 29). Tweet lawsuit: Chicago landlord sues ex-tenant over tweet complaining about apartment. *Chicago Tribune.* Retrieved June 30, 2010, from http://www .chicagotribune.com/news/local/chi-twitter-suit-29 -jul29,0,2500898.story

Microsoft Corporation. (2007a, February 15). Major cosmetics producer deploys Microsoft search technology to increase efficiency. Retrieved October June 30, 2010, from http://www .microsoft.com/casestudies/casestudy.aspx?casestudyid =201075

Microsoft Corporation. (2007b, February 20). Leading global coffee retailer improves business processes and enhances store Web portal with Microsoft Office SharePoint Server. Retrieved June 30, 2010, from http://www.microsoft.com/casestudies/casestudy .aspx?casestudyid=201085

Nielsen, J. (2006, November 6). 100 million Websites. *Jacob Nielsen's Alertbox.* Retrieved June 25, 2010, from http://www .useit.com/alertbox/web-growth.html

Preidt, R. (2008, May 2). "Virtual" health teams boost patient care. Retrieved June 30, 2010, from http://abcnews.go.com/Health/ Healthday/story?id=4777948

Prescott, L. (2010, February 10). 54% of US Internet users on Facebook, 27% on MySpace. *SocialBeat.* Retrieved June 24, 2010, from http://social.venturebeat.com/2010/02/10/54-of-us -internet-users-on-facebook-27-on-myspace

Rayport, J. (1996, December 31). The virus of marketing. *Fast Company.com.* Retrieved June 30, 2010, from http://www .fastcompany.com/magazine/06/virus.html

Reynolds, C. (2009, July 7). Smashed guitar, YouTube song—United is listening now. *Los Angeles Times.* Retrieved June 30, 2010, from http://travel.latimes.com/daily-deal-blog/index.php/ smashed-guitar-youtu-4850

Sarker, S., & Sahay, S. (2002). Understanding virtual team develop- ment: An interpretive study. *Journal of the AIS, 3,* 247–285.

Sessums, C. D. (2009, December 17). A simple definition: Web 2.0. Retrieved June 28, 2010, from http://eduspaces.net/csessums/ weblog/788551.html

Smythe, J. (2007). *The CEO: The chief engagement officer: Turning hierarchy upside down to drive performance.* Burlington, VT: Gower.

Surowiecki, J. (2004). *The wisdom of crowds.* New York: Doubleday.

Wikipedia. (2010, June 30). In *Wikipedia, the free encyclopedia.* Retrieved June 30, 2010, from http://en.wikipedia.org/w/index .php?title=Wikipedia&oldid=37089186

World Wide Web Consortium. (2008). Widgets 1.0: Requirements. Retrieved June 30, 2010, from http://www.w3.org/TR/2008/ WD-widgets-reqs-20080625

CHAPTER 6

Alavi, M., & Leidner, D. (1999). Knowledge management systems: issues, challenges, and benefits. *Communications of the AIS, 1*(Article 7).

Awad, E. M., & Ghaziri, H. M. (2004). *Knowledge management.* Upper Saddle River, NJ: Pearson Prentice Hall.

Blumberg, R., & Atre, S. (2003, February 1). The problem with unstructured data. *Information Management Magazine*. Retrieved July 9, 2010, from http://www.information-management.com/issues/20030201/6287-1.html

Business Objects. (n.d.). Expanding BI's role by including predictive analytics. Retrieved July 7, 2010, from http://ecohub.sdn.sap.com/irj/ecohub/home?rid=/hub/uuid/000b9783-cc68-2c10-2793-815b01fb135d

Business Objects. (2008). Business intelligence—Now more than ever. Retrieved July 5, 2010, from http://www.businessintelligence.com/white_papers.asp

Checkland, P. B. (1981). *Systems thinking, systems practice*. Chichester: Wiley.

Clarke, K. C. (2011). *Getting started with geographic information systems* (5th ed.). Upper Saddle River, NJ: Pearson Prentice Hall.

Economist Intelligence Unit. (2007). In search of clarity: Unravelling the complexities of executive decision-making. Retrieved July 5, 2010, from graphics.eiu.com/upload/EIU_In_search_of_clarity.pdf

Gantz, J., Reinsel, D., Chute, C., Schlichting, W., McArthur, J., Minton, S., et al. (2007, March). The expanding digital universe. *IDC*. Retrieved July 9, 2010, from http://www.emc.com/about/destination/digital_universe/pdf/Expanding_Digital_Universe_IDC_WhitePaper_022507.pdf

Larose, D. T. (2006). *Data mining methods and models*. New York: Wiley.

Leonard, D. (2006, January 30). How to salvage your company's deep smarts. *CIO.com*. Retrieved July 2, 2010, from http://www.cio.com.au/article/182425/how_salvage_your_company_deep_smarts

Levinson, M. (2010). Knowledge management definition and solutions. *CIO.com*. Retrieved July 2, 2010, from http://www.cio.com/article/40343/Knowledge_Management_Definition_and_Solutions

Lo, C. P., & Yeung, A. K. W. (2007). *Concepts and techniques of geographic information systems* (2nd ed.). Upper Saddle River, NJ: Pearson Prentice Hall.

Malhotra, Y. (2005). Integrating knowledge management technologies in organizational business processes: Getting real time enterprises to deliver real business performance. *Journal of Knowledge Management, 9*(1), 7–28.

Myatt, G. J., & Johnson, W. P. (2009). *Making sense of data: A practical guide to data visualization, advanced data mining methods, and applications*. New York: Wiley.

Pettey, C., & Stevens, H. (2009, January 15). Gartner reveals five business intelligence predictions for 2009 and beyond. *Gartner*. Retrieved July 2, 2010, from http://www.gartner.com/it/page.jsp?id=856714

Saarenvirta, G. (2004). The untapped value of geographic information. *Business Intelligence Journal, 9*(1), 58–63.

Sprague, R. H., Jr. (1980). A framework for the development of decision support systems. *MIS Quarterly, 4*(4), 1–26.

Stergiou, C., & Siganos, D. (1996). Neural networks. Retrieved July 8, 2010, from http://www.doc.ic.ac.uk/∼nd/surprise_96/journal/vol4/cs11/report.html

Swoyer, S. (2007, September 5). Unstructured data: Attacking a myth. *TDWI*. Retrieved July 9, 2010, from http://tdwi.org/articles/2007/09/05/unstructured-data-attacking-a-myth.aspx

Tapscott, D. (2008). Actionable insights for business decision makers. Retrieved July 7, 2010, from http://www.businessobjects.com/campaigns/forms/q109/apj/everyone/tapscott/BI_for_Decision_Makers.pdf

Turban, E., Sharda, R., & Delen, D. (2010). *Decision support systems and business intelligence systems* (9th ed.). Upper Saddle River, NJ: Prentice Hall.

Turban, E., Sharda, R., Delen, D., & King, D. (2010). *Business intelligence* (2nd ed.). Upper Saddle River, NJ: Prentice Hall.

White, C. (2005). Bridging the planning and business performance gap. *SAP BI Research*. Retrieved July 9, 2010, from www.sap.com/platform/netweaver/pdf/BWP_AR_BI_Research.pdf

CHAPTER 7

Brown, P. C. (2007). *Succeeding with SOA: Realizing business value through total architecture*. New York: Addison-Wesley.

Christensen, C. M. (1997). The innovator's dilemma. Boston: Harvard Business School Press.

Erl, T. (2008). *SOA principles of service design*. Upper Saddle River, NJ: Prentice Hall.

Hammer, M., & Champy, J. (1993). *Reengineering the corporation: A manifesto for business revolution*. New York: Harper Business Essentials.

Jacobs, F. R., & Whybark, D. C. (2000). *Why ERP? A primer on SAP implementation*. Boston: Irwin/McGraw-Hill.

Kumar, R. L., & Crook, C. W. (1999). A multi-disciplinary framework for the management of interorganizational systems. *Database for Advances in Information Systems 30*(1), 22–36.

Langenwalter, G. A. (2000). *Enterprise resource planning and beyond*. Boca Raton, FL: St. Lucie Press.

Larson, P. D., & Rogers, D.S. (1998), Supply Chain Management: Definition, Growth and Approaches. *Journal of Marketing Theory and Practice, 6*(4), 1–5.

Olson, D. (2004). *Managerial issues of enterprise resource planning systems*. Boston: McGraw-Hill/Irwin.

Porter, M. E., & Millar, V. E. (1985). How information gives you competitive advantage. *Harvard Business Review*, July–August, 149–160.

Taylor, F. W. (1911). *The Principles of Scientific Management*. New York: Harper Bros.

Wagner, B., & Monk, E. (2009). *Enterprise resource planning* (3rd ed.). Boston: Cengage.

Wailgum, T. (2008, January 29). Why ERP systems are more important than ever. *CIO.com*. Retrieved July 28, 2010, from http://www.cio.com/article/177300/Why_ERP_Systems_Are_More_Important_Than_Ever

Wailgum, T. (2008, April 17). ERP definition and solutions. *CIO.com*. Retrieved July 28, 2010, from http://www.cio.com/article/40323/ERP_Definition_and_Solutions

CHAPTER 8

Anonymous. (2009). CRM and social networking: Engaging the social customer. Retrieved July 31, 2010, from http://crm.dynamics.com/docs/CRM_and_Social_Networks.pdf

Anonymous. (2010). About vendor managed inventory. *Vendor Managed Inventory.com*. Retrieved July 28, 2010, from http://www.vendormanagedinventory.com/about.php

Arano, N. (2010, July 21). Canadian university offers social CRM course. *CIO.com*. Retrieved July 30, 2010, from http://www.cio.com/article/600257/Canadian_University_Offers_Social_CRM_Course

Barboza, D. (2010, July 5). Supply chain for iPhone highlights costs in China. *New York Times*. Retrieved July 28, 2010, from http://www.nytimes.com/2010/07/06/technology/06iphone.html

Breen, B. (2004, November 1). Living in Dell time. *Fastcompany*. Retrieved July 28, 2010, from http://www.fastcompany.com/magazine/88/dell.html

Dean, J. (2007, August 11). The forbidden city of Terry Gou. *Wall Street Journal*. Retrieved July 28, 2010, from http://online.wsj.com/article/NA_WSJ_PUB:SB118677584137994489.html

Edwards, J. (2003, February 15). RFID creates fast asset identification and management. *CIO.com*. Retrieved July 29, 2010, from http://www.cio.com/article/31724/RFID_Creates_Fast_Asset_Identification_and_Management

Harrison, A., & Van Hoek, R. (2008). *Logistics management and strategy: Competing through the supply chain* (3rd ed.). Upper Saddle River, NJ: Prentice Hall.

Kanaracus, C. (2009, July 9). Microsoft ties Dynamics CRM to Twitter. *CIO.com*. Retrieved July 30, 2010, from http://www.cio.com/article/496978/Microsoft_Ties_Dynamics_CRM_to_Twitter

Keller, K. (2010, June 28). iPhone 4 carries bill of materials of $187.51, according to iSuppli. *iSuppli.com*. Retrieved July 28, 2010, from http://www.isuppli.com/Teardowns-Manufacturing-and-Pricing/News/Pages/iPhone-4-Carries-Bill-of-Materials-of-187-51-According-to-iSuppli.aspx

Lager, M. (2008, April). The 2008 CRM Service Awards: Elite—JPMorgan Chase Card Services. *destinationCRM.com*. Retrieved July 31, 2010, from http://www.destinationcrm.com/Articles/ReadArticle.aspx?ArticleID=46576

Larson, P. D., & Rogers, D. S. (1998). Supply chain management: Definition, growth, and approaches. *Journal of Marketing Theory and Practice, 6*(4), 1–5.

LSG. (2010, May 11). Quantum Lightweight Trolley receives airworthiness certificate. Retrieved July 30, 2010, from http://www.lsgskychefs.com/en/press-room/information/quantum-lightweight-trolley-receives-airworthiness-certificate.html

Nash, K. (2007, October 22). Beyond Peter Pan: How ConAgra's pot pie recall bakes in hard lessons for supply chain management. *CIO.com*. Retrieved July 28, 2010, from http://www.cio.com/article/148054/Beyond_Peter_Pan_How_ConAgra_s_Pot_Pie_Recall_Bakes_In_Hard_Lessons_for_Supply_Chain_Management

Penfield, P. (2008, August 26). Visibility within the supply chain. *MHIA.org*. Retrieved July 28, 2010, from http://www.mhia.org/news/industry/7960/visibility-within-the-supply-chain

Sebor, J. (2010, March). The 2010 CRM Service Awards: The service elite—Southwest Airlines. *destinationCRM.com*. Retrieved August 4, 2010, from http://www.destinationcrm.com/Articles/Editorial/Magazine-Features/The-2010-CRM-Service-Awards-The-Service-Elite—-Southwest-Airlines-61390.aspx

Taber, D. (2009, September 28). Marketing automation: Unique kid on the CRM block. *CIO.com*. Retrieved July 30, 2010 from http://www.cio.com/article/503436/Marketing_Automation_Unique_Kid_on_the_CRM_Block

Taber, D. (2010, February 22). CRM's identity crisis: Duplicate contacts, part 2. *CIO.com*. Retrieved July 30, 2010, from http://www.cio.com/article/551313/CRM_s_Identity_Crisis_Duplicate_Contacts_Part_2

Taber, D. (2010, May 19). CRM problems come in threes. *CIO.com*. Retrieved July 30, 2010, from http://www.cio.com/article/594235/CRM_Problems_Come_in_Threes

Wagner, W., & Zubey, M. (2006). *Customer relationship management*. Boston: Course Technology.

Wailgum, T. (2008, November 20). Supply chain management definition and solutions. *CIO.com*. Retrieved July 28, 2010, from http://www.cio.com/article/40940/Supply_Chain_Management_Definition_and_Solutions

CHAPTER 9

Anonymous. (2009, October 26). Twitter "costs businesses £1.4bn." *BBC News*. Retrieved June 30, 2010, http://news.bbc.co.uk/2/hi/business/8325865.stm

Anonymous. (2010). Gartner says IT spending to rebound in 2010 with 3.3 percent growth after worst year ever in 2009. Retrieved June 30, 2010, from http://www.gartner.com/it/page.jsp?id=1209913

Anonymous. (2010, January 10). Best and worst jobs 2010. *Wall Street Journal*. Retrieved June 30, 2010, from http://online.wsj.com/public/resources/documents/st_BESTJOBS2010_20100105.html

Applegate, L. M., Austin, R. D., & McFarlan, F. W. (2007). *Corporate information strategy and management* (6th ed.). Chicago: Irwin.

Fuller, M. A., Valacich, J. S., & George, J. F. (2008). *Information systems project management: A process and team approach*. Upper Saddle River, NJ: Prentice Hall.

George, J. F., Batra, D., Valacich, J. S., & Hoffer, J. A. (2007). *Object-oriented systems analysis and design* (2nd ed.). Upper Saddle River, NJ: Prentice Hall.

Hoffer, J. A., George, J. F., & Valacich, J. S. (2011). *Modern systems analysis and design* (6th ed.). Upper Saddle River, NJ: Prentice Hall.

McFarlan, F. W., & Nolan, R. L. (1995). How to manage an IT outsourcing alliance. *Sloan Management Review, 36*(2), 9–24.

McKeen, J. D., Guimaraes, T., & Wetherbe, J. C. (1994). A comparative analysis of MIS project selection mechanisms. *Database, 25*(2), 43–59.

Porter, M. E. (1979, March–April). How competitive forces shape strategy. *Harvard Business Review, 57,* 137–145.

Valacich, J. S., George, J. F., & Hoffer, J. A. (2009). *Essentials of systems analysis and design*. Upper Saddle River, NJ: Prentice Hall.

Wheeler, B. C. (2002). Making the business case for IT investments through facts, faith, and fear: Online teaching case and teaching note. Retrieved July 15, 2010, from http://collopy.case.edu/articles/ConsumerProductsIntl

Wood, J., & Silver, D. (1989). *Joint Application Design*. New York: Wiley.

CHAPTER 10

Addison-Hewitt Associates. (2005). The Sarbanes-Oxley Act. Retrieved June 30, 2010, from http://www.soxlaw.com/index.htm

Bielski, Z. (2008, June 21). World unprepared for coming catastrophes, warn experts. *National Post*. Retrieved June 30, 2010, from http://www.nationalpost.com/most_popular/story.html?id=602830

Bocij, P. (2004). *Cyberstalking: Harassment in the Internet age and how to protect your family*. Westport, CT: Greenwood.

Burgess-Proctor, A., Patchin, J. W., & Hinduja, S. (2008). *Cyberbullying and online harassment: Reconceptualizing the victimization of adolescent girls*. In V. Garcia & J. Clifford (Eds.), *Female crime victims: Reality reconsidered* (pp. 162–176). Upper Saddle River, NJ: Prentice Hall.

Business Software Alliance. (2007). The fight for cyber space. Retrieved June 30, 2010, from http://www.bsa.org/∼/media/9CA4C9DFEDE24250AA16F16F0ED297A6.ashx

Business Software Alliance. (2010). Sixth annual BSA and IDC global software piracy study. Retrieved June 30, 2010, from http://portal .bsa.org/globalpiracy2009/studies/globalpiracystudy 2009.pdf

CAPTCHA. (2010). Telling humans and computers apart automatically. Retrieved June 30, 2010, from http://www.captcha.net

CERT. (2010). CERT Coordination Center (CERT/CC). Retrieved June 30, 2010, from http://www.cert.org/certcc.html

Champlain, J. (2003). *Auditing information systems*. Hoboken, NJ: Wiley.

Chen, H., Reid, E., Sinai, J., Sike, A., & Ganor, B. (2008). *Terrorism informatics: Knowledge management and data mining for homeland security*. Berlin: Springer.

Computer Security Institute. (2009). *CSI Survey 2009: The 14th annual computer crime and security survey*. Retrieved June 30, 2010, from http://gocsi.com/members/reports

Federal Bureau of Investigation. (2008, October 16). FBI coordinates global effort to nab "Dark Market" cyber criminals. Retrieved June 30, 2010, from http://www.fbi.gov/pressrel/pressrel08/ darkmarket101608.htm

Fitzgerald, T. (2008). The ocean is full of phish. *Information Systems Security*. Retrieved June 30, 2010, from http://www.infosectoday .com/Articles/Phishing.htm

Geers, K. (2008). A new approach to cyber defense. *Internet Evolution*. Retrieved June 30, 2010, from http://www .internetevolution.com/author.asp?id=628&doc_id=151762

Kabay, M. E. (2007). How far could cyberware go? *NetworkWorld*. Retrieved June 30, 2010, from http://www.networkworld.com/ newsletters/sec/2007/0723sec2.html

Keizer, G. (2010). Botnets "the Swiss Army knife of attack tools" (hacker militias can turn to botnets for instant cyberattacks). *Computerworld*. Retrieved June 30, 2010, from http://www .computerworld.com/s/article/9174560/Botnets_the_Swiss_ Army_knife_of_attack_tools

Leyden, J. (2002, March 27). Drive-by hacking linked to cyberterror. *The Register*. Retrieved June 30, 2010, from http://www .theregister.co.uk/2002/03/27/driveby_hacking_linked_to _cyberterror

Panko, R. (2010). *Corporate computer and network security* (2nd ed.). Upper Saddle River, NJ: Pearson Prentice Hall.

Poulsen, K. (2008, October 13). Cybercrime supersite 'DarkMarket' was FBI sting, Documents confirm. *Wired.com*. Retrieved September 1, 2010, from http://www.wired.com/threatlevel/2008/ 10/darkmarket-post

Reuters. (2006). Morgan Stanley offers $15M fine for e-mail violations. *ComputerWorld*. Retrieved June 30, 2010, from http:// www.computerworld.com/hardwaretopics/storage/story/ 0,10801,108687,00.html

Salek, N. (2008, June 24). Does cyberterrorism exist? *CRN.com.au*. Retrieved June 30, 2010, from http://www.crn.com.au/Feature/ 4652,does-cyberterrorism-exist.aspx

SearchCIO. (2007). Business continuity and disaster recovery planning guide for CIOs. *SearchCIO.com*. Retrieved June 30, 2010, from http://searchcio.techtarget.com/generic/ 0,295582,sid182_gci1206807,00.html

Stallings, W. (2010). *Network security essentials: Applications and standards* (4th ed.). Upper Saddle River, NJ: Prentice Hall.

Stallings, W., & Brown, L. (2008). *Computer security: Principles and practices*. Upper Saddle River, NJ: Prentice Hall.

US News. (2007). Top computer crimes of 2007. *USNEWS.com*. Retrieved June 30, 2010, from http://www.usnews.com/ usnews/news/badguys/070515/top_computer_crimes_of_2007_ fi.htm

Volonino, L., & Robinson, S. R. (2004). *Principles and practice of information security*. Upper Saddle River, NJ: Prentice Hall.

Weber, T. (2007, January 25). Criminals "may overwhelm the web." *BBC*. Retrieved June 30, 2010, from http://news.bbc.co.uk/1/hi/ business/6298641.stm

Websense Security Labs. (2010). State of Internet security, Q3–Q4 2009 report. Retrieved June 30, 2010, from http://www.websense .com/assets/pdf/WSL_H2_2009.pdf

Weimann, G. (2006). *Terror on the Internet: The new arena, the new challenges*. Washington, DC: United States Institute of Peace Press.

TECHNOLOGY BRIEFING

Comer, D. E. (1997). *The Internet book* (2nd ed.). Upper Saddle River, NJ: Prentice Hall.

Hoffer, J. A., George, J. F., & Valacich, J. S. (2011). *Modern systems analysis and design* (6th ed.). Upper Saddle River, NJ: Prentice Hall.

Hoffer, J., Ramesh, V., & Topi, H. (2011). *Modern database management* (10th ed.). Upper Saddle River, NJ: Prentice Hall.

Laberta, C. (2011). *Computers are your future complete* (11th ed.). Upper Saddle River, NJ: Prentice Hall.

Panko, R., & Panko, J. (2011). *Business data networks and telecommunications* (8th ed.). Upper Saddle River, NJ: Prentice Hall.

Stallings, W. (2011). *Network security essentials: Applications and standards* (4th ed.). Upper Saddle River, NJ: Prentice Hall.

Te'eni, D., Carey, J. M., & Zhang, P. (2007). *Human-computer interaction: Developing effective organizational information systems*. New York: Wiley.

Name Index

Organization Index

Time, elements of computer, 454
Time bomb, 407
Time lags and productivity, 356
Top-level domains, 115
Total cost of ownership (TCO), 359
Touch screen, 450
Trackball, 450
Training
  in customer relationship management
    (CRM), 335
  for disaster recovery, 433
  for systems implementation
    and operations, 375–376
**Transaction processing system
  (TPS), 30**
Transaction support, 148
**Transmission Control
  Protocol/Internet Protocol
  (TCP/IP), 114**
Transmission media, 110
Transnational business strategy, 72
Trojan horse, 407
Tunneling, 424
Twisted-pair (TP) cables, 473

U

Unauthorized access, 405
Uniform Resource Locator (URL), 115
Unstructured decision, 57
Uploading, 13–14
Upstream information flow, 288
USA PATRIOT Act, 402
User agent, 259
User needs, 125
Utilities, 458
Utility computing, 122–123
Utility program, 458

V

Value, 63
**Value-added network (VAN),
  470**–471
Value chain, 64, 65
  business processes and, 280–288
  organizational activities along,
    283–284
Value chain analysis, 64, 65
Value chain framework, 284
Value proposition, 85
Value system, 287
Value system framework, 288

Vanilla version, 295
**Vendor-managed inventory
  (VMI), 321**
Vendor selection, 384
Vertical market, 158
Videoconferencing, 164–165
Videoconferencing over IP, 132–133
Video input, 451–452
Viral marketing, 216–217, 225
Virtual companies, 149
Virtualization, 123
Virtual machine, 123
Virtual meeting, 207
**Virtual private network (VPN), 156,
  160, 424, 425**
Virtual reality, 202
Virtual team, 208–209
Virtual world, 201
Virus, 406
Virus prevention, 426–427
Vision loss, 76
Visual analytics, 265–266
Visualization, 262–263
Visual programming language, 462
Voice input, 451
Voice over IP (VoIP), 132
Voice-to-text software, 451
Volatile memory, 102
Volume license, 384

W

War driving, 399
Warez peddling, **414**
War spamming, 399
Watermark, 182
Web 2.0
  communication enhancement and,
    197–202
  connecting people with, 214–218
  cooperation and, 202–207
  customer relationship management
    (CRM) and, **333**, 342–343
  defining, **195**
  future capabilities of, 222
Web 3.0, 222
Web analytics, 170
**Web-based collaboration tool,
  209**–210
Web browser, 13, 114
Web cam, 165, 452
Web content mining, 252
Web crawler, 252, 260

Web development languages, 462–463
Web page, 115
Web page builder, 463
Web server, 115
Web service, 219–220, 464
Web sites, 115
  e-commerce and, 169–170
  use of databases to enable
    interactive, 240
Web spider, 260
Web usage mining, 253–254
Web vandalism, 416
Weighted multicriteria analysis, 362
What-if analysis, 255
Wide area network (WAN), 113, 470
Widget, 220–221
**Wi-Fi (wireless fidelity) network,
  113**, 399–400, 476
Wi-Fi Protected Access 2 (WPA2), 399
Wikipedia, 212–213, 232–233
Wiki, 14, 144, 211–213
WiMax, 487
Wired Equivalency Privacy
  (WEP), 399–400
Wireless access point, 482
Wireless controller, 482
Wireless LAN control, 424
**Wireless local area network
  (WLAN), 113**, 476
Wireless media, 475
Work flow software, 19
Workforce, 19
Workplace, use of Facebook
  in, 197, 292
Workstation, 108
World Wide Web, 114. *see also*
  Web 2.0; **Web 3.0**
  architecture, 116–118
  commerce capabilities of, 146
  history of, 115
Worm, 407

X

**XML (Extensible Markup
  Language), 328**–329, 464
XML tag, 328

Z

Zombie computer, 407–408